EARLY MODERN EUROPE

Early Modern Europe

Issues and Interpretations

EDITED BY

JAMES B. COLLINS AND KAREN L. TAYLOR

Editorial material and organization © 2006 by Blackwell Publishing Ltd

BLACKWELL PUBLISHING
350 Main Street, Malden, MA 02148-5020, USA
9600 Garsington Road, Oxford OX4 2DQ, UK
550 Swanston Street, Carlton, Victoria 3053, Australia

First published 2006 by Blackwell Publishing Ltd

1 2006

Library of Congress Cataloging-in-Publication Data

Early modern Europe : issues and interpretations / edited by James B.
Collins and Karen L. Taylor.
    p.   cm.
    Includes bibliographical references and index.
    ISBN 0-631-22892-6 (alk. paper) – ISBN 0-631-22893-4 (pbk. : alk. paper)
    1. Europe–History–1492–1648.   2. Europe–History–1648–1789.   3. Europe–Civilization–16th
century.   4. Europe–Civilization–17th century.   5. Europe–Civilization–18th century.   I. Collins,
James B.   II. Taylor, Karen L.

    D208.E25   2005
    940.2′2–dc22

                                        2004020758

ISBN-13 978-0-631-22892-9; ISBN-13 978-0-631-22893-6

A catalogue record for this title is available from the British Library.

Set in 10/12 Bulmer
by SNP Best-set Typesetter Ltd., Hong Kong
Printed and Bound in India
by Replika Press, PVT Ltd.

The publisher's policy is to use permanent paper from mills that operate a sustainable forestry policy,
and which has been manufactured from pulp processed using acid-free and elementary chlorine-free
practices. Furthermore, the publisher ensures that the text paper and cover board used have met
acceptable environmental accreditation standards.

For further information on
Blackwell Publishing, visit our website:
www.blackwellpublishing.com

Contents

Acknowledgments   viii

Introduction: Interpreting Early Modern Europe
Karen L. Taylor and James B. Collins   1

Part I   Evolving Early Modern Identities   **7**

Introduction   9

1   The Legacy of Rome
    Anthony Pagden   18

2   Europe and the Atlantic Slave Systems
    David Eltis   32

3   History, Myth and Historical Identity
    Karin Friedrich   41

4   The Theresian School Reform of 1774
    James Van Horn Melton   55

5   The Evil Empire? The Debate on Turkish Despotism in
    Eighteenth-Century French Political Culture
    Thomas Kaiser   69

Part II   Changes in Religion and Cultural Life   **83**

Introduction   85

6   *Ira Dei Super Nos*
    Denis Crouzet   90

7   The Charitable Activities of Confraternities
    Maureen Flynn   101

8   The Sins of Belief: A Village Remedy for Hoof and Mouth Disease (1796)
     David Warren Sabean   121

9   "Dutiful Love and Natural Affection": Parent–Child Relationships in the Early
     Modern Netherlands
     Sherrin Marshall   138

Part III   The Revolution of the Mind   **153**

Introduction   155

10   A Possible Support for Irreligion: The Sciences
     Lucien Febvre   160

11   The Material Culture of the Church and Incipient Consumerism
     Richard A. Goldthwaite   172

12   From a Culture of Science toward the Enlightenment
     Kathleen Wellman   186

13   Contesting Possession
     Patricia Seed   197

14   Ritual and Print Discipline and Invention: The *Fête* in France from
     the Middle Ages to the Revolution
     Roger Chartier   207

Part IV   The Roles of Women in Early Modern Society   **215**

Introduction   217

15   Political, Economic, and Legal Structures
     Merry E. Wiesner   222

16   Women before the Bench: Female Litigants in Early Modern Normandy
     Zoë A. Schneider   241

17   Review of *The Family, Sex and Marriage in England 1500–1800*, by Lawrence
     Stone
     Alan MacFarlane   258

18   Illegitimacy and Infanticide in Early Modern Russia
     David L. Ransel   268

19   Public Leisure and the Rise of Salons
     Deborah Hertz   282

Part V   The Rise of the Modern State System   **297**

Introduction   299

20   The Crisis in Assumptions about Political Thinking
     Felix Gilbert   305

21   From Contractual Monarchy to Constitutionalism
     Gerhard Oestreich   317

22   The Paradoxes of State Power
     John Brewer   332

23   The Power of the King
     Antonio Feros   348

24   The Royal Government, Guilds, and the Seamstresses of Paris, Normandy,
     and Provence
     Clare Haru Crowston   362

Part VI   Research Paradigms, Old and New   **377**

Introduction   379

25   The Courtization of the Warriors
     Norbert Elias   385

26   Women on Top
     Natalie Zemon Davis   398

27   The Contrasts
     Alfred W. Crosby, Jr.   412

28   Transcending East–West Dichotomies: State and Culture Formation in
     Six Ostensibly Disparate Areas
     Victor Lieberman   419

29   Introduction to *The Great Divergence. China, Europe, and the Making of
     the Modern World Economy*
     Kenneth Pomeranz   430

30   Between Carnival and Lent: The Scientific Revolution at the Margins
     of Culture
     Paula Findlen   443

Index   459

ACKNOWLEDGMENTS

The editor and publisher gratefully acknowledge the permission granted to reproduce the copyright material in this book:

1 Anthony Pagden, "The Legacy of Rome," pp. 11–28 from *Lords of All the World: Ideologies of Empire in Spain, Britain and France c.1500–c.1800*. New Haven and London: Yale University Press, 1995. © 1995 by Anthony Pagden. Reproduced with permission of Yale University Press.

2 David Eltis, "Europe and the Atlantic Slave Systems," pp. 258–62, 274–80 from *The Rise of African Slavery in the Americas*. Cambridge: Cambridge University Press, 2000. © 2000 by David Eltis. Reproduced with permission of Cambridge University Press and the author.

3 Karin Friedrich, "History, Myth and Historical Identity," pp. 71–81, 83–91, 94–5 from *The Other Prussia: Royal Prussia, Poland and Liberty, 1569–1772*. Cambridge: Cambridge University Press, 2000. © 2000 by Karin Friedrich. Reproduced with permission of Cambridge University Press and the author.

4 James Van Horn Melton, "The Theresian school reform of 1774," pp. 209–29 from *Absolutism and the eighteenth-century origins of compulsory schooling in Prussia and Austria*. Cambridge: Cambridge University Press, 1988. © 1988 by Cambridge University Press. Reproduced with permission of Cambridge University Press and the author.

5 Thomas Kaiser, "The Evil Empire? The Debate on Turkish Despotism in Eighteenth-Century French Political Culture," pp. 6–21, 33–4 from *The Journal of Modern History* 72 (March 2000), 36586. © 2000 by The University of Chicago. Reproduced with permission of The University of Chicago Press.

6 Denis Crouzet, "*Ira Dei super nos*: le révélateur de la piété panique de 1583," pp. 287–301, 305–10 from *Les Guerriers de Dieu: La violence au temps des troubles de réligion (vers 1525–vers 1610)*, trans. James B. Collins. Paris: Éditions Champ Vallon, 1990. © 1990 by Éditions Champ Vallon.

7 Maureen Flynn, "The Charitable Activities of Confraternities," pp. 44–51, 54–70, 72–3, from *Sacred Charity: Confraternities and Social Welfare in Spain, 1400–1700*. New York and Basingstoke: Cornell University Press and Macmillan, 1989.

8 David Warren Sabean, "The sins of belief: A village remedy for hoof and mouth disease (1796)," pp. 174–98, 234–5 from *Power in the Blood: Popular culture and village discourse in early modern Germany*. Cambridge: Cambridge University Press, 1984. Reproduced with permission of Cambridge University Press.

9 Sherrin Marshall, "Dutiful Love and Natural Affection: Parent–Child Relationships in the Early Modern Netherlands," pp. 13–29 from *The Dutch Gentry, 1500–1650: Family, Faith and Fortune*. Westport, CT: Greenwood Press, 1987. © by Sherrin Marshall.

10 Lucien Febvre, "A Possible Support for Irreligion; The Sciences," pp. 380–400 from *The Problem of Unbelief in the Sixteenth Century: The Religion of Rabelais*, trans. Beatrice Gottlieb. Cambridge, MA and Paris: Harvard University Press and Éditions Albin Michel, 1982, French original, 1941. English translation © 1992 by the President and Fellows of Harvard College. Reprinted by permission of Harvard University Press and Éditions Albin Michel.

11 Richard A. Goldthwaite, "The Material Culture of the Church and Incipient Consumerism," pp. 129–48 from *Wealth and the Demand for Art in Italy 1300–1600*. Baltimore and London: The Johns Hopkins University Press, 1993. © 1993 by Richard A. Goldthwaite. Reprinted with permission of The John Hopkins University Press.

12 Kathleen Wellman, "From a Culture of Science toward the Enlightenment," pp. 367–82 from *Making Science Social: The Conferences of Théophraste Renaudot 1633–1642*. Norman: University of Oklahoma Press, 2003. © 2003 by the University of Oklahoma Press, Norman. Reprinted by permission. All rights reserved.

13 Patricia Seed, "Contesting Possession," pp. 128–40 from *Ceremonies of Possession in Europe's Conquest of the New World, 1492–1640*. Cambridge: Cambridge University Press, 1995. © Cambridge University Press. Reproduced with permission of Cambridge University Press and the author.

14 Roger Chartier, "Ritual and Print Discipline and Invention: The *Fête* in France from the Middle Ages to the Revolution," pp. 13–24 from *The Cultural Uses of Print in Early Modern France*, French original in *Diogène* 110, 51–71. Princeton, NJ: Princeton University Press, 1987 (April–June 1980). © 1987 by Princeton University Press. Reprinted by permission of Princeton University Press.

15 Merry E. Wiesner, "Political, Economic, and Legal Structures," pp. 11, 13–35 from *Working Women in Renaissance Germany*. New Brunswick, NJ: Rutgers University Press, 1986. © 1986 by Rutgers, The State University. Reprinted by permission of Rutgers University Press.

16 Zoë A. Schneider, "Women before the Bench: Female Litigants in Early Modern Normandy," pp. 1–3, 5–20, 24, 26–32 from *French Historical Studies* 23(1) (Winter 2000), Duke University Press. © 2000 by the Society for French Historical Studies. All rights reserved. Used by permission of the publisher.

17 Alan Macfarlane, "Review of *The Family, Sex and Marriage in England 1500–1800*, by Lawrence Stone," pp. 103–10, 113–18, 123–6 from *History and Theory*. Blackwell Publishing, 1979. © 1979 Blackwell Publishing Ltd. Reproduced with permission of the publisher.

18 David L. Ransel, "Illegitimacy and Infanticide in Early Modern Russia," pp. 8–30 from *Mothers of Misery: Child Abandonment in Russia*. Princeton, NJ: Princeton University Press, 1988. © 1988 Princeton University Press, 1990 paperback edition. Reprinted by permission of Princeton University Press.

19 Deborah Hertz, "Public Leisure and the Rise of Salons," pp. 75–7, 95–116 from *Jewish High Society in Old Regime Berlin*. New Haven, CT and London: Yale University Press, 1988. Reproduced by permission of Yale University Press.

20 Felix Gilbert, "The Crisis in Assumptions about Political Thinking," pp. 105–11, 115, 117–19, 123, 128–31, 133–4, 136–9, 142–5, 148–52 from *Machiavelli and Guicciardini: Politics and History in Sixteenth-Century Florence*. Princeton, NJ: Princeton University Press, 1965. © 1965 by Princeton University Press. Reproduced with kind permission of Mrs Gilbert. All rights reserved.

21 Gerhard Oestreich, "From contractual monarchy to constitutionalism," pp. 166–77, 179–86 from *Neostoicism and the early modern state*. Cambridge: Cambridge University Press, 1982. © Cambridge University Press 1982. Reproduced with permission of Cambridge University Press and the author.

22 John Brewer, "The Paradoxes of State Power," pp. 137–54, 161 from *The Sinews of Power: War, Money and the English State, 1688–1715*. New York: Alfred A. Knopf, 1989. Copyright © 1998 by John Brewer.

23 Antonio Feros, "The power of the king," pp. 71–6, 78–88, 90 from *Kingship and Favoritism in the Spain of Philip III, 1598–1621*. Cambridge: Cambridge University Press, 2000. © by Antonio Feros 2000. Reproduced with permission of Cambridge University Press and the author.

24 Clare Haru Crowston, "The Royal Government, Guilds, and the Seamstresses of Paris, Normandy, and Provence," pp. 173–5, 179–93, 213–16 from *Fabricating Women: The Seamstress of Old Regime France, 1675–1791*. Durham, NC and London: Duke University Press, 2001. © 2001 by Duke University Press. All rights reserved. Used by permission of the publisher.

25 Norbert Elias, "The Courtization of the Warriors," pp. 387–97, 422–9 from *The Civilizing Process: Sociogenetic and Psychogenetic Investigations*. Oxford: Blackwell, 2000 [1994]. © 1994, 2000 by Norbert Elias Stichting. English translation © 1978, 1982 by Blackwell Publishing Ltd. Reproduced with permission of the publisher.

26 Natalie Zemon Davis, "Women on Top," pp. 124–42, 150–1 from *Society and Culture in Early Modern France*. Stanford, CA and Cambridge: Stanford University Press and Polity Press, 1975. © 1975 by Natalie Zemon Davis. Used with the permission of Stanford University Press, www.sup.org and Polity Press, Cambridge.

27 Alfred W. Crosby, Jr., "The Contrasts," pp. 3–6, 165–73 from *The Columbian Exchange: Biological and Cultural Consequences of 1492*. Westport, CT: Greenwood Press, 1972. © 1972 by Alfred W. Crosby, Jr. Reproduced with permission of Greenwood Publishing Group, Inc, Westport, CT.

28 Victor Lieberman, "Transcending East–West Dichotomies: State and Culture Formation in Six Ostensibly Disparate Areas," pp. 19–38 from *Beyond Binary Histories: Re-imagining Eurasia to c. 1830*. Ann Arbor: University of Michigan Press, 1999. Reproduced with permission of The University of Michigan Press.

29 Kenneth Pomeranz, "Introduction," pp. 3–17 from *The Great Divergence: China, Europe, and the Making of the Modern World Economy*. Princeton, NJ: Princeton University Press, 2000. © 2000 by Princeton University Press. Reprinted by permission of Princeton University Press.

30 Paula Findlen, "Between Carnival and Lent: The Scientific Revolution at the Margins of Culture," pp. 243–67 from *Configurations* 6(2). Johns Hopkins University Press, 1998. © 1998 by The Johns Hopkins University Press and Society for Literature and Science. All rights reserved. Reprinted with permission of The Johns Hopkins University Press.

Every effort has been made to trace copyright holders and to obtain their permission for the use of copyright material. The publisher apologizes for any errors or omissions in the above list and would be grateful if notified of any corrections that should be incorporated in future reprints or editions of this book.

Introduction: Interpreting Early Modern Europe

Karen L. Taylor and James B. Collins

Historiographical debates in progress since the 1960s have fundamentally redefined early modern Europe. New questions, such as the role of women in society or the nature of the relationship between Europeans and non-Europeans, drive the work of many contemporary scholars. Old questions, such as religion and politics or state-building, receive new formulations. This reader seeks to blend the new and the old, to give students a taste of the elaborate banquet offered by today's scholarship on early modern Europe.

The editors have chosen to divide the book into six parts: (1) *evolving early modern identities*; (2) *changes in religion and cultural life*; (3) *the revolution of the mind*; (4) *the roles of women in early modern society*; (5) *the rise of the modern state system*; and (6) *research paradigms, old and new*. These categories are naturally somewhat arbitrary; in each case, one can see close connections between topics treated in a given category (religious dissent) and those treated in another (colonialism). The part introductions will deliberately stress these connections.

We begin with the proposition that we need to expand the traditional boundaries of "Europe," as it is reconstructed by most textbooks and collections. We have consciously chosen to include material on the Ottoman Empire and the Polish-Lithuanian Commonwealth, as well as on a broad range of other states. Chronologically, we begin in the sixteenth century and end, with one exception, in the middle of the eighteenth. As Eugene Rice has suggested, the great changes of the late fifteenth and early sixteenth centuries – the invention of printing, the Renaissance, the integration of the Eastern and Western Hemispheres, the Reformation – laid the "foundation of early modern Europe." Europe entered a new era in the second half of the eighteenth century, both in terms of the political revolutions in the Atlantic World and the dramatic economic and social changes created by the early stages of modern capitalism.

Part I: Evolving Early Modern Identities

Early modern Europeans had to redefine themselves in every aspect of their humanity. Explorers proved to Europeans the existence of vast, heavily populated continents, hitherto unknown to them. Humanists undermined the accepted meaning of fundamental texts and writers by subjecting the sources of classical times and of early Christianity to rigorous, scholarly analysis. Scientists would soon revise people's view of the heavens, and of Earth's place in the universe, to say nothing of the laws of motion and the understanding of the human body itself. Religious reformers destroyed the seemingly immemorial unity of the European Christian community. Virtually no important institution or fundamental belief of the European world of 1450 survived intact in 1650.

Much recent scholarship has dealt with the complex construction of identities necessitated by the enormous changes in early modern European life. We have defined broadly questions of identity, choosing selections, like that of Karin Friedrich, that undermine old assumptions about "national" identity, and others, such as that of Anthony Pagden, that place "Europeans" within a global context.

Part II: Changes in Religion and Cultural Life

The Reformation disrupted European societies in a way so fundamental, so central to human existence that its passions still astound us. Yet passions with roots in ethnic (the Balkans or Rwanda), religious (Algeria, France, Ireland, Kashmir, or the United States) or racial differences cause, or deepen, many modern conflicts. In the sixteenth century, as now, passions alone do not lie behind the terrible deeds; they become intertwined with more traditional personal and political motives: territorial ambitions, *realpolitik*, and simple human greed.

The intrusion of schism into a world so militantly conscious of its religious unity, indeed, into a society that defined religion largely in terms of communal unity, led to frenzied violence all over Europe. Western Europe's Atlantic encounter, and closer contact with Africa and Asia, often reinforced the old Crusading impulses, which encouraged violence in the conquest of the Amerindian empires. Bernal Díaz, companion of Cortez, repeatedly compared the *conquistadores* to the brave knights of the *Reconquista* of Spain from the Muslims and even to Charlemagne's Franks. The ongoing struggle with the Ottoman Empire in the Mediterranean encouraged similar views; later, slave traders would use the Christian "just war" theory to excuse their foul commerce.

Many early modern Europeans could not imagine a world of religious diversity, which meant their kingdom/state had to be a Christian kingdom on earth. The Burgundian town deputies to the Estates General of France, meeting in 1560, expressed the near-universal opinion of their day: "this kingdom, which from time immemorial has been Christian, finds itself divided into several sects . . . Such division is the cause of subversion and mutation of kingdoms and the depopulation of all states."[1]

Our selections provide some sense of the variety and depth of these changes, ranging from Denis Crouzet's contribution about religious processions in northern France in 1583, to David Sabean's anthropological dissection of the ritual burial of a live bull in late eighteenth-century Rhineland Germany.

Part III: The Revolution of the Mind

During the long night of plague and war that lasted from the middle of the fourteenth century until the middle of the fifteenth, the cold plains of northern Europe felt the first warm winds of intellectual and moral change from Renaissance Italy. Many of those changes had already begun in medieval times, but Italian Humanism gave them new impetus. Areas such as Flanders absorbed the Italian artistic and cultural revolution in the early fifteenth century and then served, in their turn, as centers of diffusion. The spread of printing from Rhineland Germany into other parts of Europe after 1450/60 further accelerated the spread of new cultural norms. The Italian wars accelerated the acceptance of Renaissance ideas by the elites who participated in them, whether from France or the far-flung realms of Charles V. European aristocracy turned openly to Italian models of dress, of comportment, and of taste. Classical ideas fundamentally modified European political thought and literature, indeed all cultural life.

In the seventeenth and eighteenth centuries, the "Scientific Revolution" and the Enlightenment drove European societies in fundamentally new directions. Taken together, the Renaissance, "Scientific Revolution," and Enlightenment provided the foundations for modern intellectual life. Modern scholarship has gone beyond the traditional focus on changes among elites, seeking to reconstruct the world of *mentalités* (collective states of mind) of earlier times.

The study of *mentalités* began with the work of scholars such as Lucien Febvre, in the 1930s and 1940s, so we have included a selection from his work to give some idea of how the field has evolved. Recent scholarship, like the fascinating research of Kathleen Wellman on how seventeenth-century French intellectuals understood the science of their time, has called into question the old paradigm of the "Scientific Revolution" associated with scholars from the 1950s, like Herbert Butterfield. This new work demonstrates that the teleological view of the reception of "scientific" ideas does not make much sense. In Part VI, the selection from Patricia Seed shows the uses to which this new scientific data could be put, outside of the realm of science itself.

Part IV: The Roles of Women in Early Modern Society

Religious schism provided a critical element in the evolution of new roles for women in early modern society. Some men, like the French Protestant historian Agrippa d'Aubigné, who insisted his daughters know Latin and praised learned women to them (yet warned them against the dangers of being learned women), or the great poet Pierre de Ronsard, who placed "honor, virtue, grace, and knowledge" before "beauty" among his true love's qualities, respected and defended individual women. Yet, whether we look at legal ordinances on marriage, at official harangues about the family and the state, at the treatises of Jean Bodin or Robert Filmer, or at guild rules, from top to bottom in society, European men made a concerted effort to suppress the collective individuality of women.

Two processes were at work. First, as the generation of scholarship running from Natalie Zemon Davis's "Women on Top" (Part VI) to Merry Wiesner-Hanks's path-breaking work on women in German lands argued, women had to struggle against this renewed male assault on their legal, economic, and social position. The work of specialists on the sixteenth century, like Davis and Wiesner-Hanks, documents the first phase of that assault. Since the 1990s, however, young scholars like Zoë Schneider and Clare Crowston (Part V) have cast doubt on the validity of this model for the late seventeenth and eighteenth centuries. Every empirical study of a group of women – seamstresses, actresses, linen merchants, litigants – has found that women seized the day and empowered themselves between 1680 and 1780. In France, more women lived on their own, headed taxable households, and ran businesses; women even created new professions, like *marchande de mode* (fashion merchant), that took advantage of the burgeoning market economy. Moreover, every study of that economy, be it in England, the Netherlands, or Italy, argues that women, not men, were the buyers driving the revolution in consumption.

Early modern European states consistently stressed the special authority of fathers at precisely the moment when they stressed the special authority of the monarch. The king would have supreme authority in his kingdom; the father would have supreme authority in his family. Both authorities came from, and were modeled on, the supreme authority of God the Father. Again and again, Europeans referred to the three fathers: God the Father; the king, father of his people; the father of the family.

Male elites had to confront the possibility that one of the cornerstones of their society, the patriarchal family, had to be reformulated. The rising tide of individualism created a new threat to patriarchal society: the individual woman. Threatened in this way, men responded with a ferocious legal assault on women.

Many women, both Protestant and Catholic, used the newly fluid religious situation to create positions of power for themselves. Moreover, the central role of mothers in providing the first stages of moral education for their children gave women a particularly important new role in the *formation* of future generations. This part examines the "woman question" as it touched on various aspects of European society, from the legal activism of Norman women to the cultural dynamism of Jewish *salonnières* in late eighteenth-century Berlin. Many of the articles in other parts, such as that by Clare Crowston, illustrate the wider dimension of women's lives in early modern Europe. Women responded to the male assault with a renewed, and often successful offensive of their own.

Part V: The Rise of the Modern State System

The disorder of early modern times and the rapid growth of the royal governments called for a new political philosophy. Practical debates about lawmaking, taxation, and religion had profound theoretical consequences. The philosophic debates focused on law-making authority, turning that authority into the entity we know as sovereignty. In creating the idea of unified, inalienable sovereignty, and in juxtaposing that creation with the rise of a larger, more powerful government, the people of late sixteenth-century Europe left to the modern world one of its defining intellectual and practical characteristics: the sovereign state.

The older scholarship posited stark differences among European states, but modern researchers, like John Brewer, have found far more in common among states like England and France than earlier historians, often blinded by nationalist prejudice, had done. Thomas Kaiser's article shows how debates in eighteenth-century France helped create an image not only of the Ottoman Empire, and of "Asia," but of the French monarchy. As Felix Gilbert suggests, in one of our earliest selections, modern debates about the nature of political society owe much to the great writers of Renaissance Florence, such as Machiavelli and Guicciardini. Their writings profoundly influenced political thinkers throughout the European world.

Part VI: Research Paradigms, Old and New

Where do historians get their ideas for research? We can easily look back and see the intellectual roots of much historical scholarship in the ideas of the prominent thinkers of earlier times, above all the nineteenth and early twentieth centuries. Sociologists like Weber and Durkheim, philosophers like Hegel and Nietzsche, and political economists like Ricardo and Marx have inspired many modern historians. The great nineteenth-century historians, like Acton, Frijn, Ranke,

Solov'ev, and Michelet, created frameworks, such as chronological periodization, that still organize most historical writing. Recent historians, such as Natalie Zemon Davis, or sociologists, like Norbert Elias, have set forth broad theories that two or three generations of historians have now tested. Alfred Crosby brought the study of the environment into the consciousness of historians in a new way, lighting the fuse for the explosion of scholarship in environmental history in the 1990s.

Today's scholarship reflects the influence of these giants, but determining the direction of the next generation of research is more of a guessing game. In the selections from Lieberman, Pomeranz, and Seed we have opted for two major trends: (1) the progressive expansion of the frame of reference for "Europe," which we believe historians will view less and less as an isolated entity, and more as an integral part of a global process; and (2) the fundamental rejection of confining intellectual constructs, such as "Scientific Revolution." Scientists themselves have radically altered their view of "science," and historians like Seed or Wellman (Part III) are following suit.

The Portuguese voyages around Africa to Asia revolutionized world trade, making Europeans part of a global economy. The "voyages of European discovery" fundamentally altered European worldviews, a process already underway by means of Humanism and soon to be expanded by the religious and scientific revolutions of the sixteenth and seventeenth centuries. Historians, we believe, will soon begin to rethink categories like the Reformation, placing the contest between Catholics and Protestants into a global rather than a purely European context. The people living in the sixteenth century, especially the Protestants of northwestern Europe, viewed it so: they wrote constantly of their fears of a globalizing Catholicism overwhelming the Protestant redoubt along the North Sea. Historians of state development will take cues from scholars like Lieberman (a specialist on Asia) and begin to consider the changes in the European state system within a Eurasian, not simply European, context. Much like the people whom they study, they will find New Worlds to discover.

NOTE

1 AD Côte d'Or, C 3469, Third Estate *cahiers* for the Estate General of 1560, deputies of the duchy of Burgundy, meeting in Dijon, November 1560.

Part I

EVOLVING EARLY MODERN IDENTITIES

Introduction

Who are we? Early modern Europeans had many answers to that question, as well as to its more modern variant, who am I? The question always has multiple spatial dimensions, from the cottage next door, to the village down the road, to the Earth itself. An individual's relationship to the universe takes in both the spatial and temporal dimensions, and affects attitudes toward those separated from us by time, like the dead. Early modern Europeans included the dead within their community, as the location of their cemeteries – in the center of the village – makes manifest, just as they lived by laws that protected the future members of the group (above all the family), in matters such as inheritance.

The comforting cocoon of a world and a universe with known limits, of rural religious uniformity, suddenly burst between 1450 and 1550. Everything that been known and certain came undone: truth became falsehood, dream became reality. Little wonder that Thomas More invented Western Europe's first *Utopia* (1516) since classical times. The world took on a new shape, both literally and figuratively. At the start of the voyages of exploration, a book like *John Mandeville's Travels* could serve as a guide to Christopher Columbus on his trip into the Atlantic; by the middle of the sixteenth century, Mandeville's *Travels* had become a book of fables, not one of geography.[1] Nor did the heavens remain in place: Copernicus, Kepler, Galileo, and others removed the Earth from the center of the universe and, in so doing, redefined humankind's place in the natural order. Moreover, the European invention of printing in the 1440s (in Mainz) enabled information about the "New World" to spread to elites, who gobbled up travelers' accounts of their voyages. Scientific discoveries often spread more slowly, as Kathleen Wellman's essay (Part II) illustrates, but few genuinely literate people in eighteenth-century Europe were unfamiliar with the heliocentric view of the solar system.

Defining oneself in the world created by Columbus and da Gama, in the universe discovered by Galileo and Newton, in the fractured Christianity of Luther, Calvin, and the Council of Trent, could not have been easy. Europeans usually began their self-definition with a group, often their family. Individual self-definition became more pronounced in Europe between 1450 and 1800, a process that began in some ways with elites and in others with the lower classes, spreading from one to the other during the eighteenth century. In contemporary Western society individualism

– the belief in the supreme status of the individual – has replaced systems of belief, ubiquitous in early modern Europe as they are in many less-developed countries today, that assume the primacy of the group. Modern economists have pointed out that this ideological shift parallels an economic one, from family or household as the basic economic unit of production to the individual as that unit.

Most early modern Europeans lived on a group enterprise: a farm. In large measure because survival depended on the group, individuality had a relatively limited range of expression. People at all ranks of society viewed decisions we today would take to be individual, such as marriage, as primarily group choices. The dramatic shift in attitudes toward the marriage decision took place first with the lower classes; change moved from the bottom up. In the late sixteenth century, French couples seeking Church dispensation from the rules on consanguity invoked the wishes of the two families, the suitable station of the prospective partners, and the economic viability of the proposed household in their requests.[2] By the middle of the eighteenth century, such couples cited their mutual love and respect as the justification for the marriage. In England, as Alan Macfarlane points out (Part IV), individuals below the level of the elite often made individual marriage choices as early as the fourteenth century. Moreover, Chaucer's "Franklin's Tale" offers clear evidence that an ideology of equality within marriage already had powerful champions by the 1380s. Even allowing for greater individuality and individual choice than traditional historiography would suggest, however, the group remained paramount in early modern societies.

Early modern political theorists like Jean Bodin, writing in 1576, took rulership to mean the government of "several households"; those households, not individuals, formed the basis of civil society. Conversely, the fundamental unit of political (civic) society, of the commonwealth (*res publica*), was an individual: the citizen. The nobility, above all, had a strong sense of this dual identity: they had a profound sense of attachment to a family, and of their duties to ancestors and descendants alike. In the seventeenth century, many aristocratic families hired writers to produce a history of their family, and throughout Europe princes conducted "reforms" of the nobility, in theory to cleanse it of "dirty" commoners who had illegally usurped titles and noble privileges. Yet nobles also had a clear sense of themselves as individuals, and demanded recognition of their individuality. They resisted more strongly than any other group the efforts by central governments to treat everyone the same. Where our contemporary individualism, by definition, is intertwined with egalitarianism – we are all equal, so we all have the right to be treated as an individual; early modern nobles viewed indiscriminate egalitarianism as the greatest threat to real individuality.[3]

By the late seventeenth or eighteenth century, writers such as John Locke (*Second Treatise of Government*, 1681) or Jean-Jacques Rousseau (*The Social Contract*, 1762) had accepted the radical idea of Thomas Hobbes (*Leviathan*, 1651) that individuals created political society by means of a contract. By individuals, these writers meant men. Hobbes bluntly stated that women lacked political rights not because men "were the more excellent sex," but because men had established the commonwealths and had deliberately disenfranchised females to enhance male power. Moreover, writers such as Locke really meant men of property: "the purpose of society is the preservation of property," by which he meant "lives, liberties, and estates."[4]

The dividing line between the men of property and those without had a distinct moral overtone. In many Italian cities, like Siena, the town council was chosen exclusively from the *buoni uomini*, that is, the men of property: the good men (*hommes de bien*) were the men who had goods (*biens*). In Spain, the sixteenth-century picaresque novel *Lazarillo de Tormes* (1554) carries ironic admonishments to its hero to associate with *los buenos*, those both wealthy and good. The Calvinist doctrine of the elect, which came to suggest that worldly success was the outward manifestation of God's blessing, was thus not a radical shift in ideology, as scholars following the ideas of Max Weber have argued, but the restatement of the old idea that the men of property held a virtual monopoly on virtue.[5] Christ might have said that the poor were "blessed in spirit," and the rich may have sought out the poor for ritualized prayer (hiring poor people to mourn at their funerals, for example), but in day-to-day life, European urban elites, Protestant, Jewish, and Catholic alike, associated solid prosperity with moral rectitude.

The group–individual dichotomy had profound implications for identity, and for interpersonal relationships. The composition of a household, for example, defined the legal identity of women. The household had a legal identity, which could only be assumed by its head; logically, to royal apologists, the body politic, composed of those households, also could have only one head: the king. Everywhere, law made the adult man the head of the household, so all living under his authority had a restricted legal identity. If he died, however, and no legally adult male could take his place, then the adult woman became the legal personification of the household. Widows headed at least ten percent of European households in 1600; women headed perhaps twenty percent of them by 1780. In 1600, very few adult, never-married women headed a household; by 1780, a significant number of never-married adult urban women did so. Many a married woman also ran her own business, independent from the trade of her husband; such women had an independent legal identity almost everywhere in Europe.

On the level of the most obvious form of individual identity, gender distinction, early modern European society faced dramatic changes. The transition from a society built on groups to one built on individuals transformed the meaning of dependence, and with it the fundamental identity of women. As men struggled to define themselves as individuals, they also faced the question of whether or not women were individuals, too. This problem became manifest during the French Revolution, when the radical Jacobins simultaneously created universal manhood suffrage and destroyed women's political rights.

Perhaps men had such fears of female individualism because women so clearly took the lead in establishing personal individuality. Women were the first to buy mirrors, which spread to the mass of the population only in the eighteenth century. Mirror in hand, a woman (later a man) could make up her (his) own mind about what she (he) looked like; prior to the widespread use of the mirror, people's daily image of themselves came overwhelmingly from others. The image people, first women, projected also changed: urban women wore more colorful clothes and began to own a greater variety of garments and accessories. Aside from a few cities in the Low Countries and Italy, only the upper classes (at most, ten percent of the population) had had such sartorial variety prior to 1700. The long-term effects of democratization of dress can be seen on any street today: the modern business suit is an adaptation of the outfit worn by eighteenth-century working men.

At the same time that Europeans faced the move from a society built on groups to one built on individuals, they faced other challenges to familiar identities. All European societies rested on the assumption that people were unequal. Christian doctrine had long emphasized the spiritual equality of souls, but secular society rested on an elaborate system of dominance, often called the society of orders. Nobles dominated commoners; landowners dominated peasants; urban elites dominated countryfolk; men dominated women. Assumptions about innate inequality remained fundamental long after the period under investigation here, but the long simmering popular belief in human equality received new impetus from the Scientific Revolution. René Descartes boldly stated, in his *Discourse on Method* (1637), that all men had reason (in fact, possession of reason made them human), and were thus essentially equal. That doctrine transformed the "woman question," so long debated in places like France and England. Whereas authors had traditionally debated who was better, women or men, after Descartes, those supporting rights for women often argued that they were equal. A generation after Descartes, his disciple, François Poullain de la Barre, published *On the Equality of the Two Sexes* (quickly translated from French into English and other languages), built precisely on a syllogistic chain of reasoning that: (1) everyone agreed that all humans had reason; (2) everyone agreed that women were human; (3) therefore, as humans, women *by definition* had reason and were equal to men. Misogynists rejected this argument, on the grounds that women had less developed reason,[6] but modern feminism triumphed on precisely these grounds.

Following lines laid down by Aristotle, European societies also officially believed people were born for a certain function, and that a proper society relied on each person fulfilling that function. Those who tried to move outside their "natural" position threatened society, so they had to be repressed, or punished, or, in extreme cases, eliminated. The man who allowed his wife to run the household might have to listen to "rough music" (charivari) or take a Skimmington ride (be strapped to a pole and paraded through the village); the woman who became engaged to a man from outside her village might be collectively raped by the young male villagers; the wealthy Jew might be assaulted or his house pillaged in a riot; the leader of a demonstration might be drawn and quartered, his body parts left to dangle from trees outside the town gate for a month; the religious nonconformist might be burned at the stake. All of these things did happen, and the forces of order invariably cited attacks on the "natural" order as a justification for their action.

Yet we cannot be misled by either their rhetoric or the occasional violent outbursts of repression. Early modern Europe was a society in motion. All of the assumptions of the fifteenth century had to be abandoned. Europeans had to re-create their identities in every aspect of life. Contrary to the rhetoric of stability and order, or to the model of a stable, sedentary society promulgated by so many modern historians, the social reality was a maelstrom of change. Europeans lived in two worlds: pockets of order and stability existed everywhere, and endured for centuries; around these pockets of order, a world of movement, indeed of apparent chaos, swirled menacingly. Unable to stop it, Europeans spasmodically, violently, and futilely lashed out against it.[7]

This conflict existed in matters as simple as one's name. Europeans often expressed their individuality by adopting a nickname or public name; wandering journeymen always did so, and most market women followed the same custom. The name could be physical – Big John, Red (haired) Mary, One-Eyed Sam – or geographic – the Parisian, the Fleming. The authorities strictly forbade the use of such names and demanded that everyone, everywhere, at all times use their legal name; the records make it abundantly clear that many people did not. In villages, it would have been absurd, because so many people shared the same name and surname that nicknames were essential. Among journeymen, most of whom belonged to illegal brotherhoods, one could hardly expect them to list their legal name on the registers kept by the brotherhood.

In the realm of faith, the Catholic Church's God had a difficult three centuries. The early reformers had either failed, like John Wycliffe in England, or been restricted to a small area, like Jan Hus in Bohemia. Their ideas lived on, however; Martin Luther turned them into a spiritual revolution in 1517, when he posted his 95 Theses against indulgences on the door of the Wittenberg castle church. Soon other "Protestants," as they became known, had raised objections to the doctrines of the Catholic Church and to the moral laxity of its clergy. Reformers within the Catholic Church did much the same. By the second half of the sixteenth century, the various sides in the doctrinal disputes had created real distance among themselves, a process firmly hardened by the decrees of the Council of Trent (1543–63), which codified official Catholic doctrine.

Historians have traditionally viewed the sixteenth century as the great age of the Reformation, of the successful attack on the Catholic Church and the subsequent division of Western Christendom. Yet contemporaries often had a different view. In the middle of the sixteenth century, Catholics and Protestants alike believed in the possibility of a church council that would reconcile their differences. By the early seventeenth century, the Protestants believed themselves everywhere under siege from a resurgent Catholic Church. Protestant literature often points out the massive advances made by the Catholics *outside* of Europe, an element of early modern religious history usually ignored by the Eurocentric historiography. Millions of Amerindians converted (often under extreme duress) to Catholicism, and the Catholic Church made inroads in Africa and Asia, too. In many respects the integration of Asian believers into the mainstream Catholic Church posed as great a problem as Protestantism; the Chinese Rites Controversy, in which Jesuits in China argued that Catholic rites there had to integrate Chinese practices and beliefs, ultimately shattered the Jesuit Order and, because of the Pope's rejection of that position, slowed dramatically the spread of Catholicism worldwide.

The dichotomy between group and individual evolved in a climate of unimaginable chaos. The shattering of the unity of Western Christianity dramatically altered the relationship of neighbor to neighbor and of individual to God, thus of individual to the state. By the 1560s, strong voices argued the direct connection of the individual conscience and God and rejected forced conversion in favor of gentle persuasion.[8] These individuals pointed out that force had not worked, and that some form of concord had to be pursued. In most of Western Europe, of course, they lost the argument, leading to another century of religious war, and to a litany of cross-confessional massacre.

By the 1570s, however, one of the great powers, the Polish-Lithuanian Commonwealth, had enshrined this principle of concord in its constitution: their state was not only the Commonwealth of Many Nations, but the Commonwealth of Many Religions (Catholicism, Lutheranism, Calvinism, Orthodoxy, Judaism, Islam). Slowly, grudgingly, the Western European states came around to the same solution: Holland *de facto* in the seventeenth century; England *de facto* (with still significant restrictions on Catholics) in the middle of the eighteenth century; France in 1791. The children of European emigrants who created a new state in North America in 1787 understood the logic of the situation: they made it an article of their Constitution that the state could not establish an official Church.

Just as the unity of the Western Christian Church shattered in the early sixteenth century, so, too, did the understanding of the world itself. The European discovery of the Americas, and the integration of the Western Hemisphere into the world economy, revolutionized diets across the globe, introduced new and deadly diseases everywhere (especially among Amerindians), and made every world map in Western Europe obsolete, overnight.

Let us try to enter the worlds of a European in 1500 and in 1780. In 1500, asked to identify himself, a Frenchman might say he was Jean Charpentier, son of Pierre, and perhaps of Marie Le Brun (women did not change names at marriage), daughter of Jean Le Brun, that he lived in the village of X, worked on a given farm, tilling fields A and B (fields had names), and inhabited a certain cottage (also named). Pushed a little, he might have said he lived in a certain "country" (*pays*), meaning his tiny region, and perhaps noted that he was a subject of the King of France and of the lord under whose jurisdiction he resided. Perhaps he would have known that Jerusalem was the center of the Earth, and that the Sun and the rest of the universe revolved around the Earth. Some peasants, most townsmen would have heard of "Asia," whence came certain rare products reserved for the wealthy: silk, pepper, cloves. In some regions, Jean might have emphasized that he was a free man, not a serf; it is unlikely he would have said anything about religion, because everyone he knew practiced the same one, so there was no need to say he was a Christian, although that would have been a central part of his identity.

Men in other places might have said a few different things. Jews had been expelled from most of Western Europe by 1500: from England and France by 1400; from Spain in 1492. In 1500, many Jews lived in German, Italian, and Polish towns: tens of thousands of them lived in Provence, spread across 50 towns, but they would be expelled the following year. In those places with Jews, or on the borders touching areas of Eastern Orthodoxy or Islam, a "Christian" (Catholic) man would certainly have placed religion at the center of his identity. Given the Inquisition's persecutions of Jews and Moslems in sixteenth-century Spain, a Spanish peasant would surely have emphasized his "Christian" identity, even if (rather especially if) he was, as so many were in Valencia, a secret Muslim (*Morisco*).

Fast-forwarding to 1780, Jean Charpentier would have lost the sure identity of his forefather. He might still live on a named farm, tilling named fields, in a certain village, nestled in his little *pays*. Yet in most parts of Europe he would have to say he was a "Roman Catholic" or a "Lutheran" or a member of some other Christian Church; he would know he was a Frenchman, a subject of Louis XVI. Most people would have heard of America; many would use its products, like sugar, or grow its plants, like corn or potatoes. Townsmen would know far more about Africa, which produced the slaves to grow the sugar or coffee, and would certainly know that Jerusalem was not the center of the world, let alone the universe. Jean Charpentier (1780) also differed from his ancestors in that he knew his age: seventeenth-century French court records invariably give the ages of peasant or artisan witnesses with a phrase such as "about 40"; in the eighteenth century, every witness would give his or her exact age.[9] In the most developed parts of Western Europe, Jean would also have known how to read and write.

And what of Jeanne Charpentier, in 1500 or 1780, what would she have thought about herself? With respect to religion, occupation, and politics, she and her brother Jean would have been indistinguishable. Within these categories, their self-definitions would have remained fairly constant: for example, female–male division of labor in a household did not alter much. The Jeanne of 1780, like Jean, would have had a much greater sense of herself as an individual, and far greater freedom of action than the Jeanne of 1500.[10] Even as late as the 1680s, in the Beauvaisis region north of Paris, more than eighty percent of peasant women married someone living in their home parish; by 1750, only fifty percent did so. In the eighteenth century, far more single women moved: peasant girls came to towns to work as servants (more than ninety percent of urban female servants were rural emigrants), and saved enough money to provide their own dowry. No longer so dependent on the family for the capital to start a household, women had greater freedom to choose their own partner. The Jeanne of 1780 would have owned a mirror and far more personal items than the Jeanne of 1500. Among the richer peasant families, she would have been literate, although female literacy rates nearly everywhere lagged considerably behind those of men.

Although there had always been deep divisions between urban and rural people, by the late eighteenth century profound differences had arisen in their fundamental beliefs about how the Universe was ordered and, to some extent, why it worked as it did. As David Sabean says in his essay (Part II), describing the feelings of the peasants of Beutelsbach in 1798: "Their behavior had been shaped by the attitude of outsiders who thought that they lived in the kingdom of darkness . . . now, because of the impact of the treatment by the more enlightened and intelligent part of the nation, they had become shamed and embittered." The outside official, Belley, who conducts the investigation of the burying of the bull in Beutelsbach says, in his report, that "the villagers were not used to thinking about the connection between cause and effect," that is, in his mind, he and others who did think about cause and effect lived in the enlightened world, created by the Scientific Revolution, while the villagers did not. The rise of the pastoral in art and literature notwithstanding, urban dwellers overwhelmingly viewed rural people as savages, little understanding urban language (say German or French), and "scarcely better reason," as one French official wrote in 1675 of the Celtic-speaking Bretons.

The essays in this part speak to the multiplicity of identities held by early modern Europeans. In Thomas Kaiser's piece on "Ottoman despotism," we can see how this trope helped Europeans clearly distinguish Christian Europe, what documents of the time call the "Commonwealth of Christianity," from the Islamic world: "Ottoman Turkey was the heir to all the traditional disparaging Christian tropes regarding Islamic culture – its hypocrisy, baseness, and licentiousness – which the many crusading tracts, histories, travel books . . . endlessly repeated in their lurid narratives of cruelty, violence, ignorance, and corruption." Even when the French justified their alliance with the Turks, they accepted rather than refuted "Christian Europe's common opinion that the Turks lacked all humanity." The French merely argued that engagement, rather than estrangement was the best way to help the "savages" see the light.

Early modern times suffer from interference by their future as well as their past. Nineteenth-century historians everywhere, both consciously and unconsciously, misrepresented the history and ideas of early modern times to serve nationalist agendas of their own times. As Karin Friedrich shows, Royal Prussian local histories

> never ignored the larger dimension of the wider commonwealth . . . "it is pious work to write the history of one's fatherland." *Amor patriciae*, love of the fatherland, never entirely eclipsed the larger context . . . even sixteenth-century Prussian chronicles of monasteries and small towns never lost sight of the history of the whole Prussian province, in which such chronicles were embedded.

She draws from her Prussian sources the fundamental conclusion that nineteenth-century German historians who argued that "Danzig, Thorn, and Elbing were 'city-states' which possessed quasi-independence from the Polish-Lithuanian state" and that the German burghers of these cities lived "at odds with a foreign, hostile Polish environment, whose culture they never accepted," were completely wrong. An ethnically German burgher of Danzig had a strong sense of himself as a citizen of his city, but embedded that citizenship within a sense of being a citizen of Royal Prussia, and of the Polish-Lithuanian Commonwealth. Royal Prussian writers used the word *patria* (fatherland) to mean each of these three entities, depending on the context in which they wrote.

Those living on the Atlantic littoral, participating even indirectly in its great imperial enterprise of the sixteenth through eighteenth centuries, had to think of themselves in an even broader context. They often relied on metaphors drawn from the conflict against Islam, as when Bernal Díaz, one of the conquerors of Mexico, compared Cortez and his men to the "paladin Roland" and his companions.[11] Spanish, French, English, Portuguese, Dutch, and other texts are filled with references to bringing the one "True Faith" to the heathens of the Americas. The Spanish had to deal with far more of them – the Aztec Empire of 1519 had more than twice as many inhabitants as Spain – and had to determine the precise nature of the hitherto unimagined hordes. Bernal Díaz saw a hierarchy among Amerindians: unlike the naked savages of the West Indies, whom he regarded essentially as animals, the inhabitants of the Aztec Empire had all the attributes of real human beings: settled agriculture, a social hierarchy, fine art and craft work, and a capital city whose organization (and cleanliness) put Spanish cities to shame. Some of the Spanish soldiers, even officers, made the ultimate judgment as to the humanity of the Amerindians: they married Amerindian women, after first converting them to Christianity.

Two decades after Cortez's conquest, at the great debate about the humanity of Amerindians, held at the university in Salamanca, the Emperor Charles V himself ruled in the affirmative: Indians were human. As Anthony Pagden makes clear, this declaration of moral equality necessitated a dramatic shift in imperial thinking. It is all well and good for all men to have souls, but did they have equal reason, and equal political rights? If the Amerindians were human, then "(t)he claims to universal *dominium*, which were in the first instance the consequence of a gradually changing view of the identity of the optimal political community, necessarily involved the transfer of a definition of humanity from the moral sphere to the political." In this imperial context, Christianity could take the place that Roman law had once filled, creating "not merely political and social order," but conferring "an ethical purpose upon the entire community." At the same time, the necessity of excluding Amerindians from a political role strengthened the old idea of the Roman theorists, like Cicero, that "the *civitas*, as the sole place of human flourishing, was also, and only, the . . . political community."

This division of the human community into moral equals and political unequals proved invaluable in the denial of rights to women and in such actions as the justification of slavery in the American Constitution of 1787, or the silence of the Polish Constitution of May 3, 1791 on the issue of serfdom. David Eltis suggests that European conceptions of freedom had a direct hand both in the creation of the Atlantic world built on slave labor outside of Europe, and in the ultimate destruction of that slave system. In the period under consideration here, only the first of those processes was at work, although a powerful abolitionist movement existed, at least in the English-speaking Atlantic, by the 1750s.

The imperial question came up in a different way in East Central Europe, where the Habsburg family inherited an array of ethnically diverse territories, above all the kingdoms of Hungary and Bohemia, which they attached to their archduchy of Austria. Creating a sense of unity in such an empire proved a daunting task, as James Van Horn Melton makes clear. Empress Maria Theresa's subjects spoke more than a dozen major languages, to say nothing of local dialects. Unlike schools in late nineteenth-century France, which enforced French as the sole acceptable language, grammar schools in Maria Theresa's far-flung empire usually taught in the local language: in her Hungarian kingdom, teachers used German, Magyar, Slovak, Croat, Ruthenian, Serbian, or Romanian, depending on the language of their students. Compulsory schooling in Maria Theresa's empire thus simultaneously encouraged a sense of belonging to her empire and of being part of a distinct linguistic and religious group. The Serbian textbooks actually created a literary Serbian language, and thus gave an enormous boost to Serbian self-identity, not at all what the Empress had intended.

Maria Theresa's schools offer an outstanding example of the complexity of identities and the difficulties of fostering one overarching identity in a world that demanded (and demands) several. French or English peasants, in 1500, knew that they lived in the kingdom of France or England, in a given context thought themselves "French" or "English," yet rarely had use for such a category of identification. In his everyday life, one was an inhabitant of the village of X, spoke a local language, and practiced the same religion that every person practiced, Christianity. Other parts of Europe had stronger local identities, as in the Italian or German towns, or a more pronounced sense of religious differences, as in Balkan borderlands. German burghers, like those described by Karin Friedrich, identified with a town, with a local principality, and with a larger political community, such as the Polish-Lithuanian Commonwealth or the Holy Roman Empire. Elites had an even stronger sense of these multiple communities, particularly the larger ones. As the unity of the Commonwealth of Christianity shattered, and local communities lost power to centralizing states, senses of identity evolved. Language offers the most compelling example: sixteenth-century intellectuals wrote for an international community of scholars, in the universal language of the West, Latin; eighteenth-century members of the international republic of letters, however committed to that cosmopolitan ideal, wrote in their national languages.

NOTES

1 Fable or not, Mandeville's *Travels*, written in middle of the fourteenth century, was one of the few Western European books to argue that the world was round, hence Columbus's affection for it.

2 Canon law prohibited the marriage of those related to each other to the fifth degree – sharing a great-great-grandparent. Prior to the systematic keeping of civil registers (baptism, marriage, death), in practice few demands for an exemption extended beyond sharing a great-grandparent (for example, the bride's grandmother and groom's grandfather were brother and sister). Marriage among cousins was fairly common, especially among elites, because it enabled families to keep landed estates intact.

3 Nobles accepted other nobles as equal in a certain way, as fellow citizens, a sentiment particularly pronounced in places such as the Polish-Lithuanian Commonwealth, but did not accept the equality of a noble and a commoner.

4 Other factors, such as religion, ethnic origin, or skin color could come into play. England, later the United Kingdom, denied Catholics full political rights on the basis of their religion until the end of the nineteenth century. European states denied Jews the status of citizen, on the basis both of religion and, in some cases, "ethnicity." Political units, whether kingdoms or towns, did have naturalization procedures for immigrants. In the late seventeenth and eighteenth centuries, the question of skin color became important, especially in European colonies in the Western Hemisphere. Some European states created new rules, such as France's notorious Black Code, to exclude black people from rights.

5 The German sociologist Max Weber's *The Protestant Ethic and the Spirit of Capitalism*, published in the early twentieth century, argued that Protestantism gave rise to a new moral ethic that created the spirit of capitalism. Weber contrasted this ethic with that of other major world religions; within Europe, he contrasted it sharply with the ethic of Catholicism, which he viewed as inimical to capitalism. Few books have had so great an impact on modern historiography. Many scholars, especially in Great Britain, and to a lesser degree Continental Europe, still accept Weber's premise. The empirical evidence about early modern European capitalism suggests that Weber had the relationship backwards.

6 Europeans used this same argument against non-Europeans, such as Africans and Amerindians. Acceptance of female "equality" did not mean that a writer abandoned ideas of subordination: Poullain de la Barre placed household authority in the man's hands.

7 One might draw a contemporary parallel with respect to immigration into the United States and Western Europe. Despite the anti-immigrant rhetoric and "tightened" immigration laws, immigration into both places is at an all-time high. More immigrants entered the United States in the 1990s than in any other decade of its history. These population shifts, now as in early modern Europe, have to do with the larger forces of history, and, in the long term, have little to do with government rhetoric or policies.

8 These early efforts at concord invariably excluded atheists, and, in some cases, radical Christian groups such as the Anabaptists.

9 This difference can have two explanations: either people did not know their own age, or the courts did not care about the exact age of people of the lower classes. The former is more likely, as the courts sometimes did not give an exact age even for those of higher social status.

10 That said, women in 1500 still had unusually high wages, because of the continuing labor shortage in Europe. Women's wages as a percentage of men's peaked in about 1475 (at 80 percent in some areas), but dropped catastrophically (to 25–33 percent) by 1600, owing to population growth.

11 Bernal Díaz refers here to the legendary hero of the *Song of Roland*, a twelfth-century French epic poem about the conflict between Christians, led by Charlemagne, and Muslims, in Spain.

1

The Legacy of Rome

Anthony Pagden

> Haec est in gremium victos quae sola recepit humanumque genus communi nomine fovit matris, non dominae ritu, civesque vocavit quos domnuit nexuque pio longinqua revinxit.
>
> Claudian, *De Consulatu Stilichonis*, III, 150–4.

I

The late fifteenth century, enthused the Scottish historian William Robertson in his *History of America* of 1777, had been the period

> when Providence decreed that men were to pass the limits within which they had been so long confined, and open themselves to a more ample field wherein to display their talents, their enterprise and courage.[1]

Robertson's was a common sentiment, expressed by his contemporaries, David Hume and Adam Smith in Britain, by the abbé Raynal in France, and by the historiographer royal and Robertson's associate Juan Bautista Múñoz in Spain. In structural, political and economic terms, the colonies which first Portugal and Spain, then France and Britain, and finally, if also only fitfully, Holland, Sweden and Denmark had established in America were, as all these writers recognized, unquestionably new. Unlike their ancient predecessors, they were remote and ruled across great distances. They had been created out of a seemingly insatiable European need for precious metals, and an ambition, which the Ancients could scarcely have understood, to change the religious beliefs of their autochthonous inhabitants.

Yet for all their apparent, and much discussed, novelty the theoretical roots of the modern European overseas empires reached back into the empires of the Ancient World. It was, above

Anthony Pagden, 'The Legacy of Rome,' pp. 11–28 from *Lords of All the World: Ideologies of Empire in Spain, Britain and France c.1500–c.1800*. New Haven and London: Yale University Press, 1995.

all, Rome which provided the ideologues of the colonial systems of Spain, Britain and France with the language and political models they required, for the *Imperium romanum* has always had a unique place in the political imagination of western Europe. Not only was it believed to have been the largest and most powerful political community on earth, it had also been endowed by a succession of writers with a distinct, sometimes divinely inspired, purpose.

To understand the meaning of this imaginative dependence of the new upon the old, I shall begin by sketching in what I take to have been the determining features of the Roman empire as it came to be understood by its medieval and later by its modern commentators. . . . It is rather an attempt to capture those features which by the early sixteenth century had come to dominate the discursive practices of all who were driven to ask themselves what sort of thing an empire was, what it should be, and whether or nor its existence could be justified. These features will, in one way or another, dominate the discourse until the late eighteenth century.

II

The word "empire" is itself an elusive one, whose signification, and the contexts in which it could be employed, shifted constantly until it acquired its modern meaning in the early eighteenth century. This semantic map is still also a muddled one, and what follows is an attempt to find only one path across it.

In the first instance the Latin term "empire", *imperium*, described the sphere of executive authority possessed by the Roman magistrates, and like everything in the Roman state it had marked sacral overtones, which would survive well into the modern period.[2] It was frequently employed, particularly in the various humanistic discourses of the late fifteenth and sixteenth centuries, which borrowed their etymologies from Cicero, in the somewhat indeterminate sense which would later be captured by the word "sovereignty". The first sentence of Machiavelli's *The Prince*, for instance, begins: "All the states and dominions which have had and have empire over men . . ." ("che hanno avuto et hanno imperio sopra gli uomini . . ."). The term was also used in the more limited context, of the non-subordinate power exercised within what the Aristotelians called a "perfect community" ("perfecta communitas"). This is the sense in which it is used in the often-repeated phrase of the canonists, and later of the French jurists that, whatever the status of the emperor might be, each ruler was also an "Emperor in his own Kingdom" - *rex imperator in regno suo*.[3] As Francesco Calasso has written, this phrase "had from the beginning meant simply this: that those powers which were recognized in this period as belonging to the Emperor as 'dominus mundi', should also be recognized as those of every free king within the limits of his own kingdom".[4] "All those powers", runs the famous law code of Alfonso X of Castile, the *Siete Partidas* (Seven Parts), "which . . . Emperors have or should have over the peoples of their empires, those same, the kings must exercise in their own kingdoms" (II. i. 8).

In many instances "empire" had, by the late sixteenth century at least, become, in effect, synonymous with the earlier meanings of the term *status*, state.[5] Francis Bacon, for instance, spoke of the "Conditores Imperiorum, Founders of states and commonwealths",[6] a sense which the term retained, especially in the context of the definition of colonial relations, until the late eighteenth century. When Sir Francis Barnard, the Governor of Massachusetts Bay, declared in 1774 that "the Kingdom of Great Britain is *imperial*", he meant, as he explained, nothing other than that "it is sovereign and not subordinate to or dependent upon any earthly power".[7] As Walter Ullmann demonstrated long ago, this is also clearly the sense in which the term was used in the celebrated phrase in the Act in Restraint of Appeals of 1533: "This Realm of England is an

Empire."[8] "Empire" could also be used to express the pattern of political relationships which held together groups of peoples in "an extended system", to use J. G. A. Pocock's words, "the terms of whose association were not permanently established".[9] Such a relationship might well describe the *de facto* (and in most cases the *de iure*) relationship between Britain and her colonies. It also described the relationship between the Crowns of England, Wales and Scotland after 1707. As Thomas Pownall, Governor of Massachusetts, explained with characteristic laboriousness,

> This modelling of the people into various orders and subordinations of orders, so that it be capable of receiving and communicating any political motion, and acting under that direction as a whole is one which the Romans called by the peculiar word *Imperium*, to express which particular group or idea we have no word in English, but by adopting the word Empire. Tis by this system only that a people become a political body; tis the chain, the bonds of union by which very vague and independent particles cohere.[10]

In this context it is not insignificant that Oliver Goldsmith's *The Present State of the British Empire* of 1768 begins with 200 pages on England, Wales and Scotland.

Already by the first century CE, however, the term had also acquired something of its more familiar modern meaning. The Roman historian Sallust uses the phrase *Imperium romanum* (and he seems to have been the first to do so) to describe the geographical extent of the authority of the Roman people. And when Tacitus spoke of the Roman world as an "immense body of empire" (*immensum imperii corpus*) he was describing precisely the kind of political, and cultural, unity created out of a diversity of different states widely separated in space, and which Edmund Burke speaking in 1775 of the Spanish and British empires called "extensive and detached empire".[11] *Imperium*, in this sense, bound together different and formerly independent or "perfect" states.

Imperium could also create such states where none had previously existed. It was in recognition of this meaning of the term that, from the moment he invaded Lorraine in 869, Charles the Bald, Duke of Burgundy, styled himself "Emperor and Augustus". He may only have ruled over two territories, but to rule over more than one was, in effect, to be an "emperor". The same assumption lay behind the declaration of Alfonso VI of Castile in 1077 to be "By the Grace of God Emperor of all Spain".[12] The actual territorial ambitions of these men may have been limited but both were highly conscious of the extent to which their claims echoed those of the Roman *imperatores*, whose successor they in some sense imagined themselves to be. The greatness of states could be measured by the number and diversity of the nations of which they were constituted. "A nation extended over vast tracts of land and numbers of people", wrote Sir William Temple, "arrives in time at that ancient name of kingdom or modern of empire".[13]

All of these meanings of *imperium* survive, and sometimes combine, throughout the entire period I shall be discussing. It is only with the rise of the nineteenth-century empires, conceived as these were very largely in the aftermath of the collapse of the European colonizing ventures in America, that the term "empire" becomes limited, as it is today, to Burke's "extended empire".

III

Imperium had further, more richly nuanced, meanings still. The root sense of the word is "order" or "command".[14] In the first instance, therefore, an emperor, *imperator*, had been merely one, and generally one among many, who possessed the right to exercise *imperium*. Under the Republic the exercise of *imperium* had been restricted to the Senate, which operated in the name of the

Roman people. After the establishment of the Principate, the title became limited to a group of army commanders whose *imperium* derived not, as had that of the Republican magistrature, from the civil sphere (*domi*), but instead from the military (*militiae*). (The division between these two, Edward Gibbon was later to observe, was responsible for the corruption which finally brought the empire to an end.)[15] Augustus, although he paid due deference to the "empire of the Roman people" (*imperium populi romani*), expected the honour due to the people to be paid to him. And by the first century Roman jurists Gaius and Ulpian had both come to insist that the *imperium* of the "prince emperor" absorbed that of the *imperium populi Romani*.[16]

Since all empires began with conquests the association of "empire", understood as extended territorial dominion, with military rule has lasted as long as imperialism itself. But the Roman emperors were not only generals. In time, they also became judges, and although the famous phrase in the *Digest* (1.3.31) that the prince was an "unfettered legislator" – "princeps legibus solutus" – had originally only exempted the emperor from certain rules, it came to imply the existence of a supreme legislative authority, and was interpreted in this way by the medieval glossators on the texts of the Roman Law. The emperor may still have had a moral obligation, one which even the most absolute of early modern monarchs were to retain, to observe his own commands; but there was no legal force which could compel them, even in theory, to do so. It is easy to see how, in time, *imperium* came to donate supreme military and legislative power over widespread and diverse territories. This is why Augustus had considered taking the title Romulus, as the founder of the new Rome, although, according to his biographer, reverence for the ancestors prevented him from doing so, and why in later generations the title Augustus itself became synonymous with absolutism in this extended sense.[17] To claim to be an *imperator* was to claim a degree, and eventually a kind of power, denied to mere kings. And the theocratic dimension which *imperium* acquired during the reign of Augustus, and which was reinforced by the Christian emperors and their apologists, widened still further the distinction between imperial and royal authority.

[. . .]

The transformation of the status of the Roman emperor from Augustus to Constantine the Great effectively involved the transformation of a Roman *princeps* into a theocratic Hellenistic monarch, no matter how far removed in historical origins the Roman court might have been from those of the Macedonian monarchy.[18] In the seventh century this understanding of what it was to exercise *imperium* was identified by St Isidore of Seville with the Greek loan-word, "monarchy". "Monarchies", he wrote, "are those in which the principate belongs to one alone, as Alexander was among the Greeks and Julius among the Romans."[19] Henceforth – and this will have important consequences, in particular for Spain in the sixteenth century – the term "monarchy" was frequently used as a synonym for "empire", to describe a domain composed of a number of different states in which the legislative will of a single ruler was unquestioned, one where not only was the prince "legibus solutus", but the laws were the expression of the prince's will.

[. . .]

It was this identification with empire, understood as a diversity of territories under a single legislative authority, and empire understood as monarchy, which underpins the medieval and early-modern conflict between empire and republic. For, in principle, there was no reason why a true republic – a *respublica* – could not also be an empire, although it clearly could not, at least until Montesquieu shifted the terms of the discussion in the eighteenth century, be a monarchy. Both Athens and Rome had, of course, been republican empires. Mere size, as Alexander Hamilton pointed out in 1788, was no impediment to true republican government, so long as the various parts of the state constituted "an association of states or a confederacy".[20] Nor, as Hamilton stressed on more than one occasion, was the fact of its republican constitution any reason for preventing the United States from becoming a true empire, "able to dictate the terms of the connection between the old world and the new".[21]

The conflict between the political visions of empire and republic is based on the assumption that because all empires are founded upon conquests none, in Hamilton's terms, are in fact ever able to achieve the transition from an extended assembly of states to a true confederacy. Eventually all are destined to be ruled by single individuals exercising supreme, if not arbitrary, power, and so all are ultimately destined to transform themselves into monarchies. The Roman Principate had been responsible not only for greatly enlarging the territorial limits of the Roman *Imperium*, it had also in the process conferred upon it a new political identity, an identity which was a denial of precisely those political values – the participation of all the citizens in the governance of the state – which had been responsible for its creation. As many later commentators observed, only Sparta among the republics of the Ancient World, and Venice among those of the modern, had managed to maintain their political integrity over an extended period of time, and both had achieved this by expressly forbidding all but the most restricted territorial expansion.

Why extension should in this way lead inexorably to one or another mode of absolute rule became one of the great theoretical concerns of modern European political thinking. But whatever the answer, most European commentators had, by at least the early eighteenth century, become convinced that, as the English political and economic theorist Charles Davenant phrased it in 1701, "while Common wealths thus extend their limits, they are working their own Bane, for all big Empires determine in a single Person".[22]

IV

All these three senses of the term *imperium* – as limited and independent or "perfect" rule, as a territory embracing more than one political community, and as the absolute sovereignty of a single individual – survive into the late eighteenth century and sometimes well beyond. All three derived from the discursive practices of the Roman empire, and to a lesser extent the Athenian and Macedonian empires. It was the example of Rome, above all, an empire which had acquired an imaginative identity, a legal and political persona, which reached far beyond the contingencies of the relationship between colony and metropolis, which ensured that all future empires would be closely associated with the institution of monarchy. For by the time of the collapse of the Republic, Rome was already the largest state in the Mediterranean world, and its size, as St Augustine had remarked, was a demonstration of the far-reaching potentiality of the values of the society which had created it.

By the time Constantine the Great launched his massive and intemperate assault on the pagan – but not the Roman – world, this extensiveness had come to be identified with a certain kind of inclusiveness. There might be many kingdoms – but there could be only one empire. In the writings of Cicero, Virgil, Livy, Polybius, Tacitus and Sallust – the authors on whom most subsequent theoreticians of empire from Machiavelli to Adam Smith relied most heavily – the Roman *Imperium* constituted not merely a particular political order but, more significantly, a distinctive kind of society, whose identity was determined by what came to be broadly described as the *civitas*. In the first instance, as with Aristotle's notion of what it is to be a "political animal" (*zoon politikon*), this involved a life lived in cities. For the Ancients, both Greek and Roman, cities were the only places where virtue could be practised. They were, crucially, communities governed by the rule of law which demanded adherence to a particular kind of life, that of the "civil society" (*societas civilis*), and which were closely identified with the physical location the citizens happened to inhabit.

[. . .]

The city is also, of course, the foundational metaphor for the greatest work by a Roman Christian: St Augustine's *De Civitate Dei*, "The City of God". And, as such, it was the image which sustained much subsequent thinking about the politics of civil association. It is an image which was to be carefully nurtured by the (real) city states of fifteenth-century Italy, as much as by the architects of the (illusory) "Cities on the Hill" of Puritan New England. The *civitas*, said Aquinas, is "the perfect community",[23] and the "perfecta communitas" is here defined not merely as a politically autonomous society – although it must also be that – but as one which is "sufficient in providing for life's necessities".[24] This, too, was a definition which evoked Aristotle's notion of *autarkeia*, or "self-sufficiency", as the necessary condition of every true community, one which, to return to the language of Cicero, implied a strict adherence to the demands of the "societas civilis".[25] But the *civitas* was not only defensive. It was also itself the source of empire, if only because, as Machiavelli pointed out, the city provides both the men for the armies and the source of the authority needed to retain provinces once they have been conquered.[26] As Machiavelli also recognized – a subject about which he was particularly sensitive – for the Romans the greatness of a city was a measure of the greatness of its rulers.[27] Much of this, as we shall see, will survive, or be re-created, in the modern world.

V

For the Roman theorists, Cicero in particular, the *civitas*, as the sole place of human flourishing, was also, and only, the Roman political community.[28] Because of the close identity in all ancient political thought between what it was to be a citizen, and what it was to be a person, the Roman *Imperium*, although it was never defined as such, came to be looked upon not merely as a geographical or political expression but as a source of knowledge. As the Greek historian Polybius – who had no word with which to express *imperium* – phrased it, the "orbis terrarum" was that part of the globe which had "fallen under inquiry".[29]

The gaze of the Roman, Polybius was suggesting, had conferred upon the world an identity, and an identity which, since it was the identity of the *civitas*, was crucially dependent upon the rule of law. "O Romans," Anchises ends his famous exhortation to the new race, "to rule the nations with *imperium*, these shall be your arts – to crown peace with law, to spare the humbled, to tame the proud in war".[30] "The imperial majesty," as Justinian began his *Institutes*, "should be armed with laws as well as glorified with arms."[31] It was the Roman Law which shaped every aspect of life within the Roman world. It was the Romans' great intellectual achievement, as moral philosophy and the natural sciences had been the Greeks'. It created not merely political and social order; it also conferred an ethical purpose upon the entire community. Under the late Republic, and then more forcibly under the Principate, the legal formulation of *imperium* merged with a second-century (BCE) Stoic notion of a single universal human race, to use Cicero's phrase, a "single joint community of gods and men".[32] Zeno himself, founder of the Stoic School, had taught, or so Plutarch tells us, that

> we all should live not in cities and demes (townships), each distinguished by separate rules of justice, but should regard all men as fellow demesmen and fellow citizens; and that there should be one life and order (*koinos*) as of a single flock feeding together on a common pasture.[33]

For Greeks, like Panaetius of Rhodes (*c.*180–109 BCE) teacher and intellectual companion of Scipio Aemilius, whose lost work *On Duty* had a profound influence on Cicero's own *De Officiis*, and for the Roman moralists generally, it was a relatively easy step to think of Zeno's *koinos*, and of the Greek *oikumene* in general, as identical with the Roman *Imperium*.[34] As the world (*mundus*) constituted a "universitas" it could have but one lord to provide it with the *ratio* "of protection and jurisdiction" (*Digest* 6.1.2).[35] The law of the Roman empire thus became the embodiment of the claim to be what Aristotle had called a *koinos nomos*, a universal law for all mankind.[36] It was not merely a specific set of political arrangements, although equality before the law was a crucial part of what it was to be a *cives*; it was a true *civilization* – even if that word did not acquire its modern meaning until the second half of the eighteenth century.[37]

The civil law itself, which had been created by human reason – *ratio scripta*, in Leibniz's famous phrase – out of an understanding of the natural law, was the human law, the *lex humanus*. Those who lived by it were, by definition, "humans"; those who did not, were not. But as it was also the Roman people who were responsible for the creation of the law, there was a sense in which only the Romans could be described as human. As Suetonius tells us, the emperor Caligula (37–41 CE) – not perhaps the most impartial witness – spoke of "the Roman people, or rather, I say, the human race" (*populus Romanus vel dicam humanum genus*).[38] Those who were rational, and thus in some deep sense human, were those who lived within the limits of *the* empire, a set of associations which allowed the Roman jurists, and their medieval commentators, to contrast the "reason of empire" (*ratio imperii*) with the empire of reason (*rationis imperium*).[39] Roman and subsequently Christian social and political thinking was, and would remain, heavily dependent on the semantics of the Roman Law. Even the term "civil" itself, which remains central to all our political reflections, was used first to describe a particular kind of law, and was then applied to a particular kind of society. Similarly the verb "to civilize" meant originally to transfer a case from one branch of the law to another.[40]

Even for Cicero, whose understanding of the concept of the "republic of all the world" ("respublica totius orbis") changes markedly according to the audience he is addressing and the rhetorical tradition within which he is working, the "world" was often sharply divided into Romans and "provincials". And just as it was politically difficult for him to think of an independent territorial state, so it was difficult for him consistently to accept the existence of independent political or cultural forms.[41] The "provincials", he said in *De Republica*, are the "barbarians", rule over whom, he declared emphatically, "is just precisely because servitude in such men is established for their welfare".[42]

Cicero also had other, more humane, views on the possible social and political relationship between Romans and barbarians. But his claim that the world might be so radically divided into those whose nature it is to rule and those who are fit only for servitude draws on a real conviction of the Ancient World, one which was to have a profound influence on those who wrote about the nature and legitimacy of later empires.

The most extreme, and the most discussed, expression of that conviction is the one on which Cicero himself was implicitly drawing: Aristotle's theory of natural slavery. The natural slave – as distinct from the rational man who has been enslaved through unfortunate circumstances – a one who is bound *by nature* to a life of perpetual labour. The definition of this anomalous creature was grounded in a distinction between what, in Greek psychology, was called the "rational" and the "irrational" souls.[43] In fully developed human males, the rational invariably triumphs over the irrational. This is what it means to possess the capacity for deliberation or moral choice (*prohairesis*). Neither women nor children are, in Aristotle's view, fully rational, since the former lack what he calls "authority" (*akuron*), while the rational faculty in the latter is only partially formed. The natural slave would seem to be a wholly anomalous creature since he, while being a fully developed adult male, nonetheless has only a share in the faculty of reason, without being in full possession of it. He might be said – conveniently for his would-be enslavers – to be capable of following instructions, yet incapable of issuing them. In Aristotle's own terms, he is capable of understanding (*sunesis*) but incapable of practical wisdom (*phronesis*) for "practical wisdom issues commands . . . but understanding only judges".[44] While free he is violating what nature had intended him to be, for his master does his thinking for him, and he is himself almost literally a "living but separate part of his master's frame".[45] In practice, however, such creatures would be difficult to identify with certainty. In a crucial passage, Aristotle remarked that they might indeed be identical with the "barbarians". This was at best vague, since *barbaroi* was a general term which described all those who did not speak Greek. It would have to include, for instance, the subjects of the Persian monarchy for which, on other occasions, Aristotle had great respect. But it is clear that it is to this passage that Cicero is alluding in his description of the provincials, and that for Cicero the term "barbarian", or in his rendering "provincials", possessed some of the more nuanced meanings it has subsequently acquired. "Barbarians" were those who lacked the necessary qualities for membership of the *civitas*, and anyone who in this way did not share the Greek, and later Roman, view of the nature of the good life was an object of fear and distrust. He was an outsider, and his relationship to those who lived within the civil community could only ever be one of servitude. Being a slave for Aristotle, and sometimes also for Cicero, was thus a necessary identity . . .

This seemingly stark dichotomy between those who did and those who did not live in "the world", as defined by Athens or Rome, is perhaps not so very surprising as it might at first seem. The anthropologists have shown us that few peoples have a fully articulate sense of a single undivided genus. As Lévi-Strauss once observed, "a very great number of primitive tribes simply refer to themselves by the term for 'men' in their language, showing that in their eyes an essential characteristic of man disappears outside the limits of the group".[46] The Greeks, indeed, seem to have been unusual, if not unique, in possessing a term – *anthropos* – capable of describing the biological species, as distinct from a social category. But if this *anthropos* is taken, as it was in most ancient ethical writing, to be something more than a morphological category, and if membership of any community must ultimately depend upon recognition by that community, then the Greek and later Roman failure to recognize the *barbaroi* or the "provincials", amounted to a denial of their humanity.

Unlike, however, the "primitive" tribes described by Lévi-Strauss, or even the Greek *polis*, the Roman *civitas* was crucially a civilization for exportation, something which was already implicit in the myth of the foundation of Latium as a place where, in Virgil's formulation, "wild races have been gathered together by Saturn and given laws".[47] In Rome, although not in Athens, a slave could even be manumitted directly into citizenship. Manumission, which was fairly common after the fourth century BCE, involved, in effect, a legal transformation of a person's identity. It constituted, in Bernard Williams's words, "the most complete metamorphosis one can imagine" from an object to the subject of rights.[48] Where Aristotle's "barbarians" differed from Cicero's "provincials" was that whereas the former would seem to be immovable in their slavery – for no amount of instruction in civility could restore a man's capacity for rational understanding – the latter could clearly be educated in the ways of civil society. This is why Cicero himself, always among the most chauvinist of Romans, could nevertheless insist that the Africans, the Spanish and the Gauls were entitled to just rule, despite being "savage and barbarous nations".[49] The frontiers between the world of civil men and that of the barbarians was forever dissolving. Potentially at least, the *Imperium* was a culture without limits, which is why Terminus, the god of boundaries, refused to attend the foundation of the city of Rome.

Imperium, in this sense was, as a frequently quoted passage in Seneca's *De Clementia* implied, the *vinculum societatis* – the links in the chain which could bind together the members of widely scattered communities.[50] As the Venetian humanist Paolo Paruta noted in 1599, it had been the sheer diversity of the cultural, ethical and political elements of which it had been composed which had been the true source of the greatness of the Roman Republic. This had, he said, resulted in a society which was "ruled with such prudence and justice, that it would be almost impossible to form a more perfect royal government".[51]

Inevitably, however, there existed a tension between a strong sense of inclusiveness, derived from the peculiar importance accorded by the Greeks to the role of the community in human life, and the later Roman insistence that, in order to fulfil the purposes for which that community had been devised it had, in some sense, to include everyone there was in the world – a tension that was to persist in all later European conceptions of empire down to their final demise in the middle of this century. The community – the *civitas* which for the Roman was identical with the *Imperium* – was the only context in which it was possible to achieve one's ends as a person. But the *civitas* also had the power to transform all those who entered it. So long, that is, as you were outside it, a barbarian or a provincial, you were in some sense less than human. Once inside, you would in time become "civilized". As James Wilson was to observe in 1790, as he pondered the political significance of the collapse of the British empire in America, "it might be said, not that the Romans extended themselves over the whole globe, but that the inhabitants of the globe poured themselves upon the Romans". And this, he added, quite apart from whatever larger moral force it might have, was clearly "the most secure method of enlarging an empire".[52]

[. . .]

De iure at least, Augustus and his successors had become rulers of the world. It now required only an act of legislation, duly provided by the Emperor Antoninus Pius in the second century in the famous *Lex Rhodia*,[53] to transform the *imperator* into the "Lord of all the World": "dominus totius orbis". The concept of the *orbis terrarum* became in effect the appropriation by the political realm of the Stoic notion of a single human genus. It was, as the French historian Claude Nicolet has said of it, a "triple achievement: spatial, temporal and political".[54]

VI

After the triumph of Christianity, these notions of simultaneous singularity and exclusivity were further enforced by the Christian insistence upon the uniqueness both of the truth of the Gospels and of the Church as a source of interpretative authority. Although the secular and sacred authority was formally divided between the Pope and the emperor by Gelasian I in the fifth century,[55] the extension of Christianity remained very largely confined to what was understood to have once been the territory of the Roman world. Christianity was thought of as spatially co-extensive with the *Imperium romanum*.[56] The *orbis terrarum* thus became, in terms of the translation effected by Leo the Great in the fifth century, the "orbis Christianus", which, in turn, soon developed into the "Imperium Christianum". A century later, Gregory the Great would translate this into the "sancta respublica", a community endowed with the same simultaneous open exclusiveness which had been a feature of the Ciceronian "respublica totius orbis".

Underpinning such claims to political and territorial authority was a sense, difficult to track with any precision, that just as the *civitas* had now become conterminous with Christianity, so to be human – to be, that is, one who was "civil", and who was able to interpret correctly the law of nature – one had now also to be a Christian. By the time that Gregory the Great came to use the term "barbarus" it had already become synonymous with *paganus*, a sense which it retained in the language of the Curia until at least the fifteenth century. The *pagani* were "pagans", "unbelievers", but they were also those who were trained by "rusticitas" and who thus, as Peter Brown has characterized it, refused "to see the world as intelligible".[57] One clearly did not have to be Christian to be human, but all "barbari et pagani", for Gregory no less than for Aristotle, hovered on the very edge of inhumanity. For they were those, in the description offered by Albertus Magnus, who confused "the interrelations (*communications*) within society and destroyed the principles of justice which operate in these interrelations".[58]

Non-Christians, pagans who were also *barbari*, had to be encouraged to join the "congregatio fidelium" just as the "barbarians" had been encouraged to join the Roman *civitas*. Under the terms of the law of nature, furthermore, all men, whether pagan or Christian, had identical political rights. This belief had important consequences for the subsequent disputes over the legitimacy of the European conquest of what were, in effect, the political domains of non-Christian rulers.

So long as a people remained un-Christian, however, it might still be excluded from the more exacting definition of the term "world". Although St Thomas Aquinas and his followers insisted upon the true universality of the law of nature, they were never fully able to obliterate the earlier, more obviously Augustinian, identification of reason with belief. And Augustine himself had given more than a mere hint that he, like Cicero, might be prepared to regard some pagans as slaves by nature.[59] It certainly meant, as Richard Tuck has argued, that those inside "the world" could legitimately make the war on those outside, particularly if those on the outside were not pagans but, like the Ottomans, those – whom Aquinas had termed "vincibly ignorant" – who had wilfully persisted in their unbelief even after they had heard the Gospel. All too often the *pax christiana* was a peace for Christians only.[60] The sometimes stark difference between the ways in which the two major forms of (western) Christianity – Roman Catholicism, which from the late fifteenth century was predominantly Thomist, and the various forms of Protestantism, which were all Augustinian in inspiration – approached the question of the beliefs of others, was to have a marked impact on the different histories of the modern European overseas empires.

Christian monotheism helped to enhance this sense of singularity. Unburdened by the notion of a single creator deity, the Romans had seen no reason to confuse the observation of the law with the possession of a specific religious belief, or even the observance of a specific religious cult. For the new Christians, however, the cultural and religious diversity which had been the distinctive feature of the pagan empire was merely symptomatic of the spiritual poverty which had always underpinned the Roman concept, military and essentially secular, of *virtus*. True, Christians, from John of Paris on, allowed for a wide variety of different forms of government, local customs and laws. The "variety of things" – the *varietas rerum* – had been guaranteed by God's infinite inventiveness, and endorsed by Polybian and later Aristotelian arguments about the psychological significance of climatic variation.[61] Nevertheless all forms of civil association had to be made intelligible within a single system of beliefs. Ultimately, the image of God as father to the human family made the idea of a multiplicity of cultures, and by extension a multiplicity of states within the *Imperium*, difficult to accommodate. In terms of the same trope, if the body politic could have only one head, it could equally only have one voice and, more crucially, one set of beliefs. Christ himself, St Bernard had taught, had left Peter the government of the whole human race.[62] If this were so, if the empire was to be both unique and universal, it had in the Christian imagination also to be sacred.

The medieval empire in the West, as it is conventionally although somewhat misleadingly called, did not employ the term "sacrum" until it was added by Frederick I in 1157, yet it is clear that in the imaginative refashioning of its own history it had been a holy community from the day of Constantine's conversion. In a wider sense it had always been a holy empire, for classical Rome itself had since its foundation been endowed with both a divine origin and divine status. Virgil's Jupiter bestows upon the new city an empire without limits in either space or time. "For these [Romans] I set neither bounds nor periods of empire; *Imperium* without end I give",[63] a phrase later echoed by the fourteenth-century jurist Baldus de Ubaldis' definition of the Christian Empire as the "supreme power without limits".

[. . .]

The image of the empire as the object of successive "renovations" over time became central to the ideological forms which the later European empires were to give to their distinct projects and political identities. It is this which transformed such seemingly absurd seventeenth-century characterizations of universal empire as Tomasso Campanella's *De Monarchia hispanica*, grounded as it was upon prophetic hermeneutics and abstruse astrological calculation, into powerful political ideologies. For the Roman and medieval empires, and all those other future empires which might succeed them, were conceived as being more than simple structures of power. They were also represented as the means which God had placed on this earth for men to use in order to accomplish their ends. In this respect at least they had a strongly Aristotelian identity. The ancient *polis* had made human flourishing – *eudaimonia* – possible. By rendering *eudaimonia* as "blessedness" (*beatitudo*), Aristotle's thirteenth-century translator, Robert Grosseteste, had made that a state which it was clearly only possible to achieve within the territorial limits of the Christian *monarchia*. The idea of *monarchia* as a single system embracing the whole of Christendom became, in J. H. Burns's words, "one of the strongest elements in the political thought of the period".[64]

VII

[. . .]

The claims to universal *dominium*, which were in the first instance the consequence of a gradually changing view of the identity of the optimal political community, necessarily involved the transfer of a definition of humanity from the moral sphere to the political. This demanded the restriction of the "human" to a specific political entity which, of necessity, could only have one undisputed ruler whose status came very close to being that of a "God on Earth". The translation of the concept of the *civitas* to the Christian world reinforced the sense of the difference between those inside and those outside the Roman universal empire. It is this legacy of univer-salism, developed over centuries and reinforced by a powerfully articulate learned elite which the European overseas empires, especially that of Spain, could never quite abandon. Compelling, and for many comforting though this sense of uniqueness might have been, it also presented seemingly intractable problems both of legitimation and of representation for political projects which sought to extend the limits of the *orbis terrarum* to the point where the restraining notion offered by Bartolus' [of Saxoferrato, 1313/14–57] two genera of peoples became meaningless.

NOTES

1 William Robertson, *The History of America. Ninth Edition in which is Included the Posthumous Volume Containing the History of Virginia to the Year 1688 and of New England, to the Year 1652*, 4 vols. London, 1800, I: 55. On Robertson and Hume's view of the fifteenth century as the beginning of moder-nity see David Armitage, "The New World and British Historical Thought: from Richard Hakluyt to William Robertson," in Karen Ordahl Kupperman, ed., *America in European Consciousness, 1493–1750*, Chapel Hill, NC, 1995, 52–75.

2 For a brief account of *imperium* – and a far longer one of "imperialism" – see Rudolf Walther, *Imperi-alismus* in Otto Brunner, Werner Conze, and Reinhart Koselleck, eds, *Geschichtliche Grundbegriffe*, 7 vols, Stuttgart, 1972–92, III: 171–88.

3 Versions of this phrase were employed by Ugo de Fleury in the twelfth century to challenge the claims of Pope Gregory VII (see B. Paradisi, "Il pensiero politico dei giuristi medievali," in *Storia delle idee politiche, economiche e sociali*, ed. L. Firpo, Turin, 1983, vol. II, 211–366, 250) and by Innocent III in the decretal "Per venerabilem" in 1202, against the claims of the German emperors (Francesco Calasso, *I glossatori e la teoria della sovranità. Studio di diritto comune publico*, 3rd edn, Milan, 1957, 403). See André Bossuet, "La Formule 'Le Roi est empereur en son royaume.' Son emploi au XVe siècle devant le Parlement de Paris," *Revue historique de droit français et étranger* (1961), 371–81 and Donald R. Kelley, "Law", in J. H. Burns, ed., *The Cambridge History of Political Thought 1450–1700*, Cambridge, 1991, 66–94, 78. The concept was also employed by the Spanish and English. See in general Walther, 1976, 65–111.

4 Calasso, 1957, 22–3.

5 Machiavelli, for instance, speaks of the Venetians and the Florentines as having "cresciuto l'imperio loro" (*Principe* xii). Niccolò Machiavelli, *Il Principe*, Milan, 1960, 55.

6 "On Honour and Reputation" in Francis Bacon, *The Works of Francis Bacon*, ed. James Spedding, 14 vols, London, 1857–74, VI, 505.

7 Sir Francis Barnard, *Select Letters on the Trade and Government of America; and the Principles of Law and Polity, Applied to the American Colonies*, London, 1774, 71.

8 Walter Ullmann, " 'This Realm of England is an Empire' ", *Journal of Ecclesiastical History*, 30 (1979), 175–203.

9 J. G. A. Pocock, "States, Republics, and Empires: The American Founding in Early-modern Perspec-tive," in Terence Ball and J. G. A. Pocock, eds, *Conceptual Change and the Constitution*, Lawrence, KS, 1988, 55–77, 68.

10 Thomas Pownall, *Principles of Polity, being the Grounds and Reasons of Civil Empire*. London, 1752, 93–4.

11 Edmund Burke, *The Speech of Edmund Burke Esq. on Moving his Resolution for Conciliation with the Colonies* [22 March], 3rd edn, London, 1775, 35–6.

12 Robert Folz, *The Concept of Empire in Western Europe from the Fifth to the Fourteenth Centuries*, London, 1969, 54.

13 "An Essay of the original and nature of government", in Sir William Temple, *The Works of Sir William Temple Bart*, 2 vols, London, 1720, I, 103.

14 Moses Finley, *Politics in the Ancient World*, Cambridge, 1983, 65–6.

15 See J. G. A. Pocock, *Virtue, Commerce, and History. Essays on Political Thought and History, Chiefly in the Eighteenth Century*, Cambridge, 1985, 146.

16 Richard Kroebner, *Empire*, Cambridge, 1961, 12–14.

17 J. S. Richardson ("*Imperium Romanum*: Empire and the Language of Power", *Journal of Roman Studies*, 1991, 9) has characterized it, the "*imperium militae*, passed down from the kings through the great individuals of the Republic that had made the *imperium romanum*. . . . It was the exercise of *imperium* throughout the known world that monarchy had made its return to Rome".

18 Fergus Millar, *The Emperor in the Roman World (31 BC–AD 337)*. London, 1977, 3.

19 *Etymologiae* 9.3.21. P.L. LXXXI, 345a. "*Monarchae* sunt qui singularem possident principatum, qualis fuit Alexander apud Graecos, et Julius apud Romanos."

20 *The Federalist*, 9, in Alexander Hamilton, James Madison and John Jay, *The Federalist, or, the New Constitution*, Oxford, 1987, 121–2.

21 *The Federalist*, 11, in ibid. 133–4.

22 "An essay upon universal monarchy" in Charles Davenant, *The Political and Commercial Works of that Celebrated Writer, Charles D'Avenant LL.D.*, 5 vols, London, 1771, V:3–4.

23 *Summa Theologiae*, I–II. 90.2.

24 *De Regimine Principum*, I. 1.

25 Aristotle, *Politics*, 1252^{b}28–1253^{a}2, and see Francisco de Vitoria, *Political Writings*, ed. Anthony Pagden and Jeremy Lawrence, Cambridge, 1991, 9, n.18.

26 *Discorsi*, II. 3; Machiavelli, 1960, 285.

27 See Quentin Skinner, "Machiavelli's *Discorsi* and the Pre-humanist Origins of Republican Ideas," in Gisela Bock, Quentin Skinner, and Maurizio Viroli, eds, *Machiavelli and Republicanism*, Cambridge, 1990, 121–41.

28 *De Officiis*, I. 124. Cicero spoke of the magistrate as "assuming the role of the civitas" (*se genere personam civitatis*).

29 Quoted in P. A. Blunt, "Laus Imperii," in P. A. Garnsey and C. R. Whittaker, eds, *Imperialism in the Ancient World*, Cambridge, 1978, 168.

30   Tu regere imperio populos, Romane memento
            (hae tibi errant artes) pacique imponere morem
            parcere subietus et debellare superbos.
                  (*Aeneid*, VI, 852–3)

31 *Institutes*, Proemium.

32 "Ut iam universus hic mundus it una civitas communis deorum atque hominum existimanda." *De legibus*, 1. 22–4.

33 Quoted in Ernest Barker, "The Conception of Empire," in Cyril Bailey, ed., *The Legacy of Rome*, Oxford, 1923, 52.

34 Folz, 1969, 4. Cicero's account of an intellectual circle around Scipio Amelianus which sought to imbue *nobilitas* with the Stoic notion of *humanitas*, may indeed, as Strasburger and Finley have shown, be a creation of Cicero's imagination. But his early-modern readers did not know this. See Finley, 1983, 127.

35 See Paradisi, 1983, 308.

36 *Rhetoric*, 1. 12 1373^b, and see Blunt, 1978. The association of Roman law with Aristotle's *Koinos nomos* was the work of Aelius Aristides. See J. H. Oliver, "The Ruling Power: A Study of the Roman Empire in the Second Century after Christ through the Roman Orator Aelius Aristides," *Transactions of the American Philosophical Society*, n.s., 43, pt. 4, Philadelphia, 1953.

37 See "Le Mot civilization" in Jean Starobinski, *Le remède dans le mal. Critique et légitimation de l'artifice à l'âge des Lumières*, Paris, 1989, 15–16.

38 Quoted by Theodor Mommsen, *Le Droit publique romain [Romisches Staatsrecht]*, trans. P. F. Girard, 3rd edn, 7 vols, Paris, 1896, VI, 478–9.

39 Quoted in H. Aubépin, *De l'influence de Dumoulin sur la législation française*, Paris, 1855, 139.

40 Starobinski, 1989, 12, and Kelley, 1991, 72.

41 Mommsen, 1896, VI, 479.

42 Reported by Augustine, *De Civitate Dei*, XIX, 21.

43 For the most compelling modern discussion of Aristotle's views see Bernard Williams, *Shame and Necessity*, Berkeley, Los Angeles, and Oxford, 1993, 110–16.

44 *Nicomachean Ethics*, 1143ª11.

45 I have discussed this at greater length in Anthony Pagden, *The Fall of Natural Man. The American Indian and the Origins of Comparative Ethnology*, 2nd edn, Cambridge, 1986, 42–3.

46 Claude Lévi-Strauss, *The Elementary Structures of Kinship*, trans. Harle Bell et al., London, 1969, 46.

47 *Aeneid*, VIII, 319–23.

48 Williams, 1993, 108, citing E. Levy. See Moses Finley, *Ancient Slavery and Modern Ideology*, London, 1980, 97.

49 *Epistulae ad Quintum Fratrem*, I. 1–27.

50 Seneca, *De Clementia*, 1.4. See the observations in J. Azor, *Institutionum moralium in quibus universae quaestiones ad conscientiam recte aut prave factorum pertinentes, breviter tractantur*, 3 vols., London, 1610–16, 1066ᵇ.

51 Paolo Paruta, *Discorsi politici*, Venice, 1559, 215. Paruta claimed, however, that the collapse of the Roman state was the inevitable outcome of its over-extension in the last days of the Republic. This had led to inequality of property among the members of the *civitas*. Imperial Rome may have been the most perfect *royal* government, but every monarchy was inferior to any republic. On Paruta see Richard Tuck, *Philosophy and Government 1572–1651*, Cambridge, 1993, 96 and William Bouwsma, *Venice and the Defense of Republican Liberty*. Berkeley, CA, 1968, 285.

52 "Lectures on law: XI citizens and aliens" (1790–1) in James Wilson, *The Works of James Wilson*, ed. Robert Green McCloskey, 2 vols, Cambridge, MA, 1967, II, 581.

53 *Digest*, XIV, 2.9. Antoninus, in reply to a complaint from Eudaemon of Nicomedia that he had been robbed by the people of the Cyclades after being shipwrecked, said, "I am lord of the world, but the law of the sea must be judged by the sea law of the Rhodians when our law does not conflict with it." Justinian similarly excluded the sea from his jurisdiction (*Institutes*, II, 1.1.), which led to considerable debate in the seventeenth century. Justinian's law, *Bene a Zenone* (*Codex* VII, 37, 3) which reserves exclusive rights of property to the emperor, and subsequently to the papacy, was frequently cited together with the *Lex Rhodia*.

54 Claude Nicolet, *L'Inventaire du monde. Géographie et politique aux origines de l'empire romain*, Paris, 1988, 28.

55 Folz, 1969, 9.

56 For the authoritative definition of pagans provided by Tommaso de Vio (Cardinal Cajetan) in his commentary on St Thomas Aquinas's *Summa theologiae*, composed between 1507 and the 1520s, the only category of person which falls uncontentiously under the *dominium* of the Church is constituted by those who live on lands once under Roman imperial rule. Caietanus, *Summa Theologiae*, Rome, 1888–1906, IX, 94, commenting on IIa IIae q.66 art.8.

57 Peter Brown, *Relics and Social Status in the Age of Gregory of Tours*. Reading, 1977.

58 Pagden, 1986, 20–1.

59 *De Civitate Dei*, XIX. 21, quoting, with apparent approval, the argument from *De Republica*. See note 12, above.

60 Richard Tuck, *The Rights of War and Peace*, Oxford, 1999, 2001.

61 Antony Black, *Political Thought in Europe 1250–1450*, Cambridge, 1992, 87–92.

62 Michael J. Wilkes, *The Problem of Sovereignty in the Later Middle Ages. The Papal Monarchy with Augustus Triumphus and the Publicists*, Oxford, 1963, 412 and, more generally, 411–78.

63 *Aeneid*, I, 277–9, "His ego nec metas rerum nec tempora pono; imperium sine fine dedi."

64 Julian H. Franklin, "Sovereignty and the Mixed Constitution: Bodin and His Critics", in J. H. Burns, ed, *The Cambridge History of Political Thought 1450–1700*, Cambridge, 1991, 310–11.

2

EUROPE AND THE ATLANTIC SLAVE SYSTEMS

David Eltis

For nearly four centuries, two increasingly different labor systems evolved on opposite sides of the Atlantic. At least as they appeared in the second half of the seventeenth century, the systems grew from the same European roots, even though interactions among peoples from all parts of the Atlantic world, especially Africa, decided central issues of their geographical location and who participated in them. Why, in the very long run if slavery and freedom had the same origins, did one survive and the other wither? It is time to return to the longer view and explore how the systems of slavery and free labor affected and sustained each other in the European-dominated Atlantic world, especially after 1700. The issue has both an economic and an ideological side.

Historians have paid most attention to the material links between European slave and non-slave sectors that straddled the Atlantic. The rapid economic growth of both slave and non-slave sectors in the European Atlantic world, especially the northwest European Atlantic world, derived ultimately from the same intra-European demographic patterns, social structures, resource mobility, market values, and market institutions that placed Europe technologically and perhaps materially ahead of the rest of the world at the outset of European expansion. Initially, capital and labor flowed to the tropical Americas from Europe, presumably because the productivity of both was higher there than in Europe. The motivations behind such movements and the institutions that facilitated them were no different from those that marked similar shifts within Europe. Status and success or failure would be measured by the same standards in slave and nonslave societies. Richard Ligon and Père Labat, like most European observers visiting the Caribbean, found themselves in an alien world, but apart from the physical environment and the terms on which labor was used, it was an European milieu, despite the heavy African presence. European visitors could observe far more that was familiar and blend more easily into the society they found than could the several emissaries and children of African rulers who went

David Eltis, "Europe and the Atlantic Slave Systems," pp. 258–62, 274–80 from *The Rise of African Slavery in the Americas*. Cambridge: Cambridge University Press, 2000.

to Europe via the West Indies in the slave-trade era to reprsesent the interests of African slave dealers.

The plantation complex was nevertheless more than just the creation of merchants, plantation owners, and, less precisely, early modern capital, on which much of the literature dwells. In fact, the slave systems and what is perceived as their worst aspect, the transatlantic slave trade, were shaped as much by European consumers, African enslavers, and African slaves themselves. European consumers demanded the cheapest possible sugar, tobacco, and cotton, and for most of this period cared little for how they were produced. From the sixteenth to the nineteenth centuries the price of sugar fell so much that the product moved out of the medicinal and luxury category to become a common grocery item and, indeed, given its role as an additive, a basic foodstuff. Tobacco and cotton followed analogous paths. Given the widespread demand for these products, those promoting the slave system included almost all living in western Europe, particularly the sweet-toothed British.

It has become commonplace to point to intensifying exploitation of both domestic workers and colonial slaves brought about by the changes that reached a crescendo with the Industrial Revolution. The fact that consumers of plantation products in Europe helped create the slave systems has received less attention. Yet if the ordinary European and, more particularly, the English (for centuries, by far the largest consumers of sugar in the world) had eschewed sugar or attempted to impose a moral economy that did not allow for the consumption (and thus production) of slave-grown sugar, the slave trade would not have existed. The English rioted against engrossers and middlemen generally who were thought to raise the price of comestibles, especially bread.[1] Eventually they rose in condemnation of slavery, but only after three centuries. One of the largest riots in eighteenth-century England occurred in Liverpool in 1774 when sailors gutted slave ships and turned ships' guns on the city houses of slave-ship owners. The seamen were not expressing outrage at the slave trade, however, but rather their unhappiness at wages – the share of the income they received from the slave trade.[2] Resistance by ordinary Europeans in the form of support for abolition undoubtedly helped end the slave systems, but what needs more attention is the lack of resistance (indeed, the active support) of those same ordinary Europeans that allowed the inception and continuation of slavery and the slave trade for more than three centuries.

European waged labor and slave systems may have become more different from each other between the seventeenth and nineteenth centuries but they nevertheless continued to reinforce each other. Among the strongest (and most ironic) ties between the slave and non-slave systems of the European Atlantic are those suggested by a closer look at the "modernisation" process in England. Early English transatlantic migration was intimately connected with this process, the focal point of which was the creation of a modern labor force. English pamphlet literature circulating among the elite moved away from stressing low wages and draconian social legislation and toward the advantages of high wages in creating both enhanced worker productivity and a market for goods. Among the goods that European workers wanted were, of course, sugar, alcohol, tobacco, and, eventually, cotton goods, all of which meant slavery. Arguments stressing the advantages of high wages, some of which were used to purchase tropical produce, appear in Britain in the later seventeenth century just as transatlantic labor markets tightened.[3]

But slavery contributed in a less obvious way to these high wages. The Americas and Africa affected the English labor market by providing an alternative source of demand for labor-intensive manufactured goods. Both the Americas and Africa helped create markets both separate from Europe and with less likelihood of sudden imposition of tariff restrictions. International trade was certainly more important to the English in 1800 than in 1660. But the strongest growth between these two dates was in trade with the long-distance markets of Asia and the Americas, and in reexports of the products of these regions to the continent of Europe. Most long-distance markets afforded some protection for English goods. Transportation costs certainly acted like a tariff barrier, but at least it was a tariff barrier less susceptible to sudden changes than its man-made counterpart. It also tended to fall over the long term as transportation costs declined.[4] More important, the traditional, highly competitive continental markets for English products grew slowly, lagging behind both total trade and national income in growth, though Europe continued to comprise the largest single market for manufactured exports. In 1640, close to 90 percent of exports from London comprised manufactured goods to Europe; in the mid-1660s, the equivalent ratio was 76 percent, and in 1700, 69 percent. The major decline came after 1700. By 1785, if we take exports from Great Britain as the base instead of exports from London, manufactured goods to Europe accounted for just 28 percent of the total. Relative to national income, the figures are equally suggestive. In 1700 European purchases of English manufactured goods may be estimated at 5.2 percent of English national income; in 1785, only 2.3 percent, though of course the growth in absolute terms of all these markets was considerable.[5]

The importance of the rise of colonial markets for English wages is that as long as the continent of Europe was the market for English manufacturers, other things being equal, low wages were essential. As this market became less important so would the preoccupation with a low-wage economy. The slave system of the Americas provided a more secure market for English manufactures than did continental Europe. Thus the strong growth of the slave-based Atlantic system after the Restoration removed some of the urgent need to keep domestic wages as low as those in mainland Europe. The coincidence of this with the changing ideal in eighteenth-century pamphlets from a low- to a high-wage economy, attributed to a change in leisure preferences among English workers and improved productivity, is striking. In effect, the gradual change in the direction of English exports – from exclusive dependence on highly competitive European continental markets to the more protected environment of the British Americas and British East India markets – provided an additional stimulus to this acceptance of a high-wage economy. But there were also countervailing effects. More than three hundred thousand English came to the Americas in the second half of the seventeenth century and about the same number of Africans (allowing for mortality) arrived in English territory in the Americas. Without African slaves, wages in the colonies would have been higher and even more English would have emigrated, putting upward pressure on domestic wages. Given the relatively small importance of transoceanic trade when measured against the domestic economy, discussed further later, none of these effects could have been large.[6]

Yet small though the effect may have been, it is hard to avoid the conclusion that it was not just the European and African slave merchants that helped ensure Africans would become slaves in the Americas; it was also the aspirations of European workers. Workers turned away from transatlantic migration in increasing numbers after 1660 as wages rose, thus ensuring increased demand for African labor. Their demand for cheap plantation produce was part of a gradual, secular rise in well-being that occurred in the second half of the seventeenth century, at least in the English case, and then later elsewhere in Europe. This was accentuated by changing values on the part of the worker as plantation produce formed a part (albeit small) of the goods that the "modernised" worker was now beginning to demand, as well as by the associated willingness to respond to higher wages on the part of more English and, later, European workers. Given the European taboo against European slaves, modernisation of the English work force thus meant more slavery in the Americas for Africans.

[. . .]

The central development shaping western plantation slavery from the sixteenth century onward was the extension of European attitudes to the non-European world. If, by the sixteenth century it had become unacceptable for Europeans to enslave other Europeans, by the end of the nineteenth century it was unacceptable to enslave anyone. Put in relative perspective, before the eighteenth century Europeans, in common with most peoples in the world, were unable to include those beyond the oceans in their conception of the social contract.[7] Unlike most other peoples in the world, Europeans had the power to impose their version of that contract on others, which for three centuries meant African slavery.[8]

The emphasis here on what is ultimately a non-economic argument allows a reevaluation of the work of other scholars who have addressed the slave-free dichotomy. Generally, the position advanced here finds little echo in the historiography. The tensions posed by slavery in the Americas came to be recognized in the late eighteenth and nineteenth centuries. Given the not coincidental growth of abolitionism, the initial response to this recognition was to demonize slaveowners and slave traders, and see slavery as aberrant and certainly temporary. The conception of slavery as a "peculiar institution" was born in the abolitionist era. The Aristotelian view that some peoples were slaves by nature to which Las Casas subscribed came to be tempered by the idea that slavery was one stage through which all "uncivilized" peoples progressed toward a measure of freedom.[9] But in this form, as the influence of Ulrich Bonnell Phillips suggests, it remained widely held into the twentieth century. If slavery was a temporary condition and all peoples were potentially equal, then it might be assumed that the paradox of the extremes of slavery and freedom appearing in the Western world would be a temporary phenomenon.

From the mid-twentieth century the literature lurched toward explanations in terms of the economic self-interest of Europeans. For world-systems' scholars, slavery is associated with an early phase of European capitalism called mercantile or merchant as opposed to a later version termed industrial capital. Slavery and the slave trade have a central role in the growth of the former and therefore flourish with merchant capitalism but are incompatible with the latter and go into decline when industrial capitalism becomes dominant. But even when the former is in the ascendant, slavery is profitable only in the Americas, or periphery. In the metropolitan center of the European world system, it is always more profitable to use free labor. The pattern of slave-free use is thus explained by the self-interest of European capitalists.

The absoluteness of the barrier that prevented Europeans from becoming slaves suggests that the world-systems model in which European capitalists organized coerced labor on the periphery and free labor in the core economies is at least incomplete. We should have expected some Europeans – the prisoners of war, felons, and displaced Irish who were forced to the colonies – to have been slaves. Yet Portuguese degradados in Angola, Brazil, and Goa, French convicts sent to Louisiana and Canada, their Spanish counterparts who built the Havana fortifications, and the thousands of Cromwellian prisoners were never chattels and were always subject to "Christian usage."[10] More fundamentally the ethnic barriers, like the gender barriers that barred European women from skilled manual occupations, lead us to question all explanations of European expansion that hinge on unrestrained mercantile and mercantilist capitalism. If, as seems likely, European slaves would have been available more cheaply than Africans (as providing women with skills would have reduced the cost of skilled labor), then European merchants could not have been both profit maximizers and prejudiced (or outright racist and sexist) at the same time. Between 1500 and 1750, and no doubt beyond, European economic behavior was subordinated to major non-economic influences. At least the image of naked predatory capitalism that dominates the current historiography of early European expansion requires some modification.

Indeed, a more pecuniary or profit-maximising or "capitalist" attitude would have meant less African slavery (and greater equality for females) in the Americas.

An alternative method of dealing with the parallel evolution of more extreme forms of freedom and coercion – which also relies on the self-interest of European capitalists – rests on the argument that there was little substantive difference between waged workers and slaves. If the freedom of the waged labor market was at root a freedom to starve, freedom was therefore largely illusory. Slavery in the colonies and wage labor at home appear as two different methods of coercing workers and, as some English radicals argued in the early nineteenth century, the difference between the two was small. Abolition of slavery, when it eventually occurred, simply imposed a new form of coercion on the ex-slaves, and both the rise of slavery and its abolition thereby become less in need of an explanation. Much recent work on the post-emancipation Caribbean is consistent with this approach. From such a perspective, the economic elite, especially in north-western Europe, used different methods to reduce the economic independence of non-elites in Europe on the one hand and in the Americas on the other. By the nineteenth century it had become necessary to rely on wage labor, effectively if indirectly controlled, in all parts of the Atlantic world. Once more, the tension between Western freedom and Western slavery is reduced once we understand the true interests of European capitalists and the strategies they adopted. Variants of this draw on Gramsci, wherein slavery, or perhaps the abolition of slavery as espoused by the elite, becomes a way of legitimising the ruling classes and making the conditions of European workers seem acceptable by comparison with those of slaves.[11]

Yet the self-interest of capitalists or indeed economic motivations in general seem, by themselves, to provide an unpromising route to understanding or setting aside the paradox. Slavery was certainly an economic system offering costs well below those possible using waged labor. But if the system was so effective, why was it confined so absolutely to non-Europeans? As for the contrast (or rather lack of) between free and slave labor – there never seems to have been the slightest doubt on the distinction among slaves and free laborers, both before and after abolition, nor any hesitation in the former to achieve non-slave status, however defined and hedged – at least in the European-dominated world. Having experienced slavery, Frederick Douglass was particularly sensitive to the differences between slave and non-slave labor. To underline the peculiar awfulness of the former, he several times informed crowds he was addressing that a job vacancy had been created by his escape from slavery and that free laborers could offer their services as slaves to fill it.[12]

The various attempts to deal with the paradox – best embodied perhaps in the work of David Brion Davis, Seymour Drescher, Edmund S. Morgan, and Orlando Patterson – have tended to explore the paradox rather than attempted to resolve it in terms of class or economic interests. The cultural evolution and economic growth of the West that have shaped the modern world embody a tension between coercion and freedom of choice that may be elaborated or understood, but not reduced, dismissed, or readily explained. For Patterson, the tension long predates European overseas expansion. Freedom as a social value could not exist without slavery in the sense that in all societies what is marginal defines what is central. The conception of freedom as autonomy from personal and social obligations was perhaps possible only if an antithetical slave status defined as total dependence on another also existed. Sparta, with helots rather than pure chattel slaves, had narrower concepts of individual freedom than Athens, where slavery was extensive and closed and where the lack of rights of slaves was frequently set against the rights of adult male citizens. Both here and in Rome the appearance of full chattel slavery was associated with the disappearance of any status intermediate to the slave-free polarity – a situation with some analogies to the early modern European Atlantic world.[13]

In seventeenth-century England, the term *slavery* was applied to many situations of perceived injustice, and it already represented something devalued. The implication, clearly, was that Englishmen should be free from such restraints. Historians of North America have developed variants of this relationship to explain social cohesiveness and the ability of slaveholders to espouse an ideology in which the right of peoples to be free from oppression had a central place – "peoples" and "social cohesiveness" being for those of European descent.[14] On the other hand, historians also see a dramatic reversal in this mutually sustaining relationship helping to overthrow the slave system from the end of the eighteenth century. In the era since slavery disappeared from the Americas, western concepts of freedom have tended instead to be defined in terms of what is perceived as a lack of freedom in non-western societies, particularly the Soviet-dominated world for most of this century.[15]

Yet before the eighteenth century, these associations seem, if not invalid, somewhat overdrawn. Personal freedom in the seventeenth-century Netherlands appears much more rooted in the social structure, religion, and immigration trends of the Low Countries than in the coercive activities of a few thousand Dutchmen in Asia. The Dutch did not even enter the Atlantic slave trade until the 1630s and compared to the Portuguese and the English they remained of marginal importance until well after 1660. Likewise it would be difficult to attempt to link any of the political or religious upheavals of England in the 1640s and 1650s to a nascent slave system on one small island over 4,000 miles away, involving at most thirty thousand people in 1650, less than half of whom were slaves. Even at the time of the English Revolution, the English slave system in the Americas was of trivial importance compared to the domestic economy and society. It did not occupy a large part of the domestic consciousness.[16] In no sense did the English or Dutch live with slaves as did their counterparts in ancient Greece and Rome. In the English case, the Irish would seem more promising territory for this type of analysis, but while the Irish were conquered, expropriated, and absorbed into the English economy as thoroughly as any Mediterranean peoples into, say, the Roman Empire, they were never enslaved nor even reduced to serfdom.

After 1700 the slave empires of the Americas were of larger significance to Europe in all senses, but the rise of movements to abolish slavery in the 1780s makes it hard to evaluate the impact of slavery on freedom and vice versa. Abolition may have helped validate waged labor systems in Europe and reinforce the position of political and economic elites, but the fact remains that the slave systems themselves were abolished in the process. Moreover, in ideological terms, surely the employers of labor in England would have found it more useful to have slavery in the colonies continue rather than come to an end. Slavery would have acted as a continuing reminder to free laborers of how much worse their predicament might be and, indeed, as the mining serfs in seventeenth-century Scotland discovered, might become. In any event, in the post-1700 world, it seems that Europeans, especially the English, rather quickly outgrew any need for slavery to define concepts of freedom for themselves even supposing that they had once felt such a need.

The work of Drescher, Patterson, Davis, and Morgan has moved beyond explanations rooted in the self-interest of a European elite but, with the exception of Drescher, each of these scholars, in different ways, makes freedom in the Western world dependent to some degree on the slave systems that western Europe also developed. To these might be added the work of Robert Steinfeld on the demise of indentured servitude and the emergence of modern conceptions of free labor. For Steinfeld, the indenture contract could not survive a nineteenth-century world that had come to see slavery as immoral, at least in the United States.[17] Indentured servitude had just too many elements that parallelled slavery. The argument throughout the present work by contrast is the reverse of these positions: the rise of slavery in the Americas was dependent on the nature of freedom in western Europe.

While abolition is not a major concern here, it is also possible that the more often coercion is seen to be unconscionable for people like oneself and appropriate for others, the more likely that coercion for anyone will eventually be questioned. Awareness of the insider-outsider divide was tantamount to the ending of the slave system. In 1784 Necker, in France, reflected educated European opinion in condemning the trade, but he also found action by any single nation alone impossible to contemplate.[18] A few years later, the line was crossed when Charles James Fox posed a question in the House of Commons that he described as "the foundation of the whole business." How would members of Parliament react, he asked, if "a Bristol ship were to go to any part of France . . . and the democrats (there) were to sell the aristocrats, or vice versa, to be carried off to Jamaica . . . to be sold for slaves?"[19] After this point the number of slaves in Brazil would increase by half, those in the U.S. south would quintuple, and those in Cuba would increase eightfold. Nevertheless, when set against the backdrop of western thought, the very posing of the question – and this is the earliest documented example by someone close to power – meant that the issue was not now *whether* the system would end but rather *when*. To return to where this chapter began, abolition – the idea that no one should be a slave – was as quintessentially and uniquely western a concept as was gang labor on a Caribbean sugar estate.

The evidence discussed here thus suggests that whatever the powerful validating influences of American slave systems on concepts of freedom and, more specifically waged labor systems, of the north Atlantic, the influence of free over slave systems of the early modern world was greater than any reverse effect. There is no suggestion in any European country of a bargain between workers and ruling elite to reserve slavery for Africans and Amerindians and to guarantee at the same time wider freedoms for non-elite Europeans.[20] The real possibility of enslaving other Europeans appeared to lie beyond the serious intent of any European class or nation even before the onset of the early modern period. Slavery in the Americas was created by the freedom that Europeans had to develop resources in Africa and the Americas without the restrictions of social structures and values that held in the non-European world – the same factors that underlay the rise of waged labor systems. In stark contrast to classical times, however, this freedom of the individual against the group did not include the right to enslave other Europeans. European conceptions of the other ensured that only non-Europeans could be slaves.

NOTES

1 For the classic statement see Edward P. Thompson, "The Moral Economy of the English Crowd in the Eighteenth Century," *Past and Present*, 50(1971):76–123.
2 Gomer Williams, *History of the Liverpool Privateers* (London, 1897), pp. 555–60. I would like to thank Steve Behrendt for this reference.
3 A. W. Coats, "Changing Attitudes to Labour in the Mid-Eighteenth Century," *Economic History Review*, 11(1958–59):35–51; Stanley L. Engerman, "Coerced and Free Labor: Property Rights and the Development of the Labor Force," *Explorations in Entrepreneurial History*, 29(1992):1–29; Jan de Vries, "Between Purchasing Power and the World of Goods: Understanding the Household Economy in Early Modern Europe," in John Brewer and Roy Porter (eds.), *Consumption and the World of Goods* (London, 1993), pp. 85–132.
4 Anon, *Popery and Tyranny: or, the present state of France in relation to its government, trade, manners of the people, and nature of the countrey*, London, 1679, complained at the various subsidies and state aid to business provided by the French king. The latter was endeavoring "to make his subjects sole merchants of all Trades, as well imported as exported, and not only by the Priviledges already mentioned . . . , but also by putting all manner of Discouragements upon all Foreign Factories and Merchants by

Difficulty in their Dispatches, delayes in point of Justice, subjecting them to Foreign Duties and Seizures, not suffering them to be factors to the French or any other Nation but their own, and in case of Death to have their Estates seized as Aliens, and the countenance and conceiving the French have as to all Duty when employ'd in the service of Foreigners" (p. 13). For the importance of protected transatlantic markets to English manufacturers see Ralph Davis, "English Foreign Trade, 1660–1700," *Economic History Review*, 7(1954):150–66.

5 London exports calculated from F. J. Fisher, "London's Export Trade in the Early Seventeenth Century," *Economic History Review*, 3(1950):151–61 and Davis, "English Foreign Trade, 1660–1700," pp. 163–6; London and English manufactured exports to Europe for 1699–1701 are calculated from Davis. For 1784–86 see idem, *The Industrial Revolution and British Overseas Trade* (Leicester, 1979), Table 38. Reexports are excluded as are all trade data for the 1790s and early 1800s because of the distorting effect of war. National income data for 1700 and 1785 were interpolated from the Gregory King and Joseph Massie estimates as revised in Peter H. Lindert and Jeffrey G. Williamson, "Revising England's Social Tables, 1688–1913," *Explorations in Economic History*, 19(4)(1982):385–408. For 1785, the Lindert and Williamson estimate for 1801/3 was adjusted using the rate of growth estimates for 1780–1801 in N. F. R. Crafts, *British Economic Growth During the Industrial Revolution* (Oxford, 1985), pp. 9–47.

6 If all Africans had been replaced by English, three hundred thousand extra emigrants from England, 1650 to 1700, or about six thousand per year, would have constituted about a quarter of one percent of the English labor force in this period.

7 Seymons Drescher, *Capitalism and Antislavery: British Mobilization in Comparative Perspective*, (London, 1986), pp. 1–24. There is a striking complementarity between the shift in English perceptions outlined by Drescher and the market-driven emergence of humanitarianism that Thomas L. Haskell argues for in "Capitalism and the Origins of the Humanitarian Sensibility, Part 1 and Capitalism and the Origins of the Humanitarian Sensibility, Part 2," in *The Antislavery Debate: Capitalism and Abolitionism as a Problem in Historical Interpretation*, ed. Thomas Bender (Berkeley, 1992).

8 A somewhat attenuated version of the same process might be seen in Japan, the non-European society with the most western family and social structure before the twentieth century. Slaves in Japan were overwhelmingly Japanese (drawn from criminals and the poor) before the modern period (Orlando Patterson, *Slavery and Social Death: A Comparative Study* (Cambridge, Mass., 1982), p. 127). In the nineteenth and twentieth centuries the Japanese increasingly drew on foreign sources for slaves though the numbers where much lower than those carried across the Atlantic. Both before and after Japan imposed the abolition of slavery on Korea in 1910, Korea had come to be the major source of forced laborers taken to Japan. The absorption of foreigners into the Japanese view of the social contract – a process some would argue that is not yet complete – might account for the gradual disappearance of coercion of foreigners, though in this case there are extraneous geopolitical developments to be reckoned with in the form of world wars (Mikiso Hane, *Peasants, Rebels and Outcasts: The Underside of Modern Japan* (New York, 1982), pp. 236–7).

9 As Seymour Drescher has pointed out (*Capitalism and Antislavery*, pp. 18–20, and "The Ending of the Slave Trade and the Evolution of European Scientific Racism," *Social Science History*, 14(1990):415–50), both the proslavery and antislavery campaigns in England in the late eighteenth and early nineteenth centuries were relatively free of the biological racism that became prevalent in the mid-nineteenth century. Prior to the 1820s the abolitionist literature conveyed a strong sense that any cultural differences between European and Africans were to be explained by the ravages of the slave trade. Yet there is also a sense that Africans were at an earlier stage of development than Europeans – most clearly expressed in Henry Brougham's *An Enquiry into the Colonial Policy of the European Powers* (Edinburgh, 1803), II, pp. 507–18, which embodied the stages model of human development popular in the eighteenth century.

10 Timothy J. Coates, "Exiles and Orphans: Forced and State-Sponsored Colonization in the Portuguese Empire, 1550–1720," Ph.D. thesis, University of Minnesota, 1993, 1–31; Leslie P. Choquette, *Frenchmen into Peasants: Modernity and Tradition in the Peopling of French Canada* (Cambridge, Mass., 1997), pp. 273–7; "Order of the Council of State . . . ," Sept. 10, 1651, CSPCS, 1:360.

11 See most recently the essays by Nigel Bolland, Lucia Lamounier, and Mary Turner in Mary Turner (ed.), *From Chattel Slaves to Wage Slaves: The Dynamics of Labour Bargaining in the Americas* (London, 1995).

12 David R. Roediger, "Race, Labor and Gender in the Languages of Antebellum Social Protest," in Stanley L. Engerman, *The Terms of Labor* (Stanford, 1999), pp. 170–9.

13 T. E. J. Wiedmann, *Slavery* (Oxford, 1987), pp. 3–6.

14 Edmund S. Morgan, *American Slavery; American Freedom* (New York, 1975), pp. 338–87; Duncan J. MacCleod, *Slavery, Race and the American Revolution* (Cambridge, 1974), pp. 62–108, 183–4.

15 David Brion Davis, *Slavery and Human Progress* (New York, 1984), pp. 279–320.

16 As a test of this see the sections on "Slavery" and "Colonies" in the index and catalogue of the *Goldsmith's-Kress Library of Economic Literature: A Consolidated Guide*, 4 vols. (Woodbridge, Conn., 1976–77). Before the mid-eighteenth century the coverage of either topic can only be described as thin.

17 Robert J. Steinfeld, *The Invention of Free Labor: The Employment Relation in English and American Law and Culture, 1350–1870* (Chapel Hill, 1991), pp. 163–72.

18 *De l' administration des finances de la France* cited in Olivier Pétré-Grenouilleau, *Les Traites des Noirs* (Paris, 1997), pp. 64–5. [Jacques Necker, a Protestant Swiss financier, headed the French monarchy's finances from 1778 to 1781 and again in 1789, when he became the darling of those calling for reform. Because of his faith, he could not hold the post of Controller General, reserved for Catholics. In 1781, shortly after his first disgrace, he published the *Comptes Rendus au Roi*, a supposedly open statement of the king's finances; the book was an instant sensation and touched off a fiery debate about royal finances.]

19 *Parliamentary Debates*, 1792, XXIX, 1122.

20 Orlando Patterson argues for an implicit bargain in Solonic Greece between slave owners and non-slaves. The latter tolerated the manumission of slaves (which was a way reinforcing the slave system) because non-slaves were assured of a measure of personal and civic freedom (*Freedom in the Making of Western Culture*, 3 vols. (New York, 1991–), pp. 64–81). There are parallels here with Edmund S. Morgan's argument for an implicit alliance between rich and poor whites in Virginia against African slaves, though the Greek case appears to lack the ethnic element (*American Slavery; American Freedom*, pp. 295–337).

3

HISTORY, MYTH AND HISTORICAL IDENTITY

Karin Friedrich

Every time a society finds itself in crisis it instinctively turns its eyes towards its origins and looks
there for a sign. (Octavio Paz)[1]

Since the revival of interest in national origins during the Renaissance, prompted by the redis-
covery of Tacitus's history of the pagan tribes which challenged the decaying Roman Empire,
history steadily gained respectability as an academic subject at schools and universities. The
questioning of philosophical and theological certainties and authorities during the Renaissance
and Reformation period engendered an identity crisis, when late medieval Christian societies
were confronted with the un-Christian heritage of classical antiquity. Poland-Lithuania was no
exception; Italian and German Humanism had reached Cracow, the old Polish capital, even
before Bona Sforza (1494–1557), the daughter of Gian Galeazzo, duke of Milan, and Isabella of
Aragon, married king Sigismund I in 1518 and brought Italian artists and scholars to the Polish
court. A society as steeped in the culture of classical antiquity as that of the Polish-Lithuanian
nobility took seriously Cicero's dictum that "not to know what happened in the past, means ever
to remain a child".[2] Its sense of the past was greatly enhanced by the accumulation of political,
legal and economic privileges since the late fourteenth century, which prevented the Polish king
from collecting taxes, declaring war or passing any new laws without the nobility's consent. For
politically active citizens, the past provided a valuable set of examples and models for future action
and political legitimacy, boosting their self-confidence.

The same was true for the citizens of Royal Prussia, who regarded themselves in historical,
political and national terms as a distinct group within the Commonwealth. For the burghers
in particular, collective historical memory was patriotic scripture: being citizens of the fatherland – the city, the Prussian province or the wider Commonwealth – involved rights as well as

Karin Friedrich, "History, Myth and Historical Identity," pp. 71–81, 83–91, 94–5 from *The Other Prussia:
Royal Prussia, Poland and Liberty, 1569–1772*. Cambridge: Cambridge University Press, 2000.

responsibilities. History was a crucial instrument for the education and formation of loyal and able citizens, both burgher and noble. Since their incorporation into the Polish kingdom, the Prussian social and political elites had looked to Humanist Cracow and its university, compelled by the need to produce qualified councillors and burgomasters, secretaries and delegates to the Polish Sejm and the Prussian diets. The activities and influence of a large circle of international Humanist scholars at Cracow, many of South-German, Alsatian, Silesian or Hungarian origin, peaked in the 1520s.[3] Between 1493 and 1517, until the Reformation shattered the link, eighty-eight students from Danzig alone studied at the Jagiellonian University in Cracow, but student numbers from Royal Prussia dropped sharply after 1525 as the Prussians created their own, Protestant education system.[4] Urban Latin schools were remodelled into institutions of higher learning; from the middle of the sixteenth century, the three academic Gymnasia in Danzig, Thorn and Elbing transformed Royal Prussia into a centre of classical studies. New curricula combined Protestant theology and the traditional Humanist disciplines of philosophy, poetry, grammar and rhetoric with an emphasis on new subjects such as law, political theory and history.[5] From 1535, the Gymnasium in Elbing flourished under the leadership of the Dutch Humanist Wilhelm Gnapheus, who introduced Melanchthon's educational ideas. Danzig followed in 1558 with the foundation of a Humanist school which, in 1580, received the title of Academic Gymnasium, and became the most prominent Prussian school, particularly in the early 1600s when Barthel Keckermann, the Calvinist natural law thinker, taught there. After the decline in significance of the university of Cracow, a large number of Protestant and even Catholic nobles from all over the Commonwealth sent their children for a solid Humanist education to the Royal Prussian Gymnasia, whose attraction increased markedly until the success of Tridentine Catholicism depleted student numbers in the early seventeenth century.[6]

The Gymnasium in Thorn was reorganised in 1568, around the time when the first Jesuit schools were established in the province. Although the Protestant Gymnasia have been credited with higher educational standards than their rival Jesuit colleges, the school which the Jesuit Order opened in Thorn in 1605 enjoyed growing popularity, not only among the Polish-speaking Catholic population, but also among the families of Protestant craftsmen and day-labourers. The competition between the Society of Jesus and the Protestant schools for the hearts and minds of future citizens, especially those of Polish and Lithuanian noble extraction, became fiercer in the late seventeenth century. In 1684 the Thorn Jesuits compiled a curriculum which revealed heavy borrowing from their Protestant counterparts: Latin, Greek, rhetoric, poetry and metaphysics, as well as natural sciences and history. As a result, the Thorn Protestant Gymnasium increased its provision of Polish language classes to avoid alienating Polish-speaking Lutheran or Calvinist families. Thorn had a substantial Protestant Polish-speaking population among all groups of society, as evidenced in 1698 when the guild masters thanked the city council for cutting back the time allotted to sermons and organ-playing in the "Polish church services for Polish Protestant servant folk", so that they could go back to work sooner rather than later.[7]

Preparation for political activity in the city and the Commonwealth included training in rhetoric and oratorical skills. As Joachim Pastorius, director of the Gymnasium in Elbing from 1651–4 and history professor in Danzig from 1654–67, recommended in his letter to the son of the Danzig burgrave Adrian von der Linde, Cicero's "robust and accurate style" was best suited for political speeches.[8] The core programme of *eruditio historica* included the study of Pliny and Cassiodor, two of the most frequently quoted sources for sixteenth-century Polish and Prussian historians. Knowledge of heraldry, *Kleinodia Polona Libertatis*, for noble students was balanced with the writing of treatises on the usefulness of cities in Poland, designed for the sons of burghers.[9] Following their Order's *Ratio Studiorum* of 1599, the Jesuits in Thorn echoed the patriotic tone of Protestant teaching and similarly stressed the future role of the students as citizens of the Commonwealth, in the diet or city council's public affairs. From the mid-seventeenth century, the Jesuits carried on training their students in law, rhetoric and public speaking, while Protestant curricula started to emphasise theology, literature and mathematics.[10]

Religious differences did not prevent the burghers in the Royal Prussian cities from sharing with the nobility views on the necessity of political education. Georg Wende, rector of the Thorn Gymnasium towards the end of the seventeenth century, compared the tasks fulfilled by city councillors with those of Chinese mandarins, whose high standards of education and their noble descent made them the most suitable for state service. Wende warned that political education for the common good should not be neglected even in schools where theological education (Confucianism in China – Lutheranism in Royal Prussia) was generally preferred.[11] History and its great men were used as examples, while the knowledge of past constitutions, governments and kingdoms served as a treasure-trove of models, bad and good, for criticism and imitation.[12] Public-spirited education, intended to fortify urban burghers' pride in their citizen status, was also valued by Michael Mylius, a history professor in Elbing, who in 1642 wrote on the occasion of the death of the royal envoy and palatine of Pernau in Livonia, Count Ernst Dönhoff, of the greatest achievements of the deceased nobleman: "[He] travelled all over Europe's regions and kingdoms, especially those whose languages he easily mastered, and after his return as a great citizen of this body politic he made use of [what he had learned] for the good of the republic."[13]

Patriotic behaviour was therefore measured by the use made of education for the common good of the state and the province: Dönhoff "restored peace for God, the king and the people, for holiness, majesty and utility, *publicae salutis summam*".[14] Personal virtues and qualifications were not an end in themselves, but a means to serve – in Dönhoff's case – the city of Elbing and the Polish-Lithuanian Commonwealth. In 1651, Gottfried Zamehl, from a prominent family of burgomasters and poets laureate in Elbing, whose father had collected the manuscripts of medieval Prussian chronicles, went on a study trip to Western Europe. After his return, he summed up the patriotic purpose of his experience abroad:

> We travel to various nations and regions, but meanwhile we do not lose our love for our fatherland, nor shall we ever hold it in contempt; . . . it is not enough to live well abroad, but the motivation for all industrious activities [in foreign countries] is to come back with fame and honour to the fatherland.[15]

The hope that burghers would adopt the ideal of education recommended by the city authorities was also expressed in the appeal by the theology professor and senior pastor of Thorn, Jan Neunachbar, to appoint a local Thorunian or Prussian preacher to a vacant parish in the city: "not only do locals know the nature of their fatherland, and what is good for it, better than foreigners: but also the citizenry will be encouraged to spend something on their children and educate them for the benefit of the fatherland."[16]

Most historical works in Royal Prussia were written by burghers and disseminated from local printing presses, some of them attached to the schools. Jurisprudence ranked highly among the career choices of the urban elites, who wished to grasp the intricacies of their own constitutions and laws, the traditions of Kulm law and their ancient privileges granted by the Order and the Polish monarchy. But even law was approached from a historical angle. It was not merely historians who were sought, but lawyers who knew history, in the words of Pastorius "the parent of all sciences".[17]

Under the influence of the universities of the Empire and other European states, where the teaching of Roman law in the Renaissance had laid the foundations for the rationalist school of natural law, legal training at the Prussian Gymnasia adopted the focus on "public law". The academic preparation for public office was inspired and guided by the science of cameralism (*Kameralwissenschaften*) in the German universities of the late seventeenth century such as Jena, Halle, Frankfurt an der Oder, Helmstedt, Heidelberg and Leipzig, where many future burgo-masters and councillors of Royal Prussian cities completed their studies.[18] Prussian students and scholars who visited German universities followed the debates about Athenian democracy, the mixed constitution of Sparta and the advantages of aristocracy or monarchy; upon their return to Royal Prussia they applied what they had learnt to their domestic context, focusing on the dangers of tyranny, on the defence of their privileges and immunities inherited from previous gen-erations, on the advantages of the aristocratic and democratic elements in the polity and on the prospects for reform of the practice of government in their own state, the Polish-Lithuanian Com-monwealth.[19] German political science (*Staatenkunde*) appealed not only to Royal Prussian stu-dents: the idea that laws and constitutions had no power and meaning unless they were backed by true political power in the service of the common good held a strong attraction for seven-teenth-century Polish constitutional thinking.[20]

In such an environment, the writing and teaching of history was central to contemporary politi-cal debate, which consciously used the past as an instrument for expressing present political needs. Poland and Royal Prussia were no exception. The Dutch republic used the republican myth of Venice in the same way.[21] The Poles certainly seemed to know their origins. The mythi-cal common descent of all nations of the Polish-Lithuanian Commonwealth from the ancient Sarmatian warrior-heroes, who successfully resisted Roman attempts to conquer them, was fashioned into a statement of the Commonwealth's constitutional and political superiority over West European societies oppressed by absolute royal power. Szymon Starowolski founded his reputation as a patriotic historian early on by collecting a pantheon of Sarmatian heroes, of *bel-latores et scriptores*, who included representatives of all nations of the Commonwealth, similar to the gallery of Swedish-Gothic heroes assembled by Johannes Magnus.[22] References to great his-torical rulers and nations pointed at the imitation of past virtue. As the Goths were to the Swedes, or the Batavians to the Dutch, so were the Sarmatians to the Poles.[23] Roger Mason exposed a very similar process in medieval Scottish mythology and chronicles, expressed politically in the Declaration of Arbroath in 1320, where Sallust's idea of liberty stood godfather.[24] History, applied as a political instrument, forged a community's sense of the past by several means, including a collective name, a myth of origin and descent, a shared history and a specific political culture based on the freedom of its citizens, within a limited territory.[25]

The degree to which thinking was guided by mythical analogies was expressed by the Italian Jesuit [Antonio] Possevino, a widely travelled expert on Poland: "legends and *fabulae*, as hidden and obscure they may be, are more powerful than poems". Mythology and miracles were accepted as long as they had a purpose. The Renaissance historian Scaliger confirmed this view: no mythology was created for its own sake, all myths pointed beyond themselves to some political or didactic purpose, helping nations to identify with their own past and to apply historic virtues and values to the improvement of their present situation.[26] Although the Renaissance clearly popularised the genre of national history-writing, Kurt Johannesson has stressed that the creation of identity based on myths of the origin of peoples, cities, families or nations was not linked to one specific historical period but corresponded to a general human need to harmonise past and present.[27]

Under the influence of the Humanists, secular history was now commonly structured in *historia locorum, temporum, familiarum et rerum gestarum* – the study of an area or place, of chronological events, of dynastic and national descent, and finally of all events relating to a society and its institutions, the church, schools, governments and magistracies. Jean Bodin's attack on the German theory of *translatio imperii*, the idea of continuity between the ancient Roman Empire and the Holy Roman Empire, sparked renewed interest in other themes of history: *historia humana* (the history of secular society), *historia naturalis* (including the laws of nature), and *historia divina* (on religion and revealed truth).[28] Despite the unpopularity of Bodin's political theory, his historical methodology, focusing on historical *particularia*, suited the Prussian burghers. The historical tradition of cosmography and Sleidanus's theory of the four world monarchies, Babylon (or Egypt), Persia, Greece and Rome, had never put down strong roots in Prussia.[29] Guided by patriotism, national and provincial history was much more popular.

In the sixteenth century Danzig secretary Caspar Schütz had stressed the need for historical education. He regretted that little knowledge of the Prussian past survived, due to ignorance and lack of learning not only among the pagans, but also among the Teutonic Knights. Historians of the following century wanted to remedy this situation.[30] In *De natura et proprietatibus historiae commentarius*, published posthumously in 1613, Keckermann was one of the first Prussians to follow Bodin's history of *particularia*. In contrast to the usual Ciceronian approach, the Danzig professor did not accept rhetoric as the main instrument of history, but considered historical research a branch of philosophy and, more specifically, of logic: "nobody can write history well who is not a good logician".[31] Throughout the seventeenth century, the Royal Prussian Gymnasia included Bodin's historical methodology in their curriculum, a fact mentioned in the 1676 lecture notes of the future burgomaster Johann Gottfried Rösner, who attended the lectures of the Thorn historian Ernst König on Bodin's *Historia pragmatica*. Rösner followed Bodin's subdivision of history into new subjects, as recommended by Keckermann: the history of ethics, political economy and history, and ecclesiastical history, as well as the history of scholarship (*prudentia*) and philosophy.[32] These subjects were no longer inferior to Ciceronian rhetoric as they had been in the early sixteenth century. Not only biblical empires, but individual states, nations, peoples and even cities should be looked at from the angle of their universal significance, using the same tools and categories as ecclesiastical or world history in the past.[33] Starowolski echoed this approach in his early seventeenth-century treatise on the utility of history aimed at students at Cracow University: history only makes sense when "it reflects the deeds and events of all peoples of all times and all areas as in a great mirror".[34]

Prussian urban historians followed these recommendations. Unlike most histories of German Hanseatic cities in the Empire, Royal Prussian *Particular-Historie* never ignored the larger dimension of the wider commonwealth: "nam pius est, patriae scribere facta, labor" – it is pious work to write the history of one's fatherland.[35] *Amor patriae*, love of the fatherland, however, never entirely eclipsed the larger context. Walter Hubatsch observed that even sixteenth-century Prussian chronicles of monasteries and small towns never lost sight of the history of the whole Prussian province, in which such chronicles were embedded.[36] This is an important point, as German historians, transfixed by the power of nineteenth-century Prussia, have often argued that Danzig, Thorn and Elbing were in fact "city-states" which possessed quasi-independence from the Polish-Lithuanian state. The view behind this interpretation was that Royal Prussian burghers were at odds with a foreign, hostile Polish environment, whose culture they never accepted. A closer look at the historical and political writing of several Prussian burghers, however, reveals, a rather different picture.

Keckermann's idea of a perfect education combined patriotic with cosmopolitan values and suggests that his definition of *patria* did not end on the ramparts of his city. The fatherland, whose history one knew best, was also the place where one developed talents useful for public service and the common good. Such an endeavour made the burgher a precious and honoured member of society – his own local community, as well as human society at large.[37] The writing and teaching of history, especially at grammar school level, were therefore recognised public services for the good of the republic, and not merely an amateur's hobby-horse. Two other historians of Royal Prussia in the later seventeenth century, Pastorius and Hartknoch, wrote comprehensive guides to the history of the Polish-Lithuanian state to instil patriotic sentiments and a sense of duty among the young.[38] History-teaching had to focus on the need of young Prussians to acquaint themselves with the history and constitution not only of their cities but also of the Commonwealth. After their travels abroad, their *peregrinatio*, the young returned to the service of their *patria* as the new generation of their cities' political elite. This fatherland was the city, as referred to by fellow Danzigers or Torunians in Samuel Schönwald's travel *album*; but the *patria nostra* could also be the Commonwealth and Poland, whose historical greatness was felt to be at stake in 1655, the year of the Swedish invasion, when Schönwald and other youngsters studied abroad and discussed their anxiety about the fate of their various home provinces. Such diary entries from the 1650s demonstrate the similarity of attitudes of young burghers and nobles towards their Commonwealth, assuring mutual friendship and lamenting the war that was afflicting their common fatherland.[39] Dedication to the *respublica* was the very essence of the Ciceronian idea of the active life, shared by the Polish nobility.

The intellectual life and high educational standards in the Prussian Gymnasia, as well as Keckermann's ideals, inspired one of the Polish szlachta's most outspoken supporters of noble patriotic duty, Andrzej Maksimilian Fredro. In his educational programme of 1666 he voiced the need not only for nobles, but also for Polish burghers to imitate the Prussian cities in regularly sending their sons to foreign countries to learn languages and observe foreign customs, although Fredro did not explore why educational standards were higher in the Prussian Protestant schools. Protestant preachers had to undergo an academic training which included theological studies at a university, while Catholic priests, with the rare exception of those who could afford to go to Rome, or who received an adequate stipend, launched their careers in one of the numerous local seminaries or Jesuit colleges in Poland.[40] In many respects, however, the educational ideals of nobles shared similar requirements and a similar spirit of public duty as the education of the Prussian patriciate. Just as young burghers were prepared for public office, noble education was aimed at active participation in the political structure of the Commonwealth, as deputies to the Sejm, court officials, or even for a post as a senator. What Germany later called *staatsbürgerliche Erziehung* (civic education) was the most important element of the curriculum for a Polish or Lithuanian nobleman. History was central. A young nobleman had to be told of his origins so as to fill him with pride and a consciousness of the obligations connected with his role as a member of the noble Sarmatian nation.

Thus from the early seventeenth century the Humanist genre of history as *descriptio orbis terrarum* was replaced by a history of nations and fatherlands: the idea that the values of the past had an immediate impact on the present made anachronism a virtue. Changes in the patterns and contents of myths serve therefore as valuable tools for measuring alterations and shifts in a society's political culture. The economic and social crises in the Royal Prussian cities following the Swedish wars of the seventeenth century, the decline of their privileges and the political disappointment felt among the Prussian burghers about the behaviour of the nobility and the Polish king towards them – all this was reflected in the writing of history and in political publications. The period from early Humanism, when myths of origin were invented and first disseminated, to the eighteenth-century Enlightenment, which under the impact of the political and military crisis of the Polish-Lithuanian Commonwealth discarded many old legends, is crucial for the development of historical writing in the Prussian cities. Its citizens never turned away from history; on the contrary, when old myths no longer rang true, new myths had to be developed to account for a change in political attitudes and mentalities.

Traditions of History-writing in Poland and Prussia

Despite the hostility of Royal Prussian historians towards the legacy of the Teutonic Order after 1454, chronicles from the Teutonic period still exerted considerable influence on the political and intellectual atmosphere of Royal Prussia and the view burghers and nobles held of their Prussian nation's past. The following three traditions formed the source base for Prussian historiography in the seventeenth and eighteenth centuries: chronicles commissioned and controlled by the Teutonic Order, a separate religious chronicle tradition, and secular provincial history or *Landesgeschichte*, based mainly in the Prussian cities.

In numerous chronicles the Teutonic Knights celebrated their conquest of the Prussian lands as a victory of Christianity over the heathens. Their chronicle tradition found its first and foremost exponent in Peter von Dusburg, whose 1326 history of the Teutonic Order, based on the Order's archival material in Marienburg as well as oral tradition, not only offers a vivid description of the life, wars and political organisation of the Knights, but also attempts to explain pagan Lithuanian and Prussian society and customs to a Christian audience.[41] ... A contemporary of Jeroschin and a parish priest from Deutsch-Eylau, Johann von Posilge, left a chronicle of Prussia which also demonstrated its independence from the panegyrical school promoted by the Grand Masters of the Teutonic Order. Posilge, who was not an immigrant from Germany but a native Prussian from nearby Marienburg,[42] exerted great influence on later historians hostile to the Teutonic Order. In general, however, the majority of the Order chronicles presented a positive picture of the knights' activities in the *Ordensland*.[43] After 1454, a secular branch of chronicle-writing emerged among laymen and clergy with an interest in the pagan and Teutonic past, albeit from an anti-Order point of view. This third tradition was located in Königsberg, the capital of Ducal Prussia after the secularisation of the Order in 1525, and in the three main Royal Prussian cities, who had headed the opposition movement against the Teutonic Knights alongside the Prussian nobility. The Prussian burghers, who started to compile the history of their cities and province, continued using the Grand Masters' chronicles alongside anti-Teutonic traditions, which had the greatest impact on the chroniclers of Danzig.[44] Foreign sources, including the histories of the Livonian Order, German medieval chronicles, and ancient sources before and during the time of the migrations in Europe, were also consulted, especially on the pagan past. One of the most influential post-Reformation sources was Simon Grunau's strongly anti-Teutonic *Prussian Chronicle*.[45]

[...]

The 1520s, which saw the final victory of Poland and Royal Prussia over the Teutonic Knights and resulted in the secularisation of the Order by its last Grand Master, Albrecht of Hohenzollern, were an especially productive period for historiography in both Royal Prussia and in the newly established Duchy, from 1525 a vassal state under the Polish crown. Despite the political separation, early sixteenth-century chronicles reveal that both parts of Prussia remained intellectually very close. Grunau in Elbing and Oliwa, Hennenberger in Königsberg, and Schütz in Danzig – the three main chroniclers of the sixteenth century – all based their accounts of their pagan ancestors largely on one source: Erasmus Stella. The latter, who continued to exert a great influence on Prussian history-writing for the next 200 years, was no native Prussian. As burgomaster of Zwickau in Saxony, he was only linked to Prussia by his friendship with the bishop of Pomesania and the early sixteenth-century Grand Master of the Order Friedrich, duke of Saxony and count of Thüringen. Lacking access to the rich manuscript archives and chronicles in the possession of the Order and subsequently of the libraries in Königsberg, Danzig, Elbing and Thorn, Stella was the first historian to base his research on the Prussian past almost exclusively on the literary and historical sources of antiquity.[46] He added a new element to Prussian historiography: his chronicle aimed at a comprehensive history of the province (*Landesgeschichte*) in the context of a world history of *res gestae* from biblical times, through the age of the four world empires and the migrations, and ending in his own period. In contrast to Humanist cosmographies, history in the sixteenth and seventeenth centuries was expected to be nationally focused and complete. What could not be known had to be invented.[47]

[. . .]

According to Stella, the ancient Prussians were a branch of the Sarmatian tribes described by Tacitus (Venedi, Daci, Alani). They had come to the lands east of the Vistula and the Baltic shore as immigrants and mixed with the remnants of the Gothic peoples.[48] Impressed by Tacitus's description of the ancient Germanic tribes, who had no fortified houses, lived simply and worshipped nature, Stella attached the same attributes to the Baltic Prussians. The Saxon historian belonged to a generation of German scholars who had reacted to the Italian shunning of the Gothic-Germanic barbarians with a counter-attack: Tacitus was their weapon and proof that the Germans were not just cruel barbarians but possessed piety and a communal spirit, strength in war and nobility by merit. Rejecting the sophistication of high Roman culture as decadent, the "noble barbarians" were part of the Humanist cult of ancestor-worship which Stella introduced to Prussia.[49] Significantly, neither Stella nor his imitators in Prussia integrated the Prussians into Germanic culture, but into the Sarmatian world.

The Gothic Myth

Gothic mythology in Poland-Lithuania received a boost not only from Germany but also from Sweden, where it was even more powerfully propagated by the Magnus brothers, who used the history of the Goths by Jordanes to confirm the association of the Swedes with the Gothic tradition. The myth had expanded by the late sixteenth century, when Sigismund III, from the senior branch of the Swedish Vasa dynasty, was elected to the Polish throne. Hartknoch reports that from this time the Poles thought the Goths were in fact of Sarmatian origin like themselves. . . .

An appreciation of the foundations of Prussian mythology is vital for an understanding of the further development of Prussian historical identity. The most significant feature was not the fact that the Prussians invented their specific version of the past, but what was absent from it: the German element. There was no attempt to construct a bridge to the Holy Roman Empire, nor to the Germanic past of Tacitus's vision of *Germania* which was so valuable for German Lutheran reformers and Humanists.[50] Despite the clear recollection by Prussian burghers that most of their families originated from Germany, they not only signed an act of political and administrative incorporation with the Polish crown in 1454; they also founded a historical association with the Poles, as their historiographical tradition had to find a new home in a Sarmatian environment. The result, the creation of a highly adaptable and complex mythology which combined the Gothic-Germanic with the Sarmatian-Polish traditions, suited the political needs of the Prussian nobles as well as the townspeople.

[. . .]

As Erasmus Stella had done for Prussian history, so the German chronicler Albert Krantz, who was influenced by Tacitus and the new 1515 edition of Jordanes, effectively rehabilitated the Goths in Germany. His *Vandalia*, published in 1518, became the German historiographical credo of the century. This work considered the barbaric Germanic peoples to be the root of all Gothic-Germanic and Slavonic nations, descending from Noah as a big family of *gentes* who all originated from continental Europe. For Krantz, the Gothic-Germanic Vandals and Slavonic-Sarmatian Venedi were the same people. Krantz based his idea of Germanic Vandal-Goth unity on the old idea of a universal German monarchy – the fourth and last empire according to the biblical prophecies. This monarchy was based on *"communis ditio* (power or law) *a Germania"*, which implies that German law (Magdeburg and Lübeck law) spread widely in central and east central Europe. This legal concept, rather than culture or language – "from the river Don to the Rhine, there are many different languages" – was central to Krantz's definition of Germanic-Vandal hegemony.[51]

[. . .]

The Sarmatian Counter-myth

The Sarmatian mythological reversal turned out to be powerful. Ulewicz discovered a copy of Schedel's *Chronicon* in the Jagiellonian University Library bearing the marginal remark by a sixteenth-century hand that the Bavarians, as a Slavonic-Sarmatian people ("because their name derives from *boyars*"), were part of a Slavic realm stretching as far as the Rhine.[52] But early modern Polish authors were not content with merely turning the Gothic theory on its head. It was easy enough to replace the Goths with the Sarmatians as the great family of nations between the Don and the Vistula, Oder or Rhine – wherever the taste for expansion found its limits. The Sarmatian myth, however, was not an ad-hoc invention to counter Gothic-German or Swedish historical theories accompanying diplomatic or military warfare, but had deep roots, like Gothic mythology, in ancient and medieval chronicle literature.[53]

In the fifteenth and sixteenth centuries, on the basis of works by Herodotus, Juvenal, Ptolemy, Pomponius Mela and the Anonymous Gaul, the Sarmatians were identified in early Humanist sources as Slavonic tribes which had migrated from the Balkans or Asia Minor.[54] By the second half of the sixteenth century, the historical canon of the great Slavic-Sarmatian family which included the Poles and their brothers, the Czechs, Ruthenians, Lithuanians, Mazovians, Prussians, Pomeranians, and even the Croats and the Dalmatians, was firmly established. The ground had been laid by the Polish histories of Kadlubek, bishop of Cracow [d. 1223], and Jan Długosz (1475), and by Maciej Miechowita's history of Sarmatia (1521) and the works of his followers.

Długosz placed greatest emphasis on the biblical formulation of the Sarmatians; the story of Babylon and the descent of the Sarmatians from Japheth, who lived in Pannonia and the Carpathian mountains, continued to influence most chronicles over the following two centuries.[55] The legendary founder of the Polish nation was Lech, which explained why many foreigners called the Poles Lechitae. Maciej Miechowita's main merit was to transfer the notion of a faraway country called Sarmatia to Poland-Lithuania and to give it a fixed place on the central European map. His concept of a European and an Asian Sarmatia established great-power status for the Poles' mythical homeland and their historical identity, overcoming – as the Germans did with the help of Tacitus – the stigma of obscurity and barbarity. Still a vague concept during the first half of the sixteenth century, by the first interregnum in 1572–3 the Sarmatian theory was already influencing the Polish-Lithuanian nobility's political agenda. The expressions *Polonus, Poloni* were frequently replaced by *Sarmata, Sarmatae.* Outside Poland, foreigners started to acknowledge the identity of the Sarmatian Poles, like Melanchthon in his 1558 letter *De origine gentis Henetae, Polonicae seu Sarmaticae.*

The culture of Sarmatism has usually been accused of breeding xenophobia, narrow-minded chauvinism or plain expansionism. The development of a Polish-Sarmatian superiority-complex has been blamed for the decline or even collapse of Polish culture during the seventeenth and eighteenth centuries.[56] One of the voices considered representative of this megalomania belonged to the republican writer Stanislaw Orzechowski, himself of Ruthenian origin and a convert to Catholicism from Protestantism: "Let it be known that Lithuania cannot be equal to the Polish crown, nor can any Lithuanian, be he the most important and famous, equal the most lowly Pole – Lithuanian-born, you spend your life under the yoke – but I, as a Pole, like an eagle unbound under my king, fly freely."[57]

Although Polish and Sarmatian have frequently been used synonymously, the question is how other nations within the Commonwealth dealt with this ideology. If Orzechowski excluded the Lithuanians – officially the second nation in the republic – from the Sarmatian concept, then what degradation was in store for the Prussians? Not all Polish writers, however, agreed with Orzechowski. Aware of the discrepancies between social reality and the Sarmatian noble utopia, the Warmian bishop Marcin Kromer, like Starowolski, rejected the socially exclusive version of the Sarmatian myth, preferring to use it as a geographical demarcation between the ancestral tribes. According to Kromer, Sarmatians already lived between the Oder and the Don when Tacitus was taking great pains to decide whether the tribes between the Oder and the Vistula were Germanic or Slavonic-Sarmatian.[58] Forgiving Tacitus for his ignorance, Kromer drew a sharp line between the Germanic tribes and the Slavonic peoples at the Vistula river: the Sarmatian Slavs, settling east of it, descended from a different branch of Noah's large family, and therefore had no historical or cultural link with the Germanic Vandals or other Germanic tribes.[59] Kromer also turned Jordanes's account of the Gothic immigration from Scandinavia on its head: it was not the Germanic Goths, who, according to Tacitus, were autochthonous peoples, but the Sarmatians who came from the North. With this reinterpretation he reconciled the Sarmatian origin with the Swedish descent of the Vasa dynasty on the Polish throne and set an agenda which was respected not only by historians for two centuries to come, but also by the contemporary political establishment, as was first demonstrated in the official recognition he received as Poland's foremost historian by the Sejm.

Whether because of his commoner background or his involvement in Royal Prussian political life, Kromer exerted great influence on urban Prussian historiography, and his Sarmatian theories gained general recognition in Royal Prussia. Although he was appointed bishop of Warmia against the wishes of the majority of the Prussian estates, who rejected him as an *alienigena* and as an outspoken supporter of the heavily contested incorporation of the Royal Prussian diet into the ranks of the Polish Sejm in 1569, Prussian burgher historians frequently and affirmatively referred to his work. Throughout the seventeenth century, he was approvingly quoted as one of the best and most reliable historians and Polish sources, while Joachim Pastorius recommended his *Polonia* in a manual for the education of young noblemen as the most essential Polish history textbook.[60] Even foreign authors who were highly critical of the Polish point of view and the Sarmatian mythology, such as Hermann Conring and the Saxon professor Samuel Schurtzfleisch, knew and quoted the Warmian bishop. As a Royal Prussian senator, Kromer knew that the Prussian nobility would never have consented to being called Poles, but that as nobles they accepted the Sarmatian myth and the political privileges connected with it, the diets and noble courts, the free election of the king, and the mixed form of government. This was possible because the Sarmatian mythology was not one uniform, stereotypical concept, even though it was some times use to cover up the extreme differences that distinguished noblemen from each other in the multinational Commonwealth.

The Pomeranian nobleman van der Mylen was even more explicit: after forsaking its political independence and its past glory with the death of the last hereditary ruler of the Pomeranian dynasty, Pomerania had to suffer renewed subjection to the Saxons and the Empire, as well as partition by Sweden and Brandenburg in 1648.[61] Rejecting Schurtzfleisch's view of Pomerania's purely German character, van der Mylen asserts that the noble families (many of whom were of Slavic origin) and the mixed form of government with its privileges for the estates had once formed the essence of the Pomeranian nation. His description of such a political nation is very reminiscent of the Polish-Sarmatian mythology of noble freedoms, and it comes therefore closest to the idea of the nation that we find among Prussians and other nations (including the Polish) in the Commonwealth.[62]

The core of the disagreement between Pomeranians and Prussians concerned their differing attitude towards the Holy Roman Empire. Pomeranian historians accepted and identified with imperial rule, whereas the Prussians rejected it. While Pomeranians, Brandenburgers, Lusatians, Saxons and other peoples in the Empire divided their national consciousness into a German (and imperial) identity on the one hand, and an identification with their own territory (*Landesewußtsein*) on the other, the Prussians had no reason to assume a German identity.[63] Although they would not deny their ancestors' descent from German families, who had either immigrated or mixed with pagan Prussian families, they, unlike the Pomeranians, identified neither with the German nation nor with the Empire. Instead, in accommodating the Sarmatian myth with their own historical identity, the Prussians accepted Sarmatian citizenship not by becoming Poles but by associating themselves with the constitution and the political system of the Commonwealth. This construction produced a rhetorical tool actively used by Prussian burghers and urban elites in particular in their fight for recognition as fully-privileged citizens under the power of the Polish crown. Historical mythology therefore became the powerful basis of a Prussian burgher vision of Sarmatian history and self-definition, often used to counter their exclusion from citizenship, which the majority of the Polish nobility interpreted against them. Anyone who would listen, particularly other nations represented in the Polish-Lithuanian Commonwealth, received this message: we are Sarmatian Prussians, not subjects but free men and citizens.

NOTES

1 Quoted by Harold Berman, *Law and Revolution. The Formation of the Western Legal Tradition* (Cambridge, Mass.: Harvard University Press, 1983), p. 558.

2 "Nescire autem, quid antequam natus sis, acciderit; id est semper esse puerum", quoted by the Polish historian Szymon Starowolski, *Simonis Starovolsci Penu Historicum seu de dextra el fructuosa ratione Historians legendi Commentarius* (Venice: Zenarii Haeredes, 1620), p. 19.

3 Jacqueline Glomski, "Erasmus and Cracow, 1510–1530", *Yearbook of the Erasmus of Rotterdam Society* 17(1997), 1–18.

4 Wladyslaw Pniewski, *Jezyk polski ip dawnych szkotach gdańskich* (Gdańsk: Towarzystwo Przyjaciól Nauki i Sztuki, 1938), p. 14; M. Pawlak, *Studia uniwersyteckie mołdziezy z Prus Królewskich w XVI–XVIII wieku* (Torun: UMK, 1988), table 6.

5 For example the curriculum of 1688, *Catalogus Lectionum et Operarum Publicarum in Athenaeo Geda-nensi hoc cursu annuo expendiendarum propusito Januario ineunte* (Danzig: in Atheneo), which offered a course by Joachim Hoppe, history professor in Danzig, on "Historiam nonnullorum Regnorum publice in Jure Institutiones Juris Civilis & Canonici" (paragr. 2).

6 Janina Freilichówna, *Ideal wychowawczy Szlachty Polskiej w XVI i XVII wieku* (Warsaw: Nakladem Naukowego Towarzystwa Pedagogicznego, 1938), p. 68; Stanislaw Tync, *Dzieje Gimnazjum Toruńskiego*, 2 vols, vol. II: 1600–1660, Roczniki Towarzystwo Nauk w Toruniu (TNT) no. 53 (Toruń: TNT, 1949), pp. 82–3.

7 Ephraim Praetorius, "Kirchen-Sachen", Książnica Miejska w Toruniu (KM) 130, p. 272.

8 Pastorius started his career as a Calvinist with Arian sympathies, but ended his life a canon at Frauen-burg (Frombork): *Ad nobilium Adolesc [entem] Sigismundum de Linda, Magnifici & Nobili Viri Adriani de Linda Burgrabii & Praeco[n]s[uli] Dant[iscani] Filium Epistola, de recte eloquentia Romanae studio* (Danzig: Georg Rhetii, 1649), p. 327; Lech Mokrzecki, "Dyrektor Gimnazjum Elbląskiego Joachim Pastorius (1652–1654) i jego poglądy na historię", *Rocznik Elbląski* 4(1969), 59–83.

9 "An expediat Polonis habere civitates munitas, respondetur affirmative" (1684), Ossol. 1552/1, p. 117.

10 Stanislaw Salmonowicz, "Nauczanie prawa i polityki w Toruńskim Gimnazjum Akademickim od XVI do XVIII wieku", *Czasopismo Pruwno-Historyczne* 23(1991), 53–85.

11 Lech Mokrzecki, "Zainteresowanic historyczne Jerzego Wendego, rektora Gimnazjum Akademickiego w Toruniu 1695–1705", in Zdrojkowski, Zbigniew (ed.), *Księga Pamiakvwa 400-lecia Toruńskiego Gimnazjum*, vol. 1: *XVI–XVIIIw.* (Toruń: TNT, 1992), p. 338.

12 Lech Mokrzecki, *Studium z dziejóm nauczania historii*, Wydzial nauk spolecznych i humanistycznych 46 (Gdańsk: GTN, 1973), pp. 81, 87, 132–3.

13 Michael Mylius, *Exequiae Ill[ustrissimi] D[omini] Magni Ernesti Comitis a Dönhof, Palatini Parnaviensis Torpat[ensis] Praefecti Elb[ingensis]* (Elbing: Bodenhausen, 1642), folio A_2.

14 Ibid., folio A_4v.

15 Gottfried Zamehl, *Studiosus Apodemicus, sive de peregrinationibus studiosorum Discursus Politicus* (Leiden: Jacobi Köhleri, 1651), preface and pp. 77–8.

16 The appointment was for a pastor's position in the new town of Thorn, in 1671; Praetorius, KM 130, p. 172.

17 Joachim Pastorius, *Orationes duae quarum prima inauguratis de praeciosis Historiae Autoribus altera de potissimis eiusdem argumentis agit* (Elbing: Corell, 1651–2), folio Ev.

18 Salmonowicz, "Nauczanie prawa", 54–6; also Klaus Neumaier, *Jus Publicum. Studium zur barocken Rechisgelehrsamkeit an der Universität Ingolstadt*, Ludovico Maximilianea Forschungen 6 (Berlin: Duncker and Humblot, 1974), pp. 13–15, and Notker Hammerstein, *Jus and Historie, Ein Beitrag zur Geschichte des historischen Denkens an deutschen Universitäten im späten 17. und im 18. Jahrhundert* (Göttingen: Vandenhoeck and Ruprecht, 1972), pp. 72–6.

19 Adrian von der Linde, "Beschreibung der pohlen Art und Policey" (Bibl. PAN Gd. [Biblioteka Polskiej Akademii Nauk w Gdańsku] Nl 27.4, no. 9); David Braun, *De jurium regnandi fundamentalium in Regno Poloniae* (Cologne: Theodor Brabeus, 1722); Andreas Baumgarten, *De majestate principis* (Thorn: Coepselius, 1686); Martin Böhm, *Commentarius de Interregnis in Regno Poloniae* (Thorn: Nicolai, 1733), and numerous dissertations by the students of Hartknoch (see bibliography). On the use of republican concepts in the seventeenth century, see Wilfried Nippel, "Bürgerideal und Oligarchie. 'Klassischer Republikanismus' aus althistorischer Sicht", in Koenigsberger (ed.), *Republiken und Republikanismus*, pp. 17–18.

20 Hammerstein, *Jus und Historie*, p. 101; similarly, Kazimierz Kocot, *Nauka prawa narodów w Ateneum Gdańskim, 1580–1793*, Seria A, no. 97 (Wroclaw: Wroclawskie Towarzystwo Nauk, 1965), p. 105.

21 Eco O. G. Haitsma Mulier, *The Myth of Venice and Dutch Republican Thought in the Seventeenth Century* (Van Gorcum: Assen, 1980), p. 3.

22 Kurt Johannesson, *The Renaissance of the Goths in Sixteenth-Century Sweden* (Berkeley: University of California Press, 1991), p. 82.

23 Notable are the chronicles *Batavia* by Hadrianus Junius (Adriaen de Jonghe, 1511–1575) and Cornelius Aurelius' *Divisiekroniek* (1510) on the mythical Batavian king Bato, or the Batavian hero Claudius Civilis, who successfully fought the tyrannical Roman governor of Emperor Nero, Vitellus.

24 Roger A. Mason, "Chivalry and Citizenship. Aspects of National Identity in Renaissance Scotland", in Mason, Roger A. and MacDougall, Norman (eds.), *People and Power in Scotland. Essays in Honour of T.C. Smout*, (Edinburgh: John Donald, 1992), p. 51.

25 Kenneth Schellhase, *Tacitus in Renaissance Political Thought* (Chicago and London: University of Chicago Press, 1976), p. xiii.

26 Elżbieta Sarnowska-Temeriusz, *Świat mitów i świat znaczeń. Maciej K. Sarbiewski i problemy wiedzy o starożytności* (Warsaw: PAN, 1969), pp. 93–4, 109; see also Johannesson, *Renaissance*, p. 78 and Hans-Werner Goez, "Die Gegenwart der Vergangenheit im früh- und hochmittelalterlichen Geschichtsbewußtsein", *Historische Zeitschrift* 255 (1992), 66–8.

27 Johannesson, *Renaissance*, p. 83.

28 Werner Guez, *Translatio Imperii* (Tübingen: Mohr, 1958), p. 365; Johannesson, *Renaissance*, p. 243.

29 Johann Philippi (Sleidanus), *De quattuor summis imperiis*. On Prussia see Udo Arnold, "Geschichtsschreibung im Preußenland bis zum Ausgang des 16. Jahrhunderts", *Jahrbuch für die Geschichte Mittel-und Ostdeutschlands* 19 (1970), 83–7.

30 Caspar Schütz, *Historia Rerum Prussicarum Wahrhaffte und eigentliche Beschreybung* (Danzig: Groß, 1599), preface; Karl Kletke, *Quellenkunde der Geschichte des Preußischen Staates: Die Quellenschriftsteller zur Geschichte des Preußischen Staates*, vol. 1 (Danzig and Berlin: Schröder, 1858), pp. 73–157; Gottfried Centner, *Gelehrte und Geehrte Thorner* (Thorn: Bergmann, 1763).

31 Emil Menke-Glücker, *Die Geschichtsschreibung der Reformation und Gegenreformation. Budin und die Begründung der Geschichtsmethodologie durch Barthel Keckermann* (Leipzig: Hinrichs, 1912), pp. 124–5.

32 Rösner, "Lectiones publicae habitae in celebri Gymnasio Thoruniensi Ao 1676 et 1677 et 1678", KM 40, R 4° 16, pp. 22–3.

33 Menke-Glückert, *Geschichtsschreibung*, pp. 130–2.

34 Starowolski, *Penu Historicum*, p. 4.

35 Joachim Cureus, *Newe Chronica des Herzogthumbs Ober und Nieder Schlesien Wahrhaffie und grüntliche Beschreibung* (Eißlenben: Rätel, 1601), p. ii.

36 Walter Hubatsch, "Zur altpreußischen Chronistik des 16. Jahrhunderts", *Archivalische Zeitschrift* (Bayerisches Hauptstaatsarchiv Munich), 50/51 (1955), 429. This idea is best reflected in the German concept of *Landesgeschichte*; see Pankraz Fried, *Probleme und Methoden der Landesgeschichte* (Darmstadt: Wissenschaftliche Buchgesellschaft, 1978).

37 Keckermann, quoted by Zamehl in *Studiosus Apodmicus*, p. 84.

38 Joachim Pastorius, *Florus Poloniae seu Polonicae Historiae Epitome Nova* (Leiden: F. Heger, 1641), and Christoph Hartknoch, *Respublica Polonica duobus libris illustrata* (Lipsiae: Hallervorden, 1678).

39 A similar diary, also from 1655, is Andreas Baumgarten's "Stammbuch", APT Kat. II, XII. 12: "in this highly unhappy and most afflicted state in which our fatherland finds itself, I sign, Matthias Stanislaus Grodzki, Polish nobleman" (p. 195).

40 Henryk Barycz, *Andrzej Maksimilian Fredro wobec zagadnień wychowawczych* (Cracow: PAU, 1949), pp. 51–2.

41 Steven C. Rowell, *Lithuania Ascending. A Pagan Empire within East-Central Europe, 1295–1345* (Cambridge University Press, 1994), pp. 38–41.

42 Arnold, "Geschichtsschreibung", p. 83.

43 Hubastch, "Zur altpreußischen Chronistik", pp. 420–62, and "Deutschordenschroniken im Weichselland", *Ostdeutsche Monatshefie* 22 (1956), 713–18.

44 Arnold, "Geschichtsschreibung", p. 79. [Nicholas von Jeroschin (ca. 1290–1345), Prussian chronicler.]

45 Simon Grunau, "Preußische Chronik", in *Die preußischen Geschichtsschreiber des 16. und 17. Jahrhunderts*, vols. I–III (Leipzig: Duncker und Humblot, 1876–1896).

46 *Erasmi Stellae Libonothani De Borussiae Antiquitatibus libri duo* (Basel: Johannes Frobenius, 1518); Arnold, *Studien*, p. 118.

47 Sonia Brough, *The Goths and the Concept of Gothic in Germany from 1500 to 1750 Culture, Language and Architecture*, Mikrokosmos 17 (Frankfurt, Bern, New York: Peter Lang, 1985), p. 56.

48 *Stellae De Borussiae*, pp. 24–5.

49 According to Rowell, Dusburg had already used the example of the pagan Lithuanian "noble savages" to criticise the Roman chruch; S.C. Rowell, *Lithuania* (Cambridge: Cambridge University Press, 1994), pp. 39–40; also Johannesson, *Renaissance*, p. 87.

50 Else-Lilly Etter, *Tacitus in der Geistesgeschichte des 16. und 17. Jahrhunderts* (Basel and Stuttgart: von Helbing and Lichtenhahn, 1966).

51 Albertus Krantz, *Vandalia* (Cologne: L. Soter alias Heil et Socii, 1519), prooemium; see also Tadeusz Ulewicz, *Sarmacja. Studium z Problematyki slowiauskiej w XV i XVI wieku* (Cracow: Biblioteka Studium Slowianskiego U.J., 1950), p. 134.

52 Ulewicz, Sarmacja, p. 78.

53 Ulewicz, Sarmacja, p. 17; Stanislaw Cynarski, "Sarmatyzm – ideologia styl życia", in Tazbir, Janusz (ed.), *Polska XVII wieku. Państwo, spoleczenstwo, kultura* (Warsaw: Wiedza Powszechna, 1974), pp. 269–95; Tadeusz Mankowski, *Genealogia Sarmatyzmu Polskiego* (Warsaw: PWN, 1946); Wieslaw Müller, "Epoka baroku i sarmatyzmu", in Kloczowski, Jerzy (ed.), *Uniwersalizm i swoistość kultury polskiej*, vol. I (Lublin: KUL, 1989), pp. 217–40.

54 Ulewicz, Sarmacja, pp. 4–6.

55 Stanislaw Cynarski, "Uwagi nad problemem recepcji Historii Jana Dlugosza w Polsce XVI i XVII wieku", in *Dlugossiana – Studia historyczne w piecsetlecie śmierci Jana Dlugosza* (Cracow, Warsaw: PWN, 1980), pp. 281–90, esp. p. 286; Urszula Borkowska, "Uniwersalizm i regionalizm w Rocznikach Jana Dlugosza", in *Uniwersalizm i regionalizm w kronikarstwie Europy Środkowo-Wschodniej* (Lublin: Instytut Europy Środkowo-Wschodniej, 1996), pp. 7–26 (with English summary).

56 Cynarski, "Sarmatyzm", p. 277; Tazbir, "Ksenofobia w Polsce", passim; and S. Salmonowicz, "Prusy Królewskie w ustroju Rzeczypospolitej szlacheckiej, 1569–177", *Acta Universitatis Wratislaviensis* 945, Historia LXVI (1988): 45–56, p. 71.

57 Stanislaw Orzechowski, *Quincunx* (Cracow: Lasarz Andrysowicz, 1564), quoted by Cynarski, "Sarmatyzm", p. 275.

58 Tacitus, *De Germania*, XLVI.

59 *Poloniae sive de situ, populis, moribus, magistratibus et respublica regni Poloniae libri duo* (1575), ed. Wiktor Czermak (Cracow: Gebethner i Wolff, 1901), p. 11; see also Kromer, *De origine et rebus gestis*, p. 2.

60 D. Braun, *De Scriptorum Poloniae et Historicorum, Politicorum & J{uris} C{onsul} torum* (Elbing: Bannehr, 1723), p. 33; J. Pastorius von Hirtenberg, *Palaestra Nobilium* (Elbing: Corell, 1654).

61 Mylen, "Antiqua", in Rango, Martin, *Pomerania diplomatica sive de antiquitates Pomeranicae* (Frankfurt: Renisch, 1707) vol. III, p. 84.

62 Ibid., pp. 238–9.

63 Rainer Christoph Schwinges, "'Primäre' und "sekundäre" Nation, Nationalbewußtsein und sozialer Wandel im mittelalterlichen Böhmen", in Grothusen, Klaus-Detlev and Zernack, Klaus (eds.), *Europa Slavica – Europa Orientalis. Festschrift für Herbert Ludat* (Berlin: Duncker and Humblot, 1980), pp. 490–532.

4

The Theresian School Reform of 1774

James Van Horn Melton

Introductory Note

"The success of school reform in Austria, as in Prussia, depended not on displacing the church, but on enlisting it as a partner." James Van Horn Melton thus summarizes the failed school reform of the so-called Pergen plan, which Empress Maria Theresa dropped in January 1772. Eighteen months later, a state commission on higher education sharply criticized the Vienna Normal School, which was in charge of training new teachers. Against this backdrop of failed educational reform, Melton picks up the unlikely story of the devoutly Catholic Empress of Austria hiring the chief education reformer of her hated enemy, the deist nominally Protestant King Frederick II of Prussia.

With the Normal School in disarray and no apparent funds available for schools, Theresian school reform may well have proceeded no further. What saved the reforms was the suppression of the Society of Jesus by Pope Clement XIV in July of 1773. The significance of this event, both real and symbolic, cannot be overstated. The Jesuits had epitomized the visual, theatrical, and "plastic" qualities associated with the Habsburg baroque and Counter Reformation. More than any other single event, the dissolution of the Jesuits symbolized the end of the Counter Reformation in Austria. In 1740, the year Maria Theresa ascended the throne, the cultural influence of the Jesuits had been at its zenith. Their subsequent abolition illustrates the degree to which the reign of Maria Theresa, perhaps even more than that of Joseph, represented a genuine cultural revolution.

Beyond its broader cultural significance, the dissolution of the Jesuits was a monumental event in the history of Austrian schooling. For the expulsion of the Jesuits left not only an educational and cultural vacuum; it also left wealth. Pope Clement XIV considered the empress a valuable

James Van Horn Melton, "The Theresian school reform of 1774," pp. 209–29 from *Absolutism and the eighteenth-century origins of compulsory schooling in Prussia and Austria*. Cambridge: Cambridge University Press, 1988.

ally, and anxious to preserve the Papacy's cordial relations with the Habsburg dynasty, he ceded
to Maria Theresa all Jesuit schools, colleges, houses, and other property remaining in the monarchy. At the accession of Joseph, the total value of ex-Jesuit property was assessed at approximately
13 million florins.[1] The confiscation of Jesuit property proved timely, for it provided a source of
property and income for schools. The subsequent reform and expansion of Austrian parish
schooling would never have been possible without the wealth left by the Jesuits. It explains above
all why school reform proved more successful in Austria than in Prussia, where the Hohenzollern
monarchy benefited little from the demise of the Society. The Habsburg monarchy, although far
from enjoying fiscal health, had nevertheless derived a small financial boost from the abolition of
the Jesuits.

   The dissolution of the Jesuits infused new life into Habsburg school reform. After publishing
the abolition order in September of 1773, Maria Theresa entrusted its implementation to a commission headed by Kressel.[2] Since the dissolution of the Jesuits also necessitated the reorganization of secondary and university education, she charged the Kressel commission with developing
guidelines for a general reform of education in the monarchy. Other members of the commission
included Franz Sales von Greiner, a proponent of agrarian reform and religious toleration; the
Augustinian abbot Ignaz Müller, confessor to Maria Theresa and a reform Catholic of deep Mura-
torian convictions; and Karl Anton von Martini, professor of natural law at the University of
Vienna and a key figure in the Austrian Enlightenment. The commission symbolized the alliance
of *Aufklärer* and reform Catholics that had been so instrumental in efforts to reform censorship,
the universities, and popular religion.

   Drafted by Martini, the commission's plan of December 1, 1773 recommended that confiscated Jesuit property be used to help finance a system of universal compulsory schooling.[3]
Martini's plan called for the creation of normal schools in order to standardize curricula, textbooks, and pedagogical methods. Martini also insisted that schooling be *standesmässig* and made
a strict distinction between the curricula of urban and rural schools. Rural schools were to teach
only reading, writing, arithmetic, and religion. In town schools, which were to educate future artisans, merchants, and secretaries, a more advanced curriculum was necessary. This was to include
German, orthography, mathematics, applied arts and sciences, history, and geography. The
commission also recommended transforming many of the smaller Latin schools into elementary
schools, thereby expanding primary education while reducing the number of pupils pursuing
higher studies.

   After approving the recommendations of the Kressel commission, Maria Theresa asked [her
chief minister, prince von] Kaunitz to inquire into the possibility of bringing Felbiger[4] to Vienna
to supervise the reforms. Both Kressel and [Tobias] Gebler in the Council of State had been in
regular contact with Felbiger ever since the establishment of the Normal School. When the
Normal School fell victim to factional strife, Gebler had suggested bringing Felbiger to Vienna
to take over the institution.[5] In January of 1774, Kaunitz wrote to Gottfried van Swieten, the
Austrian ambassador in Berlin, asking whether Frederick II would grant Felbiger a brief leave of
absence from his administrative duties. On February 1, the Prussian minister Finkenstein notified van Swieten of the King's willingness to place Felbiger's talents at the disposal of the empress.
The king, assured Finkenstein, "only wishes for more opportunities to be of service to Her
Majesty and to offer proof of His genuine friendship."[6]

   Felbiger leaped at the chance to supervise what promised to be the most ambitious reform of
his century. Once Frederick had released him from his duties in Sagan, Felbiger hastily arranged
for his departure to Vienna. He arrived in the Austrian capital on May 1, 1774, and was immediately given wide-ranging authority over primary education in the monarchy. Maria Theresa,

whose confidence in Felbiger's abilities remained unshaken until her death, appointed him to the Commission on Education (*Studienhofkommission*). This agency enjoyed supreme authority over all matters relating to education.[7] She also named him to the Lower Austrian School Commission, where he enjoyed complete authority over the Vienna Normal School and all elementary schools in the city.

Felbiger's prestige as founder of the Sagan method enabled him to end the factionalism that had crippled the Normal School. At the same time, he began work on his main task, the drafting of a compulsory school edict. While working on the edict Felbiger also found time to prepare textbooks and teaching manuals for future use in the schools. By July of 1774, Felbiger had completed the edict. Following revisions by the Lower Austrian School Commission and Court Chancellery, Maria Theresa signed the General School Ordinance (*Allgemeine Schulordnung*) on December 6, 1774.

"The education of youth of both sexes," affirmed the preamble to the ordinance, "is vital to the happiness of a nation."[8] Hence schooling was now compulsory for all children between the ages of six and twelve. Rural schoolmasters were to consult parish registers to ensure that all school-age children were enrolled, while schoolmasters in larger towns and cities were to check attendance against a list compiled twice a year by the local magistrate. Pupils were to attend five days a week, with three hours of instruction in the morning and two in the afternoon. Although school was to be held year-round, pupils in the countryside were excused from school at harvest time to help in the fields. Pupils desiring to leave school before their thirteenth year had to produce a certificate, signed by their priest, attesting to their proficiency in the required subjects. The ordinance prohibited admitting boys into apprenticeships or girls into domestic service who could not produce a similar certificate. Here the edict reflected the belief, common among reformers, that guildmasters were no longer providing their apprentices with an adequate moral and religious education.

The General School Ordinance established three kinds of schools. Every town and every rural parish seat were to have at least one minor school (*Trivialschule*), which was to provide elementary instruction in those subjects deemed necessary for all classes of the population. These included reading, writing, arithmetic, and religion, the last of which was given special emphasis.

The second type of school, the so-called major school (*Hauptschule*), was an urban grammar school designed for middle-class pupils. At least one major school was to exist in each provincial district (Kreis). Major schools were to be attended both by pupils hoping to advance to a *Gymnasium* and by those desiring vocational preparation for careers as merchants, skilled craftsmen, and clerks. The curriculum of major schools included those subjects offered in minor schools, as well as courses in German composition, basic Latin, history, geography, mechanics, trigonometry, and architecture.

Finally, the edict required that a normal school be established in every province. In the future, no schoolmaster was to be hired who had not been certified by the director of a normal school. Even tutors were required to obtain normal school certification.[9] In addition to training teachers, the normal school served as the model for all other schools in the province. Patterned on the Vienna institute, the provincial normal schools served to provide uniformity in curriculum, teaching methods, and textbooks. Uniformity (*Gleichförmigkeit*) was a central theme of the reforms. In theory at least, a pupil in a Lower Austrian minor school was to receive instruction in the same subject, at the same time, using the same textbook, from a teacher using the same methods, as a pupil attending its Tyrolean equivalent.

Like its Prussian counterpart, the General School Ordinance relied on both lay and clerical school inspectors for enforcement. Supervisory duties over a minor school were shared by the local priest and a lay inspector (either a town magistrate or the deputy of the noble patron). The lay inspector was responsible for keeping the school in good repair and for ensuring that the schoolmaster, if new, was properly certified. The clerical inspector, for his part, made sure that the schoolmaster was teaching the proper subjects and using only those schoolbooks approved by the Vienna Normal School. Both inspectors were required to report annually to their district supervisor, normally an archpriest appointed by the bishop. District supervisors in turn reported to the provincial school commission, whose members were appointed by the provincial administration.

In contrast to minor schools, normal and major schools were supervised solely by lay individuals, except in the case of religious instruction, which was to be provided or supervised by a local priest. The supervisor of a normal school was the director himself, while a designated magistrate periodically inspected the major school in his town or city. Both were to report twice a year to the provincial school commission.[10]

At the peak of the administrative hierarchy was the Commission on Education. Within the commission, Felbiger's favor with the empress gave him *de facto* control over primary school policy in the monarchy. In 1777, Maria Theresa further extended his authority by appointing him supreme director of all normal schools, major schools, and minor schools in the monarchy. With this appointment, Felbiger became responsible to the empress alone.[11]

Compulsory Schooling and Educational Exclusion

A revealing paradox lay at the heart of eighteenth-century educational reform: Proponents of compulsory schooling invariably advocated socially restrictive policies at the secondary and university level. A striking example of this paradox was seen in Prussian Silesia, where Schlabrendorff's efforts to expand primary schooling were accompanied by draconian measures that prohibited children of the urban and rural poor from studying beyond the elementary level.

A similar dialectic characterized Theresian educational reform. At the very moment the General School Ordinance was being implemented, reformers were taking steps to curtail plebeian educational advancement beyond the elementary level.[12] This is not surprising, since virtually all supporters of compulsory schooling in the Habsburg monarchy favored tighter restrictions on entry into *Gymnasien* and universities.[13] Pergen's[14] attempt to "nationalize" education reflected not only a hostility toward the Jesuits, but also an attempt to regulate educational advancement more efficiently. Only in exceptional cases, argued Pergen, should the state allow children of the poor to study beyond the age of twelve: "their occupations require little else, and to do more would merely breed doubt, discontent, and unhappiness."[15] The Kressel commission, to which the empress had entrusted the administration of ex-Jesuit schools and property, shared this view. The commission's educational guidelines issued in December of 1773 advocated reducing the number of Latin schools and *Gymnasien*.

The dissolution of the Jesuits did in fact give the state an excuse to close dozens of *Gymnasien* and *Stadtschulen*. In Bohemia alone, thirty-one *Gymnasien* were closed following the expulsion of the Jesuits. Most of these never reopened, but some were transformed into major, minor, or normal schools.[16] Countless *Stadtschulen*, which occupied an intermediary rung between parish schools and *Gymnasien*, also closed. The larger ones became major schools, while smaller *Stadtschulen* were downgraded to the level of minor schools.[17] The effect of these closings was to further constrict avenues of educational advancement.

The exclusionary implications of Austrian compulsory schooling become even clearer when viewed in conjunction with the *Gymnasium* reforms of the period. Mathes Ignaz von Hess, a

Martini protégé who taught universal and literary history at the University of Vienna, submitted the first detailed proposal for *Gymnasium* reform in May of 1774. Its provisions included reducing the number of plebeian students admitted to secondary schools. "It is no loss to society," assured Hess, "if the state prevents intelligent individuals from pursuing higher studies, and instead guides them into other occupations."[18] Although the Commission on Education ultimately rejected the Hess plan for insufficient stress on vocational subjects,[19] the reforms that were finally adopted in 1776 were equally restrictive in their admission guidelines. This plan, drafted by the Piarist school reformer Gratian Marx,[20] imposed a double standard on *Gymnasium* aspirants. The children of nobles and state officials were to be granted admission automatically, but the reform imposed far more rigorous standards on plebeian applicants. The edict of 1776 affirmed that "the children of noble persons, councillors, and clerks are to be admitted even if they possess only mediocre talent and little proficiency in the necessary subjects. Children from the lower orders, however, are to be admitted only if they possess exceptional talent."[21] Moreover, by their very nature, Marx's admissions guidelines excluded most rural inhabitants. The subjects to be covered on *Gymnasium* entrance examinations included Latin, a subject that the General School Ordinance had confined to urban major schools. The system of inspection for primary schools further reinforced restrictive *Gymnasium* policies. In the major and minor schools under their charge, school inspectors were required to examine pupils twice a year in order to screen those hoping to pursue further study.[22]

Felbiger himself was careful to allay any fears that compulsory schooling might encourage the educational aspirations of lower-class pupils. He published a sequel to his primer in 1777 specifically for this purpose:

> The second part of my primer proves that happiness is possible for all classes of society as long as one is pure of heart, free of unhealthy desires, and content with one's station in life. By instilling this profound truth in our pupils, we hope to stifle any inclination to pursue further studies, thereby making them content with the station into which they are born.[23]

Ferdinand Kindermann likewise instructed Bohemian school inspectors to discourage peasant youths from reading too much, since "the welfare of society requires that the education of the common man reach no higher than his occupation. Otherwise he will no longer wish to fulfill his duties."[24] Felbiger's *Namenbuchlein*, a speller for beginning pupils, contained a song entitled "Contentment with My Station" (*Zufriedenheit mit meinem Stand*).[25] Elsewhere, Felbiger's schoolbooks mustered biblical citations to discourage aspirations for social advancement. Felbiger's primer cited *Corinthians* to prove that "each has an obligation to live in accordance with the duties and conditions proper to his station. . . . One should not frivolously aspire to a higher social position."[26] Pupils also read that Jesus listened obediently to his teachers, ate and drank moderately, and "never complained about the hardships that went with his station in life."[27] As Kindermann told an audience at the Prague Normal School, "It is more virtuous to be skilled in a humble occupation than incompetent in a higher one."[28]

The Implementation of the General School Ordinance

By February 1775, each of the Habsburg hereditary provinces had established a school commission to implement the General School Ordinance. These included Upper and Lower Austria, Austrian Silesia, Moravia, Bohemia, Outer Austria, Carniola, Tyrol, Styria, Carinthia, Gorizia, and Istria. The edict affected neither the Austrian Netherlands nor the Italian duchies of Milan

Table 4.1   Sources of primary school financing in the Habsburg monarchy, 1781

Source	Amount(florins)
Ex-Jesuit fund	28,711
Capital interest	15,600
Taxes on masked balls and comedies	11,616
Subsidies from the Court Treasury	9,243
Sale of textbooks	6,265
Contributions from provincial estates (Stände)	6,038
Ecclesiastical contributions	5,759
Inheritance taxes	4,117
Taxes on benefice recipients	3,420
Municipal contributions	679
Miscellaneous	4,007

Source: Ernst Wangermann, *Aufklärung und staatsbürgerliche Erziehung. Gottfried van Swieten als Reformator des österreichischen Unterrichtswesens 1781–1791* (Vienna, 1978), pp. 50–61.

and Mantua, since their viceregal administrations were virtually independent of Vienna. Nor did it apply to Hungary and the Banat (today southern Hungary and northern Yugoslavia), where ethnic and religious variations required separate school edicts. In the Banat, where Orthodox Serbs and Rumanians dominated, the court issued a variant of the edict in 1776. The Hungarian version of the ordinance appeared in 1777 with the promulgation of the *Ratio Educationis*. An exception was the Military Frontier, the strip extending along the Turkish border from the Adriatic to Transylvania. In this area, which was under the direct administration of the Court War Council (*Hofkriegsrat*), the General School Ordinance took effect immediately.[29]

After the creation of provincial school commissions, the most pressing need was to train teachers. By 1776, normal schools existed in Innsbruck (Tyrol), Linz (Upper Austria), Freiburg im Breisgau (Outer Austria), Brünn (Moravia), Prague (Bohemia), Graz (Styria), Klagenfurt (Carinthia), Troppau (Austrian Silesia), Laibach (Carniola), Lemberg (Galicia), Gorizia (the Duchy of Gorizia), and the City of Trieste. The creation of a normal school network, one of the most important achievements of Theresian school reform, was greatly facilitated by the use of ex-Jesuit property. Most normal schools were located in Jesuit *Gymnasien*, while interest from the sale of confiscated Jesuit property helped pay salaries of normal school teachers and supply books and teaching materials.[30] Table 4.1, which is based on figures from the beginning of Joseph's reign, demonstrates that ex-Jesuit property constituted the major source of school funding in the Habsburg monarchy. Other sources included a tax on masked balls and theater comedies. In 1775, for example, the Moravian school commission was able to collect 1,480 florins during carnival season.[31] This amount alone sufficed to subsidize more than half the annual budget of the Brünn Normal School.[32]

This investment in normal schools began to show impressive results by the end of the decade. By 1779, 546 normal school graduates were teaching in Viennese and Lower Austrian primary schools.[33] In Moravia, the Brünn Normal School had trained 344 teachers by this time, and the Prague Normal School graduated 253 schoolmasters by 1780.[34] The head of the Bohemian School Commission, Ferdinand Kindermann, also encouraged parish priests and clerical candidates to attend the Prague Normal School in order to fulfill their supervisory duties more effectively. The archbishop of Prague, Anton Peter Count Příchovský, supported Kindermann's promotion of normal school training among the Bohemian clergy. Příchovský decreed in 1776 that parish appointments were to be awarded only to those who had attended a normal school.[35] As a consequence, 179 candidates for the Bohemian priesthood had attended the Prague Normal School by 1780.[36]

The normal schools also functioned as publishing houses for the distribution of textbooks. This arrangement provided provincial school commissions with additional income, and facilitated the diffusion of inexpensive textbooks. Vienna was the first normal school to have a printing press; the empress subsequently granted publication licenses to normal schools in Prague, Brünn, Innsbruck, Freiburg im Breisgau, Linz, Graz, Laibach, and Lemberg. Textbooks were relatively inexpensive: A first-year pupil in an urban elementary school paid about eighteen kreuzer for his or her schoolbooks, roughly twice the daily wages of a nonguilded laborer in a textile manufactory.[37] The volume of sales was so great, however, that normal school presses still operated at a substantial profit. Indeed, profits were so high that school commissions began distributing one-quarter of their textbooks free to the poor of their parishes.[38] This measure doubtless improved attendance by easing the financial burden on poorer households.

Statistical evidence, though scattered and not always reliable, does show a rise in elementary school attendance. In Vienna, the number of elementary schools rose from sixty-four in 1771 to seventy-nine in 1779. More significantly, the number of children between six and thirteen who attended school increased from 4,665 to 8,039 during the same period. However, the fact that a substantial number (5,400) still received their schooling from tutors, suggests that public schools had yet to shed their unsavory reputation.[39]

School attendance also increased in the provinces. The surveys just cited showed that in Lower Austria, the percentage of children attending elementary schools rose from 16 percent in 1771 to 34 percent in 1779. In Graz, attendance among school-age children increased from 17 percent to 30 percent between 1772 and 1780.[40] In the Salzkammergut, the mountainous royal domain in Upper Austria, Maria Theresa took a strong personal interest in school reform. The Salzkammergut was a notorious center of crypto-Protestantism. Determined to eradicate heresy in the region, she founded a special fund for the creation of schools. Her efforts yielded substantial results: In 1773 only 378 out of a total of 1,580 school-age children attended a parish school, but by 1778 the number had grown to 1,044.[41] Her campaign against heresy in the Salzkammergut further illustrates the continuity between Theresian school reform and earlier Counter-Reform traditions.

Bohemia was another region in which reform proved relatively successful. With a ratio of roughly one school per thousand inhabitants in 1780, Bohemia had the most extensive network of elementary schools in the entire monarchy.[42] Bohemia boasted 1,700 elementary schools in 1776; the number had risen to 2,400 by 1790, when two-thirds of all school-age children in the province were attending Bohemian elementary schools.[43]

An important reason for the success of the reforms in Bohemia was the support they enjoyed among traditional ecclesiastical and aristocratic elites. Ecclesiastical support for the reforms in Bohemia reflected the extent to which reform Catholicism had taken root in the ecclesiastical hierarchy. Archbishop Příchovský of Prague was an energetic supporter, establishing an endowment of 40,000 florins to support elementary education in the province. By requiring all priesthood candidates to attend a normal school, Příchovský also helped to integrate the Bohemian clergy into the new system of public education . . .

Much of the credit for mobilizing aristocratic support goes to Kindermann, who headed the Bohemian School Commission. By introducing spinning into Bohemian schools, Kindermann helped meet the labor needs of Bohemian landowners. Kindermann introduced spinning classes into the Prague Normal School in 1776, and spinning was soon incorporated into more than 500 Bohemian schools. The introduction of spinning, as mentioned earlier, also improved attendance by providing economic incentives to rural families. The relatively high attendance rate (75 percent) in schools with spinning classes points to Kindermann's success in linking elementary schooling with rural industry.[44]

Obstacles to Reform

As in Prussia, there was resistance to compulsory schooling.[45] The salary of the schoolmaster remained the responsibility of the parish community, and although the free distribution of text-books somewhat reduced the financial burden, school fees remained a source of hardship for poorer families. In general, families were less inclined to send their daughters to school than their sons, although the General School Ordinance applied equally to both sexes. Theodor Janković, head of the Banat School Commission, reported in 1781 that half of all school-age boys went to school regularly, whereas only one-quarter of their female counterparts attended.[46] Attendance records from Styria, where the reforms have been studied most thoroughly, reveal that more than three times as many boys as girls attended school. This gap would narrow, however, so that by 1800, school attendance by boys exceeded that of girls by only three to two.[47]

Although compulsory schooling enjoyed widespread support among clergy of reform-Catholic persuasion, many of their more conservative colleagues distrusted the reforms. Charging that the reforms were a Protestant plot, numerous Tyrolean priests refused to cooperate. Clerical discontent in turn gave sanction to popular opposition. Riots erupted in Innsbruck in 1774, when rumors circulated that a school census being compiled by archducal authorities was actually a list of those eligible for conscription. In some Tyrolean villages, opposition to the reforms was so intense that schoolmasters and their families were physically assaulted.[48] In Bohemia, similarly, Archbishop Přichovský occasionally had to reprimand priests who condemned the reforms from the pulpit. One Bohemian priest caused a stir by charging that Felbiger's textbooks contained heretical Hussite doctrines.[49]

A particularly delicate issue among the clergy was Felbiger's "documented" catechism. Before Felbiger, the most popular catechism in Catholic Central Europe had been that of Peter Canisius, the sixteenth-century Jesuit. By Felbiger's day, the Canisius catechism was under attack for its dry, scholastic language. Catholic critics of the Canisius catechism turned to France for models, translating the catechisms of Jacques Bossuet and Claude Fleury.[50] Felbiger modeled his own catechisms on those of Fleury. Arguing that catechistic instruction must take into account the child's age and developmental level, Fleury had divided his catechism into levels of difficulty.[51] Following Fleury, Felbiger composed three catechisms, one for each school class.[52]

What was new about Felbiger's catechistic approach was the use of *Beweisstellen*, lengthy scriptural passages that provided documentary support for Catholic doctrine. Felbiger's incorporation of biblical passages into his advanced catechism reflected the move among reform Catholics to reform popular devotion by rooting it more firmly in the Scriptures. Felbiger argued that the rampant progress of unbelief among the laity required the church to rely more heavily on direct scriptural evidence: "In the present day, when unbelief waxes rife and so many show so little regard for religion, we must take care to acquaint pupils with the Scriptural foundations of faith."[53]

When Felbiger first proposed incorporating scriptural passages into his advanced catechism in 1777, he sparked immediate controversy. Previously a supporter of Felbiger, Archbishop Migazzi now protested that Felbiger's proposed use of lengthy biblical passages violated the Bull Unigenitus: "Are children or uneducated adults now supposed to consult the Scriptures on their own? Are the decrees of the Council of Trent mere paper? Then why, in this century, did the Church condemn Quesnel's proposition that 'the reading of Scripture is for all'?"[54] Although Migazzi had long advocated greater emphasis on scriptural study in the training of clergy, he feared that placing even a fraction of the Scriptures in the hands of the laity threatened the authority of the church.

Other Catholic bishops joined Migazzi, charging that the catechism itself contained heretical propositions. Maria Theresa suspended publication of the catechism while Migazzi, aided by a panel of theologians, investigated the alleged doctrinal errors.[55] Although Felbiger accepted the corrections of Migazzi and his panel, he pleaded with Maria Theresa not to expurgate the scriptural passages. Hägelin and the Lower Austrian School Commission joined in Felbiger's defense, arguing that the use of scriptural passages in the catechism would help inoculate the population against Protestantism:

> Because Protestants read the Bible, they charge Catholics with ignorance of the Holy Scriptures. Hence it would be useful to provide the peasantry with sufficient Scriptural evidence to confute opponents of the Church. Such a measure would in no way violate the teachings of the Church; on the contrary, it would enhance the influence of Catholic doctrine if the peasantry gained more insight into its sources, while the charge leveled by heretics, namely that our religion is little more than the teachings of men and cannot be proven through the Word of God, would be refuted.[56]

Hägelin's defense, cleverly couched in anti-Protestant language, helped sway the empress. Maria Theresa sided with Felbiger and urged Migazzi to consent to the publication of the catechism, scriptural passages and all. Migazzi grudgingly agreed, and by 1778, 135,000 copies of the catechism had been published and circulated throughout the monarchy.[57] Felbiger's catechisms replaced that of Canisius as the most popular in Catholic Central Europe, where they continued to be used well into the nineteenth century.[58]

School Reform in the Non-German Territories

Not surprisingly, the most serious impediment to reform was the multiethnic character of the monarchy. In an empire comprising Czechs, Slovaks, Italians, Hungarians, Poles, Rumanians, Serbs, Slovenes, Croatians, Armenians, and Ruthenes, only the most rigid and unrealistic centralist could expect the reforms to be applied in a uniform fashion. Ethnic and religious minorities naturally viewed the reforms with a mixture of fear and suspicion. Distrust was especially prevalent in Hungary and the Banat, where religious divisions among Catholics, Protestants, Orthodox, and Uniates served to exacerbate ethnic differences. Not surprisingly, then, some have viewed Theresian school reform among the non-German population of the monarchy as a thinly disguised attempt at Germanization.[59]

However, a closer look reveals that Theresian school reform was surprisingly moderate on the language question. It is true that German-speaking bureaucrats in Vienna favored the diffusion of German throughout the monarchy. Their motives, more political than national, rested on the assumption that the effective exercise of power depended on the ability of the state and its sub-jects to communicate with each other. Efforts to diffuse the German language were pursued most vigorously in Bohemia, where the state prohibited the hiring of schoolmasters who were not pro-ficient in German.[60] A knowledge of German was also required for teachers in schools on the military frontier, where military efficiency was the paramount issue. On the southwestern fron-tier, for example, German-speaking officers sometimes had to rely on Franciscan missionaries to translate orders into Slovenian.[61]

Although Theresian school reform encouraged the study of German in non-German areas, it never actually required the use of German as the language of instruction. Even where vigorously promoted, the teaching of German was designed to supplement, not replace, instruction in the native language. The Habsburg court explicitly rejected coercive measures in its promotion of German. In reference to Galicia, a Polish-speaking region, the Court Chancellery affirmed in 1780 that it would be "destructive and unreasonable to impose the German language on the Galician population. The Polish language can instill religion and morality just as effectively as German."[62] In the same conciliatory spirit, Maria Theresa exempted Slovenes on the Military Frontier from those taxes that went to support German schools.[63] This kind of ethnic pluralism was also implicit in the Hungarian version of the General School Ordinance, the *Ratio educationis* of 1777, which allowed each of the seven linguistic groups represented in the province (Magyars, Germans, Slovaks, Croatians, Ruthenians, Serbs, and Rumanians) to establish schools providing instruc-tion in its own language.[64]

Although the reforms eschewed the goal of linguistic uniformity, they did aim for uniformity of teaching methods, curricula, and textbooks. This goal could not be achieved without transla-tions of teaching manuals and textbooks. Thus numerous Italian translations were commissioned for the Italian-speaking population of the South Tyrol, Gorizia, and Istria, while in Bohemia the normal schools in Prague and Brünn translated catechisms and primers for the Czech population.[65]

A striking example of successful translation policy was the Banat, where the Serbian reformer Theodor Janković translated many of Felbiger's works into Serbian. Up until this time, Serbo-Croatian had not existed as a literary vehicle. The most literate segment of society in the Banat was the Orthodox clergy, who used a variant of Church Slavonic rather than their own vernacu-lar. In this respect, Theresian school reform constituted a major step in the emergence of Serbo-Croatian as a literary language. Efforts to diffuse the written vernacular began in 1770, when the court sanctioned the establishment of a Cyrillic press by the Viennese publishing firm of Joseph von Kurzböck. Schoolbooks were also translated for the Rumanian population, which was con-centrated in the southeastern Banat. A Rumanian version of Felbiger's *Nothwendiges Handbuch für den Gebrauch der Schullehrer in den deutschen Trivial-Schulen* appeared in 1777.[66]

In Hungary, the obstacles to reform proved all but insurmountable. Hungary's traditional posi-tion as a buffer against the Turks had forced Habsburg rulers to concede a degree of adminis-trative autonomy and religious toleration unknown in most regions of the monarchy. Hence the *Ratio Educationis* allowed each confession to use its own religious instructors and catechisms. Any intrusion by Vienna into the educational and cultural life of the province provoked the imme-diate distrust of the Protestant and Orthodox clergy. This distrust, combined with the plethora of languages in the province, greatly impeded the implementation of Theresian school reform.[67]

Religious pluralism posed similar problems in the Banat. The Orthodox religion had enjoyed statutory autonomy since the late seventeenth century, when Leopold I granted ecclesiastical self-government in exchange for military assistance against the Turks. Both lay and clerical education of the Orthodox population was in the hands of the Metropolitanate in Karlowitz.[68] Hence the success of Theresian reform in the Banat hinged upon the ability of Vienna to reach a *modus vivendi* with the Orthodox hierarchy. That such a compromise was achieved was largely the work of Janković, who had close ties with both absolutist reformers and the Orthodox clergy. Janković had not only studied under Sonnenfels at Vienna and attended the normal school, but also served under the Orthodox bishop of Temesvar before his appointment as school director for the Banat in 1773.[69] Janković was thereby able to win the trust both of the court and of the Orthodox clergy.

The school ordinance for the Banat (1776) reflected the resulting compromise. School instruction was to be in Serbian or Rumanian, although higher salaries were offered to those schoolmasters capable of providing German instruction. Although Orthodox children were required to attend a Catholic school if no Orthodox school existed, they "are not to be given the slightest injury, or compulsion in their religious belief; at the time for religious instruction they are to be released forthwith from attendance; and also, in these mixed schools, no book is to be used with confessional content."[70]

The result was a considerable expansion of primary schooling in the Banat. Janković claimed that the number of Orthodox schools in the Banat had almost doubled to 183 by 1776; the number had grown to 205 by 1778, and 452 in 1781.[71] The Hungarian Court Chancellery, which took over administration of the Banat in 1778, estimated in 1780 that most Serbian villages and more than half of all Rumanian villages had Orthodox elementary schools.[72]

In short, Theresian school reform had a significant impact on the educational level of the Banat. At the very least, as mentioned earlier, the reforms promoted the rise of Serbian and Rumanian as literary vernaculars. It is no accident in this regard that the noted Serbian playwright Joakim Vujić and the poet and translator Alexsije Vezelić, both pioneers in the rise of Serbian literature, had graduated from schools established by the reforms in the 1770s. Similarly, three of the earliest Rumanian writers to publish in the vernacular – Michael Rosu, Dmitrie Tischindeal, and Paul Iorgovici – taught in schools created by the reforms. The rise of literary vernaculars in turn helped to bring about a fundamental reorientation of the Banat away from the Russo-Byzantine East, and toward the Germanic West. By promoting the vernacular, Theresian school reform hastened the decline of Church Slavonic and thereby severed an important cultural link with the East.[73] At the same time, of course, the promotion of the vernacular would contribute to the emergence of the national, anti-Habsburg movements of the subsequent century.

[. . .]

NOTES

1 Hanns Leo Mikoletzky, *Österreich: Das grosse 18. Jahrhundert* (Vienna, 1967), p. 250.

2 Franz Kressel von Qualtenberg, director of the Vienna law faculty and member of the Council of State, was concerned that antagonizing the Roman Catholics might hinder Maria Theresa's reform projects.

3 Haus-, Hof-, und Staatsarchiv (HHStA), Alte Kabinettsakten: Studiensachen (1736–1773), Fasz. 1, fol. 602–31.

4 Johann Ignaz Felbiger was a Prussian reformer Maria Theresa brought to Austria in 1774 to prepare Maria Theresa's edict on compulsory education (*Allgemeine Schulordnung*). He was dismissed in 1784.

5 Joseph Alexander Freiherr von Helfert, *Die Gründung der österreichischen Volkschule durn Maria Theresia* (Prague, 1860), p. 308.

6 Informed that her archenemy had acquiesced, Maria Theresa drily replied, "How gallant." Ibid., p. 309.

7 The Commission on Education had emerged in the late 1750s as a department within the *Directorium in Publicis et Cameralibus*, the central body that coordinated domestic policy. Following the abolition

of the *Directorium* in 1760, the Commission became an independent agency directly subordinate to the Court Chancellery. Migazzi, who originally headed the Commission, was succeeded in 1773 by Franz Kressel von Qualtenberg.

8 The General School Ordinance (GSO) is published in Anton Weiss, ed., *Die Allgemeine Schulordnung der Kaiserin Maria Theresia und J. I. Felbigers Förderungen an Schulmeister und Lehrer* (Leipzig, 1896). For a detailed discussion see Helmut Engelbrecht, *Geschichte des österreichischen Bildungswesens*, 3 vols. (Vienna, 1982–84), 3:135–7.

9 Felbiger later published the *Vorschrift zur Unterweisung der Hauslehrer* (Vienna, 1776), a teaching manual required for all tutors. A copy is to be found in *AVA*, Studienhofkommission, Fasz. 60 (Privatlehrer, 1771–90).

10 On the system of inspection established by the GSO see Josef Stanzel, *Die Schlanfsicht in Reformwerk des J. I. Felbiger* (Paderborn, 1976), pp. 256–75.

11 Helfert, *Gründung*, p. 273.

12 On the problem of "academic overproduction" in eighteenth-century Austria, see Grete Klingenstein, "Akademikerüberschuss als soziales Problem in aufgeklärten Absolutismus. Bemerkungen über ein Rede Joseph von Sonnenfels aus dem Jahre 1771," in *Bildung, Politik, und Gesellschaft*, (Vienna, 1979).

13 A notable exception is Kaunitz. With reference to Hungary, Kaunitz favored broadening educational opportunities and increasing scholarships for promising youths, regardless of class. Here Kaunitz's educational program must be viewed in the specific context of his Hungarian policy, which attacked aristocratic particularism and sought to create a more efficient and professionalized bureaucratic infrastructure. Kaunitz's Hungarian policies are discussed in Franz A. J. Szabo, "The Social Revolutionary Conspiracy: The Role of Prince W. A. Kaunitz in the Policies of Enlightened Absolutism towards Hungary, 1760–1780," paper presented at the annual meeting of the Canadian Association of Hungarian Studies, Montreal, P. Q., Canada, 3 June, 1985.

14 Beginning in 1769, Count Johann Anton Pergen, a diplomat and later chief of the Hapsburg secret police under Joseph II, became an advocate for educational reform.

15 Allgemeines Verwaltungsarchiv Vienna (AVA), Nachlass Pergen, 1771.

16 Weiss, *Schulreform in Böhmen*, 1:9.

17 Helfert, *Gründung*, p. 402.

18 Ignaz von Hess, *Entwurf zur Einrichtung der Gymnasien in K. K. Erbländern* (Vienna, 1775), pp. 9–10.

19 See Klingenstein, "Bildungskrise," pp. 220–1.

20 Published in Wotke, *Das österreichische Gymnasium*, pp. 255ff.

21 Ibid., p. 271.

22 GSO, article 22. Joseph II would place further restrictions on plebeian educational advancement in 1784. He abolished all *Gymnasium* stipends in order, as the edict stated, "to prevent a horde of useless creatures from burdening society." Those unable to pay their tuition fees were to leave school immediately. This measure, combined with Joseph's abolition of numerous *Gymnasien*, led to a 25 percent decline in *Gymnasium* enrollment – a drop of more than 2,200 pupils – in the following school year. See Karl Wotke, "Karl Heinrich Seibt. Der erste Universitätsprofessor der deutschen Sprache in Prag, ein Schuler Gellerts und Gottscheds. Ein Beitrag zur Geschichte des Deutschunterrichts in Österreich," *Beitrage zur österreichischen Erziehungs- und Schulgeschichte*, 9 (1907), p. lxxiii.

23 Felbiger, *Nachricht von dem für die K. K. Staaten vorgeschriebenen Katechismus* (Vienna, 1777), p. 26.

24 Quoted in Weiss, *Geschichte der theresianischen Schulreform in Böhmen*, 1:261.

25 I was unable to locate this work, which is cited in Helfert, *Gründung*, pp. 510–11.

26 Felbiger, *Zweyter Theil des Lesebuches für die Landschulen* (Vienna, 1777), p. 58.

27 Ibid., p. 58

28 Kindermann, *Von dem Einflusse der niederen Schulen auf das gemeine Leben*, p. 15.

29 On the adaptation of the GSO to Hungary and the Banat see Domokos Kosáry, "Die ungarische Unterrichtsreform von 1777," in *Ungarn und Österreich unter Maria Theresia und Joseph II: Neue Aspekte im Verhältnis der beiden Länder*, ed. Anna Drabek et al. (Vienna, 1982), pp. 91–100; Moritz Csáky, *Von*

der Aufklärung zum Liberalismus. Studien zum Frühliberalismus in Ungarn (Vienna, 1981), pp. 174–5; Philip J. Adler, "Habsburg School Reform among the Orthodox Minorities, 1770–1780," in *Slavic Review*, 33 (1974), p. 34; Strahinja K. Kostić, "Kulturorientierung und Volksschule der Serben in der Donaumonarchie zur Zeit Maria Theresias," in Plaschka and Klingenstein, *Österreich im Europa der Aufklärung*, 2:855–66; Hans Wolf, *Das Schulwesen des Temesvarer Banats im 18. Jahrhundert* (Baden, 1935), pp. 178–81.

30 Helfert, *Gründung*, pp. 384–5.

31 Ibid., pp. 396–7.

32 Ibid., p. 386.

33 "Einladung zu der öffentlichen Prüfung der zwei und achtzig Schüler in der kaiserlichen-königlichen Normalschule bei St. Anna in Wien, nach geendigtem Winterkurs, 1778," in *AVA*, Studenhofkommission (Niederösterreich in genere), Fasz. 70.

34 Helfert, *Gründung*, p. 408.

35 Ibid., 410–11.

36 Weiss, *Geschichte der theresianischen Schulreform in Böhmen*, 1:15–24, 391–3.

37 On the price of schoolbooks see Helfert, *Gründung*, p. 495. Wage estimates are taken from the appendix in Bodi, *Tauwetter*, pp. 441–4.

38 Helfert, *Gründung*, p. 495.

39 "Tabellarisches Verzeichnis sämmtlicher von 5. bis 12. und 13. Jahren Schulfähigen," *AVA*, Nachlass Pergen, 1771; and "Formular zu den ferneren halbjährigen Nachweisen," *AVA*, Studienhofkommission (Niederösterreich in genere), Fasz. 70.

40 "Zustand der gratzerischen Schulen," *AVA*, Studienhofkommission, Fasz. 70 (for 1772 figures). The figures from 1780 are provided in the useful study by Walter Pietsch, *Die theresianische Schulreform in der Steiermark (1775–1805)* (Graz, 1977), p. 47.

41 Helfert, *Gründung*, pp. 409–10.

42 Pietsch, *Schulreform in der Steiermark*, p. 47.

43 Weiss, *Geschichte der theresianischen Schulreform in Böhmen*, 1:17–29; Wangermann, *Aufklärung und staatsbürgerliche Erziehung*, p. 59.

44 See Chapter 5, "From Spinning Bee to Spinning School."

45 For a general account see Engelbrecht, *Geschichte des österreichischen Bildungswesens*, 3:112–18.

46 Adler, "Orthodox Minorities," p. 44.

47 Pietsch, *Schulreform in der Steiermark*, p. 125.

48 Sebastian Hölzl, "Das Pflichtschulwesen in Tyrol ab der theresianischen Schulreform bis zur politischen Schulverfassung," Ph.D. diss., University of Innsbruck, 1972, pp. 380–9.

49 Helfert, *Gründung*, pp. 427–8.

50 Translations of Bossuet's catechism appeared in Vienna in 1758 and 1771, while versions of Fleury were published in Vienna (1766 and 1777), Strassburg (1771), and Breslau (1776). On these catechisms see Johann Schmitt, *Der Kampf um den Katechismus in der Aufklärungsperiode Deutschlands* (Munich, 1935), p. 286.

51 Ibid., p. 287.

52 In Prussian Silesia, *Römisch-Katholischer Katechismus für die erste Classe* (Sagan, 1766); *Römisch-Katholischer Katechismus für die II. Classe* (Sagan, 1765); *Romisch-Katholischer Katechismus für die III. Classe* (Sagan, 1766). In Austria, catechisms designed by Felbiger would include *Der kleine Katechismus* (appendix to the *Namenbuchlein*, Vienna, 1774); *Auszug aus dem grossen Katechismus* (Vienna, 1777); and *Der grosse Katechismus* (Vienna, 1777).

53 Felbiger, *Nachricht von dem für die K. K. Staaten vorgeschriebenen Katechismus*, p. 24.

54 Quoted in Wolfsgruber, *Migazzi*, p. 303.

55 On the controversy surrounding the *Beweisstellen* see Johannes Hofinger, *Geschichte des Katechismus in Österreich* (Innsbruck, 1937), pp. 74–106.

56 Quoted in Helfert, *Gründung*, p. 520.

57 Hofinger, *Katechismus in Österreich*, p. 104.

58　Friedrich Bürgel, *Geschichte der Methodik des Religionsunterricht in der katholischen Volksschule* (Gotha, 1890), p. 255.

59　See, for example, C. A. McCartney, *The Habsburg Empire 1790–1918* (New York, 1969), pp. 112–14.

60　Helfert, *Gründung*, pp. 469–71.

61　Felbiger, *Die Beschaffenheit und Grosse der Wohlthat welche Maria Theresia durch die Verbesserung der deutschen Schulen Ihren Unterthanen dem Staate und der Kirche erwiesen hat* (Prague, 1781), p. 83; Kostić, "Kulturorientierung," p. 852.

62　Helfert, *Gründung*, p. 483.

63　Ibid., p. 479.

64　Ibid., p. 441; Engelbrecht, *Geschichte des österreichischen Bildungswesens*, 3:130–4.

65　Helfert, *Gründung*, pp. 549–51.

66　Adler, "Orthodox Minorities," p. 36; Hans Wolf, *Das Schulwesen des Temesvarer Banats im 18. Jahrhundert* (Baden bei Wien, 1935), pp. 192–4; Kostić, "Kulturorientierung," pp. 862–4.

67　Helfert, *Gründung*, pp. 440–4; Csáky, *Von der Aufklärung zum Liberalismus*, pp. 174–5.

68　Adler, "Orthodox Minorities," pp. 24–5.

69　On Janković's activities in the Banat, see Peter Polz, "Theodor Janković de Mirijevo: Der erste serbische Pädagoge, oder, Die Theresianische Schulreform bei den Serben und in Russland," Ph.D. diss., University of Graz, 1969, pp. 33–157. Janković later journeyed to St. Petersburg in 1782 at the behest of Catherine II, where he helped supervise reforms in Russian primary education. See Peter Polz, "Theodor Janković und die Schulreform in Russland," in Erna Lesky et al., eds., *Die Aufklärung in Ost- und Südosteuropa* (Cologne, 1972), pp. 119–74. [Joseph Sonnenfels was a leading Austrian cameralist, part of a group seeking state reforms in the late eighteenth century.]

70　*Regulae directive für die Verbesserung der illyrischen und wallachischen nicht-unierten Elementar-oder Trivialschulen*, paragraph 4, as cited in Adler, "Orthodox Minorities," p. 33.

71　Ibid., pp. 31, 36.

72　The higher concentration of schools among the Serbs reflected the fact that the Serbian population tended to be concentrated in the southern and central Banat, a region of market towns and agrarian villages. In the eastern Banat, where most Rumanians lived, a more rural, pastoral economy prevailed. Ibid., p. 24.

73　Ibid.; Kostić, "Kulturorientierung," pp. 848–9, 866; Wolf, *Schulwesen*, pp. 192–4.

5

THE EVIL EMPIRE? THE DEBATE ON TURKISH DESPOTISM IN EIGHTEENTH-CENTURY FRENCH POLITICAL CULTURE

Thomas Kaiser

"From the end of the seventeenth century through all the eighteenth," Alain Grosrichard has written, "a specter haunt[ed] Europe: the specter of *despotism*."[1] If the recent historiography of pre-Revolutionary France has had any one common project, it has been to show how the French came to imagine that "despotism" threatened, in the words of Jean-Louis Carra, "to enslave this beautiful nation [of France] under the ruins of her *moeurs*, her fortune, and her liberty."[2] Notably absent from most of this work, which has focused squarely on domestic French politics, has been a sustained consideration of the diplomatic dimension; and it may now be time, not to return to the "primacy of foreign policy," as T. C. W. Blanning has recently proposed, but to heed Bailey Stone's call for a fresh examination of the interaction of international and domestic processes leading to the Revolution and beyond it.[3]

In the matter of "despotism," the case for such consideration is particularly compelling. Not only did the eighteenth-century French public pay rapt attention to events abroad when they involved French interests, but it also came to view "despotism" as a contagion that by 1789 seemed to be spreading as much outside France as within. Montesquieu and others before him had argued that "despotism" was the most common form of government in non-European societies; and however much Enlightenment "optimism" might suggest the contrary, developments in Eastern Europe by the later eighteenth century – most notably the opportunistic partition of Poland – made that region seem ever more vulnerable to the depredations of the "despots" who ruled there. In the eyes of the comte de Vergennes, French foreign minister under Louis XVI, events in Poland and elsewhere demonstrated that an "absolute disdain for the principles of justice and decency" had come to prevail in the contemporary diplomatic world, with the result that solemn treaties could no longer be relied upon to contain the avarice of sovereigns.[4] For such reasons, more than one observer in 1789 felt that "nearly everyone in Europe is wretched and in distress" and that "Europe is experiencing convulsive and more or less violent changes in all its parts."[5]

Thomas Kaiser, "The Evil Empire? The Debate on Turkish Despotism in Eighteenth-Century French Political Culture," pp. 6–21, 33–4 from the *The Journal of Modern History* 72 (March 2000), 36586.

The purpose of this article is to consider one important locus of interaction between domestic and foreign "despotism": the politics behind the French representation of the Ottoman Empire in the eighteenth century. The Ottoman Empire became a major focus of discussion and debate in French political culture, I will argue, not only because it was widely seen as the most perfect embodiment of a "despotism" common to most "Oriental cultures"[6] but also because, unlike the "despotisms" of the ancient world or modern east Asia that were remote in time or place, it played a direct, major role in contemporary European power politics and thus remained a concern of the French state and the French public at large throughout the early modern period. As one eighteenth-century observer put it, if knowledge of the ancient Greeks and Romans might be considered "pleasant" and "even useful," knowledge of Turkish politics was surely "necessary" and "nearly indispensable," since Ottoman affairs "affect us most closely."[7] The premise of this article is that both the diplomatic and the French domestic political dimensions of the Turkish "question" must be explored and interrelated in order to understand the powerful impact of the Ottoman Empire on the emergence of "despotism" as an analytic category in French political culture. In the end, just as the presence of the Ottoman Empire helped the French define the nature of their own state by providing a worst-case instance of where absolutism was tending, the Turks' gradual decline in the European power equation allowed the "despotism" it had represented for so long to appear in new guises – as both internal and foreign threats to the liberty the nation sought to defend in 1789.

As previous scholarship has shown, the French image of the Ottoman Empire prior to 1700, notwithstanding occasional references to its efficiency and military prowess, was overwhelmingly negative.[8] Established in the fifteenth century, Ottoman Turkey was heir to all the traditional disparaging Christian tropes regarding Islamic culture – its hypocrisy, baseness, and licentiousness – which the many crusading tracts, histories, travel books, and other literature on the empire, only slightly informed by firsthand experience, endlessly repeated in their lurid narratives of cruelty, violence, ignorance, and corruption. Running through these narratives was the steady theme of a society operating on the inversion of natural law, as demonstrated in a commonly repeated litany of objectionable characteristics. Decrees of the sovereign were supposedly derived not from reason, but from arbitrary will. Property belonged not to individuals, but to the sultan. Nobility not being hereditary, the natural order of ranks was routinely violated. Homosexuality being rampant, the population was on a steady decline. Women subverted the "just" rule of men, while darker races subverted the more "natural" rule of whites. Ignorance was rampant due, in part, to the state ban on printing presses. Currency, being constantly debased, held no value.

Not surprisingly, the sultan's Seraglio, which was routinely represented as a microcosm of Ottoman society for its inversion of "natural" principles, aroused particular interest. There, enveloped in unimaginable luxury and attended by a strange cast of black and white eunuchs, dwarfs, and mutes, the sultan was depicted as administering through subalterns, who were subject to immediate strangulation if they incurred the slightest disfavor. So, too, was the sultan served by hordes of captive women of Christian origin, selected to satisfy his lusts but inclined out of sexual frustration to engage in much discussed "unnatural" practices.[9] Further inciting French curiosity in the Seraglio was the mystery that surrounded it due to a partial blackout of information. For unlike the personal affairs of French kings, which were largely a matter of public knowledge, the romances of the sultan were shrouded in secrecy. One frustrated seventeenth-century chronicler of the Turkish court despaired that so little reliable information was available regarding the internal affairs of the Seraglio that one could not describe them "without . . . writing a novel," which is just what many novelists would do in the next century.[10]

As regards its political character, the Ottoman Empire was occasionally described as a legitimate form of monarchy until about 1600, but after that date subjects of the sultan were increasingly said to suffer under the "tyrannical yoke" of their "despotic" ruler, since they were obliged
to blindly obey him, his vizier, and his predatory pashas.[11] Islamic law, according to this perspective, was supposed to have the practical effect of reinforcing the political obligation to obey
the established political order, since the sultan, although theoretically subordinated to Islamic
law, had the supreme authority to interpret it however he pleased. Such a political system, based
on slavery, violence, and cruelty and approximating a Hobbesian "continual state of war," defied
the natural order, and the proof of this lay in its inherent chaos and instability.[12] As François
Eudes de Mézeray pointed out in his *Histoire des Turcs* of 1650, one might well suppose that
regimes founded on little more than violence would enjoy an immunity from internal revolution,
given that there was no popular participation in government, that public officials owed their
appointments to the sovereign, and that the people were enslaved. Yet, Mézeray argued, just the
contrary was true. Soldiers in such a state lacked faith and honor and suffered from uncontain-
able emotions, and for these reasons sultans constantly faced the threat of displacement and
murder by their palace guards, the janissaries.[13] The paradox of power later elucidated by
Montesquieu – namely, that all-powerful regimes sow the seeds of their own destruction – was
illustrated time and again by French histories of the Ottoman Empire such as Mézeray's, which
lavished great attention on the series of bloody usurpations and assassinations, many of them
organized and instigated by women, marking the succession of sultans down through the
centuries.

Indeed, so chaotic did the Turkish regime appear in these narratives that the "tyrannical" and
"despotic" category of government in which the Ottoman Empire was routinely placed threatened to collapse. For if such regimes were so unstable, they could hardly be said to exist at all,
on the grounds that no sooner would such a regime arise than its own destructive forces would
likely bring it down through revolts and other such disruptions. The very persistence of the
Turkish empire over several centuries, and most especially its ability to threaten Christian Europe
militarily, confounded French observers, some of whom could only conclude that it must be God
who miraculously sustained the empire to punish Christians for their sins; had the divinity
allowed "things to take their natural course, that Empire would not have been able to last very
long because of the seditions and revolts occurring there that are more terrible and frequent than
in any other state which has ever been."[14] To be sure, analysts adduced more secular explanations for the Turkish empire's longevity and in this cause devoted considerable attention to the
Turks' superior military machine.[15] But the sheer fact that such a "despotic" regime did not immediately self-destruct continued to pose conundrums for French observers long into the age of
Montesquieu.

For the French state, what I will call the "standard model" of the Ottoman Empire as the
epitome of despotic rule was politically problematic, given the series of diplomatic arrangements
– never, as is sometimes suggested, a real alliance – that France reached with the Ottomans starting in the early sixteenth century to counterbalance their common enemy, the Habsburgs.[16] As a
result of these arrangements, France was roasted by Habsburg propagandists, who were able to
take the ideological high ground rather easily by condemning the French for joining forces with
an infidel power having military designs on the Christian West. In response, France was obliged
to launch a rather tortured propaganda counterattack, which has not, to my knowledge, received
much scholarly attention.

What is especially worth noting here about the French justification of its diplomatic arrangement with the Turks is its adoption, not refutation, of Christian Europe's common opinion that

the Turks lacked all humanity and had "more community with animals and savages than with themselves."[17] This dark image was turned to French advantage through the portrayal of French policy as one of constructive engagement. The primary goal of French policy regarding the Ottoman Empire, went the refrain throughout the Old Regime, was the protection of Christian churches and missions of all nations. Insofar as the Turks ruled Christian lands and people "unjustly and tyrannically," the king's efforts to provide for "the comfort and conservation of Christians from all nations who would otherwise have been oppressed, ruined, and massacred" redounded all the more to his glory and reputation for piety.[18] On top of such baroque arguments, French propagandists contended that, had France not settled with the Turks, Habsburg Spain would have done so instead, thereby threatening the stability of all Christendom. For the Spanish, it was alleged, under their solemn Catholic "exterior appearance," were nothing other than ferocious "Turks" themselves, and hence any Spanish–Turkish rapprochement would lead directly to "these two Turks" carving up Europe between them.[19] Finally, maintained the French, there was no religious sanction against alliances with infidels; and if there were, Spain stood just as guilty as France, since it was allied with the princes of Persia, Calcutta, and the East Indies.[20]

The image of the ferocious, "despotic" Ottoman Empire had a second, primarily domestic political function during the Old Regime – namely, to represent a regime against which the lawful absolutism of France could be sharply contrasted. In the later sixteenth century, Jean Bodin still recognized the legitimacy of the Ottoman Empire as one of several "seigneurial monarchies" on the grounds that, even if such regimes were founded through violent conquest and characterized by the sovereign's possession of all goods and persons, they were distinct from "tyrannical monarchies." The chief difference between them, Bodin observed, was that the latter were likely to disappear though internal dissolution, because, unlike the former, they took no account of their subjects' interests.[21] But in the seventeenth century, "seigneurial monarchy" came to merge with "tyrannical monarchy." Charles Loyseau, most notably, saw no essential difference between these two types of regimes, contending that they were both "directly contrary to nature, which has made us free," since they were founded on violent conquest, their citizens were enslaved, and force alone maintained them.[22] On this basis, the Ottoman sultans were routinely and pointedly distinguished from the Christian kings of Europe. The latter, however absolute, ruled according to the laws of God, man, and nature and preserved individual liberty. If the king monopolized sovereignty in some Christian kingdoms such as France, property – a chief constituent of the early modern political personality – remained preeminently the domain of private entitlement.[23] Thus, Mézeray clearly opposed "the Monarchies of the Orient, which have almost always been despotic, and properly speaking more tyrannies than sovereignties" to "those of the West, where the kings remain within the limits of law and are content to regulate the liberty of their subjects, without wanting to suppress it."[24]

[. . .]

In the celebrated anonymous Huguenot attack on Louis XIV's monarchy, *Soupirs de la France esclave*, which explicitly drew from contemporary accounts of the Ottoman Empire, it was alleged that the royal court had become "Turk and not Christian in its maxims," that Louis was trying to "turn us into Turks," and that Colbert had sent the famous voyager François Bernier to the Ottoman Empire to study how the monarchy might confiscate all private lands and administer them in the interests of the crown.[25] (This was a curious allegation since, in his published report to Colbert, Bernier vigorously defended the French institution of private property, condemned its absence among the Turks, and went so far as to identify this as the cardinal difference between the two regimes.)[26]

By the early eighteenth century, a library of literature had appeared expressing a fundamental sense of cultural and political "difference" between Ottoman Turkey and Christian France. In such fictional works as Jean-Paul Marana's epistolary *L'Espion du Grand-Seigneur* (1684), which heavily influenced Montesquieu's *Lettres persanes*, a Turkish spy on a mission to France found himself exploring "a Nation entirely different from ours by its religion, by its inclinations, and by its customs" and was startled to find its citizens hostile to the idea that "to reign with authority and complete security" rulers must "make themselves feared and not hesitate to shed blood."[27] Reference works routinely alluded to Ottoman Turkey when defining "despotism" and its variants; thus, Antoine Furetière's *Dictionnaire universel* (1690) featured the phrase, "The Grand Seigneur [i.e., the sultan] governs *despotiquement*."[28] The Turkish example also penetrated the writing of *érudits* such as Pierre Bayle, who in an essay entitled "Du Despotisme" referred explicitly to Paul Ricaut's work.[29] With such a powerfully impressed image before their eyes, it is hardly surprising that the invocation of Turkish and other oriental "despotisms" to warn of the tyrannical tendencies of the French monarchy became a standard convention in the many critiques of Louis XIV. Even such a reform-minded royalist as the abbé de Saint-Pierre, a promoter of enlightened *despoticité* and one source of inspiration to later proponents of "legal despotism," disparagingly referred to the French state under the Sun King as a "vizierate," although it was, of course, those seeking to curb "despotism" in all its forms, like the comte de Boulainvilliers, who made much more damaging use of the juxtaposition.[30]

Over the course of the eighteenth century, "despotism" on the Turkish model ripened as a concept just as it gained currency. With Montesquieu's genius applied to the matter, "despotism" acquired a systemic nature. No longer did it designate merely an abusive regime; rather, it connoted a totalistic, aberrant form of political society that, by implication, could only be uprooted by radical restructuring of the polity. Once judicial Jansenism, which played a key role in energizing resistance of the *parlements* against the initiatives of the crown, deepened the theological and broadened the legal implications of "despotism," there emerged in France an ideological construct sufficiently powerful and widely diffused among the political public to bring down the Old Regime on the grounds that it had come to resemble the standard model of Turkey.[31]

What historians have not generally appreciated is that, while critics of monarchy sharpened the cutting edge of "despotism" as a political category, the truly fundamental reconceptualization of Ottoman society and government during the eighteenth century came not from their camp, but from defenders of the royal prerogative. Behind this reconceptualization lay, once again, a combination of domestic and foreign political factors. As recent historiography has demonstrated in detail, the monarchy was increasingly assailed over the eighteenth century by its internal critics for the "despotic" acts it committed when it endeavored to expand the tax base, suppress Jansenism, and regulate the organs of public opinion that protested against these and other initiatives. In foreign affairs, the monarchy encountered a fresh diplomatic situation, marked by a warming of Franco-Turkish diplomatic relations despite the awkwardness posed to them by the Franco-Austrian alliance of 1756. Such a rapprochement was of personal interest to Louis XV, since it bore on the tangled politics of the *secret du roi*. Support for the Turks remained an essential part of France's long-standing efforts to project power into Eastern Europe . . .

Closely associated with this diplomatic rapprochement was a cultural rapprochement that shows every sign of encouragement by the monarchy.[32] French perceptions of a softer side to Turkish and Islamic culture began with Auguste Galland's very popular translation of the *Thousand and One Nights* of 1704. Following this translation came a veritable flood of "oriental" novels, many centered around the amorous adventures of the sultan and his minions. The novels fictively penetrated the mysteries left by the more "factual" accounts of the Seraglio and filled them with imaginary romances suited to Western tastes. According to one study, novels of this genre increased in number over the first half of the eighteenth century, rising to about 30 percent of all novels published in France during the 1740s; they peaked again in the 1760s, the mid-1770s, and on the eve of the Revolution.[33] Diplomatic missions of Ottoman emissaries to France also stimulated renewed interest in Turkish culture and helped narrow the perceived divide between East and West. Commenting on the good impression made by the visiting Mahomet-Effendi, *ambassadeur extraordinaire*, and his nearly two hundred retainers in 1742 (thoughtfully reduced from six hundred out of consideration of the expense it would cause the king), the diarist Edmond Jean François Barbier specifically remarked on the ambassador's ability to speak French "as well as the rest of us," his mastery of *bienséance*, and the politeness of his entire entourage.[34] Even more striking was the fashion in Turkish clothing and the fad for portraits in Turkish costume, both of which allowed the French to see themselves literally depicted as Turks.[35] However fantastical, the portraits, like the novels, undoubtedly made Ottoman culture seem less alien to the French and, like the visit of the ambassador, inclined them to view Turks as something better than barbarians. Already in 1735 the marquis d'Argens sensed a closing of the culture gap, remarking that although "a thousand people in France [still] consider the Turks a barbaric nation to whom Heaven has given only the most ordinary and crude ideas . . . we are largely overcoming this prejudice.[36]

That the hand of the monarchy lay behind at least some of this *turquerie* is indicated by the important roles played by royal ambassadors, ministers, and members of the court in promoting it. Former attachés of the French embassy in Constantinople returned to France bearing various Turkish artifacts, some of them for the king, and displayed paintings in which they were portrayed "as honest Muslims" or depicted performing their official duties in audiences with the sultan. These representations inspired much imitation by French polite society.[37] French royal mistresses – often referred to as "sultanas" in the royal "harem" – lived up to their reputations by sponsoring music, painting, and other art forms with Turkish motifs. Mme de Pompadour commissioned Carle Van Loo to compose three paintings for her bedroom featuring sultanas in various settings, which were exhibited in the salon of 1756 and inspired print imitations that enjoyed a wide distribution. Mme Dubarry likewise commissioned Van Loo to paint scenes of the Seraglio featuring odalisques, eunuchs, and sultanas bearing a vague resemblance to her, which were shown at the salon of 1775.[38] That such efforts could be bent to suit political purposes was perhaps most apparent in the case of a production of Charles Favart's play, *Soleiman II*. Featured at the Théâtre des Italiens during a critical diplomatic juncture, the play dramatized the ties that bound French and Turkish culture. The play was based on a published story by Marmontel recounting how a French woman, who remarks on Soleiman's resemblance to a Frenchman, becomes his wife, and thereupon reforms the Ottoman Empire on the French model.[39]

The counterpart of these developments was nothing less than a highly original effort to subvert the standard model of Turkish "despotism," a project undertaken by such proroyalist writers as Voltaire, Simon-Nicolas Henri Linguet, Charles Dupin, M. Abraham-Hyacinthe Anquetil-Duperron, and others working within the foreign ministry between the 1730s and 1770s, including the onetime ambassador to the Porte and later foreign minister, Vergennes.[40] Heavily laced with antifeudal discourse, which betrayed its royalist provenance, the argument had two main parts.

The first part was a frontal attack on the highly dubious factual foundations of the standard model of Turkish despotism. Although certain critics of the standard model, notably Voltaire, remained hostile to many aspects of Turkish culture, they all contended that the blanket condemnation of every feature of Ottoman society as the product of "despotism" had engendered a perfectly imaginary, not to say absurd notion of the Turkish state as the embodiment of evil and the agent of every disaster known to have occurred under its control. "Whatever evil occurs in Asia," wrote Anquetil-Duperron contemptuously, "is always attributed to the government. Locusts have devoured a district; war has depopulated another; drought has caused a famine that forces fathers to sell their children in order to live . . . ; it is [blamed on] the government." The problem, he believed, lay in the sheer ignorance and inexperience of Western analysts and the false opposition of Western devotion to rationality and Eastern lack of it. "The traveler composes a work in Paris, in London, in Amsterdam, where one is allowed to write anything against the East. The same problems in his country, he attributes to the land, to the climate, to the nature of men, because reason has [supposedly] dictated its laws." The result was that proponents of the standard model fell constant victim to the illusions generated by what Anquetil-Duperron dismissed as "the phantom of despotism."[41]

In fact, argued the critics of the standard model, Turkish sultans did not rule arbitrarily. On the contrary, they were sworn to obey Islamic laws that protected individual rights and were guaranteed by the power of the largely autonomous muftis.[42] Sovereignty being circumscribed by a set of constitutional restraints derived from the *Koran*, the Turks lived under a legal system comparable to those of the Salic and Ripuarian Franks, by which the monarchy's "constitutionalist" critics set such store, and to the Roman Twelve Tables.[43] Religion, in other words, represented a true check on sovereign power rather than, as the standard model would have it, a mere tool of its imposition. Moreover, sultans lacked the power to dismiss their janissaries at will, to alter the coinage, or to interfere with the internal operations of private harems, and even though they could unilaterally declare war they were not likely to do so, since defeat would redound entirely to their personal discredit and threaten their security as rulers.[44]

According to these critics, moreover, private property was not constantly at risk of confiscation by rapacious sultans and their supposedly even more rapacious pashas but was if anything more secure than in Europe, with its regrettable "gothic anarchy."[45] As Linguet explained it, the sultan only rarely confiscated the estates of his private subjects; and in such cases, rather than reserving these estates for himself, he usually reassigned them to other imperial agents on the theory that they belonged to them as a corporation, much as a European king might recover a benefice held by one cleric and reassign it to another.[46] "One sees," affirmed Anquetil-Duperron, "that in Turkey the [sultan] has scarcely any more rights over inheritances than do the sovereigns of Europe."[47] In fact, government terror did not constantly threaten the civil freedom of ordinary Turks but was used merely to restrain grasping pashas and thus insure equitable administration.[48] After all, argued Anquetil-Duperron, what respect could the sultan's agents ever command if they derived their authority merely from force and never from law?[49] In fact, Christian worship was not endangered in Ottoman Turkey but was tolerated alongside other cults.[50] Moreover, few Turkish women lived in harems – fewer, surely, than French women in convents – for the simple reason that most husbands could not afford such arrangements. Women were generally more respected in Turkey than in France, where wives languished in the prison of marriage because of "barbaric" property laws.[51]

The critics concluded with a special turn of the argument, that the supposedly "despotic" Ottoman state resembled nothing so much as a "democracy," in which the conflicts among sultans, viziers, pashas, and janissaries that proponents of the standard model pointed to as proof of "despotism" served in reality as a restraint on rulers, thereby insuring adherence to law. The very instability of the Turkish political system, represented in the standard model as the necessary result of its violation of nature and as a precondition of its ultimate demise, was now ingeniously represented as proof of that system's capacity for self-correction and, thereby, for long-term self-maintenance.[52] As Voltaire explained it, Turks were loyal to the ruling dynasty if not to individual sultans, and this loyalty, in combination with the religious sanctions of the *Koran*, constituted a kind of fundamental law of the Turkish state. Hence, "the interior constitution has had nothing to fear, even if the monarch and his vizier have had much to tremble about."[53] And in cases when sultans were deposed, Linguet emphasized, they were eliminated as a result of laws they had violated, a normal political process entailing not a civil war but "a legal correction." "The state in no way suffers from the humiliation of the throne. Its dignity is neither shaken nor degraded by the punishment of the subject unworthy of occupying it. The disorder and the reform occur in an instant."[54]

Beyond attacking the factual foundation of the standard model, the critics pursued a second and equally powerful line of argument aimed at the chronic weakness of the standard model, namely its internal inconsistency. How, they asked, could the standard model account for the persistence of a regime that it condemned as altogether contrary to nature? In this regard, they were quick to discount earlier explanations requiring some deus ex machina. Predictably, Voltaire took special delight in ridiculing supernaturalistic arguments, contending that the factual case against the standard model showed that there was no miracle to be explained with respect to the Ottoman Empire, since "there is nothing but nature there."[55] Yet the real target of the critics – the dragon they knew they had to slay – was Montesquieu's celebrated conceptualization of "despotism," for it was his riveting reflections on this subject, Anquetil-Duperron observed, that had "in a way fixed ideas on the nature of Despotism" and that later works by his epigones had only repeated, though they lacked the same analytical depth.[56] In addition to pointing out Montesquieu's many errors of fact, the critics leaned especially hard on the utter implausibility of his notion of "despotism" as a common form of political society. Given its utterly vicious nature, argued the critics, one could hardly imagine how a "despotism" might originate, let alone endure. As Voltaire put it with his usual, witty sense of the absurd, "it was inconceivable that any country ever addressed its king with the words, 'Sire, we give to your gracious Majesty the power to seize our women, our children, our wealth, and our lives and to impale us according to your good pleasure and adorable caprice.'"[57] Or as Linguet put it in more ponderous terms, "there is no prince or sovereign, and it is impossible that there ever was, who governed without rules or without laws," and for this reason "despotism" had to be dismissed as a "chimera."[58]

Indeed, argued Linguet, it was perfectly pointless for Montesquieu or anyone else to undertake an analysis of the governing principles of "despotism," when the chief characteristic of that imagined kind of political society was its sheer arbitrariness, which arose out of its imputed freedom from legal constraints and its subjection to the ruler's arbitrary will.[59] To be sure, admitted the critics, there had been over the course of history all too many "despotic" rulers who had abused their powers. But this meant only that all systems of government were subject to abuse, not that "despotism" as a distinct social or political system did or even could exist.[60] Once it was conceded that even "despots" lived within systems of laws, it became impossible to draw a sharp distinction between mere monarchy and supposed "despotism." "They are two brothers who resemble each other so much that one often takes one for the other," wrote Voltaire. "Let us say that in every period they were two fat cats around whose neck the rats have tried to hang a bell."[61] The implications of this political logic were devastating: if the factual evidence acquitted the Ottoman Empire, of all regimes, from the charge of "despotism," and if virtually by definition "despotism" could not exist, then all the "constitutionalists'" dire warnings of impending "despotism" in France had no foundation. Let the Chicken Littles of this world shout all they might that France was coming to resemble the Ottoman Empire, all they would have said was that France, like the empire, was governed by rulers constrained to advance the public good.[62]

[. . .]

In conclusion, it may be said that the persistent presence of the Ottoman Empire in early modern French political culture helped to crystallize French notions of their enemies, both foreign and domestic, in complex, often paradoxical ways. Long before the Revolution, the French developed a notion of "despotic" rule and came to associate it with the Turks; but that association proved labile already in the early seventeenth century, when the French came to view the enemy Spanish Habsburgs as covert "Turks." In the early eighteenth century, Montesquieu provided a unified field theory of "despotism" that was derived from, among other materials, works examining the Ottoman Empire. He thereby provided a compelling model of misrule, which, at the same time it was used to demonize foreign opponents, also was enlisted to indict the French monarchy. Under a steady rain of accusations that it, too, had become "despotic," the monarchy waged a vigorous ideological battle for several decades against the standard model of "despotism" in hopes of dispelling the charges against itself. But neither this initiative nor any other effort to eradicate "despotism" or to make it seem acceptable on utilitarian grounds was successful. Not only had the term, a standard fixture of Jansenist/constitutionalist discourse, developed too wide a circulation and too deep a hold to be dispelled from contemporary political language, but in addition the monarchy itself found the term indispensable for purposes of distinguishing itself from "arbitrary" regimes and defaming its critics.

"Despotism" would also gain a new lease on life as a result of the unraveling diplomatic situation in Eastern Europe. One effect of the decreasing military power of Ottoman Turkey, which never entirely escaped its dubious reputation, was to make the issue of its status as a "despotic" regime almost moot except insofar as it related to its long-term viability. Another result was the repeated application of the term "despotism" to other nations – Russia, Austria, and Prussia – that had long been considered abusive regimes, but in the case of Russia and Austria now reached new depths of ignominy for having taken diplomatic/military advantage of an increasingly impotent, internally divided France. Indeed, there appears to be a correlation between the increasingly broad use of the term "despotism" and the increasing sense of vulnerability that the French felt in relation to these regimes. Of the two, Russia no doubt loomed larger as the more powerful, less manageable antagonist, but Austrian threats appeared closer to home and in some respects more insidious. For in the Austrian case, not only were there common borders to protect[63] and a costly and apparently crippling alliance to contend with, but in addition an Austrian agent in the form of the queen appeared to have seized control of the French state for purposes of exporting French wealth and revealing military secrets to her family. As early as November 1789, that kind of activity could only be interpreted as part of a plan to reimpose the authority of the king through armed intervention.[64] "Despotism," a term so debased that it no longer designated any one particular reality, seemed, paradoxically, to threaten the nation from just about everywhere, and to many observers, at least, the only recourse was revolution.

NOTES

1 Alain Grosrichard, *Structure du sérail: La fiction du despostisme asiatique dans l'occident classique* (Paris, 1979), p. 7 (my translation, as are all that follow).

2 Jean-Louis Carra, *L'orateur des Etats-Généraux* (n.p., [1789]), p. 12. Carra's call to arms against domestic "despotism" came in a work whose main purpose was to denounce the "despotic" implications of the Franco-Austrian alliance of 1756. The standard "revisionist" synthesis on the background to 1789 is now William Doyle, *The Origins of the French Revolution*, 2d ed. (Oxford, 1988).

3 T. C. W. Blanning, *The French Revolutionary Wars, 1787–1802* (London, 1996), preface and conclusion; Bailey Stone, *The Genesis of the French Revolution: A Global-Historical Interpretation*
   (Cambridge, 1994), introduction. In fact, Blanning pays much more attention to domestic factors and
   their interaction with foreign developments than his unfortunate reintroduction of the phrase "primacy
   of foreign policy" would suggest. Theda Skocpol also considers the impact of international relations in
   States and Social Revolutions: A Comparative Analysis of France, Russia, and China (Cambridge, 1979).
   For the early eighteenth century, see Peter R. Campbell, *Power and Politics in Old Regime France,
   1720–1745* (London and New York, 1996), pp. 76–82, 166–74; for the mid-eighteenth century, see
   Thomas E. Kaiser, "The Drama of Charles Edward Stuart, Jacobite Propaganda, and French Political
   Protest, 1745–1750," *Eighteenth-Century Studies* 30 (1997): 365–81.
4 Charles Gravier, comte de Vergennes, "Mémoire de M. de Vergennes sur la porte Ottomane composé
   au retour de son ambassade à Constantinople," in *Politique de tous les cabinets de l'Europe, pendant les
   règnes de Louis XV et de Louis XVI*, 2 vols. (Paris, 1793), 2:382.
5 Nicolas Ruault, *Gazette d'un Parisien sous la Révolution: Lettres à son frère, 1783–1796* (Paris, 1976),
   p. 122. On French philosophe views of Eastern Europe, see Larry Wolff, *Inventing Eastern Europe: The
   Map of Civilization on the Mind of the Enlightenment* (Stanford, Calif., 1994).
6 See the now classic Edward W. Said, *Orientalism* (New York, 1978).
7 Jean-Antoine Guer, *Les moeurs et usages des Turcs, leur religion, leur gouvernement civil, militaire et
   politique*, 2 vols. (Paris, 1746–7), 1:iv. For this reason historians need to take into account diplomatic
   sources much more than they have hitherto.
8 N. Daniel, *Islam and the West: The Making of an Image* (Edinburgh, 1960); C. D. Rouillard, *The Turk
   in French History, Thought, and Literature (1520–1660)* (Paris, 1941); Robert Schwoebel, *The Shadow
   of the Crescent: The Renaissance Image of the Turk (1453–1517)* (New York, 1967).
9 A good example is Michel Baudier, *Histoire générale du serail et de la cour au Grand Seigneur Empereur
   des Turcs*, 2d ed. (Paris, 1626). As Jacques Mallet du Pan noted, "The interior of harems [is] the first
   object of the curiosity of Europeans every time there is a question regarding Turkey." "Review of
   Mémoires du Baron de Tott sur les turcs et les tartares," *Mercure de France* 127 (1784): 160. The
   "Seraglio" referred to the entire palace of the sultan, while "harem" referred to the section of the Seraglio
   housing the sultan's women. A useful introduction to the subject is A. M. Penzer. *The Harem* (New
   York, 1993), which reviews some of the early modern literature.
10 Jean-Baptiste Tavernier, *Nouvelle relation de l'intérieur du serail du Grand Seigneur* (Paris, 1681),
   p. 312.
11 For the transition, see Lucette Valensi, *The Birth of the Despot: Venice and the Sublime Porte*, trans.
   Arthur Denner (Ithaca, N.Y., and London, 1993). Paul Ricaut, *The Present State of the Ottoman Empire*
   (London, 1668), p. 7. This work was translated into French and widely read in France. I have used the
   English edition. See also Sieur Des Joannots Duvignau, *L'état présent de la puissance Ottomane* (Paris,
   1687), pp. 48 ff. There is no room here to review how the terms "despotic" and "despotism" emerged
   in relation to "tyrannical" and "tyranny" over the course of the seventeenth century. This has been
   studied in some detail in R. Koebner, "Despot and Despotism: Vicissitudes of a Political Term," *Journal
   of the Warburg and Courtauld Institutes* 15 (1951): 275–302. Koebner shows that "tyrannical" and
   "despotic" had much the same meaning but that the former term was preferred until the end of the
   seventeenth century. "Despotic" began to be used occasionally during the Fronde and became more
   common by the eighteenth century. "Despotism" was not invoked until about 1700. See also Sven
   Stelling-Michaud, "Le mythe du despotisme oriental," *Schweizer Beiträge zur allgemeinen Geschichte*
   18/19 (1961): 328–46; Franco Venturi, "Oriental Despotism," *Journal of the History of Ideas* 24 (1963):
   133–42; Melvin Richter, "Despotism," in *Dictionary of the History of Ideas: Studies of Selected Pivotal
   Ideas*, ed. Philip P. Wiener, 4 vols. (New York, 1973), 2:1–18; Hella Mandt, "Tyrannie, Despotie," in
   Geschichtliche Grundbegriffe: Historisches Lexikon zur politisch-sozialen Sprache in Deutschland, ed.
   Otto Bruner et al., 7 vols. (Stuttgart, 1972–92), 6:651–706.
12 Ricaut, p. 3.

13 François Eudes de Mézeray, *Histoire des Turcs* (Paris, 1650), p. 39.

14 *Soupirs de la France esclave, qui aspire après la liberté* (n.p., 1689), p. 197. See also Ricaut, p. 2.

15 For one notable example, see René Lusinge, *De la naissance, durée, et cheute des estats* (Paris, 1588).

16 See Pierre Duparc, ed., *Recueil des instructions données aux ambassadeurs et ministres de France: Turquie* (Paris, 1969), introduction, for a survey history of Franco-Turkish diplomacy.

17 François I, *Translation de l'epistre du Roy Treschrétien François premier de ce nom à nostre sainct Père Paul troisième, par laquelle est respondu aux calomnies contenues en deux lettres envoyées au dict sainct Père, par Charles cinquième Empereur* (Paris, 1543), unpaginated.

18 A. Le Guay, *Alliances du roy avec le Turc, et autres; justifiées contre les calomnies des Espagnols et de leurs partisans* (Paris, 1626), p. 135; A. d'Ossat, *Lettres du Cardinal d'Ossat*, 2 vols. (Paris, 1698), 1:50; Duparc, p. 213.

19 D'Ossat, 1:415; Le Guay, pp. 111–12.

20 Jérémie Du Ferrier, *Le Catholique d'estat, ou Discours politique des alliances du Roy Tres-Chrestien contre les calomnies des ennemis de son Estat* (Paris, 1626), pp. 55–65.

21 Jean Bodin, *Les six livres de la république*, 6 vols. (n.p., 1986), vol. 2, bk. 2, chaps. 1–4. On Bodin, see Valensi (n. 11 above), pp. 60–5.

22 Charles Loyseau, *Traité des Seigneuries*, in *Les Oeuvres de Maistre Charles Loyseau* (Paris, 1666), pp. 10–11. Koebner (n. 11 above), pp. 286–7, tracks the demise of the distinction but overlooks the contribution of Loyseau.

23 See Thomas E. Kaiser, "Property, Sovereignty, the Declaration of the Rights of Man, and the Tradition of French Jurisprudence," in *The French Idea of Freedom: The Old Regime and the Declaration of Rights of 1789*, ed. Dale Van Kley (Stanford, Calif., 1994), pp. 300–39, 418–24.

24 Mézeray (n. 13 above), p. 39.

25 *Soupirs* (n. 14 above), pp. 34, 53, 19–20.

26 François Bernier, "Lettre à Monseigneur Colbert," in *Voyages de François Bernier*, 2 vols. (Amsterdam, 1699), 1:269–330.

27 Jean-Paul [Giovanni Paolo] Marana, *L'Espion du Grand-Seigneur, et ses relations secrètes* (Amsterdam, 1684), pp. 65, 307. On the importance of this work for Montesquieu, see G.-L. Roosbroeck, *Persian Letters before Montesquieu* (New York, 1936).

28 Antoine Furetière, *Le dictionnaire universel d'Antoine Furetière*, 3 vols. (1690; reprint, Paris, 1978), vol. 1, s.v. "despotiquement."

29 Pierre Bayle, "Du despotisme," in *Réponse aux questions d'un provincial*, 2 vols. (Rotterdam, 1704), 1:596–600. The first French dictionary definition of "despotism" came in the 1721 edition of the *Dictionnaire des Trévoux*; the dictionary of the Académie Française included it for the first time in its edition of 1740. Compare Grosrichard (n. 1 above,) pp. 8–11.

30 Charles Irénée de Castel, abbé de Saint-Pierre, *Discours sur la Polysynodie* (n.p., [1718]). On Saint-Pierre's political vision, see Thomas E. Kaiser, "The Abbé de Saint-Pierre, Public Opinion, and the Reconstitution of the French Monarchy," *Journal of Modern History* 55 (1983): 618–43. On Boulainvilliers and "despotism," see Henri, comte de Boulainvilliers, *Histoire de l'ancien gouvernement de la France, avec les XIV lettres historiques sur les Parlements ou Etats-Généraux*, 3 vols. (The Hague and Amsterdam, 1727), vol. 1, preface. See also Harold A. Ellis, *Boulainvilliers and the French Monarchy: Aristocratic Politics in Early Eighteenth-Century France* (Ithaca, N.Y., and London, 1988), p. 75. On the corrupting power of women in the royal "seraglio," see Thomas E. Kaiser, "Madame de Pompadour and the Theaters of Power," *French Historical Studies* 19 (1996): 1025–44, and "Louis le Bien-Aimé and the Rhetoric of the Royal Body," in *From the Royal to the Republican Body: Incorporating the Political in Seventeenth- and Eighteenth-Century France*, ed. Kathryn Norberg and Sara Melzer (Berkeley, Los Angeles, and London, 1998), pp. 131–61.

31 On the construction of "despotism," see Elie Carcassonne, *Montesquieu et le problème de la constitution française au XVIIIe siècle* (Paris, 1927): Dale K. Van Kley, *The Religious Origins of the French Revolution: From Calvin to the Civil Constitution, 1560–1791* (New Haven, Conn., and London, 1996), chaps.

4–5. On Montesquieu's selective reading of the travel literature in his construction of "despotism," see David Young, "Montesquieu's View of Despotism and His Use of Travel Literature," *Review of Politics* 40 (1978): 392–405.

32 Fatma Muege Goeçek, *East Encounters West: France and the Ottoman Empire in the Eighteenth Century* (New York and Oxford, 1987); Hélène Desmet-Grégoire, *Le "Divan magique": L'orient turc en France au XVIIIe siècle* (Paris, 1994). For a useful but incomplete bibliography, see Henry Laurens, *Les origines intellectuelles de l'expédition d'Egypte: L'orientalisme islamisant en France (1698–1798)* (Istanbul and Paris, 1987), pp. 193–237.

33 Auguste Galland, *Les mille et une nuits* (Paris, 1704), followed by many later editions. See Sylvette Lanzul, *Les traductions françaises des "Mille et une nuits": Étude des versions Galland, Trébutien et Mardrus* (Paris, 1996); Marie-Louise Dufrenoy, *L'orient romanesque en France, 1704–1789*, 3 vols. (Montreal, 1946), 2:15, 30.

34 Edmond Jean François Barbier, *Journal historique et anecdotique du règne de Louis XV*, 4 vols. (Paris, 1847–56), 2:311–12.

35 Auguste Boppe, *Les peintres du Bosphore au dix-huitième siècle* (Paris, 1911).

36 Jean-Baptiste de Boyer, marquis d'Argens, *Mémoires de Monsieur le marquis d'Argens avec quelques lettres sur divers sujets* (London, 1735), pp. 275–6.

37 For public reaction to a painting depicting one official reception, see Louis Petit de Bachaumont, *Mémoires secrets pour servir à l'histoire de la république des lettres en France depuis MDCCLXII jusqu'à nos jours*, 36 vols. (London, 1777–89), 13:98–100.

38 For public reaction, see ibid., 13:181–2.

39 Charles-Simon Favart, *Soleiman second* (Paris, 1762), based on Jean-François Marmontel, "Soleiman II," in *Contes moraux*, 2 vols. (The Hague, 1761), 1:39–65.

40 For a recent but inadequate account of the debate, see Laurens, *Origines intellectuelles*, chaps. 3–4, which overlooks Linguet's role. For one of the best studies of Voltaire's views of Islamic civilization, see Djavad Hadidi, *Voltaire et l'Islam* (Paris, 1974); on Linguet, see above all Darline Gay Levy, *The Ideas and careers of Simon-Nicolas-Henri Linguet* (Urbana, Ill., Chicago, and London, 1980). Another contributor to this position was Porter, *Observations sur la religion, le gouvernement et les moeurs des Turcs* (London and Paris, 1769).

41 M. Abraham-Hyacinthe Anquetil-Duperron, *Législation orientale: Ouvrage dans lequel, en montrant quels sont en Turquie, en Perse et dans l'Indoustan, les principes fondamentaux du gouvernement* (Amsterdam, 1778), pp. 12, 32. An early manuscript version of this work, *Le despotisme considéré dans les trois états, où il passe pour être le plus absolu, la Turquie, la Perse, et l'Indoustan*, Bibliothèque Nationale (BN) Manuscrits Français (Ms. Fr.) N.A. 453, indicates on the title page that it was submitted for inspection to Vergennes in 1776.

42 Voltaire, *Oeuvres complètes*, ed. L. Moland and G. Bengesco, 52 vols. (Paris, 1877–85), 23:530. Simon-Nicolas-Henri Linguet, *Du plus heureux gouvernement, ou Parallèle des constitutions de l'Asie avec celles de l'Europe*, 2 vols. (London, 1774), 1:26–27; Anquetil-Duperron, *Législation orientale*, pp. 112–13.

43 Anquetil-Duperron, *Législation orientale*, p. 114.

44 Voltaire, *Essai sur les moeurs et l'esprit des nations*, 2 vols. (Paris, 1963), 2:809; Vergennes, Archives du Ministère des Affaires Étrangères (AAE), Mémoires et Documents (MD) Turquie 7, fol. 170.

45 Simon-Nicolas-Henri Linguet, *Théorie des loix civiles, ou principes fondementaux de la société*, 2 vols. (London, 1767), 2:133–7; Anquetil-Duperron, *Législation orientale*, pp. 115–22.

46 Linguet, *Du plus*, 1:86–88.

47 Anquetil-Duperron, *Législation orientale*, p. 119.

48 Voltaire, *Histoire de Charles XII* (Paris, 1968), p. 142.

49 Anquetil-Duperron, *Législation orientale*, p. 15.

50 Ibid., pp. 19–22; Duparc (n. 16 above), p. 431.

51 Linguet, *Du plus*, 2:63–70.

52 The notion of Turkish "democracy" was floated by Luigi Fernando, comte de Marsigli, *L'état militaire et de l'empire ottoman, ses progrès et sa décadence*, 2 vols. (The Hague and Amsterdam, 1732), 1:31. On

Marsigli, see John Stoye, *The Life and Times of Luigi Fernando Marsigli, Soldier and Virtuoso* (New Haven, Conn., 1994). It was cited and developed by Voltaire in his *Essai*, 1:835 and 2:755–6; invoked by Anquetil-Duperron in *Législation orientale* (n. 44 above), p. 48; and recapitulated in an ambassadorial instruction (see Duparc, p. 454).

53 Voltaire, *Essai*, 1:837.

54 Linguet, *Du plus* (n. 42 above), 2:20–2.

55 Voltaire, *Essai* (n. 44 above), 1:837–8. See also in the same edition, Voltaire, *Supplément à l' Essai sur les moeurs*, 2:915–16.

56 Anquetil-Duperron, *Législation orientale*, p. 9.

57 Voltaire, *Oeuvres* (n. 42 above), 23:530. See also Voltaire, *Essai*, 1:832.

58 Linguet, *Du plus*, 1:7, 9.

59 Ibid., 1:9.

60 Voltaire, *Oeuvres*, 27:325.

61 Ibid., 30:411.

62 As Voltaire noted, "Louis XI, Henry VIII, Sixtus V, and other princes were as despotic as any sultan" (*Essai*, 1:835).

63 See Peter Sahlins, "National Frontiers Revisited: France's Boundaries since the Seventeenth Century," *American Historical Review* 95 (1990): 1423–51.

64 Florimond-Claude, comte de Mercy-Argenteau, *Correspondance secrète du comte de Mercy-Argenteau avec l'empereur Joseph II et le prince de Kaunitz*, ed. Jules Flammermont, 2 vols. (Paris, 1889–91), 2:287.

Part II

CHANGES IN RELIGION AND CULTURAL LIFE

INTRODUCTION

Children, obey your parents in the Lord, for this is right. Honor your father and mother (this is the first commandment with a promise), that it may be well with you and that you may live long on the earth. Fathers, do not provoke your children to anger, but bring them up in the discipline and instruction of the Lord.

Ephesians 6:1–9

St Paul wrote his letter to the Ephesians from a position of opposition, yet the Roman Empire's eventual acceptance of Christianity signified the rise of a religiously unified Western Europe. The schism between Roman Catholicism and Eastern Orthodoxy (1054) constituted a significant break in this unified religious culture. The next great divide in religious life came in 1517, when the German monk Martin Luther posted his 95 Theses against indulgences on the door of the Wittenberg castle church, sparking the Protestant Reformation.

The consequences of Western Europe's division into Roman Catholic and Protestant were enormous: religious wars and subsequent social and political upheaval. With the Peace of Augsburg (1555), each German State accepted the religious inclinations of its particular authority. The Edict of Nantes (1598) temporarily brought religious violence in France to a conclusion, but its revocation in 1685 precipitated the emigration of many Huguenots out of France into other parts of Europe and the New World. Religious dissent led to violence and civil war in England, not resolved until the Glorious Revolution of 1688. In the age of expansion, the development of an ideology to justify the acquiring of new "possessions" offered Europeans a stronger sense of shared cultural identity that hearkened back to the Roman Empire. A corresponding trend led to the expansion of the Roman Catholic Church abroad as missionaries attempted to convert the indigenous populations of newly acquired territories.

In posting his 95 Theses, Luther spoke out vehemently against clerical abuse of power and offered a resounding challenge to the authority of the papacy, but he did not reject authority as such, far from it. When the Peasant War broke out in 1525, peasants used Luther's words in unforeseen ways to justify their actions. When called upon, Luther supported crushing the rebellion. The freedom he spoke of was of a spiritual nature, not a political one.

The nineteenth-century German philosopher Hegel once described the "great man" in history (now a politically suspect term to evoke) as one who is able to articulate the spirit of his times. Luther spoke out at a moment when a significant segment of society was prepared to meet the challenge of greater personal responsibility in developing a relationship with God. The rise of individualism in the early modern period, in the midst of older concepts of social identity, played a role in the Reformation as well. Many people responded to the sense of dignity inherent in a movement that called for the "priesthood of all believers."

> In the first place, men of the Church commit many abuses against the holy decrees and ordinances in dissolute habits, gaming, taverning, possessing arms and in hunting. Furthermore, they spend most of their time scandalously, and have women and girls in their houses under the pretense of domestic service, by whom they have children.[1]

The good people of Troyes were not alone in protesting the dissolute habits of the clergy in their *cahiers de doléances*, drawn up for the meeting of the Estates General in 1614. If the general populace had reason for complaint against the clergy, the Roman Catholic Church, too, felt frustration at the habits of the laity, particularly in rural areas. Parish visitation records often mention that men and women frequent taverns on Sundays, do not partake of the sacraments, and display attachment to superstitious, if not pagan, beliefs. Peasants lit great bonfires on the eve of the feast of St John the Baptist, a religious holiday that falls at the summer solstice. In many parts of France this originally pagan tradition lives on today. In seventeenth-century Brittany, the Church cracked down on peasants who used the cemetery to play *boules*, dry their laundry, or hold markets. Young couples were told not to live together during the period between their engagement and the marriage ceremony.[2]

The Roman Catholic Reformation, or Counter-Reformation, which found its origins in the Council of Trent, constituted a combination of that institution's response to the Protestant Reformation and spontaneous spiritual movements within the Church. One of the primary goals of the Council was to clarify Roman Catholic dogma in the face of Reform Protestantism. A less overt aim of the Council was to draw the laity into conformity with Roman Catholic doctrine as a means of social control. By promoting the centrality of the parish as a means of regulating and supervising the habits and beliefs of the laity, the Church intended to impose conformity on religious behavior, hence, religion became a mediating force in shaping communities. As a result of these efforts, the Church began to intervene in new ways in the sphere of family life. If, in the sixteenth century, it was still common for a young couple to consummate their marriage on a promise of betrothal, by the late seventeenth century, the Church had largely succeeded in imposing the sacrament of marriage as the only legitimate means of sanctifying conjugal life.

The success of the post-Tridentine Church in imposing uniformity on religious behavior could only have been possible within the context of clerical reform. The local parish priest could no longer live openly with his concubine and their mutual children, although some people argued that they should. He could no longer mumble unintelligible prayers over mass. He must teach the catechism to his young parishioners. By the late seventeenth century, the average cleric was better educated, strict in his adherence to clerical rules, and actively engaged in parish life.

Tridentine reform of the Church paralleled contemporary trends in state-building and society. In clarifying Roman Catholic dogma, for example, the Church shifted increasingly to the image of paternity, thus recognizing both obedience and authority within a paternal and hierarchical social structure. The Protestant Churches, too, accentuated obedience to authorities within and outside of the home. Beyond the concern for conformity to orthodoxy, there was another, less tangible aspect to religious reform. For both reform movements, Catholic and Protestant, earlier traditions in spirituality such as the Modern Devotion and Northern Piety provided impetus in the sixteenth and seventeenth centuries and laypeople responded enthusiastically. It seems ironic that the Roman Catholic Church should try to increase spirituality by imposing uniformity in religious practice. In fact, spirituality did increase in the seventeenth century.

Women played a particularly important role in the rise of spiritual movements. At various times throughout history, women have sought to change their lives via religious channels; often, it seems, by the possibilities offered through new religious movements. Just as thirteenth-century women responded to the broader opportunities for participation in spiritual life offered by the heretical Cathar movement, royal and aristocratic women embraced Protestantism in sixteenth-century France. The Reformed Church held tremendous appeal to "ordinary" women as well. The Civil War sects of seventeenth-century England likewise offered new opportunities to women.

Michel Foucault introduced us to the notion of how society may define gender and the ways in which such definitions are played out through the mechanism of power and pleasure. According to Foucault, power structures tend to mask the mechanisms allowing them to manipulate the system to their own benefit.[3] Yet, there is also a reciprocal and symbiotic relationship between the individual and society that is manifested in a number of ways. Society may dictate appropriate behavior, through dress or rules of etiquette, but it would be foolish to accept outward signs as the sole means of reading into their meaning. Conformity, be it religious, social, or political, may mask what lies beneath the surface. Men and women of the early modern period, both Roman Catholic and Protestant, used religion as a means for personal growth, self-expression, and activism within their communities. The spread of print culture, commercial trade, religious movements, and community activism, all contributed to an increasingly vibrant cultural life in the early modern period. This proliferation of new ideas contributed, too, to the "civilizing process."

Civility may be defined as external behavior controlled by generally accepted social rules. Over the course of the early modern period people began to eat with both forks and knives. They were urged not to spit on the floor or break wind in public. Increasingly elaborate notions of civility developed, along with new notions of intimacy. Intimacy was associated with quiet, prayer and reading, and was reflected in domestic architecture. The early modern period witnessed the increasingly distinct separation of public and private space, yet both communal and public space came to be governed by emerging notions of good taste in behavior. The broader processes by which notions of civility spread throughout early modern society reflect the heightened sense of individualism we have been tracing over time. The heightened sense of the self, as defined by personal over social identity, is revealed in literature, particularly the popularity of memoirs and journals. The very act of keeping a journal is a manifestation of the individual's self-creation or "self-fashioning."

In public space, too, behavior was governed by the group through a kind of disciplining that led to the reproduction of social norms. Interest in civility was revealed in numerous treatises and textbooks often produced for pedagogical purposes. Many such works were derived from Erasmus's *Manners for Children* (1530), designed to instruct children in appropriate public demeanor. Erasmus's text was based largely on tradition. One might equally consider Alberti's *Four Books on the Family* (1434–7), or one might reach further back to Cicero's *On Duties* (44 BCE). Earlier behavioral manuals were intended for the aristocracy. Erasmus's text was different in that it was intended for a broader audience. Civility was beginning to spread throughout society. Manuals of conduct established standards of behavior in a period when traditional norms were breaking down through Reformations, religious wars, and rapid social and political change. In a period of social and cultural realignment, civility became one of the new unifying features of European society.

In the first reading, Denis Crouzet vividly depicts the great penitential processions in France that took place in 1583–4. Dressed all in white, tens of thousands of French men, women, and children, from all walks of life, marched to holy places in shared religious fervor. Pointing to the connections between religious, political, and economic life, Crouzet urges the reader to remember that this was a society whose foundation lay in faith. Drawing on the concept of the body politic, the white penitents challenged the monarchy's claim to *direct* society towards its collective salvation. At the same time, Crouzet wisely encourages the reader to consider the processions as more than "spontaneous" manifestations of a spiritual crisis. Recalling the violent fervor of Catholics on St Bartholomew's eve in 1572, he suggests that the penitential processions of the 1580s were, in effect, the reverse side of the same coin. The failure to rid society of its impurities through the massacre of Protestants contributed to a redirection of religious fervor inward in a period of eschatological fear.

Maureen Flynn's work reveals another arena in which early modern Europeans sought the spiritual well-being of society. Flynn focuses on Spanish confraternities, but these voluntary charitable organizations arose across Catholic Europe. Despite attempts by the Tridentine Church to enforce uniformity in devotional practices, confraternities retained a degree of autonomy in providing a form of insurance to their members, while continuing to offer charity to members of the community at large. Hence the confraternities served as a system of social welfare in a period prior to the rise of the modern state. Flynn's work, too, underscores the importance of salvation to early modern believers. Based on a concept of universal Christian brotherhood, charitable acts brought grace and salvation both to oneself and to others. That concept, however, broke down at the end of the early modern period with the notion of "deserving" and "undeserving" poor. The unifying medieval worldview began to unravel as questions of social order and disorder rose to the fore.

Like Flynn's work on the confraternities, David Sabean's *Power in the Blood*, too, illustrates popular culture at work. By 1796, however, the response of the villagers to misfortune no longer led to penitential movements such as we saw with Crouzet's "warriors of God." When a German village was beset with an epidemic of hoof and mouth disease, its inhabitants drew on a past tradition and sacrificed a communal bull by burying it alive at a crossroads outside the village. The bull, owned by the community as a whole, was sacrificed to eradicate a danger that came from outside. Sabean suggests that the incident may be analyzed in terms of the conflict between eighteenth-century Enlightenment thought and superstition. Village life was governed by social knowledge rather than rationalized knowledge as represented by outside officials. The sacrifice of the bull represents the villagers' manipulation of circumstance and of knowledge in their own interest. It thus reveals the dynamics of power relationships within the village itself and with the outside world. Finally, when state officials arrived to investigate the charge of cruelty, incomprehensible to peasants whose view of animals is that they exist to satisfy human needs, they attempted, not entirely successfully, to impose a new *rational* moral order on village society.

The theme of social order runs through all of these readings. In the century of the Reformation, impurities that threatened the community were, for the most part, conceived of in religious terms. Either one must remove the outside, alien element (Protestant or Catholic depending) or one must repent for one's own sins and the damage they may bring to society at large. By the seventeenth century, the definition of menacing social impurities had begun to change. The undeserving poor, beggars and vagabonds, endangered social order and stability. Seventeenth-century

Dutch images and emblemata exhorted people to cleanliness because of its association with order and godliness. Drawing on a tradition in political theory dating back to classical antiquity, one especially strong in sixteenth-century Europe, the Dutch viewed the household as the microcosm of the body politic. Order and cleanliness within the home ensured good order in the commonwealth. Not only did a well-maintained home symbolize a well-ordered commonwealth, cleanliness formed part of a set of behavioral codes and cultural values that helped shape group identity.

Sherrin Marshall's "Dutiful love and Natural Affection" focuses on parent–child relationships in the early modern Netherlands. Marshall explores the complex system of reciprocity in parent–child relations and thus challenges the traditional argument that "affective individualism" did not develop until late in the seventeenth century. Marshall's analysis of wills, family registers, and personal correspondence offers compelling evidence of real affection between parents and children. Moreover, her research suggests that numbers of children per family and child spacing allowed for the development of strong affective bonds within the nuclear family. Finally, the classical Humanist education gentry parents sought to ensure for their children gave them the means to compete with well-educated non-noble families for important positions.

NOTES

1 *Cahiers de doléances*, bailiwick of Troyes, 1614. Cited in Jean Delumeau, *Catholicism Between Luther and Voltaire; A New View of the Counter-Reformation* (London, 1977), 155.
2 James B. Collins, *Classes, Estates, and Order in Early Modern Brittany* (Cambridge, 1994), 281.
3 Michel Foucault, *The History of Sexuality*, vol. I (New York, 1990), 86.

6

IRA DEI SUPER NOS

Denis Crouzet

There is an evident discrepancy between the object of recent historical research on the Catholic League, the analysis of its social, economic, or political causes, and the major upheaval that shook France in 1583: a great cycle of processions. Just before the creation of the League, a spectacular wave of eschatological anxiety swept through France; in my opinion, this wave is more central to understanding the complexity of the League than has been thought, as we shall see. More than ever before, the Second Coming of the Son of God to the World was thought to be imminent. There is an undeniable continuity with the thinking of the mid-sixteenth century, but certain elements are markedly different.

Once again a History without God: On the Problematics of the League

Anyone who dips into the historiography of the League, as earlier with that of the Reformation, cannot help but be struck by the positivist nature of historical approaches, which, however complementary they may sometimes be, often come to contradictory conclusions. In its ontological tensions, a society which has opened itself to another Being, and whose entire existence has no sense other than to prepare its people for another life, outside of time and the world, is analyzed like a contemporary laicized society, closed in on itself and its secularity, and completely self-contained. It is thus not the substance of the analyses of the League – which from H. Drouot to E. Barnavi and R. Descimon show remarkable perspicacity and extreme sensitivity – which seem to me to be worthy of criticism, but rather the fundamental principle of these analyses: that the imaginary, in this case the relationship between man and God, cannot act out history or the causes of events. Writing about the history of a crisis, which is manifestly a religious crisis, leaves out any mention of God.

Denis Crouzet, "*Ira Dei super nos*: le révélateur de la piété panique de 1583," pp. 287–301, 305–10 from *Les Guerriers de Dieu: La violence au temps des troubles de réligion (vers 1525 – vers 1610)*, trans. James B. Collins. Paris: Champ Vallon Editions, 1990.

The problematics of the League primarily concern the life of man in the world, and the frustrations or struggles of that life. The League tension over the adoration of God can only be a means for Catholics of affirming that the world, as it would evolve or as they would feel it evolve, was in conflict with their aspirations and ideas.

In fact, from an economic point of view, the mobilization of Catholics was chronologically concomitant with a series of years of bad weather that aggravated the dramatic impact of the ravages of the civil wars. One result of this was a movement into the cities of the homeless poor, who were difficult to control, especially with the continual lowering of the living conditions of urban society which began in 1578 due to the increase in the price of a bushel of wheat, a price that peaked in 1587.[1] But is it not paradoxical to record that the key events in the history of the League, the Day of the Barricades and the break away from the king of January 1589, took place in a period when price controls were being relaxed? Might not the merchant classes also have been affected, suffering as they did the effects of a prolonged slump, due to the hindering of free circulation of goods by the quasi-institutionalization of a predatory war; merchants who, it is true, were numerous, even predominant, especially from 1588 to 1591, in the Parisian League in all its guises?[2] In this causal perspective, the steady rise in power of the League movement tallies with the logic of a crisis which affected all layers of the urban population, and of the crystallization of frustrations on the image of a king suspected of reconciliation with the Huguenots and accused of squandering the resources furnished by taxes that were at the same time rising considerably.

Thus, in 1588, owing to the steadily worsening economic crisis, there would have been a "typical pre-revolutionary situation."[3] Yet this is a relatively anachronistic perspective, for within the mindset of the Late Renaissance, such events did not have the immediate quality of being negative or positive; they were signs from God, intrinsically stripped of autonomous or temporal meaning. They were theophanic [related to the appearance of God to man], set forth by God, who, while damning man, led him into sin and corruption. In this climate of fear, the economic sphere, like the social and the political ones, did not exist as a distinct category, so that those who suffered its effects were able to vent their frustration. One spoke only of God, of His anger, of which man was the barometer, of the divine requirement that man should transform himself through his relationship with the Sacred. Upsetting the balance, whether through war, plague, famine, or poverty, thus operated as God's theater. And was not the League, in its acts and its discourse, a response to these signs, a phenomenon of eschatological conscience, which a deductive analysis alone can decode?

On the other hand, from the social point of view, some historians have theorized several conflicting dynamics.[4] The League has been examined as a temporary union of towns and nobles, which, insofar as the nobility are concerned, tends to reduce to a schematic certainty the multiplicity of situations and tensions inherent in a heterogeneous social stratum, divided by clientilism, by family or clan antagonisms, and by hostility toward the handful of nobles who participated in Court life and benefited from royal largesse. Economic factors would have been in play, at the level of the aristocracy as well as that of the petty nobility. J. Jacquart estimates that the petty squirearchy around Paris was the victim of an acceleration of the financial crisis, which had long threatened it. The group of royal officers were found in the first rank of its beneficiaries. Many minor noble lords joined the League.[5] The current work of J.-M. Constant,[6] while insisting on the "feudal dimension of the League," would seem to show, however, that it would only have been a minority of nobles who would have returned to the League[7] (which confirms the numerous League libels and pamphlets calling for the mobilization of the nobility or trying to discourage the nobles from engaging with the royalists). The League, within the framework of a political interpretation, would on the other hand have supported a traditional, "feudal" reaction, by means of certain attempts at disassociation in principalities close to the Court (for example, that of Mercoeur in Brittany). A struggle against the principle of "absolutist" authority, through the exaltation of faith, it was to return to the double myth of autonomy and aristocratic control. Along with R. Descimon, we must ask if this interpretation is not largely anachronistic in the second half of the sixteenth century (the actions of the great "Politique" lords, like Damville in Languedoc, could also seem to bear witness to a desire for aristocratic autonomy).[8]

I do not think the involvement of the nobles in the League can be understood in ideological terms, inasmuch – as J.-M. Constant has judiciously noted[9] – as the breaking up of the kingdom into feudal and urban units risked being far less favorable than one might think to a systematic war to eradicate heresy. Was not the League, objectively, beyond the standard rhetoric of its pamphlets, an anti-feudal reaction seeking primordially to cement the different ranks of society in a sacred Union? Was it not primarily the sphere of power, rather than power itself, that was the object of its criticism? Did not the regrouping of the nobility around the House of Guise mean a rejection of the way royal policy was moving, a policy whose aim was to transcend the system of clientilism based on lineage through the creation of a monarchic system that would rival aristocratic ones,[10] a system directly dependent on the king for its social rise and its financial existence, and developed by the Joyeuse, the Epernon, and the *mignons*?[11] The modernization of the state under Henry III was an ambiguous phenomenon. Did not discontent mitigate against a process of relative state feudalization of the monarchy, which would have broken the image of a royalty mystically united to its nobility, all its nobility: "As for the nobility, Sire, it is the strength of your state, the sinews of your kingdom, the security of your country . . . it is the arms of your body; arms which naturally delight in defending your Head, and spare no effort, no property, no life [to protect it]", say the *Memoires de Deputez de la ville de Paris aux estaz tenuz a Blois en l'an 1588* . . . [*Memoirs of the deputies of the city of Paris for the Estates (General) held at Blois in 1588* . . .]?[12] A process that would have been, for the monarchy, the means of preserving its power at a time when the nobility was facing a financial crisis aggravated by political instability and war, as well as by the economic difficulties unique to the creditors involved, most of them merchants and royal officers.[13]

To be sure, for Henry III, the creation of a group of nobles personally close to him was a defensive move, seeking both to impose a stable Court nobility and to prevent the isolation of central power, as at the start of the first Wars of Religion, in the midst of an active and invasive interplay of aristocratic rivalries.[14]

But, in the end, was not what would have counted in the commitment in the League the sacred conception that the nobility could have of its social existence, of its active participation in the mystery of royalty – which we perhaps incorrectly call "modernization" of the state – would have tended to eliminate or marginalize? Was it not the "white robe imbued with loyalty and affection" in which Blaise de Montluc loved to be arrayed which lets us define what might be the ideal of an "absolute choice" to be in the active service of a king appointed by God?[15] Was not social identity seen through the belief in an osmosis between this particular group of nobles and the soteriological [related to salvation mediated by Jesus Christ], sacred nature of its king, as well as in the frenetic existential quest for achievement through the struggle, both necessary and willed by God, to reestablish a single religion? Did not the warlike utopia that exalted earlier kings, fighting with their nobles in Italy, make concrete the myth of a vital dispensation lived together? The question of nobles belonging to the League is thus badly put, because it is asked in reverse. A religious awareness of social status and function would have been of prime importance for the nobility, a mystical sense of participation in the salvation of earthly society ruled by the king.

[. . .]

In truth, there is no politics in the modern sense of the word; politics during the Wars of Religion, from the viewpoint of a prophetic civilization, is the work of religion. The *Respublica* [political Commonwealth, made up of its citizens] was considered as something which had to function as a whole for the greater glory of God. Civil society was built on religion, which was its principal preserver, its Law, and there was no civil office, at whatever level, which was not considered a religious duty, by the accomplishment of the type of justice that defined it.

[. . .]

In my opinion, what Robert Descimon does not consider in his fundamental study of the Sixteen [the radical group who ran Paris under the League] is that this urban unity and sense of civic responsibility which showed itself through service in the bourgeois militia and through the accession to "posts of responsibility," and which became sacred through "zeal," was only political at base level. Or rather, politics was not an end in itself for the Leaguers, but only a means which allowed each of its protagonists to take part as intensely as possible in the accomplishment of God's will; it was duty, a work of piety, the divine order of justice assumed by those whose faith assured them they lived in a union with God, and not confiscated or monopolized by a minority, corrupted through office. Zeal thus made civic responsibility sacred, and its object, the purified city, placed all the zealots in a position to procure the salvation of men. But, from this certainly anguished desire for the rapprochement of the earthly and heavenly cities, arose the idea that the major event of the League would be a crisis of eschatological adoration, whose manifestation was the mobilization of Catholics, and into the reasons for which it would be worth inquiring. The typical member of the League, living at a time of eschatological imminence, was a man driven by an extreme concern for temporal *work*, of personal engagement in the service of God.[16]

And is not God, once again, the missing part of the problematics of modern scholarship, the center that contemporary historiography bypasses or avoids, because it arbitrarily postulates that there were "social forces and political stakes" "beneath the cloak of religion"?[17] My working hypothesis is the opposite. It could be considered a methodological archaism, to be sure; but from the start, its very concept shows that a phenomenological approach, allowing a reconstitution of the mindset on which the League was constructed, is more adapted to the analysis of sixteenth-century French religious conflicts than a structuralist investigation. What is more, I believe that one must try to move away from the imperialist, even totalitarian, frame of a socioeconomic or sociopolitical causality which, through its conception of a single historical truth, ferociously casts anathema upon all analytical processes that do not stem from its original premises. The writing of History does not seem to me to have for its goal the attainment of a mythic truth of the forces producing events, but the elaboration of an explanatory system whose sole truth is coherence, if not systemization.

[. . .]

With this obsession of everyone – which I believe can be discerned – with collective salvation, with being saved through participation in the urgent construction of the heavenly city, can we not say that at bottom, beyond the simple "associative surface" (Michel Foucault) of its own translation into events and of that elaborated by its adversaries, the League was lived as a substitute for a failed period of corruption and vice, of a sequence of collective adoration prefiguring an ahistorical time of punishment and resurrection, of reconciliation with God?

We cannot explain the League economically, socially, or politically. Nor can we analyze it as ritual violence – unlike the involvement of militant Catholics during the early troubles [of the 1560s].

What we must therefore try to research, in a sort of archaeology of soteriological adoration, are the mindsets which had formed the League, of that pressing necessity felt by the subjects of the king to take part in a reform of his kingdom, and to participate in the restoration of a world more in harmony with divine demands. A work of Justice. I believe I have found one of these mindsets in the White Processions of 1583–4.

The White Processions of 1583–4: An Attempt at Spatial Reconstruction

My attention was first drawn to a mention in the *Journalier* [day book] of Jean Pussot, who described a curious phenomenon which suggests a change of pace in the days of collective piety: "this year [1583] the people of France and especially of this region [Champagne] were much carried away by devotion, to the extent that everyone, in town and village, made grand processions. They began around mid-July and continued until the end of October: the people were neatly dressed in white linen. The processions carried the *Corpus Domini* [Body of the Lord; the usual phrase one might expect from a sixteenth-century Catholic would be *Corpus Christi*, the Body of Christ], the people always sang various songs, prayers, litanies, psalms, and prose verses, like the *Ave Maria*, the prose songs of the Nativity and Assumption of Our Lady, *Deus benigne*, *stabat Mater*, *Christi fideles*, *Averte faciem*, and many other things of great devotion . . ." The intensity of all this made an impression because of the immediate recognition of a change to the usual practice: "in such a way that it was an admirable thing, so much so that many 'great' Catholics, typically cold in their devotion, became much more inflamed with devotion."[18]

No study exists of the White Processions, no doubt because of the extremely scattered nature of the sources and their selective nature, as well as the problem of their symbolic anti-structure and "liminality."[19] Nonetheless, they fired the imagination: at the start of his interrogation on November 14, 1602, Jean Caille, of Chateaubleau, accused of rape, declared that he was born "in the year of the White Processions."[20] Only the comparative reading of day books drawn up in north and northeastern France can show the extent of an extraordinarily devout compulsion that, in my opinion, allows us to put the League back into the context of a crisis of divine adoration.[21]

"... From the Frontiers of Germany ..."[22]

The geography of the White Processions is problematic. Most of the chroniclers of the time limit them to Champagne and Picardy, with the exception of a widely circulated pamphlet, *Le vray Discours des grandes processions qui se font depuis les frontiers d'Allemagne jusques á la France, dont jamais n'en fut faicte de semblables et comme plus amplement vous sera montré dans le Discours* [The true Discourse of the great processions taking place from the frontiers of Germany to France,[23] of which no one has ever seen the like, as you will read in this Discourse], which was published in Paris in 1583[24] and which is interesting in that it had been read by or was known to several contemporary writers of memoirs: the chronicler of Beauvais knew that the White Processions began "at the said time, in the Germanies."[25] Pierre de l'Estoile [a famous Parisian diarist] knew that the first "penitents" came to Reims and Notre-Dame de Liesse from the "districts of the Ardennes."[26] In his *Memoirs* the chief officer of the local tax district of Neufchâtel-en-Bray, Adrien Mitton, sets forth a slightly different version of the story of the *True Discourse*, which perhaps takes into account a mode of oral transmission that reinforced the printed one and had much more potential to spread its message; he reports that in September and October 1583 "the people on the borders of Germany" dressed in white and made their way to the sanctuaries of Lorraine and the Ardennes, "so that the inhabitants of Picardy, Champagne, and Upper Normandy spent the summer of the said year walking in procession, dressed as I have said."[27] The Bordelais François de Syrueilh is closer to the raw information, telling us that in the month of August "seven or eight thousand men dressed themselves all in linen from head to toe . . ." and that great processions took place "with great devotion and penitence."[28] This movement of men and women "from one place to another, the one following the other," and which caught the imagination, was something extraordinary.

The map one can piece together of the number of devout processions places its origins in Lorraine, thus lending meaning to *The True Discourse*. . . . Perhaps the "year of processions" might have had its ritual beginnings in the bailiwick of Bar-le-Duc.[29] On June 23, 1583, the day of the Feast of God, a procession whose avowed goal was to implore God to grant rain to his faithful took place. At first glance, nothing could have been more traditional. All of the corporate groups of Bar went to Behonne. The next day, the Feast of St John the Baptist, a date of great importance in the cycle of agrarian festivals, the inhabitants of Bar and of the parishes of Behonne, Savonnières, and Tannoy marched together in procession to Longeville.[30] On Sunday, June 26, the residents of Ancerville processed to Bar. The white apparel did not appear until the next day, with the restriction that only those most susceptible of incarnating purity wore it: on the Monday (June 27) the procession from Bar to the church of Naives was marked by the presence of young girls and children dressed in "monastic clothing" [that is, robes usually worn by either monks or nuns], according to the local Annals.[31] A system of collective movements, spreading like wildfire, had begun. On July 3, the inhabitants of Revigny and other villages arrived at Bar, while the faithful of Bar left for Ligny, "carrying two crosses and banners of Our Lady." Over the next two weeks, those marching for God flooded the city, to the extent "that so many arrived each day that one could not count them." The area covered by the processions expanded considerably on Sunday, July 17, when the Barrois, led by the bailiff [chief judge], his family, and urban notables, headed for St-Nicolas-du-Port, sanctuary of the patron saint of Lorraine. Young girls were dressed in bridal white and carried processional candles, followed by men holding torches. In the Barrois, processions followed one upon the other until September, at least as far as we can make out.[32]

An Epicenter: The Diocese of Reims

Nonetheless, the explosive center of the processions was the diocese of Reims, in which, systematically, an entire Catholic population penitentially took the route of hierophantic [mystically religious] sanctuaries. Thanks to the list of processional arrivals at Reims published by the canon and theologian of the cathedral of that city, which covers the period from Friday, July 22 through Tuesday, October 25, it is possible to better understand the workings of this devotional zeal.

First of all, in terms of numbers: we know that 72,409 pilgrims went to Reims.[33] In comparison with the Barrois, there was a gap of about a month in the explosion of zeal in the faithful of the towns and countryside of Champagne. The chronological moment of maturation was very brief: from July 22 to July 28, about 1,600 pilgrims (2.2%) arrived, but in the following week 6,125 (8.6%) did so. From August 5 to September 8, there were massive arrivals: 42,153 marchers (58.4%), or an average of over 1,200 daily arrivals. In reality, the apogee came around August 15 [the feast of the Assumption of Mary, still a national holiday in France], with 13,350 arrivals between August 10 and 15 (18.5%). The White Processions seem to go hand in hand with an explosion of Marian piety. The liturgical calendar was important, because over 63 percent of the pilgrims came to Reims on a Saturday or a Sunday. Beginning with the second week of September, and up to October 21, there was a clear overall decline in weekly arrivals (ranging between 2,222 and 3,674 pilgrims per week), with the exception of a peak of 7,190 pilgrims from September 30 to October 6 [September 29, as noted above, was St Michael's Day, a major holiday at the time], then a rapid falling off, owing perhaps to the demands of agricultural work.

The map [of the processions] does not seem to me to permit us to judge if the processions in Champagne were spontaneous or organized phenomena. I will opt, at this point, for spontaneity, because of the nature, both infectious and discontinuous, of the geography of the departures, a spontaneity perhaps carried along in a second phase by a password. The White Processions appeared first to be a country matter, of villages seized by the need to go to pray in the great sanctuaries and take to the road together, on the same day (which did not exclude individual departures before or after the departure of nearby villages). But the processions were also an urban phenomenon, often spurred by the arrival of the country folk. First of all there was a White Procession inside the city, like that which the Cardinal of Guise decreed should be organized in Reims itself, in order, according to local scholar Dom Guillaume Marlot, "to give them more authority," the second Friday in September, precisely when the system of rural parish processions began to lose momentum. Moreover, there were processions of city-dwellers to the most prestigious urban or rural sanctuaries, and it is this model that seems to predominate in the months following the great White Processions of Champagne. . . .

A Ritualized System

Everywhere, entire communities seem to have taken the road to the sanctuaries: the procession from the city of Bar-le-Duc was led by the bailiff René de Florainville, accompanied by his wife and children. Some rustic processions show the presence of "gentlemen and their families," who marched alongside the Holy Sacrament. During the processions from the villages of Lambercourt and Myannay, "they followed Monsieur de Ligny, Monsieur de Hornoy, his son-in-law, and eight or nine other gentlemen dressed in linen like the others, carrying the cross." The marching order was the same for the processions from the villages of Saint-Jean-des-deux-Gémaux and Ussy-en-Brie, who entered Paris followed by "two gentlemen of the said villages," dressed also in white and riding on horseback. Their "ladies were dressed in the same fashion," riding "in a small coach." Hubert Meurier confirms this mixing of the classes on the march: no one was "ashamed" to wear white; "great Lords," gentlemen, town governors, or legal men; merchants, artisans, plowmen, and peasant wine-growers did not hesitate to leave their work for several days.[34] Nursing mothers brought their babies with them. "In short, I could see that no one wished to absent himself, it if were possible, as if not to be present would lead to excommunication." The clergy were strategically placed. For small rural processions, the parish priest carried the Holy Sacrament. The great urban processions witnessed the participation of the bishop, surrounded by all his clergy, wearing sacred capes, preceded by the people, who marched in two rows (the pilgrims who marched from Dreux to Chartres "marched four by four, in orderly fashion").

The Ritual Geography of the White Processions: A Working Hypothesis

If one places a map of the 1583–4 processions over a map of the ecclesiastical divisions of northern France, it is obvious that it was those dioceses subject to the archbishop of Reims which took part in the White Processions. Whence the hypothesis that the White Processions, although they did not spring from an identifiable decision – "and we – became general thanks to and were supported by the ecclesiastical hierarchy . . ." Without wishing to read too much into this, I get the impression that the dynamism of this "white piety" was completely channeled and achieved its apogee under the ecclesiastical hierarchy. The White Processions began a short time after the archdiocesan council, held at Reims in May 1583 at the instigation of the cardinal of Guise [also archbishop of Reims], decided to follow the decrees of the Council of Trent.[35] The bishops of Soissons, Laon, Beauvais, Châlons-sur-Marne, Noyon, Amiens, and a deputy of the bishop of Senlis attended the council. It is striking to note that the bishop of Boulogne was absent, and it was in his bishopric that no trace of White Processions can be found, while in the other bishoprics, penitential marches were practically institutionalized by an official ceremony of welcome for pilgrims, even, sometimes, by the participation of the bishops themselves in the processions. Did the council of May 1583 have anything to do with the instigation of the White Processions or with their spread? The council had affirmed the necessity of reestablishing the "former vigor of the ecclesiastical state of this province by uprooting vices and regulating morals by using the discipline of our fathers."[36]

In the White Processions, do we detect from later events the first stirrings of the second League (December 31, 1584 to January 16, 1585)? Does not the map of the regions crisscrossed by the penitents correspond to that of the League strongholds of 1589? Some contemporary authors were conscious of a certain link of cause and effect; the chronicle of the Protestant, Buffet, after having noted the processions of 1583, declared that "the League was, in fact, founded soon afterwards."[37] Did not the historiographer of Meaux give credence to a tradition when he wrote that the League members "invented what one calls the White Processions"? If one reads the last lines of Meurier's third sermon, it seems that the story, which begins with the White Processions and is deciphered through the penitential adoration of men and women, is very close to what would become the program of the League: ". . . that we cannot hope for anything but a thorough reform of all estates, and consequently the softening of all troubles, the entire extirpation of heresies, and finally a perfect reestablishment of all things, with a good peace everywhere"?

In consequence, do we not deduce that a study of the pilgrims of 1583–4 would reveal the mindset in which the League developed?

The White Processions, as mass rituals, allow us to identify the thinking behind the Holy League. They prove that the years following the St Bartholomew's Day Massacre (1572) once again plunged the people into a state of eschatological anxiety.

NOTES

1 An analysis of the subsistence crisis of 1586–7, by M. L. Pelus-Kaplan, "Marchands et échevins d'Amiens dans la seconde moitié du XIVe siècle: crise de subsistances, commerce et profits en 1586–7," *Revue du Nord*, 44(252), Jan.–Mar. 1982, pp. 51–71, which completes M. L. Pelus-Kaplan, "Une crise de subsistances à Amiens (1586–1587)," *Annales historiques Compiègnoises*, 15, July–Sept. 1981, pp. 4–11. The major work on this topic is J. Jacquart's, *Société et vie rurale dans le sud de la région parisienne du milieu du XVIe siècle au milieu du XVIIe siècle*, Service de réproduction des theses, Université

de Lille III, 2 vols, esp. vol. I, pp. 218–300. P. 227: "following the bad harvest of summer 1586, prices rose sharply on two markets: a *mine* of wheat in Beauvais rose from 68 sols in the fall of 1586, to 92 and then 140 sols in spring 1587, meanwhile in Paris a *setier* of wheat rose from 17 livres in August 1586, to 39 livres on July 27, 1587."

 2 Cf. E. Barnavi, *Le parti de dieu: étude sociale et politique des chefs de la Ligue parisienne, 1585–1594*, Brussels and Louvain, 1980, pp. 112–20 and R. Descimon, "La Ligue à Paris (1585–1594): une revision," in AESC, 37(1), Jan.–Feb. 1982, pp. 72–111 and ibid., pp. 122–8, "La Ligue: des divergences fondamentales." "Réponse à Robert Descimon," by E. Barnavi, pp. 112–13. Essential texts. R. Descimon, however, distinguishes within the market the cautious position of the Parisian silk trade, devoted "to the needs of the Court and ready to collaborate in an aulic and statist project."

 3 The point of view, for example, of A. Lebigre, *La révolution des curés 1588–1594*, Paris, 1980, pp. 73, 93–5.

 4 Which mistakenly ignores the peasant world, certain rural revolts having accompanied the League or having been salvaged by it, like the Gautiers in Normandy (report presented by M. Foisil in D. Richet's seminar at EHESS, "The League in Normandy").

 5 Jacquart, *Société et vie rurale*, vol. I, pp. 266–9, and on the purchase of land by officers, p. 298.

 6 J. M. Constant, *Les Guise*, Paris, 1984, p. 123.

 7 Ibid., pp. 216–17: "nevertheless, the nobility as a whole did not massively mobilize for the Guises. There was an active minority that imposed itself by force or made more noise than adherents . . . So one could say that the political struggle, like the civil war, only concerned a tiny elite from among the ruling classes of this era." Equally, J. M. Constant, *Nobles et paysans en Beauce aux XVIe et XVIIe siècles*, Lille, 1981, and *La vie quotidienne de la noblesse française aux XIVe–XVIIe siècles*, Paris, 1985, D. Bitton, *The French Nobility in Crisis, 1560–1640*, Stanford, 1969, R. R. Harding, *Anatomy of a Power Elite, the Provincial Governors of Early Modern France*, New Haven and London, 1978, and E. Schalk, "The Appearance and Reality of Nobility in France during the Wars of Religion: an Example of how Collective Attitudes can Change," *Journal of Modern History*, 48(1), pp. 15–31.

 8 The "Politiques" were those who remained Catholic, but supported the Protestant king, Henry IV, prior to his conversion in 1594. Damville was Henri de Montmorency, constable of France, governor of the large southern province of Languedoc, whose capitals were Toulouse and Montpellier. On Damville, F. C. Palm, *Politics and Religion in Sixteenth-Century France. A Study of the Career of Henry of Montmorency-Damville, Uncrowned King of the South*, Boston, 1929 and M. Wilkinson, *The Last Phase of the League in Provence*, London, 1909.

 9 Constant, *Les Guise*, p. 148.

10 The problem of the noble clan and political choice in J. M. Constant, "Clans, parties nobiliaires et politiques au temps des guerres de religion," in *Genèse de l' état moderne. Prélèvement et redistribution*, Paris, 1987, pp. 221–6, and the analysis of royal policy in P. Champion, "La légende des Mignons," *BHR*, 6, 1939, esp. 495–527.

11 Crouzet refers here to the middling nobles, like the Joyeuse and Epernon families, raised to the ranks of duke by Henry III (ruled 1574–89). Henry's favorites were called his *mignons*, or "sweeties."

12 "Le cahier de doléances de la ville de Paris aux Etats généraux de 1588," ed. E. Barnavi, *Annuaire-bulletin de la Société de l'Histoire de France*, 1976–7, p. 111. Also in M. Orlea, *La noblesse aux Etats généraux de 1576 et 1588*, Paris, 1980, in particular on the divisions and the phenomenon of League disengagement among the nobility, which are subtly depicted by M. P. Holt, "Attitudes of the French Nobility at the Estates-General of 1576," *Sixteenth-Century Journal*, 18(4), 1987, pp. 489–504.

13 The example of the House of Nevers, drawn in after the League attempt owing to a second royal financial rescue (after a first during the 1560s), could demonstrate that the problem for the Catholic aristocracy was the inaptitude of the monarchy to take charge economically; as a result of which the king could only press a limited segment among them. The result was a pseudo-feudal method of government which, for want of financial means, could only attract a fraction of the nobility: cf. D. Crouzet, "Recherches sur la crise de l'Aristocratie en France au XVIe siècle: les dettes de la maison de Nevers," *Annales: histoire, économies, sociétés*, 11, 1982, pp. 7–50. Critique of the notion of a noble crisis by J.

Russel Major, "Noble Income, Inflation, and the Wars of Religion in France," *American Historical Review*, 86, 1981, pp. 21–48 and J. B. Wood, "The Decline of the Nobility in Sixteenth and Early Seventeenth-Century France, Myth or Reality?," *Journal of Modern History*, 48, 1976, and *The Nobility of the Election of Bayeux: Continuity through Chang, 1463–1660*, Princeton, 1980. Analysis of the overall problem by J. H. M. Salmon, "Storm over the Noblesse," *Journal of Modern History*, 53, 1981, pp. 242–57.

14 The French Wars of Religion lasted intermittently from 1562 until 1627, with the heaviest fighting in the period between 1562 and 1598. Crouzet refers here to the rivalry among the three great aristocratic families of the 1560s: the Guise, head of the Catholic party, the Bourbon, head of the Protestant party, and the Montmorency, usually identified with the Politiques.

15 Crouzet here uses the word *élu*, meaning elected or chosen, playing on the special meaning of "election" – chosen by God to be among the eternally saved – typical of sixteenth-century writers. Cited in A. Jouanna, *L'idée de race en France au XVIe siècle et au début du XVIIe siècle (1498–1614)*, Université de Lille III, 1976, vol. II, p. 643. On the noble quest, to combat and by combat, for the at once similar and different virtues of glory and nobility, see W. L. Wiley, *The Gentleman of Renaissance France*, Cambridge, 1954, p. 39.

16 R. Descimon, *Qui étaient les Seize?: mythes et réalités de la Ligue parisienne (1585–1594)*, Paris, 1993, pp. 71–3.

17 Crouzet here emphasizes work to highlight the Catholic emphasis on the importance of faith and works for salvation. Protestants believed humans were saved "by faith alone."

18 E. Barnavi – R. Descimon, *La sainte Ligue le juge et la potence, l'assassinat du president Brisson (15 novembre 1591)*, preface by D. Richet, Paris, 1985, p. 263.

19 Jean Pussot, *Journalier ou mémoires*, ed. Henry et Loriquet, Reims, 1858, Rés. Lk^7 8208, pp. 18–19.

20 The exception is two pages in A. N. Galpern, *The Religion of the People in Sixteenth-Century Champagne*, Cambridge, 1976, pp. 184–5. For England, R. C. Finucane, *Miracles and Pilgrims. Popular Beliefs in Medieval England*, London, 1977. On pilgrimage as symbolic anti-structure, see V. Turner, *Dramas, Fields and Metaphors. Symbolic Action in Human Society*, Ithaca and London, 1974, pp. 182–97.

21 I owe this reference to Al Soman.

22 Here I am taking up, and modifying, an article published under the title "Recherches sur les processions blanches, 1583–1584," *HES*, 4, 1982, pp. 511–63.

23 "Germany" here would mean the Holy Roman Empire. In the late sixteenth century, the border between the Holy Roman Empire and the kingdom of France lay much further to the west than the current boundary of France and Germany. The border ran down the "four rivers": the Scheldt, Meuse, Saône, and Rhône. In the northeast, Champagne, today well inside of France, was a frontier province; Alsace was well inside the Empire, whose western edge in this region lay close to the cities of Metz and Verdun.

24 "France" here has its ancient meaning, the area just northeast of Paris, often called the Île-de-France.

25 *Le vray Discours des grandes processions qui se font depuis les frontiers d'Allemagne jusques à la France, don't jamais n'en fut faicte de semblables et comme plus amplement vous sera montré dans le Discours*, à Paris, 1583, Lb^{34} 215, which gives 10 August as the date of the first procession, the inhabitants of the German borders going to Saint-Hubert and then Saint-Nicolas-du-Port. On August 15, 7,000 of the faithful from the area around Saint-Nicolas arrived at Notre-Dame de Liesse, returning via Reims and Notre-Dame de l'Epine.

26 *Récueil memorable d'aulcuns cas advenus depuis l'an de salut 1573 tant à Beauvais qu'ailleurs – Documents pour servir à l'histoire de Beauvais et du Beauvaisis au XVIe siècle*, ed. V. Leblond, Paris and Beauvais, 1909, 4° Lk^4 2775, p. 12.

27 L'Estoile, *Mémoires-Journaux*, ed. Brunet, Paris, 1875, vol. II, pp. 135–45.

28 Adrien Mitton, *Mémoires d'Adrien Mitton, président en l'élection de Neufchâtel-en-Bray et des environs (1520–1640) – Documents concernant l'histoire de Neufchâtel-en-Bray et des environs*, ed. F. Bouquet, Rouen, 1884, Lk^{7}24351, p. 45.

29 *Hommes* in French can, like the English "men," carry the meaning either of "males" or "humans." François de Syrueilh, *Journal de François de Syrueilh de l'an 1568 à l'an 1585. Publié par M. Clément-Simon*, Bordeaux, 1873, p. 115.

30 There were two bailiwicks of Bar; the one in question here, as its name suggests, belonged to the duke of Lorraine. The duchy of Lorraine formed part of the Holy Roman Empire. The leaders of the radical Catholics in France, the Guise family, descended from one of the younger sons of an early sixteenth-century duke of Lorraine, so this region had very close ties to the Catholic League, founded by the Guise. As the subsequent narrative makes clear, the movement spread to the region of Champagne, also dominated by the Guise, both as royal governors and as archbishops of Reims.

31 The Feast of John the Baptist, June 24, was one of the four great agrarian/religious festivals of medieval and early modern times. These festivals – Easter, John the Baptist's Day, St Michael's Day (September 29), and Christmas – marked the changing of the seasons; festivals associated with the change of seasons naturally long antedated Christianity, which coopted preexisting holidays by assigning major religious festivals to them. Every farm lease in France involved payment of some rent and dues on June 24, and French people everywhere celebrated the eve of St John's Day with large bonfires. In "pagan" times, these bonfires welcomed the summer sun; the French clergy unanimously denounced the bonfires of St John's Eve as pagan festivals and demanded their abolition. They survive today in some areas, such as Burgundy, where town fire companies supervise the bonfires, and in the German Rhineland, where bonfires dot the hillsides on the evening of June 23.

32 L. Davillé, *Bar-le-Duc à la fin du XVIe siècle*, Bar-le-Duc, 1917, pp. 219–21.

33 *Ibid.*, on September 7, Madame de Vaudemont came, together with the parishioners of Koeur and neighboring villages, as far as Bar.

34 Hubert Meurier, *Traicté de l'institution et vray usage des processions tant ordinaries, qu'extraordinaires, qui se font en l'Eglise Catholique, contenant un ample discours de ce qui c'est passé pour ce regard en la Province de Champaigne, depuis le 22. de juillet jusques au 25. d'octobre, 1583, Divisé en trios sermons, faits en la grande Eglise de Rheims, par H. MEURIER, doyen et chanoine theologal dudit lieu*, A Rheims, chez Jean de Foigny, à l'enseigne du lion, 1584 (the dedication to Dame Renée de Lorraine, abbess of Saint-Pierre de Reims, is dated November 2, 1583), D. 12992: "What follows is the catalogue and number of persons who processed to Reims, dressed in white and carrying a cross, from July 22, 1583 to October 25 of the same year. The final figure given by Meurier is 72,409: my calculations only reach 72,089, from which the percentages have been calculated.

35 Dom G. Marlot, *Histoire de la ville cité et université de Reims*, Reims, 1846, vol. IV, p. 472.

36 *Récueil memorable*, p. 13.

37 Meurier, *Traicté de l'institution*, p. 28.

7

The Charitable Activities of Confraternities

Maureen Flynn

Drawing upon the notion of the *vita activa* and rejecting the contemplative tradition of the cloister, confraternities organized the pursuit of salvation through the practise of good works. Preeminent among the good works were those of mercy, and it is my contention that in observing merciful works as devotional exercises, confraternities created one of the first "institutions" of social welfare in western history. To understand how private gestures of charity, today only a minor and ephemeral part of the welfare process, could have formed the core of traditional poor relief requires that we enter the spiritual consciousness of the past. We must in the first analysis recognize the powerful stimulus provided by the Christian faith to charitable giving.

In the attainment of salvation, the medieval church accorded varying degrees of credit to both grace and works, but it was the notion of works which chiefly manifested itself in Christian social ethics and which particularly interested commonfolk in confraternities. Their corporate statues were concerned not so much with setting private inner standards of belief over members as with regulating collective behavior for the purpose of stimulating communal piety and earning spiritual merits. As Pierre Chaunu has remarked, medieval Christianity was expressed not as much through beliefs as through deeds.[1]

For theologians concerned with guiding the faithful in their achievement of merits, the crucial Scriptural text was Matthew, chapter 25, on the Last Judgment. Conditions necessary for salvation were delineated in the key verses 34–6:

> Come blessed of my Father, take possession of the kingdom prepared for you from the foundation of the world; for I was hungry and you gave me to eat; I was thirsty and you gave me to drink; I was a stranger and you took me in; naked and you covered me; sick and you visited me; I was in prison and you came to me.

Maureen Flynn, "The Charitable Activities of Confraternities," pp. 44–51, 54–70, 72–3, 155–62 from *Sacred Charity: Confraternities and Social Welfare in Spain, 1400–1700*. New York and Basingstoke: Cornell University Press and Palgrave Macmillan, 1989.

The Biblical image in Matthew of God as a hungry, thirsty, naked and homeless pauper, ushering the blessed to his right side on the basis of their generosity to him, and damning misers and inhospitable folk to his left, was invoked before the public in sermons to stress the value of charity. Theologians considered almsgiving the most worthy expression of love for God and for neighbors. It was, they believed, the most effective manner of obtaining spiritual purification. Medieval and early modern Catholic theologians discussed charity in terms of its redemptive value.[2] According to Friar Tomas de Trujillo, "he who gives charity, extinguishes hunger, and covers nakedness, extinguishes his own faults and covers his own sin".[3] Paraphrasing Ecclesiasticus 3:30, the confraternity of San Ildefonso announced its charitable activities with the declaration that "charity kills sin as water puts out fire".[4]

From the early centuries of Christianity, charitable deeds worthy of divine recognition were incorporated into literature and sermons on the proper Christian life. Augustine was among the first of the church fathers to cite specific acts of mercy for the instruction of Christians. In his discussion of faith and works in the *Enchiridion*, Augustine presented almsgiving as a way to atone for sin. To make up for the commitment of serious sins, he argued that charity must be performed during one's lifetime, for these transgressions cannot be redeemed by purgatorial fire after death.[5] Augustine offered a long list of spiritual acts to be practiced in obtaining forgiveness of sin. This list included feeding the hungry, giving drink to the thirsty, clothing the naked, offering hospitality to the stranger, sheltering the fugitive, visiting the sick and incarcerated, ransoming the captive, bearing the burdens of the weak, leading the blind, comforting the sorrowful, healing the sick, guiding the lost, counseling the perplexed, providing for the poor, correcting the unrighteous and pardoning the offender.[6] To these imperatives he later added the burial of the dead.[7]

Augustine's list was refined in the Middle Ages and eventually assembled into a moral code. One of the earliest expressions of this was contained within the Benedictine rule which commissioned several acts of charity for observance by the monastic community.[8] In AD 802 a Carolingian capitulary entitled "Admonitio generalis" which dealt with the basic precepts of Christianity enjoined the practice of charitable acts with the injunction that "faith without works is dead". To follow the ideal of treating others as oneself, the capitulary prescribed feeding the poor, taking pilgrims into one's home, and visiting the sick and incarcerated. As works which would clean away sins, it mentioned redeeming captives, assisting those unjustly persecuted, defending widows and orphans, ensuring justice, preventing iniquity, curbing prolonged anger, and avoiding excessive drinking and banqueting.[9]

By the late eleventh and twelfth centuries, the acts of mercy were established as formulae for lay spiritual behavior. Pedagogical texts such as the 1093 cartulary of Mas-d'Azil advised Christians to "keep charity always in your heart", by calling into fraternal peace those who complain, supporting the poor, visiting the sick and also burying the dead.[10]

In the *Siete Partidas*, Alfonso X's law code compiled in the second half of the thirteenth century, a section concerned with managing beneficence in society divided the acts of mercy into spiritual and corporal types. It considered the spiritual acts of pardoning the injurer, punishing the wicked, and instructing the ignorant superior to the material forms of mercy, likening them to the souls' superiority over the body. The corporal acts consisted of feeding the hungry, giving drink to the thirsty, clothing the naked, and visiting the sick and imprisoned.[11]

The earliest thirteenth-century Latin catechisms reduced the acts of mercy to seven for easier memorization. Once cast into seven, a number that held special ritual significance in Christian thought,[12] the merciful acts remained spellbound to the present day. In Juan Ruiz's fourteenth-century account of the acts of mercy in the *Libro de buen amor*, they had become something of a talisman for the faithful. Ruiz argued that these charitable acts could conquer the evil forces of the world, the devil and the flesh.[13] Regularly to feed the hungry, house the wayfarer, dress the naked, give drink to the thirsty, visit the sick, dower orphans and bury the dead might fend off impurity and preserve the soul, sanctified by baptism, for entry into heaven.

In the catechetical treatise of Pedro de Veragüe, the merciful acts were introduced with the warning that

> Esperança perderás
> E la feé quando serás
> Delante Dios, berás
> Con gran liberalidad
> Fas obras de caridad
> Que la linpia boluntad
> La caridad es tan alta
> Que todos bienes alcança
> De quien non resçibio falta[14]

In the catechism, seven spiritual acts had been added to the corporal, and in time this dual moral code became the standard format of the merciful works presented in Catholic educational texts. The spiritual acts, invoked less frequently, included teaching the ignorant, counseling the doubtful, admonishing sinners, bearing wrongs and adversity patiently, forgiving offenses willingly, comforting the afflicted and praying for the living and the dead. Among the corporal acts, dowering orphans was permanently replaced with burying the dead, and cited along with feeding the hungry, giving drink to the thirsty, clothing the naked, lodging the homeless, visiting the sick, and ransoming the captive. These seven acts were versified in Latin as "pasco, poto, coligno, tego, visito, librero and condo".[15]

The merciful acts were propagated along with the Creed and the Ten Commandments as part of the attempt to turn late medieval and early modern Europe into a Christian society. One finds them in confessional manuals and mystical literature, among preachers' sermons and lay devotional guides. They were painted and sculpted in church interiors and posted on church doors.

As the charitable works were standardized in written religious treatises and catechisms, they became formalized in practice. The seven corporal works took on stereotypical dimensions in the charitable work arranged by benefactors. Every testator aspired to perform an act of mercy upon his or her death. Wills of the late medieval and early modern period are filled with carefully formulated bequests in demonstration of the donors' charitable virtues in order to ensure the safety of their souls. Even testators from small villages, where one might have expected poor understanding of catechetical precepts, revealed a striking familiarity with the seven acts of mercy. In 1545, Juan Gregorio ordered the sale of all his clothes in order to buy simple woven garments to distribute to the poor.[16] A townswoman of Zamora, Catarina Alvarez, chose to feed the hungry by giving two pounds of bread to four needy people every Sunday.[17] Francisco de Verástigui, resident of the village of Calabazanos, named most of the acts of mercy in his testament in 1554, making donations to the confraternity and hospital of the royal court and to a confraternity in charge of caring for poor orphans in the place where he would die. He left 50 ducats for the redemption of captives, 50 ducats to free a pauper from jail, and provided for dressing and giving money to 13 paupers who accompanied his body to the grave.[18] Any one of the merciful works – freeing a prisoner, or clothing the poor – carried with it the explicit message that the service was holy, offered to the needy in the image of Christ.

Enshrined as religious ritual, the acts of mercy possessed a significance transcending the utilitarian functions that they served. It was the religious meaning attributed to the merciful works
that accounts for their influence in social custom and that ensured their continuous observance
by the populace. The performance of an act of mercy was a means of acquiring grace, a wholly
efficacious rite that communicated with God even as it relieved the physical discomfort of one's
fellow Christian. But the practical role of charity should not be obfuscated by the formality with
which it was exercised. As the anthropologist Victor Turner has said of many communal rituals,
"a creative deed becomes an ethical or ritual paradigm".[19] Almsgiving was commuted in Zamora
into a religious paradigm and in this routine became all the more effective as a program of daily
welfare. Beggars required feeding every day, three times a day if they could get it. Whenever they
sat at a resident's doorstep at dinnertime they represented an opportunity to exercise one of these
charitable virtues.

The acts of mercy became institutionalized as soon as they attained the status of ritual.
Zamoran confraternities, in their concern for the sanctification of members' souls, adopted the
merciful acts among their earliest activities. The first documentary references to confraternities
in the city in the thirteenth century are, in fact, private deathbed donations of blankets to them
for distribution to the needy.[20] In later centuries, confraternal statutes explicitly declare that their
objective was to pursue charity. A standard introduction to the individual programs of charitable
confraternities proclaims that they were "founded primarily to accomplish the 'obras de misericordia', that is, true charity, which is the principle upon which all similar confraternities ought
to be founded". The reason given for such work – "so that the living grow in devotion and that
the dead never lack divine offices" – equated almsgiving with soul-saving.[21] Mercy propagated
graces among the community for the collective sanctification of souls.

In pursuing acts of mercy, confraternities worked in conjunction with private individuals,
canons, priests, friars, nuns and *beatas* to create a comprehensive welfare program for society. At
a time when the government was unable or unwilling to allocate aid to the indigent, who constituted a significant proportion of the total population (almost 30 per cent of Zamora's residents,
a figure that most Castilian towns matched[22]), these individuals and private religious organizations shared responsibilities for relief. Their actions were conditioned not merely by the needs
of society and the means of assistance at their disposal. They meticulously observed the merciful works when turning to care for paupers. It was the imitative quality of their charitable gestures that gave direction to almsgiving in Catholic society. Religion ritualized relief to the poor,
creating a welfare system with its own distinct organization and rhythms. Alms were by no means
given in the spontaneous and haphazard manner in which traditional scholarship has portrayed
pre-industrial attempts to administer to the poor. The methods adopted to provide poor relief in
the past were standardized by the acts of mercy. Let us see how this operated.

"To Feed the Hungry, Give Drink to the Thirsty, Visit the Sick and Clothe the Naked . . ."

The management of hospitals was one of the most ambitious ways that confraternities chose to
observe the merciful works. At least thirteen confraternities in the city of Zamora ran their own
hospitals. Others assisted monastic infirmaries and privately endowed hospitals where their devotional concerns were applied to the permanent care of the sick and homeless. Although it has
been recognized in the literature on poor relief that medieval health care facilities owed their existence to religious organizations and pious individuals in the service of God,[23] what remains to be
clarified is the manner in which religious preoccupations conducted actual nursing services.

One of the oldest hospitals in Zamora was called the Hospital of Shepherds. Established in the twelfth century by a group of merchants, the hospital was taken over by furriers of the Cofradía de Santa María y San Julián from the mid-fourteenth to the mid-fifteenth centuries.[24] It was located in the church of San Julián at the entry to the city from the bridge over the Duero, where it welcomed pilgrims passing through from the south. Pilgrims were considered particularly worthy recipients of charity due to their homeless status, and the confraternity sought to provide them with food and shelter along their journey. The hospital also cared for the sick, housing patients until they were fully cured and able to earn a living. An attendant living on the premises supervised patients and ensured that they received communion and made confession. By late medieval standards the hospital was relatively well supplied with fourteen beds and twenty-five wool blankets.[25] In addition, twenty-five sets of used clothing were reserved as burial garbs for those who might die within the hospital. The clothing was donated by furriers from their personal wardrobes at their deaths, a ritual of charity pledged by all members upon entering the Cofradía de Santa María y San Julián. This contribution of clothing to the needy, referred to as a "falifo", was shared by other confraternities in the province of Zamora for the maintenance of their hospitals and earned them the name "cofradías de los falifos".[26]

Collective almsgiving supplemented these private donations of clothing and food to provision patients. Once a year, in ritual profession of clothing the naked, the furriers of the confraternity gave to each of their patients a cape of coarse goat's hair, a fur robe, and shoes. In compliance with their commitment to feed the hungry, on major feast days they distributed to patients portions of rabbit and pork with bread and wine. Together, food produced by the furriers' own hands and clothes offered from their own backs entirely supported the health care facilities of the hospital.

Not all confraternities concocted such imaginative rituals to furnish hospitals but they all offered equally intimate gifts and services. Aristocrats of the two most extensive welfare facilities in sixteenth-century Zamora, Nuestra Señora de la Candelaria and Nuestra Señora de la Misericordia, went out into the streets to find homeless paupers to lodge in their hospitals. They then visited patients, bringing along food and firewood for their needs. On a more modest scale, cofrades of the Ciento extended hospital care to sick clerics, and commoners in other confraternities worked in their own small institutions, furnished with only a couple of beds, when needy members required special nursing attention. These private hospitals brought cofrades into direct contact with the poor and infirm, offering them opportunities to perform religious services through countless daily ministrations.

People gave what they had to supply the institutions. Antonia Martín donated two small pillows "for paupers who are well behaved".[27] In 1566, a cleric, Francisco Aguilera, gave to one of his confraternities two ducats to buy its patients bread and to another confraternity he donated two ducats for clothes.[28] It was particularly common for members to offer their bedding to hospitals at the time of their deaths. Leonor de Cormega gave a mattress, a blanket, two sheets and two pillows to the poor of the Hospital of the Candelaria, and a mattress and a blanket to the Hospital of the Misericordia in 1546.[29] Such careful allocation of the goods of one's estate, each gesture crafted to imitate an act of mercy, constituted the sole source for provisioning some of the tiny confraternal hospitals.

Due to the personal nature of endowments, administration of health care in these hospitals was extremely cumbersome. Beds, clothing and food rations provided by individual bequests were saddled with special stipulations and could not always be allocated efficiently. Confraternities were bound by law to preserve the intention behind each donation and to protect the integrity of the pious endowment with corporate funds. Imposing a degree of order over these multiple sources of funding was the most serious challenge faced by hospital management.

[...]

Additional opportunities for pious lay people to perform good works existed at the large pilgrims' hospital of the Catholic Monarchs in Santiago de Compostela. Construction of the hospital in Santiago began in 1503 by Queen Isabella, who had been informed of the pressing need for a large hospital to accommodate paupers and pilgrims who gathered from all over Christendom to visit Santiago's shrine. The Queen promised that anyone who joined a confraternity dedicated to Santiago and its hospital, or donated one twentieth of a ducat to the institution, would enjoy remissions of their sins through future masses said by the confraternity in a chapel of the hospital. Men and women from all estates throughout Spain and France joined the Cofradía de Santiago and with the authorization of the Emperor Maximilian and Archduke Carlos in 1508, its membership expanded to include Germans.[30]

A major responsibility of the confraternity was to hear masses regularly for the souls of cofrades, the monarchs and the poor, which yielded indulgences and graces for all who contributed to the hospital. It was also responsible for publishing notices of collective indulgences and encouraging donations. Initially, rental income provided by the Catholic Monarchs supported hospital services, but by 1511 the regent Juana was compelled to seek additional donations from the public to cover increased costs. She distributed among cofrades licenses to preach and solicit charity in parishes on Sundays and holy days.[31] In the following years, cofrades throughout Spain organized a comprehensive campaign to collect funds by sending out letters soliciting donations to major cities and increasing their own private membership fees.

Except for volunteer services offered by cofrades, nursing and medical care was performed by hired personnel and clergymen. They too carefully followed the prescriptions of the acts of mercy, for despite monetary reimbursement they considered their work holy. In addition to treating the sick, they fed beggars who came to the door for alms, cared for abandoned children and offered hospitality to pilgrims in need of lodging.[32] The hospital had three separate infirmaries in the mid-sixteenth century, each with six of its beds reserved for pilgrims. It was expected that only one person would occupy each bed, although over-crowding periodically forced patients to share facilities. In 1568, two additional infirmaries opened to admit more patients and the hospital sent out German and French chaplains to search the streets and churches of Santiago de Compostela for foreigners in need of nursing care.

It is apparent in Santiago's hospital that the act of mercy of sheltering the homeless was closely allied in practice with caring for the sick. Many pilgrims to shrines were seeking cures for illnesses and disabilities, and required medical attention. Late medieval Zamora supported at least five confraternal hospices (the term *hospital* referred to both hospices and hospitals) along major thoroughfares and near bridges for the convenience of travellers. City residents who sought to assist travellers donated to Santa María y San Julián, Santa María de Tercia, Santa María de los Alfares, Nuestra Señora de la Misericordia, and San Juan de Acre, the groups in charge of these hospices. Again, the main burden of administrators was to co-ordinate the idiosyncratic wishes of private donors to the needs of the poor. Only the most street-wise of the city's beggars knew, for instance, that every Saturday and Sunday cofrades of Santa María de Tercia distributed bread to each pilgrim in their hospice and to travellers and paupers who gathered outside the doors for charity.[33]

More extensive than the institutional nursing care provided by cofrades was the private care that they extended to sick people in their homes. In pursuit of the act of mercy of visiting the sick, virtually all confraternities developed policies for attending to their own members when they became ill. A system of vigils was set up whereby cofrades took turns caring for sick brothers and sisters. The usual custom was to have two cofrades attend at one time. Beginning with those who resided nearest to the home of the invalid, members rotated visits day and night to maintain constant attention at the bedside. Cofrades brought candles, food, medicine, the eucharist, and, if necessary, oil for the Last Rites, seeking to comfort the sick and nurse him back to health or ensure a Christian death. Many of the confraternities of commoners, unable to afford charitable programs for paupers hardly worse off than themselves, concentrated solely on aiding each other in this manner.

While non-members were obliged in receiving charity to recompense benefactors with spiritual services, brothers and sisters received help without incurring the duty to reciprocate. In delivering charity to members as a right of fellowship without strings attached, cofrades were less concerned with literally fulfilling the acts of mercy and came up with ingenious methods to assist each other. The aristocratic confraternity of San Ildefonso paid debts of members unable to meet their obligations. Rural confraternities formed their own type of mutual assistance network, aiding impoverished member by permitting them use of the corporation's land, providing wheat, and sending hands to aid in the cultivation of farms for those unable to work. The Cofradía de la Vera Cruz in the village of Villalcampo stipulated that its cofrades would hand over a day's earnings to a sick member who called upon it for aid. It also guaranteed that if a cofrade fell ill outside the village without means to support himself or people to nurse him, the confraternity would retrieve him, journeying up to a day at the cost of the organization.[34] One of the most useful functions of the rural confraternities was to act as agencies supplying seed to needy farmers.[35]

By breaking away from ritual, the assistance programs to members met circumstances in a manner creative and flexible enough to prevent as well as to alleviate poverty. During the sixteenth and seventeenth centuries, craft confraternities in more industrially advanced areas such as Madrid developed sophisticated insurance programs for their members. Antonio Rumeu de Armas provides fascinating information on confraternities that subsidized members through periods of sickness, joblessness, and, in the case of a few confraternities consisting solely of women, of help with pregnancy and early childcare. A confraternity of cobblers in late sixteenth-century Madrid furnished sick members the services of a doctor and a barber-surgeon as well as medicine (except for women), and seven *reales* a week in indemnity payments for time that they lost at work while ill. The Cofradía de Nuestra Señora de las Nieves y Jesús Nazareno and the Cofradía of San Antonio Abad in the same city extended extraordinary support for risks associated with motherhood. These two confraternities allocated sums of money to cofradas upon the birth of children, giving lower amounts for miscarriages. Subsidies for miscarriages were delivered only if the fetus were at least three months old, confirmation of this to be made by an experienced member. If women fell ill after giving birth, they received daily allowances for periods up to one month.[36]

"To Offer Hospitality to the Homeless . . ."

As part of the fulfillment of the prescription to aid wayfarers, some confraternities took upon themselves the duties of maintaining bridges for safe passage across the countryside. According to Marjorie Boyer, medieval churchmen had encouraged the widespread notion that bridge construction and repair were pious activities by demanding that travel across them be gratuitous and forbidding fortification on bridge premises.[37] In fact, these strategic nexus of communication were endowed more frequently with chapels and shrines than with parapets in the Middle Ages. Clerics' sermons also invoked the sanctity of bridges by employing imagery of the viaduct in drawing a connection between the material and spiritual worlds. The most famous analogy was, of course, Bernard of Clairvaux's depiction of the Virgin as an aqueduct of grace from the heavens to individual souls.[38] A sixteenth-century Spanish treatise propounding the spiritual rewards of charity commented that "the bridge to the glory of paradise is mercy",[39] a figurative statement that the Zamoran confraternity of the Animas of San Simón manifested quite literally by painting images of souls on bridge walls near its almsbox to stimulate donations for souls in purgatory.[40] It was a culture and a period that took symbolism seriously.

Brotherhoods of bridge-keepers lined the roads of major pilgrimage routes in the Spanish peninsula as well as in parts of England and France.[41] The oldest appeared in the late eleventh and early twelfth centuries in the valleys of the Rhône and the Loire rivers, performing the functions of bridge construction and repair, charity collection, and accommodation for travellers.[42]

The most active bridge-keeping confraternity in the province of Zamora was located in the northern village of Rionegros. Dedicated to Nuestra Señora de la Carballeda, it was commonly known as the "Cofradía de los Falifos". According to the confraternity's papal bulls, the earliest of which dates from 1342 and attests to the existence of the organization during previous pontificates, the confraternity participated in extensive poor relief programs for pilgrims throughout the province of Leon. The bull of Pope Eugene IV of 1446 recognized its pious activities, claiming that since its establishment, the confraternity had erected 35 bridges over "several different and dangerous rivers for the greater security of pilgrims who travel to visit the temple of the Apostle Santiago and other pious places, and founded 30 hospitals for the lodging and sustenance of the frail, of abandoned children, and of sick people and orphans".[43] In 1538, Paul III conceded to its members numerous indulgences and complete pardons of ecclesiastical penalties to encourage support of its estimated 20 hospitals, its many bridges and roadways, and its dowry programs for young girls and education of abandoned children.

The pious activities of Nuestra Señora de la Carballeda were financed completely by voluntary donations of members from villages in the north of the Zamoran province. According to the organization's statutes, revised at the end of the eighteenth century, cofrades sustained the work for many centuries "without further resources than charity and the contribution of the Falifa, that is, a piece of the best clothing that they had, like a cape, a coat, a jacket, a petticoat, a doublet or whatever was the style in the territory". The clothing was used by the poor or sold on the market for money to finance bridges and facilitate the travels of pilgrims in inhospitable regions of the province.[44]

"Offering hospitality to the homeless" was not a rigid prescription. It was pursued in many forms. Besides hospices and bridges, orphanages were also constructed to heed the call of this particular holy deed. Care of foundlings and orphans became an important concern of Spanish confraternities in the sixteenth century, when several organizations under the advocacy of Mary or Joseph were established specifically for rearing homeless children. In addition, many medieval confraternities that once had been dedicated to aiding travellers and sick people began to focus on the young as pilgrimages to Santiago declined in popularity. In the early modern period, Nuestra Señora de la Carballeda transferred funds which had been directed towards the maintenance of bridges and hospices to care for foundlings and poor children in the village of Rionegro and its countryside. Hospitality to infants abandoned at its chapel doors involved hiring wetnurses to raise the minors until they reached the age of seven, when they were placed in schools and trades.[45]

Foundling confraternities were established in Salamanca and Valladolid in the sixteenth century to care for unwanted children in the southern realms of Leon-Castile. The Cofradía de San José y Nuestra Señora de la Piedad in Salamanca offered protection to foundlings deposited at the Door of Pardon of the cathedral, sometimes left by parents who travelled several dozen miles. The confraternity hired wetnurses, primarily Portuguese peasants, at approximately 5000 *maravedís* a year for the care of each child.[46] It also provided the women regular provisions of baby clothes and shoes and covered baptismal costs. Between September 1590 and July 1596, the confraternity recorded expenses on 500 children, the vast majority of whom died within the first year of their care by the hospital.[47]

Funding for these services depended heavily on public support, and the confraternity called upon the assistance of the citizenry of Salamanca in yearly demonstrations. Parades have always served as means to rally popular support, and the confraternity excelled in utilizing them to further their charitable cause. Once a year the children of the orphanage circulated through the city streets brandishing candles and incense and holding in their hands a few *reales* of charity as tokens of the care accorded them by the confraternity. At the head of the procession, cofrades of San José mounted their icon of Nuestra Señora de la Piedad on a scaffold over their shoulders and several dozen priests carrying crosses surrounded the patron saint. Steadily pounding kettle-drums, cofrades called the attention of the public to their holy work.

In Valladolid the Cofradía del Niño Jesús y San José that raised infants set out at doors of churches and wealthy homes found a no less grandiloquent way to attract public attention. It sponsored local theatrical productions and utilized the proceeds to support annually an average of 100 children with wetnurses, dowries and religious and educational services. In 1638, the crown conceded to the foundling program additional revenue from taxes on oil consumed in Valladolid.[48]

In the city of Zamora, canons of the cathedral assumed responsibility for raising foundlings,[49] assisted by several confraternities dedicated to dowering poor orphans once they reached mar-riageable ages. Dowering orphans had long been recognized as a charitable deed in Spain, although in the formal listings of the acts of mercy, it had been replaced by ransoming captives or burying the dead. Dowries remained nevertheless one of the most popular forms of charity because donors visualized their gifts protecting the virtue of poor girls from prostitution. The 1389 testament of Gomez Martínez, for example, attests to the sentiment of piety surrounding this particular act. He ordered his cousin "to look for four poor virgins in Zamora for God and for the souls of my father and mother and brothers", and to help find them husbands with money donated to their dowries from his estate.[50]

Of all charitable offerings, dowries permitted donors the greatest opportunities to exercise their personal preferences in the choice of recipients. Donors dictated the moral character of the women who were to receive the gifts, and frequently specified the family lineage or neighborhood from which they were to be chosen. It is with the dowries that we see the patronage system of old regime society most grievously manipulating with private prejudices the fate of the poor.

Eighty members of the aristocracy formed the confraternity of San Nicolás to dower young women and reap the spiritual rewards of this act of charity. The process of selecting candidates was long and rigorous, characterized by a great deal of publicity and ostentatious display. In one of their programs, members of San Nicolás chose four cofrades to examine young women for the dowry provided by a Franciscan friar, Rodrigo de Villacorta, who left 200 gold ducats, 12 bushels of wheat and one bushel of barley for marrying a woman every year. The four deputies distrib-uted application forms among the preachers in the city and posted notices in public places to inform all who might know of poor orphans wishing to marry to bring their names and places of residence to the attention of the confraternity.[51]

The four deputies carefully reviewed qualifications of the nominees, questioning neighbors and acquaintances as to their moral standing and reputation. In making their choices, they fol-lowed criteria set up by the confraternity which established that they give priority to women with noble blood over commoners, and to residents over non-residents. These standards also obliged that deputies give preference to nominees without parents or relatives who might provide for them "because the intention of our confraternity is to help the poorest who live in the most licit and honest state".[52] In addition, they gave an advantage to older candidates whose time for child bearing was running out. If more than six women remained eligible after this screening process, deputies wrote the names of the candidates on slips of papers and threw them into a container for a child, whose innocence and impartiality in the matter could be assured, to draw six final-ists. At a mass held near the end of May, the six names were put again into a container and placed on an altar. Cofrades commended the lottery to Christ in the hope that the final choice might be the woman in most need. After services, the presiding priest reached into the basin and pulled out the name of the woman who was to be married that year.

Immediately after the drawing, the mayordomo and deputies of the confraternity called upon parents or relatives to select a husband for the winner. On the day of San Nicolás, she and her fiancé were married during high mass at the church of Santa Olaya in the presence of all cofrades and parishioners. In this elaborate and prolonged preparation for marriage under the confrater-nal system, the woman's own wishes were never consulted, nor was it assumed that she would feel anything but gratitude in fulfilling the spiritual obligations asked of her by the father of the fund. Every Sunday for a year following the wedding she took on the task of offering bread, wine and candles provided by the confraternity at the sepulchre of Friar Rodrigo in the monastery of San Francisco. The following year, the duties were taken over by another newly-wed woman, ensuring continual attention over the grave of the donor. In this manner his dowry gift, designed to protect and ensure woman's virtue through marriage, capitalized on the sanctifying powers of the prayers of the pure.

The concern to regulate the sexual morality of the poor was just as obvious in the confrater-nity of Nuestra Señora de la Anunciación. Founded by the bishop of Zamora, Diego Meléndez de Valdés, in the early sixteenth century, it was modelled after the Anunciata established in Rome in 1460 for the purpose of dowering poor women.[53] The choice of advocacy was not an arbitrary one. The Annunciation honored the miraculous conception of Jesus by Mary, "announcing" her favored status in the eyes of God. To Catholics the Annunciation represented the supreme achievement of marriage and motherhood, when mortal woman became vessel for the God-head. Unable ever to attain a similar position, young women nevertheless were asked to recognize the Virgin as their role model.

The 110 members who first joined the Anunciación in Zamora consisted of both clerical and lay men and women who claimed for themselves "pure Christian lineage". Special privileges of the confessional that were conceded by the papacy permitted members to elect their own con-fessor, who had the power to absolve them of all their sins and to commute almost any vow or act of penance imposed on them in the past into the performance of an act of mercy.

The pious works of the confraternity began with the will of its founder, who donated 200,000 maravedís to buy land and possessions for rental income applied to a permanent dowry fund. The mayordomo and ten elected deputies managed the program. They selected recipients for the dowry among nominees offered by other members of the Anunciación. The eleven cofrades granted gifts to as many "poor, honest and well-reputed" women as could be endowed, estimat-ing that at least 160 bushels of wheat in rent were necessary to put together a dowry for one woman.[54] To guarantee objectivity in choosing among eligible candidates, the committee was instructed not to favor daughters or servants of members, nor to admit well-to-do women before poor ones. Moreover, women living with their parents and relatives or patronesses were favored over those working for wages outside the city, and once again natives of Zamora were given pri-ority over those born elsewhere. Requirements tightened in the seventeenth century, a tell-tale sign of a growing austerity during the Counter Reformation, when deputies began to examine rigorously the reputations of the women in question and inspect baptismal records for certification of age and place of birth. Revised ordinances of 1644 reveal a growing preoccupation with the morality of the poor. Since "the life span of people is shorter now", the organization despaired, "evil enters at a much earlier age". Cofrades decided to reduce the age of eligibility from 18 to 16 in an effort to reach innocent young girls "before they destroyed themselves" through promiscuity.[55]

Many other confraternities acted as supervisors of small dowry funds provided by their members or by parishioners of their church. A chaplain of the cathedral asked the confraternity of the Misericordia to marry one orphan girl for his soul every year with a perpetual *fuero* of 3,500 *maravedís*.[56] Women were particularly active as donors of dowries. The widow Leonor Rodríguez left to the confraternity of the Santíssimo Sacramento de San Antolín 28,864 *maravedís* in annual rents to dower an orphan girl on the day of Nuestra Señora de Septiembre every year. She authorized the confraternity to buy more property for the dowry fund with additional rental money and asked it to inspect her possessions every two years to ensure that they were in good repair.[57] To the same confraternity in 1592, Francisca Valderas left 400 *reales* to be given to an orphan in quantities of 10,000 *maravedís* yearly on the anniversary of Nuestra Señora de Septiembre, asking cofrades to pray for both her own and her husband's soul.[58] Several women contributed to dowry funds handled by the confraternities of the Ciento, Las Huérfanas de San Bartolomé, and Nuestra Señora del Rosario.[59]

It is impossible to quantify the number of needy women married by confraternities in the city each year in order to assess the relative economic importance of this particular act of mercy because dowry money, like other charitable donations, varied from year to year. Every parish had at least one marriage program to offer neighborhood residents, but none of them possessed funds sufficient to cover all the city's poor women. Unlike the wealthy confraternity of the Encarnación in Seville, which alone dowered over 100 women every year,[60] the modestly funded Zamoran confraternities generally offered only one or two annual dowries. The significance of these marriage gifts was as much moral as economic. Poor young women would wait for years in expectation of a dowry, and all the while their reputations were on the line. Their dependence on dowry money to marry gave society an important tool with which to discipline and control their sexuality.

"To Redeem Captives . . ."

From the bridal altar to the jail cell the acts of mercy followed the needy. The prescription to "ransom prisoners" involved either assisting local folk in city jails or captives in foreign lands. For the latter, the large crusading orders of the Santísima Trinidad and the Merced had been established in Spain.[61] For prisoners at home, the confraternity of Nuestra Señora de la Piedad y Pobres de la Cárcel had been founded to free those in the public jail. This confraternity accumulated donations and rents for the purpose of assuming debts of poor people and providing them with food, clothing and firewood in jail. Its property extended into small villages of the province, having been donated by wealthy individuals concerned with helping the indebted, who always included peasants from the countryside.[62]

Contributors to the acts of mercy of freeing prisoners frequently made discriminate selections of recipients. Juan Vázquez de Zeynos and his wife María de Zarate offered the rents of houses in the village of Fuentes to the confraternity "to redeem from Zamora's public jail those held for

debts, on Christmas and Easter". The couple insisted that the funds be used for no other purposes and asked that the confraternity delegate one of its members to keep accounts without
salary. Eight days before Christmas and Easter a record of prisoners in jail was to be taken and
as many prisoners as possibe to be freed, beginning with those held for the smallest amounts.
The debts of farmers were to be paid before those of city people, with first priority to those
from the rural area of Madridaños. Cofrades were instructed not to free prisoners accused of
stealing or of crimes of infamy, and those whose debts were taken over had to have been jailed
for at least 15 days. The money was deposited in the cathedral of Zamora, and if the Pobres de
la Cárcel failed to fulfill its duties, the sum was to be transferred to the Misericordia for the same
purpose.[63]

Most major towns in Spain had confraternities similar to the one in Zamora attached to jails
for the care of prisoners . . . In Salamanca 24 noblemen, who aspired personally to visit and
redeem prisoners, founded in 1500 the Cofradía de Caballeros Veinte y Quatro de las Reales
Carceles . . . In the early years of its foundation, the confraternity was supported solely through
the charity of members and the public, and by the turn of the century it had accumulated an enormous amount of rental income in money and kind which vastly surpassed expenses in the jail.
By then it had become one of the wealthiest and most prestigious charitable organizations in
Salamanca. Even officials of law and order applauded its work in freeing prisoners, no doubt in
part because it reduced the number of inmates lodged in crowded quarters and improved living
conditions for the rest. But in language more appreciative of the religious than the practical
accomplishments of the confraternity, city officials praised its "divine services" on behalf of the
souls of cofrades.[64]

"To Bury the Dead"

Of all the merciful acts, the burial of the dead was considered the holiest.[65] It was the last rite of
corporal mercy that the community could offer its members, and thereafter only the spiritual act
of prayer for the dead remained to assist souls to paradise. Virtually all confraternities offered
funeral services to members, their families and the poor. The principal burial society in Zamora
was the Misericordia, one of a category of large and prestigious confraternities throughout Europe
dedicated to caring for paupers who could not afford the costs of Christian rites. The
Misericordias earned the designation of arch-confraternities by affiliating with two brotherhoods
operating in Rome, the white penitents, established in 1264, and the black penitents, founded in
1488. Both of these had gained papal approval along with special indulgences for their work.
The white penitents assumed responsibilities for treating the sick and offering dowries to poor
girls as well as burying the dead. The black penitents buried dead paupers found within the limits
of the Roman campagna and consoled criminals condemned to death. Their duties, according
to accounts of Hippolyte Hélyot (1660–1716), a Third Order regular of St Francis, were especially lugubrious. When judges sentenced persons to death, they notified the black penitents who
sent four of their number to condole with the condemned in prison and help them make general
confessions. The four members remained with prisoners all day and night until their call to execution, when the rest of the brothers gathered to escort them in procession amid crosses draped
in black cloth. Slowly and solemnly cofrades moved with lighted candles chanting the seven
psalms of penitence until they reached the gallows, where they dressed the convicts in confraternal robes, symbolically turning them into brothers, then attended their executions and burials,
and prayed for their souls.[66]

By emulating these activities, Misericordias outside the Papal See shared in the same indulgences granted to the Roman penitents. In the Spanish peninsula, the black penitents were noted for their presence at *autos de fe*. The white penitents, always more numerous, followed their Roman counterparts by engaging in a variety of charitable services. They found especially favorable conditions in Portugal where the Crown gave approval to the establishment of 114 Misericordias between 1498 and 1599.[67] The work of Portugal's white penitents included all 14 acts of mercy, both spiritual and corporal, which they channelled through almshouses and hospitals.

Zamora's Misericordia was known by travellers throughout the province for offering lodging to the homeless and burying dead paupers. It operated a hospital in the parish of San Martin to shelter those seeking beds and warmth in the winter and administered to them the sacraments. Since its principal duty was to bury the dead, it provided funeral services for all those unable to afford rites, including the patients of the poor leprosarium of San Lázaro outside the city walls. Cofrades regularly searched the inner city and its suburbs for sick and dying paupers, prepared to carry them to the hospital or arrange proper Christian deaths for them. During years of pestilence cofrades were particularly active, coming out two by two into the streets with wooden planks and coffins to recover plague victims and bury them in cemeteries.[68]

The Misericordia also provided burial services for well-to-do persons who commended their bodies to it at death, especially non-residents who had no other confraternity to administer to their needs. During an illness which kept him hospitalized in Zamora, Juan Gáez de Segura from Vitoria commended his body to the Misericordia. "Since I am a stranger", he expressed his wish, "that it bury me and spend the wax, and say the masses that it is obliged to perform, and customarily performs, for other strangers . . ."[69] María del Valle, a poor woman from the city without money for burial services, asked the Misericordia to bury her in any manner in which its cofrades saw fit.[70] Amaro Hernández de Losada was similarly obliging. In 1577 he arranged in his testament that at his death the "cofrades of the holy Cofradía de Nuestra Señora de la Misericordia take pity on my soul and do that which it is obligated to do . . . and bury my body in the church of Santa María la Nueva, and perform that which it usually does for other poor persons".[71]

[. . .]

What was done for society's wretches was done with heightened enthusiasm for a brother or sister of one's own confraternity. The dying cofrade counted on his brotherhood to attend to his burial by setting up funeral processions and offering prayers. Customarily members gathered together at the home of the deceased dressed in special funeral garbs to accompany the body to mass. Draping the coffin with a pall designed in a color distinctive of their brotherhood, cofrades carried the body to burial. The number of candles held by mourners as they bore the soul through the city streets was a matter of utmost importance. They carried only half as many for a servant or child under the age of 14 as for a full-fledged member. Similarly, the number of requiem masses and prayers that cofrades offered during the subsequent mourning period depended on the deceased's membership status.

Special procedures were followed for burials at the pilgrimage shrine of Santiago de Compostela. When a pilgrim died in Santiago's hospital, a cofrade walked through the city's main streets ringing a small bell to announce the impending funeral to anyone who wished to go to the service. If the deceased should happen to have been an affiliate of the brotherhood of Santiago, all members present in the city were obliged to attend the funeral and they were called by the ringing of a bell larger than that used on behalf of non-affiliated pilgrims. Any cofrade who died in another city could be buried in the hospital's cemetery if he wished his body carried back to

Santiago. There he received all the honors and religious services promised by the confraternity to Santiago's members.[72]

Except for this international pilgrimage confraternity which extended burial services to members residing outside the seat of Santiago de Compostela, confraternities restricted their burial services to members who were residents of their own town. So important was the home base that if a member died outside the confines of the town, cofrades had the obligation to journey only to the edge of municipal limits to greet the body and carry it back inside for funeral services. And if the deceased had wished to be buried outside the town, members were obliged only to accompany the body in procession to the urban walls, leaving the burial to others.[73] In contrast to this concern that funeral ceremonies be held within the neatly circumscribed spatial setting of the city, the remains of the body itself were not always required for the execution of a funeral. If a member died in a distant place, services would be offered in town for his body *in absentia*. The soul apparently could be saved anywhere, as long as loved ones prayed on its behalf at home.

A widespread and curious custom practised at funerals in Zamora tells more about popular religious ideas concerning death and the afterlife. Offerings of food called *limosnas* and *animeras*, usually consisting of bread and wine, were placed over sepulchres or graves of the dead immediately after the burial. Later in the day, they were consumed by relatives, paupers and priests. What the rituals meant for mourners is something of a puzzle. Possibly the bread and wine represented the body and blood of Christ that brought the redemption of mankind. Such an interpretation is suggested by the arrangement of straw baskets containing bread, two liters of wine and four candles that the confraternity of the Ciento customarily offered to members who died.[74] But why did some people request that additional foodstuffs be placed before their graves? Catalina Fernández furnished her Cofradía de Santa Ana with property for purchase of a bushel of wheat, 60 *maravedís* worth of bread, six decanters of wine, a pair of rabbits and some wax to offer on the day of her burial.[75] A not uncommon request was for fruit and cheese. The large quantities and peculiar choices of items intimate that the offerings may have derived from an old pagan custom of distributing food at tombs for sustenance of the dead.[76]

In fact, during the early years of the Christian church, theologians had recognized a similarity between the offerings of Christians over graves of the dead and traditional pagan burial rituals. Both Augustine and Ambrose condemned the custom called *refrigerium* of feasting over the graves of the dead. Pagans thought that the deceased were actually present and partaking in the food of the living at the meal.[77] Augustine attempted to eradicate the heathen element in the funeral banquet by bringing the offerings in line with orthodox views on the resurrection of the body with the soul after death. He also wanted to reduce the opportunities for excessive drinking and eating that the ceremony engendered. So he recommended that Christian mourners share only moderately-sized meals at tombs, and then insisted that a portion of the aliments be distributed to the poor.[78] In the form of alms, the funeral banquet was transfigured into a cult act consistent with Catholic belief in the power of charity to assist the souls of the dead to heaven.

But old habits return. Church synods in medieval and sixteenth-century Castile continued to regulate distribution of burial food to paupers in order to preserve its character as alms. The bishopric of Astorga agreed to honor the disposal of 'caridades perpetuas' of the dead because it was traditional in the area, but carefully apportioned amounts to their proper sources. One third of the charity was delivered to paupers, one third was given to the church's accounts of the dead and another third went to the local council.[79] The church found it repeatedly necessary to caution relatives of the dead not to impoverish themselves, for in addition to offering food over gravesites, they began to distribute doles to paupers outside the doorway of the deceased's home on interment day.

Alms were the food that nourished blessings and prayers for the dead. Testators who requested funeral meals for the welfare of their souls '*como de costumbre*' may have been taking advantage of the goodwill which, as they undoubtedly had experienced, accompanies a feast. Or perhaps they were exploiting the sense of gratitude and the desire to recompense that all guests feel toward their hosts. In any case, heirs of the dead faithfully fulfilled obligations to wish a safe and speedy delivery of souls to heaven during feasts. On All Saints' Day the populace in Aragon, Catalonia and Valencia developed elaborate memorial uses for the *rosca*, a wreath of bread made of wheat and oil topped with sugar and honey. After mass, mourners placed a large lighted candle inside the *rosca* and carried it to gravesites where they sat and prayed until the candle burned down and extinguished itself, melting the sugar on top of the *rosca*. Then celebrants consumed the loaf.[80] The name of this dish, *almitas*, is strikingly similar in meaning to the Zamoran funeral offering of *animeras*. Both referred to the soul. Identical sentiments underlie All Saint's Day ceremonies in Galicia and Asturias, where mourners prepared plates of chestnuts in amounts corresponding to the number of souls that they wanted freed from purgatory.[81] Such rituals have been interpreted by scholars in various ways, as expressions of solidarity, gratitude, renewal, even, Mikhail Bakhtin suggests, toasts to the health of the dead.[82] But running through all the rituals is the theme of alms as a means of transporting the soul to paradise. We have seen that cofrades employed the currency of charity in many imaginative forms, but nothing quite surpassed the extraordinarily graphic ritual use of it at the last stage as souls left the community of providers and recipients at funerals.

The Confraternal Welfare "System"

In late medieval and sixteenth-century Castile, religious beliefs generated welfare practices singularly different from modern secular programs to fulfill basic material needs of society. Catholic ideology and ritual provided a common framework in which individual neighborhoods arranged charitable assistance. Welfare in Zamora and surrounding population centers was delivered, to use Clifford Geertz' term, through communal ritual 'thick' with symbolism. Principal among the sacred symbols were the seven acts of mercy which dramatized Biblical history. The merciful acts simulated Matthew's exhortation to provide for the needy, and their constant repetition by lay and religious people constituted the praxis of medieval Christian poor relief. This shared meaning created a uniform pattern for charitable activities, producing what might be called a poor relief "system". How was Biblical metaphor translated into an active moral code that reflected Christian precepts so precisely that no one could mistake its meaning? The representative power of the written word in traditional society was unlike anything known today, as Michel Foucault has explained so breathtakingly to us in *Les Mots et les choses*.[83] To find in the natural world resemblances of metaphysical concepts was considered the pathway to knowledge in the medieval period. The pious Christian believed that the legible words of Scripture should stamp visible marks over the surface of the body. To emulate in gesture was to "know" Scripture.

[. . .]

The charity practiced in Zamora offers an excellent example of how thoroughly a society's culture affects the lifestyles, even the chances of survival, of its members. Within a regime of privilege in which the distribution of property itself was sanctioned by cultural codes, the only mechanism that ensured a flow of goods to sectors in critical need was religion. Catholicism orchestrated the rhythm of charity by ordaining certain holy occasions for the dispersal of alms. Then it further keyed the content of charity to the tune of the seven acts of mercy. Most importantly, Catholicism created the instruments, so many confraternities, through which lay charitable services were played out.

[. . .]

NOTES

1 Pierre Chaunu, *Le Temps des deux réformes de l'Eglise* (Paris: Fayard, 1975) p. 172. Gabriel Le Bras has said that late medieval confraternities were oriented less toward the practise of the sacraments and more toward the liturgy and acts of mercy and piety. *Introduction à l'histoire de la pratique religieuse en France* (Paris, 1942–45) vol. 1.

2 The duties of almsgiving were by no means a peculiarly Christian phenomenon. All major world religions have shared a similar evaluation of charity, including the idea that charity propitiates the gods. Edward Westermarck, *The Origin and Development of the Moral Ideas* (London, 1906), chapter 23 on "Charity and Generosity". For a discussion of the attitudes of the early church fathers to charity, see Boniface Ramsey, OP, "Almsgiving in the Latin Church: The Late Fourth and Early Fifth centuries", *Theological Studies*, XLIII, 2 (June 1982) 226–59.

3 Tomás de Trujillo, *Libro liamado Reprobación de Trajes y abusos de juramentos con un traiado de limosnas* (Estella, 1563) 225.

4 Archivo de la Mitra de Zamora (AMZ), *Ordenanzas de San Ildefonso*, of 1503, p. 522.

5 Augustine, *Enchiridion*, Chapter 19:67–9, in CSEL, XLIV, 48, English edition in *The Library of Christian Classics* (Philadelphia, 1955), VII, pp. 378–81.

6 *Enchiridion*, Chapter 19:72.

7 Augustine, *In. Ep. Ionn.* 8:9, in Migne, *Patrologia Latina*, XXXV, col. 2040.

8 Those which repeated Augustine and were adopted as formal acts of charity were: to relieve the poor, to clothe the naked, to visit the sick and to bury the dead. *The Rules of St. Benedict*, chapter 4: "The Tools of Good Works".

9 *Monumenta Germaniae Historica*, ed. George Pertz, (1835) *Legum, tomus 1, Karoli Magni capitularia.* 802. "Admonitio Generalis", Lines 16–29.

10 Michel Mollat, *Les Pauvres au Moyen Âge, étude socials* (Paris, 1978) pp. 112–13.

11 Alfonso X. *Las Siete Partidas, Partida 1, tit.* XXIII, *ley* IX.

12 They paralleled here the seven sacraments, the seven theological and cardinal virtues, the seven cardinal sins and the seven gifts of the Holy Spirit (wisdom, understanding, counsel, fortitude, knowledge, piety and fear of the Lord.)

13 Juan Ruiz, Arcipreste de Hita, *Libro de buen amor* (Madrid: Espasa Calpe, 1974) pp. 257–63.

14   [Hope and faith you will lose
                                     when before God
                                     you stand, wait and see
                                     with great generosity
                                     offer acts of charity
                                     that your with be pure
                                     The greatness of charity
                                     is that it fulfills all needs
                                     and be who receives it not shall pass Heaven by.]

Pedro de Verague, *Doctrina de la discreción* in Florencio Janer (ed.), *Biblioteca de Autores Espanoles* (Madrid: 1864) LVII, pp. 373–8.

15 "El catecismo de Albórnoz", in *Studia Albomotiano* (Cartagena, 1972) ii, p. 225. The verse is also included in the *Summa Theologica* of Thomas Aquinas, Part. II, Q. 32, Art. 2.

16 Archivo Histórico Provincial de Zamora (AHPZ), Protocolos, no. 80, *fol.* 348.

17 AHPZ, Protocolos, no. 80, *fol.* 249.

18 AHPZ, Protocolos, no. 130, *fols* 239–44v.

19 Victor Turner, *Dramas, Fields and Metaphors* (Cornell, 1974) p. 249.

20 Archivo de la Catedral de Zamora (ACZ) , *leg.* 18, doc. 2; *leg.* 17, no. 1; and *leg.* 12, no. 14.

21 AMZ, *Ordenanzas de San Ildefonso*, p. 512; AMZ, Archivo de los Cientos, *Ordenanzas de Nuestra Señora de la Antigua* of 1566, page 3.

22 According to official censuses in the AG Simancas, Hacienda, *leg.* 205.

23 Fundamental studies of the history of hospitals in Spain are: Fermin Hernández Iglesias, *La beneficencia en España* (Madrid, 1876); Antonio Rumeu de Armas, *Historia de la Previsión Social en España* (Madrid, 1944); María Jiménez Salas, *Historia de la Asistencia Social en España en la edad moderna* (Madrid, 1958); and the articles deriving from a conference in Portugal, compiled in *Actas das los Jornandas Luso-Espanholas de Historia Medieval* (2 vols, Lisbon: 25–30 September 1972). For Europe in general, and especially France, see the recent study by Michel Mollat, *Les Pauvres au Moyen Age, étude sociale* (Paris, 1978).

24 There is no available evidence that the merchants formed a confraternity in the twelfth century. ACZ, no. 1419, *leg.* 13, no. 26. In the mid- to the late-fifteenth century, the confraternity of Nuestra Señora del Caño took jurisdiction over the hospital.

25 ACZ, *leg.* 16, no. 46.

26 A detailed study of the origins of the word "falifa" by Manuel García Blanco attributes it to Arabic origins; this usage appeared first in the thirteenth century, and by the fourteenth century the new meaning of a pledge of clothing was common in these parts of Spain. Manuel García Blanco, *La lengua española en la epoca de Carlos V* (Madrid, 1967) pp. 135–67.

27 AHPZ, Protocolos, no. 118, *fol.* 143.

28 ACZ, *leg.* 239.

29 AHPZ, Protocolos, no. 36, *fols* 320–1; 17 September 1546.

30 Archivo de la Universidad de Santiago, Archivo de los Reyes Católicos, Serie 3, Libro 1, *Libro de la Real Cofradla de Santiago, 1503–04*; and *leg.* 63, no. 27. Donations increased to a sixth of a ducat to cover building and repair costs, nos 42-48.

31 Ibid. *leg.* 63, nos 28, 42–8.

32 Ibid., *Section 6, libro 1. Libro de cabildos de la Real Hospital.* fol. 26v. Little is known about the medical treatment provided in the hospital. Generally, only patients with non-contagious diseases were allowed into the hospital. Medicine bought at the fairs in Medina del Campo was used, and barber-surgeons performed bloodletting and cleaned and shaved pilgrims as they entered. In 1557, a severe outbreak of the plague in the city compelled the hospital to accept children stricken with buboes, considered symptoms of a contagious disease. The children were treated with medicaments and purged in a manner done "without sticks". Ibid., *libro 2.*

33 AMZ, Archivo de Santa María de la Horta. Santa María de la Horta, no. 41 (1).

34 *Ordenanzas de la Cofradia de la Vera Cruz de Villalcampo* in Luis Calvo Lozano, *Historia.*

35 Archivo parroquial de San Frontis, *Libro 33.*

36 Antonio Rumeu de Armas, *Historia de la previsión social en España* (Madrid, 1944) pp. 587–97, and pp. 242–4 on security against dangers of maternity.

37 Marjorie Nice Boyer, *Medieval French Bridges: A History* (Cambridge, Massachusetts: Medieval Academy of America, 1976) p. 31. Mircea Eliade discusses the universal use of the concept of bridges in *The Sacred and the Profane, The Nature of Religion*, translated by Willard R. Trask, (New York and London, 1959) pp. 181–3.

38 St Bernard, *Sermo de Aquaeducto. In Nativitate Beatae Mariae Virginis*, in Migne, *Patrologia Latina*, vol. 183, col. 1013–14.

39   Alexandro Anglico, Dr. *Tratado muy útile de las obras de misericordia*, translated from the Latin by Pero
     González de la Torre (Toledo, 1530) *fol.* 6.

40   AHPZ, Desamortización, *Caja* 138.

41   For the distribution of hospices along the road to Santiago in Burgos, see the article by Pedro Carasa
     Soto, "La asistencia socialy las cofradias en Burgos desde la crisis del Antiguo Régimen", *Investiga-
     ciones Históricas*, vol. III (University of Valladolid, 1986) pp. 179–229. Hospitals and hospices depen-
     dent on confraternities in Leon, Astorga, Zamora, Salamanca, Cuidad Rodrigo and Palencia are
     examined by José Sánchez Herrero, "Cofradías, Hospitales y Beneficencia en algunas diócesis del valle
     del Duero, siglos XIV y XV", *Hispania*, CXXVI (January–April 1974) 34.

42   The attribution of pious motives to bridge-building in the twelfth century accelerated bridge construc-
     tion after a period of relative abandonment in the central Middle Ages according to Marjorie Nice Boyer,
     Medieval French Bridges, p. 31. One of the earliest bridge confraternities appeared in 1084 in France,
     near Bonpas, over the Durance river. "Confréries", DDC (Paris, 1935–65) col. 142. In England,
     Stratford-upon-Avon had two brotherhoods of bridges, that of the Holy Cross and of the Assumption.
     See J. J. Jusserand, *English Wayfaring Life in the Middle Ages* (London, 1961) p. 32.

43   The bulls were republished in 1806 in Valladolid in "Bulas y Brebes de diferentes sumos Pontifices,
     las que contienen varias concesiones y gracias en favor del santuario y cofrades de Nuestra Señora de
     Carballeda". For graciously providing me with copies of the bulls and ordinances of the Cofradía de los
     Falifos in Rionegro del Puente, I thank Don José Prieto Carro, of the village of Rionegro.

44   *Constituciones de la Cofradia de Nuestra Señora de la Carballeda*, published in Valladolid, no date;
     approved by the council of the confraternity in 1785 and by Carlos III in 1787. Introduction, *fols* 2v
     and 3; chapter 11, *fols* 10 and 10v; and the bulls, pp. 3, 15 and 16.

45   *Constituciones de Nuestra Señora de la Carballeda*, *fols* 5v and 6; chapter 13, fol. 11; chapters 21 and
     22, *fols* 14 and 14v. In Madrid, the Hospital de los niños expósitos, or la Inclusa, began to take in chil-
     dren by 1572 after devoting itself to convalescents. In 1600, the Asilo de los niños Desamparados was
     also established in Madrid for children. Jacques Soubeyroux, 'El encuentro del pobre y la sociedad:
     asistencia y represión en el Madrid del siglo XVIII', *Estudios de Historia Social*, 20–1 (1982) 21.

46   In the last decade of the sixteenth century, 5000 *maravedis* would have been equivalent to the value of
     10 bushels of wheat.

47   Archivo Municipal de Salamanca, uncatalogued, *Libro del recibo i gasto de los niños expósitos de la cofra-
     dia de San Joseph y Nuestra Señora de la Piedad*.

48   Teófanes Egido, "La cofradia de San José y los niños expósitos de Valladolid", *Estudios Josefinos*, 53
     (Valladolid, 1973) 83–5 and 95–9; and Archivo Municipal de Valladolid, *Libro de Actas*, 23 July 1597,
     fol. 245.

49   ACZ, *leg.* 255. *Libro de Niños expósitos.*

50   ACZ, *leg.* 18, no. 24.

51   *Ordenanzas de la Cofradia de San Nicolás*, in Fernández-Prieto, *Nobleza de Zamora*, p. 397.

52   Ibid., p. 397.

53   AMZ, *Ordenanzas de la Cofradla de Nuestra Señolo de la Anunciación*, or Valdés, *fols* 40v and 41v; and
     ACZ, *leg*, 239 and 208.

54   AMZ, Documentación Valdés. *Libro de Acuerdos*, *fol.* 83v. 2 December 1638. By the end of the eigh-
     teenth century, the total amount of property owned by the confraternity of San Nicolás brought in 2845
     bushels of wheat and barley in yearly income. AHPZ, *Desamortización Caja* 102, no. 8.

55   AMZ, *Ordenanzas de la Cofradia de Nuestra Señora de la Anunciación, fols* 29–29v, and 37.

56   AHPZ, Protocolos, no. 353. *fol.* 253.

57   AHPZ, Diputación, *leg.* 69.

58   Ibid.

59   AMZ, Archivo parroquial de Santa María de la Horta, Santa Lucía, No. 29. Archivo parroquial de San
     Ildefonso, No. 19. And AHPZ, Protoeolos, no. 348, *fols* 172 and 185v; no. 331, *fols* 241–2; and no.
     287, *fols* 3v–4.

60   Pablo de Espinosa, *Teatro de la Santa Iglesia metropolitana de Sevilla* (Seville, 1635) 71.

61 Ellen Friedman, *Spanish Captives in North Africa in the Early Modern Age* (Madison, 1983); and James William Brodman, *Ransoming Captives in Crusader Spain: The Order of Merced on the Christian-Islamic Frontier* (Pennsylvania, 1986).

62 AMZ, Archivo parroquial de Santa Maria de la Horta, Archivo de San Julián (4). ACZ, *leg.* 19, no. 6.

63 AHPZ, Protocolos, No. 69. *fols* 502–508v; and ACZ, *leg.* 19, no. 6.

64 Salamanca, Archivo del Ministerio de Sanidad y Seguridad Social. *Cofradfa de Caballeros (XXIV) Viente y Quatro, de las Reales Carceles de esta culdad* (Salamanca, 1915).

65 The point at which burying the dead entered the ranks of religious duties is obscure. It had been highly valued in ancient cultures, but was not cited in Matthew's description of holy works. St Augustine recognized it as a charitable act, and medieval commentaries on Matthew's passage since at least the thirteenth century added the burial of the dead to the list. It was named as an act of mercy in the cartulary of Mas-d'Azil in 1093, and Jean Beleth, a Parisian theologian and liturgist, cited it in his description of the acts in his *Summa de Ecclesiasticus officiis* of the late twelfth century. Nicolas of Lyra, *Biblia Latina*, and Hugonis de S. Chara, *Biblia Latina*. Jean Beleth, *Summa de Ecclesiasticis officiis*, chapter 77 in *Corpus Christianorum*, vol. XVI (Tunholti, 1976). Philippe Arlès believes that burying the dead as an act of mercy was a product of the late Middle Ages. *L'homme devant la mort* (Paris, 1977) pp. 184–5.

66 Hippolyte Hélyot, *Histoire des Ordres Monastiques* (Paris, 1719) vol. VIII, pp. 262–3; and Maurice Bordes, "Contribution à l'étude des confréries de pénitents à Nice aux XVIIᵉ–XVIIIᵉ siècles", *Annales du Midi: Revue Archéologique, Historique, et Philologique: Revue de la France Méridionale*, xix 139 (July–December 1978) 384.

67 Fernando da Silva Correia, *Origen e formação das Misericórdias portuguêsas: Estudios sôbre a História da Assistência* (Lisbon, 1944).

68 AMZ, *leg.* 1097, No. 1; Archivo parroquial de San Lázaro, no. 1; and Archivo parroquial de San Juan de la Puerta Nueva, *Libro* 12. In Lima, Peru, the Confraternity de la Caridad y Misericordia performed essentially the same functions, burying the dead, caring for paupers, attending to the sick and dowering orphans. See Olinda Celestino and Albert Meyers, *Las cofradías en el Perú: Región central*, p. 116.

69 AHPZ, Protocolos, no. 128, *fols* 223–3v.

70 AHPZ, Protocolos, no. 264, *fol.* 130.

71 AHPZ, Protocolos, no. 449, *fol.* 155.

72 Archivo de la Universidad de Santiago. Archivo de los Reyes Católicos, *leg.* 63, no. 32, *fols* 4, 8, and 8v.

73 AMZ, Archivo de los Ciento, *Ordenanzas de la Cofradía de los Ciento*, *fols* 23v–24; *Racioneros, fol.* 15; and *San Nicolás*, in Fernández-Prieto, *Nobleza in Zamora, fol.* 389.

74 AMZ, Archivo de los Ciento, *Constitutiones de la Cofradia de los Ciento, fol.* 25.

75 Archivo Histórico Nacional, Madrid (AHN), Clero, *leg.* 8373, testament of 1478.

76 Th. Klauser, "Das altchristliche Totenmahl nach dem heutigen Stande der Forschung", *Theologie und Glaube*, xx, (1928) 599–608; A. Parrot, *Le refrigerium dans l'Au-delá* (Paris, 1937); A. Stuiber, *Refrigerium Interim. Die Vorstellungen vom Zwischenzustand und die frukchristliche Grabeskunst* (Bonn, 1957). P. A. Fevrièr, "À-propos du repas funéraire: cult et sociabilité", *Cahiers archéologiques* xxvi (1977) 29–45; M. Meslin, "Convivialité ou communion sacramentelle? Repas mithriaque et Eucharistie chrétienne", *Paganisme, judaisme, christianisme . . . Mélanges offerts à Marcel Simon* (Paris, 1978) 295–306. For the practise of *refrigerium* in the early Middle Ages and legislation regulating it, see Oronzio Giordano, *Religiosità popolare nell'alto medioevo* (Bari, 1979) pp. 67–71.

77 Augustine, *Confession*, VI, 2; and J. Quasten, "Vetus superstitio et nova religio. The Problems of *refrigerium* in the ancient Church of North Africa", *Harvard Theological Review*, xxxiii (1940) 253–66.

78 Augustine, *Epistularium*, XXII, 6, *Corpus Scriptorum Ecclesiasticorum Latinorum* (CSEL), xxxiv, pp. 58–9.

79 The eleventh-century Council of Coyanza limited participation at funeral ceremonies and offertory meals to clerics, paupers and "the weak", and prohibited banqueting by the laity around sepulchres. Alfonso García Gallo, *El Concilio de Coyanza* (Madrid, 1951) pp. 24–5, 318–19. Biblioteca Nacional

de Madrid. *Constituciones Synodales de Avila*, *fol.* 110v, capitulo 12; and AMZ, *Constituciones Synodales de Astorga, const.* XVI capitulo 6.

80 N. Hoyos Sancho, "Luz a los muertos", *Las Ciencias*, xxiv (1959) p. 933; and Violet Alford, *Pyrenean Feslivals* (London, 1937) p. 262.

81 L. Hoyos Saínz, "Folklore español del culto a los muertos", *Revista de Dialéctologia y Tradiciones Populares*, 1 (Madrid, 1945) pp. 30–53.

82 Mikhail Bakhtin, *Rabelais and his World*, trans. Helene Iswolsky (Cambridge, Mass., 1968; originally published in Moscow, 1965) pp. 79–80; see also Arnold van Gennep, *Manuel de Folklore Français contemporain*, 1 (Paris, 1946) p. 777; Claude Dolan-Leclerc, "Cortège funebre et societé au XVIe siècle à Aix-en-Province: Le presence des pauvres", *Le sentiment de la mort au Moyen Age* (Montreal, 1979) p. 107; Deschamps, *Les Confréries au moyen âge* (Bordeaux, 1958) p. 96; P. Ariès, *L'Homme devant la mort*, p. 33; J. Huizinga, *Homo Ludens: a study of the play-element in culture* (Boston, 1955); and Harvey Cox, *The Feast of Fools; a theological essay on festivity and fantasy* (Cambridge, Mass., 1969).

83 Michel Foucault, *Les Mots et les choses*, first French edition, 1966 by Editions Gallimard; published in English as *The Order of Things* (New York, 1971).

<h1>8</h1>

THE SINS OF BELIEF: A VILLAGE REMEDY FOR HOOF AND MOUTH DISEASE (1796)

David Warren Sabean

For the life of the flesh is in the blood; and I have given it for you upon the altar to make atonement for your souls; for it is the blood that makes atonement, by reason of the life.

Leviticus 17.11

> Beutelsbach, Zwiefalten, Napoleon,
> What's the rhyme and reason?
> In Beutelsbach, they bury the bull,
> In Zwiefalten, they play the fool,
> And Napoleon is not – notoriously extravagant.
> That's the rhyme and reason.[1]

The people from Beutelsbach are called "bull lynchers".[2]

In 1796, the villagers of Beutelsbach in the Württemberg District of Schorndorf, faced with an outbreak of hoof and mouth disease, decided to make a sacrifice to the epidemic.[3] They buried the communal bull alive outside the village under the crossroads leading to Endersbach. Rumors of the outbreak of superstition and cruelty reached the officials in Stuttgart, who in due course sent a special commissioner in the person of *Canzlei Advocat* and *Amtsschreiber* Bolley from Waiblingen to investigate. He took evidence from various villagers over the period 24 October to 5 November, finally turning in a 209-page summary of the testimony together with a report.[4] Conflicting testimony, unexpected lapses of memory, evasion, and prevarication made it impossible to get at the "truth" of the matter, which for the commissioner amounted to assigning clear responsibility to the actors in the drama. However, what was a problem from Canzlei Advocat Bolley's perspective is for us particularly helpful, because the multilayered testimony provides a great deal of insight into the processes of village decision making and the workings of popular

David Warren Sabean, "The sins of belief: A village remedy for hoof and mouth disease (1796)," pp. 174–98, 234–5 from *Power in the Blood: Popular culture and village discourse in early modern Germany*. Cambridge: Cambridge University Press, 1984.

culture. There is no better way to begin than by simply relating the testimony as it was taken down by Bolley, letting the story emerge bit by bit until we can see how he himself put it together.

The first witness was the twenty-seven-year-old Lieutenant Johann Friedrich Reinhard, at that time Substitut in the village Rathaus. According to him, the burial took place at the insistence of the villagers (Bürger), who believed that the same means had been used to bring a cattle epidemic to an end in Neckarrems a hundred years previously. The deed took place in Beutelsbach on 4 September and was carried out by three men, the cowherd Hans Jerg Becker, Hans Jerg Knauer, and Friedrich Ritter. Although they had shared one and a half *Mass* (a little more than two liters) of wine together, they were by no means drunk. The Schultheiss ordered that when the bull was brought to the grave, it was to be shot in the head and then buried. Although Reinhard was not a witness, he heard that 200 people attended the event and that apparently the bull had not been shot. In fact, it took three attempts to get the bull into the grave. Felling so sorry for the animal, the lieutenant had not asked any further about the matter, except to enquire why it had to be done. The cowherd, Schultheiss, and Bürgermeister had all told him the story about the cattle epidemic in Neckarrems a hundred years previously. In addition, the cowherd (Becker) had also reported several days before that the bull had contracted the disease. Everyone thought that the burial had to happen in the way it did in order for its magic (*zauberisch*) power to have effect (*äussern*). The lieutenant felt he had to point out that no one had ever thought to bury a sick cow alive. In fact, the central government had ordered that sick cows be slaughtered and buried with skin and hair.

The next witness was the sixteen-year-old Incipient in the Gerichtsschreiberei, Abraham Mayer, son of the pastor in Steinenberg. He testified about the three men coming to the Rathaus to get some wine. The cowherd appeared a while later to fetch a rope to tie the bull with, at which time he told Lieutenant Reinhard that the Schultheiss had given the order to shoot the bull. Nothing else was said then except that the animal was sick. Four days later, the *Feldschütz* Knauer told him that as the cowherd Becker was leaving, the Schultheiss, standing in the doorway, had cancelled the order to slaughter the animal first.

One of the members of the village Gericht was the fifty-year-old surgeon, Christoph Barchet. When it came time to discuss the issue in the Rat he had left the village rather than take part in the resolution. He was aware that as a surgeon, well versed in physics and philosophy, he could be expected to oppose superstition. In fact, he had had a set-to with the Schultheiss on the Rat over just that issue. About eight days before an official from Stuttgart had come to give instructions about the epidemic, the *Dorfschütz* had been sent to a blind shepherd in Kirchheim to get him to help heal the cattle.[5] Barchet expressed the opinion that the shepherd could not be of much use unless he came to the village, to which the Dorfschütz replied that he had helped other people already even when he was not present – one did not have to worry any more. As far as sympathetic means were concerned, the surgeon held them for useless, and the notion that they could have effect as pure superstition. But the Schultheiss in a very offensive manner said that Barchet did not know everything. One of the Räte present noted that a French doctor at Endersbach had ordered the burial of a bull after it had mounted a sick cow. And then the Schultheiss mockingly said, "That, of course, Barchet would believe." Although Barchet did not stay around the village to discuss the matter further, he was able to say that the decision was taken in the Rat on Sunday after the morning church service. Customarily during the church service, the Schultheiss invited Rat members to gather together when there was anything to discuss.

Johannes Schwegler, aged forty-three, another surgeon in the village and member of the Rat, testified that over a hundred head of cattle had died so far in the epidemic. At the meeting of the Rat on Sunday after church, the Schultheiss had informed them all that the bull was sick. He also related that various villages in the region had learned that if a bull was buried at a crossroads, the epidemic would be snuffed out. The question was put as to whether Beutelsbach should give the method a try. Some were of the opinion that it would do little good, but it would not hurt to try anything. In any event, there was no decision, and Schwegler was no longer able to say who in the Rat was for the measure and who was against it. Furthermore, he never heard anything about the burial of a *live* bull and was sure that it had always been a question of killing the bull first. It could be that he had missed something, since as a member of the Rat and not of the Gericht he did not attend all of the meetings. He also did not attend the execution of the bull. When Bolley expressed great skepticism over his testimony, he noted that all four of his cows had died, and he therefore had little to expect from any action. In all probability, he had thought to himself that such means would not be of very much use. He had to admit that the official document about superstition during a cattle epidemic had been read in church before the burial of the bull took place.

In order to clear up a few details, the surgeon Barchet was recalled. He said that in one assembly of the Gericht and Rat, a live burial had been discussed. He could not say whether pressure for the burial came from the villagers (*Bürgerschaft*) or who was responsible for starting the idea in the first place. He observed people going by his house on the day of the event itself with buckets full of earth to bury the bull, but he could not recall any particular names. He also heard that two members of the Rat were there but did not know which ones.

The schoolmaster, Matheus Eberhard Hammer, happened by chance to be in a field near the burial. He heard a noise and saw a lot of people, but by the time he came along to investigate, the bull was already buried. In any event he heard absolutely nothing about the stupid prank beforehand. Except for the three men who did the deed, he could not think of anyone he saw at the time. The schoolmaster then said that he was against the deed but was of the opinion that once the sacrifice was made, that would bring an end to the matter. He also did not think that the burial place was a real crossroads. One of the "roads" was more of a path that lost itself among the fields. He heard later that the Schultheiss had been asked by several villagers to do what had been done.

The court recorder (Gerichtsschreiber), August Ludwig Billfinger, had been absent from the village when it all happened. According to him, it was the general opinion (*Gerücht*) that such a burial was a means of curing a cattle epidemic.

Johannes Kuhnle, thirty-seven, son-in-law of the oldest Richter, Bernhard Koch, actually attended the burial. He noted that it was very dangerous to try to kill a bull in an open field. Even though several people had axes, it was found to be too dangerous to use them. But as luck would have it, the bull slipped into the grave accidentally – otherwise it certainly would have been slaughtered.

Michael Ellwangen, forty-five, was in his field but came along when he heard the noise. By the time he got there, the bull had already been buried. It had slipped into the grave. All there was to observe was a great tumult of women and children – nothing important – so he went on. Although he had never heard the story about burying a live bull, he had to say that he ignores all such tales anyway.

Already having lost eight cattle, the miller and Richter, Augusten Raff, was against the decision to bury the bull. For him, the epidemic was a judgment of God that no one could escape. He was also unable to say how anyone voted, although most did vote in the affirmative. It was not decided under which crossroads the bull was to be buried, nor was it expressly said that it should be buried alive. The story was that the "sympathetic" means involved would have their effect after the bull had mounted a sick cow. At the time of the council discussion, the bull was not yet sick. He further said that he did not approve of the magistrates being called together to a meeting on Sunday, which happened all too often in the village.

Friedrich Koch, son of the Heiligenpfleger and himself Richter, came along once the bull was in the grave. Because it had fallen in by itself, it was impossible to slaughter it. He had never heard anything about such a burial being able to prevent a cattle epidemic.

One of the village butchers, Leonhard Vollmar, fifty-six, had gone along to slaughter the animal and was there from the beginning. Indeed the bull had slipped into the grave, but it was then dug out because it was standing up. He could not say what happened after that because he left. Not having been asked to slaughter the animal, he had no other reason to be there.

At this point, the commissioner Bolley went to view the spot where the burial took place and concluded that it really was a crossroads. He then continued questioning various people, several of whom had passed by at the time but were unable to say anything about the matter.

One of the oldest members of the Gericht, Wendel Gaupp, seventy-seven, said that he was out there in the field at the time. He wanted to get a look at what was happening, but there were so many people that he could not get to the grave. He had indeed heard the superstition about a live bull and had in fact believed it. The Schultheiss certainly had a good intent, and many people would have held it against him if he had not carried out the burial. People would have been able to say, "so was it with the Philistines, they did not believe". Gaupp was not able to point to any individual who demanded the burial, rather it was a question of a rumor (*Sage*) in the village.

Further testimony was taken from various villagers. Jacob Vollmar III, who was getting potatoes from his field, was not believed when he said that he had not been interested enough to go along and see what was happening. He said he was not as curious as other people. As for the rest, there were the same contradictions about who had helped and who had seen what. Michael Ellwangen said it was quite unreasonable to expect the truth from a single villager. One would risk having one's windows broken in, and no one would pay for them.

Then Bolley got to the actual men who had carried out the deed. The cowherd Hans Jerg Becker, thirty-two, had been the caretaker (*Pflegevater*) of the bull. He buried it so that the cattle epidemic would stop. This method had been suggested by David Langenbach, who had worked as a journeyman mason in Schwetzingen. There, an epidemic among the swine had been ended by burying one at a crossroads. Since the bull in Beutelsbach was sick, he had been told by the Dorfschütz to take it out and bury it at a crossroads. As for himself, he did not want to watch, but in any event it was never a question of burying the bull alive. After going over all of the steps of the burial, he maintained that it had been impossible to kill the bull. The third time it fell into the grave, it broke its neck. At the end of the testimony, Bolley suggested that he was full of contradictions and that although the story from Langenbach was about the live burial of a sow, Becker now tried to maintain that there definitely was no order to bury the bull alive. Hans Jerg Knauer, fifty, who also took part, similarly denied that there had been any order about burying the bull alive. Friedrich Ritter, mason, forty-four, also related the story about the swine epidemic. According to him, the bull in Beutelsbach was sick. He thought it had broken its neck when it fell into the grave.

Wendel Gaupp was brought back, together with Heinrich Breuning, who had given testimony that has not been summarized here. Gaupp said that the generally accepted story (*Sage*) was that the bull had to be buried alive. That, of course, is why he went along to watch. The bull would have been killed before the burial if the superstition had not dominated. Breuning also said that from beginning to end it was a question of burying the bull alive, for otherwise the epidemic would not end. That was the general opinion (*Stimme*).

Bolley then put the various witnesses together against each other and forced them to tell their versions in the presence of those who contradicted them – a so-called "confrontation". Friedrich Ritter finally said that he had offered to fetch his gun when the bull came to the grave, but everyone had said that the bull must be buried alive. All those who were there to slaughter the bull were sent away. Then he contradicted himself and admitted that from the beginning it was a question of a live burial. He had been given his order by Knauer. Bolley put as much pressure as possible on Knauer to get him to reveal who had given him the order, but he talked so confusedly that no sense could be made from what he said.

The source of the story about the buried sow, David Langenbach, said that he had never suggested that a living pig had been buried. Anyway, he had told the story only after the incident with the bull. Friedrich Birkenmaier, member of the Gericht, aged seventy-five, as an old man seldom went to church, and he could not remember anything about an assembly of the council. He seemed to be able to recall something about the burial of a bull. The oldest Richter, Koch, was too sick to come to testify. Hans Jerg Breuning, senior, Richter, eighty-six, was sure that in the council the notion about a live burial had been discussed. He had ventured the opinion that it would not help very much, but since he had no cattle himself, he did not follow the matter. In the discussion, the Schultheiss gave as his source for the story the knocker in Neckarrems. He himself did not hold much for the idea, but because the bull was sick and the order had been given to bury it with skin and hair, he was willing to give it a try so as not to have to suffer from the criticism of the community. Breuning was unable to say what decision had been made. Some had argued for the burial in order to keep the villagers happy. Others said that it would not help. Another Richter, Jacob Becker, was also at the meeting but did not remember any longer what was dealt with. Some villagers probably wanted the burial and some probably did not.

Hans Jerg Knauer was questioned again about the origins of the order to bury the bull alive. He finally said that the cowherd Becker gave the order. He had never said anything before because it had only just occurred to him. After various confrontations and denials, the cowherd Becker said he gave the first order to Knauer and that he did it off his own bat. If it had been so wrong to do such a thing, then the minister and vicar from the village of Schnait would not have watched. Besides, several other villages and towns had done the same thing, namely Neckarrems, Schorndorf, and Weiler. Then he said, in a brutal manner, that the bull was his and he could do as he wished with his belongings.

The vicar Jäger from Schnait said he happened "by chance" to be walking along the path with his brother-in-law, the pastor Bilfinger, when they came upon the scene. By that time, the bull already had three feet of earth on it. He said something suitable to the occasion and went sadly away. Pastor Bilfinger asked rhetorically, "Do you people think that brutality exercised on an animal will help you?" Although the schoolmaster there agreed with his opinion, most of the people told him it was none of his business.

Another Richter, Philipp Lenz, denied that anyone talked about the burial place in terms of curing the epidemic. He asked how that method could help in any way, for the epidemic was a misfortune from God that one was powerless to turn aside. There was no superstition mentioned at the Rathaus.

After several others were called to testify, Bolley got to the Schultheiss, Johannes Schuh, who he was sure was the source of the order to bury the bull alive. Schuh testified that everyone agreed to bury the bull with skin and hair according to the law. Some Richter had related various stories at one meeting or other of the Gericht or Rat about burying an animal at the crossroads. He had said that he did not hold anything for the idea and would not give a pinch of tobacco for it. But the bull belonged to the community, and they could do with it as they wanted. During the epidemic, he had scrupulously followed the orders of the prince, often against the opinion and will of the villagers. As for the magistrates, it was all the same to them whether the bull was buried here or there. Out of necessity people often play false tricks (*Misstreiche*). Some of the Räte and Richter considered the whole matter to be superstition. During the discussion, no record was kept, and there was no real decision taken. It seemed a matter of no import where the animal was buried, and in any case, there was never a question of live burial. The Schultheiss suggested that people had given false information at various times because "they did not know how to remember".

The Schultheiss was unable to mention any specific villagers who wanted the bull buried. Among the common people (Bürger), superstition was very strong. He had found himself in great difficulty because so many cases of misfortune were piling up, and they were all simply in despair. Villagers gave many examples where this method had helped: Schwetzingen, Hebsack, Neckarrems, Schorndorf. In fact it would have been impossible not to carry out the burial for the very reason that the animal was already sick. Contrariwise, nothing was sacrificed, and no one ever thought of a live burial, which would have been too gruesome. What the Schultheiss had in mind was to use the burial as a means of stamping out superstition or of preventing an outbreak of it. Furthermore, if various people had not brought the matter up in the council meeting, he would not have mentioned it. He could not remember who had suggested the idea. He himself was far from being superstitious, which brought up the matter of the altercation between himself and the surgeon Barchet over the blind shepherd. Although he had said that Barchet did not know everything, he could not remember what the Dorfschütz had said in the first place to prompt the reply. The shepherd had a great reputation as a veterinarian, but the Schultheiss did not know beforehand what sort of methods he used. True, mistakes are sometimes made, but there is a difference between sins of wickedness and mistakes which one is driven to out of great necessity.

After taking all of the testimony, Bolley made his summary report on 7 November. He had experienced how many difficulties were in the way of anyone wanting to investigate the truth of any happening whose consequences extended over an entire village, especially where the only witnesses were the people from the village itself. He could only find a few people who were capable of telling the truth.

The first conclusion that the commissioner came to was that the bull really had been buried alive. Secondly, there were two men there to bury the bull – Friedrich Ritter and Hans Jerg Knauer. The cowherd Becker was believable when he said that he was only supposed to lead the bull to the grave. In fact, the sad fate of the bull lay on his heart. There were conflicting stories about whether Knauer was there the whole time or not. During the hearing, he got Becker to change his testimony. Bolley suspected some deeper meaning from the fact that Knauer was never willing to admit where he was. Without support from other people, the three were probably not capable of carrying out the deed themselves. According to the most reliable testimony, at least five other men helped throw the bull into the grave. While many of those named denied it, the matter was not pursued, since in most cases it was a question of simply jumping in to help.

Bolley encountered the opinion among many people from Beutelsbach that they were empowered to dispose of their own bull arbitrarily. They were not responsible to anyone. However, part of their attitude stemmed from the great publicity that the matter had received and the constant teasing which the villagers had experienced ever since the event. Their behavior had been shaped by the attitude of outsiders who thought that they lived in the kingdom of darkness, even though at the moment of carrying out the deed, their interest in the event was completely different. But now, because of the impact of the treatment by the more enlightened and intelligent part of the nation, they had become shamed and embittered. This brought Bolley in danger of personal threats, and he had had to be careful and cunning (and threaten the villagers with military force). With this mood in the village, it was somewhat undesirable to make the number of people guilty of the actual execution of the deed very large.

Bolley's third conclusion had to do with whether the bull was buried alive with intent. It was hard to see how it could have happened otherwise. In the end, Bolley obtained confessions on certain points. But the problem was that all the people he interviewed were in constant communication with each other. The facts were these: the bull was taken to the grave by the cowherd. There he was tied by the feet and pulled from the other side and thereby thrown into the grave. Unfortunately, the first time he landed on his feet, which meant that a way had to be dug to get him out. The second time he landed on his back but directly jumped to his feet. The third time, after landing on his back, he was immediately covered with stones and earth so that he could not get up again. As for Johannes Kuhnle's story that the bull slipped in, Bolley did not believe it. He pointed out that he was the son-in-law of the oldest Richter. The other son-in-law, Michael Ellwangen, said that it was too much to expect one Bürger to tell the truth. In the end, anyway, Ritter and Knauer admitted that the intent was to bury the bull alive from the very beginning.

The fourth point of the report had to do with the reasons for doing the deed. Everyone pointed out that the bull had been sick, even those who were against the burial. Bolley was not able, however, to venture how sick – it had certainly not been sick for fourteen days as the cowherd said. At least it had enough strength to get out of the grave, and if it had been so sick, then slaughtering would not have been so dangerous. It seemed clear that the bull was not buried because it was sick. Also there was no doubt that the bull was buried at a crossroads. This was done to stop the epidemic, and no one dared to say otherwise.

Much of the commissioner's interest was taken up with the fifth point, namely how the order was given and by whom. The matter was dealt with at the meeting of the Gericht on Sunday, 4 September. There the Schultheiss announced that the bull was sick and brought up the notions that had been mentioned at previous meetings. From all of the testimony, it was not clear who first put forward the idea. The Schultheiss proposed burying the bull at the crossroads, but he said that at the meeting he made it clear that he did not believe in its curative powers. Several people supported this part of his testimony, although most did not remember. There seemed to be no way to find out who was for or against the proposal. Almost all of them were indifferent to the matter of burial and raised no protest. There was no formal vote or decision taken. Only Hans Jerg Breuning, senior, said that the discussion was about a live burial from the beginning.

The question narrowed down to the events just before the burial and the orders given at that time. The cowherd Becker said that there had been no order at all – it should be noted that he lived in the Schultheiss's house. It is clear that only he came to get a rope from the Rathaus and that only he was given an order to shoot the bull. On the other hand, the Bürgermeister, Heiligenpfleger, and Schultheiss all say that Knauer came and not Becker. Thus the question of whether Knauer stayed at the grave during the whole event is linked to whether he came back for another order. Or, on the other hand, if he was not there, the whole thing could appear as an accident, or a demand on the sport from the Bürger who were present. In the end, however, Knauer said that the intent was to bury the bull alive, and then the whole set of inventions lost their value. However, Knauer still maintained that he had received no order. Scribent Mayer's testimony that an order had been given in the doorway on the way out can be collated with the fact that more than 200 Bürger at the graveside heard Knauer speak of an order. It is unimaginable that Knauer and Ritter would have carried out the deed without an order. Still Knauer denies that he had one.

Many people went to the show because the bull was to be buried alive, and the superstition had to do with a *live* burial. It would seem that since the Schultheiss ordered the burial, he also ordered its exact manner. Since the whole event took more than an hour and several members of the Rat were present, the only conclusion that could be reached was that the live burial was done with the permission of the Schultheiss, Gericht, and Rat. But the actual matter of the order remained full of contradictions. For one thing, many people were there with buckets full of earth and stones, ready to suppress the bull right away. Yet all of the Richter said that they had never heard that a live burial was necessary. One of them said that there was nothing unusual about a great crowed of people; it happened every day.

The Schultheiss said that the demand for burial at the crossroads came from the villagers (Bürgerschaft) with vehemence, and that he would never have made the proposal if he had not lost hope. He was pushed into a corner by their unreasonable expectations. On the other hand, he was unable to name anyone who had made the demand. None of the deputies from the community (Gemeinde) were brought in to take part in the decision, nor was a meeting of the whole village called. Heinrich Breuning maintained that if the village (Bürgerschaft) had been asked, the deed would never have taken place. It appears that many Bürger never learned anything about the matter and most were not even interested in it. Indeed, some were angered by this outbreak of superstition under public authority. Yet one can assume that many people wanted the attempt made, and many were hopeful at the time. And there must have been a large part of the village which did not disapprove.

Canzlei Advocat Bolley reflected that superstition was still common among the educated class of people, and the common man had a very crass grasp of religion. For them, there was little receptivity for purer notions. Both classes demonstrated their superstitiousness in the belief in the magical power of a church in the Remstal. As for the lower stratum, there was a great tendency to be receptive to the supernatural and the extraordinary. They would run after the hawkers of secret remedies, charlatans, and quacks, and were not used to paying any attention to the relationship between cause and effect.

Since the villagers thought that the bull was lost, they thought that by its horrible death their cows could be rescued. When they wondered about the thoroughness of the investigation, they often said that after all it was only an animal. What was done was probably not a violation of the sensitivity of many of them – here Bolley noted that he had a great deal to do with peasants, and so he knew. He was unable to say whether their wishes were communicated to the Schultheiss in any way or if they got him to take the first step. Perhaps there simply existed a tacit agreement between the villagers and the Schultheiss, and necessity led to the decision. The commissioner finished by noting that if the teasing by the neighbors did not stop, there could be a number of serious incidents.

After due consideration by the High Council, the reluctant Bolley was sent back at the end of the year to investigate further.[6] This time he concentrated on the exact events surrounding the supposed order made just before the burial. When he talked to Knauer, the latter was rude, kept wandering out of the hearing to check with people outside, and continually changed his testimony. There was also a great deal of interest in the rope that was fetched from the Rathaus because it was considered that this could have had no other purpose than to pull the bull live into the grave. Finally, the Schultheiss was questioned again and warned sternly to tell the truth. He said that he had been brought up to tell the truth and would continue to do so. Bolley said that all of the witnesses pointed to the fact that Knauer gave the order at the grave and that he had just come from the Rathaus. It was also known that the *Wildschütz* Böhm was there with a gun and would have shot the animal if allowed. There could be no other conclusion than that the Schultheiss had given the order to bury the bull alive. However, the Schultheiss said he gave the order to kill the bull, and began to cast blame on the Heiligenpfleger Koch and a council member, Joseph Breuning, who were both at the burial. There was no way of shaking the testimony of the Schultheiss.

Some of the solidarity of the villagers seems to have been shaken a bit, and a few strange incidents took place. The cowherd had apparently said at one point that the matter would have gone quite differently if Koch and Breuning had not been at the graveside. In fact, Koch's son, when he was drunk, had a document made out saying that those who had carried out the deed would be "taken care of" for hushing up the problem of who had given the orders. Later, young Koch pleaded that he was too drunk to know what he was doing, and Becker began to fear that he was now going to be the scapegoat. The Schultheiss came along again later in the hearing and repeated his accusation about Koch, and began to suggest that other witnesses were untrustworthy because of deeds that they had committed in the past. Friedrich Ritter, for example, was a knave (*Spitzbube*) who had sat out a term in jail for stealing wine. Finally Heiligenpfleger Koch said that he was not the only one involved in the event. After all, one should believe an honorable man a little bit. Those behind it were the whole magistracy. He came back a few days later and said that the Schultheiss had sent him to Endersbach fourteen days before the burial, to a French doctor who prescribed buried live bull for the epidemic. Not finding any such doctor there, he was informed by the local Schultheiss that it was all empty talk. On his return, he told most of the magistrates that it was a matter of shooting the bull.

On 10 December, Bolley made his second report. He pointed out that Ritter had informed him that as soon as the Schultheiss had told him *where* to dig the grave he knew that the bull was to be buried alive. Bolley considered the Schultheiss to be somewhat of an enthusiast (*Schwärmer*). As for Koch, he appeared to be a good and sensible man but with a tendency to superstition. Both Ritter and Koch considered the Schultheiss to be a knave (*Spitzbube*), while others considered him crafty.

In January of the following year, Bolley again made his way to Beutelsbach, this time to force those who appeared to be principals in the burial to take an oath.[7] The ceremony was preceded by a sermon in which perjury was explained. The Schultheiss, Heiligenpfleger, Knauer, Becker, and Ritter were all warned several times and told how small the gain from perjury was in comparison with the terrible consequences. When they would not be moved, they were forced to take a physical oath. The Schultheiss swore that he had never ordered or intended a live burial. He swore that he told Knauer to kill it. The other oaths were similar in content. Knauer swore that he never received or passed on an order. He had repeated gossip as a mere rumor, but he could not give the origins of it. Becker swore that he had not received an order from the magistrates but thought that Knauer gave the order off his own bat. Ritter swore that from beginning to end the order came from Knauer. He would have shot the bull if allowed to.

With the oath-taking, the affair seemed ended; at least there are no indications in the reports that the men were punished in any way. From later information, the men who actually took part in the "execution" apparently all received fines. However, in 1801 the whole affair flared up again with various accusations, changes of testimony, and attempts to unseat the Schultheiss. It all began in September when the former cowherd Hans Jerg Becker was put into the tower in Schorndorf on bread and water for six days.[8] He had broken into a neighbor's house in Beutelsbach with an open knife in his hand and carried out various "excesses". At the end of his jail term, he took the opportunity when summoned before the officials to say that he had sworn a false oath four years previously. Since then, he had had no peace. At that time, he had sworn that the whole village (Bürgerschaft) in Beutelsbach had demanded a live burial, but it had just been a case of the Schultheiss's order. Ritter and Knauer had also sworn false oaths.

In the several weeks that followed, a faction developed inside the village that tried to bring charges against the Schultheiss. Heinrich Geywitz and Jacob Vollmar petitioned to have the affair opened up again and to let several deputies of the village (Gemeinde) take part.[9] On 5 September, a petition argued that the largest part of the Bürgerschaft requested that the authorities rescue their honor. They wanted the responsible people in the famous bull burial affair to be publicly punished. It was pointed out that the bull was buried alive as an offering to the epidemic. The execution of this work of superstition was an act carried out by the enlightened village magistrates alone, and had no other effect than to bring the village of Beutelsbach into ridicule for a long time both inside and outside Württemberg. They had experienced in the previous investigation how the magistrates tried to pass off the work of superstition and folly on the whole village (Bürgerschaft), and indeed Knauer, Becker, and Ritter were misled into taking an oath that the famous act came from the will of the entire community. Becker now says that he was led astray by the Schultheiss on the grounds that it was only over an animal that they would have to swear. For over five years, people had been patiently waiting for the Schultheiss and magistrates to be punished, but they were still in office with their honor maintained. Finally to rescue what honor could be rescued and to punish those responsible, a questioning of the whole village was requested.

The immediate investigation which this petition caused was, however, into the motives of the two petitioners.[10] Apparently they had not gone through the proper channels, which involved forwarding their petition to the central authorities in Stuttgart by way of the district officials of the *Oberamt*. Unfortunately, they had sent it directly to Stuttgart, and then upon questioning alleged that they did not know about the rules. It was pointed out that the order regarding petitions had been read to all of the Bürger in the village. All that they could reply was that at the time of the publication of the ordinance they had no petition and did not pay any attention. When told that they were responsible for the details of every such communication and that this one had been sent out many times, Vollmar and Geywitz then pointed out that they had not been to church for a long time and so must have missed it all. Handing in a list of 129 Bürger who had signed the petition. Vollmar said that when Becker returned from jail in Schorndorf, he alleged that the whole community would be fined 1600 fl.[11]

Canzlei Advocat Bolley arrived in the village at the end of September and took fresh testimony.[12] The former cowherd Becker now related the story that on the Sunday before the burial, Ritter was sent by the Schultheiss to find a crossroads to bury the bull alive. Having found a place where no one would notice, the Schultheiss then ordered the job to be done late at night. However, Becker had refused to help, and one of the Richter talked the Schultheiss out of it. On the following morning, Becker started to take the bull to join the other sick animals which were to be slaughtered, but the Dorfschütz ordered him not to do anything on his own responsibility. The bull had to be buried alive at a crossroads. Knauer and Ritter, who were to dig the grave, first had a drink in Becker's living room, which was in the house of the Schultheiss. Becker was sent for and given the order from the Schultheiss to take the bull to the grave, tie him up, and throw him into the grave alive. But the cowherd was only willing to lead the bull there. When he arrived without any rope, he got into a dispute with Heiligenpfleger Koch, who then sent the Dorfschütz to get one. As the bull went into the grave the second time, Leonhard Vollmar wanted to shoot it, but Friedrich Koch and Johannes Breuning who came fresh from the Rat would not allow it. But as the second attempt misfired, everyone there called to have the animal shot so that it would not have to suffer any more. Knauer then went to the Schultheiss to get fresh orders, but while he was gone the Richter present insisted on a live burial, which was accomplished before Knauer returned. In any event, he came back with orders to bury the bull alive. The Schultheiss said the bull was to be buried with its feet towards heaven and its head towards the village of Stetten.

Becker said that at the previous hearing everyone had been coached by the Dorfschütz before testifying. Before taking oaths, the Schultheiss had warned them all to be firm. They would only be threatened with an oath but would never be forced to take one because of an animal. In any event, the Schultheiss promised to make good any costs to the participants. Becker was threatened with ejection from his house if he failed to remain constant. In the end, he got an 8 Reichsthaller fine, which the Schultheiss did not pay for him. When Bolley suggested that this new testimony came only from hate and revenge against the Schultheiss, Becker maintained that he had not had peace since he took the false oath. Unfortunately for Becker, Ritter remained by his previous testimony and maintained that the Schultheiss had ordered the animal to be slaughtered. Knauer said that he had too strong a conscience to be moved to taking a false oath just for his own advantage.

Bolley's personal opinion was that the whole affair was full of contradictions and no one seemed trustworthy. In his report, he pointed out that Becker had had to pay his own fine. Also, the Schultheiss had kicked him out of his house, taken away his job as cowherd, and recently fined him for some misdemeanor. In addition, Becker could not be trusted because he had sworn a false oath. He seemed to be motivated by revenge and hostility against the Schultheiss. If one decided to expand the investigation to question all the villagers, little would be gained since the problem was not whether the bull was buried alive but who gave the order. None of the leaders of the anti-Schultheiss faction were eye-witnesses. In one of their petitions, they mentioned that Breuning had sworn a false oath, but in fact he had sworn no oath at all. Since Breuning's son got Becker's post as cowherd, it would seem that the entire affair was resolving itself into petty quarrels of personal advantage.

At the end of the file of documents, a short report from the High Council was forwarded to the prince.[13] Bolley was commended for an excellent investigation. It was pointed out (as it had been by the commissioner) that Becker had never sworn that the whole village (Bürgerschaft) had demanded a live burial. With this major inconsistency, his denunciation of the Schultheiss and magistrates was very suspicious. As for the Schultheiss himself, his consistency throughout spoke in his favor – if not for his rectitude, then for his cleverness and subtlety.

. . . There is a certain eighteenth-century flavor to the discourse between the commissioner and the villagers – enlightenment versus superstition and ignorance. Certain themes which had exercised villagers in the seventeenth century seem to have disappeared, especially that of penance. Although some villagers saw the epidemic as a visitation of God's judgment, none of them seem to have called for a show of remorse and a wave of conversion to ward off the consequences of sin. One pietist seemed resigned to the fact that God's punishment was inexorable, but another suspected that one could get round God and obtain results in another way. However, that would have been an even greater offense. In the earlier metaphor of penance, an implicit exchange relationship was implied. Although Lutherans always had to struggle with the original notion of Luther that there was no way in which people could earn their salvation, the notion of penance, even when it meant mere receptivity, introduced a more-or-less implicit reciprocity. In the story of the buried bull, the dominant theme is sacrifice, which at first glance seems finally to introduce a clear element of exchange, although this time outside the Christian tradition.

To understand the nature of the metaphor of sacrifice, it is necessary to take a close look at the symbolism of the burial. First of all, it took place at a crossroads outside the village. It was from the outside that the epidemic came, and the place of burial represented an open route, a crossroads suggesting communication in general. No one thought of burying the bull under the crossroads at the center of the village; rather the place chosen was acceptable precisely because it was outside. In this way, it was not a metaphor expressing exchange but was a seal against transaction altogether. Nor were the categories of sacrifice those which suggest exchange – not across species but within, a pig for pigs, a bull for cattle. Contrasting sharply with the Hebrew-Christian tradition, the sacrifice involved no shedding of blood.[14] All of the drama surrounding the burial during the actual event centered on the issue of suffocation versus the shedding of blood. No one was allowed to sacrifice the bull by shooting, hacking, or bludgeoning. In short, the nature of the sacrifice differed precisely from the Christian notion in its bloodlessness and consequent lack of exchange: "without the shedding of blood, there is no remission of sins" (Hebrews 9.22).

By not modeling relationships with the outside in terms of exchange, villagers were expressing the arbitrariness and unpredictability of some of the relationships which the village had with the wider world. And the notion of a live burial was conceived of as a sacrifice made to the disease, not to God. The only time He was brought into the matter was to say that His judgment could not be questioned; there was no use trying to placate Him. Perhaps the conspicuous absence of the Beutelsbach pastor in the whole investigation suggests that everyone saw the matter as simply outside his domain.[15] In any event, the sacrifice was to the disease and was associated by many people explicitly with cruelty and horror. The village was in fact communicating with the outside – with the epidemic – along the model of inflicted pain, a sacrifice, a destruction – through the mediation of the bull. The pastor from Schnait posed the right question when he asked if the villagers thought that exercising brutality on an animal would help them. It seemed reasonable to them because relations with outsiders – the recruiter, the quarter-master, the tax collector, the huntsman, the *rentier*, the debt collector – were frequently modeled along the lines of just such a sacrifice.

Another aspect of the metaphor of the bull lies in the puzzle posed by the story of sows being sacrificed to bring a swine epidemic to an end. In that story, a female pig was thought to suffice for female pigs. But no one considered the possibility of sacrificing a cow for the cows in Beutelsbach – it had to be the bull. The significance of the bull lies in the fact that it stood for the whole collectivity of the village in a way that no boar could do. In the eighteenth century, it was very unusual for a village to have its own boar, while almost every village had a bull.[16] In the transformation from one story to the other, the figure of the bull as representative for the village was therefore emphasized.

A central part of the story as it unfolded in the various testimonies is the notion of the village collectivity. One never spoke of the "Dorf", the village as such, but of the "Gemeinde" or the "Bürgerschaft", often suggesting a corporate group but sometimes just the people who happened to live within the boundaries of Beutelsbach. Most frequently, the corporate meanings of the terms were used for the collectivity as it stood against the Schultheiss or the group of magistrates. Although officials were chosen with at least the partial agreement of the villagers, they were not the "representatives" of the villagers, that function being left to the *ad hoc* village *Deputierte* questioned from time to time on this or that mater. There was the will of the Gemeinde and the will of the magistrates, both being corporations in their own right. The links between the two are complicated, but the example offered in the documents here helps to make a few points clear.

Perhaps the basic model can be understood by reference to other corporations such as "master and college", "dean and chapter", "abbot and monastery". Once elected, the head figure fulfills his office without direct reference to the opinions of his "subjects"; or better, he has the prerogatives of Herrschaft which he can and does exercise. In this case, however, the Schultheiss constantly referred to pressure from the Bürgerschaft, and the way he conceptualized the relationship is a clue to the nature of the community, at least in terms of its internal government and the dynamics of Schultheiss/Gemeinde. Various witnesses suggested that the villagers would have held it against the Schultheiss if he had not carried out the deed. Schultheiss Schuh himself said that before burying the bull, he had been acting against the opinion and will of the villagers. He found himself in great difficulty because so many cases of misfortune were piling up. Indeed, he felt himself pushed into a corner. The problem lies in how he considered himself answerable to the community. Since his position carried life tenure, one would have to look elsewhere than the mere threat of dismissal for the sanctions that could be brought to bear on him.

In fact, the authority exercised by a Schultheiss depended on certain important moments of consensus. After all he was, as most village heads were, a native of the village, a landowner, farmer, and family member. His position was tied up with all of the relationships that bound people together as neighbors and kin. More importantly, the success of his office rested to a large degree on his ability to get people to follow his lead. The denial to any powerful group of what they considered their just demands could make a village essentially ungovernable. A small example must suffice.

It was quite usual for the prince or state of Württemberg to have the rights to the tithes, which once belonged to the church.[17] By the eighteenth century, a usual procedure was to auction off the collection of the tithes to a bidder or several bidders from a village in the following way. Before the harvest, an auction was held with prospective bidders estimating what the size of the harvest was likely to be. They would offer a price for the whole tithe, expecting to make a profit on the margin between the price bid and the actual amount collected. Whether there was one bidder or several and whether the bid was for the present harvest or extended over two or three years, many people were bound together to make a profit. Sheaves had to be inspected, grain brought in, stored, threshed and delivered, all of which involved administration, policing, and labor. Of course, it was to the advantage of whoever won the bid to keep the price as low as possible. This was done by making an arrangement with the Schultheiss beforehand, so that various interest groups each got their turn at offering the low bid. Although a public auction was held, with perhaps visiting officials as observers, and minutes of the transaction were kept – everything running perfectly to form – in fact the central government was being short-changed. Of course, such ruses were part of the everyday life of a village and could only have been carried out by tacit consent, which in turn rested on a sense of mutual advantage and fair distribution. No faction could be excluded from important resources – at least no faction which "counted". The fact that knowledge which was generally available in any community could be communicated to the outside for use in destroying a Schultheiss is not the most interesting point, although village magistrates often left office under such conditions. The more important insight is into how the Schultheiss had to balance between factions, and how his skill was related to his prestige and power. A key word in the village vocabulary was *parteiisch*, rooted in the interest of a complex spoils system.

But the Schultheiss did not just balance different factions, he also balanced different sources of power: the secular and the sacred. By the nature of his position, he carried secular authority. He was the agent of the Württemberg state, and its most direct link to the subjects. He was the magistrate whom villagers had to deal with on a day-to-day basis. On the other hand, his power in the religious realm was substantial. He always sat on the church consistory, which among other things dispensed punishments for swearing, violations of the sabbath, and immorality of all kinds. He had the most prestigious seat in the church, was empowered to deliver an annual judgment on the pastor at the superintendent's visitation, and was always a central figure for good or evil in the formation of opinion vis-à-vis the pastor, popular piety, and village moral life. But this is mostly on the formal side; more loosely, his authority and power were related to the way he was tied to the village notions of the sacred and the supernatural.

How Schultheiss Schuh played both sides of his power base offers instruction on the way the system functioned. On the one hand, he seemed to have placed a screen over his "true" beliefs. No one was sure whether he really believed in the efficacy of the buried bull or not, or whether he was an "enthusiast" or enlightened, acting from his own beliefs or those of the village. He seems to have planted himself squarely in the area of "perhaps". In fact, he stood to win no matter what happened. If the epidemic had stopped, that would have increased the non-secular side of his power base, perhaps emphasizing the charismatic aspect of his official personality. On the other hand, if the epidemic had continued, then he had recourse to the argument that he had not really believed in the magic. He had simply done his best for a superstitious lot of people. All of this, of course, did not take into consideration the interference from the outside. What had been an issue of power and authority was turned into one of belief. As Canzlei Advocat Bolley said, the villagers were not used to thinking about the connection between cause and effect, but *he* was – and about the connection between belief and action. And just there he failed to understand the situation by searching for a belief/action nexus, when the issue was the relative power position of the Schultheiss and other members of the community.

Perhaps we can see the situation a little more clearly by turning our attention to "knowledge" as it was processed by the community. It always came in the form of generally received notions, rumor, tradition, report, opinion – *Sage, Gerücht, Stimme*. Knowledge in this sense is social knowledge, worked out in the give-and-take of discussion between neighbors, friends, and family members. It is emphatically not a single "truth", a coherent story with only one version, but rather a continuing discussion around a single theme, a reckoning of the probabilities, a fluctuating judgment. It is by its very nature a basis for *practical action*. It is part of the various strategies which determine that actions of village members are coherent and understandable to all the actors. There was, of course, room for individual interpretation, disguised self-interest, skill, stupidity, and conservatism. Judgment always comes after the fact and is based on the success of an action, whether a person emerged with honor, power, or esteem, and one could choose to lose materially while gaining other forms of capital – symbolic or social. The link between Sage – as social knowledge – and action, and between them both and success should make it clear that this kind of knowledge is always tied to power, and that as "discourse" is not composed of a discrete set of ideas. Nor can the Sage be the belief of a whole village, as Bolley sometimes seemed to think. Many paid absolutely no attention to the reports, and even those who believed in them took various attitudes and gave them varying degrees of credence.

Given the structure of village knowledge, there was a basis for many different kinds of action. What the Schultheiss did was to throw his "comment" into a running discussion. He had to be seen as acting from the Sage, for only then would his action have political meaning inside the village. As Gaupp testified, he could not afford to put himself totally outside the range of village reality – to become a foreigner, a "Philistine", a "non-believer". When his conspicuous lack of success emerged as the village became the laughing stock of the whole region and subject to a very irritating investigation, then people tried to deny him the protection of the Sage. Some pointed out that no deputies from the Gemeinde had been consulted, nor had the Bürgerschaft been assembled, suggesting thereby that the Schultheiss himself was not even a part of the culture, which was patently untrue. Those who petitioned for a further investigation in 1801 put the Schultheiss outside the bounds of village discourse by ironically calling him "enlightened", but more significantly coupled the superstition of the burial to its effect – which was to bring the village into ridicule. That is, the act became superstitious for the villagers in retrospect because of its disastrous outcome. Since such a result could not have arisen from the "will" of the entire community, then the community could not have been said to be superstitious. Even Schultheiss Schuh could never mention anyone in the village who held the idea which he imputed to them. Although this probably came partly from the fact that he would never reveal something like that to an outsider, it was more certainly from the fact that no one held the idea as a *belief*. Practical knowledge is of the sort: "one says . . .", "I have learned . . .", "I don't think there is much to it, but . . ." It is a basis for action, not for abstraction, and arises from the collective weighing of probabilities and trial and error.

The Sage of the village and the rationalized knowledge of the bureaucrat or journalist, theologian, or academic thus contrast quite sharply. Ideas from which one can stand back dispassionately and analyze on the model of the written text are not part of the world of the village. With this contrast, we can see why the surgeon Barchet, because of his position as philosopher, medical student and "physicist", rooted in a notion of knowledge not subject to processing in the Sage, had to leave the village altogether when the matter was discussed. The Schultheiss tested his power against Barchet by denying him the sanction of village discourse. When he said that the surgeon did not know everything, he was arguing that his kind of knowledge did not cover all cases. It was not a denial of the effect and usefulness of rational knowledge but a denial that the rational could judge its own terms: it too was evaluated by the effects it produced, by its usefulness for practical action.

Both Canzlei Advocat Bolley and the surgeon Barchet had a model of communication based on ascertainable facts, clear ideas, and a direct access to truth. For the villagers, truth was instrumental, and the specificity of the ideas not so important. Whether the bull first mounted a sick cow or whether it was itself sick – or dead – the exactness of detail was not so impelling as the necessity to act. In a sense there was a truth for normal times and one for moments of desperation, a point which the Schultheiss repeated several times. Similarly, another distinction between implicit and explicit truth is clearly to be made and helps to explain an essential problem for Bolley. If the Schultheiss acted on the basis of an internal village belief structure, then there was no "fact" to be obtained. The search for an explicit order was bound not to end in the location of a "corpus delicti". Communication modeled on the Sage is implicit; it shares the structure of the metaphor rather than that of the declarative sentence.

In part, the commissioner was unable to penetrate the village because the knowledge contained in it was not subject to being made explicit. On the other hand, the village systematically denied him access to what they knew because they did not know what use he was going to make of it. They were amazed at the thoroughness of the investigation, which after all was "just about an animal". Feeling justified in using an animal for human ends, the villagers nonetheless knew they were not particularly prone to cruelty. The cowherd Becker felt sorry for the animal and was always referred to as its guardian-father (*Pflegevater*). At the grave, many people had had enough when they saw the bull actually suffering. Nonetheless, they quite rightly feared opening their values to inspection from outside.[18] There was a considerable amount of lying in order to create a screen of confusion, although probably no one thought of a concerted plan, even though there had been some coordination of testimony. Confusing the outside was part of a long ingrained habit based on the experience of domination. Since for the villagers there could be no knowledge

---

136 DAVID WARREN SABEAN

which was not tied up with power, it would have been foolish to give those in a position of domination something to dominate them with. In addition, it was unclear and unpredictable how knowledge given to the outside would change the power situation inside the village. In the end, a serious fight broke out after the balance of power had been tipped. The faction attacking the Schultheiss could not imagine how the Schultheiss, having so clearly failed in his linking the Sage with action, could nonetheless have emerged with his power and honor enhanced. Whenever outsiders mixed into village affairs, the situation veered off into absurdity.

For the Reformation and for the moral philosophers of the Enlightenment, the accent was always on right belief. Justification, after all, came from faith, which, whatever the nuance of position, brought a noetic element to the first rank. When moral philosophers became concerned with reform, they attacked from the outset crass religious beliefs, uneducated conscience, or corrupting ignorance. Whatever the degree of optimism, it was necessary to attack these matters first before good practice on the part of the mass of the population could follow. Württemberg villagers, on the other hand, were more worldly wise, or perhaps saw under the mask of reforming notions the realities of social discipline and domination; they were more apt to see belief as a kind of matrix from which different sorts of action could flow. This was so because practical action grew out of the situation; it was part of a strategy directed towards maintaining or enhancing one's position in a web of social relationships. A story, a theory, a coherent structure of ideas could be shaped and reshaped in village discourse without anyone necessarily giving assent to them in any specific way. Community members could describe village opinion on a certain point without implying belief or the willingness to take any specific action on the basis of that opinion. What was thought to be the case and what people did were not linked in the definite way that a simplistic hermeneutic would expect. In fact "mistakes of belief" were considered to be of very secondary importance and carefully distinguished from "sins of wickedness", the latter being imputable largely to past actions in the light of how they worked out, and in terms of the social relationships that were rearranged.

NOTES

1 The poem comes from Karl Steiff, *Geschichtliche Lieder und Sprüche Württembergs* (Stuttgart, 1912), no. 288, pp. 1009–10, and is entitled "Die letzte Hoffnung Demokratie" or "Wie reimt man das zusammen?". It was composed in October 1850. The original contains many verses, each involving a rhymed wordplay which is left blank and then substituted with a harmless phrase. In the original stanza, the missing word is *Sparren*; that is, Napoleon (III) has a screw loose. In my translation, I have rather ineptly rhymed "bull", "fool", and the missing word, "normal".

> Beutelsbach, Zwiefalten, Napoleon,
> wie reimt sich das zusammen?
> In Beutelsbach begrabt man den Farren,
> In Zwiefalten sind die Narren,
> und Napoleon hat einen – sparsamen Geist.
> So reimt sich das zusammen.

2 Hugo Moser, *Schwäbischer Volkshumor. Neckereien in Stadt und Land, von Ort zu Ort*, 2nd edn (Stuttgart, 1981), pp. 346–7. The original term is *Hommelhenker*.

3 Württemberg Hauptstaatsarchiv in Stuttgart (WHSA) Series A214 (*Kommissionen des Oberrats (1579–1817)*), Büschel 810, entitled "Commissarische Untersuchung wegen lebendig Begrabung eines Farren zu Beutelsbach."

4 *Ibid*, Protocol dated 24 October to 5 November 1796 and report dated 7 November (document 10A).

5 For an overview of the regulations and ordinances, see A. L. Reyscher (ed.), *Sammlung der württem-bergischen Geseze*, vol. 14 (Tübingen, 1843), pp. 1110–11.

6 WHSA A214, 10 December 1796 (document 13).

7 *Ibid*, 7 January 1797 (document 15).

8 *Ibid*, 29 September 1801 (document 19).

9 *Ibid*, 20 August 1801, 22 September 1801 (documents 21, 22).

10 *Ibid*, 14 September 1801 (document 23).

11 *Ibid*, 14 September 1801 (document 25).

12 *Ibid*, 1 October 1801 (document 25).

13 *Ibid*, unnumbered and undated.

14 Vanessa Maher called my attention to this point. See the essays collected together by M. F. C. Bourdillon and Meyer Fortes (eds.), *Sacrifice* (London, 1980), especially J. W. Rogerson, "Sacrifice in the Old Testament. Problems of Method and Approach", pp. 45–60, and S. W. Sykes, "Sacrifice in the New Testament and Christian Theology", pp. 61–83.

15 In fact, he was a very old man, dying just after the first investigation at the age of seventy-nine. The new pastor was appointed in December 1796. *Schwäbische Merkur* (23 November 1796), p. 347; (26 December 1796), p. 375.

16 In Neckarhausen, for example, a boar was first purchased for the village in the 1860s. The growth in the number of pigs kept by villagers and attention to breeding came as a result of farming new root crops after the agricultural revolution.

17 The example is taken from an investigation into the criminal activities of a Schultheiss in the village of Neckarhausen during the first decade of the nineteenth century; WHSA A214 Bü 746.

18 Useful reading on knowledge as power inside a community and the necessity for strategies of concealment and dissimulation can be found in Juliet Du Boulay, *Portrait of a Greek Mountain Village* (Oxford, 1974), pp. 179–229. What she says about communication among villagers is also relevant for that between the inside and outside.

9

"DUTIFUL LOVE AND NATURAL AFFECTION": PARENT–CHILD RELATIONSHIPS IN THE EARLY MODERN NETHERLANDS

Sherrin Marshall

Relationships between parents and children in past times have been the object of considerable scrutiny by historians in recent years. It has become a historical truism that childhood, within the context of what Lawrence Stone has described as "affective individualism," only appeared late in the early modern period. Stone, writing on "Family History in the 1980s," sets the date at about 1680.[1] Prior to that time, children died "so frequently that it was difficult to take them seriously," states one reviewer of a recent book, and even when they survived, they were "lost in the primacy of the community."[2] Other historians take an even more dismal view of the child's place in the world. Lloyd deMause puts it bluntly in his influential essay, "The Evolution of Childhood": "The history of childhood is a nightmare from which we have only recently begun to awaken. The further back in history one goes, the lower the level of child care. . . ." For the early modern period, deMause's grim documentation includes the virtual abandonment of children to wet nurses, and extended periods of swaddling.[3] The lineage was all; the child was a null, and affective feelings were by and large nonexistent: this is only a slight overstatement of the perception instilled by such views in the student of history. The previously quoted reviewer also notes that "after infancy, children wore the same clothes and spoke the same language as adults." In short, this corollary truism says they were miniature adults.[4]

Such views fail to grasp the complexity of the early modern period. Children kept the lineage alive, and that was indeed one extremely important function. The future of the core family and its inheritance rested with its children. Recognition of these realities shaped relationships within the core family: the child had a future responsibility to the core family, but the core family, by the same token, had an immediate responsibility to the child. Reciprocity was an important principle underlying relationships within the core family from birth on, and this principle manifested itself in a variety of ways. The relationships between parent and child are revealed as considerably more nuanced and intricate than is customarily believed.

Sherrin Marshall, "Dutiful Love and Natural Affection: Parent–Child Relationships in the Early Modern Netherlands," pp. 13–29 from *The Dutch Gentry, 1500–1650: Family, Faith and Fortune*. Westport, CT: Greenwood Press, 1987.

Primary evidence for the reciprocity of parent–child relationships in the sixteenth- and seventeenth-century Netherlands appears, first, in excerpts from the mid-sixteenth-century customary law:

> The children of Husband and Wife stand under the authority of their Father, as long as they are underage.

> Goods which the said underage children receive by inheritance, gifts, legal acts, or other means, remain in full possession of the said children, without their Father receiving any legal right to the said possessions.

> No real property of underage children can be alienated. . . .

> And thus when the children come of age, or come to marry, so that they are free of the authority and trusteeship of their said Father, they may administer their goods themselves, and enter into contracts, and stand before the law . . . as if they had no Father.

> Father and Mother may give their underage children goods, feudal as well as personal.[5]

Customary law offers one important type of evidence for the historian of the family and childhood. Children were protected under law through their position as future inheritors; their inheritances were similarly guarded. This legal evidence must be weighed against the first legal statement, which reminds us that until they came of age, children were theoretically under their father's absolute authority.

Coming of age, or attaining one's legal majority, was a momentous event in the individual's life. Under the Roman law that prevailed in the north Netherlands, it occurred at age twenty-five.[6] Young men were customarily not called to sit with the States, a second measure of maturity, before the age of twenty-four. The suitable age for marriage, a third important indicator of adulthood, was referred to in a number of documents, such as a marriage contract of 1571. The bride-to-be was a widow with children from her first marriage, and the document specified how long the estate would be responsible for them. According to those terms, males could marry at age twenty and females at age eighteen.[7] A court case that involved the minor Anna van Meerten van Essesteyn had been brought in part because she was approximately thirteen years old at the time, and her relatives considered that to marry at that age was, in their words, "against law and nature." We might conclude that such an argument was used, cynically, to thwart her marriage to an individual of whom they disapproved, because Anna was wed only two years later to a much more suitable candidate, Willem, Baron of Gent. (The couple's contemporary, Arend van Buchell, noted in his diary that the bride was "young in years, but very rich.")[8] Regardless of these speculations, back in 1582 the argument of Anna's immaturity had carried legal weight.

Children in the north Netherlands therefore had a lengthy period of time during which they were considered children, legally, politically, and socially. There was also sufficient space between children to make family bonding and nurturing possible. In a randomly selected sample of 54 children born into the total gentry and gentry-connected families between 1504 and 1611, for whom exact birthdate as well as place in the family are known, an average of 19.9 months separated the births of children. An average of 4.3 children per marriage were born into 796 marriages contracted between 1510 and 1629. Furthermore, of a sample of 141 of those marriages, only 13 produced more than 6 children. Small core families were the norm for the gentry. There were a number of results from this, such as the provision of a larger inheritance for each child. In this context, however, the important point is that both ultimate family size and spacing between children affected developmental patterns which allowed for family nurturing and bonding. Each

Table 9.1   Infant and Child Mortality in Gentry Families, 1510–1629

Date of Marriage	Marriages	Children born	Children surviving
1510–1529	7	47	37
1530–1549	16	117	66
1550–1569	12	52	40
1570–1589	8	36	27
1590–1609	12	55	36
1610–1629	7	31	19

child mattered. Not only was the average core gentry family small, but infant and child mortality were high. Out of the sample of 54 children born between 1504 and 1611, 19 died before age 21. If 4.3 children was the average in these property-holding families, parents were just able to reproduce themselves. The impact of infant and child mortality can be seen in a different way. Sixty-two marriages contracted between 1510 and 1629 were chosen at random. Comparing the number of marriages contracted, number of children born into those marriages, and number of surviving children yields the results shown in Table 9.1. In the ill-fated second cohort, almost half of all children born died before reaching adulthood, and in all the other cohorts, mortality was at least 21 percent. In such circumstances, anxiety over the survival of offspring ran high.

The concern felt for each child also appears in testamentary dispositions. These furnish additional legal evidence, but of a more personal and individual sort, in contrast to the abstract customary law. Legal documents such as the highly conventional 1625 testament of Henrick Tuyll van Serooskerke and Jacobmina van Wijngaerden can provide a second type of evidence for the reciprocity of parent–child relationships.[9] This testament was drawn up, said the parents, "for the benefit of our children that we will leave behind, which possessions we distribute here . . . through the dutiful love and natural affection which we bear for one another as well as for our children." The emphasis in the testament on the words "nature" and "natural" along with "duty" was no accident. Just as relationships were reciprocal, duty and nature were in balance. And the way in which these words are connected informs us that the writers saw no dichotomy between them. Duty did not diminish love, it modified it. Affection was "natural," that is, inherent within nature and expected.

But are these only words? After all, a testament is by definition a formal document. How much insight do these words yield into what life was really like, and what feelings family members had for each other? An understanding of daily life is more difficult to reach in any period. Predictably, relatively few documents pertaining directly to affective feelings are extant from the sixteenth and early seventeenth centuries, but there are some which can help us to a better understanding of this complex interrelationship between parents and children.

The children of Johan van Ewsum and Anna van Burmania wrote frequently to their parents from school in Munster during the late 1560s.[10] They went into their feelings in some detail, in words that would not appear unusual today, except, perhaps, for the respect expressed for parents. Jurgen van Ewsum wrote, for example, in 1569:

> It seems from your letters that you are both in good health, and we hope that God almighty grants, dearest father and mother, that you will so remain. We wish, too, that our dearest father and dear mother could come to Munster some time for a visit, and be able to look over our life and house-

hold here. I hope that will happen, dear mother. Because we live very well here in Munster; this is an exciting place because our street is in the center of everything.[11]

Jurgen was about twelve or thirteen years old at the time. His youngest brother, Joost, was only five, and his letter was briefer and more plaintive: "I hope that my dear father and dear mother can come to visit me soon. . . . please thank little sister for sending me the sugared almonds. . . . since I don't know what else to write I will wish you, dearest father, dearest mother, and dear sister, a hundred thousand good nights."[12]

One might suspect that affective feelings were not very strong in this family after all, since Joost was away at school in Munster at the age of five. But our awareness of what was happening in the Netherlands in 1569, linked with the van Ewsums' known Protestant proclivities (especially through Johan van Ewsum's brother, Christoffel) indicates that it may have seemed imperative to send the children to some impeccable refuge.[13] Further, Johan had had no success in finding what he, who had studied at Leuven (Louvain) in 1532 and Cologne in 1534, deemed suitable educators to instruct the children in Groningen.

Johan evidently took the education of his children seriously from the time they were very young. Moreover, that concern was coupled with his care for their physical well-being. The short-lived attempt to find a *pedagogo* close to home led to an exchange of letters which not only dealt with the subject matter of lessons, but specified that the Ewsum sons should have clean linens and a room with a working fireplace.[14] Johan's devotion to education extended beyond his own family. He served as guardian for the children of Sybolt Bywema between 1538 and 1553, and the account books record receipts from a bookseller, circa 1550, for purchases including Aesop's fables, two volumes in Latin of the humanist Rudolph Agricola, a Greek lexicon and several volumes of Greek literature, along with exercise books.[15] Johan's own children did not become notable scholars, although they learned the fundamentals and the eldest could express himself fluently in Latin. They did, it appears, learn to love and admire their father.

In 1570, two years after his studies in Munster and by now in the service of Maximilaen van Hennin, Count of Bossu, Jurgen learned of his father's death. He wrote to his mother, Anna van Burmania: "that I, my dear brothers and sister can bemoan at length that we have lost our dear lord father far too soon. How much good that does is obvious, my dear mother, but we are doing it anyhow, since we don't know better than that, and to pray to God almighty for his living soul."[16] Jurgen had learned a number of lessons from his parents which helped to shape his faith and aspirations, too. As his letter continues: "I hope, my dear mother, that my prayer can be to live daily with a faithful and true heart, and I pray and beg of you my very dearest mother, to put all frenzy from your heart, for God's will must appear above all things." Jurgen's father would surely have approved of such sentiments, as he would have approved, possibly even with an indulgent chuckle, of the way the letter continues:

> Please forgive me, mother, for not writing sooner; I wrote as soon as I heard. I should also mention that they have an excellent organist here, who can play wonderfully, and I have enormous desire to learn myself. He has promised me that he will teach me for a *daler* per month. In my opinion that is very little, for if I were still in school I would be costing much more. It is my hope to send you before long a letter written in French. . . . I hope God will keep and preserve you for a long time, that we can all live together in happiness. . . . Jurgen van Ewsum your obedient son.[17]

Such a letter is an excellent testimonial to where Jurgen stood in his life, and what had been inculcated by his parents. He expresses genuinely deep sorrow over the loss of his father, but is also able to empathize with his mother's feelings of loss. Jurgen was at once a product of his time and his father's educational practices, but he also voices thoughts that a present-day thirteen- or fourteen-year-old would not find unusual: he would like to learn to play the organ; he hopes to be able to write soon in French. Both of these aspirations, the youth knows, will please his mother, which is one reason why he puts them in his letter. But his request for a *daler* to pay for the organ lessons makes it plain who is still footing the bills; "not very much," he adds ingenuously, "for if I were still in school I would be costing much more."

The Ewsum children wrote in Latin to their father. Even the five-year-old Joost tried his hand with *"meus pater bene pater,"* while the older children were able to manage lengthy and legible epistles.[18] They wrote, separately, to their mother in Dutch, as was the letter of condolence from Jurgen. Their Latin letters were not atypical. As they reached an educational level where it was practicable, adolescent males corresponded in Latin with fathers and friends. Philibert van Serooskerke wrote to his father in Latin in 1550: *"Domino in Moermont et Wellant, patri amantissimo,"* he addressed it, signing himself, *"tuus obedientissimus filius."*[19]

Mothers interested themselves in the moral and intellectual growth of their children as fathers did. Elisabeth van den Boetzelaer tot Toutenburg, "born van Mervelt," as she signed herself, wrote to her son Willem Jacob and another youth who was apparently his roommate, in 1599 while the two youths were studying in Emmerich: "I hope you are both studying hard, so that you will grow in wisdom and understanding, and I send you the following words: *A sapientia qui ex ore altissimi prodidisti . . . fortiter et suaviter disponensque omnia, veni ad docendum nos viam prudentie."*[20] (You who, from your wisdom, sent forth [your words/the word] from the depth of your mouth, setting forth all courageously and sweetly, come to teach us the way of foresight.) She reminds them to attend church and treat everyone politely, hopes that God's grace and goodness will be with "my dear children," and adds that she is not certain when she can come for a visit, since, as she says, "the road is far." Therefore, she concludes, "I am sending each of you your own package of six Utrecht cakes, wrapped in paper, so that each of you can have his own packet. Take this as a token of love, and I'll try to do better next time."[21] The tone, concerns, and sentiments of this letter are modern and warmly parental, and illuminate affectionate feelings, openly expressed. Significantly, this aristocratic mother was able to append a moralistic Latin quote. Chance preserved these documents. The letter from Elisabeth van den Boetzelaer is the only personal letter in the family archives. We could not conclude, as a result, that the boy's father cared nothing for his intellectual and moral development.

Other types of documents also show the importance of children from birth on for both the core family and the lineage. Personal handwritten genealogies were sometimes written in a family Bible, especially in Protestant families, sometimes written out separately, especially in Catholic families. In addition to a list of children's names, such genealogies note date of birth, through which we can chart the spacing of children, and sometimes date of death. Further, the day of the week and precise hour of birth were often noted. Godparents were registered. A comparison of several genealogies provides an overview of conclusions which can be drawn.

First, genealogies make it possible to see the fate of all children born, including the stillborn and those who died in infancy. All children, except the stillborn, were named and baptized. In one case, a named child who died eight days after birth had the notation: "died and was buried, but first, hastily baptized." In another instance, a genealogy noted: "this child [named] died young; his mother still lay in childbed." The events did not pass unnoticed. A fundamental level of caring was expressed in these records.

Second, genealogies provide additional information on child-spacing patterns. There was no significant difference in spacing of children even when the stillborn are taken into account.

Twenty months remains the average between live births. One possible conclusion from the statistic is that some gentry mothers, at least, nursed their children. This is contrary to what historians have guessed, and in fact we would expect that they would have had wet nurses for their children.[22] As the evidence stands, however, the space between children is significantly high. The twenty-month interval would have allowed a substantial period of infancy for each child. Death of a newborn or infant meant that the interval between the previous child and the following birth was even more substantial.

Finally, genealogies yield important insight into the choice of godparents. From a survey of godparents named between 1552 and 1656, godmothers came most often (48.7%) from the core family. Godfathers, on the other hand, were chosen almost equally from the core family (35%) and from the group categorized as "other," such as friends and patrons (37.8%). Did being named as "godmother" have more sentimental value for a member of the core family—a grandmother, for example? The choice of a godmother from the core family, especially if such sentimental ties were developed and strengthened, was very likely to provide for a surrogate mother, should the birth mother die. By the time grandchildren appeared, moreover, the chances were greater that grandfathers were deceased. When members of the core family are named as godfathers, they are most often brothers of the infant's mother or father; of the extended family, they are most often uncles—all surrogate fathers themselves, but without a grandfather in such a role. (See Figure 9.1.)

Adriaan van Renesse van der Aa began his entries in his family's Bible (which dated from 1332) with the year 1552. This coincided with the birth of his first child and son, Gerrit. For Renesse, that meaningful event marked the beginning of his own contribution to the lineage. Renesse carefully noted the date, day of the week, and hour of the child's birth. He also registered the names of Gerrit's godparents. There were two godfathers: Gerrit van Renesse, maternal grandfather, for whom the boy was probably named, and Seger van Arnhem, Adriaan's uncle; the godmother was the boy's maternal grandmother.[23] Eight children were born within twelve years, the last in 1564. Their father recorded the same information for the other five sons and two daughters, and we can conclude that for him at least, order of birth was a more important determinant in the selection of godparents than was the sex of the child. The second child, daugh-

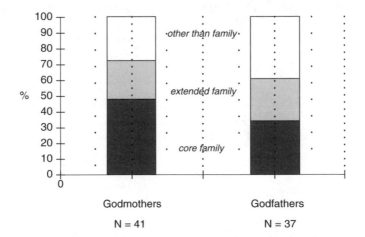

Figure 9.1   Selection of Godparents in Gentry Families, 1552–1656

ter Sophye, had as godparents Adriaan's brother and two sisters. (See Table 9.2.) By the time the eldest son, Gerrit, was eight, he stood as godfather to the sixth-born child, Albert. Although children were not considered as adults, they participated in familial rituals and shared the communal life of the family.

After Adriaan's death in 1586, the Bible apparently found its way into the possession of his youngest child, Johan. Johan eulogized his brothers Frederick and Gerrit, who had both died in 1609 (allowing him to inherit the Bible), and went on to record the births of his own children. By now there was an important addition: the minister who baptized them.[24] All of the godparents chosen by the Renesse van der Aas were either family members or close friends. Although Gerrit and Johan were both heavily involved in Utrecht politics, the role of godparent was not utilized politically by them. Through her/his godparents, infants in this family were linked more closely to the network of kin, particularly the core family, and friends.

Patrons were also chosen as godparents, and ordinarily the children were then named after them. When Eleonora Micault was baptized in 1513, her godmother was "the sister of the Kaiser Charles V and she was named after her." The fact was proudly noted by her daughter Geertryud in the latter's genealogy of 1575.[25] Nonaristocratic patriciate families often honored their patrons in similar fashion. Jasper von Kinschot kept a family register from 1578 to 1601 which recorded the births of thirteen children between 1580 and 1598.[26] Kinschot, an only child, had studied at Cologne and Douai, where in 1571 he received the degree of Doctor of Law. He became coun-

Table 9.2   Selection of Godparents, Van der Aa Family, 1552–64*

Name of child; birthrank	Date of birth	Godmother(s)	Godfather(s)
1 Gerrit	12 – 9 – 1152 (21 months)	m. g'mother	m. g'father p. g'uncle
2 Sophye	26 – 6 – 1554 (17 months)	p. aunts, 2	p. uncle
3 Jan	11 – 11 – 1555 (20 months)	m. g'aunt	m. g'uncles, 2
4 Frederik	7 – 3 – 1557 (19 months)	p. aunt	p. uncle; pastor of der Aa
5 Bernt	28 – 10 – 1558 (17 months)	fam. friend	fam. friends, 2
6 Albert	14 – 5 – 1560 (31 months)	p. aunt	m. uncle; brother Gerrit
7 Agnyesse	24 – 11 – 1562 (14.5 months)	fam. friends,	2d cousin
8 "Young" Jan	4 – 2 – 1564	p. aunt	p. uncle; brother Gerrit

Key

m.	= maternal
p.	= paternal
(– X months –)	= space between two children

*The *mother* of these children, Agnes van Renesse van Wulven, died 10-7-1567, not in childbirth, as far as we know.

The *father*, Adriaen van Renesse van der Aa, died in 1586. He did not remarry. Agnes was his first wife.

cillor to the Merode family, and Merode's daughter Marguerite, Marquise of Bergen-op-Zoom, attended his wedding party in 1578.

One miscarriage in 1579 preceded the first birth, and five of the thirteen children failed to survive their first birthday, providing a good example of a family in which infant deaths allowed noteworthy spacing between children. The deaths also undoubtedly made the surviving children even more important to the core family and lineage. The first son, Adam, had Jasper's father-in-law and stepmother as godparents. But by the seventh child, daughter Maria, Kinschot had shifted patrons and Maria van Nassau, Princess of Orange, was godmother; the eighth, Maurice, had Count Maurice of Nassau as godfather. Louise de Coligny, widow of William of Orange, was godmother to the eleventh. The presents given by these illustrious personages and the numbers in attendance (Maria van Nassau's whole court turned out to visit) were all carefully recorded by Jasper van Kinschot. His choice of godparents not only indicated his allegiance, but cemented relationships. Kinschot bound his children into his patronage network from birth.

Kinschot only notes feeling for his children on one occasion. After the death in 1601 of his first wife, Josine Pyll (daughter of Nicolas Pyll, councillor and commissioner of the house of Berghen), Kinschot remarried in 1603. His reason, he said, was simple: "taxed with the responsibilities of my household and the rearing of my children I sought in marriage Joffvr. Maria de Chantraines, called de Bruesant, born in Brussels, who had [as husband] for approximately fourteen months Sr. Geleyn de Best a very wealthy merchant of London in England . . . and thanks be to God for the love and affection we have shared and for the good and christian upbringing with which my dear children have been provided."[27] Educational goals were of paramount importance to Kinschot; they had defined his achievements and position.

Gentry and nonaristocratic families shared a concern for the rearing of children, and a genuine interest in their education. This indicates, I believe, some overlapping of their educational values, although this conclusion is controversial. H.F.M. Peeters, writing on *Childhood and Youth at the Beginning of the Modern Period*, makes the point that humanistic learning with "its one-sided language-oriented instruction" made "no sense for the ordinary nobility—that of the blood." Peeters concludes that in fact an anti-humanistic tendency existed throughout Western Europe, with the possible exception of "individual German lands."[28] Admittedly, he notes, there were exceptions. Philip Marnix van St. Aldegonde, the gentleman who was the friend and advisor of Prince William of Orange, wrote *De Institutione Principium ac Nobilium Puerorum* (*Of the Education of Princely and Noble Youths*). In it, he argued that through classical training the nobleman had the opportunity to use his skills in public, to give good counsel or advice, to lead his soldiers at the battlefield, or to serve a foreign nobleman. Since Peeters concludes that in the aristocratic milieu children received practical preparation which would enable them to fill their aristocratic roles, he suggests that classical training such as the famed humanists and Marnix van St. Aldegonde proposed had little meaning.[29]

The reality was otherwise. Hendrik van den Bergh had considered the "art of war" and the "art of scholarship" to be linked. Success in one field was predicated upon competency in the other. Johan van Ewsum provided his sons with the best classical education that he could. (His daughter was excluded from this program, but perhaps that omission lay with her mother, for Johan died when his daughter Susanna was no more than six.) At the same time, Johan studied plant and animal husbandry assiduously to encourage his estates to yield a profit. In a remarkable journal, he recorded the names, growing habits, and rates of success of a large number of fruits. Supposedly he exchanged plant cuttings with others who were interested in scientific farming techniques.[30] These practical attitudes owe something to the fact that the gentry was more modern, closer both to the realities of working the land and to the urban patriciate, than were the members of the high nobility. Knowledge was put to practical ends. The gentry saw no inconsistency in wedding these two objectives of pursuing higher learning and using their knowledge to turn a profit. Hilde de Ridder-Symoens has studied aristocratic educational patterns extensively; her question is whether they regarded university study as "humanistic ideal or bitter necessity?"[31] That is, did the aristocrats pursue further study solely because they had determined that otherwise, non-noble members of the educated urban patriciate would crowd them out of lucrative posts which called for (primarily) legal training? Her astute conclusion is that "the humanistic ideal removed the bitterness of the necessity," and that in any case in the Low Countries the "integration between the nobility of birth and the nobility of service or profession was a very flexible process." The Italian humanistic ideal of the *uomo universale* produced a new type of nobleman.[32] Parents such as Johan van Ewsum felt that they were giving their children the best possible educational experience not only for their youth, but also to prepare them for adulthood through the inculcation of those ideals.

The Netherlandish interpretation of the "new learning" frequently owed as much to a pragmatic perception of the realities of aristocratic life, at least among the gentry, as to the Italian humanists. This pragmatism was also influenced by the gentry's connections with the urban patriciate, particularly before the mid-seventeenth century, and that had also impacted noticeably on childrearing practices. Cornelis van Lockhorst and his wife Geertruyd Spoor made their will and testament on March 19, 1602. Their sons were named as universal legatees, and the surviving parent was charged with providing guidance for them until they reached maturity or marriage:

> [We wish to] . . . commend to them the state of matrimony, so that the survivor of us should support them with a dowry, with consent, with advice, with such goods as are in his or her control and discretion . . . we testators trust one another faithfully, that the survivor of the two of us, shall not shortchange the children, but on the contrary will seek to give them every advantage and profit.[33]

Cornelis, a successful Amsterdam merchant, did not die until 1617. By then he and Geertruyd had endowed Adam's marriage in 1613 with 32,000 guilders, purchased seigneuries for both sons, and perhaps most important, given their children a healthy respect for the realities of life and finance.[34] Cornelis used Adam as his business representative in Frankfort and Brandenburg in 1611 and 1615, and Cornelis junior as his representative in Frankfort in 1614.[35] It was not until twenty-five years after the elder Cornelis' death that this branch of the family was recognized as noble. The sons had long since repaid their parents' devotion by doubling their mother's fortune between their father's death and hers in 1624.[36] Adam and Cornelis very obviously owed what they became to their parents, and it should not surprise us that neither ever fit the traditional aristocratic mold of monetary fecklessness. Adam, for example, kept his own complex account books all his adult life, down to a thorough reckoning of every expense at his wife's funeral.[37]

In these cases, the interests of parents and children seemed to dovetail. But then, as now, there was always the possibility that parents and children would not see the mutuality of interests. As children reached maturity, such possibilities would seem to increase. The choice of marital partners also had the potential to cause parent–child conflict. One might expect arguments or court battles over inheritances. There were relatively few. The legal provisions for minors inheriting lands may have contributed to a feeling of security and thus fewer squabbles, at least while the parents were alive. Beyond that, sensible parents tried to ensure a peaceful division of property while they were still alive. The *magescheid* (division among relatives, as such a settlement was known) was a binding legal document designed to eliminate family feuds.

In early modern gentry families, adult children remained at home, living within the family circle, far longer than expected. Those who moved out were often close by, frequent visitors who might take their meals at home. Relationships between parents and children were permanent and continuous in nature. A group of depositions arising out of the Spanish occupation of Utrecht provides a striking example of one such family, and allows us to see the relationships between these grown children and their parents. In 1571, Spanish troops were billeted with private citizens in Utrecht. This was, in part, an ongoing punishment for what the central government in Brussels considered disloyalty on the part of Utrechters during the "first Revolt" of 1566–67. The soldiers were predictably unruly, the citizenry predictably maltreated by them. On November 25, the soldiers were celebrating the Spanish victory over the "infidels and Turks" when one got into an argument with Maerten, the twenty-five-year-old son of the Utrecht burgomaster, Johan Taets van Amerongen.[38] Maerten was allegedly slashed with a knife on his face. This was not the last of the family's problems with the soldiers, however. Two days after this incident, a Spanish soldier came to the burgomaster's house to arrange for a room for himself. The depositions of the Taets van Amerongen family show first, their everyday life, and second, how that life was further disrupted:

[testimony of] Johan Taets van Amerongen burgomaster of the city of Utrecht, approximately 55 years old . . . declares that this midday as he, deponent, sat with his wife and children and some friends at the table for the midday meal, the doorbell rang, and his servant Peter opened it . . . whereby he [Peter] came to the table and said there were two Spaniards, and Octavian his servant went into the hall to attend to them . . . returning, he [Octavian] told this witness and his assembled company that there was a sergeant requesting a chamber of his master . . .[39]

[testimony of] Marten van Amerongen, son of burgomaster Amerongen, approximately 25 years old . . . declares that he was at the table for the midday meal with his father and mother . . . when the said Octavian came to inform them of the sergeant seeking a room, and his father said to Wouter van Gaesbeeck, who was at the table, to go with the maid and show him to the room; the witness's father [Johan van Amerongen] went into the hall when the maid called him . . .[40]

[testimony of] Johan Taets van Amerongen . . . the said Sergeant with another soldier returned to him to say that they should open instead the downstairs chamber, or he would break the door in half . . . that he was a servant of his Majesty . . . and that the ordinance said he was to have the best room, and the said Sergeant said, do it or I'll see you in prison, whereby he drew his rapier . . .[41]

[testimony of] Marten Taets van Amerongen . . . upon which the family heard the uproar, and the children and friends rushed into the hall, where I saw Wouter van Gaesbeeck, and took out my own rapier so that I could protect my father . . .[42]

[testimony of] Johan Taets van Amerongen, Canon of St. Maria, Utrecht, approximately 26 years old . . . I was at home in the house where I live with my parents in the immunity of the said Church, eating with my parents . . . it is my understanding that the Spanish soldier threatened my father and my bastard uncle . . .[43]

Although the sergeant was disarmed, there were two reasons for the elder Amerongen's sworn complaint. One was that he now feared to go to the Town Hall to conduct business; the other was that he feared for the safety of his children. The two children, it should be noted, were twenty-five and twenty-six years old; still unmarried, still living at home, still, by form of address, identified in the parent–child relationship. Assuredly, the younger Johan was unmarried because of his religious vows. But we would not, therefore, expect him, much less his twenty-five-year-old brother, to be living with his parents, unless such living arrangements were commonplace. Although the younger Johan had religious title and position, Maerten's status was derived through his father: "son of burgomaster Amerongen." Further, it could be concluded that the same reciprocal relationship formed in childhood continued to exist after the children grew to maturity: "I took my own rapier so that I could protect my father," said Maerten; "I feared for the safety of my children," said burgomaster Amerongen. Here, we have no reason to doubt the sincerity of the words. This is no formalized testament, but a deposition given under oath, where the words must be persuasive.

There were a number of areas wherein parents had and felt responsibility for their children. In general terms, the first and most important goal was to provide for their good upbringing, whether specifically Christian or not. There were, inevitably, prescriptive advice-books on how to do it. The most famous of such works in the early modern north Netherlands were those of Jacob Cats, himself a seventeenth-century patriciate success story who became (Grand) Pensionary of Holland. "Father" Cats, as he was known, wrote a large number of fables, tracts, and proverbs, and his work was as widely read as the Bible, for the simple reason that his moralising was palatable. Although moralistic meaning was implanted in his writings on child-rearing practices, he also wrote entertainingly and with commonsensical insight: "The child who goes out to play, tells how it is in his home each day." "when children are quiet, they've gotten into mischief." Cats impressed upon his readers with whom child-rearing duties ultimately lay:

> In the event that a youth gets into trouble,
> Don't place the blame on him.
> The father deserves the punishment himself,
> He who didn't teach his child any better.[44]

But Cats also believed that children had a reciprocal responsibility to their parents to behave properly. The rationale for this was equally clear: "To my understanding, it was well said in olden times, Better that the child should cry than its mother."[45] The fundamental parental responsibility was to provide children with the right norms and behavioral models. Caspar Barlaeus, Leiden professor and writer, penned the following sentiments to Adriaen Ploors van Amstel and his wife Agnes on the birth of their daughter Maria Odilia in 1636:

> That she should survive her first days of life without any illness,
> That she should cut her teeth painlessly,
> That as a girl she should be pretty, not too desirable, but also not undesirable,
> That as she reaches the age of marriage her beauty should be pure, modest, and pious,
> That when she is married she should not command her husband but should also not serve him,
> That she should not as mother either love her offspring to distraction, or neglect them,
> That as she reaches old age she can trust in a better life and with full awareness carry her life to
>   its end.[46]

Thus, the norm of reciprocity was socialized from a very early age, as was that of the ideal of balance in all personal relationships.

Once children were grown, the duty of the parents was to launch them into adult life as best they could. This might mean the purchase or passage of lands and possessions, assistance in the choice of a marital partner, and helping to make a "good" marriage. All of these applied for male and female children. Planning for further training and education – university study, for example, or military service to another nobleman – were forms of parental assistance given only to youths.

In 1550 Adolph van Rutenberg's father, Jan, arranged for him to enter the service of Goert van Reede, the lord of Saesfeld.[47] Adolph would "serve my noble Lord of Zaesfeld faithfully for at least a period of four years, in all that my lord wishes him to do . . . with such company, by night or day, as he [van Saesfeld] wishes. . . ." The tone of such a document harked back to an earlier feudal period, although the relationship itself was still common enough in the sixteenth century. Placing adolescents in a nobleman's service was clearly not the only acceptable form of training for them by the sixteenth century, however. There was a fight over family possessions following the murder of the Gelderlander Johan Mom in 1574. Two uncles from the maternal lineage (Pieck) swore that Johan's eldest son, Frederick, was already fourteen years old and could decide for himself who should exercise the crucial familial responsibility of overseer of the Land van Maas en Waal. Infuriated, the deceased Johan's brother initiated proceedings in the provincial Court of Gelderland, stating that the youth was not yet fourteen and would be better off in school or as esquire in training with a knight.[48] In other words, both options were equally acceptable for the adolescent.

Even in desperate circumstances, parents tried to fulfill their responsibilities to their children. It is possible that they saw those responsibilities as synonymous with their obligations to the lineage, but I did not find that attitude expressed even once in so many words. What emerges, rather, are sentiments such as those articulated by Adriaen de Wael, Lord of Vronesteyn, as he was about to be executed: "begs that my lord the Count of Montfoort and my lady his wife, [will see] that Frederick [his eldest son] can be reared suitably outside this country, and schooled properly, so that he may be qualified . . . ," and from "his friends, that Lubbert [his second son] can attend school for as long as is possible."[49] And for his youngest child, daughter Engeltgen, de Wael "hoped that she might enter the convent at Oudwyk, there to be clothed and professed, insofar as she wishes it, and otherwise, not. And if not, then he [de Wael] wishes that all of his children share equally in what is left of his estate." In other words, de Wael's anxiety was for his core family, and the eleventh-hour arrangements he attempted were directed at his children.

Once the children reached legal adulthood, the parents' task was officially complete. Wills and testaments show that for many parents, however, the bonds of "dutiful love and natural affection" continued to be felt. The testament of Hieronimus van Serooskerke in 1570 indicates that every one of his children continued to warrant consideration.[50] Hieronimus was a widower; although he asked to be buried in Bergen-op-Zoom, he said it should be "in such a place as my children shall consider good." His oldest son, Philibert, "shall manage his father's estate to the behalf and profit of his brothers and sisters." Hieronimus also specified first the possessions which Philibert would receive. He went on to list his next two sons and their respective inheritances, and then began with his eldest daughter, Geertruyt, followed by three more daughters in order of age. This was above and beyond the family goods which each girl had received on her marriage. As executors, Hieronimus named his eldest son and his son-in-law, Bruininck van Wijngaerden, married to Hieronimus' youngest daughter, Marie. Once again, allocation of family goods provided a powerful incentive to hold the family together, and the family was defined in terms of the core family by marriage as well as by birth.

When children did not live up to parental expectations, the disappointment was keenly felt. Henrica van Egmont van Meresteyn wrote in the *Album amicorum* which Reynout van Brederode kept in 1588: *Mon deul ne dys.* ("My grief cannot be expressed.")[51] By that time, two of her sons had been killed in the Eighty Years' War. Two more children, one of whom was the famed Admiral of Holland, Johan van Duvenvoorde, had become Protestants. The other of those two, her youngest daughter, had been first a nun at the convent at Rijnsburg. After leaving religious life, she had been married twice to Protestants. Henrica apparently remained on good terms with all the children despite these issues. She had coped, too, with the tragic loss of life brought by war. But she had witnessed enough to encourage her to express her feelings with a pessimistic motto.[52]

The child's responsibilities to his or her parents did not necessarily end with adulthood. When distances were not far, they continued to have frequent contact with their parents and were expected to provide for their parents and for the continuation of a core family unit, as their parents had provided for them. It does not appear that there was a great difference in these attitudes between Protestant and Catholic. Johan van Ewsum supposedly remained Catholic; his brother Christoffel turned Protestant. Hieronimus van Serooskerke was a Catholic. By his grandson's time the family had become Protestant. Cornelis van Lockhorst fled the Low Countries at the beginning of the Eighty Years' War in search of religious freedom, but he returned and amassed a fortune. One legacy to his children was that of religious toleration; his will provided funds— administered by his widow, Geertruyd Spoor—-for a meeting place for the Amsterdam Mennonites.[53] These attitudes of interfamilial reciprocity, then, crossed religious lines during the sixteenth and early seventeenth centuries in the north Netherlands.

Yet, based on the fragmentary evidence of sixteen wills and testaments, there was a difference in the testamentary disposition for male and female children. In families which were identifiably Catholic, the male children figuratively and literally came first. They were listed first in their parents' wills and they received more in the way of core family and lineage possessions. In families which were identifiably Protestant, on the other hand, children were ranked in order of birth. Both sexes were endowed with possessions at marriage, as in the Catholic families. But the wills of Protestant parents made additional provisions for female as well as male children. Finally, in both groups, boys received the bulk of the estate.

It is impossible to correlate these differences in property dispensation with a variation in parental attitudes toward children, except indirectly. No differences in the responsibilities felt by children can be openly detected, either. Adam and Cornelis van Lockhorst shared the responsibility of caring for their aged mother and ensuring that her last years were secure. "You have always been my dear good sons," Geertruyt Spoor wrote in the document wherein she granted permission for them to administer her financial affairs.[54] As the family possessions were a sacred responsibility, the delegation of their administration symbolized the older generation's faith that the younger shared its concerns. The raising of children was similarly seen as a sacred responsibility. "A record of the birthdate of the children of myself, Gerard de Wael van Vronesteyn, by Jof. Wilhelma van Amstel van Mynden, lent [to us] by the Almighty," de Wael wrote as he began the genealogy in 1609.[55] His preface was no literary convention, but the simple truth, as he saw it. There is ample evidence that the relationships between gentry parents and children were loving and close, rather than cold and perfunctory. We have also seen that the interests of the individual within the core family, and the core family within the lineage, were similarly reciprocal and meaningful. The mutuality of dutiful love as well as natural affection continued across generations.

NOTES

1 L. Stone, in *Journal of Interdisciplinary History* XII (1981), 74–5.
2 Anatole Broyard, Review in *The New York Times* (August 28, 1982), of Neil Postman, *The Disappearance of Childhood* (New York, 1982).
3 In *The History of Childhood* (New York, 1975), 1. Many recent works share this bias to some extent; see, for example, K. Arnold, whose careful work *Kind und Gesellschaft in Mittelalter und Renaissance*

(Munich, 1980) combines substantial selections from literary documents with a short analysis which tends to follow Philippe Ariès, *Centuries of Childhood: A Social History of Family Life*, trans. R. Baldick (NY, 1962), see 16; H. Peeters, *Kind en Jeugdige in het begin van de Moderne Tijd* (Meppel, 1975), makes some extremely sensible points regarding iconography and children's games (see chap. 2, esp. 90) but relies on the same general arguments and reaches the same general conclusions.

4 Broyard; for a different viewpoint see also V. Suransky, *The Erosion of Childhood* (Chicago, 1982), part 1.

5 J. van de Water, *Groot Placaatboek vervattende alle de placaten, dordonnantien en Edicten . . . der Stadt Utrecht*, 3 vols. (Utrecht, 1729), vol. 1, 426.

6 B. Hermesdorf, "Romisches Recht in den Niederlanden," in *Ius Romanum Medii Aevi*, vol. 5, 5a (Milan, 1968); R. Van Caenegem, "Boekenrecht en gewoonterecht, het Romeinse recht in de zuidelijke Neder-landen op het eind der middeleeuwen", *Bijdragen en Mededelingen van het Historisch Genootschap* 80 (1966), 12–38, suggests the ways in which laws were interpreted, but ends with the fourteenth century and deals only with the southern Netherlands.

7 Rijksarchief Utrecht, Arch. Slot Zuylen, no. 55. Although the archival register states that this is the bride's first marriage, that conclusion proves incorrect upon a careful reading of the document.

8 Rijksarchief Utrecht, FA Zoudenbalch, 8; Van Buchell, *Diarium* (1560–99), G. Brom and L. A. van Langeraad, eds. (Amsterdam: Werk. Hist. Genootschap, 3d ser., 21), 114.

9 Rijksarchief Utrecht, Arch. Slot Zuylen, 70.

10 For background on this very interesting family, see M. Hartgerink-Koomans, *Het Geslacht Ewsum* (Groningen, 1938); W. Formsma et al., *De Ommelander Borgen en Steenhuizen* (Assen, 1973); J. J. Woltjer, "Van Katholiek tot Protestant," *Historie van Groningen* (Groningen, 1976), 214–18.

11 Rijksarchief Groningen, FA Ewsum, 189, I (XIV).

12 Ibid., 189, I, (XII).

13 Hartgerink-Koomans believes that Johan chose Munster because he sought a "good Latin school" (256). However, Christoffel van Ewsum's Protestant leanings and his connection by marriage with other known Protestants forced him into exile, and Johan also lived in a state of uneasy tension for years.

14 Rijksarchief Groningen, FA Ewsum, 130.

15 Ibid., 131.

16 Ibid., 189, I (XXXVI).

17 Ibid.

18 Ibid., 132, XI, [M].

19 Rijksarchief Utrecht, Arch. Slot Zuylen, 58.

20 Ibid., Amerongen, II, 59.

21 Ibid., fol. 59v.

22 *NL* 33 (1915), 306.

23 Ibid., 307–8.

24 Ibid.

25 Rijksarchief Utrecht, Arch. Slot Zuylen, 54 (unnumbered folio).

26 *NL* 23 (1905), 209–12.

27 Ibid., 216–17.

28 Peeters, 136–7.

29 Ibid., 184–7.

30 Rijksarchief Groningen, FA Ewsum, 277.

31 H. de Ridder-Symoens, "Adel en Universiteiten in de zestiende eeuw. Humanistisch ideal of bittere noodzaak?" *Tijdschrift voor Geschiedenis* 93 (1980), 410–32.

32 Ibid., 420–9, esp. 429.

33 Archief van Hardenbrok, Cothen, Utrecht (Arch. H'broek), 1391.

34 Ibid., 1348–50, 1405.

35 Ibid., 1500–01, 1611.

36 Ibid., p. 1400 contains their accounts from 1617 to 1626.

37 Ibid., 1551–9.

38 Algemeen Rijksarchief, Brussels, Aud., *339*, fols. 191–2, 222–4, 226–7.

39 Ibid., fol. 228.

40 Ibid., fol. 232v–233v.

41 Ibid., fol. 228.

42 Ibid., fol. 233r.

43 Ibid., fol. 234r.

44 *Spiegel van menselijk leven in prenten en verzen van Jacob Cats*, G. van Es, ed. (Amsterdam, 1962), 55–6.

45 Ibid.

46 Quoted in J. Ploos van Amstel, "Adriaen Ploos van Amstel, 1585–1639," *Jaarboek Oud-Utrecht* (1980), 73–4.

47 Rijksarchief Utrecht, Arch. Slot Zuylen, 54.

48 H. van Heuningen, *Tussen Maas en Waal* (Zutphen, 1971), 68–9.

49 Algemeen Rijksarchief, The Hague, Arch. Heereman van Zuydtwyck, 1935.

50 Rijksarchief Utrecht, Arch. Slot Zuylen, 48.

51 A. G. van der Steur, "Johan van Duvenvoirde en Woude (1547–1610), heer van Warmond, admiral van Holland," *Hollande studiën* 8 (Dordrecht, 1975), 203.

52 Ibid., 204.

53 Arch. H'broek, 1394–5.

54 Ibid., 1399.

55 J. Kleijntjens, "Het Huis 'Vronstein,'" *De Navorscher* 71 (1922), 196.

Part III

THE REVOLUTION OF THE MIND

Part III

The Devolution of the Adam

Introduction

For Copernicus never discusses matters of religion or faith, nor does he use arguments that depend in any way upon the authority of sacred writings which he might have interpreted erroneously. He stands always upon physical conclusions pertaining to the celestial motions, and deals with them by astronomical and geometrical demonstrations, founded primarily upon sense experiences and very exact observations.

Galileo Galilei, *Letter to the Grand Duchess Christina*, 1615

The foundation of modern intellectual life rests on the conviction that truth may be discerned through the application of reason. While we normally associate an emphasis on reason with the Enlightenment, the origins of modern thought lie in the intellectual and cultural developments of the Renaissance, the Reformation, and the Scientific Revolution, developments that we now associate with a corresponding rise in individualism.

As Renaissance thinkers explored classical texts, their voices rang out in praise of the power of the human mind and human creativity. Created in God's image, humanity would refashion society along new lines and in accordance with values drawn from those earlier texts. Castiglione's *Book of the Courtier* (1528), Marguerite de Navarre's *Heptameron* (1560), and Erasmus of Rotterdam's *Manners for Children* (1530) all reveal the belief that it is possible for the individual to determine him or herself, signifying the beginning of a break from a rigid corporate structure of society that was based more firmly on social than personal identity. The Protestant Reformation could not but contribute to emerging notions of the relationship between the individual and society. Many people were attracted by Protestantism's emphasis on the dignity of the individual, the value of his or her labor, and the possibility of developing a more personal relationship with God.

The invention of the printing press made a great contribution to the spread of new ideas that emerged from the Renaissance and Reformation as well as from the age of exploration and expansion. New technology in shipbuilding and navigation made the voyages of men like Columbus possible. New technology also drove the Scientific Revolution. Yet the development of the scientific method did not signify a sharp break between faith and reason. God blessed Columbus's voyage for the glory of the Catholic Spanish Crown. The Inquisition persecuted Galileo.

In the letter with which we began this introduction, Galileo continued, "[Copernicus] did not ignore the Bible, but he knew very well that if his doctrine were proved, then it could not contradict the Scriptures when they were rightly understood." Galileo and Copernicus did not deny the validity of scripture, but they questioned the notion that it could provide a basis for understanding the mechanisms of the natural world. They met with opposition from the Church and popular thought because they challenged the Aristotelian-based medieval worldview that had served for centuries as the foundation for understanding both the structure of the universe and human society. That worldview offered a psychologically secure picture of the world and mankind's place in it. If, as Galileo argued, the surface of the moon was uneven, if Jupiter had moons, if the planets did not revolve around the Earth in perfect spheres, then the heavens were not sublime and incorruptible, associated with divine perfection. If the universe was heliocentric rather than geocentric, then this called into question the relationship not only between man and his surrounding environment but also between man and God.

Copernicus, Galileo, Kepler, Newton, and others began to create a new understanding of the structure of the universe based on empirical research. Yet another aspect of the Scientific Revolution was the development of new ways of understanding knowledge. Francis Bacon theorized on the new experimental method, arguing that knowledge results from empirical, experimental research. Galileo, Copernicus, Kepler, and Newton had all practically applied the scientific method in their research. Bacon offered a theory that served as a formalization of the empirical method. In contrast to Bacon, whose reasoning was inductive, René Descartes's *Discourse on Method* (1637) was based on deductive reasoning. Descartes believed that knowledge is only attainable through reason. He believed that human beings cannot accept something as true unless they clearly and distinctly perceive it. Only the application of reason gives certainty. One cannot even trust the senses because they too may deceive us. Descartes's skepticism, however, confirmed rather than denied the existence of God. If something is self-evident to one's reason, then it exists. For Descartes, the existence of God was self-evident.

John Locke's *Essay Concerning Human Understanding* (1690), introduced yet another empirical theory as to how human beings learn and form ideas. According to Locke's theory, all knowledge is derived from experience. At birth, the human mind is a blank slate (*tabula rasa*); the environment informs a person's understanding and beliefs. Education and social institutions determine human development.

A combination of Renaissance and Reformation faith in the power of the human mind and the birth of a critical scientific method meant that reason and sense began to challenge the traditional authority of a canon of literature that had governed Western thought for centuries. Thinkers such as Bacon, Descartes, and Locke differed from earlier thinkers in that they began their discussions on scientific methods, whether inductive or deductive, with their own theories.

The empirical approach of the scientific method, along with broader developments in epistemology based on the primacy of sense experience, led to momentous changes in Western thought. We must not think, however, that such transitions occurred smoothly. Older beliefs in magic and alchemy, for example, coexisted with new scientific discoveries. The discovery of the arcanum for porcelain was the by-product of a state-sponsored search for the method to make gold. In the eighteenth century, part of the problem of trying to calculate longitude was based on an intellectual hurdle which was difficult to surmount because it, too, challenged the remnants of that Aristotelian-based worldview with which we began. Newton himself continued to believe in the regular motions of the clockwork universe. Rather than precision measurement, the answer to the mechanisms governing the natural world must be found in the divine perfection of the heavens.

Yet even as old and new forms of belief continued to coexist, the publication of Newton's *Principia Mathematica* ushered in the Enlightenment. In theory, nothing was to be accepted on faith; rather a rational, critical, scientific way of thinking was to be applied to all manner of investigation. The Scientific Revolution constituted a major influence to this new worldview. Enlightenment thinkers believed that the scientific method would reveal the laws governing not just the natural world but also human society. The economy and society are ordered, as is the natural world.

In French, the *Siècle des Lumières*, the Enlightenment represented emancipation from ignorance and superstition, led by Reason – the power of light over darkness. Enlightenment philosophers questioned traditional authorities. In the seventeenth century, progress had meant intellectual progress. For the most part, seventeenth-century thinkers did not bring science into direct conflict with religion, although that was sometimes how their work was perceived. By the eighteenth century, some thinkers were beginning to question whether religious truth could ever be known with any certainty. One need only think of the writings of David Hume. Still, thinkers like Hume were on the cutting edge of society. Enlightenment philosophers, generally speaking, formed an unusual group in both their nonreligious and philosophical views and reading habits. Their views on religion, for example, were not representative of society as a whole.

Influenced by Locke, Enlightenment philosophers believed that human beings could create better societies and better people. For some Enlightenment thinkers, arts and trades offered a model for progress. An increase in human knowledge was the best way to achieve progress. Hence, an emphasis on education was also a significant aspect of Enlightenment thought. The goal of the *philosophes* was the spread of knowledge. They asked fundamental questions about life, God, human nature, good and evil. They wanted to use their ideas to influence society – economic and social – elites, and, to a degree, they were successful.

Enlightenment philosophers engaged in a common undertaking to influence society. The *Encyclopedia: The Rational Dictionary of the Sciences, Arts, and Crafts* (completed in 1772) was perhaps their greatest project. Initially banned by the French government, this work, edited by Denis Diderot and Jean d'Alembert, professed to offer a compendium of all human knowledge. It praised science and the arts while questioning religion and authority. It criticized intolerance, legal injustice, and social institutions. Its authors believed that greater human knowledge would lead to greater human happiness. Yet we should not think of the *philosophes* as democratic. While they believed in the spread of knowledge and the power of education to improve society, Enlightenment thinkers by no means recommended this for all people.

For Enlightenment thinkers, education was a means of reform but also social control. The leaders of this intellectual movement remained, by and large, suspicious of the common people's ignorance and superstition. Enlightenment thinkers took a utilitarian approach to education, frequently arguing that education should be geared to socioeconomic standing. Old and new ways of thinking continued to coexist. Even as eighteenth-century thinkers developed a new appreciation for the lower classes and a broader definition of "citizen," theirs remained a society based on inequality and privilege. As Robert Nye has pointed out, "there were many competing discourses in the eighteenth century, some of which appear to fit badly with our notions that this era broke decisively with older traditions, embraced scientific materialism and progress, and advanced the cause of political and social equality."[1]

The seventeenth-century revolution of the mind involved significant changes in European mentality, but recent scholarship has asked us to rethink the relatively recent idea of a "Scientific

Revolution." That idea had its clearest early formulation in Herbert Butterfield's 1951 classic, *The Origins of Modern Science, 1300–1800*, which has remained one of the foundational texts for students of the early modern period. Butterfield argued that the "Scientific Revolution" of the seventeenth century dwarfed the importance of movements such as the Reformation because it changed humanity, marking the beginning of modern thought. Butterfield emphasized the secularization of thought that accompanied this intellectual movement. He also took what we would now consider an inappropriately Eurocentric approach to this subject. More recent scholarship, like the pieces by Paula Findlen (Part VI), Patricia Seed, and Kathleen Wellman, has challenged many of Butterfield's assumptions.

Lucien Febvre's thoughtful study, *The Problem of Unbelief in the Sixteenth Century*, helps us to understand why Butterfield and other historians of science may have viewed the Scientific Revolution as such a watershed in Western thought. Febvre reveals the complexities of early modern thought in the period prior to the development of the scientific method. He argues that, prior to the seventeenth century, early modern society did not yet possess the mental tools necessary for the development of a critical, analytical approach to the natural world. "Just as it had no tools, science had no language," he observed. Moreover, early modern Europeans had no concept of precision. To the modern mind, they lived in a paradoxical world where the concepts of synchronic and diachronic time overlapped. In addition, because scholars tended to work in isolation from one another, knowledge was not diffused systematically and one scientist's "opinion" was equally worthy of another's. Febvre subtly reveals both the intricacies and charm of early modern thought while challenging the notion of objective truth. In this respect, the early modern tendency to accept paradox and inconsistency as normal has come full circle in late twentieth-century movements focusing on the relativity of truth, even in scientific thought.

The selection from Kathleen Wellman's book on the monthly meetings of the leading scientists and scholars of Paris in the late 1630s and early 1640s offers an historian's venture into this new world of science. Wellman finds that the most learned men of that time did not always interpret the scientific discoveries of their time as we do today. Many times, those defending the "conservative" view of a question relied on "scientific" method, whereas those supporting the "modern" perspective could rely on tradition, and eschew scientific discoveries. Her work, and that of many other scholars, makes it impossible any longer to believe in a nice narrative accretion of scientific knowledge. No longer a direct superhighway, the path of modern science resembles more an Alpine switchback road.

Building on Febvre's work, Paula Findlen (Part VI) rewrites the narrative of the Scientific Revolution using a comic trope. She, too, sees historical writing as subject to both the perspective of the individual historian and his or her given subject. The "plot" may differ from one telling to another. Just as Febvre reveals to us the ways in which religion and "irrational" ways of thinking were deeply embedded in early modern society, Findlen elaborates on this theme by looking at the Scientific Revolution as caught between two conflicting modes of cultural expression inherent in early modern society, Carnival and Lent. Findlen sees this conflict as a metaphor for a clash between official and unofficial culture, representative of the struggle between passion and reason. As the culture of Lent came to dominate, the element of play, or the quixotic and paradoxical nature of early modern thought, slowly died out.

Roger Chartier's piece on ritual and print discipline fleshes out this contrast. The playful and passionate character of the early modern mentality revealed itself in traditional rituals such as the *fête*, some of which were connected to Carnival. Such events, he argues, were "situated at the crossroads of two cultural dynamics." If Lent represents official, rationalized culture, the *fête* embodies the spirit of popular culture. Popular rituals and celebrations also offered an opportunity for society to work through social, religious, and political tensions. By the eighteenth century, the carnivalesque *fête* as a spontaneous celebration by the populace to commemorate local traditions had died out, replaced by official ceremonies that were fundamentally didactic in nature.

The dialectical movement between religious and secular thought played out in a number of social arenas. Chartier and Findlen focus on ritual celebrations. Richard Goldthwaite traces this development through visual images. Since the end of the Middle Ages, religious images had stimulated piety and even mystical experiences. By the fifteenth century, the rich tapestry of Italian visual arts had expanded beyond religious themes to incorporate secular subjects as well. Religious images increasingly came to share public and private space with secular images with a similar didactic purpose. Everywhere, Italians were confronted with a feast of visual stimulation. Yet images might also be dangerous: sixteenth-century priests argued that the power of the image might "threaten the moral health of the soul."

The appetite for images transcended religious boundaries. Certain groups, like Dutch Calvinists, might ban images of Jesus and Mary, or of "saints" (they rejected the concept of saint), yet they would purchase art with human figures in pastoral settings, or households, or even in church interiors. Catholics bought countless images of Jesus, or of Jesus and Mary, as well as lesser quantities of images of saints, above all John the Baptist and Mary Magdalene, arguably the most human of the saints.

These two saints show us the intricate interplay of the religious and the secular in early modern culture. Images of the Magdalene could range from Donatello's harrowing statue of the aged ascetic, clothed in her hair shirt, to Titian's reclining prostitute, to the series of deeply spiritual portraits by the seventeenth-century French painter Georges de la Tour (1593–1652). His "Repentant Magdalene," gazing at a skull that blocks a direct view of the candle that illuminates her, offers stunning witness to the power of the inner light in early modern spirituality. They are a visual counterpoint to the ideas of the great French mathematician, Blaise Pascal, who argued that "the heart has reasons of it own, that reason understands not."[2] As for John the Baptist, his feast day, June 24, closely coincided with the summer solstice: for centuries, the institutional Catholic Church fulminated against the bonfires lit on St. John's Eve as vestiges of pagan cults welcoming the summer sun. Those wondering if the spoilsports won the day need only take a drive in the Catholic areas of the German Rhineland on June 23 to see that people shape religious faith just as it shapes them, and that worldviews, scientific or otherwise, do not always follow the straight and narrow path.

NOTES

1 Robert A. Nye, "Forum: Biology, Sexuality, and Morality in Eighteenth-Century France – Introduction," in *Eighteenth-Century Studies* 35.2 (2002): 235–8.
2 Wellman emphasizes in her book that those participating in the conferences organized by Renaudot spoke anonymously, but she strongly believes Pascal attended some of the sessions.

10

A POSSIBLE SUPPORT FOR IRRELIGION: THE SCIENCES

Lucien Febvre

There are times when we sneer at the science of the period. We make fun of this one's unicorn horns, that one's old wives' remedies, everyone's superstitions, ignorance, and credulity. At other times we feel respect. We extol a heroic effort and find ourselves agreeing with the old myth of the Renaissance. And we are right to fluctuate in this way.

The Old Myth of the Renaissance

It is an old myth that is still alive, despite much criticism. It starts with antiquity and the science of the ancients, the fertile Hellenic inventiveness that created the geometry of Euclid, the mechanics of Archimedes, the medicine of Hippocrates and Galen, the cosmography and geography of Ptolemy, the physics and natural history of Aristotle – an entire body of knowledge that was able to pass from the Greeks to the Romans. After that, a descent into night, the dark night of the Middle Ages. The ancient treasure was forgotten, if not lost. For centuries, nothing but syllogistic reasoning and sterile deduction. Not one fruitful achievement in doctrine, not one technological discovery of any importance.

This lasted until once again, at the end of the fifteenth century, a revolution was set in motion. Men became aware of their intellectual impoverishment and set out in search of the vanished treasures. One by one the scattered pieces were found in attics. To make use of all these riches they once more, through a superb effort, learned how to read real Latin, classical Greek, and, beyond that, even Hebrew, which had no utility for scientific knowledge but was indispensable for biblical exegesis. Then there was a drunken orgy. Gorging themselves on all this ancient provender suddenly placed within their reach, the humanists set to work. They were helped by printing, which had just come into existence. They were helped by the new geographical maps they had

Lucien Febvre, "A Possible Support for Irreligion; The Sciences," pp. 380–400 from *The Problem of Unbelief in the Sixteenth Century: The Religion of Rabelais*, trans. Beatrice Gottlieb. Cambridge, MA and Paris: Harvard University Press and Editions Albin Michel, 1982, French original, 1941.

recently acquired that suddenly expanded their mental horizons as much as their physical ones. Copernicus grafted himself onto Pythagoras, Kepler onto Copernicus, and Galileo onto Kepler, while Andreas Vesalius added to the fruits of experimentation those of the Hippocratic tradition.

All of this, which seems logical, simple, and coherent, we hardly believe anymore.[1] Not that it is enough for us to know that "the men of the Middle Ages" were far from ignorant of all of ancient culture. What counts in our eyes is not that Brother John or Brother Martin of the Dominican order or the venerable Benedictine brotherhood might have been acquainted with some manuscript fragment or other of an ancient classical text around the year 1280. What counts is the way Brother John and Brother Martin read that fragment, the way they really were able to read it. Did they read it as we do? Certainly not. Their Christianity did not limit itself to putting to rest all the great metaphysical anxieties troubling the faithful. It animated and inspired the great *summae* of the time, its *Mirrors of the World, Faces of the World*, and so on, and took man over completely, accompanying him in all the undertakings of his life, public as well as private, religious as well as secular. It armed him with coherent conceptions about nature, science, history, morality, and life. And it was through these conceptions, without worrying about putting in place historically what he read, that he read, interpreted, and appropriated the ancient texts. Sometimes, by accident, he rather amazingly managed to understand a fragment or remnant of them.

And, on the other hand, what about the humanist revolution? What exactly were the effect and influence of humanism on scientific concepts and their revival in the time of the Renaissance? Many knowledgeable people – Thorndike, to name but one[2] – have believed it possible to reduce that effect to nothing, or almost nothing. They have maintained the thesis – a plausible one – that humanism and science developed separately, without any direct reciprocal effect. On one side was humanism, nurtured by books and authors – nurtured exclusively by books and authors. Humanism read Pliny the Elder just as it read Pliny the Younger, citing both the one and the other with veneration, referring with just as much respect to the uncle's knowledge as to the nephew's graceful pen, and creating alongside the scholastic tradition of Bartholomew the Englishman and Albert of Saxony (who vied with each other in being printed and reprinted by the best publishers) a classical tradition, above all an Aristotelian tradition, that was no renewal, that renewed nothing. On the other side was reality: discoveries, inventions, and technology, along with the skills and reflections they set in motion, which would later become the skills and reflections of authentic scientists.

Thus there were few or hardly any contacts between bookish knowledge and practical knowledge. Yet there was the example of cartography, of the comparison presented in atlases between the detailed and accurate drawings along the sides, provided by the portolanos, those masterworks of navigation, and the scholarly Ptolemaic maps based on a network of coordinates. Wasn't there something in this example to give encouragement to the men of the time? There was nothing, however – or almost nothing. We are given over to astonishment and wonder when we find in a book devoted to the Venetian navy of the fifteenth century[3] an unexpected reference to an attempt made at the beginning of the century to marry theory and practice. Even more astonishing, it was an attempt that succeeded. In 1525 and 1526, when the Venetian Senate was deliberating about a type of vessel suitable for the destruction of pirates, Matteo Bressan, a venerable master of the trade who had been brought up entirely on practice, presented them with a type of round boat. But Victor Faustus, public lecturer on Greek eloquence in the city of Saint Mark – Victor Faustus the humanist, brought up on Greek mathematics and Aristotelian mechanics – dared to venture on practical ground and submitted to the Senate his learned plans for a quinquereme. And the marvel was that in the competition the quinquereme carried off the prize against the boats made by artisans – this, as one can imagine, to the great enthusiasm of the humanists, eager to extol the new Archimedes.

It was practically a unique example, until the day that Vitruvius began to dictate the projects of master masons – who suddenly became "architects." In 1539 Robert Estienne included the word in his dictionary, thus giving his approval to the development.[4] No matter that Faustus's quinquereme was, incidentally, unable to stay in favor with the Venetian sailors for long. A tradition had been established. And when the problem once again presented itself later on, the Venetian Senate turned, not to the master craftsmen, but to a learned professor of mathematics. The name of that professor was Galileo Galilei.

That was a different time. While waiting for it to arrive slowly, nothing changed. Bold explorers and daring sailors had long since crossed and recrossed the equator (1472–3), but the learned physician Alberti Carrara, who died in 1490, was still teaching in 1483 and 1490, in his *De constitutione mundi*, that on this very equator there existed a barren, empty zone, quite uninhabitable, the preface, as it were, to a southern hemisphere completely covered by water. It was the same with the scholar Alessandro Achillini, who did not die until 1512. He seriously considered in his turn the question of how to know whether the equatorial regions were inhabited or not, and it was with the help of ancient and medieval citations (Aristotle, Avicenna, Pietro d'Abano) that he imperturbably resolved it, without any reference to the Portuguese explorations. Then there was Jacques Signot's *Description du monde*, which was published by Alain Lotrian in 1539; the book was reprinted in 1540, 1545, and 1547 in Paris and in 1572 and 1599 in Lyon. There is no mention of America in it. And in the same year, 1539, there was the *Recueil de diverses histoires des trois parties du monde*, translated into French from a work by J. Boemus. It was, as the title said, about the three parts of the world. There was no mention of America in this often reprinted compilation. The question of the equatorial zone was not to be resolved in accordance with experience until 1548, when [Gasparo] Contarini's posthumous *De elementis* appeared.

These were closet geographers and cosmographers, who lagged behind the open-air geographers and cosmographers. But, as Duhem has clearly shown, it was the same in the domain of what was then called, in a poorly defined term, physics. The humanists were actually behind the Paris scholastics who based their study of dynamics on fruitful principles: Jean Buridan, Albert of Saxony, and others. The humanists continued to swear by Aristotle. They stayed with his physics – for example, among the French, Lehèvre d'Etaples and the men of his circle. If it was necessary to give it some support (and it was), they turned to the metaphysics of Nicholas of Cusa. Later, when the disciples of Melanchthon felt the same need, they would invoke the words of Holy Writ, further prolonging the era of confusion.

Having said this, there you have it. Today we hardly speak at all anymore, we speak less and less, of the Dark Night of the Middle Ages – and this has been so for some time now. Nor do we speak of the Renaissance as if it were poised like some victorious archer scattering the shadows of that night once and for all. This is because good sense has prevailed and we are no longer really able to believe in the total suspensions we used to be told about: the suspension of human curiosity, of the spirit of observation and, if you will, of invention. It is because we have finally told ourselves that when an epoch had architects with the breadth of those who conceived and built our great Romanesque basilicas (Cluny, Vézelay, Saint-Sernin, and so on) and our great Gothic cathedrals (Paris, Chartres, Amiens, Reims, Bourges) and the powerful fortresses of the great barons (Courcy, Pierrefonds, Chateau-Gaillard) – what with all the problems of geometry, mechanics, transportation, hoisting, and handling of material that such construction presented, and the whole wealth of successful experiments and observed failures that this work both necessitated and encouraged – it is contemptuous to deny to such an epoch, en masse and indiscriminately, the spirit of observation and the spirit of innovation. On closer examination, the men who invented – or reinvented or adopted and introduced into our Western civilization – the chest harness, the horseshoe, the stirrup, the button, the watermill, the windmill, the carpenter's plane, the spinning wheel, the compass, gunpowder, paper, printing, and so on, served the spirit of invention, and humanity, with distinction.[5]

Printing and Its Effects: Hearsay

So when we are told that the spirit of observation was reborn in the Renaissance we can answer: No, it did not need to be reborn, to reappear. It had never disappeared. It only took new forms, perhaps. And it certainly equipped itself mentally. For in order to construct great summations, theories, and systems it is first necessary to have material, a great deal of material. The Middle Ages never had such material at its disposal.

For them the tremendous effort of the ancient compilers had been as good as lost. Here and there a manuscript preserved a few portions, a manuscript known to a small number of men. There may have been another manuscript a hundred leagues away. There was no way of bringing them together, comparing them, setting one alongside the other, without a dangerous, precarious journey.

Then came the birth of printing. At the same time, the scattered fragments of ancient learning were beginning to emerge a little everywhere. Thereupon printing got to work. It reassembled, collected, and transmitted. As early as 1499 the basic collection of the "old astronomers." Greek and Latin – *Scriptores astronomici veteres* – was published in Venice by Aldus Manutius. The same Aldus had already published his five folios of the Greek text of Aristotle between 1495 and 1498. Volume III contained the *De historia animalium*, volume IV the *Historia plantarum* of Theophrastus together with the *Problemata* and *Mechanica*. Ptolemy's *Cosmography* had already come off the presses in 1475, minus the charts, then in 1478 in Rome with the charts wonderfully engraved on copper. In turn, Hervagius in Basel issued the first edition of Euclid's *Elements* in 1533 and then the first edition of Archimedes' works in 1544. Galen had been published in Greek by Aldus in the form of five small folios in 1525, and the Greek text of Hippocrates had been published in 1526, also by Aldus. They had been preceded by Avicenna (1473, 1476, 1491), and Pliny, published in Venice by Johannes de Spira in 1469 (then in 1470, 1473, 1476, 1479, and so on), had come ahead of everyone else. Thus the geometry, mechanics, cosmography, geography, physics, natural history, and medicine of the ancients were brought within everyone's reach. One was armed, equipped for study. One worked on solid foundations. From now on one could interpret, perfect, and comment on what the old masters had taught. Or, rather, one could have done so if one did not venerate them so.

The work of altering, completing, and readapting started. With a passion that was at once furious and calm, Konrad von Gesner of Zurich undertook to catalogue all the animals he found mentioned in any work. It was an enormous undertaking thankless and a little naive, since it placed real beings and fabulous ones side by side. He filled four huge folios that were published in Zurich in the middle of the century (1551). There were others who catalogued plants with the same passion. In 1530 in Strasbourg appeared the first volume of the earliest illustrated flora, the wonderful collection by Otto Brunfels, *Herbarum icones ad naturae imitationem effigiatae*.

This was followed in Basel in 1542 by the *De historia stirpium* of Leonhard Fuchs, and soon afterward by Rondibilis's *Fishes* – the learned Rondelet – first in Latin, as was proper (1554), and then in French (1558) with its wonderful woodcuts. At almost the same time (1555) Pierre Belon of Le Mans published his *Fishes* and his *Birds*, "together with their descriptions and true portraits drawn from nature." The whole of living nature. To this Georg Agricola added inanimate nature, the minerals. In 1546 his *De ortu et causis subterraneorum* appeared in Basel. In 1555, also in Basel, appeared the magnificent folio of *De re metallica*. Scholars were able to put in long working days. They now knew their labor would not be in vain; printing was there to make it bear fruit throughout the world. And Rabelais, who stoutly counted himself among these great makers of inventories, who when he was in Rome felt the urge to catalogue all the ruins and remnants of antiquity, was able in his *Gargantua* and his *Pantagruel* to intone a hymn to science, to men's limitless knowledge.

That was Rabelais in *Gargantua* and *Pantagruel*. But in 1564 *Book Five* of *Pantagruel* appeared, and we will no doubt never know to what extent it was or was not the reworking of what had been sketched out by Rabelais. In *Book Five*, chapter 31, we find the astonishing allegory of Hearsay, the misshapen old fellow who is blind and palsied but all covered with ears that are always wide open and supplied with seven tongues that move at once in his furnace-door mouth. Through all his ears he receives incongruous and crude information from books and newspapers, and through all his tongues he communicates it to gaping listeners who never verify, criticize, or examine it, no matter what it is. "And all by hear-say" is the refrain of the passage, punctuating the nasty remarks; a Molière-like refrain we would say if it were not Rabelaisian. Is the irony forced? No, this is both ironic and fair. For if the men of that time made compilations, if they made compilations above all and to the exclusion of almost everything else, it was because for conquering the world's secrets, for forcing nature out of her hiding places, they had nothing – no weapons, no tools, no general plan. They had only a tremendous will – their will, and nothing else.

The Lack of Tools and of a Scientific Language

As far as physical tools are concerned, they were still unacquainted with the most ordinary instruments of today, those that are familiar to everyone and, furthermore, those that are the most simple. For observing they had nothing better than their two eyes, aided at the most, if they needed it, by eye-glasses that were necessarily rudimentary. Certainly neither the state of optics nor of glassmaking made any others possible. There were no lenses of either glass or cut crystal that were suitable for enlarging very distant objects like the stars or very small ones like insects and seeds. It was not till the beginning of the seventeenth century, in Holland, that the astronomical telescope would be invented and Galileo would be able to observe the stars, discover the mountains of the moon, add to the number of stars, count thirty-six Pleiades instead of seven, and contemplate the ring of Saturn or the moons of Jupiter. And it was likewise not till the seventeenth century, also in Holland, that Leeuwenhoek of Delft, with a magnifying glass and then with a rudimentary microscope, was able to conduct the first research on the internal structure of tissues and reveal to astounded naturalists the amazing fecundity of the Infusoria. But once an observation was made, what was there to measure it with? There was no clear and well-defined nomenclature, there were no guaranteed, precise standards adopted and cheerfully assented to by all. What there was was an incoherent multitude of systems of measurement that varied from city to city and village to village – whether dealing with length, weight, or volume. As for taking temperatures, that was impossible. The thermometer had not come into existence and was not to do so for a long time.

And just as it had no tools, science had no language.[6] It is, of course, true to say that in its final glow before being extinguished the Greek genius had created algebra. But it was an algebra for calculating, an algebra whose ambitions were limited to guaranteeing conveniently automatic calculations, whereas to us algebra is only secondarily a mechanical means of solving problems, and is also only secondarily a way of calculating with symbols. If algebra can be defined as the point where mathematics contemplates relation in all its nakedness without any support other than the symbol for the relation itself, the point where arithmetic is transformed into logic, a logic more exact, richer, and deeper than that of the dialecticians, then algebra had not come into existence in Rabelais's time. It was not to come into existence until the very end of the sixteenth century, with François Viète's *Isagoge*. Viète was from Poitou, born in Fontenay-le-Comte, where that other François had lived for so long in a monastery. At any rate, it was Viète who took a technique, a collection of practical rules and recipes for the use of those who liked mathematical games, and made of it, not a true science (that was the work of the Italians Tartaglia, Cardano, Ferrari, and Bombelli), but a language linked to a science, linked in such a way that every improvement in the science brought about an improvement in the language, and vice versa.

Of course, anyone who opens up the *Summa de arithmetica, geometria, proportioni et proportionalità* by Lucas Pacioli, published in Venice in 1494 – the first mathematical treatise that printing made widely known – will find some algebraic concepts there: *algebra, almucabala, arte maggiore*, presented as a method of calculation necessary for arithmetic and geometry. But it is a strange algebra, still ignorant of mathematical signs $(+, -)$, whose place is taken by letters; of the very convenient use of x and y; of the practical symbols x, x^2, x^3, x^4, whose place is taken by expressions like *cosa* to mean the unknown or *censo* to indicate the unknown squared.[7] To Viète goes the honor of having introduced the use of letters to indicate both known and unknown quantities, and of having likewise adopted a practical notation for expressing powers. In anticipation of this, Pacioli did teach how to solve quadratic and certain higher-degree equations with rudimentary tools, but the general solution of third-degree equations remained unknown to him. It would be the collective achievement of a whole series of great Italians, among them Tartaglia and Cardano.

There was no algebraic language. There was not even an arithmetic language that was convenient, regular, and modern. The use of the numerals we call Arabic because they are Indian, the gobar numerals that came into western Europe from Spain or Barbary, was far from common, although Italian merchants had been acquainted with them ever since the thirteenth and fourteenth centuries. If there was a rapid spread of the practice of using these symbols in calendars for ecclesiastics and in almanacs for astrologers and physicians, it met strong resistance in everyday life from Roman numerals – or, to be more exact, the slightly modified minuscule Roman numerals that were called *chiffres de finance*. They appeared grouped according to categories, separated by dots: tens, twenties superscribed by two Xs, hundreds superscribed by a C, and thousands superscribed by an M – all as poorly contrived as possible to permit the execution of any arithmetical operation no matter how elementary.

There were also no written calculations – those procedures that seem so convenient and simple to us and that still seemed fiendishly difficult to men of the sixteenth century, suitable only for the mathematical elite. Before laughing, let us remember that in 1645, more than a century after the appearance of *Pantagruel*, Pascal was still insisting on the extreme difficulty of written calculations when he dedicated his calculating machine to Chancellor Séguier. Not only do they constantly force us "to keep or borrow the necessary sums," whence come innumerable errors (and he might have added that it was precisely because of these errors[8] that the Arabs had invented checking by casting out nines), but moreover they demand of the unfortunate

calculator "deep attention that tires the mind in a short time." Actually in Rabelais's time counting was done mostly and almost exclusively with the help of counting boards or "exchequers"
(which gave their name to the ministers of the treasury on the other side of the Channel) and
counters, which were used with greater or lesser dexterity in the Ancien Régime up to its decline.[9]

In any case, did those men figure better in their heads than with pen in hand? I am always
reminded of the lovely story about the secretary of a president of the Chambre des Comptes who
was rudely called upon by a gang to open his door: "If you don't open, there are fifty of us here,
and we will each beat you a hundred times." He who was summoned answered at once, in terror.
"What? Five thousand blows!" And Tallement des Réaux, who tells the story, is filled with
wonder: "I admire the man's presence of mind, and it seems to me one needed to be secretary
to a president of the Comptes to make the calculation so adroitly!"[10] The impossible calculation:
100×50.

Moreover, the techniques and methods of written calculation were still far from uniform. Addition and subtraction were done from left to right. Our present procedure only started to be used,
in part, around 1600. Pacioli, the great authority, gave his readers a choice of three methods of
subtraction and eight of multiplication, each having its own name. Their difficulty seemed to be
such that efforts were bent to find mechanical means that would allow novices to avoid them –
for example, Napier's famous "bones" at the beginning of the seventeenth century. But it was
division that of all the operations had the worst reputation. Rival methods made claims on the
student, and the one we use today was not the one held in most repute – far from it.

There were no established methods, there were insufficient symbols. In 1489 the signs + and
– were found, to be sure, in Johannes Widman of Eger's *Mercantile Arithmetic*, but as abbrevia-
tions, not operational symbols. In 1484 the Parisian Nicolas Chuquet, working for the merchants
of Lyon, was still using the notations p and m to abbreviate "plus" and "minus" in his *Triparty*.[11]
As a matter of fact, Viète was the first author who is really known to have employed these signs
consistently, starting in 1591, and little by little he promoted their use. The equals sign =, introduced in 1557 by Robert Recorde in a treatise that remained in manuscript for a long time, was
not in general use, either, until the seventeenth century. The "multiplied by" ×, employed by
Oughtred in 1631, did not prevail right away; Leibniz still indicated multiplication by the sign.
As for the sign ÷ (divided by), it also dates from 1631. Need I add that logarithms were not
invented until 1614 by Napier – and that Rabelais's contemporaries had not the slightest notion
of any of this?

At which we ought not smile and ask: Is it really necessary to possess these signs in order to
reason correctly?[12] It is surely not by divine right that the cross means "plus" and the Saint
Andrew's cross "multiplied by." The reverse convention could have been adopted. But to do
arithmetic or algebra in a useful way without some such system of signs is impossible. And a man
who does not have them at his disposal, who is therefore living in a world in which mathematics
is still elementary, has not had his mind formed in the same way as one who, even though he may
be ignorant or unable – or unconcerned – to solve an equation himself or do a more or less complicated problem, lives in a society that is on the whole subjected to the rigor of its modes of
mathematical reasoning, to the precision of its modes of calculation, and to the correctness and
elegance of its ways of giving proofs.

"All of our modern life is as though impregnated with mathematics. Men's everyday actions
and their structures bear its mark – and we do not escape its influence even in our artistic pleasures or our moral life." A man of the sixteenth century would not have been able to subscribe
to this statement by Paul Montel. We are not surprised by it. It would have caused him, quite
rightly, to be totally incredulous.

Fluid Time, Stagnant Time

Let us apply these reflections to the measurement of time. People were often still content to approximate it as peasants do – estimating daytime according to the sun and nighttime, or rather the end of night, by listening for the rooster's crow. It is interesting to read from the prolific pen of the Reformer of Lausanne, Viret, words of praise for the roosters that men-at-arms always took with them when they went off to war: "which at night served them as clocks."[13]

The fact is that there were very few real clocks, most of them for public use. Furthermore, it was a rare town that could pride itself on a true clock, either without chimes or, wondrous to behold, with chimes, like the oldest one of all, the one ordered by Charles V and placed on the tower of the palace in 1370 – it still gives its name to the present-day Quai de l'Horloge. They were sturdy, rudimentary machines. It was necessary to wind them several times in the course of twenty-four hours. We would know that from Froissart's *Horloge amoureuse* even if city archives from the end of the fourteenth century did not speak a great deal about the one who "regulates the clock" (*gouverne le reloige*) and about his consumption of grease, iron wire, wood, and rope for the said clock, its hammer, and its wheels: "A clock cannot go by itself or move, unless it has one to watch it and care for it: a clockmaker, who administers to it carefully when necessary, lifts its weights, returns them to their duty, and makes them move in an orderly way."[14]

There is no need to say that those clocks did not sound the hours. Every time the hand passed a new hour, a pin fixed to the driving wheel released a lever that set in motion a hammer that sounded an alarm on a bell. The watchman, thus alerted, with the aid of the hammer then struck the necessary number of strokes on the bell of the tower. But there was no question of indicating the hour's subdivisions. And besides, in many instances the night watchmen were provided with the hour only approximately, by means of hourglasses using sand or water that they were responsible for turning. They cried out from the tops of towers the information these furnished them, and guards repeated it on the streets. As for individuals, how many in Pantagruel's time owned a clock? The number was minimal, outside of kings and princes. They were proud and considered themselves privileged if they possessed, under the name of clock, one of those hourglasses that used water rather than sand, to which Joseph Scaliger offered pompous praise in his second *Scaligerana*: "horologia sunt valde recentia et praeclarum inventum."[15]

On the whole, they were the ways of a peasant society, which accepted the fact that it would never know the exact time except when the bell rang (assuming it was set properly) and otherwise referring to plants and animals, to the flight or song of some bird. "Around sunrise" or else "around sunset": these are the most frequent indications by Gilles de Gouberville, a gentleman of Normandy, in his diary.[16] Sometimes, rather curiously, he refers to the behavior of a bird he calls a *vitecoq*, which must have been a kind of woodcock. "It was the time of the *vitecoqs'* flight," he will say, "when I came home" (November 28, 1554) or, again, he will note that on January 5, 1557 (os), after vespers the bachelors of the parish started playing pall-mall with the married men; they were at it "till the *vite-coqs'* flight."[17] And yet Gouberville had a clock, a great rarity, which he sent to an armorer in Digoville in January 1561 (os) for repairs.[18] And he delighted in taking note of the hours, always prefacing this with a modest and prudent "around": they returned "around an hour before daybreak" or "we came to take several glasses, around half an hour" – which has a precision that was entirely abnormal.

Thus we find fancifulness, imprecision, inexactness everywhere, the doing of men who did not even know their ages precisely. Countless are the historical personages of the time who have given us a choice of three or four birth dates. When was Erasmus born? He did not know, only that the event took place on the eve of Saints Simon and Jude. What year was Lehèvre d'Etaples born? We try to deduce it from very vague hints. What year was Rabelais born? He did not know, Luther? We are in doubt. The month was generally known – a month in a year that was itself poorly organized, since the vernal equinox had moved back little by little from March 21 to March 11. The family and the parents remembered that the baby had come into the world at haymaking time, at the time of the wheat harvest or grape harvest; there had been snow, or else it was the month "when the ears of wheat began to come out . . . and the stalks were already starting to grow": these rustic details are in John Calvin.[19] So a family tradition was established: François was born on November 27, and Jeanne on January 12 (how cold it was when she was carried to the font!). Sometimes even the hour was known, in a more or less general way – "around," as the Sire de Gouberville would say. The mother did not forget the hour; it was the date, an abstract notion, that went beyond the sphere of ordinary concerns. To find birth certificates in good order we have to turn to the world's great – or the sons of doctors and learned men, those for whom a horoscope was cast and whose birth, as a consequence, was surrounded with astonishingly accurate details. They knew (or rather their astrologers provided for them) the year, the day, the hour, and the minute, not only of their birth, but of their conception. We are informed of this by Brantôme, who was an intimate of Margaret of Navarre through his mother and grandmother. The princess had been born "under the 10th degree of Aquarius when Saturn was separated from Venus by the quartile aspect on the 10th of April, 1492, at 10 o'clock in the evening at the castle of Angoulême – and had been conceived in the year 1491 at 10 hours and 17 minutes before midnight on the 11th of July."[20] Now, that is being precise! Cardano himself was no less well informed about his entry into the world. He gives the year, day, and hour, but to within the quarter.[21]

With these exceptions, the great mass gave up all concern for precision. "There is nothing," wrote Thomas Platter in his memoirs, "that I can vouch for less than the exact time of each circumstance of my life" – which did not prevent him from telling wonderful stories about his mother's father, who lived to the age of 126 and at over 100 married a girl of 30 by whom he had a son, but naturally no one knew the date of his birth.[22] What good was such precision to a Valais mountaineer? Men had not yet been forced to precision by the harsh discipline of time that we know: civil time, religious time, school time, military time, factory time, railroad time – so much so that in the end everyone has to have a watch. Just think, in 1867, at the time of the Paris International Exposition, there were still barely four million watches in France, and twenty-five million in the whole world. That was very few, but it was already a lot, since it had been necessary to overcome so much resistance and instinctive aversion. "I never tie myself to hours," solemnly declares the abbot of Theleme, Friar John. "They are made for the man, and not the man for them."[23] But a hundred years later Sorel's Francion, describing his arrival at the College of Lisieux, groans, "I was obliged to appear at divine services, at meals, and at lessons at certain hours, to the sound of the bell, by which all things were marked."[24]

In the main in the sixteenth century, in the great longstanding duel fought between experienced time and measured time, it was the first that kept the advantage. "Chapter XXIII. How Gargantua was instructed by Ponocrates, and in such sort disciplinated, that he lost not one hour of the day." Not to lose an hour a day: horrible ideal of new times! How much happier good King Charles V had been; he had a taper that was divided into twenty-four parts, and from time to time someone came to tell him "to what point the candle had burned down."

Chronology imposes a tough abstract rule. Can we ourselves claim to have submitted to it fully and rigorously? When we evoke our own past and then compare our memories with the calendar, what disharmony there is! It is obvious that we remake the past according to our dispositions, often telescoping the years and constructing out of events that are sometimes very widely separated in time coherent wholes that we find pleasing. If this is true of us, men of today, who do not know how to live without a watch, a watch carefully set according to astronomical time, what was it like in the sixteenth century? For how many men had the astronomical calendar already become the true measurement, the true regulator, of time? Even in the religious realm? Can we really believe that for measuring time, for slicing it up, peasants then had any means of measuring and marking but particular circumstances that were important to the life of the group and capable of arousing it to paroxysms of activity or of passion?

Just think how even today the concept of time easily becomes hazy, despite the number and rigor of the marks we have with which to measure it. It takes the child a while to pin it down, while a sick person easily makes mistakes about it. As we go back a dozen generations we find ourselves in the midst of the era of fluid time. Among the uneducated, "before" and "after" were two concepts that did not yet strictly exclude each other. Death did not prevent the dead from living and coming back. It was the same with space. In Rabelais's time many objections were raised to accepting the idea that a man could occupy two places at once – two spots in a space that was still poorly organized, where each thing was not yet the rightful occupant of an exclusive place, a place that could be instantly located at any moment.

Are we therefore surprised that men of the past lacked a historical sense? That, to take only one example, they never raised the problem of the age of the world in any of their writings? That the absolute figure of 4004 years from the creation of the world to the birth of Christ was never a subject for discussion?[25] And that, finally, it was with no discomfort at all that they saw their painters depict the besiegers of Jericho in the garb of the men-at-arms of Marignano or clothe the bystanders at Golgotha in slashed doublets? The great step backward, the great movement in reverse as humanity gradually retook possession of the trenches from which it first set out to conquer what it calls progress, had not begun. It is still going on before our eyes and scores new successes every day. For many men of that time the historical was confused with the mythical. In the indefinite past that they called "former times" or "olden times" or "a very long time ago" without more precision, who knows how many still accepted without much difficulty the presence of mythical personages existing side by side with "mythified" (if I may say that) historical personages in a sort of fluid promiscuity that shocks us but did not bother any of them? All of this went a very long way; it involved all of life and the total behavior of the era.

Do we need one last indication? If time was not measured with accuracy, if no one bothered to keep track of it, reckon it, or regard it in an exact way, how could it have been treated as a precise commodity to be saved, managed, or used effectively? In its works the sixteenth century, the heir of the fifteenth century in this respect, was in fact one of the biggest wasters of time that a century ever was. That was the period when the architects of churches, castles, and palaces squandered a prodigious outlay of days, months, and years in complicated ornaments, tracery, and flourishes; when buildings in the Flamboyant style, carved Burgundian chests, and cut and slashed garments – even dishes cooked with a knowing, cruel slowness – seemed like so many huge strongboxes in which men who kept no reckoning hid away bundles of time that did not produce interest.[26] It was a far cry from our unadorned, sleek buildings, all flat surfaces without moldings or sculpture, rising into the air in three weeks – the air into which a skyscraper rises in three months is the same air in which the Tour Saint-Jacques, with its festoons and arches, could be seen growing for years, course upon course, every day becoming more and more carved and ornate.

It would take much time, much research that is now lacking, tools we have not been provided with, to complete this picture of the conditions of thought of a century we think we can still reach out and touch but which is, however, already so far away both in its mental habits and its social structure. Yet are we not well enough informed by now to think, without too much presumption, that if these were the conditions of existence to which the men of that time were subjected, their thought could not really have had conclusive force nor their science compelling power?

NOTES

1 See, in volume XVI of the *Encyclopédie française*, 21 vols. (Paris, 1935–66), the articles by Joseph Bédier on "Le Moyen Age" (pp. 16'10-3–16'10-9) and by Lucien Febvre on "La Renaissance" (pp. 16'10-13–16'12-1).

2 Cf. Lynn Thorndike, *Science and Thought in the Fifteenth Century* (New York, 1929).

3 Frederic C. Lane, *Venetian Ships and Shipbuilders of the Renaissance* (Baltimore, 1934). Reviewed by Lucien Febvre in *Annales d'Histoire Economique et Sociale*, 7 (1935), 80–83.

4 Earlier the word had been used by Lemaire de Belges (1510) and Geoffroy Tory (1529). Rabelais launched its use in *Pantagruel*. Francis I conferred the title on Serlio in 1541. Likewise see references from Amiens in Lucien Febvre, "Ce qu'on peut trouver dans une série d'inventaires mobiliers," *Annales d'Histoire Sociale*, 3 (1941), St: trans. in *A New Kind of History*, ed. Peter Burke (New York, 1973).

5 See Marc Bloch, "Les 'Inventions' médiévales," *Annales d'Histoire Economique at Sociale*, 7 (1935), 634–43, and, in general, the whole November issue of that year on technology, "Les Techniques, l'histoire et la vie."

6 On what follows, see Moritz Cantor, *Vorlesungen über Geschichte der Mathematik*, vol. II: *Von 1200–1668*, 2d ed. (Leipzig, 1900), especially ch. 53 on counting boards, ch. 57 on Pacioli, ch. 58 on Chuquet and Lefèvre, ch. 68 on Viète. See likewise W. W. Rouse Ball, *A Short Account of the History of Mathematics*, 4th ed. (London, 1905), chs. 11, 12; and Augustin Cournot, *Considérations sur la marche des idées et les événements dans les temps modernes*, ed. François Mentré, 2 vols. (Paris, 1934), I, ch. 3: II, ch. 1.

7 Which he abbreviated as *co* (*cosa*), *ce* (*censo*), and *cu* (*cubo*). Regiomontanus (1436–76), for his part, called the unknown *res* and its square *census*. To solve a problem *per artem rei et census* meant to solve it by means of a quadratic equation.

8 "Errors in calculation were the general rule. It was exceptional for an addition to be correct. The divergences were often considerable, sometimes exceeding 100,000 *livres*." Roger Doucet, *L'Etat des finances de 1523* (Paris, 1923), p. 12.

9 On these usages see, in addition to Cantor, Albert Dupont, *Formes des comptes et façons de compter dans l'ancien temps* (Paris and Vienne, 1928). The whole development of arithmetic and even of elementary algebra took place in association with advances in bookkeeping. On these, see Raymond de Roover, "Aux origines d'une technique intellectuelle: la formation et l'expansion de la comptabilité à partie double," *Annales d'Histoire Economique et Sociale*, 9 (1937), 171–93, 270–98.

10 Gédéon Tallement des Réaux, *Historiettes*, ed. Antoine Adam, 2 vols. (Paris, 1960–1961), II, 470.

11 On Chuquet, see Cantor, II, 318, and Aristide Marre, "Notice sur Nicolas Chuquet et son *Triparty en la science des nombres*," *Bulletino di Bibliografia e di Storia delle Scienze Matematiche e Fisiche, Pubblicato da B. Boncompagni*, 13 (1880), 555–92, followed by a reproduction of the text of the *Triparty* (593–659, 693–814).

12 See the observations by Abel Rey on this subject in his *La Science dans l'antiquité*, 5 vols. (Paris, 1930–48), III, 371 ff. Which is not to overlook the important reflections in Cournot, I, 35: "If, however, the Greeks had been acquainted with our arithmetical notation, there is no doubt this would have given a different direction to their studies, even the purely speculative ones."

13 Pierre Viret, *Instruction chrestienne*, II: *Exposition de la foy chrestienne* (Geneva: Rivery, 1564), p. 179 (dialogue IX).

14 [Paraphrase of II, 927–934 of Jean Froissart, "Li Orloge amoureus" in *Oeuvres de Froissart: poésies*, ed. Auguste Scheler, 3 vols. (Brussels, 1870–1872), I, 79–80 – Translator.] See Alfred Franklin. *La Vie privée d'autrefois*, 23 vols. (Paris, 1887–1901), IV: *La Mesure du temps*, passim.

15 "Clocks are very recent, and a wonderful invention." He goes on: "The Water clock, *hydrologium* – I have one . . . Those using water are less durable and more accurate, since the sand sometimes piles up or gets damp . . . Finely broken enamel is better than sand . . ." S.v. "Horloge," *Scaligerana ou bons mots . . . de J. Scaliger* (Cologne, 1695), p. 198.

16 For example, "about an hour after sunrise" (Aug. 1553), *Le Journal du Sire de Gouberville*, ed. Eugène de Robillard de Beaurepaire (Caen, 1892), p. 28; "It was about sunset when we arrived" (Sept. 1553), ibid., p. 34.

17 Ibid., pp. 139, 398. On January 4, 1562, Gouberville presented a friend with "a brace of *vitecoqs*" (p. 857).

18 Ibid., p. 747.

19 "Quand les blés commencent à jeter, . . . que déjà le tuyau commence à s'élever." *Joannis Calvini opera quae supersunt omnia*, ed. Baum, Cunitz, Reuss, and Erickson (Corpus Reformatorum), 59 vols. (Brunswick, 1863–1900), XXVII, col. 371. There was a strange step backward: at the height of the century of scientific precision, of the measurement of the meridian and the invention and strict definition of the meter, a "quantitative" [Febvre probably means qualitative – Translator] calendar was again to be seen, and by the grace of Fabre d'Eglantine the months greened and flowered: Floréal, Prairial, Messidor. And the ten days of the decade were given rustic names: grape, saffron, chestnut, horse or colchicum, and so on.

20 Pierre de Bourdeille, Seigneur de Brantôme, *Vie des dames illustres* in *Oeuvres complètes*, ed. Ludovic Lalanne, 11 vols. (Paris, 1864–1882), VIII, 123.

21 Jerome Cardan, *The Book of My Life*, trans. Jean Stoner (New York, 1930), p. 4. The hour's subdivisions were poorly organized. Systems varied: 4 points, 10 minutes, 15 parts, 40 movements, 60 ostenta, 22,560 atoms, said Hrabanus Maurus; 4 points, 40 movements, 480 ounces, 5,640 minutes, said a thirteenth-century text cited by Littré (s.v. "Minute"); 4 points, 10 minutes, 40 momenta, 22,560 atoms, said Jean Michel Albert (d. 1450). See Thorndike, p. 221.

22 Thomas Platter, *Lebensbeschreibung*, ed. Alfred Hartmann (Klosterberg and Basel, 1944), p. 24.

23 *Gargantua*, ch. 41.

24 Charles Sorel, *Histoire comique de Francion*, ed. Emile Roy, 4 vols. (Paris, 1924–31), I, 172.

25 Geoffroy Atkinson, *Les Nouveaux Horizons de la Renaissance française* (Paris, 1935), pp. 270, 416–17.

26 The cage in which the Duke of Nemours was kept at the castle of Pierre Scize in Lyon by order of Louis XI (1476) had required, apart from the ironwork that took the largest expenditure of time, 139 days' work by master and journeyman carpenters, we are told by Deniau. See Arthur Kleinclausz, *Histoire de Lyon*, 3 vols. (Lyon, 1939–52), I, 348. On all of this see Adolf Loos, "Ornament and Crime," (1908), in Ludwig Münz and Gustav Künstler, *Adolf Loos, Pioneer of Modern Architecture*, trans. Harold Meek (New York, 1966), pp. 226–34. What was a paradox then is a truism today.

11

THE MATERIAL CULTURE OF THE CHURCH AND INCIPIENT CONSUMERISM

Richard A. Goldthwaite

Beginning in the thirteenth century, Italy experienced an increase in the production of liturgical apparatus, from altars with the entire panoply of utensils, furnishings, and accessories, to the full complement of the necessary buildings; and the pace of this production continued to rise through the fourteenth to seventeenth centuries. This increased production was due not so much to liturgical innovation as to all the exogenous forces reviewed here arising out of the structural evolution of the church and the greater demand for its services.

These forces were all part of a phenomenon that has been called here a spiritual restlessness among the laity and that resulted in a process of the laicization of religion. This process began in the thirteenth century and continued until the Counter Reformation, when the secular clergy once and for all reasserted its secure control over lay religious practices and sensibilities. Laicization consisted, on the one hand, of greater efforts by the clergy to incorporate the laity into its own institutions and, on the other, of initiatives by the laity to appropriate sacred space for itself. The mendicant movement taken in its entirety – its emergence in the thirteenth century as a new kind of clergy distinct from the regular and secular varieties; the organization of Second Orders for women and of Third Orders for the laity in general; the proliferation of these orders, the rapid and widespread propagation of houses, and their internal divisions – all this represented a gigantic effort by the church to reach out more energetically to the laity, particularly the masses crowding into the growing towns and cities. Likewise, the doctrine of purgatory, with its practice of commemorative masses for the dead, and the cult of the saints, with its further possibilities for divine intercession, aroused the demand of the laity for church services. What is more, these doctrines gave laypersons the wherewithal to take more initiative themselves to satisfy their religious needs. For example, the cults of many of the new saints who won their way into the hearts of Italians arose as local lay movements independent of official canonization. With the confraternal movement, groups of laypersons went so far as to create sacred space for themselves, and private

Richard A. Goldthwaite, "The Material Culture of the Church and Incipient Consumerism," pp. 129–48 from *Wealth and the Demand for Art in Italy 1300–1600*. Baltimore and London: The Johns Hopkins University Press, 1993.

persons went further, both by buying into churches and by carving out consecrated liturgical space for themselves in their private domestic worlds. An extreme lay initiative was the practice of devotions that grew up around religious objects, especially pictures, that people bought in ever-greater quantities for the privacy of their homes – a practice that threatened to take religious sensibilities altogether outside the orbit of the church's control and into the hands of the individual.

This spiritual restlessness among the laity at the end of the Middle Ages impinged mightily on the demand for all those things that constitute the material culture of religion in late medieval, Renaissance, and Baroque Italy. Demand in the market for religious artwork soared to new heights as more and more individual and institutional consumers crowded into it. If institutional proliferation within the church theoretically meant the fragmentation of the church's wealth in the hands of more clerical consumers for the liturgical apparatus, in fact the propagation of new foundations occurred at a time when the church was able to tap more and more of Italy's immense wealth by generating demand for its services. The dynamic growth and transformation of the institutional infrastructure of the church in fact occurred largely because new foundations had the possibility of scrambling to get their share of these outside sources of wealth. The result was direct investment from the private sector in the enlargement or renewal of the church's physical plant. In fact, the soaring demand from the laity, both individually and collectively in confraternities, for commemorative and votive masses and for its own private liturgical space in churches provided much of the wherewithal to sustain the real costs of building, remodeling, and enlarging the physical facilities of the church and of filling churches up with the necessary liturgical equipment, not to mention private forms of devotional art – to pay, in short, for all the religious artwork produced in the Renaissance. Another result of the church's success in marketing its services through goods, however, was the extension of possessiveness of lay persons into the material world of religion; and their direct participation in the market for religious goods exposed religious sensibilities to an incipient consumerism.

The Expansion and Filling Up of Liturgical Space

Statistics to document the filling up of liturgical space and to measure the rise in the production of artwork are hard to come by. For some places we have figures for the increase in the number of churches. Florence, one of the largest cities in Italy, had 126 institutions with something that might be called a church at one time or another before the Black Death, including about 50 parish churches. Notwithstanding the demographic disasters of the fourteenth century, the physical plant of the Florentine church continued to expand. Over the next three hundred years, during which time the city regained barely three-fourths of the population it had had at the time of Dante, about 75 older churches were extensively rebuilt and about 65 new ones built. In 1427 there were 17 monasteries within the city walls and 12 more in the suburbs just outside. At the same time, convents numbered 27 in the city plus 21 in the suburbs; by the end of the century they numbered 37 in the city and 17 outside the walls; and in 1552 they totaled 56. Between 30 and 35 hospices of one kind or another can be counted at any one time in the fifteenth century. Confraternities numbered 43 in the mid-fourteenth century and 96 a century later; 156 have been identified as having existed at one time or another before 1500. Monastic houses numbered 19 in the fifteenth century, with most of the orders and Observant movements represented.[1]

Odds and ends of figures from other places confirm the pattern. In the provincial town of Borgo San Sepolcro, the population growth to about 5,000 in the thirteenth century was accompanied by an increase of ecclesiastical institutions from 3, all monasteries, to 16 with the addition if 2 secular churches, 4 male mendicant houses, and 7 convents, to which must be added 1 major confraternity and 8 hospices; and then 14 more confraternities sprang up in the first half of the fourteenth century. In the fifteenth century, towns that had been much larger before the Black Death still had an extraordinary number of churches: Treviso, with about 9,000 inhabitants, counted 19 churches besides its cathedral, 12 religious houses, and 15 hospices; Pistoia, reduced to half the size of Treviso, had 29 parish churches and 11 hospices; and Prato, about the same size as Pistoia at the time, had 9 parish churches plus 5 monastic foundations (and 5 more arose in the sixteenth century).

Moreover, in many places the number of churches tended to grow from the fifteenth through the sixteenth centuries even though the population did not return to earlier preplague level. Genoa in 1535 had 76 churches, 23 oratories, and 35 religious houses; a century later there were 90 churches, 19 oratories, and 53 houses, most of which were new or completely rebuilt structures. Bologna in the thirteenth century, a much smaller place than Florence and Genoa at the time, had 94 churches; in the early seventeenth century, according to a guide to the churches of the city (which was approximately the same size as Florence at that time but now an administrative center in the papal states), the number had grown to 188, of which 62 were associated with religious houses and 32 either were new or had been largely rebuilt since the mid-sixteenth century. During the next century the total number grew to 270 – a 50 percent increase – and the list gives us a more precise designation of their use: 24 belonged to colleges, schools, and *monti*, 42 to convents, 32 to monasteries, 68 to confraternal organizations, and 24 to guilds. In Verona, a city of about 25,000 to 30,000 inhabitants, the number of churches went from about 70 in the fifteenth century to 90 at the middle of the seventeenth century. In the mid-seventeenth century Naples had almost 100 male houses alone; and in the next century remote towns in Sicily with no more than 10,000 inhabitants could have from 15 to 20 religious houses and as many as a dozen parish churches.[2]

Comparative figures for cities outside Italy are hard to come by. Lyon in the mid-sixteenth century, the third largest city in France with a population of 60,000 to 70,000, had, besides its cathedral, only 7 parish and 4 collegiate churches and 9 male houses. In the thirteenth century, before the rise of the mendicants, Cologne, the largest city in Germany with a population of about 40,000, had a cathedral, 16 parish and 11 collegiate churches, and 10 monastic houses (including nunneries); but many important German towns – Frankfurt, Bamberg, Wurzburg, Ulm – had only 1 parish church. On the eve of the Reformation the great imperial city of Nuremberg, whose population of about 20,000 ranked it among the top half-dozen cities in Germany, had only 2 parish churches (along with 2 other churches, 2 hospitals, 2 convents, and 8 monasteries); and Strasbourg (about the same size) had 7 parish and 5 collegiate churches and 19 religious houses. A better count has been taken for a much smaller place at the same time: Biberach in southern Germany, which, with a population of about 5,000 inhabitants, was about the size of Prato and Pistoia. It had only 10 churches, of which 1 was a convent (there were no monasteries) and several little more than chapels; and there were no more than 38 altars all together. The principal church was the single parish church with its 18 altars.[3]

While Italian churches increased in number, they were also filling up with altars. Additional altars had begun to appear in major churches from the eleventh century onward largely as a response to the need to accommodate more priests, but in the course of the thirteenth century altars began to proliferate at a much higher pace to satisfy the new popular demand for more commemorative and votive masses and to provide local cults and confraternities with their own liturgical identity. According to a panegyric of Milan written in 1288, there were 200 churches with 480 altars in the city and 2,050 churches with 2,600 altars in the countryside – a low ratio of altars to churches compared with the situation a century and a half later, when Alberti threw up his hands in dismay at the contemporary practice of crowding the churches with altars, interrupting his text at this point to say that it was useless to continue on with the subject.[4] Yet another century later, when bishops were fired by Counter Reformation zeal to bring some order to the centuries' accumulation of liturgical apparatus in many churches, they must have shared the experience of the bishop of Brescia, who, on journeying into the countryside to assess the state of the cult in his diocese, found churches cluttered with myriads of altars, some attached to columns and some also in the vestibules. No wonder Carlo Borromeo issued instructions for cleaning out these unsightly accretions of time and restoring dignity to the place of the cult, insisting that each alter be placed, if not in its own chapel, at least in a framed niche to define it architecturally in its own space.[5]

In the towns of north and central Italy the density of churches, and of altars within them, must have been far higher than in any other part of Europe, not counting also chapels in private palaces and the dense stratum of semipublic chapels on private estates throughout the countryside. Notwithstanding the increase in demand for secular painting, the major part of the output of almost all Italian painters, including the very greatest, was directed to meeting the demand for religious pictures. To the enlightened reformers of the late eighteenth century, intent on weeding out inefficiencies, the excessive number of churches and religious houses in relation to the population more than justified the vigor with which they closed down so many of them, cleaning them out of their centuries' accumulation of artwork – an act that ruthlessly uprooted and dispersed throughout the world art market a large part of Italy's huge artistic patrimony.

The Internal Dynamics of Demand

Demand has its own internal dynamics. The very energy of an expanding consumer society such as the one described here can generate other forces that are released within the confines of the market itself and amplify demand. If one consumer does something that catches the attention of others so that they are inspired to follow his or her lead, that consumer's behavior is said to have a demonstration effect in the market that arouses further demand. If in the attempt to outdo one another consumers go beyond imitation, competition becomes an even more powerful force in generating demand for new things, more expensive things, or simply more things. If, finally, the terms of competition are enlarged to include taste, which then begins to change with ever-greater frequency as consumers seek to keep ahead of one another, another powerful dynamic – fashion – is introduced into the market, assuring a continuing renewal of demand so that it is able to maintain and even increase it momentum. In other words, the demonstration effect can set off a kind of chain reaction, releasing new forces such as competition and fashion that converge into, and amplify, demand.

Throughout the Middle Ages the demonstration effect was operative in the market for religious artwork. The development of Gothic architecture in the cathedrals of the Ile de France is generally seen in these terms, and it has been shown how innovation in mosaic decoration of thirteenth-century Roman churches led to attempts to update older work.[6] Many contracts surviving from the later fourteenth century in Italy document explicit instructions for the imitation of an existing work. In a traditional preindustrial economy in which the role of the artist was not yet highly developed, the client could point to something close at hand that represented more or less the model to be followed. Contracts of this kind do not necessarily mean that exact imitation was required; the intention was probably to give only general indications of what was desired in the easiest way possible. For example, when in 1546 Count Giovanni Antonio Caracciolo made provisions in his will for the decoration of his family chapel in Naples, he cited a sculpted image and two tombs, each in separate chapels in other churches, to give an idea of what he wanted.[7]

In this kind of market the appearance of something new or arresting in its difference caught the attention of other potential consumers. For example, an altarpiece painted by Foppa in Genoa about 1483 was designated the model in two subsequent contracts for altarpieces in other churches in the city; likewise, the *Coronation of the Virgin* Ghirlandaio painted for a Franciscan church in provincial Narni around 1485 immediately aroused other houses of the order in the vicinity to commission copies, including a convent near Perugia that twenty years later commissioned the young Raphael to do a picture like it.[8] When documentation is otherwise lacking, this pattern of the diffusion of imitative or similar works through the network of a religious order can often be accounted for in this way. The fresco cycles in the great church of Saint Francis at Assisi were obvious models for other churches in the order; and in Siena the polyptychs that appeared in Franciscan and Dominican churches in the early fourteenth century seem to have set a fashion for a new art form that subsequently not only spread through provincial houses of these orders but also was taken up by other orders that previously had shown no interest in multipanel paintings. Similarly, the wall-type rood screens frescoed by Foppa in two Observant Franciscan churches in Lombardy were widely imitated within the order throughout the region at the end of the fifteenth century.[9]

It is just one step from imitation to open competition, but it can be a big step for the further growth of an already expanding and crowded market. As far back as the fifth century, inscriptions attest that competition was a strong motive for church building.[10] Raul Glaber thought competition explained why there were so many beautiful churches in the eleventh century, and not long afterward the great abbot–builder Suger admitted as much about his own motivations. This competitive impulse has also been inferred from the sequence of Gothic cathedrals whose vaults rose higher and higher – at Paris, Chartres, Rheims, Amiens – until finally (in 1284) at Beauvais they came tumbling down. In the context of Italian urban civilization, public buildings that were particularly expressive of status figured in the rivalries among communes; and the formulation of the concept of magnificence in the Renaissance fully rationalized open competition among private builders.

As a result of internal factions within religious orders as well as rivalry among individual institutions for popular support, the spirit of competition also permeated the market for religious artwork. As laymen appropriated church space for their own altars and chapels, or acquired benefices with control over an entire church, demand got an additional boost from all the obsessions and rivalries of the social and political worlds. It has been inferred from some of the contracts of the kind cited above, in which consumers clearly had an eye on other works, that competition was indeed lurking behind these envious glances, although few are as explicit as Raphael's 1505 commission to paint a picture like the one Ghirlandaio had done twenty years earlier but "of higher perfection, if it is possible."[11] As this instance of patronage by a Franciscan house indicates, not even the mendicants, with their disdain for wealth, were immune to the competitive spirit. In 1422 the Dominicans of Santa Maria Novella in Florence, becoming only too conscious of the building going on all around them, appointed a committee to consider extensive rebuilding "in order to imitate the other churches and to work for the embellishment of the monastery";[12] in 1521 the Dominicans of San Niccolò in Venice successfully blocked the plans of Observant Franciscans to erect a church they felt would have been too near their own.[13]

Confraternities, too, felt the pressures to outdo one another, especially on the occasions of the public processions in which they participated on great holidays, when they could conspicuously demonstrate their status – occasions that gave social and political overtones to the performance of a basic religious function. This competition with others could consume so much of the patrimony of confraternities that a marked concern with the problem came to be written into later statutes.[14] In Venice the government injected a strong civic spirit into the rivalry among those confraternities it recognized as having the special status of *grande*, thereby committing them to ambitious building programs to outdo one another; but also among the dozens of small confraternities in Venice, competition has been cited as the most important motive for the commissioning of ambitious altarpieces.[15] Rivalry among such patrons is one reason that they sometimes sponsored formal competitions among artists to get the best products possible.

Once released in the marketplace, competition amplifies demand by setting new standards for consumption that usually involve greater magnitude of expenditure. The cathedrals of Siena, Florence, Bologna, and Milan in the fourteenth and fifteenth centuries are notable examples of competition among communes to have a bigger building or one built with more expensive materials or with more elaborate and monumental sculptural decoration. The Florentines, besides trying to outdo them all in their grandiose program for free-standing, greater-than-life-sized sculptures on the façade and campanile and for colossal figures high up on the drum of the cupola, declared yet other grounds for competition – daring technology – when they decided to accept Brunelleschi's plan for covering the crossing of their cathedral. Once they got their new cathedral, they continued their extravagance inside with luxurious and innovative internal appointments. Competition can thus account for a powerful disposition to spend more and more for religious artwork, and these expenditures can take several forms depending on what the stakes of competition are – size, quantity, inherent luxury, craftsmanship.

Introduce, finally, taste into this complex of notions about what the stakes are, and a dynamic for change dependent on fashion is released that can further amplify demand. When the desire arose, in the thirteenth century, to have a picture on the high altar of their cathedral, the Sienese were content to transfer an altar front to the altar table; but once such an object enjoyed so much public prominence, the desire arose to increase its grandeur – and so by the end of the century they commissioned the great *Maestà* by Duccio. In fifteenth-century Venice, where pictorial style changed rapidly, guilds who had chapels in major churches and saw their colleagues put up altar tables in more up-to-date styles felt the pressure to follow suit even when they had had a picture painted not too many years earlier. In sixteenth-century Florence the grand duke took advantage of Tridentine reforms calling for the cleaning out of the centuries' accumulation of clutter in church interiors to justify the refurbishing of both Santa Croce and Santa Maria Novella according to the latest aesthetic criteria, which dictated side altars evenly spaced and of equal size.

Fashion arouses demand not necessarily for more things or something of greater magnitude but for something different; and if the new object is in fact cheaper, its replacement frequency following rapid change of fashion may stimulate growth of productive forces that more than make up for its decline in value. Taste is therefore a dynamic above all for renewal, and it possesses its own momentum. This momentum counted for much in the history of secular art in the Italian Renaissance, eventually constituting a good part of the demand factor – to the point that, perhaps for the first time in the history of art, artists themselves were in a position to move in aggressively and win a commanding position over the market. Domenico Veneziano's famous letter to Piero de' Medici in 1438 is perhaps the earliest extant expression of how for both producer and client competition was beginning to impinge on the market: he promises to produce a picture as marvelous as any that could be done by other prominent painters, and he is sure his work will bring Piero much honor.

Painters of religious pictures, moreover, realized the considerable potential of their products for variation as pictorial forms responsive to changing fashions and taste and to changing ideas, attitudes, and sentiments arising from religious sensibilities. Painting had the potential for rendering images with infinite variety; and once this capability was exploited to enhance the efficacy of images in inviting the observer to respond, powerful new rhetorical possibilities opened up. Panel paintings in particular, by freeing the painted image both from the strictly liturgical context of the altar and from the narrative context of mural painting, had a potential for psychological meaning heretofore unknown; and the change toward naturalism, realism, and secular subject matter gave painting of all kinds a new social role outside the performance of the liturgy. Thus charged with all kinds of cultural and psychological meaning, painting became responsive to an enormous variety of influences – doctrine, popular spiritual movements, political propaganda, social values, psychological needs. Painting, therefore, became the ready instrument of a new kind of mass religion. Its history in the later Middle Ages is very much the story of how it realized its market potential as a popular art form responsive to devotional movements and freed from the control of the church.

This enlargement of the content of painting gave the artist greater possibilities for developing new techniques of representing images and refining his own style. All these elements increasingly went into the taste for a picture. The content of art thus broadened considerably; and as a result of this extraordinary sensitivity to changes in the larger world, the pace of change within the pictorial arts accelerated from the fourteenth century onward. Moreover, to the extent that these influences vary over time, they increased the susceptibility of art to change and variety; hence taste, including fashion, came increasingly to the fore in the art market. In short, the industry was successful in meeting the growing demand through product and process innovation – by introducing new and accessible, useful, malleable, and changeable products.

The market potential for the pictorial arts was enormous: for mural decoration it was nothing less than the walls of every church, for altar pictures nothing less than all the altars in those churches, and for panel painting nothing less than every home and even every room in the home. Murals and painting on wood were relatively inexpensive compared with the earlier pictorial forms of mosaics and sculpted images made from materials with high intrinsic value or requiring intensive labor input, and costs of the materials of painting fell lower as time wore on – that is, as the market expanded. The industry was highly flexible in its organization; and by introducing new and cheaper products, it was successful in arousing demand to levels never before achieved. By the sixteenth century, artisans were enjoying an expanding market in which, to a greater degree than ever before in the history of the West, a premium was put on innovation and invention. Vasari observed this situation with great insight: his concept of progress in the arts was rooted in his understanding of what was happening in a marketplace in which artisans struggling for a living kept raising the ante in their competition to capture more of the market. Once the producer takes the initiative and is able to shift control of the market from the demand to the supply side, the consumer economy is born.

The Generation of Pictorial Culture

From the end of the thirteenth century onward, as Italians found their religious experiences focused increasingly on new pictorial forms, their lives came to be filled with images. Theirs was a pictorial world much more dense with images than that known by most other Europeans. Johan

Huizinga, commenting on northern attitudes toward art at the end of the Middle Ages, remarked that the craving for symbolism and allegory became an obsession to convert every mental concept into a pictorial image, so that at all levels of society "art in these times was still wrapped up in life." For the Italians more than for other Europeans, however, the converse was also true: life was completely wrapped up in art.

In the Byzantine world icons were a source of spiritual powers associated with the holy people and emperors they represented. When they were imported into Italy in the thirteenth century, they brought something of their mystery with them; but images in the West did not have the sanctity they had in the East, where they were closely tied to the liturgy. As pictorial forms evolved in the looser religious society of the West, therefore, new rhetorical possibilities opened up. The didactic function of pictures was developed by the friars in association with their preaching mission, and devotional images such as the Pietà appeared that had nothing to do with the narrative tradition of the Bible or with any liturgical function. Along with these iconographical innovations, figures of Christ, the Madonna, and the saints became humanized in their depiction, so that the observer could establish a personal and emotional relation with them. All this enriched the pictorial culture of Europeans – and nowhere more so than in Italy.

By the end of the fifteenth century, production of pictorial decoration of churches in Italy had reached a much higher level than in most other parts of Europe. The painted altarpiece, in contrast to the sculpted form so much more common in northern Europe (except for Flanders), probably became a standard fixture; and today it is hard to imagine an Italian church without pictures at its various altar tables. The growth in the size of these pictures is itself impressive: the evolution of the typical altarpiece from the end of the thirteenth century onward, until it reached the enormous proportions of the pictures sixteenth-century artists painted in the normal course of their work, can be replayed by a walk through the chronologically organized galleries of any major museum.

As no other Europeans, including the Flemish, Italians became accustomed to seeing the walls of their churches covered with images. Within a century of the first great fresco cycles, mendicant churches in many Italian towns were entirely frescoed from floor to ceiling; and the painting of walls extended deep into the inner recesses of monasteries – to refectories, chapter rooms, cloisters – converting interior architecture into pictorial decoration.[16] If frescoed walls are not so much in evidence today as altarpieces, it is chiefly because so many were painted over as the result of the new architectural aesthetic that came to dominate taste in the fifteenth century. Yet, however successful Renaissance architects were in recovering the blank wall for their own aesthetic, the pictorial impulse broke through again in the sixteenth century – apparently first in a major way at the Cathedral, San Sigismondo, and other churches of Cremona. Moreover, vaulted ceilings and cupolas along with wall surfaces were appropriated for pictorial decoration that dissolved architecture and enveloped worshipers with images now in an illusionistic way they had never experienced in the earlier mendicant churches. Some major sixteenth-century artists spent most of their time painting extensive chapel cycles. Domenichino worked almost exclusively on just one project, the Cappella del Tesoro in Naples, for the last decade of his life.

The communal ethos also found outlets in the representative arts of painting and sculpture. Sacred images proliferated in the street and squares not just to incite private devotion but to enlist the holy in the effort to maintain public order.[17] Beginning in the thirteenth century, painted rooms in public places depicted the values underlying good government and commemorated historical events in the life of the commune. In the fourteenth and fifteenth centuries residents of some towns – above all, Florentines – expressed their public indignation against convicted enemies of the public interest – bankrupts, debtors, forgers, traitors – by having them painted, so that they were fully recognizable, on the exterior walls of government buildings at street level for all to see, making the place into what has been termed a "negative church" where sinners of all kinds were displayed.[18] By the later fifteenth century people in the streets also encountered images on a grand scale in the frescoes and graffiti that decorated entire palace façades in many cites. These major art forms, along with the *pittura infamante* on communal buildings, have long since been lost (and therefore hardly studied) through the wear of time, so that it is impossible for us to re-create the extensive pictorial world that engulfed many Italians as they went through the streets on their daily tasks.

Finally, with the rise of devotional piety and the diffusion of inexpensive panel paintings throughout the marketplace, Italians could take pictures home with them and into their private lives. At the beginning of the fifteenth century the cardinal Giovanni Dominici emphasized the importance of having paintings in the home, especially pictures of child saints and young virgins, for the religious edification of children; he would "make the home like a temple with paintings." Contemporary inventories from Florence reveal how common – and how numerous – pictures came to be in the workshops and homes of people of modest wealth, often showing up in every room, including the kitchen; and servants owned them as well. The surviving record book of Neri di Bicci documents the profitability of this popular market for one of the painters who supplied it, and the careers of Lorenzo Lotto in the Marches and of the Bassano in the Veneto are evidence that the popular taste for painting had spread also into the provinces.

By the fifteenth century, images in the private world of the upper classes, as in the public world, began to become secularized. The tradition of decorating palaces with chivalric scenes and gardens populated with great personages and ancestors goes back at least as far as the papal palace at Avignon and continued in Verona, Ferrara, Pavia, Mantua, and other princely centers at the end of the fourteenth century. A 1414 contract for fresco decoration in the home of Nicolò Grimaldi in Genoa refers to similar scenes in three other houses in this merchant city,[19] and interior frescoes survive from the fifteenth century in Florence (all in villas), Ferrara, Mantua, and elsewhere, not to mention the increasing literary references to them by such writers as Sabadino degli Arienti. By the sixteenth century the rich and powerful were much possessed by the fashion for decorating the interior walls and ceilings of their palaces with vast scenes filled with historical and literary materials of some significance to their own lives. Advisors helped them work out learned programs of all kinds, and in his manual of 1587 Armenini included a section on the appropriate subjects for decoration of private palaces. The Campi worked extensively in private palaces of Cremona; Nosadella was known above all as a fresco painter of private houses, although most of his work is lost; and Prospero Fontana spent most of his time as an interior decorator traveling around northern Italy to Genoa, Bologna, Florence, Parma, and Rome. These and other sixteenth-century painters, like Pordenone, made the major part of their living frescoing private homes both inside and out. Meanwhile, in the fifteenth century, pictures with secular subject matter began to appear on chests (a principal item of furniture at the time) and then increasingly in panel paintings on walls – a subject we shall return to below. Finally, many of the other art forms developed in Renaissance Italy – painted and transparent smalto, niello, maiolica, wood intarsia, ecclesiastical garments, stained glass – were perfected largely as pictorial forms laden with illustrative material in a naturalistic style that was a virtuoso defiance of the inherent physical limitations of these media, so strong was the pictorial impulse of the age.

This expansion of the pictorial arts beginning in the later thirteenth century and the extent to which Italians eventually found themselves encountering images in churches, on the streets, in their homes, and even on dishes at the dinner table have never been adequately assessed. Pictures had a profound effect on the religious mentality by sharpening the sensibility to images and even conditioning modes of expression. Italians found their religious lives increasingly caught up in a pictorial world that came to exist on its own terms as a new kind of reality located somewhere between this world and God's realm. Images, once they were isolated on panels and detached from both a liturgical context and larger decorative schemes, could invite contemplative penetration into the holy realm, involving the viewer in an intimate and private psychological experience: they acquired miraculous powers and commonly came to speak to observers, to act on them, and to react to them. Saint Giovanni Gualberto and Saint Francis underwent conversions while contemplating the crucifix, and many visionaries from Saint Catherine of Siena in the fourteenth century to the Counter Reformation saints of the later sixteenth century were influenced if not in fact stimulated by pictures.[20] Images could, of course, also work miracles, especially images of the virgin; and the large number of new churches constructed in the fifteenth century and variously dedicated to Santa Maria – delle Carceri, della Consolazione, delle Grazie, della Quercia – attests the frequency of such events. By the fifteenth century Italians commonly expressed their private gratitude for the miraculous intercession of saints in the solution of their personal problems by leaving a picture as an ex-voto recording the event at the appropriate shrine, usually a highly frequented pilgrimage site. Not surprisingly with this kind of pictorial sensibility, people on their deathbeds wanted to fix their attention on images of holy figures, and confraternities sprang up to minister to criminals condemned to death by brandishing holy images before their eyes even as they ascended the scaffold.[21]

The importance of the image for the ritual of prayer within one's own household, where in the private exercise of their religious devotions Italians found their attention increasingly fixed on pictures, has been illustrated by Richard Trexler's analysis of evidence from fifteenth-century Florence. Giovanni Morelli describes in his record book how he concentrates on images, weeps before them, kisses and embraces them, and then prays to them. Contemporary anecdotes (which, if not reporting reality, reflect a certain verisimilitude) illustrate how, as in any human relation, tension could arise between the image and its interlocutor: a shoemaker, angered by a picture of Saint John because it had given an unsatisfactory answer to a question about his wife's faithfulness, defiantly expresses his deep sense of betrayal after years of devotion to the image, curses it, and announces his abandonment of it; another man whose son died despite appeals to an image of Christ hurls his rage at the image, telling it he would have done better to have appealed to another image of Christ nearby.[22] With the secularization of the pictorial world in the Renaissance, images could also threaten the moral health of the soul, if we can accept the suggestion of Carlo Ginzburg that by the sixteenth century priest-confessors had come to regard sight as the sense most susceptible to sin and images as the occasion for the most serious sin they had to deal with – lust.

The expanding pictorial world of the Italians was also one in which they themselves entered. Frescoes – from the *pittura infamante* on the external walls of the town hall to major scenes decorating the interiors of both princely palaces and churches – were crowded with contemporary portraits, including often the artist himself peering out at the public. Ghirlandaio's numerous fresco cycles in the Sassetti chapel at Santa Trinita, the Tornabuoni chapel at Santa Maria Novella, and elsewhere are the most notable examples of religious scenes transformed into group portraits. In his discussion of how to compose a painted scene, Alberti advised the insertion of portraits of well-known persons so that the viewer could have greater empathy with the picture. No scene – historical or contemporary, secular or religious – was out of bounds. Court personalities and citizens at Milan under the Sforza got themselves depicted in Leonardo's *Last Supper* (as Antonio de Beatis remarks in his travel journal of 1517–18), and Michelangelo put himself and others into his *Last Judgment* in the Sistine Chapel. Nor has any society ever gone in so enthusiastically for portraiture as a separate form. After religious works, portraits constituted the most important output of many artists and the most numerous kind of picture found in many homes. Scholars have never been able to explain satisfactorily just what Italians saw in these kinds of visual representations of themselves – propitiation, family piety, propaganda, pride, remembrance, introspection – but obviously their sense of themselves was conditioned by the experience of occupying a world of representational art and by the knowledge of being ever on view even apart from their personal presence.[23]

Before the elaboration of secular art in the Renaissance, painting in the religious tradition aroused an awareness of the pleasure in beauty. Communal documents from the early fourteenth century explicitly state this criterion for public projects, and the history of Giotto's fame in fourteenth-century Florence testifies to the extent such sensibilities were diffused throughout society. The impact painting began to make also on intellectuals as a special kind of activity is manifest in the reputation Giotto enjoyed already within the generation following his death. Boccaccio recognized a distinction in the ways the artist appealed to the ignorant and to the wise; and in his testament Petrarch observed that the ignorant were incapable of appreciating the beauty of the picture of the Virgin by Giotto he owned.

Beginning with Alberti in the fifteenth century, the art of painting – still primarily a religious medium – came in for serious intellectual discussion. In the medieval tradition pictures and symbols had long been regarded as a necessary adjunct to reading in the way they acted on the memory and hence helped in the recollection and even comprehension of a text,[24] but now the humanists enlarged the power of the image by incorporating them into their literary culture. On the one hand, they loaded images with complex ideas to raise them above the level of mere representations or symbols with simple correspondences to become charged with abstract meaning; hence they elaborated emblems, imprese, hieroglyphs, and other such devices whose highly compressed complexity revealed "a higher reality whose very presence exerted its mysterious effects."[25] On the other hand, the recognition of the power of the visual image to convince and to impress itself on the mind led intellectuals to refine the rhetorical device of creating pictorial images with words to put ideas across to readers and auditors. Following this course, painting allied itself with literature; and once painting was admitted to this rhetorical culture of the imitative arts deeply steeped in the classical tradition, the first claims were made for it as a higher intellectual activity that separated it from the mechanical arts and placed it as a sister art alongside poetry. The secularization and privatization of painting opened the way for an infinite range of subject matter and a corresponding enlargement of its rhetorical possibilities. While the visual arts were thus winning a way into the intellectual's world, artists themselves began to assert intellectual claims on their own terms. As a consequence, artists had greater range for innovation, and patrons in turn enlarged their aesthetic experiences. This venture of Italians into a seemingly infinite pictorial world thus led to the discovery of art as a particular realm of human activity, where the mind was elevated to a new sphere of operation.

When, in the sixteenth century, the cry of iconoclasm began to be heard north of the Alps, it fell on deaf ears in Italy. The pictorial world, along with the luxury of the entire liturgical apparatus, was too solidly in place. Art and the artist had won impressive credentials with the intellectual and social establishment outside the church. Zwingli's condemnation of holy images on the ground that, having been made by man himself, they are unworthy of his veneration could hardly make sense in a culture that was venerating them, at least in part, for the very reason that these things were in fact made by men – men with special, artistic talents. More important, images had worked their way into the very heart of religious practices and sensibilities. Italian writers who rallied to the cause of religious imagery against the attacks from Protestant reformers hardly made a defense at all, largely ignoring the iconoclasts' arguments, so much did they take it for granted that imagery had made an indelible impression on the Italian subconscious. Images, according to Bishop Paleotti, the author of the most celebrated tract on the subject, were "the strongest, most efficient instrument" for dominating, even ravishing, the senses; for the Jesuits, images inspired mystical contemplation and thereby enhanced spirituality. To remove them would have threatened the stability of the social order.[26]

It has been too little observed that the iconoclasm of the Protestant north was part of a larger program to rid the church not only of images but of the entire material culture of luxury that had grown up around the liturgy and to redirect that wealth to the poor. The iconoclasts' objections to much of the traditional liturgical apparatus was that it was sensuous in its luxury, it absorbed too much church wealth, and it deprived the poor of needed sustenance. Reformers were concerned about the monetary value of liturgical utensils, including candles as well as pictures; and in clearing out their churches of all these things, they were often explicit that money saved should go to the poor. As Zwingli saw it, man himself, especially the poor, should be the proper object of veneration, since people are made in God's image.[27]

The success of the Protestants' policy against the traditional material culture of the liturgy, and the little attention the Counter Reformation church in the north seemingly gave to the subject – to judge from recent studies of Speyer and the Palatinate, of Lyon and its environs, and of Champagne – indicate rather different traditions in the north and in Italy. In any case, in Italy, for all the Tridentine sumptuary legislation directed against luxury in the personal lives of the clergy, there could hardly be any pulling back from the use of luxury to enhance the entire liturgical apparatus and from the further development of the pictorial arts to appeal to religious sensibilities. The material culture of worship built on the propositions that God needs to be venerated and admired and that the visible convinces was too embedded in tradition. Reform orders such as the Capuchins and the Jesuits who, like the Cistercians, Franciscans, and a host of others before them, had originally wanted severely stark churches eventually found themselves operating in rich and sumptuous places. That most zealous of reforming prelates, Carlo Borromeo, did not hesitate to call for marble and other precious objects in his instructions for endowing churches with the splendor and decorum proper to holy places. The Baroque church, presenting itself as a completely orchestrated program of extravagantly rich decoration and profuse imagery extending throughout the entire space, was a logical outcome in the history of the material culture of Christianity. By this time a veritable consumerism in the religious sphere had been defined and fully endorsed by the church itself.

Italians, therefore, made little of the argument that the wealth incorporated in the liturgical apparatus could be better used to help the poor. Some church thinkers, confronted with mounting cries from reformers for charity to the poor, defended extravagant expenditures on the grounds that, quite simply, God comes first.[28]

Michelangelo felt that the "most noble science" of painting came from heaven and that, although it therefore belonged to no country, it in fact just happened to be Italian. A powerful tradition of romanticized notions subsequently grew up to place art more firmly in the Italian character; and many would agree with Martin Wackernagel that a "deeply underlying fact" of Italian civilization was "the powerful need to look at images that was alive in all levels of the population; . . . the directly artistic aspect of the work of art, of form's powers of aesthetic stimulation and attraction [figures] only in the last place [as almost a] side effect, and not always an absolutely necessary one."[29] To explain this "need for art" and why the Italian artistic tradition is so extraordinary in comparison with that of other European countries, however, it is not enough to postulate, with Wackernagel and so many others, "an elemental instinctive drive." Instead, if Italians underwent some kind of profound transformation in their basic modes of perception, it was because they were engulfed in images and luxury; the "need for art" was the result of a historical process in which the changing world of material goods conditioned the modes of perception of an entire population.

NOTES

1 Estimates of the number of institutions and their population have been attempted by J. Henderson, "Religious Confraternities and Death in Early Renaissance Florence," in *Florence and Italy*, ed. P. Denley and C. Elam (London, 1988), p. 384; and Charles de la Roncière, "Les confréries en Toscane au XIV et XV siècles d'après les travaux récents," in *Confraternite romane: Esperienza religiosa, società, commitenza artistica*, ed. Luigi Fiorani (Rome, 1984); for religious houses, see Gene Brucker, "Monasteries, Friaries and Nunneries," in *Christianity and the Renaissance: Image and Religious Imagination in the Quattrocento*, ed. T. Verdon and J. Henderson (Syracuse, 1990); and Roberto Bizzocchi, *Chiesa e potere nella Toscana del Quattrocento* (Bologna, 1987), p. 31.
2 Giorgio Doria, "Investimenti della nobiltà genovese nell'edilizia di prestigio (1530–1630)," *Studi storici* 27 (1986), 18 n.; Matteo Mainardi, *Origine e fondatione di tutte le chiese . . . di Bologna* (Bologna, 1633); Luigi Montieri, *Catalogo di tutte le Chiese . . . di Bologna* (Bologna, n.d. [but during pontificate of Benedetto XIV]); Giorgio Borelli, *Città e campagna in età preindustriale, XVI–XVIII secolo* (Verona, 1986), p. 360; Luigi Pesce, *La chiesa di Treviso nel primo Quattrocento* (Rome, 1987), 1:142–59 and vol. 2, apps.; Maria Rosa, "Chiesa e la città," in *Prato, Storia di una città*, vol. 2, ed., E. Fasano Guarini (Prato, 1986); James R. Banker, *Death in the Community: Memorialization and Confraternities in an Italian Commune in the Late Middle Ages* (Athens, Ga., and London, 1989), pp. 21–32; David Herlihy, *Medieval and Renaissance Pistoia: The Social History of an Italian Town, 1200–1430* (New Haven, 1967), pp. 244, 248; Enrico Bacco, *Naples: An Early Guide*, ed. and trans. E. Gardiner (New York, 1991), pp. 50–54.
3 Philip T. Hoffman, *Church and Community in the Diocese of Lyon, 1500–1789*, (New Haven, 1984), pp. 11–16; John B. Freed, *The Friars in German Society in the Thirteenth Century* (Cambridge, Mass., 1977), p. 80; Gerald Strauss, *Nuremberg in the Sixteenth Century* (New York, 1966), p. 157; Thomas Brady, *Ruling Class, Regime, and Reformation at Strasbourg* (Leiden, 1978), p. 217; Christopher S. Wood, "In Defense of Images: Two Local Rejoinders to the Zwinglian Iconoclasm," *Sixteenth Century Journal* 19 (1988), 25–44.
4 Leon Battista Alberti, *L'architettura*, ed. Giovanni Orlandi (Milan, 1966), 2:628; the Milanese text is cited in Giorgio Cracco, "La 'cura animarum' nella cultura laica del tardo Medioevo (lo specchio delle 'laudes civitatum')," in *Pievi e parrocchie in Italia nel Basso Medioevo (Sec. XIII–XV)* (Rome, 1984), 1:561.
5 Daniele Montanari, *Disciplinamento in terra veneta* (Bologna, 1987), p. 93; Maria Luisa Gatti Perer, "Cultura e socialità dell'altare barocco nell'antica Diocesi di Milano," *Arte Lombarda*, 42-3 (1975), pp. 17–18.
6 William Tronzo, "Apse Decoration, the Liturgy, and the Perception of Art in Medieval Rome: S. Maria in Trastevere and S. Maria Maggiore," in *Italian Church Decoration of the Middle Ages and Early Renaissance: Functions, Forms and Regional Traditions* (Bologna, 1989), pp. 167–93.
7 Maria Antonietta Visceglia, "Corpo e sepoltura nei testamenti della nobiltà napoletana XVI–XVIII secolo," *Quaderni storici* 17 (1982), 605.
8 Jocelyn Ffoulkes and Rodolfo Maiocchi, *Vicenzo Foppa of Brescia, Founder of the Lombard School: His Life and Works* (London and New York, 1909), pp. 133–34; Roger Jones and Nicholas Penny, *Raphael* (New Haven, 1983), pp. 16–17.
9 Alessandro Nova, "I tramezzi in Lombardia fra XV e XVI secolo: scene della Passione e devozione francescana," in *Il francescanesimo in Lombardia* (Milan, 1983), pp. 197–215.
10 Bryan Ward-Perkins, *From Classical Antiquity to the Middle Ages: Urban Public Building in Northern and Central Italy, AD 300–850* (Oxford, 1984), pp. 75-7.

11 Vincenzo Golzio, *Raffaello nei documenti, nelle testimonianze dei contemporanei e nella letteratura del suo secolo* (Vatican City, 1936), pp. 11–13.

12 Gene Brucker, *Renaissance Florence* (Berkeley, 1969), p. 34.

13 Rona Goffen, *Piety and Patronage in Renaissance Venice: Bellini, Titian, and the Franciscans* (New Haven and London, 1986), p. 5.

14 Roberto Rusconi, "Confraternite, compagnie e devozioni," in *Storia d'Italia: Annali*, vol. 9 (1986), p. 497.

15 Patricia Fortini Brown, "Honor and Necessity: The Dynamics of Patronage in the Confraternities of Renaissance Venice," *Studi veneziani* 14 (1987), 207; Peter Humfrey, "Competitive Devotions: The Venetian *scuole piccole* as Donors of Altarpieces in the years around 1500," *Art Bulletin* 70 (1988), 401–23, p. 405.

16 A process never systematically studied, according to Wolfgang Braunfels, *Monasteries of Western Europe* (London, 1972), p. 142.

17 Edward Muir, "The Virgin on the Street Corner: The Place of the Sacred in Italian Cities," in *Religion and Culture in the Renaissance and Reformation*, ed. S. Ozment (Kirksville, Mo., 1989), p. 25.

18 The characterization comes from Samuel Y. Edgerton, "Icons of Justice," *Past and Present* 89 (1980), 28–38.

19 Antonia Borlandi, "Pittura politica e committenza nel primo Quattrocento genovese," *Renaissance Studies in Honor of Craig Hugh Smyth*, ed. A. Morough et al. (Florence, 1985), 2:71.

20 Millard Meiss, *Painting in Florence and Siena after the Black Death* (Princeton, 1951), ch. 5; Mario Fanti, "Voglia di Paradiso: Mistici, pittori, e committenti a Bologna fra Cinquecento e Seicento," in *Dall'avanguardia dei Carracci al secolo barocco: Bologna, 1580–1600*, ed. Andrea Emiliani (Bologna, 1988), p. 90.

21 Samuel Y. Edgerton, "A Little-Known 'Purpose of Art' in the Italian Renaissance," *Art History* 2 (1979), 45–61.

22 Richard Trexler, *Public Life in Renaissance Florence* (New York, 1980), pp. 119–21, 176–80; Hans R. Hahnloser, "Culte de l'image au moyen âge," in *Cristianesimo e ragion di stato: L'umanesimo e il demoniaco nell'arte*, ed. Enrico Castelli (Rome, 1953), pp. 225–33.

23 Enrico Castelnuovo, "Il significato del ritratto pittorico nella società," in the Einaudi *Storia d'Italia*, vol. 5 (Turin, 1972), pp. 1033–94, offers little discussion of function and does not resolve the problem of the popularity of this form.

24 Mary Carruthers, *The Book of Memory: A Study of Memory in Medieval Culture* (Cambridge, 1990), pp. 221–9.

25 E. H. Gombrich, "*Icones Symbolicae*: Philosophies of Symbolism and Their Bearing on Art," in his *Symbolic Images: Studies in the Art of the Renaissance* (Chicago, 1972), p. 179.

26 This is the theme of Giuseppe Scavizzi, "La teologia cattolica e le immagini durante il XVI secolo," *Storia dell'arte*, no. 21 (1974), 171–212.

27 Lee Palmer Wandel, "The Reform of the Images: New Visualizations of the Christian Community at Zürich," *Archiv für Reformationsgeschichte* 80 (1989), 105–24.

28 Scavizzi, "Teologia cattolica," pp. 201–4.

29 Martin Wackernagel, *The World of the Florentine Renaissance Artist: Projects and Patrons, Workshop and Art Market* (Princeton, 1981), pp. 7–8.

12

From a Culture of Science toward the Enlightenment

Kathleen Wellman

"A model of our civilization and a mirror of human life" – so Charles Sorel expressed his appreciation of the comprehensive and inclusive character of Renaudot's conferences. They provided a model of civilization because of their open, accessible, and inclusive form of intellectual exchange. They mirrored human life in the range of topics they covered, from the natural to the political.

This conclusion begins then, with the unique character of Renaudot's conferences. By Renaudot's deliberate design, there can be no protagonists in this history. Because of his highly unusual notion that the most appropriate way to convey knowledge is to have anonymous speakers make presentations in a group as large as the room could hold, the efforts of historians to attach concrete biographical data to any of the participants or to provide a sociological analysis of the group and its ideas have been thwarted.[1] We know no better at the end of this study who attended the conferences than we did at the beginning. Even if more evidence ultimately comes to light about individual participants, it would nonetheless remain impossible to assign specific speeches to them. So this history is populated by the ideas of those who attended. Those ideas are naked, without the robes of external authority. Only the intellectual antecedents so significant that they could be mentioned without violating the spirit of Renaudot's injunction against sustaining one's argument through the authority of others – Aristotle, Plato, Cicero, Montaigne, Ficino – appear in this history and then only as venerated shades. Participants did not embellish their remarks with extensive quotations, so even the intellectual context is more suggestive than concrete. The disembodied character of these conferences frustrates the historian's occupational proclivity to anchor ideas in a concrete context.

Despite the limits of the historical analysis one can bring to bear, these documents belong in our histories of the seventeenth century. They illuminate virtually every topic they address, from science to gender. Because they treat such a broad array of topics in such an undogmatic way, they better represent contemporary opinion than do elite academies. Because they took place in

Kathleen Wellman, "From a Culture of Science toward the Enlightenment," pp. 367–82, 426–7 from *Making Science Social: The Conferences of Théophraste Renaudot 1633–1642*. Norman: University of Oklahoma Press, 2003.

the 1630s and 1640s, crucial decades in the development of the new science and absolutism, they add important dimensions to our understanding of the early seventeenth century. But their import is even greater. They amplify – and in some cases provide counter-narratives to – conventional accounts of the history of France, its intellectual history, and particularly the history of early modern science.

The lacunae in our historical knowledge of this group were quite deliberately created: sociological knowledge was not as significant as what they discussed; it would only distract the reader from the ideas, precluding the ultimate recognition of and assent to truth. So, to our surprise, participants did not consider the experiments they performed worth publishing and recording, although such records would better integrate them into the history of science and would enhance their modern reputation. Instead it was important to publish multiple views on the questions raised. The participants produced an extensive record of their conversations to edify their contemporaries, to provide the service of comprehensive (by their lights) public knowledge so that truth would out. This truth would only be clouded by such extraneous information as the name, status, and reputation of the participants.

The conferences deliberately intended to treat a full range of questions, to present a veritable seventeenth-century encyclopedia. They frequently raise these issues as questions (often conventional questions within the *quodlibetal* tradition), and the knowledge presented is quite deliberately polyvalent. They do not mean to offer one, definitive answer, so their notion of an encyclopedia is somewhat different from that of the grand *Encyclopédie* of d'Alembert and Diderot. This encyclopedia stands as a monument to eighteenth-century thought – and indeed it would be unthinkable for historians to deny that role to the *Encyclopédie*. But in many ways Renaudot's conferences are better examples of encyclopedic knowledge and are perhaps even more revealing of their age, because of the great variety of views they present. Conference pieces were not written by carefully selected experts. They were not commissioned by the editors to offer a like-minded perspective or to present a single, authoritative view. Instead, Renaudot and his conferees were more interested in presenting an open view, unconstrained by any editor's proclivities or ideology. As we have repeatedly remarked, not even issues of the greatest interest to Renaudot (chemical medicine, for example) go unchallenged. The conferences encourage as free and open a presentation of opinions as could be elicited from the audience.

Despite their truly encyclopedic character, the conferences did not fulfill Renaudot's hopes that they would serve posterity, be useful, and stand as an encyclopedia of seventeenth-century knowledge. Although they do in many ways epitomize these hopes for modern historians seeking to understand the seventeenth century, they did not immediately serve posterity; they were not recognized by Renaudot's successors as having established an encyclopedic basic of knowledge nor did they have a pronounced effect on the next generation. Several short-lived groups, like that of Pierre Bourdelot, tried to replicate the form of the conferences, but they could not flourish without the kind of protection that Richelieu had afforded Renaudot. There are other, more compelling reasons that Renaudot's group did not exert much influence or have direct followers in the succeeding generations. The open, egalitarian notion of scientific discussion promoted by Renaudot was foreign to the world of state-sponsored science, like that of the Académie des Sciences. Renaudot's conception of public discourse, where ideas were presented without editorial comment and without crediting the speaker, was antithetical to the self-promotion and the jockeying for position and patronage necessary to succeed in the much more rigid, stratified, society under Louis XIV. Renaudot's idealization of the anonymous presentation of ideas was out of step with the desire of scientists and philosophers to use their ideas to establish their reputations and then to use their reputations to gain patronage, position, and status.

Not only did the practice of science and its venues change dramatically from the period of Renaudot's conferences to that of the Académie des Sciences, the very nature of science changed. Cartesian mechanism swept Paris. It offered the features we more typically associate with the culture of science – the professionalized scientist, a mathematical understanding of nature, and the use of carefully measured experiments. Mechanism narrowed the scope of science to physics (although it was quickly applied to other areas like chemistry and medicine) and narrowed the method of science to mathematics.[2] The late seventeenth century responded to its crisis of knowledge by privileging mathematics, by rejecting the deductive and the empirical as only probable.[3] But these were the very kinds of inquiries most central to Renaudot's gatherings.

Perhaps most significant, the mathematization of science professionalized its practitioners. Science, as the stuff of sequestered academics competing for funding and for election to academies, became remote from the culture of the ordinary educated person. This newer culture of science combined with the culture of the court not only changed the nature of scientific discussion, it decisively separated science from culture at large – that is to say, science became more specialized and divorced from broader cultural issues. As Descartes forcefully insisted in the *Discourse on Method*, science was irrelevant to broader cultural concerns, especially the controversial subjects of religion, politics, and custom. Cartesian mechanism both privileged physics and separated science from the human sciences. Thus the science cultivated by Renaudot's group was too inclusive to be credible later in the century. The method practiced, if indeed one can be deduced from their very eclectic conversations, was too polymorphous, anecdotal, descriptive, and inconclusive. And science as understood by Renaudot's group was both essential and integral to social analysis. Their approach was rapidly superseded by a more rigid, hierarchical, state-controlled culture, which fostered a science clearly at odds with the conferees' understanding of science, especially its utility in social analysis. The conferences thus have no obvious intellectual heirs in the culture of absolutism and state-sponsored academic science.

It is ironic that, although mechanism divorced science from social concerns, it also made scientific prestige central to the culture and popularized science more accessible to the layman.[4] It fostered a new scientific culture in which scientists competed for what might be called the entertainment dollar of absolutist culture under Louis XIV and Louis XV – public experiments, demonstrations, and dissections could vie with plays and musical entertainments to attract seventeenth-century audiences.[5] These kinds of activities brought science to the layman, but in most cases the purpose was not to move the understanding but to delight the imagination. The scientific experiment was like the deus ex machina of classical theater; it defied expectations and provoked astonishment at the marvels of technology. Science, it can be argued, became not the common coin of discourse, as it was for Renaudot's conferees, but a method of demonstration.

The conventional recounting of the scientific revolution heralds the arrival of a mechanical science shaped by a rigorous method, produced by an increasingly professional group whose ways were too specialized for ordinary understanding. It is not surprising, then, that a group of conferees seeking to make knowledge public and accessible, to apply science as a method of rational analysis to all aspects of culture, and to break down, at least to some degree, social barriers to the acquisition of knowledge in the old regime would not be viewed as venerated ancestors by proponents of a new, narrower notion of scientific culture. The openness of Renaudot's group – with its implicit iconoclasm, both intellectual and social – makes it distinctive in the culture of the old regime. By the 1660s such iconoclasm would have been almost unimaginable in the meticulously hierarchical society of the court of Louis XIV. Both the organization and the mission of intellectual gatherings like Renaudot's are thus antithetical to the culture of absolutism. Although it had some modest and short-lived successors, Renaudot's group demonstrated a degree of intellectual independence that would not have been possible later. Its form – open, inclusive, unconstrained, egalitarian – could not be adapted to the dictates of classical style or to the social protocols of the court. The reformist agenda of Renaudot and the distinctive fusion of science and human science his group presented did not conform to the new science of the scientific revolution; the fluidity of its form did not correspond to the rigidity of culture in the court of Louis XIV.

Later in the seventeenth century, Renaudot's conferences could not have been as unconstrained in content as they were. To a degree unimaginable under Louis XIV, Renaudot's group avoided censorship or prohibition of the topics they discussed (though they themselves claimed to eschew religion and politics).[6] Their conversations were not stifled by a monarch like Louis XIV, who was both concerned with the expression of opinion and able to constrain opinion within the range he deemed acceptable. French intellectual life had not yet felt the chilling effect of the Fronde. That revolt, which took place from 1648 to 1653, began as a revolt by the parlementary judges of Paris but soon spread to involve the nobility and their troops. It made such an impression on the young Louis XIV that he removed his court to Versailles where he could both control the nobility and make royal patronage the source of most cultural productions. But because the conferences occurred in a less constrained environment, they could explore unconventional and even politically suspect ideas. Renaudot's group does not resemble the culture and science of the next generation and very likely would not have flourished or perhaps even survived in it.

Largely because his interests were so uncharacteristic of the culture of absolutism, Renaudot has only just begun to warrant mention in histories of the seventeenth century. Many use the period of Louis XIV as the standard for discussing the entire century. Most histories of philosophy in the seventeenth century take Descartes as a starting point, and histories of science move along the classic line from Galileo to Descartes to Newton.[7] The culture of the 1630s and 1640s, which Renaudot's conferences show was quite rich and creative, is considered significant only as a forerunner to the culture of absolutism or mechanism. Renaudot's conferences suggest that this period should be reassessed to explore at greater length the connections between science and culture, precisely because this period was less constrained by absolutism or mechanism. Renaudot's conferences sustain a different reading of the connections between science and culture than is standard. This counter-reading suggests that the reign of Louis XIV with its espousal of mechanism, absolutism, and classicism should be seen as anomalous rather than characteristic of the early modern period. Just as Renaudot's conferences have greater affinity with the reactions against the culture of absolutism in the Enlightenment than with the period that immediately followed, so too the history of early modern France might better be understood as a period of cultural complexity, vitality, and critical acuity, interrupted by the long but unusual period of absolutism – the reign of Louis XIV.

Treating Louis XIV's reign as anomalous rather than as characteristic of early modern France can be productive in many respects. It allows up to focus on the great intellectual dynamism and the myriad forms of intellectual life that characterized France in the aftermath of the wars of religion, illuminating a rich embodiment of the republic of letters.[8] Such a reorientation also allows us to recognize the vitality of French scientific discussion. (The French academic tradition has not cultivated its own history of science and, with the significant exception of Descartes, the anglophone tradition has largely neglected it.) If absolutism is not considered the end point of early modern culture, we can see in the early seventeenth century concerted and productive social analysis and the application of a growing fascination with science to such analyses. If these analyses are not dismissed as unproductive because of subsequent absolutist constraints on such inquiries, they can be acknowledged as offering, at the very least, important antecedents of Enlightenment social science.

Renaudot's conferences sustain these arguments for the significance of the early seventeenth century in all these respects and in quite specific ways. The broad notion of science as the basis of a shared culture, both advocated and demonstrated by the conferences, most persuasively and logically ties them to the social sciences of these later periods. In these conferences, participants deploy scientific knowledge in new ways. They move beyond the Renaissance ethos and toward the Enlightenment, beyond the humanistic invocation of "nature" and toward the more definitive uses of nature as a foundation for understanding society.

Other connections can be productively drawn between Renaudot's group and the Enlightenment. Renaudot's group can reasonably be considered as an early forerunner of the culture of the republic of letters, and its members as antecedents to the philosophes of the French Enlightenment. This is not to say that the philosophes are directly indebted to Renaudot, but rather that his conferences suggest greater affinities between the early seventeenth and mid-eighteenth century than one might expect. Renaudot's conferences seem quite remote from the spirit and structure of classicism. The affinities between Renaudot's group and the philosophes should causes us to reflect on the supposed reliance of the Enlightenment on Newtonian science as a source of social criticism or the general belief that the mechanical sciences are the source or model of the social sciences. Many of the fundamental attitudes often identified with the Enlightenment are found in this very early group with only minimal exposure to the new mechanical philosophy – and of course no familiarity at all with Newton.

There are good reasons that Renaudot's group took positions akin to those taken later by Enlightenment philosophes. Philosophes reacted against the constraints of an established classicism and absolutism. Although their crusade was much more explicitly reformist and progressive, the greater openness they sought resembles that practiced by conferees. Like members of Renaudot's group, the philosophes could maneuver more effectively, better evade censors, and act with greater intellectual independence than intellectuals under Louis XIV. Despite their greater autonomy, they too chafed against a rigid social hierarchy and sought new audiences, appealing as Renaudot had done to a broadly inclusive understanding of the public.

The nature and character of science in the conferences has great affinity with sciences of the Enlightenment. Lorraine Daston's characterization of Enlightenment science suggests some very telling comparisons between Enlightenment science and the approach taken by Renaudot's conferees. Because Enlightenment science was so rich and diverse, she identifies certain expectations of science as the unifying ground on which these diverse manifestations can best be understood. Above all, the enlightened emphasized utility; they extolled science as the basis for material improvement and were "passionate for the moral and material improvement of the human estate." The Enlightenment was also, as Daston terms it, a veritable "echo chamber" of constant discussion of scientific topics in many venues.[9] These very attitudes are fundamental to Renaudot's conferences and perhaps most accurately describe their import as well. Both Renaudot's conferences and Enlightenment science were conducted with a concern to weigh ideas and information by the standards of utility and to disseminate them. Conferees thus pursued a goal of public enlightenment as well as offering, initially, a focused "echo chamber" of scientific and cultural discourse and then one broadly disseminated through print. Like the proponents of enlightened science, conferees were united more by shared values than by professional expertise, and they, like the philosophes, advocated the open dissemination of knowledge.

The Enlightenment has often been presented as the result of a more or less simplistic application of Newtonian science to the social sphere. But as the study of Enlightenment science has developed, it has become increasingly evident that this science was much more complex, diverse, and sophisticated than the conventional view suggests. When one probes beneath the surface, it is clear that Enlightenment science was extremely wide-ranging and diverse. It did not simply focus on the mathematical sciences but also became increasingly preoccupied with the earth sciences and the biological sciences, just as Renaudot's conferees had been. The annals of Enlightenment science record, although some histories of science do not much emphasize them, the works of Georges Buffon, Benoît de Maillet, and J.-B. Robinet. Enlightenment figures, like Renaudot's conferees, were students of nature, captivated by the study of natural phenomena. Although mechanism still retained a great hold over the scientific imagination and practice, it had also, by the first decades of the eighteenth century, begun to provoke some criticism as too narrow and too rigid.[10] Even such a devoted proponent of the "geometrical method" as Fontenelle recognized that "some room must be allowed for the empirical study of nature," and as early as 1753, Diderot bemoaned the tyranny of mathematics over the investigation of nature.[11]

Renaudot's group offers a well-developed, early modern manifestation of these more diverse interests, which will again occupy many eighteenth-century figures not only in France but also throughout Europe. Conferees discussed an array of natural phenomena and explored the sciences with a sense of nature's amplitude, incorporating natural history, geology, and chemistry. In other words, they looked to the actual world of nature, which mechanism tended to neglect. This is not to say that scientific discussion in the Enlightenment returned to as broad and diverse a theoretical base as Renaudot's conferees were willing to explore. But some of the areas that early eighteenth-century thinkers were most interested in were no more than slightly amenable to mechanism, and these were just the areas of investigation that Renaudot's group pursued: geology, physiology, the natural sciences, and medicine. But the continuing propensity of historians of science to privilege the physical sciences and to idealize a mathematical method has distorted the understanding of both early seventeenth-century science and the Enlightenment. Perhaps (as Renaudot's group suggests) the earth sciences, physiology, the natural sciences, and medicine should be recognized as of far greater significance to the development of social science and Enlightenment thought than historians generally concede.

Of course, science, as Renaudot's group uses it, is full of contradiction and competing theories in virtually every subdiscipline, and these competing theories offer useful explanatory devices extending far beyond conventional applications of science. For conferees, science – whatever model one held – could be used to comment effectively not only on scientific but also on social concerns. These conferences stand at a critical point of transition in the use of science as means of social analysis, demonstrating how the application of science to social topics could fundamentally alter the tenor of discussion. That analysis is neither as progressive as one might hope in a time of increasing absolutism, nor as focused and reform-minded as the analysis of the philosophes. Nonetheless, using science as a touchstone for discussing ethics, social practices, and political issues alters the character of discussion – religious arguments are excluded and arguments from authorities discouraged, so much so that the tenor of the conferences is strikingly distinct from that of other contemporary documents.

Many scholars have pointed to the greater secularism of the Enlightenment as a defining characteristic of the movement, especially in conjunction with an emphasis on science at the expense of theology. Whether or not it was the intention of Renaudot's group, their discussions serve to separate decisively religion from science, and (perhaps equally significant) religion from social analysis. This group was overtly opposed to religious explanations (though a few participants gave them), disinclined to credit tradition and authority, and inclined to favor instead the experiential, the pragmatic, and the demonstrable. Participants were acutely aware that science could both privilege arguments and give them a new authority to wield against old authorities. The "scientific perspective" was brought to bear on issues that would previously have been treated rhetorically, theologically, or metaphysically, and this produces a striking secular feel to these conferences. The cultivation of science per se was proclaimed as progressive and utilitarian. Like the philosophes, conferees recognized that unenlightened opinions could harden into prejudice.

The absence of appeals to religion in the conferences calls into question Paul Hazard's famous remark distinguishing the late seventeenth century from the Enlightenment. He described a revolutionary change of perspective: "One day the French people almost to a man were thinking like Bossuet. The day after they were thinking like Voltaire."[12] The conferences vividly demonstrate that, long before the advent of the Enlightenment, scarcely a single participant in Renaudot's conferences thought like Bossuet, and some shared attitudes that would later characterize the philosophes. The conferences also fostered attitudes essential to the development of the Enlightenment by eroding religious authority in specific ways. For example, a staunch reliance on the theory of temperaments undercut the significance of the soul in understanding human beings – an approach common among eighteenth-century physicians and physiologists. Like many Enlightenment figures, conferees demonstrated an appreciation for the relativity of customs and cultures. The model physician of the conferees – moderate, perhaps disinterested, and certainly not fanatical, immune to prejudice and thus able to evaluate evidence dispassionately, unfettered by religious or political restrictions, guided instead by empirical and pragmatic considerations – conjures up the philosophe.

Conferees and philosophes share similar epistemological positions. In some respects, the conferences prefigure Immanuel Kant's clarion call to Enlightenment, *sapere aude* (dare to know). Kant's first injunction to his contemporaries was to leave behind intellectual immaturity, which he defined as the incapacity to use one's mind without the guidance of others. Conferees, because of their willingness to cast aside the weight of the authorities of the past, demonstrate many of the same approaches to knowledge that the philosophes espouse. Both groups assume that nature can be known, that man should be placed in relationship to nature, and that nature prescribes the social.[13] D'Alembert rejects skepticism in favor of science, an attitude he shares with conferees, when he urges, "Therefore let us believe without wavering that in fact our sensations have the cause outside ourselves which we suppose them to have; because the effect which can result from the real existence of that cause could not differ in any way from the effect we experience."[14]

Although conferees effectively apply science to social analysis, such applications have impressed historians as strikingly progressive only when the analysis is based on the application of the "true science" of mechanism or Newtonianism. It has been easier for historians to discount the disconcertingly eclectic science of groups like Renaudot's than to recognize it as a significant, early modern application of science to society.

Much recent literature cites the Enlightenment as the source of the embryonic social sciences, although to avoid anachronism in talking about the origins of the social sciences, historians have used the term *human sciences* instead.[15] One can, for example, readily connect early eighteenth-century moralistic preoccupations with human nature to the origins of the social sciences. Those who developed the human sciences considered human nature and the nature and roles of women, tried to integrate man into nature, detached politics and ethics from tradition and religion – all with the aid of science. The early explorations of the "human sciences" during the eighteenth century return to points raised and concerns expressed by Renaudot's conferees.

Various Enlightenment authors proclaimed they were turning their attention, as none had done before, to the science of man. Ultimately, they are credited with the development of anthropology, sociology, psychology, and like sciences. Although it is certainly legitimate to point to the eighteenth century as the period when these issues became central intellectual concerns, this study makes clear that a century earlier Renaudot's group was preoccupied with the same issues. Their discussions can thus be used to trace further back into the early modern period the emergence of the social sciences.[16] It is perhaps peculiar, by our lights, that Renaudot's participants considered their rather inchoate understanding of science to be a sufficient basic for discussion of the human sciences. Even if they do not articulate as clear a social scientific agenda as the philosophes, they nonetheless consistently demonstrate their sense that science provides the best evidence and means of analysis of the social.

The conferences look ahead to the Enlightenment not only in content but also in form. The scientific community as defined by Renaudot has much in common with the later republic of letters. There are tantalizing connections suggested by the recent intense historiographical discussion of the phenomenon called the republic of letters. We are well aware of the appeals of the philosophes to a "republic of letters" during the eighteenth century as an idealized, fictional location where merit would prevail over privilege, equality over hierarchy, independence of mind over appeals to tradition. This eighteenth-century manifestation of the republic, unlike earlier incarnations, privileged the French language and thus French intellectuals.[17] This vision has elicited both contemporary and modern criticisms. Robert Darnton has highlighted the discontents of second-generation philosophes, like Mercier and Brissot, who could not gain admittance.[18] Others have pointed to the aristocratic composition of this reputed republic and questioned the intellectual independence of a republic whose members were funded by patronage. Regardless of its limitations, the notion allowed eighteenth-century men of letters to construct an idealized form of intellectual exchange and a community that challenged the more hide-bound and elitist institutions of the past.

This distinctive, eighteenth-century French manifestation of the republic of letters drew on earlier notions of the republic, which had developed chiefly in England and the Netherlands around the practitioners of print culture. As Anne Goldgar has demonstrated, this incarnation was characterized, as her title reinforces, by "impolite learning" and an emphasis on hierarchy within the new print culture.[19] (An even earlier French incarnation of the republic in the late seventeenth century was closely tied to court culture and could be considered neither independent nor egalitarian.)

It is the later development of the republic of letters among the philosophes that most emphatically illustrates just how much ahead of its time Renaudot's group was.[20] What explicitly connects Renaudot's group to later formulations of the republic of letters? The conferences demonstrate great openness, which Fontenelle contended was the identifying characteristic of the republic of letters. The conferences, like that republic, are rooted in the academic culture of Renaissance humanism. They appeal to the wider public both as audience and as potential adjudicator of opinion; they are offered without editorial comment, laying before their audience and readership a rich fare of scientific and cultural commentary. Renaudot's group did not simply pay lip service to egalitarianism; its forum was as universal, inclusive, and democratic as any in the early modern period, so much so that the gatherings offered no possible basis for hierarchy or the advancement of participants.

Although Renaudot defined the notion of an intellectual community in a strikingly original way for the seventeenth century, his definition becomes much more familiar if it is placed in a later context. His group probably included professionals, but its membership was not defined in terms of professional expertise, and even more significant, it was not defined by privilege. Its operating assumptions were more like those of an intellectual "republic" and thus antithetical to more formal academic institutions. The group emphasized consensus through the open presentation of multiple perspectives rather than individual endeavor. It was cooperative rather than competitive, anonymous rather than based on the credibility of participating members. It was open both in terms of its membership and its receptivity to eclectic ideas. In some ways these characteristics make it even more idealistic than any of the actual incarnations – and even conceptions – of the republic of letters. (This greater idealism might well have impeded the quest for professional success of members as intellectual figures, which was certainly a goal of many participants in later incarnations of the republic of letters.) The notion of intellectual community embodied by Renaudot's group might have been too inclusive even for the Enlightenment republic of letters; it suggests a model of science and medicine open to all educated men (and potentially women as well). It was not restricted to the traditional educated elites. It was iconoclastic and potentially subversive. Instead of suggesting, as scientists frequently did, that science transcended social and political concerns, this group provided a model of science as an effective means of social analysis.[21]

The progressive egalitarianism of the conferences suggests certain affinities between these anonymous individuals who gathered to discuss intellectual issues for nine years on one hand and the collective enterprise of the encyclopedists on the other. Conferees obviously share a sense of the pursuit of knowledge as a collective endeavor, perhaps fulfilling, as the English translator of the first two hundred conferences proclaimed, the agenda for science set by Francis Bacon – a claim d'Alembert more famously made later for the *Encyclopédie*. Because they attempted to break with their cultural antecedents or at least leave them unacknowledged and unspecified, they were able (as indeed were the philosophes) to claim science and the prospects it entailed as a new approach to social issues. Because they did not extensively cite their cultural antecedents, they could appeal to science as the new foundation for their analysis of culture; thus they had both a scientific agenda and a unifying platform. Like the encyclopedists, Renaudot's conferees understood knowledge to be progressive, but their expectations were less sanguine and less overtly positive. It is one thing to believe that knowledge is liberating and that the truth will out. It is another to believe that one already has the foundation for knowledge that will inevitably yield progress. In other words, conferees shared attitudes with the encyclopedists but did not express them with such self-assurance. They did not have as clear a definition of science or vision of what it could accomplish; nor did they have the experience of the mature absolutism of Louis XIV to give them a clear social and political agenda. Thus the social analysis of the conferees, while rooted in science like that of the Enlightenment, was less developed both because they were not united in concerted opposition to absolutism and because their sense of science provided a less uniform foundation.

This group's discussions offer a unique perspective for future research because participants critically reexamined received wisdom and thoughtfully employed scientific positions to comment on their culture. They provide ground on which it is possible to engage current historiographical debates on the new roles of intellectuals in the transformation of discourse in the public sphere, the relationship between intellectual and social history, and the relationship between science and gender. They raise issues of ethics, morals, and social values and shed light on broader perspectives such as the history of mentalities or moral economics. The conferences document that culture under Louis XIII has been understood too much in terms of the absolutism of Louis XIV. They show the earlier period's vibrancy and affinities to the Enlightenment's full-blown application of science to social issues.

The present study supports much larger contentions as well: that intellectual issues are crucial in constructing social reality for any modern social group, and that the intellectual issues of the early modern period are neither as static nor as uniform as the contours of traditional intellectual history suggest. It exposes the insufficiently explored congruencies of the history of science and intellectual history; it contests the remnant positivism that still adheres to some histories of science; it sheds light on the nature and character of science in the age of the scientific revolution. We must conclude, ultimately, that Renaudot's conferees did leave an important but neglected legacy. By discussing and weighing all the seventeenth-century sciences, they extended the sense of the relevance and the range of the application of science. They not only fostered a culture of science and the early development of the social sciences; they also created a set of expectations about the interpenetration of nature and culture that constitute the basis of modern civilization.

NOTES

1 One would like to have the wealth of specific information for Renaudot's conferees as was deployed in David Sturdy in *Science and Social Status: The Members of the Académie des Sciences, 1666–1750* (London, 1995).

2 See Peter Robert Dear, *Discipline and Experience : The Mathematical Way in the Scientific Revolution* (Chicago: University of Chicago Press, 1995).

3 For a discussion of the implications of this development see Rhoda Rappaport, *When Historians Were Geologists, 1665–1750* (Ithaca, NY: Cornell University Press, 1997).

4 This is the social implication that most conventional accounts of early modern science chose to emphasize in discussing the social ramifications of mechanism.

5 See Geoffrey V. Sutton, *Science for a Polite Society: Gender, Culture, and the Demonstration of Enlightenment* (Boulder, CO: Westview Press, 1995).

6 It is worth wondering, although impossible to know, how avant-garde Renaudot's group would have been, had they been free to discuss religion.

7 For example, the new *Cambridge History of Seventeenth-Century Philosophy*, edited by Daniel Garber and Michael Ayers, 2 vols (Cambridge: Cambridge University Press, 1998), begins with Descartes and treats the previous period only as background to Descartes.

8 George Huppert argues in *The Style of Paris: Renaissance Origins of the French Enlightenment* (Bloomington and Indianapolis: Indiana University Press, 1999) that the late Renaissance has great affinity with the Enlightenment.

9 Lorraine Daston, "Afterword: The Ethos of Enlightenment," in William Clark, Jan Golinski, and Simon Schaffer (eds.), *The Sciences in Enlightened Europe* (Chicago: University of Chicago Press, 1999), 495–504.

10 See the physiologically based works of La Mettrie and Diderot, written in the 1740s: Julien Offray de La Mettrie, *L'Homme plante, L'Homme machine*, and *Le Système d'Epicure*, in *Oeuvres Philosophiques* (Berlin, 1774), 3 vols; Denis Diderot, *Pensées Philosophiques* and *Lettre sur les aveugles*, in *Oeuvres philosophiques*, ed. P. Vernière (Paris, 1964), 9–79, 81–149.

11 For Fontanelle, see Rappaport, *When Historians Were Geologists*, 43, 51. Diderot, *De l'Interprétation de la nature*, in *Oeuvres philosophiques*.

12 Paul Hazard, *European Mind: The Critical Years, 1680–1715* (New Haven, 1953), 7.

13 The philosophes, like many writers from the Renaissance on and including the conferees, used "nature" as a prescriptive term. For just several of many examples, see Jean Le Rond d'Alembert, *Preliminary Discourse to the Encyclopedia of Diderot*, trans. R. Schwab (Indianapolis, 1963), 11–12.

14 Ibid., 9.

15 See Christopher Fox's introduction to Fox, Roy Porter, and Robert okler (eds.), *Inventing Human Science: Eighteenth-Century Domains* (Berkeley: University of California Press, 1995), 1–30; Sergio Moravia, "The Enlightenment and the Sciences of Man," *History of Science*, XVIII(18), 1980, 247–68.

The History of the Human Sciences 6 (1993) is an issue dedicated to the eighteenth-century development of the human sciences. See also Richard Olson, *The Emergence of the Social Sciences, 1642–1792* (New York, Twayne, 1993).

16 Eighteenth-century figures wanted to extend to the study of man the certainty and accuracy of the physical sciences, Major studies of the history of this correlation include Georges Gusdorf, *Les Sciences humaines et la pensée occidentale*, 6 vols (Paris: Payot, 1966–73); Michèle Duchet and C. Blankaert, *Anthropologie et histoire au siècle des lumières: Buffon, Voltaire, Rousseau, Helvétius, Diderot* (Paris: Flammarion, 1995); and Keith Michael Baker, *Condorcet, from Natural Philosophy to Social Mathematics* (Chicago: University of Chicago Press, 1975).

17 Dena Goodman, *The Republic of Letters: A Cultural History of the French Enlightenment* (Ithaca, NY: Cornell University Press, 1994).

18 Robert Darnton, *The Great Cat Massacre and other Episodes in French Cultural History* (New York: Basic Books, 1984), and *The Literary Underground of the Old Regime* (Cambridge, MA: Harvard University Press, 1982).

19 Anne Goldgar, *Impolite Learning: Conduct and Community in the Republic of Letters, 1680–1750* (New Haven, CT: Yale University Press, 1995).

20 In the eighteenth century republic of letters, there was little explicit discussion of what a "republic" meant even by those who considered themselves members. (Perhaps they saw it more clearly in terms of what it was not – the terms with which I began this discussion.) Members of Renaudot's group also offer only the vaguest appreciation of a republic as a source of greater freedom, although in practice the group provides a compelling model of an intellectual community that was quite egalitarian.

21 Descartes' *Discourse on Method* is perhaps the most striking example of this claim, which Margaret C. Jacob has developed for many leading figures of the scientific revolution, in *The Cultural Meaning of the Scientific Revolution* (Philadelphia, PA: Temple University Press, 1988).

13

CONTESTING POSSESSION

Patricia Seed

But having discovered new stars and a new sky, how did one possibly own or "take possession" of the heavens above and the seas below? The answer, of course, was that there was no way to own the seas and the stars, only ways to own the knowledge of how to sail across them, how to note the passage of time on the night seas by the movement of constellations, and how to keep track of position on the open seas by techniques of navigation.

In the twentieth century, we do not own outer space, the stars, the planets, the moon. What we have is the knowledge and the science to travel there – the rocket designs and spaceships, just as the Portuguese had the ship designs and the caravels, ocean-going vessels invented to sail the South Atlantic. Likewise in our century we have created the techniques of navigation in outer space using mathematics and scientific instruments, just as the Portuguese developed the mathematics and instruments of high-seas navigation. In their disputes with other European powers, Portuguese officials claimed a right to exercise a commercial monopoly over regions inaccessible without their techniques. While the moon has no apparent commercial advantages, if it did, it would not be surprising that the United States would claim a right to a monopoly on grounds that they had pioneered the means of navigating to its surface.

D. João III of Portugal claimed in a letter to his trade representative in Flanders in 1537 that

> the seas that can and should be navigated by all are those which were always known and always known by all and common to all. But those others [such as the South Atlantic] which were never known before (*sabidos*), and never even appeared navigable, these seas (that) were discovered by such great efforts on my part [i.e., the Portuguese crown] may not [be navigated by all].[1]

The Portuguese did not claim exclusive rights to all the seas, only to those for which they had pioneered the means of sailing. Furthermore, the king called the process of ascertaining the characteristics and means of sailing these seas "discovery."[2]

Patricia Seed, "Contesting Possession," pp. 128–40 from *Ceremonies of Possession in Europe's Conquest of the New World, 1492–1640*. Cambridge: Cambridge University Press, 1995.

The term *discovery* (*descobrimento*) in its contemporary scientific sense, means to obtain knowledge for the first time of something previously unknown. The waters of the South Atlantic had not been navigated previously, making the Portuguese indisputably the first to learn of these seas and, furthermore, the first to provide precise nautical descriptions of them. The process of discovery signified a deliberate effort involving the expenditure of considerable energy and funds.[3] In the earliest surviving navigational itinerary for sailing to the Indies, the author, Duarte Pacheco Pereira, described how the kings of Portugal "ordered discovered" the West African coast by sailing the South Atlantic:[4]

> Due to the intelligence of our princes . . . and the courage of their hearts, they spent their treasure in the discovery of these lands. . . . The discovery of these Ethiopias (Africa) cost . . . the deaths of many men and much expense. . . . It is with no small effort that we have written of the laborious way and greater difficulty of discovery than might appear. Our princes who undertook this did not spend their (country's) lives and treasures in vain.[5]

The concept of a right to what they had discovered stemmed from the "laborious" nature of the effort the Portuguese had undertaken, and the "greater difficulty of discovery." It stemmed from the cost in human lives, and in financial terms as well – "their (country's) lives and treasures."

The argument is a familiar contemporary one. The person (or corporation) who pays the salary, provides the equipment, and organizes the scientific project owns the right to a patent on the ideas that are discovered. The individual scientist – who created the idea – is not the owner of the right to exploit it; rather it is the company that provided the money for the laboratory and laid out the tools and equipment that has a right to receive an income from the discoveries. The Portuguese claims, repeatedly voiced in international conflicts, that they had right to a commercial monopoly on the seaborne trade with the new lands was an explicit claim that because of their vast expenditures on developing the science and technology of high-seas navigation, they had a just right to compensation.

Other competing powers were unwilling to accept Portuguese claims for a monopoly on sea routes in exchange for their discoveries. Grotius exaggerated the Portuguese claim, stating that they claimed to rule the entire ocean, rather than simply the regions to which they had discovered the navigational means of access.[6] He also added that the Portuguese had no boundaries save "an imaginary line."[7] Since all mathematical lines are imaginary, Grotius thereby rejected the entire mathematical and scientific basis of Portugal's claims to discovery.

A different set of objections emerged from English competitors. In 1562, Queen Elizabeth had stated that Portugal had no dominion over "places *discovered*," to which an irritated Portuguese ambassador had replied that "his master *has* absolute dominion . . . over all those lands already discovered."[8] In a scientific sense, discovery created rights of dominion for the Portuguese, but did not do so for the English.

Some Frenchmen were unsympathetic, while others had a certain amount of respect for the Portuguese position. On the one hand, the Dieppe captain Jacques Parmentier declared, like Grotius, that the Portuguese possessed an "excessive ambition" and "it seems that God only made the seas and the land for them, and that other nations are not worthy of sailing."[9] André Thevet, on the other hand, wrote that the Portuguese do not easily tolerate the French in Brazil "because they assess and attribute ownership of things [to themselves] as first possessors, which considering that they have made the discovery, is true."[10]

Because Portuguese claims to the New World and to West Africa were founded upon the creation of knowledge, they left few physical markers as signs of discovery, since it was the knowledge of means – not the ends – that they claimed to possess. While the Portuguese primarily marked their discovery of regions by latitude numbers, recorded in logs and transferred to maps, they sometimes noted their discoveries by an object on land – a stone pillar or a cross.

Crosses were the traditional objects Europeans planted during their travels to new regions, but their actual cultural and political significance varied widely. For the English they were mere markers of presence, signs that Englishmen had once passed that way, while for the French, Spanish, and Portuguese alike, they were political indicators of a claim upon a region.[11] For the Frenchmen taking possession of the Amazon, they were the symbol of a political alliance between the natives and the French king; for the Spanish they had been a physical manifestation of the idea that the area was now under Christian (i.e., Spanish) command. But for the Portuguese, their meaning was and had been historically distinctive.

Beginning with Gil Eannes's first rounding of the navigationally treacherous Cape Bojador in 1434, Portuguese explorers had often erected crosses on the land they had attained, indicating the southernmost reach of their voyage.[12] Sailing southward down the west coast of Africa, Portuguese explorers continued the custom of placing crosses. But after crossing the equator, the Portuguese began a distinctive practice of recording the southernmost limit of their navigational discoveries, by planting tall stone pillars.[13] These pillars were six- to eight-foot-tall columns each topped by a square stone on which were carved in Latin and Portuguese the year and the names of the king and expedition leader. Perched on top of the square was a cross, slightly taller than the square.

Such pillars had been prevalent in medieval Portugal.[14] Planted on tall hilltops on the African, Indian, and, later, American continents, such pillars were directed at other passing European seaborne observers rather than natives. In placing these giant stone markers on African shores, the Portuguese were principally noting their discoveries of regions previously unknown to Europeans. The inscriptions on the stone were quite specific. They were records of discovery. "In the year 6685 of the creation of the earth and 1485 after the birth of Christ," reads one, "the most excellent and serene King Dom João II of Portugal ordered this land to be discovered and this padrão to be placed by Diogo Cão, nobleman of this house."[15] More than simply an indication of having passed through, the stone pillar proclaimed the Portuguese technological achievement. Thus, the Portuguese began recording the discovery (literally "uncovering") of lands hitherto unknown to Europeans on the African continent. The prominent Portuguese legal scholar Seraphim de Freitas argued that "the Portuguese were the first to investigate and open the new navigational path to the Indies, which is why they acquired the right to it."[16] He continued that "Vasco Da Gama communicated this understanding by placing stone columns in some ports, as testimony of Portuguese lordship."[17]

The Portuguese notations of discovery were visibly fixed upon tall stone monuments and occasional crosses. But in so marking their progress across the oceans to new lands, the Portuguese were also mapping a grid – an imaginary network of numbers – latitudes noted by astronomers and pilots, recorded both in the subsequent guides and fixed upon the land by the visible symbols of stone pillars and occasional crosses. For the stone pillar did not occupy a place or a territory the way a house or a fort did; rather most importantly it marked a point, a location. The actual fixing of the point was done by numbers – degrees and minutes – which were calculated on the basis of the height of the polestar and later the sun, written down, forwarded to the crown, and then incorporated into the pilots' guides. The coordinates of the pillar, carefully recorded in subsequent guides, could be used by sailors at sea to check their location. The *padrão*, like a giant pin stuck into the earth, was the visible and prominent fixing of a position, which could be then used by pilots to check their onboard records against the known coordinates of the giant pillar.

By fixing large landmarks atop promontories visible from the ocean, they also noted the exact extent of their previous achievement and provided a potential benchmark for future expeditions. The Portuguese discoveries mapped space with a network of numbers, rather than describing or occupying a place.

Alone among Western Europeans, the Portuguese carried out an astronomical ritual upon arrival that bore political significance. Unlike the elaborate ceremonies of the French, the construction of house sites and gardens by the English, and declarations to native people by Spaniards, the Portuguese established their claim to dominion through discovering numbers that fixed the place on earth by the position of the sun in the sky.

Before the fleet bearing Master John departed from Brazil, back across the South Atlantic to India, a small ceremony was arranged to accompany the planting of a cross which had been cut from some local wood. After a discussion about "where it seemed to us that it would be better to plant the cross, *so that it might better be seen* . . . the cross was planted with the arms and devise of Your Highness which we first nailed to it" (emphasis added). Then just as they departed, Nicolau Coelho placed tin crucifixes around the necks of all the natives present. Like the wooden cross, placed where it was most visible from the ocean, the tin crosses around the natives' necks also served as visible reminders to the Portuguese presence. Individuals wearing or owning those crosses could be identified as having prior contact with the Portuguese (or the natives they had met). These were not the only crosses used in the first Portuguese contact. There was also the cross in the sky above, described in the only other lengthy account of the discovery known to have reached King Manuel,[18] the first description of the Southern Cross, the astronomical discovery of a "new sky and new stars."

While subsequent history has tried to make the first Mass celebrated into the founding moment of Brazil, it was not so regarded at the time.[19] King Manuel sought information not about a religious ceremony, but about the stars and the skies. Indeed, the clergy (and their actions) were relegated to a minor role in the course of the discoveries.

Clergy played no role in the first thirty-five years of the Portuguese presence in Brazil – nor were there any early efforts to claim or Christianize indigenous peoples.[20] The first settlement plans for Brazil contained no mention of any role for clerics. The first time that clerics became involved in a political role in Brazil was in the middle of the sixteenth century, when the first governor-general, Tomé de Sousa, was sent with a contingent of Jesuits.

Clerics traditionally played a far more constrained role in Portuguese political affairs than anywhere else in Western Europe. Alone in Western Europe, medieval Portuguese coronation ceremonies had no role for clergymen. In 1438 the Papacy tried to force Portuguese monarchs to establish such a ceremony, but to no avail. Eventually the pope backed down and the clergy remained without a role in legitimating Portuguese royal power.[21] In the absence of a legitimate political role for the clergy, anti-Semitic sentiments were not mobilized into violent action until well into the sixteenth century. In fourteenth- and fifteenth-century Spain and Aragon, clerical leadership legitimated violence against religious minorities.[22] The attacks on Seville's Jewish communities which began the pogroms of 1391 were led by powerful clerics, including the acting archbishop of the city. The equally anti-Semitic Portuguese clergy historically had little influence on politics.[23] Elsewhere on the Iberian peninsula during the fourteenth and fifteenth centuries, clerics successfully enacted legislation banning Jews from positions of political power or influence. Portuguese clerics alone failed to secure such legislation.[24]

Excluding the clergy from political power also permitted Portuguese monarchs to practice the religious toleration that permitted them to pursue mathematical and scientific goals. When Catholic clergymen played a role in the technical advances, they did so because of their mathematical skills rather than their traditional clerical ones. João II, for example, is reported to have selected priests for voyages to southern Africa on the basis of their mathematical rather than their religious skills.[25] Unlike Isabel of Castile, who soon founded Spanish dominion upon the imposition of a foreign religion, Portuguese rulers initiated their claims to the New World through science, which had been created for them by Jewish astronomers based upon the heritage of the Islamic era.

Portuguese leadership in scientific navigation began to grind to a disastrous halt at end of the fifteenth century. The fanatically intolerant Catholic Kings of Spain demanded that Manuel expel the Jews before being allowed to marry their daughter. In this way the Catholic monarchs not only ended the centuries-old tradition of Moslem and Christian tolerance in Spain, they in effect forced Portugal to do so as well.

Between December 1496 and April 1497, Jews were given the Almohad option of conversion or exile. But then the pressure was increased. In April 1497, all children under fourteen were to be forbidden to leave the kingdom, so many parents converted so as not to lose their children. They were known as New Christians, or *conversos*. Thus, Jewish scientists such as Abraham Zacuto departed for North Africa and eventually Israel, while Master João was forcibly converted, as was Pedro Nunes, the man whom even the chronicler of D. João III's reign described as "the great Portuguese mathematician, who in his time had no equal" – the man who had characterized Portugal's contribution as the "new sky and new stars."[26]

Dom Manuel had high regard for his converted Jewish scientists, including Master John who established the latitude of Brazil and the first accurate drawing of the Southern Cross. But Manuel's expulsion and forcible conversion decrees effectively sanctioned outpourings of anti-Semitic violence among his subjects. In 1506 the first pogrom erupted in Lisbon, causing the death of 2,000 converted Jews.[27] The peace and toleration of Portugal began to disappear. Dom Manuel's offspring followed the example of their fanatically intolerant Spanish grandparents rather than their more tolerant father, bringing the clergy into politics, establishing the Inquisition, and in 1543 burning the first Portuguese at the stake.[28] While personally protected by powerful patrons, even the grandchildren of the famous cosmographer Pedro Nunes were harassed by the Inquisition.[29]

The expulsion of the Jews was widely lamented at the time and seen by many of Portugal's elites as a catastrophic mistake. By 1513 there was a shortage of astronomers in Portugal. By the 1520s the scientific and technological edge that Portugal had enjoyed was eroding, the claim to making new discoveries coming to an end.[30] The exiling of its mathematical and scientific talent effectively put an end to the scientific experimentation that had rendered Portugal the pioneer in the science and mathematics of modern navigation.

The technologies that they had developed through the 1530s came to be widely shared by sailors throughout the world. When Master John landed on the coast of Brazil, only the Portuguese could accurately describe a place using latitudes. Soon all Europeans were able to do so. The mariner's astrolabe, first created by Abraham Zacuto for Vasco da Gama on his first voyage to India in 1497,[31] soon was widely adopted in Western Europe. Spanish sailors adopted it by the 1550s; twenty years later English mariners acquired it, and by the 1580s Dutch sailors were using it on their voyages to the East, having learned how while sailing on Portuguese vessels. Once this knowledge became widely known, as it inevitably did, Portugal no longer exclusively held the instruments or the technologies needed to sail the high seas. Nor was it continuing to innovate in these areas.

By the 1560s scientific leadership in navigation passed to the hands of the Dutch. Superior astrolabes began to be made in Louvain.[32] Many of the most educated Portuguese Jews fled to

Antwerp, and then after its fall to Amsterdam, bringing their knowledge with them.[33] Dutch sailors traveling regularly on Portuguese ships became familiar with Portuguese nautical and oceanographic guides (called *itineraries*). Jan Linschoten modified the Portuguese guides and published them as *Itineraries*.[34] Portuguese navigators' observations of variations in terrestrial magnetism came into the hands of Simon Stevin, who wrote a well-known treatise on the subject.[35] Even the solutions to mapping nautical routes were inspired by Portuguese science.

Upon returning from Brazil in 1532, Martim Afonso da Souza observed to Pedro Nunes that when sailing east or west along the same latitude his boat appeared to be heading to the equator but in fact, never reached it. Nunes responded that using a compass to sail east or west along an identical latitude was different than following a great circle course. The compass-driven course, Nunes remarked, was actually a sequence of separate great circle courses. Nunes then drew a picture of the compass-driven course, the first depiction of the loxodromic curve,[36] and subsequently mathematically described these curves.[37]

To eliminate the problem of the loxodromic curve on a navigator's map was the problem that Gerardus Mercator (1512–94) later solved. Latitude lines lie parallel to each other, with the distance between lines virtually identical at the equator as at the poles.[38] Lines of longitude, however, resemble cuts in the rind of an orange, farther apart in the center, but converging at the ends.[39] In 1569 Mercator increased the spacing between latitude lines the further they were from the equator, thus making all loxodromes appear as straight lines.[40] While there are inevitable distortions of sizes of landmasses closer to the poles,[41] Mercator's map allowed pilots to draw a constant compass course in a straight line – solving the problem originally identified by a converted Portuguese mathematician and first observed on a voyage to Brazil.

Many of the Portuguese scientific and technological achievements remain to this day. Trigonometry is still widely used in both mapping and navigation, applications discovered by the Portuguese. But perhaps Portugal's most important legacy is how its mariners and cartographers changed the way in which the world is seen. Where medieval European maps had envisioned a world with Jerusalem at its center, the Portuguese reinvented the world as a uniform set of latitude coordinates, the form in which we know it today. They reimagined the globe as a single object where any place could be described and located by a number. The uniform latitude scale may be marked on globes but it is not visible anywhere. Latitudes are a set of imaginary lines that people the world over recognize and treat as real. They form the continuing legacies of Portugal's adapting its Islamic and Jewish scientific heritage to solve the problems of high-seas navigation.

Over the course of centuries, millions of other peoples in the southern hemisphere had seen the stars near the celestial pole; two large groups had even chosen it for navigation. Navigating Arabs called it a geometric shape – the quadrilateral; some of their Polynesian counterparts called it "the net," others the "sacred timber."[42] Aborigines trekking through the vast spaces of the Australian outback named the guard stars "the two brothers" and the cross "the lance"; nomadic peoples of the Sahara called one of the guards "the weight." Naming involves selecting an object the stars resembled from one's own cultural catalog – a Polynesian fishing net, a timber crucial to the construction of ocean-going canoes, an aboriginal hunting lance, a trading nomad's commercial weighing device.[43] But the Portuguese picked a different symbol from their catalog – a cross.

Like other Europeans, Portuguese represented their particular political ambitions and interests in the southern hemisphere as the expression of a global Christianity. In sailing over the oceans they were establishing dominion for a Christian power – not converting the people – but by dominating the seas and using the stars above to achieve that goal.

Naming the sky above by the cross in a sense takes possession of it. The stars oversee the ocean itself, the movement of ships as they sail from point to point. The rotation of stars across the heavens marks the time of watches on board ship; their position guides the navigators checking the course through the nighttime sky. Naming the constellation the Southern Cross expresses an imperial ambition, but the cross above, like those planted on land, designated not a place but a point in space.

Because other Europeans learned their navigational astronomy from the Portuguese, they borrowed their nomenclature as well.[44] The Portuguese named the Southern Cross; a Portuguese pilot first drew it for the European world. Thus, in the nighttime skies above the southern hemisphere, lies the principal legacy of Portuguese claims of possession – the Southern Cross – as Pedro Nunes said nearly five centuries ago, a new sky and new stars.

Ships that glide silently over the seas leave no traces, no permanent marks on the face of the earth; even their remains, buried at thousands of fathoms beneath the surface of the sea, are erased from visibility, from permanency. The measurements of the height of the sun and other stars left no visible traces; the mathematical lines which divide our world exist nowhere except in our minds and imaginations. The luffing of the sails, the creaking of the wood, the rush of the wind, the sounds of men's voices all are gone. The legacies of the once vast Portuguese empire are in the names of the stars above and, occasionally, in the sounds of ships navigating below.

NOTES

1 D. João III to Rui Fernandes (*feitor* of Flanders) May 2, 1534, quoted in Carvalho, *D. João III*, 64.
2 The twentieth-century debate about discovery (from 1940 to the early 1960s) used the phenomenological criterion of the intention of the sovereign individual *actor* to "discover," rather than on imperial or official intentions. Samuel Eliot Morison, *Portuguese Voyages to America in the Fifteenth Century* (Cambridge, Mass., 1940), 5–10; Edmundo O'Gorman, *La idea del descubrimento de América* (México, 1951); Marcel Bataillon and Edmundo O'Gorman, *Dos concepciones de la tarea histórica: Con motivo de la idea del descubrimiento de América* (México, D.F., 1955), trans. as *The Invention of America: An Inquiry into the Historical Nature of the New World and the Meaning of Its History* (Bloomington, Ind., 1961); Marcel Bataillon, "L'idée de la découverte de l'Amérique," *Bulletin Hispanique*, 55 (1953): 23–55; Wilcomb Washburn, "The Meaning of 'Discovery' in the Fifteenth and Sixteenth Centuries," *American Historical Review*, 68 (1962): 1–21.
3 "Discover" and "Discovery," *OED*; Serafim da Silva Neto, *História da língua portuguêsa* (Rio de Janeiro, 1952–7), 450. Before the Portuguese voyages, the word *discover* in English merely meant reconnoiter or divulge a secret (§ 4, 5) rather than "bring to fuller knowledge" (§ 8, 9).
4 Pacheco Pereira, *Esmeraldo* (Lisbon, 1892), 2–4, 100–1, 105. Identical language in Gaspar Correa's prologue to his *Lendas da India* (Lisbon, 1858–66) describing Dom Manuel as having ordered "the discovery of India," and in chap. 1 as "endeavor[ing] to discover and conquer."
5 Pacheco Pereira, *Esmeraldo*, 141, 146, 152. Similar sentiments were expressed by D. João III in Jan. 16, 1530, letter to his French ambassador, João da Silveira, in M. E. Carvalho, *D. João III e los francezes* (Lisbon, 1909), 182, 184. In these, as in many Portuguese writings of the time, the discovery was attributed not to the private citizen who had actually embarked upon the voyage, but to the royal official who subsidized and sanctioned the voyages of discovery. Thus, Prince Henry is characterized as the discoverer of the regions of West Africa even though he never traveled on any of these voyages. João de Barros, *Ropica pnefma* (1532), writes, "With the importance of the worlds the enlightened kings of Portugal have discovered." Quoted in Godhino, *Les découvertes* (Paris, n.d.), 56.
6 Hugo Grotius, *De iure praedae commentarius*, trans. Gwladys L. Williams (Oxford, 1950). Chap. 12 is the slightly revised treatise *De mare liberum*. He argued that the Portuguese did not "discover" these

routes but rather that they "pointed them out (242). He objects to the size of the ocean claimed by the Portuguese as "immoderate power" (239).

7 Ibid., 240.

8 Answer to the Portuguese ambassador, June 15, 1562, *Calendar of State Papers*, 95. Second replication of the Portuguese ambassador, June 19, 1562, ibid., 105 (emphasis added).

9 Paul Gaffarel, *Histoire du Brésil français* (Paris, 1878), 84–112.

10 André Thevet, *Les singularitez de la France Antarctique* (Paris, 1878; orig. pub. 1558), 308.

11 The 1580 English expedition searching for a northeast passage through Europe to Asia described a cross upon which "Master Pet did grave his name with the date of our Lourde . . . to the end that if the William did chaunce to come thither, they [*sic*] might have knowledge that wee had beene there." "The Discoverie Made by M. Arthur Pet and M. Charles Jackman of the Northeast Parts," in Richard Hakluyt, *Principal Navigations, Voyages, Traffiques, and Discoveries of the English Nation* (Glasgow, 1904), 3: 288. For other examples, see Patricia Seed, "Taking Possession and Reading Texts: Establishing the Authority of Overseas Empires," *William and Mary Quarterly*, 49 (1992), 183–209, at 193–4.

12 When west winds blow, the waves can reach fifty feet, and from October to April thick fogs are usual. Antonio de Oliveira Marques, *History of Portugal*, 2 vols. (New York, 1972), 1: 149. When "Gil Yanez attempting what none durst before him passed beyond Cape Bojador, and there planted a Crosse," Manuel Faria y Sousa, *The History of Portugal* (to 1640), trans. John Stevens (London, 1698), bk. 4, chap. 3, 274. Upon reaching Cape Branco, Diego Affonso "caused to be erected on land a great cross of wood that his partners might know he was going on before them." Gomes Eanes de Zurara, *Discovery and Conquest of Guinea* (London, 1896–9), 103.

13 The voyages of Diogo de Cão in approximately 1471 were the first during which the massive stone pillars were planted. This was approximately one decade after the first Portuguese voyage south of the equator. Paulo Merêa, *Novos estudos del história de direito* (Barcelos, 1937), 27n27.

14 Placed on the boundaries of property they signified the boundaries, but also had historically signified that the land was not subject to taxation by the king. Hence the markers (and in some cases crosses) signaled royal revenue agents to keep off the property. Revenue agents of other European powers were thereby presumably put on notice of Portuguese economic intentions, if not their actual accomplishments. Alexandre Herculano, *História de Portugal*, ed. José Mattoso, 4 vols. (Amados, 1980–1), 2: 245, 386. This commercial dimension entered into Portuguese use of the pillars in the sixteenth century.

15 Translation given in Luís de Albuquerque *et al.*, *Portugal–Brazil: The age of the Atlantic Discoveries* (Lisbon, 1990), 67.

16 "Portugueses . . . foram os primeriros a investigare a abrir o caminho da navegação da India . . . quer porque adquiriram o direito da predita navegação." Seraphim de Freitas, *Do justo império asiático* (Lisbon, 1959–61), chap. 3, para. 14, 1: 127.

17 "Conforme Gama o deu a entender, colocando, em alguns portos, colunas de pedra que fossem testemunhos do domínio lusitano." Freitas, ibid., chap. 8, 13, 1: 293. The identical understanding also appears in João de Barros, *Asia* (Venice, 1562), dec. 1. liv. 3, cap. 2, 79–80. See also Gaspar Correa, *Lendas da India*, prologue.

18 There is another account reportedly written by Ayres Correa, but to date no copy of this has been found in the Portuguese archives. Abel Foutoura da Costa, *Os sete únicos documentos de 1500, conservados em Lisboa, referentes à viagem de Pedro Alvares Cabral* (Lisbon, 1940).

19 The association was probably created later because in Portuguese the word *ceremonia* most usually refers to a religious occasion. The Mass was celebrated as the founding of Brazil most memorably in the nineteenth-century painting "A Primeira Misa no Brasil" by Vitor Meireles at the Museu Nacional de Bellas Artes in Rio de Janeiro. But celebrating Mass was part of the customary Sunday activities on long ocean voyages; masses were also customarily said prior to departure. See Alvaro Velho, *Journal of the first voyage of Vasco da Gama* (London, 1898), 96. Neither the words *possession* nor *taking possession* were mentioned in connection with the cross-planting, whereas they were frequently invoked in connection with the padrões.

20 Religious issues were not given a priority anywhere in the Portuguese empire until 1532 when João III (el Rey Piadoso) created the Mesa da Consciência. Antonio Baiao et al., eds., *História da expansão portuguesa no mundo* (Lisbon, 1937), 2: 74. Freitas subsequently rewrote this history in order to justify Portuguese dominion on the basis of the papal bull. Freitas, *De justo imperio asiático* (Lisbon, 1959–61), 156.

21 The Portuguese monarchs constituted themselves by proclamation and oaths of loyalty. Marcelo Caetano, *Lições de história do direito português* (Coimbra, 1962), 225.

22 Thomas Glick sees this process as beginning in the eleventh century. *Islamic and Christian Spain* (Princeton, 1979), 160.

23 For anti-Semitism among clergy, see Alexandre Herculano, *História de Portugal* (Lisbon, 1846 53), 2: 164.

24 Albert A. Sicroff, *Les controverses des statuts de "pureté du sang" en Espagne du XVᵉ au XVIIᵉ siècle* (Paris, 1960).

25 Joaquim Bensaude, *L'astronomie nautique au Portugal à l'époque des grandes déconvertes* (Berne, 1912), 196–7. For sixteenth-century critiques of the role played by clergymen in the expansion, see Luís de Camões, *os Lusiadas*, canto 10, stanzas 85, 108–19, 150.

26 For Nunes, see Bensaude, *L'astronomie nautique*, 63; António Baião, *Episódios dramáticos da Inquisição portuguesa*, 2 vols. (Lisbon, 1936), 1: 163–5; "Grande matemático português Pêro Nunes, que em seu tempo não teve igual." Frei Luís de Sousa, *Anais de D. João III*, ed. M. Rodriges Lapa, 2 vols., 2d ed. (Lisbon, 1954). 2: 193, parte 2, liv. 1, cap. 15.

27 A. H. de Oliveira Marques, *History of Portugal* (New York, 1972), 1: 213; Meyer Kayserling, *História dos judens em Portugal* (São Paulo, 1971 [1867]), 127–32.

28 Oliveira Marques, *History*, 1: 207; Kayserling, *História dos judeus*, 145–207.

29 Nunes managed to escape the persecution, but not through royal protection. As Luís de Albuquerque has shown, Nunes was the teacher of the Inquisitor General Cardinal D. Henrique and was protected in that way. Luís de Albuquerque, *As navegações e a sua projecção na ciência e na cultura* (Lisbon, 1987), 61. Nunes's grandchildren, however, were scrutinized by the Inquisition. Baião, *Episódios dramáticos da inquisiçao portuguesa* (Lisbon, 1924–[vol. I, 1936]), 1: 163–5.

30 M. Gonçalves Cerejeira, *O Renascimento em Portugal*, 4th ed. (Coimbra, 1974), 333: Baião, *Episódios*, 305; I. S. Révah, *La censure inquisitoriale portugaise au XVIᵉ siècle* (Lisbon, 1960), 8, 33; Rodolpho Guimarães, *Les mathematiques en Portugal*, 2d ed. (Coimbra, 1909), 26; Jaime Cortesão, *Os descobrimentos portugueses*, 2 vols. (Lisbon, 1959–61), 2: 362, chap. 12; M. Gonçalves Cerejeira, *O Renascimento em Portugal* (Coimbra, 1918), 132; Reijer Hooykaas, *Humanism and the Voyages of Discovery in Sixteenth Century Portuguese Science and Letters* (Amsterdam, 1979), 58: Bensaude, *L'astronomie nautique*, 214–15. On Portuguese efforts to create a Christian astronomical and mathematical tradition (and the persecution that good astronomers faced on suspicion of being Jewish), see Luís de Albuquerque, *Crónicas de História de Portugal* (Lisbon, 1987), 144–8.

31 Bensaude, *L'astronomie nautique*, 40, 79; Barros, *Asia*, dec. 1, liv. 3, cap. 2, 1: 126–127, describes it as "3 palmos" in diameter but does not mention that Zacuto was its creator. Modern equivalents of these dimensions are from Roger C. Smith, *Vanguard of Empire: Ships of Exploration in the Age of Columbus* (New York, 1993), 56. Fourteenth-century astrolabes were usually more than double this size, 7 palmos. José M. Millás Vallicrosa, *Las tablas astronómicas del rey don Pedro el Ceremonioso* (Madrid, 1962), 67–9. Besaude calculated the Arabic astrolabe of 95 to 125 mm in diameter, weighing 1 kilo; and that of 1632 being 184 mm in diameter and weighing 3.84 kilos. The Arabic ones are 360 degrees, the nautical ones go four times from 0 to 90 degrees. Bensaude, *L'astronomie nautique*, 79. The "new astrolabe" described by Camões as a "sage and wise invention" is thought to refer to Zacuto. Camões, *Os Luisadas*, canto V, stanza 25.

32 By the mid-sixteenth century, the Louvain had become the center for the manufacture of scientific instruments, including astrolabes. Astrolabe manufacturers trained at the Louvain school dispersed throughout northern Europe. A. S. Osley, *Mercator: A Monograph on the Letter of Maps, etc. in the Sixteenth Century Netherlands* (New York, 1969), 91–7.

33 Kayserling, *História dos judeus*, 233–6.

34 Jan Huygen van Linschoten, *Itinerario, voyage ofts schipvaert*, 3 vols. (Amsterdam, 1596).

35 Luís Mendonga de Albuquerque, *Curso de história da naútica* (Rio de Janeiro, 1971), 214–15; idem, *História de la navegación portuguesa* (Madrid, 1991), 238; Simon Stevin, *Principal Works*, ed. E. Crone et al. (Amsterdam, 1955–66); vol. 3, *Navigation*. The English editor of Stevin's treatise mentions only two of the three Portuguese treatises on measuring magnetic variation.

36 *Loxodrome* derives from the Latin translation of the Dutch word for curved line (*kromstrijk*), which appeared in Stevin's analysis of Nunes's description. W. G. L. Randles, "Pedro Nunes and the Discovery of the Loxodromic Curve," *Revista da Universidade de Coimbra*, 25 (1989): 123, 129. "Tratado que ho doutor Pero Nunez fez sobre certas duvidas da navegação" (1537), in Nunes, *Obras* (Lisbon, 1940; original edn 1537), 1: 166; A. Fontoura da Costa, *A marinharia dos descobrimentos* (Lisbon, 1933), 225–49. To change from a compass-driven to a great circle course Nunes drew upon Jabir ibn Aflah's theorem that the sines of the angles of a spherical triangle are in inverse proportion to the sines of the arcs opposite them. Nunes, "Tratado em defensam," in *Obras*, I, 176–178; Randles, "Nunes," 125.

37 Idem, in *Opera* (1566) bk. 2 chap. 23 cited in Randles, "Nunes," 129. Mercator never provided a mathematical explanation of this projection. See note 40.

38 At the equator a degree of latitude is 68.7 miles, while near the poles it is 69.1 miles, a discrepancy of 0.4 miles or 1.1 kilometers.

39 Technically called meridians, they are arcs of a great circle connected at the poles. The distance between meridians is zero miles at the poles, but 69.2 miles (111.3 km) at the equator.

40 "Text and Translation of the Legends of the Original Chart of the World by Gerhard Mercator, issued in 1569," in *Hydrographic Review*, 9 (1932): 7–45, esp. 11. Mercator's solution was visual, although Nunes's description of the solution for sailing was mathematical. J. A. Bennett, The *Divided Circle: A History of Instruments for Astronomy, Navigation, and Surveying* (Oxford, 1987), 61, attributes the mathematical explanation to Edward Weight in 1599.

41 Distances are distorted at higher latitudes, but the direction remains a straight line. Costa, *Marinharia*, 225–49. See also Daniel J. Boorstin, *Discoverers* (New York, 1991), 273. Most European sailing in the age of expansion took place between 45° north and 45° south. The unequal landmass critique is frequently made. See Marshall Hodgson, "The Interrelations of Societies in History," *Comparative Studies in Society and History*, 5 (1963): 227–50.

42 The Polynesian names are those given by the Anutans in Richard Feinberg, *Polynesian Seafaring and Navigation: Ocean Travel in Anutan Culture and Society* (Kent, Oh., 1988), 101. Another Polynesian names for the constellation is Newe. The Arabs called the pole star Gah. Costa, *Marinharia*, 63.

43 Guiseppe Maria Seta, *The Glorious Constellations*, trans. Karin H. Ford (New York, 1992), 299.

44 Henri Lancelot-Voisin, sieur de La Popellinière, in *Les trois mondes* (Paris, 1582), describes "that we call the Star of the South, and the others of midday, around which there are some others in a Cross that is called the Southern Cross." He then also describes finding the height of the sun at midday with the astrolabe (6–6v).

14

RITUAL AND PRINT DISCIPLINE AND INVENTION: THE *FÊTE* IN FRANCE FROM THE MIDDLE AGES TO THE REVOLUTION

Roger Chartier

Any historical reflection on the *fête* must depart from the observation of its actual conditions of existence, in order to understand the veritable "festive explosion" that has marked the historiography of this last decade. Although it is not specifically historical, the emergence of the *fête* (and in particular of the traditional feast) as a preferred subject of study leads one in effect to wonder why, at a given moment, an entire scientific class (in this case, French historians) felt attracted by a theme which until then was treated only by collectors of folklore. Seemingly, three reasons, which pertain as much to the recognized function of the historical discipline as to its internal evolution, may be cited. It is clear, above all, that the increased research into the traditional feast constituted a sort of compensation, in terms of understanding, for the disappearance of a system of civilization in which the *fête* had, or rather is considered as having had, a central role. Historical analysis has therefore been charged with explaining, in its idiom and with its technique, the nostalgia exuded by a present that has eliminated the *fête* as an act of community participation. On these grounds, it then becomes possible to rediscover one of the major functions assigned – implicitly or overtly – to history today: to restore to the sphere of knowledge a vanished world, the heritage of which contemporary society feels itself a rightful but unfaithful heir. That the process of understanding is difficult to separate from the fabrication of an imaginary past collectively desired is, in the end, insignificant, unless it is meant to underscore those things that, by being the most neglected by our present age, have become the most symptomatic of a world we have lost. The *fête*, evidently, is one of these.

On the other hand, the *fête*, at least as an object of history, has benefited from the rehabilitation of the specific event. After massive scrutiny of time's long courses and its stable flow, historians – particularly those of the *Annales* tradition – have turned their attention toward the event. In its transitoriness and its tension, it may in fact reveal, just as well as long-term evolution or social and cultural inertia, the structures that constituted a collective mentality or a society. The

Roger Chartier, "Ritual and Print Discipline and Invention: The *Fête* in France from the Middle Ages to the Revolution," pp. 13–24 from *The Cultural Uses of Print in Early Modern France*, French original in 110, Diogène, 51–71. Princeton, NJ: Princeton University Press, 1987 (April–June 1980).

battle has been among the first to benefit from this reevaluation. Removed from narrative history, it can set up a suitable observation point for apprehending a social structure, a cultural system, or the creation of history or legend.[1] In the same manner, the festival has abandoned the shores of the picturesque and the anecdotal to become a major detector of the cleavages, tensions, and images that permeated a society. This is particularly evident when the *fête* engendered violence and the community was torn apart, as in Romans in 1580: "The Carnival in Romans makes me think of the Grand Canyon. It shows, preserved in cross section, the intellectual and social strata and structures which made up a *très ancien régime*."[2] The geological metaphor clearly illustrates a perspective in which the festive event is indicatory and the extraordinary is charged with speaking for the ordinary. Even when a *fête* does not generate excesses or revolt, it is amenable to this kind of approach. It always produces that singular albeit repeated moment when it is possible to grasp the rules of a social system, even though they are disguised or inverted.

A final reason has helped to focus historians' attention on the *fête*. It is, in effect, ideally situated at the nub of the debate that has dominated French historiography for the last ten years, the study of relations in the sphere of conflict or compromise between a culture defined as popular or folkloric and the dominant cultures. The *fête* is an exemplary illustration of this contest. To begin with, it is clearly situated at the crossroads of two cultural dynamics. On the one hand, it represents the invention and the expression of traditional culture shared by the majority of people, and on the other, the disciplining will and the cultural plan of the dominating class. One can then quite rightly apply to the *fête* the analytic methods that Alphonse Dupront applied to the pilgrimage, which underline the tensions between the vital impulse of collectivity and the discipline imposed by institutions.[3] Furthermore, the "popular" festival was quickly looked upon by the dominant cultures as a major obstacle to the assertion of their religious, ethical, or political hegemony. Thus it was the target of a constant effort aimed at destroying it, curtailing it, disciplining it, or taking it over. The *fête* was therefore the stage for a conflict between contradictory cultural realities. Thus it offers a taste of "popular" and elite cultures at a moment of intersection – and not only through an inventory of the motifs which are supposedly their essence. The festival was one of the few scenes in which one may observe popular resistance to normative injunctions as well as the restructuring, through cultural models, of the behavior of the majority. From this the *fête* derives its importance for a history of mental attitudes that concerns the analysis of specific and localized cultural mechanisms.

Having thus acknowledged the reasons which have given the *fête* a priority in historians' work, it is possible, considering a well-defined period (France between the fifteenth and eighteenth centuries), to summarize the achievements of and problems posed by retrospective interpretation. In order to do this, a good method appears to be to consider a certain number of case studies, both original and borrowed. Finally, as a last preliminary, the great ambiguity inherent in the usage of the word *fête* must be kept in mind. Its apparently single meaning revolves, in fact, around manifold differences, often reflected through a series of oppositions: popular/official, rural/urban, religious/secular, participation/entertainment, etc. As it happens, these cleavages, far from aiding a clear typology of festive ceremonies, are themselves problematic, since nearly always the festival is a blend which aims at reconciling opposites.

On the other hand, *fête* carries in itself the definition – theoretical or spontaneous – with which each of us has invested the word. By blending memory and utopia, by affirming what the *fête* must be and what it is not, these definitions will certainly be highly personal and idiosyncratic. Consequently, it becomes impossible to reconstruct the *fête* as a historical object with well-defined contours. In an attempt to halt this shifting, fleeting, and contradictory reality momentarily, we will accept here as *fêtes* all those manifestations which are described as such in traditional society, even though festiveness occurred outside the *fêtes* (and perhaps especially outside).[4]

The first and fundamental premise is that the traditional festival, far from being an established fact – capable of description within static limits – was, from the end of the Middle Ages until the Revolution, the object of many modifying influences which must, before anything else, be ascertained. Ecclesiastical censures were without doubt the oldest. The Church's condemnation of festivals and popular rejoicings supplied material for an uninterrupted series of texts from the twelfth to the seventeenth century. The literature of the *exempla*, which provided material for homilies, is the first example of those admonitions later relayed by the massive corpus of conciliar decrees, synodal statutes, or episcopal ordinances. From the end of the seventeenth century, the abundance of this material was such that it could serve as a basis for theological treatises responsible for transmitting Church tradition and entrusted with informing the priesthood – such as the two works by Jean-Baptiste Thiers.[5] These ecclesiastical interdictions were all the more important inasmuch as they were often adopted by civil authorities, *parlements*, and municipal councils. A typical example of this alliance among the organs of power was the struggle against itinerant festivals in the seventeenth and eighteenth centuries in the jurisdiction of the *parlement* of Paris.[6] These festivals, which were held on Sundays and holy days of obligation and were often associated with a fair marked by traditional rejoicings (dances and games), were banned by a decree of the *Grands Jours d'Auvergne* in 1665. Two years later, this pronouncement was extended to the entire jurisdiction of the *parlement*. Further, during the last decade of the *ancien régime*, one finds this general ban extended by some fifty particulars. Everywhere the mechanism was identical: A complaint was deposited by the parish priest with the general prosecutor of the *parlement*, who then asked the local judges to open an inquiry. Often, if not always, his information resulted in a decree of interdiction. Such an organized and predetermined attack attests simultaneously to the intractability of the rural populace toward the injunctions of established authorities and to convergences between the Christianizing will of the clergy and the magistrates' efforts to enforce control over morals.

The objective of the Church was twofold: to obtain mastery over time and over peoples' bodies. The control of festive times was thus a point of primary confrontation between folk culture and the Church. Very early, as far back as the thirteenth century, the literature of the *exempla* revealed the deep conflict which enmeshed the cycles of Easter and Pentecost.[7] According to the folklore, that particular time of year was above all the time for those festivities that initiated youngsters into society, from the aristocratic tournaments to the dances of the *chevaux-jupons* in a popular environment. For the Church, however, this time of glorification of the Holy Spirit had to be for procession, pilgrimage, and crusade. This conflict for the possession of time occurred on a daily scale as well. The Church acted unceasingly to prevent nocturnal rejoicings and to eradicate the concepts which permitted such events. It tried to eliminate the partition between daytime, which belongs to the Church, and nighttime, the dominion of the people.

Aiming to discipline the flesh, the Church understood festive behavior according to the same categories which were conceived for the designation and description of superstitious conduct. Thus, a triple condemnation of the traditional *fête*: It was illicit, or even "popular" in the sense of Thiers's use when he suggested it as the opposite of catholic. Festive behavior, in fact, varied infinitely; it was not at all dependent upon ecclesiastical authority, but rather was rooted in specific community customs. It was therefore opposed, point by point, to the Catholic spirit which was universal, officially backed, equal for all. This theological condemnation was strengthened by a second, psychological one. For the Church, the popular *fête* was identified with excess and intemperance, with the irrational expenditure of body and wealth. It was situated, therefore, exactly opposite to authorized practices, which were necessary and carefully meted out. Finally, from a moral stand-point, the *fête* signified indecency and license. In it, the rules which formed the basis of Christian society were forgotten. Emotion was bestowed without control, modesty lost its standards, and the flesh let itself go without reverence for the Creator. Considered the abode of spontaneity, disorder, and dishonesty, the *fête* became, in the eyes of Christian moralists, the epitome of anticivilization. It combined, they felt, the different traits which tainted criminal practices as contrary to the true faith, to due propriety, and to Christian modesty. From all of this, it is not surprising that festivals have long been among the major targets of the Church's effort to Christianize the population.[8]

Strategies to censure the *fête* were diverse. The most radical tended to prohibit them – as, for example, in the case of the *Fête de Fous*, generally celebrated on the Feast of the Holy Innocents and characterized by the inversion of the ecclesiastical hierarchy, by the parody of religious ritual, and by manifold rejoicings (theatrical games, dances, feasts, etc.). A *fête* with strong religious connotations, unfolding essentially within the religious sphere, the *Fête des Fous* was the object of age-old condemnation, often reiterated and seemingly effective. In his *Traité des Jeux et des Divertissements*, Thiers reviews the texts that banned both the *Fête des Fous* and the Feast of the Holy Innocents. His series begins in 1198 with the decree of the Bishop of Paris and comprises three texts of the thirteenth century, seven of the fifteenth, and ten of the sixteenth.[9] Such persistence seems to have paid off, since the *Fête des Fous* disappeared at the end of the sixteenth century and by the mid-eighteenth century was already the object of history, but a history so far removed and strange that it was almost indecipherable: "The *fêtes* of which I undertake to recount the history are so extravagant that the reader would have difficulty in giving them credence were he not instructed on the ignorance and barbarism that preceded the renaissance of belles-lettres."[10]

Often this strategy of eradication was not possible and had to give way for compromises in which the festive apparatus passed under religious control. As in the case of the pilgrimage, the Church aimed at imposing its order on the spontaneous, at controlling popular liberty, and at extirpating its intolerable manifestations. Thus this is how one must understand the tenacious battle fought by the churches (both Protestant and Catholic) against dance, an essential element both symbolical and jocose of the traditional *fête*, which they saw as a practice possibly present in ceremonies of very different natures. Here again, Thiers cites various authorities to condemn dance as a school of impurity and weapon of the devil: "How few are those who, dancing or seeing others dance, will not bear within themselves some dishonest thought, will not cast an immodest glance, show an indecent posture, pronounce a lewd phrase, and, finally, will not form a certain desire of the flesh, which the Holy Apostle says?"[11] By deforming the body, dance distorts the soul and inclines it to sin. Thus it must not contaminate the authorized festivities.

A third clerical strategy was that of selectivity. The aim of Christianization was to separate the licit core of the *fête* from the superstitious practices deposited around it. A typical example of this perspective may be found in the religious discourse concerning the fires of Saint John.[12] The *fête* and its fires, which were meant to celebrate the birth of the saint, were considered legitimate, but only on the condition that they would be strictly confined and controlled. The ceremony was to be brief; the bonfires had to be small to avoid any surplus or excess; the dancing and feasting which accompanied the fires were forbidden; and the superstitious practices which they engendered were prohibited. The fires of Saint John nourished, in effect, a great number of beliefs in which superstition was visible to the naked eye, since all were based on the illusive relationship that existed between a gesture (throwing grass on the fire, keeping the embers or the charcoal, going around the fire in certain turns or circles, etc.) and its supposed effects (to divine the hair color of one's future bride, to guarantee freedom from headaches or kidney pains for a whole year, etc.).[13] Between the licit festival and its superstitious and immoral perversion the dividing line was unclear, as is clearly witnessed on the local level by the difficult relationship established between communities and their parish priests.[14] Tolerance and condemnation lived side by side, as much to avoid open conflict, often litigious, as the intolerable infractions. Two cultures faced each other in the *fête*: one clerical, which aimed at organizing behavior to make of the *fête* an homage to God, the other, of the majority, which absorbed the religious ceremonial in an act of collective jubilation.

Although unquestionably the most constant and the most powerful, ecclesiastical pressure on the *fête* was not the only pressure brought to bear. Between 1400 and 1600, in fact, the urban festival (and especially the Carnival) had to face other interference as a result of growing municipal constraint. Everywhere municipal governments tried to curb the town *fête* by controlling its financing, its itinerary, and its program.[15] More and more, toward the dawn of modern times, the *fête* became supported by municipal finance and not only by the head of the confraternity that traditionally organized it. Progressively, private charity gave way to public financing. Thus the municipality gained tighter control of the ceremonial itineraries and so granted a privileged place to certain locations which were the emblem of public identity and power (for example, Town Hall or the market place, occasionally even the municipal magistrates' residences). Thus also, the municipality began a more and more determined intervention in the elaboration of the festive program, which until then had been the exclusive responsibility of the organizing confraternities, the youth "kingdoms," or the *abbayes folles*.

This municipal control had an evident objective: to express, through the idiom of the *fête*, an ideology at once urban and secular. The composition of the processions is a prime example of this scope. They assembled, symbolically and in reality, all the principal corporations and guilds which composed the town, as in Metz in 1510 and 1511.[16] Assembling all hierarchically, the festival expressed the unity of the urban community. It also created an urban legend, which instilled the town's past with a prestigious history, ancient or biblical. In Metz on Torch Sunday, 1511, the eminent citizens disguised themselves to personify David, Hector, Julius Caesar, Alexander the Great, Charlemagne, and Godefroy de Bouillon, all of whom legitimated the power of the city and the authority of its oligarchy. The urban festival thus became a political tool that allowed the town to assert itself against the sovereign, the aristocracy, and neighboring towns. Through expenditure and ostentation, the *fête* demonstrated the town's wealth, and thus instituted a diplomacy of competition which was not without influence on the festive calendar. In order to authorize mutual assistance to the town representatives for the carnivals, the towns of Flanders and Artois in effect rescheduled their festivities. One can observe here how a political ideology is capable of inflecting, defining, or transforming ancient rituals to subvert their meaning.

Censured by ecclesiastical authorities and diverted by municipal oligarchies, the traditional *fête* did not therefore manifest itself except through the distortions progressively imposed on it by the authorities. It would seem impossible to rediscover, beneath these deformations and mutilations, an original base, appropriately "popular" or "folkloric." The raw materials of the *fête* in the sixteenth and seventeenth centuries, as we understand them today, were always a cultural mix, the components of which it is not easy to separate, whether we attempt to organize them by dividing popular from official festivity or by tracing the change over time, in which dependence (on Church and municipal authorities) replaced an earlier spontaneity. That is why it has appeared legitimate to me to set down first the modifications effected on the festivals by the authorities rather than to attempt an illusory description of a festival supposedly free of doctrinal contami-

nation. But this composite material is itself the object of a history which may perhaps be elucidated with a case study that focuses on the system of the *fêtes* in Lyons from the end of the Middle
Ages to the Revolution.[17]

The scheme of this evolution is clear: It shows the succession from *fêtes* based in community
participation to *fêtes* conceded to the populace. During the Renaissance the system of *fêtes* in
Lyons was composed of two major elements: *fêtes* of all the citizenry and gregarious, spontaneous
fêtes. The former presupposed the participation of the entire population of the town in the same
rejoicing, even though this participation was hierarchical and occasionally conflictive. This was
obviously the case of the religious festivals born of the Merveilles festival, which disappeared at
the beginning of the fifteenth century, such as the pardons of Saint John's Day, the processions
of Rogations, and the feasts of patron saints. This was also the case of the royal entries, such as
the many into Lyons between the end of the fifteenth and the beginning of the seventeenth
century: 1490, 1494, 1495, 1507, 1515, 1522, 1548, 1564, 1574, 1595, 1600, 1622 – exactly
twelve entries in 125 years, to which should be added all those that were not royal. Each triumphal entry presented a reciprocal spectacle: The citizens became spectators of the royal procession and the king and his court spectators of the urban procession, in which participated all
the city dwellers, including artisans, assembled in corporations (until 1564) and by wards thereafter. The entry was also a plural festival par excellence, in which multifold elements overlapped:
processions, cavalcades, theatrical games, *tableaux vivants*, fireworks, etc. The iconographic and
scenographic material thus shown offered many readings, certainly as diverse as the different
social and cultural groups, but at least unified within a ceremony that assembled the town
together.

The other essential component of the *fête* in Lyons of the sixteenth century was those *fêtes*
which can be defined as "popular," on the condition that "people" not be too narrowly defined.[18]
Some of these *fêtes*, taken in hand by the *confréries joyeuses* – in this case the twenty abbeys of
Maugouvert – founded their activity upon close relationships within the neighborhood. The same
was true of the charivari that ridiculed beaten husbands under the guise of a donkey ride. Organized by the world of artisans and merchants, these rejoicings were also spectacles that might be
offered to the aristocratic visitors; such was the case with the cavalcade of 1550 and also with the
one of 1566, which was to figure in the triumphal entry of the Duchess of Nemours.[19] On other
occasions, the leading role belonged to the *confréries joyeuses* of the guilds, particularly that of
the printers. The confraternity of La Coquille (The Typographical Error), which may also have
been the organizer of donkey cavalcades (as in 1578), was responsible for the parodic processions which marked Shrove Sunday. Between 1580 and 1601, a half-dozen pamphlets "printed
in Lyons by the Seigneur de la Coquille" attest to the vitality, in both merrymaking and criticism,
of the group of printing guildsmen.[20]

The beginning of the seventeenth century, however, saw the breakdown of this system of festivals founded on popular participation or initiative. Two dates are symbolic historical turning
points: In 1610, for the first time, the pamphlet printed on the occasion of the Shrove Sunday
festival mentioned neither the *abbayes joyeuses* nor the confraternity of La Coquille; and in 1622,
Louis XIII was the last to receive a triumphal entry in the old manner. The following ones, such
as that of Louix XIV in 1658, were nothing more than simple receptions by the municipal authorities and did not imply the participation of the local population. The change brought about was
therefore threefold. First of all, popular organizations (*abbayes*, confraternities), traditionally the
organizers of the festivals, died away. Second, the *fêtes* of the urban population, the triumphal
entries, and the religious ceremonies lost their force. A good index of this decline is a comparison of church jubilees in Lyons in 1564, 1666, and 1734. From the sixteenth to the eighteenth

centuries, the amount and the ostentatiousness of decoration in public celebrations seems to have grown in inverse relation to popular participation. Thirdly, the *fête*, conceded to the public and reduced to a display, became the norm. Thus, in the sixteenth century the artisans offered to the eminent members of society the spectacle of donkey cavalcades, but in the eighteenth century it was the authorities who offered fireworks to the populace. Over the passage of time, popular initiative vanished and the *fête* became standardized. Whatever the occasion, whoever the organizers – aldermen or lords-canon of Saint John – the ceremony was the same, reduced to a fireworks display in which the original meaning of the traditional bonfire – the *feu de joie* – was totally obliterated. The *fête* transmitted and instituted an order of separation in the city, which lost its consciousness as a unified citizenry in which each member participated at his own level.[21]

NOTES

1 G. Duby, *Le Dimanche de Bouvines, 27 juillet 1214* (Paris, 1973), in particular 13–14.

2 E. Le Roy Ladurie, *Le Carnaval de Romans. De la Chandeleur au mercredi des Cendres, 1579–1580* (Paris, 1979), 408. (Mary Feeney, trans., *Carnival: A People's Uprising at Romans, 1579–1580* [New York, 1979], 370).

3 A. Dupront, "Formes de la culture des masses: De la doléance politique au pèlerinage panique (xviiie–xxe siècle)," in *Niveaux de culture et groupes sociaux* (Paris, 1967), 149–67.

4 M. de Certeau, "Une Culture très ordinaire," *Esprit* 10 (1978):3–26.

5 J.-B. Thiers, *Traité des Jeux et des Divertissements* (Paris, 1696) and *Traité des Superstitions selon l'Écriture Sainte, les Décrets des Conciles et les sentiments des Saints Pères et des Théologiens* (Paris, 1679; 2d ed. in 4 vols., Paris, 1697–1704). On the latter text, see J. Lebrun, "Le *Traité des Superstitions* de Jean-Baptiste Thiers, contribution à l'ethnographic de la France du xviie siècle," *Annales de Bretagne et des pays de l'Ouest* 83 (1976):443–65, and R. Chartier and J. Revel," Le Paysan, l'ours et saint Augustin," Proceedings of the Conference *La Découverte de la France au XVIIe siècle* (Paris, 1980), 259–64.

6 Y. M. Bercé, *Fête et révolte. Des mentalités populaires du XVIe au XVIIIe siècle* (Paris, 1976), 170–6.

7 J. C. Schmitt, "Jeunes et danse des chevaux de bois. Le Folklore méridional dans la littérature des *exempla* (xiiie–xive siècle)," *Cahiers de Fanjeaux* 11 (Toulouse, 1976), 127–58.

8 J. Delumeau, ed., *La Mort des Pays de Cocagne. Comportements collectifs de la Renaissance à l'âge classique* (Paris, 1976), 14–29.

9 Thiers, *Traité des Jeux*, 440–51.

10 J. B. du Tilliot, *Mémoires pour servir à l'histoire de la fête des fous qui se faisait autrefois dans plusieurs églises*, cited in Y. M. Bercé, *Fête et révolte*, 140.

11 Thiers, *Traité des Jeux*, 331–41. Like the dance, carnival masks are doubly to be condemned: They disguise the body of man and consequently blaspheme against his Creator. They authorize ribaldry of the most dangerous kind both for the good order of society and for its morals. As proof, two texts. First the synodal constitutions of the Diocese of Annecy (1773 edition): "We finally exhort Their Lordships the Archpriests, Parish Priests, and their Curates, especially in the towns and Cities, to eradicate the abuse of the masquerades which are nothing but a shameful relic of Paganism. To succeed, they must rise against it in their sermons and teaching, especially from Epiphany until Lent; they must demonstrate its absurdity and danger, showing the people that such disorder is injurious to God whose image is disfigured; that it dishonors the members of J. C. by lending to them burlesque and out-of-place characters; and that it encourages licentiousness by facilitating that which impairs modesty" (cited in R. Devos and C. Joisten, *Moeurs et coutumes de la Savoie du Nord au XIXe siècle. L'Enquête de Mgr. Rendu* [Annecy and Grenoble, 1978], 120). Second the preamble of a decree of the Magistrat of Lille in 1681: "Considering that each year sometime before Lent such disorders and inconveniences occur, detrimental to the welfare of souls and the public good, caused by the licentiousness which many people of one or the

214 ROGER CHARTIER

other sex employ in going through cities masked or otherwise disguised . . ." (cited in A. Lottin, *Chavatte, ouvrier lillois. Un Contemporain de Louis XIV* [Paris, 1979], 322).

12 J. Delumeau, *Le Catholicisme entre Luther et Voltaire* (Paris, 1971), 259–61. (English translation: *Catholicism between Luther and Voltaire: A New View of the Counter-Reformation* [Philadelphia and London, 1977].)

13 These superstitions are reported in Thiers, *Traité des Superstitions*, 1:298 (1712 ed.) and 4:404 (1727 ed.).

14 T. Tackett, *Priest and Parish in Eighteenth-Century France. A Social and Political Study of the Curés in a Diocese of Dauphiné, 1750–1791* (Princeton, 1977), 210–15, and D. Julia, "La Reforme posttridentine en France d'après les procès-verbaux des visites pastorales: ordre et résistances," in *La Società religiosa nell'età moderna* (Naples, 1973), 311–415, in particular 384–8.

15 M. Grinberg, "Carnaval et société urbaine, xive–xvie siècle. Le Royaume dans la ville," *Ethnologie française* 3 (1974):215–43.

16 Ibid., 229–30.

17 The basic materials for such a study are collected in the catalogue *Entrées royales et fêtes populaires à Lyon du XVe au XVIIIe siècle* (Lyons, 1970).

18 N. Z. Davis, "The Reasons of Misrule," in *Society and Culture in Early Modern France* (Stanford, 1975), 97–123.

19 *Entrées royales et fêtes populaires*, 49–50. Two documents cited, one by Davis ("Reasons of Misrule," n. 70), the other in the Lyons catalogue (no. 22), permit one to see into one of these *confréries joyeuses*, which met in 1517 on the Rue Mercière.

20 N. Z. Davis, "Printing and the People," in *Society and Culture*, 218.

21 R. Chartier, "Une Académie avant les lettres patentes. Une Approche de la sociabilité des notables lyonnais à la fin du règne de Louis XIV," *Marseille* 101 (1975):115–20.

Part IV

THE ROLES OF WOMEN IN EARLY MODERN SOCIETY

INTRODUCTION

Civil and political liberty is in a manner of speaking useless to women and in consequence must be foreign to them. Destined to pass all their lives confined under the paternal roof or in the house of their marriage; born to a perpetual dependence from the first moment of their existence until that of their decease, they have only been endowed with private virtues. The tumult of camps, the storm of public places, the agitations of tribunals are not at all suitable for the second sex. To keep her mother company, to soften the worries of a spouse, nourish and care for her children, these are the only and true duties of a woman. A woman is only comfortable, is only in her place, in her family or in her household. She need only know what her parents or her husband judge appropriate to teach her about everything that takes place outside her home.

Louis-Marie Prudhomme, *On the Influence of the Revolution on Women*[1]

The Czech writer Milan Kundera once wrote: "Western society habitually represents itself as the society of the rights of man, but before a man could have rights, he had to constitute himself as an individual, to consider himself such and to be considered such."[2] The phrase "the rights of man" is one historians often associate with that great document of the French Revolution, *The Declaration of the Rights of Man and of the Citizen*. The Revolution gave birth to modern politics and an understanding of human rights that has extended well into the twentieth and twenty-first centuries. Yet, the rights of man articulated in 1789 did not extend to women. As the Jacobins argued, women's duties were restricted to the domestic sphere.

Women's work within the home and in the raising of children was necessary to the maintenance of the family, the symbol of the body politic, going back at least as far as Aristotle's *Politics*. The ambiguity of women's roles in Western society as well as society's understanding of women's nature has equally distant roots in the history of Western thought. For Aristotle, women were imperfect men, the result of something that had gone wrong at the moment of conception: perhaps the parents were too young, or too old, or too diverse in age. Perhaps one of them had not been healthy. Woman is thus a "deformity" but one which occurs in the ordinary course of nature. Aristotle, along with his heirs, saw a woman's role within the household as substantial.

However, because he saw them as intellectually and physically subordinate to men, their primary function was procreation, not companionship. Plato went even further: only with another man could one develop a truly fulfilling intellectual (and loving) relationship.

In early modern times, such was the traditional understanding of a woman's role; hers is the private and domestic sphere. Recent scholarship, however, has forced us to reconsider how that domestic sphere ought to be defined. Household duties then differed radically from those of today and an early modern woman's domestic responsibilities naturally differed in accordance with her social status. A woman from a wealthy family probably did not cook and clean herself, yet she would have directed the activities of her household servants and accounts. For a large household to run efficiently, its mistress would need to know how each task was carried out, even if she did not do it herself. Even in a wealthy peasant family, the mistress of the house would have had assistance from children and/or servants in the fulfillment of daily domestic tasks. A woman's domestic responsibilities combined economic activities with family chores. Contemporary injunctions on a woman's role in society often fail to reveal how women participated in the economy in significant ways. Rural men, hardworking though they were, did not produce much cash. Women's spinning and their sales of garden vegetables and domestic animals at market brought the cash necessary for survival into the household. Recent scholarship shows that many women went beyond the limits of the traditional understanding of women's economic activities and demonstrates the need to redefine the domestic sphere.

Marriage often tended to restrict women's legal roles. Still, a husband's control of his wife's property could be modified by the marriage contract, giving her legal ownership of her dowry. In many parts of Europe, a woman was assured a certain portion of her husband's estate. In some regions in the late Middle Ages and the early modern period, women gained legal and economic independence from their husbands if they carried out business on their own or with their husbands. Women might even declare themselves "single" for legal purposes.

Court records indicate a range of women's economic activities, including the management of property and carrying out of legal transactions. Widows, in particular, continued their husband's business, sometimes participating in guilds, although guild structures increasingly excluded women. The following readings reveal the sometimes surprising disparities between legal theory and practice as they pertained to women. Moreover, they reveal disparities in the presentation of women's juridical and economic status in earlier historiography and that of more recent scholarship.

Despite prescriptive legal restrictions, working women continued to participate in the public sphere. The paradox of women's roles in society is equally revealed at the upper levels of society. With the rise of salons, first in the seventeenth and again in the eighteenth centuries, women patronized writers and the arts and held intellectual debates in their homes. Influenced by Renaissance thought, the earlier salons contributed to the rise of *précieuse* culture, emphasizing eloquence and good manners. The *précieuse* women, ridiculed by Molière, the seventeenth-century French playwright, were considered ludicrous because of long-standing views about women's intellectual inferiority. Women should not pretend to be learned people because they only made themselves appear absurd. Yet, again, there is the paradox of the central role of mothers in providing the moral education of their children. The seventeenth-century rise of female education focused in part on preparing women, Catholic and Protestant, to fulfill this role.

The woman question may be linked to broader socioeconomic and political issues. In this case, the critique of learned women was connected to concerns about social transition. Not all of the women involved in salons came from the highest nobility. Some came from wealthy bourgeois families. The *précieuses* believed nobility of spirit was more important than nobility of birth. Since women were dominant in the salons, controversy over their role in society came from the fact that the salons encouraged an opening up of polite society to new categories of the elite, to those not strictly traditional nobility, by promoting a new value system that approved of *mésalliances*, ennoblements through office or wealth, and acceptance of those who adopted a noble lifestyle. The blurring of lines between traditionally distinct classes or orders brought the controversy out into the open. At the heart of the debate was the fear of social disorder resulting from changing social structures.

This situation was further complicated by women's roles in court factions. The centrality of patron–client relationships to court politics by no means denied women a participatory role. Patron–client relationships were central to an individual's power base, and noble women were a part of these struggles. Although women could not benefit directly from appointments to government positions, they might possess royal offices, or use their position at court to vie for the king's attention for their own clients or for their own profit. Women acted as brokers of royal patronage in the interest of their husbands, lovers, sons, male relations, or clients.

Moreover, we know from the example of Maria Sibylla Merian's work that women did function outside the confines of the domestic sphere in other ways as well. Merian's life as an artist and writer who produced remarkably detailed and naturalistic representations of flora and fauna offers yet another example of a woman "going public." According to the traditional paradigm, learned women may have been subject to ridicule in some instances, but there were clear exceptions to the rule. Recent scholarship has revealed that, as the seventeenth and eighteenth centuries progressed, conditions improved and women such as Merian and the *salonnières* were not such exceptions after all.

In the passage with which we began, Kundera argued that a *man* must first constitute himself as an individual before he could have rights. The long-term processes at work in European society over the course of the early modern period contributed to the rise of the individual, defined in part by the watershed of the French Revolution. The paradoxical nature of social debates over the role and nature of women in this same period reveals as much about women as it does about the struggle between individualism in the context of the rise of the modern state and the decline of Old Regime society.

The following readings span a wide geographic range. They, likewise, reveal a number of issues central to the early modern debate on women. Natalie Zemon Davis's *Women on Top* (Part VI) examines sexual symbolism and role reversal in the early modern period. Sexual role reversal, "the world turned upside down," allowed for social criticism of the patriarchal family as a metaphor for the body politic. It is not surprising that the image of the "unruly woman" should be connected to riotous social criticism. Society had long viewed women as sexually voracious and incapable of controlling their passions. In taking on the role or image of women, men took advantage of the assumption that women were weak and therefore not accountable for their actions. Davis not only lays out the historiographical debate on the *querelle des femmes*; she subtly reveals how women's status is more ambiguous than it seems at first glance.

By the eighteenth century, Enlightenment themes had come to dominate European intellectual and cultural life. As Deborah Hertz's work shows, the rise of public cultural events like theater performances opened up new experiences to broader segments of society, but such events did not always satisfy the needs of intellectuals seeking more serious discourse. The eighteenth century witnessed the rise of salons, secret societies, and discussion clubs, often focusing specifically on the Enlightenment and its definition. By the end of the century, secret societies were banned and many discussion clubs were closed to women. Yet, as we see in Hertz's work, for a time, the great Berlin salons, often led by women, ushered in a new sort of egalitarianism by allowing women and Jews to participate actively in the richness of Berlin cultural and intellectual life.

To a degree, all of these readings help us to understand the difference between theory and practice. In an admittedly highly litigious culture, Zoë Schneider's article, "Women before the Bench," reveals the degree to which women's role in the court system is indicative of their participation in public space. Focusing on Norman legal codes that were often misogynous and limited women's legal and economic rights, Schneider shows us the ambiguity of women's legal status. There were both advantages and disadvantages to women's status and, as we see in the case of the "Pitiless Sister," exceptions to legal restrictions.

The problem of deconstructing the unclear relationship between women and the law in the early modern period leads us to an understanding of the historian's potential pitfalls. Legal codes and city ordinances are prescriptive documents. They do not necessarily tell us how things really were, only how authorities at the time thought they should be. Alan Macfarlane's review essay of Lawrence Stone's *The Family, Sex and Marriage in England, 1500–1800* reveals other hidden obstacles for the historian. Macfarlane objects to Stone's division of the early modern family into neat phases: the "Open Lineage" family (1450–1630); the "Restricted Patriarchal" nuclear family (1550–1700); and the "Closed Domesticated" nuclear family (1640–1800). Macfarlane indicates that the problem is not so much with Stone himself, as with a whole generation of historians who have accepted an approach to understanding social history from a historical determinist perspective, often without even realizing it. The reader may or may not agree with Macfarlane or Stone on the rise of individualism in the West, but Macfarlane's judicious critique of Stone's use of sources not only anticipated recent trends in the history of the family but also allows the reader to peel away the many layers of critical analysis necessary to solid historical research.

David Ransel's *Mothers of Misery* allows us to turn to the periphery of Europe. His comparative analysis of infanticide in eighteenth-century Russia discloses the social displacement of women as a result of outside social pressures. Ransel begins by stating that the problem of infanticide was a subject of *government* concern in the eighteenth century. As he draws a picture of the issues related to child abandonment in Russia, the reader notices social classes unfamiliar to the student of early modern Western Europe: slaves and "assigned peasants" (serfs). Any social reform in eighteenth-century Russia would necessarily be "top down," raising interesting questions about the relationship between the individual and the state in an autocratic regime.

Like the passage from Ransel, the excerpt from Merry Wiesner's *Working Women in Renaissance Germany* shows how a focus on women may reveal broader socioeconomic and political issues. Wiesner's study begins with an examination of the political, economic, and legal factors in six German cities that played into women's opportunities and restrictions in the world of work. Moreover, to understand those structures of authority, it is first necessary to consider the consequences of the Reformation and the role of guilds in the exercise of political power in the German states. Wiesner shows how the family indeed served as the foundation of the body politic, yet not always in the interest of the patriarchal order. Together with Schneider, Wiesner's work shows how individual women and their families found ways to "get around" the law in order to protect their economic interests.

The historiographical debate about women in early modern society really began in 1919, when the Englishwoman Alice Clark published her seminal study of the working life of women in seventeenth-century England. Clark argued that, in the seventeenth century, the shift toward capitalist industry had a negative impact on women's status. According to Clark, women's productive capacity was greater in the period prior to industrialism, precisely because of the varied economic activities in which women engaged. Clark argued that women's domestic work had been overlooked because women never received wages for the work they produced; everything was for family consumption. We now know that such was not the case; women often produced goods for the market. Clark argued that the increasingly gendered division of labor, linked to the rise of sharply differentiated public and private space, confined women to a domestic sphere and led to a Marxist alienation from the product of their labor. She believed such alienation never existed in the earlier period, when families worked together for subsistence. In many ways, Clark's work laid out the traditional argument that, in Macfarlane's view, trapped Stone in his study of the family in the early modern period. Other historians see the process of industrialization as contributing in the long term to women's emancipation from the drudgery of unappreciated labor in the domestic sphere. Regardless of which side of the fence one falls, Clark's pioneering work, with its synthesis of processes leading into the modern era of mechanized economic production, framed a debate that has lasted for more than 80 years, and that still remains unresolved. The exciting prospect offered by the work of historians like Hertz, Schneider, Crowston (Part V), and Findlen (Part VI) is that a more thorough examination of the diverse lives of early modern women will lead us to a new synthesis that offers a better explanation not simply of the lives of women, but of European social development.

NOTES

1 (February 12, 1791) in Lynn Hunt, ed. and trans., *The French Revolution and Human Rights* (Boston and New York, 1996), 131.
2 Milan Kundera, *Testaments Betrayed* (London, 1995), 8.

15

POLITICAL, ECONOMIC, AND LEGAL STRUCTURES

Merry E. Wiesner

The work women did in any early modern city was determined to a great degree by the political, economic, and legal structures of that city. Any understanding of the changes in women's work requires some idea of those larger structures. Important, too, are both variations among the cities and things working women shared in all of them. Therefore this chapter begins with short sketches of the relevant political, religious, and economic developments in each city and ends with a more general discussion of citizenship, women's legal personality, and the guilds.

Frankfurt was a free imperial city, ruled by a city council made up of two-thirds city patriciate and one-third guild masters, which also had control over the guilds. At the beginning of the sixteenth century, it had a population of 11,000–12,000 and an economy based on agriculture, crafts, and local trade; only at the time of the fair, twice a year, was it a major trading center. During the sixteenth century the city encouraged immigration, especially by Dutch and Walloon (*welschen*) clothmakers, who brought new methods of cloth production with them, so that by the end of the century the city's population was about 18,000, one-fifth of whom were not Germans. Empty places in the city were filled in, and trade blossomed year round. The population declined somewhat as a result of the Thirty Years' War, although the city fared better in that conflict than most south German cities.

After a revolt in 1525 involving both religious and political demands, and further conflicts between Lutherans and Zwinglians, the city finally settled for Lutheran Protestantism in 1535. This led, later in the century, to conflicts with the Calvinist Welschen and also with Catholics who wanted to remain in the city. The city also had a large (2,000) Jewish population, all of whom lived on one tiny ghetto street. They were often involved in money lending and thus often the target of persecution; in 1612 in the Fettmilch Aufstand, a revolt with a wide range of demands, the Jews were thrown out of the city completely, although they were allowed back in shortly afterward under imperial protection.

Merry E. Wiesner, "Political, Economic, and Legal Structures," pp. 11, 13–35 from *Working Women in Renaissance Germany*. New Brunswick, NJ: Rutgers University Press, 1986.

Most crafts in the city were carried out by the 130 guilds, but during the course of the six-teenth century, more and more crafts began employing pieceworkers and day laborers in their shops. This was particularly true in the new industries, such as silk production, but occurred in older industries as well. Wages and hours for these workers were extremely low, especially in com-parison to food prices, which rose quickly during the sixteenth century despite the city council's attempts to control them. Taxes also rose, especially indirect taxes on basic goods, which hurt the poor most of all, so there were numerous causes for social and economic grievances.

Political power in the city was increasingly concentrated in the hands of the old patriciate, which was really an urban aristocracy, as it lived from rents and had closed its ranks to new-comers. This group set itself off sharply, not only from the guilds, but also from the major mer-chants and traders, who were often the wealthiest city residents.[1]

Strasbourg was also a free imperial city, ruled by several different city councils, whose members also filled most of the official and supervisory posts in the city. Like many German cities Strasbourg had seen conflicts between the old patriciate – the *Constoffler* – and the guilds during the fourteenth century, and the guilds had gained significant representation on all city governing bodies. By 1482 the city's constitution was set, with political and economic power concentrated in a small group of merchants, guild masters, and professionals.

The guilds were also increasingly rationalized and regulated during the fifteenth century, with power concentrated more and more in the hands of the masters, to the detriment of the jour-neymen. The number of guilds in the city was set at twenty, with various occupations joined together into one guild. Every citizen had to "serve" (*dienen*) a guild, either actually doing the work of the guild (*leibzünftig*) or simply paying a guild for the privilege of belonging (*geldzünftig*).

The city's economy was broadly based – shipping on the Rhine, grain and wine from Alsace, the manufacture of a wide variety of goods, and especially regional commerce and trade. The level of commerce and manufacturing varied with good and bad harvests, local wars, and competition with other cities. In general the economy was healthy and growing during the early sixteenth century, suffered increasingly from the general inflation during the latter part of that century, and was then disrupted and depressed by the Thirty Years' War, a pattern found in most south German cities. The city's population followed this pattern as well, growing from about 15,000 during the fifteenth century to over 30,000 by 1620 but then shrinking again because of the war and several outbreaks of the plague to about 25,000 by the mid-seventeenth century.

The city accepted a very tolerant Protestantism in the mid-1520s in a movement first sup-ported by intellectuals and the general populace and then gradually co-opted and adapted by the ruling elite. By the end of the sixteenth century, tolerance had been replaced by a stringent Lutheran orthodoxy, with Calvinists as well as Catholics and Jews no longer welcome in the city. During the course of the Reformation, the city councils also took over the administration and oversight of primary and secondary education, reorganized the system of poor relief, and expanded the city hospitals. The ruling patriciate thus assumed control of all the major political, economic, intellectual, and religious institutions in the city, a control which, despite social, eco-nomic, and political grievances, was unchallenged to 1789, though the city itself was annexed to France in 1681.[2]

Nuremberg was one of the three largest cities in early modern Germany – along with Cologne and Augsburg – and enjoyed a cultural and artistic importance that was perhaps unsurpassed. Although there is great dispute about the population size, it lay somewhere between 30,000 and 50,000 and seemed to be increasing throughout the period. Its economy was based on an enormous variety of products – leather, cloth, metals, gold, and later, books – and on commerce with all of Europe.

Nuremberg was a free imperial city, governed by a city council made up of twenty-six active members, all of whom were chosen from a very small circle of families. Entrance to this elite group was somewhat open in the fourteenth and fifteenth centuries but was closed tightly in 1521 and limited to forty-three families. The council (*Rat*) made all political, military, economic, and later, religious decisions in Nuremberg, down to the most trivial. Unlike the other cities I studied, Nuremberg had no independent guilds; after an abortive artisans' revolt in 1349, the council never allowed any craft independent powers of supervision or regulation. Anything which hinted at guildlike activities, such as workmen's drinking clubs (*Trinkstuben*), endowments limited to members of one craft, or extraordinary requirements for becoming a master, was quickly suppressed. Many crafts were increasingly regulated, with series of ever-more-explicit ordinances promulgated from the fifteenth century on, but these ordinances were always issued by the council, not by the craft itself.

Despite a lack of political power, artisans and craftspeople in Nuremberg were well off economically until about 1550, as the paternalistic government maintained economic policies which benefited the entire city by promoting local manufacturing, the production of luxury goods, and a steady volume of trade. After the mid-sixteenth century the city began a slow economic decline owing to local wars, shifts in patterns of international trade, and increasing competition.

The council began to take over the administration of public welfare in the city as early as the late fourteenth century, establishing funds for orphans, indigent expectant mothers, lepers, the elderly, and others, and in 1522 it reorganized and rationalized the whole system. In 1525 the city became officially Lutheran, and the council assumed control of church lands and institutions, often using them to expand the municipal welfare system. Of all the cities I studied, Nuremberg was the most conservative and slow to change, for the city council was careful to weigh the effects of any change on the "public good."[3]

Memmingen was a small free imperial city with a population of about 4,100 in 1450. Its economy was originally based on the salt trade, for it stood where the salt road from Switzerland to Bavaria crossed the road from Ulm to Italy. During the fifteenth century it also became a center of fustian (a coarse blend of cotton and linen) weaving, wine production, and regional trade, with a wide variety of crafts.

As the result of an artisans' revolt in 1347, the guilds forced the town patriciate also to form a guild, the *Grosszunft*. The city council was from that year until 1551 about half artisan, half patrician, with the two groups alternating in holding the office of mayor. In 1551 as a result of the city's participation in the Schmalkaldic War, the emperor ended guild hegemony, and the municipal government from then on was purely patrician.

During the Peasants' War, leaders from three large peasant armies gathered in Memmingen, where they adopted the Twelve Articles, the basic list of peasant grievances. Shortly afterward the city threw out the peasants, who were not able to take the city. The Zwinglian Reformation had been introduced early, and in 1530 Memmingen was one of the four cities bringing the Confessio Tetrapolitana to the Diet of Augsburg, a confession which strongly emphasized biblical authority and sharply attacked ceremonies.

The city reached its zenith economically and politically in the mid-fifteenth century and remained relatively strong until the outbreak of the Thirty Years' War; by 1618 the population had grown to about 6,000. During the course of the war, however, the city was first occupied by Wallenstein's army and then besieged and taken alternately by the Swedes, the imperial forces, the Swedes again, and finally the Bavarians. By 1648 the city had only 1,500 inhabitants and was never able to regain its commercial or cultural importance.[4]

Besides these four free imperial cities, I also investigated two ducal cities. Stuttgart was a typical ducal capital, with few organs of self-government and many lower level nobility who had land, or even lived, in the city. Its population had grown from about 4,000 to 7,000 in the fifteenth century and continued to grow to about 10,000 by the beginning of the seventeenth century. Its economy was based on the agricultural and natural products of the surrounding Württemberg countryside – wine, grain, flax, timber, fish – on long-distance trade in salt, and on a variety of crafts, many of which produced luxury goods for the ducal court.

During the early sixteenth century Stuttgart was caught in frequent warfare under the long rule of Duke Ulrich, who also introduced the Reformation to Württemberg. The duchy became officially Lutheran in 1534, and the Reformation was further consolidated over the next several decades under the leadership of Johannes Brenz. The Thirty Years' War brought disaster to Stuttgart, as the city was occupied by imperial forces and suffered several outbreaks of the plague, reducing the population to half its prewar level.[5]

Munich was a very unusual ducal capital, as it had been granted a city charter and a number of market privileges in the mid-fourteenth century, during the imperial reign of Louis III (Ludwig der Bayer), a member of the Wittelsbach family, who was also the duke of Bavaria. Though these privileges, such as controlling tolls and market regulations and enjoying an independent city council, were usually reserved for free imperial cities, Munich had its charter reconfirmed by each new emperor until 1641. In governmental structure and political history Munich in the late Middle Ages was thus more like the free imperial cities than the pure territorial capitals such as Stuttgart.

Munich saw a long dispute between the artisans and the patrician city council in the late fourteenth century, which resulted in a short-lived takeover by the artisans' party and eventually in a compromise constitution, the Wahlbrief von 1403, which lasted until the eighteenth century. This agreement marked the beginning of a century-long golden period for Munich. Her patricians grew as wealthy as the nobility in the surrounding countryside, primarily from regional trade in salt, grain, wine, cloth, and metals; trade with Venice; and the east–west trade in building materials. In 1500 the city, with about 13,500 residents, reached a high point of self-rule because the Wittelsbach dukes had very few privileges.

Gradually during the sixteenth century the court began to take over more and more power in the city, assuming control of the salt monopoly and other city privileges. In the 1520s some old Munich families were attracted to Lutheranism, but the dukes remained staunchly Catholic, bringing in the Jesuits in 1559; religious tribunals in 1569 and 1571 broke all Protestant influence in Munich. Economically, the city remained strong in the sixteenth century, not only in regional and long-distance trade but also in the production of Loden, a coarse woolen cloth, and of fine manufactured goods, such as jewelry, clocks, armor, and musical instruments. As the Wittelsbachs increased their power, they began to transform Munich into a cultural and artistic capital, which attracted a variety of artisans to the city. By 1600 the population had grown to over 20,000.

Like every other city in south Germany, Munich suffered during the Thirty Years' War, from the Swedish occupation in 1632, even more from the plague the Spanish army brought into the city in 1634; about one-third of the population died. The city had to provide a number of forced loans to the dukes throughout the war, which ruined it financially. Munich would not reach its prewar heights in trade and manufacturing again until the nineteenth century.[6]

As these short descriptions indicate, the six cities varied in population, political structure, economic development, and religion. I had originally intended this study to be a comparative one, as I expected women's work to be viewed and regulated differently in the different cities. As the research progressed, it became apparent that the similarities were more striking than the differences. Though some types of occupations were found in only some cities, the work that most women did could be found in all communities. Women's work was restricted not only in cities with declining economies and shrinking opportunities but also in those with booming economies and steady immigration from the rural areas. It was restricted in cities occasionally ruled by noblewomen as well as in those whose governing body was elected. City councils with heavy guild membership limited women's work, but so did pure patrician councils, to whom working women represented no status or economic threat. Religious differences also played a lesser role than I expected. Though they disagreed on so many other issues, Protestant and Catholic men united in their growing opposition to women working in certain occupations. It became clear to me that the economic, political, and cultural forces which determined women's work were shared ones.

The institutional structures providing the background for women's work were also shared ones. Every city made clear distinctions between citizens and noncitizens, giving citizens great legal and economic advantages. Every city had law codes which enumerated the rights and responsibilities of city residents and controlled their actions. Every city had some form of guild or craft organizations which regulated some occupations and also had certain occupations not controlled by any guild. Within all of these structures distinctions were made between men and women; distinctions were also made among women according to their marital status, which rarely made a difference for men.

Citizenship was the fundamental institution on which all others were based. As cities had grown during the Middle Ages and had won their independence from feudal overlords through negotiation, purchase, or revolution, they had become legal entities, corporate bodies made up of all those living within the city walls. It was therefore extremely important that everyone living within the city, or at least those owning property, renounce all allegiance to other authorities, if the city was to maintain legal and economic independence. Cities therefore required all propertied persons to formally assume citizenship if they moved into the city and to formally renounce it if they left permanently. Cities backed these requirements with taxation demands; noncitizens often paid much higher taxes, and persons renouncing citizenship were often fined heavily as the cities attempted to discourage them from leaving.

Citizenship entailed both obligations and privileges, and cities increasingly denied citizenship to those who could not carry out the obligations or else simply quit requiring everyone living in the city to become citizens. Servants coming in from the countryside to work in the households of citizens were not required to become citizens, nor were wage laborers or pieceworkers who did not maintain their own households. Those seeking citizenship had to prove they were of legitimate birth, free status, and "honorable reputation" (*wohl Verhaltens*) and often had to pay a citizenship fee.[7] By the sixteenth century noncitizens often outnumbered citizens within the city walls, though the privileges accorded to citizens remained. If one wanted a political voice or economic power, one had to become a citizen.

In most cases regarding citizenship, cities treated men and women relatively equally. Unmarried women or widows moving into a city were required to purchase or earn citizenship in ways similar to men and to prove that they were legitimate, free, and had good reputations. They swore an oath on first becoming citizens and were required in most cases to provide soldiers and arms for the city's defense.[8] The number of men and amount of equipment women were required to provide were assessed according to the value of the property they held, exactly as they were for male heads of household.[9] Citizens' wives and daughters often did not swear an oath, as the citizens' oath was only taken by the head of household. After a male citizen died, his widow was often required to take an oath, thus indicating her new status and responsibilities.[10]

Occasionally women were granted citizenship without paying the normal fees, usually if they were maids who had served a long time – then, fifteen, or twenty years – and "as long as they behaved honorably and without causing any aggravations." Often these women had to swear that they would not ask for public support during their first five years as citizens. This was also true for widows who paid normal citizenship fees; in addition to the fee they had to prove they owned enough property to support themselves without working.[11] Cities also attracted midwives by offering free citizenship to them and their husbands in the same way they offered citizenship to physicians.[12] Women who felt they had performed a special service to city residents occasionally requested a grant of citizenship, as a case in Memmingen in 1571 notes: "She says that she served the people during the Schmalkaldic Wars with her cooking and other services."[13] Such cases were decided individually.

Women also used religion as a means of obtaining citizenship. With the coming of the Reformation, and especially with the Peace of Augsburg, there was an upsurge in those renouncing citizenship and moving elsewhere. In Nuremberg, for example, the decade of the 1510s saw 66 persons giving up their citizenship; the 1520s, 131; and the 1530s, 383.[14] (Nuremberg officially became Protestant in 1525.) Where did these people go? In many cases, to nearby Catholic cities, such as Munich. A woman requested that she and her husband be allowed to become citizens of Munich again, as they could no longer stay in Nuremberg; the Munich city council wanted proof that she "had always held the Catholic religion" even while living in Nuremberg before it would allow them back in. In this case, they only asked about her religious practices, not those of her husband, perhaps because she was making the request. Another refugee from Nuremberg, also Catholic, offered to nurse "sick and infected persons" if Munich would grant her citizenship. Again the city council requested that she bring proof from religious authorities that she had always been a Catholic.[15] Religion was also an acceptable justification for a woman to remain in a city after her husband had left. Even in cases involving the most gruesome wife beating or cruelty, city councils usually ordered women to remain with their husbands; the councils would even try to find men who had deserted their families in order to send the family to them! If the man left for religious reasons, however, the family was often allowed to stay, as long as they agreed to follow the religion of the city.[16]

In some cases involving spouses of differing faiths, a clear double standard emerged in city councils' decisions about whether to allow the couple to remain in the city. In 1631 the Strasbourg council considered whether citizens should lose their citizenship if they married Calvinists. It decided that a man would not "because he can probably draw his spouse away from her false religion and bring her on to the correct path." He would have to pay a fine, though, for "bringing an unacceptable person into the city." A woman who married a Calvinist would lose her citizenship, however, "because she would let herself easily be led into error in religion by her husband and be led astray."[17]

In some cases, cities allowed women to stay without obtaining citizenship at all, usually if they were extremely poor or very old or sick. The city council still wanted to know who and where these charity cases were and sent inspectors out to each quarter of the city. Foreign women who had not received special permission but who were found living in the city were fined, as were the citizens who housed them.[18]

If a woman moved out of the city permanently, she was expected to renounce her citizenship formally and pay the often quite substantial tax (*Nachsteuer*) demanded by the city council. Occasionally she was allowed to retain her citizenship if she married a foreigner and moved away, but only after receiving special permission and under special circumstances, such as the city council's recognition that the new husband was quite elderly and the woman would most likely be moving back into the city after his death. All citizens, male and female, were usually required to live in the city and could lose their citizenship for staying too long outside its walls.[19]

Women, like men, could also lose citizenship for a variety of reasons. One of the most common punishments for a crime was banishment, usually a specific distance away from the city walls. As cities began to enforce stricter moral legislation in the sixteenth and seventeenth centuries, they used the threat of loss of citizenship as a weapon in the battle against adultery and fornication. In Strasbourg in 1620 any citizen-woman, widowed or single, who let herself get pregnant before her wedding was to lose her citizenship once the pregnancy was discovered. This was during the Thirty Years' War, and the city council was especially horrified at the prospect of soldiers impregnating city residents. In 1623 the city council even considered extending this to any male citizen whose wife became pregnant before marriage, although so drastic a step was never taken.[20] Couples who married before they had enough money to set up a household, and thus were likely to become public welfare cases, were also threatened with loss of citizenship.[21]

As cities began to tighten their citizenship requirements, they tried to prevent women from marrying "unacceptable" foreigners. In 1557 the Strasbourg city council forbade citizens' widows or daughters to marry foreigners without its express permission. If they did, they and their husbands would have to leave the city. Memmingen also granted citizenship rights to maids who had served faithfully for many years, but on the condition that if they married, it would be to a citizen "so that two foreign persons do not come into the city in this way." Augsburg, as well, often accepted a woman as a citizen with the note "on the condition that she doesn't marry, unless it is to a citizen." In 1613 Strasbourg sharpened its earlier restrictions and required a male foreigner who wanted to marry a citizen's widow or daughter to obtain citizenship rights on his own before he even became engaged.[22] The situation was the same in Frankfurt. According to a regulation passed in 1614, if a woman married a foreigner who had not received citizenship rights on his own, she would lose her citizenship and be forced to leave the city. In 1623 this was extended to male citizens who married foreign women:

> It has been discovered in the case of citizen's sons and widowers, that many of them marry foreign, propertyless, and even slovenly suspicious female persons and then bring them in [to Frankfurt] and that these persons receive citizenship through this marriage: when the husband dies they then marry someone similar [i.e., a foreigner] and the city and the common good are brought all kinds of problems and difficulties. So we are caused and moved to extend the previous ordinance to include male persons, widowers, and citizen's sons. Therefore they are earnestly admonished that from now on no one is to marry, or even offer to marry or become engaged to, any foreign female person without first bringing us proof of her legitimate birth and her property and means of support. If the marriage is then allowed, these persons are required to purchase citizenship according to the amount of property they own as the law requires.[23]

In regard to the basic rights, obligations, and duties of citizenship, then, cities made little distinction between men and women. Beyond that, however, there were clear legal restrictions on what the female half of the population could do. Some of these restrictions, and the majority of legal cases in which women were involved, concerned private and family matters, so I do not specifically discuss them here. Others concerned legal and economic matters which affected all women, for example, witnessing, inheritance, and guardianship, thus providing the legal setting within which women could operate on public matters; these I mention briefly. Still others primarily concerned working women and are examined in greater depth.

Women could serve as *witnesses* in civil cases if no male witnesses were available and could appear in criminal cases, though their rights in the latter were somewhat limited.[24] A woman could report stolen goods and could report that she had been raped, although she would usually have to prove that she had tried to resist and that she had a good reputation. Pregnant women were given special rights as witnesses; along with other "dangerously ill" people, they were allowed to give their testimony before a case had been officially opened, in case they were no longer available once it had.[25]

If a woman was ordered to appear before a court as a defendant or witness and refused, she was to be banished. In the case of a married woman, if the refusal was with her husband's knowledge, he was to take the punishment; if he did not know or approve, she was to take it. A married woman was also required to accept a court order that her husband appear; if she refused to take it or took it and then did not tell her husband, she was to be arrested herself.[26]

If there was any suspicion about a woman's character or motivation, however, her testimony in any case was to be discounted: "If a woman is of a timid disposition and fears her husband, then she is to be disdained. If she is a brave woman, who only wants to hide her feelings from her husband out of consideration, then she should be accepted, as long as she is found to have a good reputation [*guten Leumundts*]. Also, if the opposition party will allow her to speak, then she is not to be ignored."[27]

Women could freely make their own wills, although they generally could not serve as witnesses for anyone else's will. In Nuremberg girls could make a binding will at the age of twelve, while boys had to wait until they were fourteen. In the Duchy of Württemberg the legal age for both boys and girls was sixteen. In general, no special requirements were placed on women making wills; the procedure varied from town to town as to the number of witnesses required and the way in which a will had to be registered but was the same for both men and women. This was also the case with inheritance laws. These were often extremely complicated, as they sought to cover every possibility – multiple marriages, stepchildren from a previous marriage, grounds for disinheritance, adoption, and so on – but were roughly the same for men and women. The only interesting difference is that in some cities a son could be disinherited at any time for entering into a marriage against his parents' will, but a daughter could not if it was shown that the parents had not found her a husband before she was twenty-two or twenty-four.[28]

A clear difference between the legal status of men and women emerges in the issue of guardianship. When a man died, his children, even if their mother was living, were usually given a male guardian responsible for their welfare until they came of age. Usually, although not always, the widow was given a guardian (*Vogt*) as well. He was to represent her in court cases and act as her agent if a male voice was needed. Here again, though, there was a difference between legal theory and practical reality. Widows were frequently represented by their guardians but also appeared in court to present their own cases.

For a variety of reasons cities began to tighten up their systems of guardianship beginning in the late fifteenth century. I found it possible to trace this process in Strasbourg and see some of the motivation behind it. In 1465 four members of the city council recommended that a guardian be appointed for every widow within one month of her husband's death:

Who is to give her useful and well thought out advice: also every widow responsible to provide a horse for the city [i.e., whose property was above a certain value] should not have the right to give away or sell more than 20 gulden worth of her property or goods without the knowledge and approval of her guardian. Every widow should also make a yearly report concerning her property to her guardian. If the widow marries again the guardianship is to be ended.[29]

But the system was not to be limited solely to widows:

> All unmarried women who have come of age but who no longer have a father and mother are to be given a guardian as well. Also if a man or boy who owns property comes of age and handles this property in such a way that he is bringing himself to ruin, which the council can clearly see, then the council will appoint him a guardian from among his own relatives or in some other manner help him to take care of his own interests.[30]

Thus, with the patriarchal attitudes so common among city councils, these four members recommended that those judged to be incapable of handling their own affairs be given guardians "for their own good." Men who were unable to deal with their own inheritance were to be treated exactly like women.

Although at first glance the city council appeared to be protecting gullible widows and spendthrift young men, their real motivation emerged in a discussion six years later. Again the council recommended that all widows and unmarried women be given guardians, but this time expressly to prevent their going into convents and deeding all their property to the convent, "by which their relatives are disinherited and the city loses people who provide it with horses [i.e., taxpayers]." The guardian was to approve any agreements the woman made regarding her property, although she could complain to the council if she felt he was treating her unfairly. If she wanted to go into a convent, she was free to go but could only take in enough property to support her during her lifetime; at her death no more than fifty pounds was to be given to the convent, with the rest to go to her heirs. Covering all angles, the council also noted that women who gave up their citizenship but then came into one of the city's convents were also to follow these rules, "for giving up their citizenship shall not allow them to escape them."[31]

The council adopted these regulations shortly afterward, but not without opposition. One of the most vocal opponents was the preacher and moralist Geiler of Kaisersberg, who saw the regulations as an infringement on individual women's opportunity to do works of charity. In a sermon from 1501 he commented:

> Arranging a guardian for widows who are responsible and sensible persons is a novelty that has arisen in this city supposedly for the common good. In truth, as I will report, it was a self-seeking move by those who were in power. Strasbourg has long stood and been governed without such an inappropriate law. The decline of the city cannot be attributed to it, but to many other things as I have often said before. Everyone who is bothered by something always says it harms the common good, but it really involves his own affairs.
>
> The opposite is shown to us in the advice of God and the practice of the holy saints, like Saint Elizabeth, who gave two thousand marks at one time to the poor for the building of a hospital, or Saint Paula, who lost everything that she had, and many others too numerous to tell. The Gospel tells us directly: if you want to be saved, go out and sell everything you have and give it to the poor. It does not say to give it to your heirs and relatives. This law is totally against the word of Christ. It is a mockery of God, a haughty service of the devil to forbid a pious person to give everything that she owns for the will of God.[32]

In this and other sermons Geiler constantly stressed the freedom and right of both men and women to do what they wanted with their own money. It is clear, of course, that the underlying dispute is an economic one. The city felt it was losing too much money to the convents; the convents, that they had a right to the property of the women who entered them. What happened as a result of this dispute, however, was that the power of guardians over widows and unmarried women in all economic matters, not simply their going into convents, was increased.[33] As is so often the case throughout this study, restrictions on women came about as a by-product of a dispute between two groups over political and economic power.

The power of guardians was similarly increased in other cities throughout the sixteenth century. In 1578 Augsburg ordered that all widows report to the official in charge (*Oberpfleger*) within one month of the death of their husband, make an appraisal of all goods and property, and choose two men who were not heirs to act as guardians. If the widow did not, the city council would choose these for her "because so often out of stupidity and inexperience, especially in these difficult times, widows have diminished the estate of their children and even sunk into total poverty." The women of Augsburg were apparently not ready to admit to their stupidity or inexperience, however, as this ordinance was reissued in 1615, with the added threat that if any woman out of "disobedience or mischief" did not follow it, she was to be clapped in irons.[34] In 1668 it was reissued again, as a new problem had emerged. Widows had claimed that since their guardians, and not they themselves, swore an oath that the appraisal was complete, they could not be held liable if it were not. After all, they were only inexperienced women who might easily forget to include something. The city council responded by adding the clause that the widows, as well as their guardians, had to swear all oaths, whether they appeared in court or not.[35]

Throughout the entire period, widows frequently took their guardians to court when they felt their rights had somehow been violated. All the city codes allowed them to do so, and city councils were quite willing to order a guardian to take better care of a widow and her children or to appoint a new guardian if the first one was creating problems.[36] In these cases, the widow herself, not some male relative, appeared before the city council to argue her case. Thus, though the power of guardians steadily increased during the period, women were never totally at their mercy.

Along with a strengthening of the role of guardians over widows, the sixteenth and seventeenth centuries saw increasing restrictions on widows' rights to their own children. In a number of cities it was up to the guardians whether a woman should retain control of her children if she remarried. Even with very young children, the deceased husband's father often had more to say about their future than their mother did. Only women whose children were illegitimate had full fatherly force and could appear in court on behalf of their children in all cases.[37]

In addition to these limitations on their ability to be witnesses, make wills, serve as guardians, and handle inheritance, women were often specifically forbidden to make contracts or own, buy, and sell property. The guiding force behind many of the restrictions was the concept of *weibliche Freiheit*, "female freedom" in exact translation. Basically this meant that women had the "freedom" to declare their signature invalid on contracts and agreements in cases where they were acting for any third party, including their husbands. They could simply say that they had been misled or pressured or had not understood what they were doing and thus should not be held liable.[38]

In some cases, weiblich Freiheit acted as protection for a woman. She could even claim it on loans from her own husband and say that he had pressured her into making an agreement. Only if two of her male relatives were present could she legally give up this right, "because wives are so easily persuaded into making such dangerous promises through the duplicity of their husbands."[39] In some cities two impartial judges could be substituted for the relatives.[40]

Generally, though, weibliche Freiheit acted as a protection for the husband, for it meant his wife could not legally pledge his goods or property to pay back any debts.[41] The husband's knowledge and agreement was needed on any major financial decision which involved property held jointly: "Whoever loans a woman money without the knowledge of her husband, be it man or woman, Christian or Jew, shall not have the right to demand it, and her husband will be able to retrieve the letter or pawn for five pounds. Before this, he must prove the debt was made without his knowledge."[42]

There were, however, a number of ways a woman could get around this weibliche Freiheit and make legally binding contracts. First, if she was acting in her own interests, handling her own property, the principle did not apply at all. Even a married woman who owned property in her own name – and this was very common in the sixteenth century – was free to do with it as she wished, to buy, sell, loan, or pawn without the knowledge or approval of her husband.[43] Widows and unmarried women could also handle their property without a co-signer.

Second, if a woman had acted deceitfully (*"gefährlich und betrüglich"*) or had made money off the contract, she could not later plead weibliche Freiheit. This was a protection for those who lent a woman money under the understanding that she would not later claim weibliche Freiheit, only to have her attempt to do so anyway. Cities added this limitation, despite the fact that weibliche Freiheit was a right protected by the emperor, because they found that "good and honorable people, in all good faith" were loaning money and then losing it when a woman refused to pay them back.[44]

Third, a woman could also willingly and specifically give up this right in the presence of two witnesses who were her relatives. In Frankfurt this agreement was to be made in the presence of a Bürgermeister, and the clause noting her renunciation was written into the contract. In Nuremberg she could also do this in the presence of two of her husband's friends and a notary.[45]

Fourth, and most important for this story, exceptions were made for women whose occupations required that they buy and sell goods or loan and borrow money. The earliest city law codes (e.g., Lübeck 1200–1226) made no mention of such occupations, but usually by the late fourteenth century, exceptions were being made for all sorts of women. In Lübeck these women were described as "those who have market rights [*kopschat*], and who loan and sell independently." The Munich city law code from 1340 states simply: "A woman who stands at the public market and who buys and sells has all the rights that her husband does." An Augsburg ordinance from 1432 notes that all female marketwomen (*Krämerin*) lost their weibliche Freiheit.[46]

In the late fifteenth century many cities began to define more precisely who was and who was not a market woman, making exceptions for them in suing and inheritance cases as well. A Nuremberg city ordinance notes: "Also no bailiff may summon a married woman. And no judge or summoner can issue a suit against any married woman. If a suit is written against a married woman, her husband shall be without penalty and can free his wife from any suit with a payment of thirteen pfennige, except for female tailors, shopkeepers, money changers, innkeepers, and market women."[47] Frankfurt and Stuttgart used similar language, and as a case in 1505 in Frankfurt indicates, married market women, not their husbands, were imprisoned for their own debts.[48]

The special status of market women is evident in inheritance laws. On the death of a spouse, most cities allowed the survivor to separate all his or her goods from those of the deceased and pay off the heirs and creditors only from the goods of the deceased. By doing this, the surviving spouse also gave up any claim to a share of the estate of the deceased but was assured of retaining something if the debts were larger than the estate. This was intended primarily as a protection for women, who could thus at least take back and live off their dowry and any other goods they owned separately, rather than see them go to pay off their husband's creditors. This "renunciation and separation" had to be done within a month of the death, and the surviving spouse had to swear that he or she had not taken anything from the estate of the deceased.

Market women were not allowed to do this renunciation and separation. The Nuremberg Reformation from 1564 spells this out: "If a couple practices a craft or business together, with buying and selling, like cloth cutting, money changing, running a stand at the market and the like, or are public innkeepers or wine handlers, then both spouses are obliged to pay all debts in the same manner. Because the wife in such occupations is in the same danger of loss, an equal share of the profits shall also belong to her."[49]

The Frankfurt Reformation from 1578 gives a more elaborate justification for excluding market women:

> Because in selling and at the market stands, the two spouses carry out a common business – the wife as well as the husband goes through the streets or sits at the market stall, sells and buys, takes in and gives out money, keeps the books, and other such things. Also, with people who keep a public inn or hostelry, or a common wine stand, it is difficult to divide or separate the goods. So that the people who do business with them will not be deceived or injured, we have decided that in such cases both spouses will be responsible to pay back all debts in full.[50]

In Frankfurt and Lübeck the common business even included the woman's dowry; if she was a market woman and carried out a common business with her husband, she could make no marriage contract which excluded her dowry from the final reckoning of debts. The reasoning of the Lübeck authorities is illustrative on this point:

> Because this city of Lübeck is a merchants' city and dedicated to trade and commerce [Handel und Wandel], honor and trust must always be present, which the oldest and first laws clearly recognized. Thus it is better that private persons, especially women, are somewhat harmed in their inheritance and goods than that the trust needed in trade is weakened or even destroyed in this city, which would bring decline and disaster.[51]

The Frankfurt Reformation, like that of Nuremberg, gave her the slight solace that "because the woman in this sort of common business must stand in the same danger and chance of loss, it is also just [billich] that all profits from such business belong equally to her."[52]

Frankfurt later extended this restriction to include wives of "craftsmen, vineyard workers, day laborers, and the like." Why? "Because what they produce and purchase for their craft (with which both spouses support themselves) is common property and is often even acquired without purchase (i.e., by barter with the neighbors, or made by one spouse), and one as well as the other is responsible to pay all debts."[53] With this, the city council recognized that neither spouse would have brought much, if anything, into the marriage and that both worked to produce or purchase any goods, so that dividing things between the husband and wife would have made little sense. Though this is a compliment to the wife of a laborer, as it recognizes her vital contribution to the family income, it actually worked to her detriment, for she was often left with nothing on her husband's death because their debts were so often greater than all the property held.

Strasbourg had passed a similar ordinance in the early sixteenth century, but one vague enough to cause constant problems. In 1552 the city council decided to spell things out more clearly:

> Because a large number of tiresome legal cases have come up frequently between creditors and widows, as to whether these women are market women or not, and on both sides there have been appreciable expenses, we have decided that from now on, all women are to be recognized and seen as market women if they are in business by themselves or alongside and with their husbands (either in salted or other wares, in grain or other things, with nothing excluded). Whether they sell inside or outside the city of Strasbourg, on market or fair days, whether they buy or sell wholesale or retail, or exchange goods for other goods and thus carry out public business (öffentliche Gewerbehandel).

> Those who sell wine, fruit, grain, or other things from their own fields at harvesttime are not to be considered [as market women], but only those who handle these goods as their primary business and derive most of their support from this.[54]

Strasbourg was somewhat more narrow in its consideration of the wives of craftsmen than Frankfurt was: "And as to whether the craftspeople who buy wares and then later distribute, sell, or trade these goods are to be considered market people: so in the same manner if a craftsman or his wife buys other wares and sells them along with the things they have made themselves, she is to be considered a market woman."[55] The council also reserved the right to decide in those cases in which the woman's status might still be in dispute.

Just such a case was brought to the Strasbourg XV, the body which handled all internal affairs, in 1584. This case points up several aspects of the whole issue of weibliche Freiheit and the status of market women. A butcher's widow wanted to separate her goods from those of her husband, a proposal opposed by his creditors, who argued "that the widow, while her husband was alive, stood at the butcher's counter herself, weighed out the meat, took in money, melted tallow, made candles, sold the candles, and other things. After his death she also slaughtered four head of cattle and received the money for them; therefore she is to be considered a market woman." The widow answered them that she had not stood at the counter or sold at the market. The council asked its lawyers about what to do in the matter, questioned the other butchers, and finally decided that she had not been active enough to be considered a market woman. What is striking about this case is that the woman was playing down her own role, arguing that she had less of a part in the family business than she probably had. It was to her financial advantage to assert, or to pretend, that she knew nothing about butchering.[56]

Thus the whole question of weibliche Freiheit and its limitations takes a very ironic twist. Originally, it appears that any woman could claim weibliche Freiheit, no matter what her occupation. Gradually city councils realized (or claimed) that women were using the privilege to their own advantage in order to make contracts and then break them. The women most likely to have done this, the market women, were gradually excluded from weibliche Freiheit and forced to take full responsibility for all their economic activities. Because in many cases, like that of the butcher's widow, it was detrimental to the woman involved to be considered a market woman, she was forced into the position of denying her own competence and knowledge about the family business.[57] A Munich case from 1595 is a good example. A man demanded payment for a horse from the widow of a butcher, who answered him that she "knew nothing about her husband's business or what he had contracted for." She knew very well, however, that this man had not been there when all her husband's creditors had been ordered to appear shortly after his death to make their claims against his estate.[58] In most such cases, the city councils recognized that such women were economically active and relatively independent; the women themselves tried to deny it in order to claim weibliche Freiheit. What few women's statements there are about their own activities are therefore not always creditable; the creditors may actually be more accurate when they report that certain women did everything their husbands did in running a business.

Though law codes mention only the four exceptions to weibliche Freiheit already noted (women acting in their own interests, women specifically giving this right up, women deceiving their creditors, and market women), actual court proceedings involve many more women. Women were making contracts, buying, selling, and trading land and goods all the time without specific male approval or the co-signature of their husbands. Perhaps some implied renunciation of weibliche Freiheit was understood in each case, or else the whole principle was frequently ignored.[59]

This distinction between theory and practice appears in many types of legal cases involving women. Despite theoretical restrictions on their ability to appear in court, women appeared as plaintiffs and defendants fairly frequently. Many of these cases involved marriage and family issues, but others were strictly economic. Women brought suits to demand repayments for debts owed them, usually quite small but occasionally as high as one thousand florins; to ask for extensions on loans they owed to others; to demand that pawnbrokers return goods they had paid off; or to demand that former or present employers pay them the salary owed them.[60] Though the law distinguished between single, married, and widowed women, women of all marital statuses brought cases to court, evoking no comment that this was somehow unusual.

The difference between theory and practice points out the ambiguity of women's legal position. Women were simultaneously independent legal persons (they owned property, inherited wealth, received wages, paid taxes) and dependent parts of a legal entity, the family, whose financial decisions they did not officially control. On marriage, a woman gave up some of her legal rights in return for greater security and an established status, but not all of them. At no point in the sixteenth and seventeenth centuries did a woman completely lose her legal identity when she married. She could also use the institution of the family to defend her status and rights against other male-controlled institutions, or even against her own husband. On widowhood, a woman's legal status changed again, and not simply back to what it had been before marriage, for the widow's status brought additional responsibilities and opportunities.

This ambiguity stems from the aims and motivations of the men making the laws and also from their views of women. They viewed women as less competent and weaker than men, needing both guardians to protect them and protection from those guardians, should the guardians turn out to be unscrupulous and crafty. City councils also realized that women could be just as unscrupulous and crafty as men, so laws were needed to protect society from women as well as to protect women themselves. The family was seen as the foundation of society, with the husband as its proper head; when strengthening the power of the husband was perceived to strengthen the family, lawmakers built up his power. If his personal interests worked to the detriment of the family, however, the wife's interests might be strengthened. City councils aimed at both social control and full city treasuries, aims which came into conflict when they had to decide whether to allow widows and single women to work independently.

If there were ambiguities in women's general legal status during the early modern period, there were even more surrounding their rights and responsibilities in the workplace. Most production in 1500 was organized by craft guilds, which had grown up in most German cities during the twelfth and thirteenth centuries. During the fourteenth century these guilds began to demand that they be allowed to participate in city government, which was generally controlled by a small number of merchant families. These merchant families, often termed "patricians," dominated the economy of the city and were the only ones allowed on the city council.

The guild demands varied from city to city but generally included seats on the city council, an end to the patricians' special privileges, some control over defense of the city, rights to determine taxation levels and the tax structure, control of the gates into the city, and other economic and political rights. The guilds were often joined in their opposition to the patriciate by day laborers and the poor, and the conflicts were often violent. In some cities, such as Strasbourg and Memmingen, the conflict resulted in the guilds' winning some participation in the city government. In other cities, such as Nuremberg, the guilds were totally defeated, and the city council forbade any independent guilds from that point on; production in Nuremberg was organized by the "sworn crafts," which were completely controlled by the council.[61]

Conflicts between the guilds and the city councils continued throughout the early modern period and frequently involved women's work or, more specifically, whether the guilds or the city council would control what work women would do and when exceptions would be made. Women were rarely actors in these conflicts, for with the exception of a few female guilds in Cologne and

Basel, the guilds in Germany were male organizations.[62] They were structured according to the male life cycle. One studied for a set number of years as an apprentice, then became a journeyman and theoretically worked under a number of different masters to perfect one's skills, then finally made a masterpiece. If it was judged acceptable by the current masters (and they felt there was business enough to support another shop), one could settle down and open a shop.

The guilds recognized, however, that a master could not run a shop on his own, and in many cities they required that the master be married. The master's wife and daughters thus often learned some of the skills required for that particular craft, though they were not officially part of the apprenticeship structure. In addition, a master craftsman might hire maids or female pieceworkers during busy seasons, so there were often women working in the shops alongside the journeymen and apprentices. Most workshops were small and attached to the master craftsman's house; thus women could easily divide their time between domestic duties and work in the shop. Women could spend a great deal of their time in production-related tasks, for there was relatively little housework in early modern homes. Clothing and furnishings were few, simple, and rarely cleaned, and a maid or maids assisted in the cooking and washing.[63]

Because women were not officially part of the guild structure, however, their work in guild shops was not dependent on their own level of training but on their relation to past, present, and future guild masters. The work changed when the woman's status changed from daughter to wife to mother to widow, and thus it followed the female life cycle. Because these status changes were personal ones and might occur at any time, it was difficult for working women to perceive themselves as a group with common interests. Unlike apprentices and journeymen, they did not have a clear peer group. Because of the informal nature of women's participation in the guild system, there were no formal institutions which protected their rights in the workshop. Individual women might be granted the right to work at a particular occupation, but there were no blanket statements allowing women per se to work.

Masters' widows were a particular problem for guilds. On the one hand these women were generally skilled at running a shop, and the tools, raw materials, and workers were already in place. In addition, the guilds wanted to make sure that masters' widows and orphans were supported, for they were fraternal welfare organizations as well as economic institutions. On the other hand the widow had not received official training, and by operating a shop she often prevented another master from being allowed to join the guild and open a shop. The fact that she was now giving orders to apprentices and journeymen also contradicted commonly held notions of the proper place of men and women. Guilds thus had to resolve a variety of conflicting aims in their treatment of masters' widows.

The guilds themselves were also in the process of change during the period. Particularly in cloth production, but also in other industries, the independent household-workshop was being replaced by the household whose labor was hired by a merchant investor who owned the raw materials. The investor might hire many households, both in the city and in the surrounding countryside, and his trading network was often international in scope. Guilds often felt threatened because they could not produce products as cheaply, and so they sharply limited the number of workshops by restricting widows or by allowing a journeyman to become a master only if he could inherit an existing shop.[64]

As the opportunities for journeymen to become masters decreased, they became permanent wage workers rather than masters-in-training (*Gesellen* rather than *Knechte*) and formed separate journeymen's guilds. These guilds demanded the right to determine who would work in a shop by refusing to work alongside those who did not have their approval. At first this meant those who were of illegitimate birth, but gradually it came to include women. Journeymen first demanded that masters' maids be excluded from all production-related tasks, then that wives and daughters be excluded as well.[65] Guild shops became increasingly male, as even the master's wife retreated more and more from actual production.

The new capitalist industries offered employment for women, but this was also problematic in the eyes of local authorities. When women – and young male workers as well – worked in guild shops, they generally lived in the master's household and were under his control. When workers were simply hired by the day or by the piece, they might live independently, not under anyone's control. Local and state authorities considered such "masterless" persons a threat to public order and passed laws restricting their movement from town to town or even prohibiting them from living on their own.

Concentrating on guilds and capitalist industries, on economic structures, can, however, be somewhat misleading. Most women worked in occupations which were not highly regulated or in sales and service occupations not directly affected by the rise of capitalism. Even for someone involved in an industry which did change, such as cloth production, the transition may have meant little. The working conditions of a spinner in the home of a master weaver, or in a small workshop organized by a major cloth merchant, were no different. She may have been called a "maid" in the former situation and a "piecework spinner" in the latter, but a close look at her daily tasks shows the two to be identical. An overemphasis on changing economic structures may lead away from the realities of most women's work lives.

This qualification must be kept in mind when analyzing any of the legal and economic restrictions on women during this period. Law codes and guild regulations are only a framework, only a theoretical description of the way one group of men would have liked things to operate. They are not a picture of reality – in fact, they are often the opposite. Any move by a city council or a guild usually came in response to something people were already doing. These bodies were inherently conservative and made changes only after extended grumbling and long considerations. This is certainly the case with women's economic activities; if something was forbidden, it is certain a number of people were doing it. The more frequently a prohibition was repeated, the more often the law was being broken. One must examine, then, not only changes in laws and ordinances, but if and when and why these changes were enforced.

. . . As this chapter has pointed out, generalizations which lump all women together are very dangerous. Women's experience varied according to social class, economic status, and citizenship status – factors traditionally taken into account in social and economic history – but also according to age, marital status, family size, and life span – factors rarely considered. In some cases, the sex of a working person is not an important factor in analyzing the impact of change. More often, however, no matter how much variation there was among women, the fact that they were women was the most important determinant of what work they would do.

NOTES

1 Carl Bücher, *Die Bevökerung von Frankfurt am Main im 14. und 15. Jahrhundert*, Tübingen: ocial-statische Studien, 1886; Friedrich Bothe, *Geschichte der Stadt Frankfurt am Main in Wort und Bild*, Frankfurt, 1913; Hans Mauersberg, *Wirtschafts- und Sozialgeschichte zentraleuropäischer Städte in neuerer Zeit. Dargestellt an den Beispielen von Basel, Frankfurt a. M., Hamburg, Hannover und München*, göttingen, 1960; Gerald Lyman Soliday, *A Community in Conflict: Frankfurt Society in the Seventeenth and Early Eighteenth Centuries*, Hanover, NH: University Press of New England for Brandeis University Press, 1974; *Frankfurt um 1600: Alltagsleben in der Stadt*, Frankfurt am Main: Historisches Museum, 1976.

238 MERRY E. WIESNER

2 Julius Rathgeber, *Strassberg im 16. Jahrhundert. 1500–1598. Reformationsgeschichte der stadt Strassburg ... Bevorwortet von K. R. Hagenbach*, Stuttgart, 1871; Ulrich Crämer, *Die Verfassung und Verwaltung Strassburgs von der Reformationszeit bus zum Fall der Reichsstadt (1521–1681)*, Frankfurt: Elsass-Lothringen Instituts, 1931; Franklin L. Ford, *Strasbourg in Transition, 1648–1789*, Cambridge, MA: Harvard University Press, 1958; Miriam U. Chrisman, *Strasbourg and the Reform: A Study in the Process of Change*, New Haven, CT and London: Yale University Press, 1967.

3 G. W. K. Lochner, *Die Einwohnerzahl der ehemaligen Reischstadt Nürnberg*, Nuremberg, 1857, 19; Caspar Ott, *Bevölkerungsstatistik in der Stadt und Landschaft Nürnberg in der ersten Hälfte des 15. Jahrhunderts*, Berlin, 1907; Willi Rüger, *Die Almosenordnungen der Reichsstadt Nürnberg*, Nuremberg, 1932; Rudolf Endres, "Zur Einwohnerzahl und Bevölkerungsstruktur Nürnbergs im 15./16. Jahrhunderts," *Mitteilungen des verein für Geschinchte der Stadt Nürnberg*, 57 (1970): 242–71; Otto Püchner, "Das Register des Gemeinen Pfennigs (1497) der Reichsstadt Nürnbergs als bevölkerungssgeschichtliche Quelle," *Jahrbuch für fränkische Landesforschung* 34/35 (1975), S. 909–48.

4 Oscar Westermann, "Die Bevölkerungsverhältnisse Memmingens in ausgehende Mittelalter," *Memmingen Geschichtsblätter* 2 (1913); Karl Bosl, ed., *Handbuch der historischen Stätten Deutschlands – Bayern*, Stuttgart: Kröner, 1961.

5 Erich Keyser, *Wüttembergisches Städtebuch*, Stuttgart and Berlin: Kohlhammer, 1939–74; Max Miller, ed., *Handbuch der historischen Stätten Deutschlands*, Stuttgart, 1965.

6 Bosl, *Handbuch*, 464–84; Fridolin Solleder, *München im Mittelalter*, Munich and Berlin, 1938.

7 Memmingen Bürgerbücher (BB); Nuremberg Amts- und Standbücher (AStB), nos. 299–300, 305–6; Augsburg BB.

8 Benno Schmidt and Karl Bücher, *Frankfurter Amts- und Zunfturkunden bis Zum Jahre 1612*, 512. Frankfurt Bürgermeisterbücher (BMB): 1495, fol. 26a; 1505, fol. 15b. Beata Brodmeier, *Die Frau im Handwerk*, Forschungsberichte aus dem Handwerk, vol. 9, Münster: Handwerkswissenschaftlichen Institut; 1963.

9 The idea that women did not swear oaths or assume any military responsibilities and were thus a kind of second-class citizens can be found in a number of authors. Where they got this idea remains a mystery, however, as the sources are full of women swearing all kinds of oaths – as witnesses, officials, citizens – and providing all kinds of horsemen, armor, and archers and even working themselves on city walls and fortifications. They certainly took as active a part in the city's defense as any older male citizen, who would also simply have provided soldiers and not buckled on his old, rusty armor himself. Female citizens did not vote for city officials, but then, neither did a large share of the male citizenry. As with Bücher's contention that the imbalance between the sexes must have ended in the sixteenth century, this may be another example of an imaginary justification for legal and economic restrictions on women. It may also be the result of extrapolating backward from the actual situation in nineteenth-century Europe.

10 Munich Ratsitzungsprotokolle (RSP), 1544.

11 Quote is from ibid., 1610, fol. 180. Similar cases in Augsburg BB: 1559, 1562; Memmingen Ratsprotokollbücher (RPB), October 13, 1570; Munich RSP, 1600, fol. 92.

12 Frankfurt BMB, 1471, fol. 141; Nuremberg Ratsbücher (RB), 3, fol. 198 (1482); Nuremberg AStB, nos. 305–6.

13 Memmingen RPB, March 23, 1571.

14 Nuremberg AStB, no. 306, fols. 206–7.

15 Munich RSP: 1601, fol. 24; 1598, fol. 171.

16 Memmingen BB, 269/1.

17 Strasbourg XXI, 1631, fol. 40.

18 Strasbourg XV, 1580, fols. 5, 95.

19 Memmingen BB, 269/1; Augsburg Schätze, vol. 16, fol. 379 (1632).

20 Strasbourg XXI: 1620, fol. 53; 1623, fol. 250.

21 Memmingen BB, 269/2 (1583); Munich Ratsmandata, vol. 60B3 (1628).

22 Strasbourg Statuten, vol. 18, no. 3, fol. 74; reissued 1594, 1627, 1687. Memmingen RPB: June 21, 1602; March 13, 1616. Augsburg BB, 1580 and elsewhere. Strasbourg XXI, 1613, fol. 392.

23 Frankfurt Ver, vol. II, no. 57 (July 31, 1623).

24 Frankfurt Gerichtssachen, Ugb. 51, no. 27 (1691); Stuttgart Stadt Cannstadt, no. 1098 (1532–49).

25 Otto Reiser, "Beweis und Beweisverfahren im Zivilprozess der freien Reichsstadt Nürnberg," J.D. dissertation, Erlangen University, 1955.

26 "Kaiser Ludwigs Rechtbuch 1346," in Maximilian Freiherr von Freyberg, ed., *Sammlung historische Schriften und Urkunden*, nos. 56–9.

27 Joseph Baader, ed., *Nürnberger Polizeiordnungen aus dem 13. bis 15. Jahrhundert*, Bibliothek des Litterarische Verein, Stuttgart: Litterarische Verein, 1861, 29–30.

28 Reiser, "Beweis," 74; Nuremberg Stadt, *Der Statt Nürmberg Verneuerte Reformation*, sec. 29:4; Stuttgart Polizeiakten, A38, Bu. 5, "Fürstemthumb Württemburgs Gemeinen Landtrecht" (1576), secs. 1:36, 2:29; Maximilian Freiherr von Freyberg, ed., *Sammlung historischen Schriften und Urkunden*, Stuttgart and Tübingen: J. G. Gotta, 1834, no. 104.

29 Strasbourg Statuten, vol. 24, fol. 62 (1465).

30 Ibid.

31 Ibid., vol. 18, fol. 104 (1471).

32 Johannes Geiler von Kaisersberg, *Die aeltesten Schriften*, Freiburg in Breisgau: Herder'sche, 1877.

33 Strasbourg RB, vol. 1, no. 89 (1522): "Wie es mit dem ungeerbten aussgohn hinfuhrter gehen soll."

34 Augsburg Schätze, vol. 16, fols. 164–6 (1578), 272–3 (1615).

35 Augsburg Gedruckte Verordnungen, "Erneuerte Witwen und Waisenordnung" (1668).

36 Strasbourg XXI, 1606, fol. 42b; Strasbourg XV, 1633, fol. 26; Frankfurt BMB, 1509, fol. 136b; Munich RSP, 1522; Stuttgart Polizeiakten, A38, Bü. 1, "Witwen und Waisenordnung (1540)."

37 Munich RSP, 1522; Augsburg Schätze, vol. 16, fol. 164 (1578); *Frankfurt um 1600*, 77, quoting 1611 Frankfurt *Eherecht*; Bertha Kipfmüller, "Die Frau im Recht der freien Reichsstadt Nürnberg: Eine rechtsgeschichtliche Darlegung auf grund der verneuerte Reformation des Jahre 1564," J.D. dissertation, Erlangen University, 1929.

38 Memmingen RPB, February 16, 1618. This is similar to the English principle of coverture, although in England the husband was then responsible for the debts; in German cities, as I show later, the creditor had simply lost his loan.

39 Strasbourg RB, vol. 1, no. 108.

40 Ibid., vol. 2, no. 133.

41 Sec. 73 of "Ansbach Landrecht," in Freyberg, *Sammlung*, no. 350.

42 Baader, *Polizeiordnungen*, 29–30.

43 Stuttgart Polizeiakten, A38, Bü. 5, "Furstemthumb Württemburgs Gemeinen Lantrecht" (1576); Nuremberg Stadt *Nürmberg . . . Reformation*, sec. 29:5

44 *Der Statt Frankfurt erneuerte Reformation*, sec. 2, tit. 16:9.

45 Ibid.; Baader, *Polizeiordnungen*, 29–30.

46 Wilhelm Ebel, *Forschungen zur Geschichte des lübischen Rechts*, Veröffenthohungen zur Geschichte der Hansestadt Lübeck: Max Schmidt, 1950; quotations are from Luise Hess, *Die deutschen Frauenberufe des Mittelalters*, Beiträge zur Volstumforschung, no. 6, Munich: Neuer Filser, 1940, 52. This was also the case in London. A married woman who conducted business on her own was declared a "femme sole" and was thus responsible to pay all rents and debts. She could even be imprisoned for debts, and her husband was untouched, both in person and property (A. Abram, "Women Traders in Medieval London," *Economic Journal* 26, June 1916, 280). Market women also received special consideration in Denmark, though the exact nature of their position is not spelled out as clearly as it is in London or the German cities (Inger Dübeck, *Købekoner og konkurence*, Studier over Myndigheds Ehrhvervørettens Udvikling med Stadugt Henblik pa Kvindens historiske Retøstilling, Copenhagen: Juristforbundets, 1978, 184).

47 Baader, *Polizeiordnungen*, 29–30.

48 Frankfurt BMB, 1505, fol. 118b.

49 Nuremberg Stadt *Nürmberg . . . Reformation*, sec. 28:6.

50 *Frankfurt . . . Reformation*, sec. 3, tit. 7:12.

51 Ebel, *Forschungen*, 121.

52 *Frankfurt . . . Reformation*, sec. 5, tit. 5:6.

53 Ibid.

54 Strasbourg RB, vol. 1, no. 89 (1552).

55 Ibid.

56 Strasbourg XV, 1584, fols. 128–9.

57 Munich Stadtgericht, 867, 1598; Ebel, *Forschungen*, 10.

58 Munich Stadtgericht, 867, 1595.

59 The same situation existed in London during the fifteenth and sixteenth centuries. Women could make public declarations that they intended to trade as "sole merchants" – *femmes sole* – but the number of women designated as such far exceeded those who actually made such a formal declaration (Marian K. Dale, "The London Silkwomen of the Fifteenth Century," *Economic History Review* 4, October 1933, 328). Perhaps the public declaration in both German cities and in London simply served as a way of assuring creditors that one was really a market woman or *femme sole*, so that one could borrow more easily, but was not absolutely necessary. In both areas this again points up the gap between legal codes and legal practice.

60 Munich Stadtgericht, 867, 1592–1600; Frankfurt BMB, 1609, fols. 78a, 55b. 88b; Frankfurt Gerichtssachen, Ugb. 69, no. 5; Friedrich Bothe, *Beiträge zur Wirtschafts- und Sozialgeschichte der Reichsstadt Frankfurt*, Altenburg: Stephan Geibel, 1906, 129, 161.

61 Hans Planitz, *Die deutsche Stadt in Mittelalter*, Graz and Cologne, 1954; Erich Maschke, "Verfassung und soziale Kräfte in der deutschen Stadt des späten Mittelalters, vornehmlich in Oberdeutschland," in *Städte und Menschen. Beiträge zur Geschichte der Stadt, der Wirschaft und Gesellschaft 1959–1977* (VSWG Beiheft 68), Wiesbaden, 1980, S. 170–274; Karl Czok, "Die Bürgerkämpfe in Süd- und Westdeutschland im 14. Jahrhundert," *Esslinger Studien* 12/13 (1966/7): 40–72.

62 For studies of the all-female guilds, see E. Dixon, "Craftswomen in the Livre des Mètiers," *Economic Journal* 5 (June 1895), 209–28; W. Behagel, "Die gewerbliche Stellung der Frau im mittelatlterlichen Köln," *Abhandlungen zur mittleren un neueren Geschichte*, no. 23, Berlin and Leipzig: Walter Rothschyild, 1910; Helmut Wachendorf, *Die wirtschaftliche Stellung der Frau in den deutschen Städten des späteren Mittelalters*, Wuackenbrüuck: C. Trute, 1934; Margaret Wensky, *Die Stellung der Frau in der stadtkölnische Wirtschaft im Spätmittelalter*, Quellen und Darstellungen zur häsische Geschichte: Cologne: Böhlau, 1981.

63 Dora Schuster, *Die Stellung der Frau in der Zunftverfassung*, Quellenhefte zum Frauenleben in der Geschichte, no. 7, Berlin: Herbig, 1927.

64 Peter-Per Krebs, "Die Stellung der Handwerkswitwe in den Zünft von Spätmittelalters bis zum 18. Jahrhundert," J.D. dissertation, Regensburg University, 1974; Rudolph Wissell, *Das alten Handwerks Recht und Gewohnheit*, 2 vols, Berlin: Colloquium, 1971, 1974; Karl Bosl and Eberhard Weis, *Die Gesellschaft in Deutschland*, Munich: Lurz, 1976; George Unwin, *Industrial Organization in the Sixteenth and Seventeenth Centuries*, New York: Kelley, 1963; Hermann Kellenbenz, *The Rise of the European Economy*, London: Weidenfeld & Nicolson, 1976.

65 Wilfried Reininghaus, "Zur Entstehung der Gesellengilden im Spätmittelalter," Ph.D. dissertation, Münster University, 1980; Ernst Mummenhoff, "Frauenarbeit un Arbeitsvermittelung: Eine Episode aus der Handwerksgeschichte des 16. Jahrhunderts," *Vierteljahrschrift für Sozial und Wirtschaftsgeschichte* 199 (1926), 157–65; Paul Kampffmeyer, *Vom Zunftgesellen zum freien Arbeiter*, Berlin: Dietz, 1924; Georg von Schanz, *Zur Geschichte der deutschen Gesellenverbände*, Leipzig: Duncker & Humblot, 1877.

16

WOMEN BEFORE THE BENCH: FEMALE LITIGANTS IN EARLY MODERN NORMANDY

Zoë A Schneider

In the early fifteenth century, Christine de Pisan advised propertied gentlewomen to "cultivate good will among lawyers," a class of acquaintances that was assuming increasing importance for women. Noting that women could expect to be entangled in the details of legal business throughout their lives, she went on to recommend that they form amicable relationships with their "bailiffs, provosts, and all those concerned with the administration of justice.[1] By the late seventeenth century the abbé François de Salignac de Fénelon, in his *Traité de l'éducation des filles*, felt it necessary to prescribe an even more rigorous legal education for women: nothing less than a thorough grounding in customary law codes and legal practice would protect their interests. He strongly advised taking daughters into the law courts for a real education in the "chief principles of the law, as for example the difference between a will and a donation, what is meant by contract, entail, and partition among coheirs, the chief rules of the law and customs of the region in which one lives. . . . If they get married, virtually all their chief concerns will turn on matters of this type."[2] By Fénelon's time, these maxims for female litigants could be extended to almost all women, noble or otherwise, with property to manage.

Fénelon and de Pisan point us toward the hidden iceberg of female judicial activity in the ancien régime. Women's civil litigation in France has sometimes been obscured by the more traditional focus on their criminal prosecution for witchcraft, infanticide, or prostitution. Although both colorful and important, criminal cases by their nature represent only a small fraction of cases involving female litigants, typically fewer than 5 percent.[3] Among historians who have studied civil litigation, fruitful work has been done on the creative use of family law and marriage contracts by both men and women, expanding our knowledge of the positive engagement of ordinary families with the courts.[4] Yet we still know relatively little about the extent and nature of women's use of the court system in France. A full statistical examinations of women's legal activity in the lower courts as litigants, arbiters, and seigneurs *haute justiciers* can help to shed new light on their public role in the judicial system as a whole, and in property law in particular.[5]

Zoë A. Schneider, "Women before the Bench: Female Litigants in Early Modern Normandy," pp. 1–3, 5–20, 24, 26–32 from *French Historical Studies* 23 (1) (Winter 2000). Duke University Press.

Understanding women's roles in the judicial system can also help to nuance our understanding of their position within the French state. Despite the very real erosion of women's stature in both royal law and political theory over the sixteenth and seventeenth centuries,[6] the courtroom dossiers tell a more subtle story about women's practical legal position. The majority of women were engaged with the judicial system in the French *bailliage*, *vicomtal*, and seigneurial courts, and there women were overwhelmingly judged not by royal laws or abstruse theories, but by provincial customary codes and usages.[7] On the whole, the records of these local benches mitigate the impression of sharp decline left by royal law codes. Legal practice and customary law in some cases devolved in favor of women in the seventeenth and eighteenth centuries, particularly in the inheritance of royal offices and in female curatorship of family property. Certain women also maintained their rights to appoint seigneurial judges, act as binding arbiters or lay judges, and select qualified occupants for the judicial offices they sold. Nevertheless, the customary regime handed down from the middle ages was unusually rigorous toward Norman women, and indeed placed clear obstacles in the path of both legal participation and property control.

In a sample of 1,220 cases taken from the lower royal and seigneurial courts of upper Normandy in the years 1680–1745, the statistical skeleton underlying de Pisan's and Fénelon's advice becomes clear. Nearly a quarter of the principal parties (plaintiffs and defendants) to court cases were women, and more than half of these women were plaintiffs who initiated suits in active pursuit of their interests in the village and bourg courts.[8] In excess of 95 percent of women's suits were civil cases that turned on critical matters of property, family, and honor, thus paralleling men's uses of the lower court system (table 1). But women's judicial activity was also distinct from men's: they operated under a substantially different set of customary laws that required female litigants to use extraordinary strategies to protect their interests.

[. . .]

From the air, the Caux appropriately looked something like a golden loaf of risen bread, set in a water bath bounded by the Atlantic in the north and west and the Seine in the south. One of the most densely populated rural areas in France, the high plain with its seven hundred or more villages was traditionally an area of intensive wheat and flax cultivation. By the late seventeenth century, its mixed economy was shifting into high gear for textile production in cotton and linens, transforming the region into a bellwether of protoindustrialization.[9] The complex economy and dense population in turn kept the wheels of the courts spinning with an abundance of litigation. Indeed, the Caux was so blessed with disputatious villagers that it might have inspired Racine's character Petit-Jean, who warned that one would have to learn to "howl with the wolves" to go to court with a Norman.[10] The daily cases these energetic litigants brought before the bench help illuminate for us the reality, as opposed to the mask, of legal practice.

Normandy, with its severely misogynist local laws, provides an admirable laboratory to test observations about the practical ability of women to use both the law and the court system in France under the most unfavorable technical conditions. As the legal historian Jean Yver has noted, "the Norman régime constituted the most severe situation of inferiority" for women in all the French customs.[11] Early modern jurisconsults agreed with Yver: the eighteenth-century Parisian commentator Henri Basnage went so far as to call the unreformed Norman custom "barbarous" with regard to women, and some of his colleagues were not much more charitable toward the reformed 1583 edition of the *Coutume de Normandie*.[12]

[. . .]

Table 16.1 Female Plaintiffs and Defendants in Norman Royal and Seigneurial Courts, 1680–1745

Court	Date	Total number cases	Number female cases	Percent female cases	Number female plaintiffs	Percent female plaintiffs	Number dames or noblewomen	Percent dames or noblewomen
Cany-Caniel (high justice)	1694	248	63	25.4	34	53.9	18	28.5
Cany-Caniel (high justice)	1707	375	79	21.0	38	48.1	18	22.7
Cany-Caniel (high justice)	1727	200	64	32.0	35	54.6	11	17.1
Cany (royal *bailliage*)	1680	149	21	14.0	11	52.3	5	23.8
Cany (royal *bailliage*)	1710	87	6	6.8	3	50.0	1	16.6
Cany (royal *bailliage*)	1730	51	15	29.4	10	66.6	5	33.3
Grainville-la-Teinturière (royal *bailliage*)	1698–1745 (All)	110	40	36.3	22	55.0	2	5.0
Total cases	1680–1745	1,220	288	23.6	153	53.1	60	20.8

Source: Archives départementales, Seine-Maritime (see n. 8).

Customary law in Normandy was synonymous with property law, and property meant nearly everything in daily life in the Caux. Access to marriage partners, social status, and sheer survival hinged on it. Most property in rural society still moved through family lines, above all through inheritances, donations, dowries, and dowers. The royal and seigneurial courts were thus over-whelmingly involved with regulating the family and with the transmission of village property. Family and property are also where one must seek most of women's activities in the courts, and where women faced the greatest challenges in overcoming the legal presumptions against them. Yet the records confirm that through property women played a fundamental role in the lower royal and seigneurial court system, and thus in the public space where justice and the state most closely touched ordinary Normans.

The Letter of the Law: Women in the Norman Customs

[. . .]

Virtually all Norman customary laws affecting women, with the exception of a few provisions like those on spousal battery, dealt with property. Customary laws throughout Europe typically concerned transmission of property, but there was an additional impulse behind the interest in women's property: "Where women receive land, the basic means of production, either as dowry or as part of their inheritance . . . the social implications are greater because its ownership is dras-tically reorganized at every generation."[13] As a result, "inheritance involves the transmission of rights in the means of production . . . a process critical to the reproduction of the social system itself."[14] Under those conditions, a large part of provincial and local jurisprudence was naturally focused on controlling, defining, and limiting the reorganization of property through the distaff side.

[. . .]

Legal commentaries on the Norman *Coutume* underlined this deep attention to the problem of women and property. In [David] Houard's commentary on royal offices (one of the most important categories of property in the province, and one whose functions could only be exer-cised by males), almost the entire four-page entry was devoted to women's property rights in offices through dower portions and successions.[15] He dedicated more than fifty pages to the prop-erty of women who were separated, widowed, or married; the only topic that earned more ink in his volume was property in fiefs (175 pages). Thus the family, and above all the position of women within the family, was endlessly and almost compulsively reconfigured as a property-transmitting institution in the *Coutume*. The discrepancy between de jure and de facto treatment of women and property made these extensive commentaries necessary. As Houard demonstrated in his entry on royal offices, it was extraordinarily difficult to pin down the de jure nature of different types of property like royal offices; women's de facto access to these forbidden types of property only complicated matters.

Women and their families typically confronted five major property issues over the course of their lives: (1) inheritances and dowries as daughters, (2) marital property and acquisitions (*acquêts*) of the marriage as married women, (3) lineage property (*propres*) as separated wives, (4) dowers (*douaires*) and usufruct as widows, and (5) tutorship and curatorship (*tutelles* and *curatelles*) as widowed mothers. Their access to property changed with their civil status over their life, and generally changed more dramatically than men's access to it.

From birth, customary law placed Norman women under two unusual property disadvantages. While most French customs exercised strict control over noble succession, Norman law applied equally to commoners and nobles. This parallelism affected female accession to inheritance in all social classes, not merely among the nobility. In Article 248 the law further split inheritors by gender, which stated that "as long as there are males or descendants of males, females or descendants of females cannot succeed."[16] As Jacqueline Musset summarized, "one of the essential principles of the Norman law is, without contest, the exclusion of all girls, noble and commoner, from the succession of their father, mother, and all ascendants.[17] This exclusion set a keynote for women's limited access to property later in their lives, as sisters, wives, mothers, and widows, and even from beyond the grave through their wills. The specific exclusion from lineage property – all property that had been held in the family for at least one generation – in fact limited their access to almost all property. By law all *acquêts*, or newly acquired property, became *propres*, or lineage property, with the first person who inherited it.[18] In ancien régime society, where new wealth was generated only very slowly, almost all property fell under lineage rules.

[. . .]

Once married, daughters had no legal right to a dowry. Dowering a daughter in Normandy was a natural obligation, not a legal one.[19] If the father did not give his daughter a dowry, he could set aside a reserve share of the inheritance for her in her marriage contract, as long as it conformed to the inheritance rules.[20] Once given a reserve share, the daughter could not pretend to any additional part of succession upon the death of the parents.[21] This law would seem to exclude daughters from returning their reserve share on the death of the parent in exchange for sharing in the succession, a common practice in other provinces.[22] Moreover, if a father had promised nothing to his daughter in the way of either dowry or reserve succession at the time of the marriage, then she had no claim on either. "If nothing was promised to her," the *Coutume* stated tartly, "then she shall have nothing."[23]

The *Coutume* made one exception in matters of dowry, for a woman who had been orphaned and left under the tutelage of her brother or other tutor. He was obligated to procure her a suitable husband and expected to provide a *dot* or dowry, and could not contract a *mésalliance* for his sister to profit himself. In an unusual departure, the *Coutume* explicitly stated that the orphaned young woman could address herself to justice after the age of twenty, if her eldest brother or tutor refused to fulfill his obligations to marry her off within a year and a day of her request. If she was still not married by the age of twenty-five, she could find a husband for herself and make a claim against her brother's inheritance for the dowry. On the whole, the orphaned woman enjoyed quite powerful rights relative to most women in Normandy.[24]

Once married, a woman found herself under the power of another famous originality in the Norman code. Custom denied community property between spouses in the province. According to Article 389 of the general *Coutume*, "those joined in marriage are not common in property."[25] A wife therefore had no permanent claim over the *acquêts* (property that the couple acquired in common after their marriage), and marriage contracts were powerless to alter this law. Marriage contracts were also powerless to increase the widow's dower in Normandy. This made such contracts far more rare than under customs like those of Orléans, where the will of the contracting parties was considered superior to that of the law, thus encouraging couples to reconstruct marital property arrangements in ways that seemed good to husband and wife.[26]

Yet despite its apparently draconian nature, certain articles of the law offered hidden options for women. One of the most outstanding features of the Norman custom as a whole was the more than ordinary care taken to preserve property in its original lineage, marking "an extreme point in the protection of lineage" among the customary laws of France.[27] This insistence on lineage property did have some benefits for women in extreme circumstances. The custom granted Norman wives property separations (*séparations des biens*) from indebted or wasteful husbands to protect the property belonging to their lineages, and judges were unusually vigilant in upholding these separations in court. In one of the *placités* published by the Parlement of Normandy in 1666, which slightly modified customary usage, a separated wife could sell or put a mortgage (*hypothèque*)[28] on her mobile property, no matter how valuable, as well as any real property she acquired after the separation. Any real property she had before the separation or that came to her through inheritance, however, could only be sold with the advice and consent of her relatives. Practically speaking, few women acquired real property after their marriages and outside of inheritance, which made these liberties of limited value.[29]

As Houard noted, separated wives also regained as a result of their restored ownership other rights that were not all specified in the *Coutume*, including the right to dispose of their property through a will, and their right to become their husband's first creditor on his death.[30] He noted that Norman women could make civil separation a condition of the marriage contract, in which case they reserved some rights to alienate, donate, and will their lineage property throughout marriage.[31] This practice offered an important exception to the standard marriage regime. There is no indication that it was often or ever used by commoners in the Pays de Caux, however, and it may have been largely the territory of noble or very wealthy urban families. The law also provided some protection for wives against marital violence, although with an important condition. "A wife may render a complaint to Justice for an injury made to her person, and pursue it even if she is disavowed by her husband," the law explained, "as long as the injury is atrocious.[32]

On becoming widows, women in Normandy as elsewhere acquired extensive rights over their own persons. In Normandy, however, they remained under strict control regarding their property. Women were entitled to a dower – the usufruct of up to one-third of the property the husband brought to the marriage – and of up to one-third of the *acquêts*, or fruits of the marriage.[33] The marriage contract could reduce her portion to less than one-third, but it could never augment it. There could also be a "painful or humiliating condition" attached to a woman's dower portion. If the family charged that the widow had behaved immodestly during her mourning, for example, she could be stripped of her property rights altogether.[34]

The local *Coutume* of the Pays de Caux was uncharacteristically liberal about widows' property: it allowed them the usufruct of one-half the property acquired during the marriage, whereas the general *Coutume* allowed only one-third.[35] Norman women had no permanent property in their share of the acquisitions of the marriage unless the husband had no children from any bed.[36] In essence, a Norman widow acted as a temporary depository for the "real" heirs of the couple's property, and could be sued by the eventual heirs if they felt she was dissipating their inheritance. Not even English common law, which also denied community property, was as stringent in denying women use of the acquisitions of the marriage once widowed. In England, both widow and widower retained a life interest in their property, through mechanisms known as male curtesy or female free bench.[37]

Legal practice, however, often lightened this disability. Widows could be, and often were, granted certain financial rights over the management of their children's lineage property, including the two-thirds share of the usufruct which they were not technically allowed. Courts often appointed widows as both tutors and curators of their children. The seventeenth-century

Norman parlement felt compelled to revisit and extensively relegislate the matter of tutorship and curatorship, one of very few areas of customary law in which it intervened. The *Placités* of 1666 modified and extended customary laws, and later the *arrêt* du 7 mars 1673 laid out an eighty-article regime on tutorship, an equally rare royal intrusion into customary practice.[38] The parlement reiterated, among other things, that a widow who remarried could be forced to give up control of her children's property by either the deceased's relatives or by her new husband, who could then proceed to elect a new curator.[39] The repetition of numerous articles suggests that women's control of property through their minor children was both vital for family stability and often troublesome. The law also assumed that women were normally given the curatorship of their children's *biens*, which gave them temporary control of significant real property.

Custom did protect the widow's own lineage property by making her her husband's first creditor for the restitution of her dowry, which could be taken first out of the mobile property and then out of the marital acquisitions if need be.[40] The *Coutume* also made a brief social provision for a new widow: she was owed forty days of nourishment, forty days of residence in her principal habitation, and her mourning clothes while the dower was being settled. (This was perhaps an optimistic estimation of how long it could take to settle a contested dower in the court system.) The widow's weeds were less for her own sake than for the sake of fulfilling her public duty to her husband, since "the wife was obliged to demonstrate by exterior signs her regrets for the loss she had sustained." They were part of the *pompe funèbre*, and to be regulated "less by her taste and her fortune, than by the rank her husband had occupied in society."[41]

Even at her death, the *Coutume* restrained a woman's control over property, forbidding her to make a testament without first obtaining her husband's or heir's permission. The *Coutume* specified that even if the woman obtained permission from a judge to make a will or donation, to transfer a gift between the living, or to alienate property, the act was invalid without the husband's consent.[42] If permission was granted by her husband or established in the marriage contract, she could designate up to one-third of her property to go to younger children. Both men and women were forbidden under most circumstances to draw up a will that donated or willed immovables away from the natural heir designated by the *Coutume*, even properties they had acquired through their own efforts during their lifetimes.[43] Men were free to disinherit some sons and all daughters by a testament, or to further advantage the eldest son at the expense of his siblings, but only within the limits allowed by the *Coutume*.

There were a few other bright spots in this otherwise gloomy legal picture for Norman women. One of the most important was that Normandy conformed to a basic lineage principle of most French customary laws. The rule of "paterna paternis, materna maternis" dictated that a woman's property always return to her birth lineage if there were no direct descendants. This clause gave the woman and her own family a certain permanent interest in the lineage property that she had brought to the marriage.[44] They retained the default ownership of this property, and the law therefore took a real interest in protecting this property from dissipation. As a result, Normandy developed a strong regime of property separation for women whose lineage property was threatened by their husband or their husband's creditors. Lineage property also gave a woman important allies in her bid to control property: her brothers, father, uncles, and other males of her lineage. These court cases did not simply pit individual women against individual men, but family against family.

Norman parents did sometimes attempt to even out their children's inheritances, male and female, by converting some of their immovables or real property into cash or into fictive immovables like offices, which the *Coutume* controlled less strictly. This follows a similar pattern observed by Ralph Giesey in the region covered by the Parisian *Coutume*, and may have given daughters greater access to family property.[45] Husbands and wives in Normandy did occasionally draw up illegal *contrats entre mariés* that transferred goods between husband and wife and allowed them more equality in property.[46] The Custom also treated property in town, or *en bourgage*, as a less essential form of property than rural land and buildings, a distinction that allowed women to take a larger share of immovables held within the walls of bourgs and cities as their inheritances.[47]

Finally, some daughters enjoyed a property advantage in Normandy that had enormous practical consequences. If the daughters were the only surviving children, they inherited lineage property as if they were the male heirs. According to Article 240, if the eldest male had a daughter only, she had an "equal right to the prerogative of the eldest . . . by representing her father in the direct line."[48] This article provided a particularly interesting departure from the insistence on male inheritance, since some French customs specified that male heirs be sought outside the immediate family and down through several degrees of kinship if necessary. Article 272 further specified that if there were more than one daughter, they shared equally in the succession.[49] Female inheritance of the whole property was also the only circumstance in customary law when noble fiefs could be divided upon succession; a full *fief de haubert* could be divided into eighths to make even lots for daughters in default of male heirs. This right of inheritance was perhaps the single most important property right accorded to women in the *Coutume* of Normandy, and it gave women in prominent Caux families like that of the marquis de Becdelièvre and the duc de Longueville effective control over enormous titled properties, seigneuries, high justices, cash, and royal offices.[50]

Trends in Female Litigation: Practical Uses of the Law

Out of the day-to-day flow of court cases involving women, common legal patterns emerge from the static background of written law, revealing the often hidden and important exceptions to enforcement of the Norman customs. Just as women participated in 23.6 percent of the 1,220 legal cases studied here, so, too, they provided 23 percent of the annual property pleges to the seigneury of Cany. It is precisely this level of property control that should make us wary of assuming that women had little role in a court system dominated by property cases. Women thus not only used the courts frequently, they used them for the same purposes men did: to protect property, rights, and family. What is also notable is that nearly 80 percent of the women in court were commoners without sieuries or seigneuries in their families. The lower border of what Alain Margot has called the "legal country" usually began with women in the strata of propertied *laboureurs* and rural merchants.[51] Although most *laboureur* families in the Caux leased, rather than owned, the majority of their land, they were active as small-scale bankers, lending cash, grain, and mobile property to other peasants. They also had important property to fight over in inheritance cases. Even women below the level of substantially independent peasants appeared in court as plaintiffs from time to time, prosecuting thieving sergeants, grasping relatives, and, in very rare instances, their social betters and landlords. Although there were significant variations from year to year, the percentage of women using both royal and seigneurial courts appears to have risen slowly between the last decades of the seventeenth century and the early decades of the eighteenth century: in the high justice of Cany, up from 25.4 percent in 1694 to 32 percent in 1727; in the royal bailliage of Cany, doubling between 1680 (14 percent) and 1730 (29.4 percent).[52]

Women were, however, far less likely than men to be in court answering criminal charges. Of the cases involving women, only 2.4 percent (7 of 288) were criminal in nature, whereas the overall criminal caseload of the courts typically ranged between 10 and 15 percent of the total.

Women's use of the courts for all non-property-related cases (principally unwed pregnancy declarations or *déclarations de grossesse* and crimes) were less than 5 percent. Even that percentage masked many property issues. The *déclarations*, for example, were all made by mothers who included a claim for financial restitution or upkeep for the child from the father.

[. . .]

The rise in court use can perhaps be partly correlated with rising female literacy rates in the Pays de Caux and in the province as a whole. The Caux had been an area of striking female illiteracy in the seventeenth century, despite the relatively high literacy rates enjoyed by the Norman province. Literacy rates among women were only 4 percent in the late seventeenth century; and although they had only risen to 34 percent by the late eighteenth century, it represented an eightfold increase.[53] Some of the growth in court use may have come from social strata where women had been on the margins of literacy before, particularly among families of *laboureurs* or substantial peasants. Nevertheless, illiteracy had never proved a firm barrier to court use among either men or women in the Caux, and other factors must be sought as well. The changing Caux economy may have provided an equally important spur to female litigation. The prosperity of the drapers' and dyers' guilds in Cany and other large bourgs, particularly after large-scale cotton spinning was introduced to the Caux in the early eighteenth century,[54] raised the numbers of families and women involved in commerce or artisanal production.

Inheritance was the most contested and most financially important business that crowded the court dockets of the Pays de Caux. Death redistributed the patrimony of a family not only to the family's own survivors, but often to the entire rural community of creditors: landlords, moneylenders, merchants, and lawyers. Rural notables watched the movements of inheritances and property with the same avidity as investors watch the modern stock market or corporate mergers. Women played a pivotal role in this ever-changing landscape, holding approximately a fifth of all landed property as noted above. Women's possession of mobile property, including cash and offices, may have been significantly higher since the customary law allowed women greater access to these actual or fictive moveables. The inheritance of property, particularly in cases of daughters without brothers, and the usufruct of property as widows and curators often made women into landlords and lessors in the Caux.

[. . .]

Beyond their roles as plaintiffs and defendants before the bench, women were also invaluable witnesses and even arbiters in the courts of the Caux. Traditionally, courts gave women's testimony equivalent status only to that of criminals or minor children, and male parties occasionally attempted to have evidence thrown out on the grounds that it came from women. But several practical factors helped to dilute the common legal presumption that women's oaths or testimony were suspect. In the royal and seigneurial courts of France, hearsay was admissible evidence in a trial, which meant that informal circuits of village communication could be tapped for testimony. Certain kinds of cases, such as attestations of a woman's previous chaste behavior when suing for marriage or restitution from a seducer, or those requiring physical examination in cases of suspected abortion or infanticide, virtually required the affirmation of female witnesses, such as midwives.[55]

[. . .]

Outwitting the System: The Case of "The Pitiless Sister"

The real limits of female control over inheritances, offices, and property, as opposed to the theoretical limits imposed by strict provincial *coutume*, were tried in the courts. The most intriguing example is an appellate case that reached the Parlement of Normandy in 1715 after extensive litigation in the *vicomtal* and *bailliage* courts of Pont-L'Evêque. Moreover its protagonist, Marguerite Chauffer, shows us unsuspected paths to property and legal influence open to women who were neither noble nor widows: she was an unmarried woman in her thirties, still living in her father's household, when she wrested away control of much of her elder brother's inheritance in offices and property.

The Chauffer case began in the *vicomtal* and *bailliage* courts thirteen years before it reached the sovereign court at Rouen. In 1702, M. Chauffer, a receiver of the *tailles* in Pont-L'Evêque, became a paralytic confined to a room in his house in the bourg. For eight years, until his death, his role as head of household was reduced to signing his name at the bottom of papers placed in front of him. From the beginning of Chauffer's incapacity, his wife, his daughter Marguerite, his elder son François, and his younger son entered into a battle for authority over the family properties and royal office. Marguerite won the early skirmishes in the king's court and at home, keeping possession of some of the family's land and manor houses in the country. Most surprisingly, she retained control over her father's royal office, which she then sold to a qualified candidate who was her personal choice for the post, despite her brother's violent objection. Her battle demonstrated that women could breach certain holes in the strict letter of the law on female inheritance, using both the royal courts and the court of public opinion to press their case.

The elder son François appealed these lower-court decisions to the parlement. In a legal *factum* that he had printed and distributed at his own expense, he grudgingly credited his sister with enormous legal resourcefulness. Marguerite was the eldest of the three children, and, from the beginning of her father's illness, according the François, she had conceived the plan of despoiling François of his property. She first wrote up a reserve share of the property for herself, setting aside the main house, with its receipts, revenues, and effects, using one of the blank pieces of paper that had been signed by her father. At the same time, Marguerite and her mother conspired to take the management of the whole estate into their hands. François accused them of a premeditated design to exile him from his paternal house from the time of his father's paralysis in 1702, in order to "usurp his authority, and the administration of his property and his business." These included "cash, effects, revenues, papers and blank documents" signed by his father.

Other witnesses confirmed that mother and daughter did in fact administer all aspects of the family property until the father's death, and in the absence of the eldest son. In one of the earlier *bailliage* trials in 1704, the tax collector of the parish of Roncheville affirmed that when he arrived to collect the tax, it was the mother and daughter who received him in their office. Other witnesses affirmed that rents, *lettres de change*, merchants' bills, taxes, the *finance* of the syndic's office and of the clerk of the rolls, and the leases and revenues of their estates were all dealt with by the two women. They noted that the sister remained in possession of the keys of the *armoire*, the *comptoire*, and the office, the surest sign that she was in control of the family finances.

According to notarial contracts, Marguerite was also active in the land market. She used a highly resourceful strategy to buy land near Pont-L'Evêque, by passing money to a noble widow and having the contracts of purchase signed in her name. In April 1707 and again in July 1708, Catherine Voisin, madame la présidente de Bacquemare, widow of a distinguished *parlementaire*, passed a contract before the notaries in Paris for purchase of a field in the parish of Bonneville sur Tocque. The contract stated that the land was acquired for and to the profit of Demoiselle Marguerite Chauffer, "who has only borrowed her [Voisin's] name." Marguerite gave Catherine 700 livres cash, as a down payment on the 2,200 livre price of the property. Madame de Bacquemore then received the balance of 1,500 livres in silver *louis* from Marguerite's agent.

Here we have an unusually clear example of a woman who was still living at home under *puissance paternelle* (although no longer a minor), and legally barred from engaging in property transactions without consent, doing exactly that.[56] She was able to use the legal rights of a widowed noble woman as a cover to transact business and acquire property in her own right. Although it would require long searching in notarial records to confirm whether or not this was a standard arrangement between women in the ancien régime, the utility and ingenuity of this end run around customary law is apparent. The legal advantages of some women, particularly propertied widows, could make them useful property agents for women still under paternal or marital authority

The key to Marguerite's success, François's appeal reveals, was twofold. She had been able to manipulate legal documents, contracts, and customary laws, and she had been able to maneuver public opinion, including the courts' opinion. In some awe, his *factum* charged that his sister had worked the court system from the village *vicomté* up to Versailles in order to pillage his moveable and immovable property and then acquire his father's office. François complained that she initiated so many trials in the *vicomté*, in the *bailliage* . . . , in parlement and in the council against her unhappy brothers, that they were stripped of their rights, and obliged to abandon them to this pitiless sister." She lost one of these suits in the *vicomté* of Pont-L'Evêque in 1711, when she was condemned to reimburse her brothers for the value of their father's office – but not condemned to give it back. She delayed the execution by demanding accounts of their inheritance first, and in the meantime sold the office to another *sieur*, who remained in undisputed possession of it.

François charged that Marguerite trumped him in the court of public opinion as well. In a paragraph full of unintended revelations, he complained that women could unfairly manipulate public opinion, and by implication manipulate royal judges and attorneys, into sympathizing with their plight. His sister had taken the offensive before the bench and portrayed herself as a victim of customary law, a woman "reduced to that sad servitude of all the girls of Normandy." Many lawyers and judges had been tricked by her complaints, the brother asserted, "notably those who are plainly instructed in the spirit of the provincial *Coutume*, where the eldest son is the object of all liberalities, and where the daughters must submit to them." Curiously, François believed that attorneys and officers who were best instructed in the rigors of the Norman custom would be precisely those who were most swayed by Marguerite's arguments and complaints. His statement indicates that there was a certain public sympathy with women's treatment under the *Coutume* by legal practitioners, which in fact is borne out by a few of the better known commentaries of the eighteenth century.[57]

There were deeper reasons as well why the courts sided with Marguerite on most occasions. These reasons bring into play social goods which the courts were charged with protecting, even if it meant occasionally siding against custom and with women. These goods included filial obedience, paternal authority, and the protection of family property. François had been away from the household for at least two years during his father's paralysis, completing his law studies in Paris. His mother and older sister necessarily took charge of the household finances, as did many Norman women who found themselves widowed or effectively widowed through marriage to absent soldiers, distant officials, or men no longer competent to manage their affairs through illness or mental incapacity. Not even François charged that they had mismanaged the family patrimony, except that they had commandeered it for themselves. Numerous royal officers and town merchants, who had dealt with the two women as the head of the Chauffer household and as landlords and as taxpayers for eight years, appeared in court to testify as much.

François, in the meantime, had incurred the wrath of his father. A bourgeois witness from Pont-L'Evêque, Jean Domin, testified in the family's 1708 trial that François had been refused table and bed by his father on his return from Paris, and had been forced to live very poorly in a rented chamber. The elder sieur Chauffer had violently objected to his son's intended marriage the following year, in 1709. The rebellious son then sought an *arrêt* in the parlement to permit him to marry against his father's wishes. Evidently the community also knew of some complaint against her brother; when François filed another suit two years after his father's death, in 1712, Marguerite successfully attacked his personal integrity and his conduct in court. The lower courts continued to find in Marguerite's favor on most points.

Although the final outcome of the case is unfortunately lost, we do know some of the legal arguments and the intermediate decisions that led to Marguerite's success. François charged that Marguerite had come into possession of two-thirds of the revenue of the succession, or about six thousand livres per year in rents. She also acquired possession of her father's office, worth twelve thousand livres income per year, leaving only forty-two hundred livres per year in income for her brother. (The partial list of property involved indicates that he was exaggerating his disabilities.) François argued in court using Article 271 of the *Coutume*, which stated that sisters could take none of the fields and manor houses in the countryside as their succession unless there was also a manor for each brother. Therefore, François argued that he and his brother should be able to take two manors from their mother's succession and two manors from their father's. Since there were only two manors in the successions of each parent, François and his younger brother were entitled to all four, with none left over for the sister. François argued that Article 271 was expressly made for women, to prevent them from succeeding to rural property.[58]

Marguerite cited Article 356 in her defense, which indicated that the eldest could take the *preciput* from the father's succession, but was not necessarily entitled to a *preciput* from both mother and father, and in any case had to recompense the younger siblings for their share in the mother's property. She conceded her brother's case in their father's succession, but not in their mother's succession. The outcome of other court cases indicates that her argument was often considered legitimate by the courts. The mother's inheritance was often distributed more evenly than the father's, as long as his was the most sizeable portion or contained the principal house and its attached land.

Perhaps the most important issue raised by the Chauffer case was whether royal offices could be passed to women as inheritances or dowries. As the most important form of real property next to land in the later ancien régime, this was a critical question for contemporaries. Office was also a public dignity, a function that partook of the government of the French state, which contemporaries recognized as a political issue. Widows were legally allowed to inherit only the partial usufruct of royal offices from their husbands, which they either leased out or held in trust for their minor sons. Under the Norman *Coutume*, a widow was entitled to the usufruct of one-third of the value of the office, as long as this did not exceed one-third of the total marital property she was allowed to use during her lifetime.[59]

But this case opens a rare window onto legal reality in the court system. Women did in fact begin taking offices as final inheritances from their fathers and husbands, despite the clear presumption of customary law against it.[60] Commentators on the Norman *Coutume* spilled a great deal of ink on this issue, but by the late eighteenth century experts agreed that women inheriting offices had become usual practice in the courts. Houard's legal discussion of royal offices, for example, is taken up almost entirely with the discussion of women's rights to inherit public property in office. According to the *Coutume*, offices were considered *immeubles*, that is, similar to land or real property. But judges frequently decided that they were only fictive immovables, and should in fact be treated like cash or moveable property. Widows could take their husband's entire office as part of their dower portion, and daughters could take them as part of their reserve share of their inheritance.[61] As a result, both noble and non-noble women increasingly claimed royal offices as their inheritance portion by the later seventeenth century. Here as in other areas of property law, the seemingly inflexible face of custom was constantly modified in local practice.

Between Theory and Practice: Women's Shifting Roles in Ancien Régime Justice

The erosion of the position of women in French royal law over the sixteenth and seventeenth centuries has been a matter of interest to both social and legal historians in the past few decades. The increasing restrictions on both women's persons and property, as well as on their access to public power, are notable features of royal law codes from at least the time of Henry II. The strengthening of laws against infanticide and abortion during his reign, and the reaffirmation of the Salic Law in 1593, are but two well-known examples. Sixteenth-century political theorists like Jean Bodin and seventeenth-century practitioners like Cardinal Richelieu elaborated theories for women's exclusion from public and even private power.[62] But the lower court records indicate the potential hazards of extrapolating actual practices from royal law codes and political theories. Prescriptive rather than descriptive, they often mask the volume and extent of women's involvement in real property, and thus in a lower judicial system largely designed to manage both property and family. Indeed, as James B. Collins has suggested, the need to pass repeated laws controlling women indicates that neither they nor their property were thoroughly under control.[63]

The *Coutume* of Normandy indeed laid a heavy hand on both women's property and persons, yet some of the most important presumptions of civil law and society in the ancien régime gave a certain amount of real power back to women. The inviolability of contracts was one of these concepts: whether the contract held by a woman was a dowry, a lease, or a loan, it had to be honored if civil chaos was not to ensue. The inviolability of family property was another such concept. The desire to prevent the dissipation of a woman's family capital or her children's inheritance led the courts to regularly give women de facto control over family property. Civil separations from spouses, the right to act as *femmes libres*, and the curatorship of their children's inheritance restored women to authority over property that legal and political theorists in principle denied. Finally, the crucial decision to allow daughters to inherit the patrimony in lieu of living brothers in the *Coutume de Normandie* opened an unexpectedly wide door to female ownership of land, offices and moveables in the Norman province.

Contrary to the legal trend at the top of the state, the Norman customary laws redacted in the sixteenth century had in fact lightened some of the social and legal disabilities imposed on women by the medieval *Coutume*, although the property regime remained severe with regard to women. Moreover, two widespread changes in seventeenth-century Norman legal practice were both in women's favor: the presumption of maternal tutorship and usually curatorship, and the right of women to take royal offices as final dowries or inheritances.

These provincial legal practices matter in the larger sense, because property was organically linked to the exercise of public authority in the ancien régime. At the top of the social scale, propertied Norman women were able to exercise secondary public power in the judicial system through their roles as binding arbiters, their inheritance of the monetary value of judicial offices, their curatorship or ownership of high justices, and their right to appoint seigneurial judges and lesser officials to these still vital courts. Equally important, women of lesser means were regularly accepted into the court system of the Caux as litigants, to protect identical social good: family stability, the orderly transmission of lineage property, and social order. Women's active role in the courts serves as a welcome reminder that ordinary villagers of all stripes played their part in the local justice system. In doing so, they took a small but vital role in the public arena where the state became rooted in village and town life.

NOTES

1 Christine de Pisan, *A Medieval Woman's Mirror of Honor: The Treasury of the City of Ladies*, trans. Charity Cannon Willard (New York, 1989), 109–10.

2 Abbé François de Salignac de Fénelon, *Traité de l'éducation des filles*, in *Fénelon on Education*, ed. H. C. Barnard (Cambridge, 1966), 84–5.

3 On women in *bailliage* and *vicomtal* criminal cases, see particularly Malcolm R. Greenshields, "Women, Violence, and Criminal Justice Records in Early Modern Haute Auvergne," *Canadian Journal of History* 22 (1987): 175–94; for Normandy, see also Alain Margot, "La Criminalité dans le bailliage de Mamers, 1695–1750," *Annales de Normandie* 3 (1972): 185–224; Bernadette Boutelet, "Etude par sondage de la criminalité dans le bailliage de Pont-de-l'Arche (XVIIe–XVIIIe siècles): De la violence au vol: En marche vers l'escroquerie," *Annales de Normandie* 4 (1962): 235–65; and Marie Madeleine Champin, "Un Cas typique de justice bailliagier: La Criminalité dans le bailliage de Alençon de 1715 à 1745," *Annales de Normandie* 1 (1972): 47–84.

4 On the family and law, see Nicole Castan, "La Criminalité familiale dans le ressort du Parlement de Toulouse (1690–1730)"; *Crimes et criminalités en France sous l'Ancien Régime, XVIIe–XVIIIe siècles* (Paris, 1971); Nicole Castan and Yves Castan, *Vivre ensemble: Ordre et désordre en Languedoc (XVIIe–XVIIIe siècles)* (Paris, 1981); Mark Cummings, "Elopement, Family, and the Courts: The Crime of Rapt in Early Modern France," *Proceedings of the Western Society for French History* 4 (1976): 118–25; Bernard Derouet, "Les Pratiques familiales, le droit et la construction des différences (15e–19e siècles)," *Annales HSS* 2 (1997): 369–91; and Paul Ourliac and Jehan de Malafosse, *Histoire du droit privé*, vol. 3 of *Le Droit familial* (Paris: 1963).

5 On property law, see particularly Barbara Diefendorf, "Women and Property in Ancien Régime France: Theory and Practice in Dauphiné and Paris," in John Brewer and Susan Staves, eds., *Early Modern Conceptions of Property* (London, 1994), 170–93; Jack Goody, Joan Thirsk, and E. P. Thompson, eds., *Family and Inheritance: Rural Society in Western Europe, 1200–1800* (Cambridge, 1976); Emmanuel Le Roy Ladurie, "A System of Customary Law: Family Structures and Inheritance Customs in Sixteenth Century France," in Robert Forster and Orest Ranum, eds., *Family and Society* (Baltimore, Md., 1976); Daniel Lord Smail, "Démanteler le patrimoine: Les Femmes et les biens dans la Marseille médiévale," *Annales HHS* 2 (1997): 343–68; and Robert K. Wheaton, "Affinity and Descent in Bordeaux," in Robert Wheaton and Tamara K. Hareven, eds., *Family and Sexuality in French History* (Philadelphia, Pa., 1980).

6 See Adrianna Bakos, ed., *Politics, Ideology, and the Law in Early Modern Europe* (Rochester, N.Y., 1994); Gordon Schocket, *Patriarchalism in Political Thought: The Authoritarian Family and Political Speculation and Attitudes, Especially in Seventeeth-Century England* (New York, 1975); Roland Mousnier, *The Institutions of France under the Absolute Monarchy, 1598–1789*, 2 vols. (Chicago, 1979), 1:85–91; Sarah Hanley, "Engendering the State: Family Formation and State-Building in Early Modern France," *French Historical Studies* 16 (1989): 4–27.

7 The reformed civil and criminal codes of 1667–70 had little effect on daily legal practice in Normandy. The civil code was primarily a collection of administrative regulations focused on reforming the judiciary itself, and as a practical matter, the crown was more or less helpless when it came to altering deeply embedded property or customary laws. Nor did it necessarily wish to do so; local order was well served by the existing system. On the restricted effects of the criminal and civil codes and of positive royal laws on lower court cases, see Zoë Schneider, "The Village and the State: Justice and the Local Courts in Normandy, 1670–1740" (Ph.D. diss., Georgetown University, 1997): 77–8.

8 The lower court cases examined here were drawn from the Archives départementales, Seine-Maritime (henceforth ADSM). 13 BP 9–57, vicomté et bailliage de Cany; ADSM, 71 BP 8–15, vicomté et bailliage de Grainville-la-Teinturière; ADSM, 46 BP 13–29, haute justice de Cany-Caniel; and ADSM 71 BP, 1–7, haute justice de Grainville-la-Teinturière.

9 Rouen, Bibliothèque municipale, Ms. Y 169, Intendant de Vaubourg, *Mémoires des généralités*; Edmond Esmonin, *La Taille en Normandie au temps de Colbert, 1661–1683* (Paris, 1913); and Guy LeMarchand, *Le Fin du féodalisme dans le Pays de Caux* (Paris, 1989), 8–16.

10 Jean Racine, *Les Plaideurs*, in *Théatre de Racine*, ed. Pierre Mélèse (Paris, 1951), 131–32.

11 Jean Yver, "La Rédaction officielle de la Coutume de Normandie (Rouen, 1583): Son esprit," *Annales de Normandie* 1 (1986): 24. See also R. Genestal, "La Réforme de la Coutume de Normandie à la fin du XVIième et au cours du XVIIième siècle," *Revue historique de droit* 5 (1926).

12 Henri Basnage, *Commentaires sur la Coutume de Normandie*, 4 vols. (Rouen, 1709, 1778), 2:389.

13 Goody, "Inheritance, Property, and Women," in Goody, Thirsk, and Thompson, *Family and Inheritance*, 10.

14 Ibid., 14; see also Ralph E. Giesey, "Rules of Inheritance and Strategies of Mobility in Pre-Revolutionary France," *American Historical Review* 82 (1977): 271–89.

15 Houard, *Dictionnaire analytique*, 4:373–6.

16 *Coutume de Normandie*, Art. 248: "Tant qu'il y a mâles ou descendans des mâles, les femelles ou descendans des femelles ne peuvent succeder."

17 Jacqueline Musset, "Les Droits successoraux des filles dans la coutume de Normandie," in *La Femme en Normandie: Actes du XIXe congrès des sociétés historiques et archéologiques de Normandie* (Caen, 1986): 53–4.

18 *Coutume de Normandie*, Art. 247.

19 Musset, "Droits successoraux des filles," 53–60. Although it is probable that many daughters did receive voluntary dowries from their parents, as they did in other provinces, the law sharply curtailed the transfer of real property (that is, land or houses) to daughters who had brothers.

20 *Coutume de Normandie*, Art. 258.

21 *Coutume de Normandie*, Art. 358.

22 Houard, *Dictionnaire analytique*, 264–5. The local custom of the Pays de Caux did grant a daughter the right to renounce her reserve share, if it was loaded with debt or otherwise carried prejudice to her.

23 *Coutume de Normandie*, Art. 250; similar provisions can be found in Arts. 252 and 363.

24 *Coutume de Normandie*, Art. 261, 264, 267–8, 298.

25 *Coutume de Normandie*, Art. 389.

26 Yver, "Rédaction officielle," 31; as he pointed out for the Norman custom, "C'était dénier au contrat de mariage la force constructive qui lui est reconnue dans les autres coutumes." See also Robert Vivien, *De l'usage des contrats de mariage en Normandie* (Paris, 1909); and Georges Bloc, *De la communauté entre époux en Bourgogne* (Dijon, 1910).

27 Yver, "Rédaction officielle," 20.

28 *Hypothèque* in ancien régime law can be best translated as "mortgage," but because property rights were seldom absolute or vested in one individual, the *hypothèque* was often more complicated in practice than modern mortgages or secured loans.

29 Arrêt de mars 1666, Parlement de Normandie, "Les Placités," in *Coutume de Normandie, avec l'ordonnonce de 1667, & celle de 1670* (Bayeux, 1773), Art. 126, which modified Art. 541, *Coutume de Normandie*.

30 Houard, *Dictionnaire analytique*, 266–67.

31 Houard, *Dictionnaire analytique*, 259–66.

32 *Coutume de Normandie*, Art. 543.

33 Women without children were allowed usufruct of one-half under the general custom as well.

34 Pierre Cinquabre, "Le Statut juridique de la femme normande aux XVIIe et XVIIIe siècles," in *La Femme en Normandie*, 43–51.

35 Although a one-third or one-half usufruct was not necessarily a hardship for wealthy widows, for many it entailed dependency upon adult sons or upon the curator of the children's *biens*, if curatorship were given to a male relative.

36 Unlike most customary laws, the Custom of Normandy did not recognize *partage des lits*, or the split-ting of inheritances according to which bed the children came from. All children descended from one male were recognized as part of the same family for inheritance purposes.

37 Goody, "Inheritance, Property, and Women," 11.

38 Arrêt du 7 mars 1673, "Election des tuteurs; Placités de mars 1666," in *Coutume de Normandie, avec l'ordonnonce de 1667* (Bayeux, 1773).

39 Arrêt du 7 mars 1673, Art. 10.

40 *Coutume de Normandie*, Art. 365.

41 Houard, *Dictionnaire analytique*, 279.

42 *Coutume de Normandie*, Art. 417; Houard, *Dictionnaire analytique*, 259–66.

43 *Coutume de Normandie*, Art. 285, 417.

44 For further discussion of lineage property, see Giesey, "Rules of Inheritance," 271–89, and Diefendorf, "Women and Property," 170–93.

45 Giesey, "Rules of Inheritance," 275.

46 Cinquabre, "Statut juridique," 44–48.

47 *Coutume de Normandie*, Art. 271.

48 *Coutume de Normandie*, Art. 240.

49 *Coutume de Normandie*, Art. 272.

50 Although there are no exact statistics available on the percentage of families in which no son survived to adulthood, there are enough examples among the Caux nobility to indicate that it was not a rare event.

51 Alain Margot, "La Criminalité dans le bailliage de Mamers (1695–1750)," *Annales de Normandie* 22 (1972): 223.

52 ADSM, 1 ER 1084, "De Becdelièvre gages-pleges," unpaginated. In 1734, for example, seventeen of the seventy-two *gages-pleges* in the seigneurie of Cany-Barville, or just over 23 percent of the *masures* and land parcels held by *roturiers*, were noted as being held "à cause de sa femme" or "ayant épouzé la herit-tier." See also James B. Collins, "Economic Role of Women in Seventeenth-Century France," *French Historical Studies* 16 (1989): 436–70, for similar statistics on Burgundy.

53 See Muriel Jéorger, "L'Alphabétisation dans l'ancien diocèse de Rouen au XVIIe et au XVIIIe siècles," in François Furet and Jacques Ozouf, eds., *Lire et écrire: L'Alphabétisation des Français de Calvin à Ferry* (Paris, 1977), for a discussion of literacy trends in upper Normandy.

54 Archives departementales de la Seine-Maritime (ADSM), 1 B 5528, Parlement de Normandie, arts et metiers: filasiers, toiliers.

55 The Parlement of Paris had an official midwife whose testimony was used in cases involving infanticide or abortion.

56 Women reached their majority at age twenty-five under the Custom of Normandy. In Marguerite's case, she still had to seek paternal consent before alienating any of her own capital assets, and certainly before buying property with what were still her father's assets.

57 See, e.g., N. Pesnelle, ed., *Coutume de Normandie*, 2d ed. (Rouen, 1727).

58 ADSM, 1 B 5699, Parlement de Normandie, Factums: M. François Chauffer vs. Demoiselle Marguerite Chauffer, 1715.

59 *Coutume de Normandie*, Arts. 367–411.

60 Royal legislation created considerable ambiguity about their status as well. Extensive legal precedent gave rights to those who had financed an officer's purchase of his position or of its *droits*. The financial backer, rather than the officer, "owned" the portion of the office – or *droit* – he or she had financed.

61 Houard, *Dictionnaire analytique*, 373–6.

62 Jean Bodin, *Six Livres de la République* (1583; rpt., Geneva, 1961) 1:2 lays out the classic statement of the paternal-familial model of the state, arguing for absolute authority of fathers and husbands over children and wives. Cardinal Richelieu restated the dangers of allowing women access to public authority in his *Testament politique* (Paris, 1947), 328, on the basis of women's natural cruelty and injustice. See also n. 5.

63 Collins, "Economic Role of Women," 469–70.

17

Review of *The Family, Sex and Marriage in England 1500–1800*, by Lawrence Stone

Alan Macfarlane

This is an important book. It deals with subjects of considerable topical interest and great complexity about which we know little. It claims to make statements about both the past and the present. Professor Stone argues, for example, that the modern Western family system is "geographically, chronologically and socially a most restricted and unusual phenomenon, and there is as little reason to have any more confidence in its survival and spread in the future as there is for democracy itself" (687). It makes very general comments on the nature of preindustrial life and cites another discipline, anthropology, in support of these claims . . . It is a massive work of eight hundred pages with some thirteen hundred footnotes. The author claims that he has used "every possible type of evidence" in order to "pick up hints about changes in values and behaviour at the personal level" (10). The combination of topic, academic reputation, and size of book is likely to ensure that not only will it be widely read but that its central arguments will be accepted by specialists and the general public alike.

That the book is already on the way to such acceptance can be seen from the early reviews. Keith Thomas makes some serious criticisms but predicts that there "is no doubt that the book deserves the widest possible readership or indeed that it will get it."[1] He points to the "many merits of Professor Stone's absorbing if occasionally wayward book," believing that his "argument may yet prove to be substantially right," and that, even if he is mistaken, Stone "has offered an indispensable chart . . ."[2] Joan Thirsk predicts that there "will be quibbling over small details, but no major disagreement, I think, with the general perspective."[3] J. P. Kenyon writes that "in the last analysis the accumulation of random evidence is impressive, and most of it fits together. His picture of pre-modern man, so very different from what most of us would have expected, will be subject to amendment in many of its details, but I expect its main outlines to stand."[4] Rosalind Mitchison has a number of reservations about the book, but concludes that "on its main theme, the rise of individualism, there can be no doubt that it is firmly founded."[5] The only major dissenting voice so far is that of Edward Thompson; even he is apologetic about being so "cross."[6]

Alan Macfarlane, "Review of *The Family, Sex and Marriage in England 1500–1800*, by Lawrence Stone," pp. 103–10, 113–18, 124–26 from *History and Theory*. Blackwell Publishing, 1979.

The reception for the book would not be so assured if it was not based on a general theory of the development of modern English society which historians and sociologists find attractive. This is the real justification for a long review. Stone has stated bluntly what many have assumed but never said. Furthermore, his book provides an interesting example of the way in which a set of assumptions shapes the historian's evidence. The dust-jacket claims that this is a "book whose hypotheses challenge much conventional wisdom about English social evolution, and its relationship to religion, politics, capitalism and industrialization." In fact, the central hypotheses concerning the gradual growth of individualism in the sixteenth to eighteenth centuries are all anticipated in the works of Marx and Weber and have been reiterated in various forms by historians since then. Stone takes for granted the gradual transformation of a traditional, group-based, kinship-dominated society into the modern capitalistic system, a change most notably described by R. H. Tawney. The general outline of the shift in the nature of English economy and society between 1400–1750 appears to be well established. In this period the following occurred: the invention of private, absolute property and the destruction of group ownership; the destruction of the household as the basic unit of production and consumption; the growth of a money economy; the rise of a class of permanent wage-laborers; the upsurge of the profit motive and the unending accumulative drive; the rise of modern industries and large towns; the elimination of "magical" and "irrational" forces which prevented economic accumulation; the undermining of small, closely-meshed communities with the growth of geographical and social mobility. England changed from a society in which the individual was subordinated to a group of some kind, whether the family, village, religious congregation or estate, to that depicted by Hobbes in the seventeenth century in which society was composed of autonomous individuals.

Specifically in relation to the family and kinship, Max Weber laid down many of the foundations upon which Stone builds. Weber describes the gradual erosion of wider family groupings. Societies all originated in a stage where kinship dominated all life and large clans absorbed the individual. In China and India this phase continued into the nineteenth century. In Western Europe, a combination of Christianity, feudalism, and the growth of towns began to erode these large groups. Protestantism was especially important in shattering the "fetters of the kinship group." The Puritan divines further stressed the nuclear family and the importance of marriage as a period of affection. The power of the head of the household as a patriarch was also stressed by the Puritans. Gradually the subservience of women began to be challenged and the individual began to assert himself against his parents. The nature of this general shift in family structure, as well as the reasons why it occurred – the rise of acquisitive individualism – appear to be well established.[7]

The general theory of the changes in economy, society, and politics predicts that when one turns to sentiments as expressed in family life, marital arrangements, and sexual behavior there should be a gradual evolution along the lines documented by Stone. Thus his picture of the past is just what one expects to find. The only cause for surprise is that the medieval and early modern period was even more cruel and beastly than one might have anticipated. Thus there might be arguments about whether Stone has exaggerated certain changes. Yet there can be little doubt that we would expect to find that his claim to have described "perhaps the most important change in *mentalité* to have occurred in the Early Modern period, indeed possibly in the last thousand years of Western history" will be borne out (4). Thus, as Thompson states, his central argument is "not original," but " Stone is the first to isolate its – Affective Individualism's – familial and sexual consequences in English history in this way."[8] Thus Stone's book helps to confirm and add depth to the current paradigm of the development of the first industrial nation. It reveals remarkably clearly the current consensus on the nature of the transition which is supposed to have occurred between the fifteenth and eighteenth centuries. Stone has set dates and given labels to the various shifts in domestic life which occurred alongside the evolution toward the modern capitalist economy. The three main stages in the history of the family, for example, he describes as the "Open Lineage Family," which lasts from approximately 1450–1630; then the "Restricted Patriarchal Nuclear Family," from about 1550–1700; and finally the "Closed Domesticated Nuclear Family," from about 1640–1800.[9]

There is only one major difficulty. While Stone manages, on the whole, to make the past fit into his scheme, putting forward a theory of the various stages through which England's inhabitants passed, his description of life in the Early Modern Period bears little resemblance to the society which is revealed to a number of us who have studied the period. For example, I have been working for fifteen years on court records, village documents, diaries and autobiographies, pamphlets and tracts, sources which Stone uses and also others which he has failed to investigate. None of these supports his general evolutionary framework. Furthermore, as a social anthropologist who has lived and worked in a contemporary non-industrial society, I find that his assertions about the basic nature of life before the advent of industrialization are largely misleading. What appears to have happened is as follows. Stone was faced with an awkward choice, of which he may or may not have been fully aware. His training and basic assumptions, the whole weight of a century of historical research, led him to expect a gradual progression of social life in a certain direction. The historical evidence either flatly contradicted the predictions, or failed to fit them neatly. He thus either had to jettison the whole set of interlinked assumptions which have their roots in Marxist, Weberian, and Whig history, or else he had to ignore or misinterpret the evidence. It is not surprising that he should have taken the latter course. His massive effort to fit the material into an inadequate scheme provides a compendium of the distortions produced when a tenacious but false paradigm blinds the historian.

In order to assess the value of Stone's contribution, we may first of all examine four central assumptions in the book. The first is that sentiment is intimately related to demography. Stone repeatedly argues that affection and love were, on the whole, impossible before the eighteenth century because the conditions of preindustrial life were so insecure that one would not dare to enter into a deep relationship for fear of it abruptly ending. This is bluntly stated by Stone when he writes that the "value of children rises as their durability improves . . ."; nowadays "Children no longer die, and it is worth while to lavish profound affection upon them . . ."; "to preserve their mental stability, parents were obliged to limit the degree of their psychological involvement with their infant children"; "high mortality rates made deep relationships very imprudent" (420, 680, 70, 117). Marriages were loveless for the same reason. Stone argues that marriages only lasted for an average of seventeen to twenty years in "Early Modern England," and marriage was "statistically speaking, a transient and temporary association" (55). Consequently, relations between husband and wife were affectionless. The conjugal family, based on unloved children and unloving husband and wife was therefore "very short-lived and unstable in its composition. Few mutual demands were made on its members, so that it was a low-keyed and undemanding institution which could therefore weather this instability with relative ease" (60). Furthermore, because parents did not love their children, they let them die, hence increasing insecurity and leading to further neglect: "the neglect was caused in part by the high mortality rate, since there was small reward from lavishing time and care on such ephemeral objects as small babies. It was a vicious circle" (81).

There are at least four major objections to this central psychological assumption. Firstly, an awareness of anthropological literature would immediately have provided cases of societies without modern medicine and with low standards of living in which people are enormously loving toward their children, despite frequent deaths in infancy.[10] Secondly, no study is cited to show that people consciously work out the expectation of life of their children or the likely duration of their marriage and tailor their emotional lives accordingly. In any case, a marriage lasting for an average of over seventeen years can hardly be dismissed as "transient." Thirdly, there is abundant evidence, as far back as personal records have survived, that people did love their children or their spouses and feel despair when they died. Fourthly, as Stone admits, there is no correlation whatsoever between mortality rates and the supposed development of the feelings and affection which he tries to chart (82). The supposed growth of love, particularly in the eighteenth century, does not fit with any known changes in the expectation of life or duration of marriage. Thus one of the fundamental axioms upon which much of Stone's speculation is based is of dubious value.

A second assumption is a form of economic determinism. There are frequent generalizations which are based on the belief that social institutions, feelings, and attitudes can be deduced from technology and the level of wealth in a society. It is assumed that the material world determines the culture in a fairly simple one-to-one way; and, consequently, that as affluence increases, so will feeling. We are told that in the past a large part of the population was so poor and miserable that there was no time or energy for an emotional life. Stone writes concerning the eighteenth century that there "are levels of human misery at which the intensity of the struggle to satisfy the basic need for food and shelter leaves little room for humane emotions and affective relationships." Propertyless wage-laborers failed to help their parents because "their houses would be too small to accommodate them, and their incomes too marginal and precarious to have any surplus with which to feed and clothe them" (476, 421). Sexual norms are to be explained by the distribution of property: "the principle of premarital female chastity and the double standard after marriage are, therefore, functional to a society of property owners, especially small property owners"; "the higher ones goes in the society and the greater the amount of property likely to change hands with a marriage, the greater the stress on pre-marital chastity" (637, 504). Thus the rise in pre-marital sexual intercourse was a result of the "rise of the proportion of the propertyless with no economic stake in the value of their virginity . . ." (641). Economics also determined the choice of a marriage partner: "economic considerations bulked large in motivating mate selection . . ." among the lower middle classes in the eighteenth century, as among the gentry (392). As the economic stake in marriage rose, so did the status of women: the "seventeenth century saw a sharp rise in the size of marriage portions paid by the bride's parents to the groom's parents. This rise meant an increase in the economic stakes in marriage, and so enhanced the position of the wife" (330). Numerous other examples could be cited.

Yet any familiarity with the literature on modern non-Western societies, where standards of living are often far lower than those enjoyed by the English in the preindustrial period, would have shown that emotions, the care for parents, sexual norms, the arrangement of marriage, and the status of women vary enormously. They cannot be explained by economic factors. If Stone were right, the benighted peoples of the Third World and most of the past would have lived lives devoid of emotion, moved merely by the scramble for a livelihood. His assumption is extremely naive. It can again be challenged on the grounds that it neither fits the chronology of the supposed development of emotion which he believes in, nor does it fit with what we know about other societies, nor with the evidence for England from the fifteenth century.

A third assumption is that there has been a gradual evolution in history from simpler, more "backward," "lower" periods through a series of stages "up" to the present. Although on several occasions Stone makes general remarks disclaiming any simple linear development, writing for example that "even if the trend [that is, from *Gemeinschaft* to *Gesellschaft*] has been correctly identified, it has not been a constant linear movement" (661), the whole book is based on the evolutionary model described earlier in this critique. Of course there were reversals, as in the nineteenth century, but the picture is one of inexorable "progress" along the lines envisaged long ago by Macaulay. As Thompson has also noted, "despite disclaimers of any normative intent, Stone cannot prevent 'the modern family' from becoming the hero of his book."[11] This can be seen in the words that are used to describe changes in the past: things are constantly "rising" toward the present; where something has not yet risen, the country is "backward." For instance, "England was more advanced than France in most respects, but more backward in a few" (480). It can also be seen in the portrayal of the period up to the sixteenth century and beyond as one which was inhabited by cruel, unfeeling, smelly people. It was filled with parents who were "cold, suspicious, distrustful and cruel"; the "late sixteenth and early seventeenth centuries were for England the great flogging age"; there was "a low general level of emotional interaction and commitment" (194, 170–1, 95). Gradually there emerged the loving, caring society where dirt, cruelty, and disease were eradicated. There is a striking similarity to some nineteenth-century anthropology, where "savages" were regarded as children, without fully developed minds or emotions, who gradually "grew up" into civilization. Behind the details there is the same feeling that England was gradually "growing up" and renouncing childish ways.

A fourth assumption is that the wealthy and powerful provide the leading sector in change; their morality was "seeping down" to the lower orders because the rich were the "pace-makers of cultural change" (374, 12). Consequently, the emotional and intellectual life of the ninety percent of the population below the gentry was even more "backward" than that of the elite. Stone justifies his lack of interest in what he patronizingly calls the "plebs," partly on the grounds that they merely followed their masters, partly because he believes that "the historian is forced to abandon any attempt to probe attitudes and feelings, since direct evidence does not exist" (603). His allusions to those below the level of the gentry are brief, usually a few lines at the end of sections on the wealthy. Yet a lack of interest and consequent lack of evidence does not inhibit Stone from making a number of assertions about the sentiments and behavior of such people. We may look at a sample of the types of generalizations made; none of them is supported by any solid English evidence. The poor "had no economic incentive to have many children" in the eighteenth century; "they procreated extensively, partly because of social tradition and partly for lack of forethought and self-control"; the "poor seem in general to have been both more prudish and less imaginative about sex than the leisured classes"; "the poor were very much dirtier than the rich"; "among the mass of the very poor, the available evidence suggests that the common behaviour of many parents towards their children was often indifferent, cruel, erratic and unpredictable," though this may partly be excused "because they needed to vent their frustration on somebody" (421, 488, 487, 470). As Thompson remarks, these "hypotheses reproduce, with comical accuracy, the ideology and sensibility of 18th century upper class paternalists."[12] Since no evidence is given in support of these views, there is clearly no need to take them seriously.

[. . .]

Yet it is above all in his treatment of evidence that Stone shows his dilemma best, and it is to this we may now turn. In order to support a thesis which stemmed directly from the conventional view of the major transition from feudalism to capitalism, but which seemed difficult to prove, Stone is driven by his largely unexamined general theory to distort the past. He ignores or dismisses contrary evidence, misinterprets ambiguous evidence, fails to use relevant evidence, imports evidence from other countries to fill gaps, and jumbles up the chronology. This enables him to confirm that his expectations were right and to show to his own satisfaction that the past moved in the way it should have done. The fact that he was driven to such extremes is itself strong evidence that the fit between general framework and the historical material is very bad.

The first weakness, the ignoring of contrary evidence, is best displayed in Stone's treatment of literary material, particularly poems and plays. Stone is committed to the proposition that love and affection were largely the creation of the eighteenth century. They must not, therefore, exist before that date. The problem for him is that there is a vast literature, from medieval love poetry and Chaucer, through the Elizabethan sonnets, Shakespeare, Donne and the metaphysical poets, to Restoration drama and poetry, which seems to point to the opposite conclusion.

[. . .]

Another example of the ignoring of contrary evidence may be less conscious. It concerns the overlooking of a very great amount of material that does not fit the chronological framework, occurring too early, and which is therefore not mentioned. On numerous occasions Stone states that something is new and revolutionary, particularly in the eighteenth century. On almost every occasion it is possible to find the same view or trend present several hundred years earlier. On one occasion Stone comments that "as early as 1741 Baron de Pollnitz was struck by the greater liberty English women enjoyed than those in his own country" (318). This is used as evidence that women in the eighteenth century were being given greater freedom and treated with affection for the first time. A more careful reading of the literature produced by travellers would have shown that people were astonished at the liberty and loving treatment of wives not just "as early as 1741" but from at least the sixteenth century. Thus, as Mildred Campbell wrote long ago, referring to the writings of various foreign travellers in England between 1558 and 1614, "English women were held, in general, better off than their sex elsewhere. Hentzner, a German travelling in England in 1598, declared they were fortunate above all women in the world. Other foreign travellers expressed similar views, as did contemporary English writers."[13]

[. . .]

The ignoring of evidence that does not fit the schema, combined with rapid reading, is a fatal flaw. An example of a slightly different kind may be cited. It is just possible that Stone did not read the tracts, or at least the pages, alluded to above. But he certainly did read my book *The Family Life of Ralph Josselin*, since he uses it on a number of occasions in order to support his argument. Yet there is a great deal in the book, and even more in the full edition of the Diary, which has now been published by the British Academy, which flatly contradicts the general thesis. Ralph Josselin exhibits a warmth and depth of grief which Stone believes should not have existed. The treatment of such awkward evidence is revealing. Stone dismisses the evidence from Josselin, as well as the not inconsiderable works on family life by Morgan, Demos, and Hunt, in a footnote, since their combined view that marital relations were often warm and loving does not fit with his hypothesis (700, fn. 35). Yet it is his treatment of the parent–child relationship which is particularly interesting. As an example of the attitudes toward children's deaths in a "middling" family, Stone cites Josselin, who he believes had "much the same cold-blooded attitude" toward his children's deaths as he alleges is shown by Adam Martindale. Stone writes that "Ralph Josselin was not particularly upset either by the death of his ten-day-old child, or that of the thirteen-month-old one" (113). The actual description in my book conveys resignation and loss: "my deare Ralph before midnight fell asleepe whose body Jesus shall awaken; his life was continuall sorrow and trouble; happy he who is at rest in the Lord."[14] Although this was a controlled sadness, it is far from a "cold-blooded" lack of feeling. In the next paragraph of my book I then describe the death of Mary, the eight-year-old child. The account is still very moving indeed, after all these centuries; it shows a depth of sorrow which it would be impossible to fit with Stone's central thesis.[15] Stone therefore pursues the only possible course; he totally omits Mary and moves on to the older children.

This example verges on the second major weakness of Stone, namely the misinterpretation of evidence. Stone's main sources are autobiographical accounts. We have seen what he can do with a diary, and the same way of dealing with evidence can be seen in his treatment of another genre, namely account books. It would appear to be self-evident that since account books in the past, as in the present, were written in order to list income and expenditure, one would not expect them to be expressive. They would not be the place to find the revelation of deep feelings. I keep an account book, and if a child of mine died, my heart might almost break but the entry would probably read, "Funeral costs for my child – £20" or some such wording. I would be horrified to think that a future historian would try to deduce anything about my feelings for my children from this. Yet this is exactly what Stone tries to do. He believes that "Between upper-class parents and children, relations in the sixteenth century were also unusually remote . . . [there was] a degree of indifference and casual unconcern which would be inconceivable today. The most one normally could expect from a father at that time was the laconic entry in the account book of Daniel Fleming of Rydal in 1665: 'Paid for my loving and lovely John's coffin: 2s. 6d.'" (105). Allowing for the context, this appears to be far from "laconic," but more seriously, to use such evidence as proof of lack of affection appears unwarranted. It is part of a general fault which has been noted by several reviewers, namely the frequent tendency to interpret lack of evidence as indicative of lack of feeling. Silence cannot be treated as synonymous with apathy or hostility. Nor can modes of address, the naming of young children, the treatment of children at school be interpreted in the brusque and straightforward way employed by Stone. It would be easy to prove almost anything about contemporary society if we took its etiquette and rules of behavior at their face value.

A third method which helps to keep the past within the strait jacket imposed by Stone is the failure to cite or use material which should have been included in such a study. There are two major examples of this. The first concerns the treatment of the backdrop to the work, the later medieval period up to the middle of the sixteenth century. Since Stone's whole argument rests on the movement away from the supposed characteristics of this initial position, it is extremely important to know what kind of society England was between about 1350–1550. Stone does indeed spend a good deal of space describing this "traditional society" which was "eroded" by the new sentiments and the market economy as time passed (29). In contrast to the later periods there was a "more simple semi-tribal, feudal or community" organization in medieval England; it was a period when "privacy, like individualism, was neither possible nor desired"; marriage among the property-owning up to the sixteenth century was "a collective decision of family and kin"; "inside the home the members of the nuclear family were subordinated to the will of the head, and were not closely bonded to each other by warm affective ties" (152, 6, 87, 7). Accounts are given of medieval marriage, which resulted in a situation where, at the lower levels, "the habitually casual ways of the population" conspired to "make the medieval approach to marriage and sex very different from that of seventeenth-century England" (30 ff., 605). For instance, we are told that the "three objectives of family planning were the continuity of the male line, the preservation intact of the inherited property, and the acquisition through marriage of further property or useful political alliances" (42). Since Stone is here repeating a number of the conventional views about late medieval society, it is possible that he felt no need to document his pages of assertion or to look at a single original document, either in manuscript or in print, before 1500. Yet if he had looked more carefully at the Paston Letters, Chaucer, manor court rolls, or the recent spate of detailed studies of particular villages, he would have been in for a shock, for to the unbiased observer they seem to indicate a society very different from his stereotype . . .

The other type of omission concerns the main period of his study. If one is to undertake a serious study of the family, marriage, and sexual behavior in the period between 1500–1800, there are a number of very obvious primary manuscript sources, other than the autobiographical material used by Stone. The richest sets of manuscripts are the records of the courts, not only the ecclesiastical ones which supervised morality, but also Quarter Sessions, Assizes, Chancery, King's Bench, and many others. A second major source is testamentary material, particularly wills. A third is the assembled collection of other local records, particularly manorial documents and parish registers. There is no evidence in this book that Stone has ever looked at a single manuscript source in any of these categories for the purpose in hand.

[. . .]

There is a further reason why the book is unconvincing. Even if Stone were correct about the general nature of the change which is supposed to have occurred, he offers no plausible theories as to why the transformation in feeling should have happened when it did. He believes that the main reasons for the harsh brutality and lack of feeling in the earlier period was high mortality, economic insecurity, and the absence of "learned cultural expectations." Therefore he would need to show how there was a sudden change in all these factors in the eighteenth century. Yet he admits that mortality fluctuated in a way that did not fit with sentiment, that economic security did not suddenly emerge in the eighteenth century, and that literary and educational pressures had been just as great in the seventeenth as in the eighteenth century. His task of sorting out the causal chain is not made easier by his confusion of "capitalism," factory work, and "industrialization." Thus on several occasions he slides from one to the other as if they were synonyms (646, 661). As Thompson points out, Stone must surely know that these are separate entities which "are not identical and are not historically coincident . . ."[16] To equate them adds another dimension to the inadequacy of the discussion of causation.

We may conclude by giving our solution to the question posed by Thompson, namely how it is that a man who has read so much and worked for so long on England in this period could have written such a book: "there must be some ulterior theoretical explanation for this disaster."[17] For however much we may admire Stone's energy, exuberance, wide knowledge of the upper-class literature and power of synthesis, as well as the other virtues which it has not been necessary to point out since most reviews are full of them, there is a problem. Whatever the considerable merits of certain sections of the book, the final judgment on it can hardly be other than that it is indeed a "disaster." Thompson believes that it can be explained by Stone's isolation of the "family" as an institution, thus taking it out of its embedded context. Certainly this is a cause of a certain shallowness, but it is not a sufficient explanation for the basic inadequacy of the book. The answer lies at a deeper level and, ultimately, has nothing to do with Stone. It would appear that historians of England have for the past hundred years or so developed a general model of the nature of economic and political change in England from the medieval to the modern period which is constituted of a whole set of assumptions about progressive evolution from the past. Such a model seems plausible as long as we keep to the external world of politics and economics and as long as the detailed evidence from certain sources is not used. The works which have appeared concerning social and economic life at the local level in the medieval period onward, particularly in the last twelve years, do not fit at all with the predictions of the model. We are therefore either forced to scrap much of the old framework and to start again, or we can try to force the evidence into the older mold. Stone is quite correct. If Marx, Weber, Tawney, *et al.* were right, the past should have developed in the way he describes. If we take away his hyperbole, the transition in feeling and the rise of individualism should have occurred exactly as he describes it. This is why, on the whole, unless they are made irate by his handling of the "plebs," historians are likely to find his story innately convincing. They may dispute details but will find it hard to disagree fundamentally with his general picture.

I have suggested elsewhere an alternative interpretation of the general transition from a supposed "traditional" to a "modern" society in England.[18] Oversimplifying a complex argument, I have suggested that in relation to England, Marx and Weber were wrong and consequently that most of the edifice which has been built on their work is also defective. Those self-evident and obvious shifts in basic economic and social structure between 1400 and 1700 did not occur at all; they are an optical illusion created largely by the survival of documents and the use of misleading analogies with other societies. England in 1400 was roughly as follows. The concept of private, absolute property was fully developed; the household was not the basic social and economic unit of society but had already been replaced by the individual; a money economy was fully developed; wagelabor was already widely established, and there was a large class of full-time laborers; the drive toward accumulation and profit was already predominant; the "irrational" barriers toward the isolation of the economic sphere were already dismantled; there were no wide kinship groups, so that the individual was not subordinated to large family structures; natural "communities," if they had ever existed, were gone; people were geographically and socially highly mobile. If this were the case, we may wonder what the consequences would be for the speculations concerning the supposed massive emotional and psychological transition which Stone believes occurred between 1400–1800. Such a major change would no longer be expected. We would predict that from the very start of the period there would be some loving parents and some cruel parents, some people bringing their children up in a rigid way, others in a relaxed atmosphere, deep attachments between certain husbands and wives, frail emotional bonds in other cases. Of course there would be variations in the social and legal relations, in customs and fashions, both over time and between different socioeconomic groups. But the idea of a massive transformation from a group-based, brutal, and unfeeling society to the highly individualized and loving modern one would not need to be documented. My reading of the historical evidence for England suggests that such a general framework fits the evidence far better, leading to far less distortion, than that which Stone has inherited. It is a picture based on co-existing and varying "modes," similar to that adopted for the study of child-rearing and religious experience from the seventeenth to nineteenth centuries in England and New England in a recent book.[19] The alternative offered here would probably not work for France or a number of other European countries. It is based on the fact that, for as yet unexplained reasons, England seems to have been peculiar in that, from at least the fourteenth century, it was inhabited by individuals with highly stressed legal, economic, political, and religious rights and duties.

NOTES

1 Keith Thomas, review of Stone, *Times Literary Supplement* (21 October 1977), 1227.
2 *Idem.*

3 Joan Thirsk, review of Stone, *Times Higher Education Supplement* (28 October 1977), 16.

4 J. P. Kenyon, review of Stone, *Observer Review* (4 September 1977).

5 Rosalind Mitchison, *The New Review* 4 (February 1978), 42.

6 E. P. Thompson, review of Stone, *New Society* (8 September 1977), 501.

7 This summary of Weber's views is based on Max Weber, *General Economic History*, transl. Frank H. Knight (New York, 1961), 50–1, 54 ff., 173; R. Bendix, *Max Weber: An Intellectual Portrait* (London, 1966), 70–1, 74, 77–9, 114–15, 139, 330, 417.

8 Thompson, 499. Likewise, commenting on an earlier summary of Stone's central thesis, Christopher Lasch not only found it unoriginal, but wrote that Stone "outlines a curiously old-fashioned argument" concerning the decline of kinship (*New York Review of Books*, 11 December 1975, 53).

9 As will be seen below, Stone alters some of these dates as the book progresses.

10 The general works by Erik Erikson and Margaret Mead contain numerous instances of a loving attitude toward young children in societies with non-Western demographic patterns. Specific instances of love could be cited from most anthropological accounts; two instances from an area I know are the Garos (R. Burling, *Rengsanggri: Family and Kinship in a Garo Village* [Philadelphia, 1963], 106) and the Nagas of Assam (C. von Fürer-Haimendorf, *Morals and Merit* [London, 1967], 112).

11 Thompson, 499.

12 *Ibid.*, 501.

13 Mildred Campbell, *The English Yeoman* (New Haven, 1942), 261.

14 Alan Macfarlane, *The Family Life of Ralph Josselin* (Cambridge, 1970), 165.

15 The full description is even more moving than that quoted in *The Family Life*; see *The Diary of Ralph Josselin*, ed. Alan Macfarlane (Oxford, 1976), 201–4.

16 Thompson, 500.

17 *Idem.*

18 Alan Macfarlane, *The Origins of English Individualism: The Family, Property and Social Transition* (Cambridge and New York, 1978).

19 Philip Greven, *The Protestant Temperament: Patterns of Child-Rearing, Religious Experience, and the Self in Early America* (New York, 1977).

18

Illegitimacy and Infanticide in Early Modern Russia

David L. Ransel

The exposure and killing of infants first became a matter of government concern in Russia at the beginning of the eighteenth century. Peter I issued a decree in 1712 deploring this needless waste of human life. "Children of shame," as he called them, were being left in various places to die or were being killed outright soon after their birth. He ordered the establishment of hospitals (*shpitalety*) in every province, places where mothers of illegitimate children could deposit them in secret and thus avoid "committing the still greater sin of murder."[1]

A half-century later, Ivan Betskoi (of whom much more will be said later), with Empress Catherine II's encouragement, spoke eloquently about the fate of unwanted children. In a decree of 1763 that he composed for the empress, Betskoi told of many children abandoned in the streets of Moscow, left by their mothers to cruel fortune, and the majority of these children died. An even bigger problem, in Betskoi's view, was outright child murder. However great might be the number of children exposed in the city, he wrote, "it is indisputable that an incomparably greater number, barely having managed to draw their first breath, are deprived of it secretly by merciless mothers and their inhuman accomplices."[2] The solution undertaken by Catherine's government was to build two large foundling homes, one in Moscow and another in St. Petersburg, which would collect and care for unwanted children of those cities and the surrounding countryside.

This decision to allocate substantial resources to deal with child abandonment and infanticide is somewhat puzzling. It was not a response to a public outcry. Apart from the isolated work of a few clergymen, the initiative belonged exclusively to the central government. An explanation of this concern has to rest on three alternative premises. It is possible that before the eighteenth century, infanticide and child abandonment were so rare and aberrant in Russia as not to constitute a serious problem. If this was so, circumstances must have changed in the late seventeenth and early eighteenth centuries so as to produce a large number of cases in a short time, and these new conditions alerted the government to the need for action. It is also possible that in early times, exposure or direct killing of infants was common but took place in the woods and marshes

David L. Ransel, "Illegitimacy and Infanticide in Early Modern Russia," pp. 8–30 from *Mothers of Misery: Child Abandonment in Russia*. Princeton, NJ: Princeton University Press, 1988.

of rural Russia and did not come to general notice. In this case, conditions would have had to change in a way that concentrated the practice in a public sphere and made it visible to the authorities. Finally, the disposal of unwanted infants may have been customary and accepted in early Russia and therefore evoked no particular concern on the part of either the government or the people. If this was the case, the initiation of actions to combat this loss of life should be attributed to a shift in values, a new appreciation of infant life. Validation of one or another of these explanations is difficult, owing to the thinness of the documentary record of social behavior in early Russia . . .

The Legal Evidence

The lack of social data with which to test these hypotheses leaves scholarship at present with little more to go on than the surviving legal record. Though normative rather than descriptive, laws are still worth investigating for the clues they may contain about official attitudes and general constraints.

The legal record makes the nature of the old family regime clear. In pre-Petrine Russia, parental and, in particular, paternal authority was all but absolute. Characteristically, the law even allowed parents to sell their children into slavery. This provision, common in Asia and the Middle East as well, could be seen as evidence that children had value at least as commodities, but it did not suggest an especially high level of parental attachment to children. It is probably also significant that secular law in medieval Russia dealt with murder in a way that excluded consideration of the killing of one's own child. Murder subjected the killer to vengeance from the relatives of the deceased or to a payment (and, according to later texts of Kievan codes, to a monetary payment alone), the amount of which was linked to the social position of the deceased. Infants had no social position and therefore little or no value in the eyes of the law, whoever killed them. If a child was killed by an outsider, relatives might want to exact vengeance or monetary recompense as in an ordinary murder, but in the case of a child murdered by its own parents, no legal issue arose, since no one could claim the right to avenge the act or to demand monetary compensation for the loss. In short, the ordinary system of justice placed virtually no restraint on the disposal of one's own child.

Children were not entirely defenseless, however. Just as in the West, until the sixteenth century the protection of children and of others not provided for in secular law was left to the church. The first references to infanticide in early Russia therefore appeared in canon law, specifically in the ecclesiastical statutes associated with the names of the Kievan grand princes Vladimir and Iaroslav. Unfortunately, these largely procedural codes yield little social information.

The Vladimir statute merely mentions child murder as one of several crimes within the jurisdiction of the church.[3] The Iaroslav statute is somewhat more revealing: it commands, in article 6, that "if a woman conceives a child without a husband or with a husband and later kills it or throws it to the swine or drowns it, take [her, after she] has been convicted, into a convent: and her clan must redeem her."[4] At first glance, this seems to be a straightforward condemnation of infanticide, with the church acting as protector of unwanted children. The Soviet specialist B. A. Romanov has placed precisely this construction on it.[5] But this interpretation is surely wrong. A closer look indicates that the article was aimed not at infanticide but at fornication, for the immediately preceding and explicitly linked article prescribed the very same punishment for unmarried women who fornicated, even if these women did not harm any children that might result. Article 5 said: "If an unmarried woman fornicates or conceives a child when living with her father or her mother or as a widow, take [her, after she] has been convicted, into a convent."[6] The inclusion of a legally married woman in article 6 ("or with a husband") does not contradict this interpretation but rather indicates a sanction against gratuitous indulgence in intercourse, just as Western canon law condemned any form of sexual gratification without the intention of conception.[7] In other words, the law viewed infanticide not as child murder but as a belated form of birth control. The common basis of all these crimes was unsanctioned sexual activity.

Given the church's attitude toward sexual indulgence, the emphasis was well placed. Infanticide is clearly first and foremost a population-control measure, indeed the most efficient such measure. If modern societies with low levels of infant mortality and high expectations of survival and longevity can afford the luxury of control early in the reproductive process, especially contraceptive control, people living in subsistence economies with high mortality benefit from the fine tuning that infanticide allows. By exercising control at the end point of the reproductive process, they maintain sufficient fertility to assure population replacement and yet are able to trim the number of infants in response to periodic subsistence crises. As contrasted with abortion, infanticide has the additional advantage of providing greater protection for the mother's life. It also allows families to select the sex of offspring and to remove weak, crippled, or deformed products.[8]

The first evidence that infanticide was considered something other than population control appeared in an addendum to a sixteenth-century Muscovite law code, the *Sudebnik* of Ivan IV. The issue of a child murder was not mentioned in the code itself, but the addendum, which was a borrowing from Byzantine law that apparently had practical application in Russia, drew a clear distinction between abortion and infanticide. It treated abortion more harshly than earlier statutes had treated infanticide but as something less than a capital crime: "If a woman is pregnant and lays hands on her womb so as to lose the product of conception, she is to be beaten and confined."[9] At the same time, the addendum instructed that "the killer of a child shall be tried as a murderer."[10]

It is difficult to know if this was a general prescription, since it neglected the striking distinction between legitimate and illegitimate children that was made in the comprehensive seventeenth-century code, the *Ulozhenie* (1649) of Tsar Aleksei Mikhailovich. Although the Ulozhenie carried forward the distinction between abortion and infanticide, its differential treatment of legitimate and illegitimate children made explicit the concern with sexual license rather than with the life of the child. According to the Ulozhenie, if a woman gave birth to an illegitimate child and either killed it or conspired with another to have it killed, she was to be sentenced to death without mercy. The article even included the didactic note that "seeing this, others would not take part in this foul and illegal act and would cease fornicating."[11] On the other hand, if the victim was a legitimate child killed by its father or mother, the law prescribed merely a one-year prison sentence followed by a public confession in church, and it even explicitly forbade the application of the death penalty to parents convicted of killing their own child.[12] It is also significant that the article about killing an illegitimate child appeared in the code in connection with an article on pandering and not together with other homicides. This bracketing is further evidence of the lawmaker's concern with sexual matters rather than with the life of the child.

European Influences and Russian Evolution

The harsh condemnation in the Ulozhenie of infanticide by an unwed mother may have been an echo of the treatment of the "fallen woman" in western and central Europe, where, from the late

Middle Ages to the Enlightenment, efforts to confine sexual activity to marriage brought increasingly ferocious sanctions against the unwed mother who exposed or killed her child. The Ulozhenie article in question was a direct borrowing from the Lithuanian Statute of 1588, which in turn seems to have drawn on practices then current in Germanic law.[13] In view both of this derivation and of some instructive parallels in the development of Western and Russian societies in the early modern age, it would be helpful to consider the European situation.

[. . .]

The punishment for infanticide became caught up in this rising spiral. Until the high Middle Ages in the West, there seemed to be some tolerance of nonmarital sexual activity, and perhaps fairly high levels of infanticide were also tolerated, in the interests of keeping population in line with economic resources.[14] But after the Council of Rome in the eleventh century, the church began stressing the importance of confining sexual indulgence to marriage, an emphasis that was strengthened toward the end of the Middle Ages and carried forward even more vigorously by the Reformation. As a result, the position of the unwed mother became increasingly isolated and precarious. She faced social ostracism and hence the prospect of having to turn to prostitution or other unsavory means of staying alive . . .[15]

The crusade against extramarital intercourse and its products, the illegitimate child and infanticide, gained particular momentum in the sixteenth century. In several European countries, unmarried servant women were regularly inspected to see if they had breast milk. The presence of milk in the breasts justified, according to article 36 of the *Constitutio Criminalis Carolina*, introduced in the Holy Roman Empire under Charles V in 1532, the application of torture to discover the cause.[16] A still more draconian provision appeared in article 131 of the code. It was evidently too easy for a woman found to have borne an illegitimate child that later turned up dead to declare that it had been stillborn or had died of natural causes. Accordingly, article 131 introduced a presumption of guilt for murder in cases in which an unmarried woman was alone at the time of birth and hid the newborn child, and the baby was later found dead. Unless the woman could prove that the child was stillborn or died naturally, she was to be convicted of infanticide.[17] Effective prosecution demanded this unusual presumption in an age when medical practitioners had no convincing method for demonstrating the cause of infant death.[18] After its appearance in the *Carolina*, the rule was written into French law in 1556 and confirmed in 1586 and again in 1708. Presumption of guilt based on similar or slightly modified conditions, usually involving the failure to register an extramarital pregnancy, subsequently found its way into the codes and practices of many other European countries, including England in 1624, Sweden in 1627, Württemberg in 1658, Denmark in 1683, Scotland in 1690, and Bavaria as late as 1751.[19] The punishment for infanticide varied from place to place. Denmark even then was relatively more humane in requiring only a simple beheading. In Sweden, women were cast into a fire. The *Carolina* more typically called for burial alive and a stake to be driven through the woman's chest, a punishment applied in Prussia as recently as the early eighteenth century.[20]

After the witchcraft hysteria of the seventeenth century, the harsh persecution of deviant women spent its force, and the next century saw a sharp downturn in indictments and convictions for infanticide. In England, a rapid decline set in during the first decades of the eighteenth century.[21] The change came somewhat later to central Europe. In a letter of 1777 to Voltaire, Frederick II of Prussia could still declare that in Germany infanticide accounted for more executions than did any other crime.[22] But, as Frederick's concern itself testified, the "humanitarian revolt" was on its way to shaping a new, more tolerant attitude toward the unwed mother, and legislators soon modified the cruel treatment of these women, eventually abolishing the death penalty for infanticide.[23]

In Russia, matters never went so far as to fix in law a presumption of guilt for an unwed mother whose child had died. Perhaps the massive slaughters during Ivan IV's reign, the Time of Troubles, and the church schism exhausted the urge for bloody sacrifices in that age and spared Russia the witch hunts and other misogynous assaults that punctuated west European history in the sixteenth and seventeenth centuries. A misogynous impulse was nonetheless at work in Russia during this period, and for a time the monastic clergy succeeded in promoting a social regime based on a combined fear and loathing of women.

Before the sixteenth century, Russian women in their role as representatives of powerful families had on occasion figured prominently in political and economic life. But with the retreat of the great families before the centralizing autocracy, the public sphere became confined to state service, in which women took no part. The autocracy drew strength from its alliance with the monastic brotherhood, and the monks in turn used state authority to spread their views on the wickedness and incompetence of women. As a result, leading families learned to cloister their women, subject them to a life of celibacy, and shut them off from a public role. For families lower on the social scale, cloistering was impractical. The rules for these people were expounded in the *Domostroi*, a document associated with the monk Silvester which exuded contempt for women and advised confining them to the household (but had to recognize their important role in the household economy).[24] It was during this time of monkish rule, when official values most nearly mirrored the misogyny of the West, that Russia also came closest to the harsh Western treatment of unwed mothers by adopting in the Ulozhenie of 1649 the differentiation between the killing of a legitimate and an illegitimate child.

Although Western women endured more suspicion and persecution in this era than did Russian women, the Western attitude toward infant life may have been more solicitous than the Russian. In the West, the laws on registration of pregnancies and the presumption of guilt in cases of death after concealment of the pregnancy and birth reflected concern for the life of the child. Russian law before the eighteenth century did not express the same degree of interest in the life of the child, be it legitimate or illegitimate. (The distinction may have been more formal than practical, but it is worth noting nonetheless, because the practical similarities did not favor protection for the child.) In Russia, the differential value attached to the lives of various family members in medieval times persisted right into the late seventeenth century, and the sharpest difference was in the meager protection afforded a child. The Ulozhenie prescribed various punishments for the killing of relatives, but in every case the crime called for substantial penalties – except when the victim was a child. A wife who killed her husband received the grim fate of burial alive, in some cases after being tortured with fire.[25] Killing of parents also brought death. Even a husband had to pay for murdering his wife; although the code remained curiously silent about wife murder, the courts apparently treated this crime seriously, varying the penalty with circumstances. Only the killing of children was regarded as something of a misdemeanor. The more severe penalty for killing an illegitimate child cannot be taken as evidence to the contrary; it revealed a shift since Kievan times not in attitudes toward infanticide but in the penalties for non-marital sexual indulgence. The object of the law was not to save the life of the child but, as it said explicitly, to persuade others to "cease fornicating."[26]

The influence of the monks in Russia was brief, and the Ulozhenie's article on infanticide survived for only a half-century. A different set of values emerged under the rule of the "tsar reformer," Peter the Great (1689–1725). Historians credit Peter with introducing a major change in official attitudes toward women. Peter certainly opposed the previous cloistering of women, and he quickly set about dismantling the barriers to female participation in society. He also showed little respect for moral and religious strictures on illegitimacy. Yet in ending the distinction between the killing of a legitimate and an illegitimate child, Peter displayed no charity toward the unwed mother who murdered her child. His military articles of 1716 simply rendered the legal status of the child moot by imposing an equally severe penalty for killing any infant, legitimate or illegitimate. The punishment for child murder became equivalent to that for the premeditated murder of a father, mother, or military officer – namely, to be broken on the wheel and left to die.[27] Peter's main interest lay in preserving and expanding the nation's population. He was conversant with Western ideas about the importance of "human capital." No doubt the continual manpower shortages suffered in his armed forces and building projects did even more to convince him of the need for practical measures to increase population size.

Interestingly enough, although he set aside the Ulozhenie's distinction between legitimate and illegitimate children, Peter replaced it with a distinction between infants and older children. In editing the draft of the article in the military code that called for death on the wheel for child murder, the tsar inserted in his own hand after the word "child" the qualifier "in infancy."[28] Although Peter wanted to break down the old Russian family regime – in a sense, to pry it open and make it a public asset rather than a private haven – he was not ready to undermine paternal authority. A tension remained in Russian law between the goal of preserving life and the right of a father to maintain control. A court later interpreted the article to mean that if a man accidentally killed his child (or wife) in the course of disciplining him or her, the homicide was not a capital offense. Even if he killed his child intentionally for misbehavior, the penalty should be no more than simple execution by beheading.[29] In this regard, Westerners have no reason to feel superior, since in most other European countries, including England and the American colonies, courts afforded similar protection to murderously abusive parents; as noted earlier, the distinction between Russia and the West in this area may have been more formal than real.[30] This interpretation indicates, nevertheless, that so far as child murder was concerned, the military articles of Peter I treated only the killing of an infant as a special case deserving of a sterner penalty than was imposed for ordinary homicide. In one sense, then, Peter restored the pre-Muscovite prescriptions of the Iaroslav statute, since his law also ignored the legitimacy of the victim and viewed infanticide primarily as a population-control measure. However, in Peter's code the emphasis was different. The Iaroslav statute sought to restrict gratuitous sexual indulgence, whereas Peter wanted to increase the number of his subjects. His action was both a sign and a consequence of a new appreciation of infant life.

[. . .]

Increased Incidence and Visibility

The preceding discussion does not answer the question of whether the concern expressed about infanticide in the eighteenth century arose from an increased incidence of child exposure and murder. The absence of social data or even of reliable observations of child murder prevent analysis of this type. One exception to this generalization is the recent discovery by Richard Hellie of substantial female infanticide among slave populations in the seventeenth century.[31] In view of the startling nature of this evidence, scholars must scrutinize it carefully. Still, it could scarcely be doubted that Russians availed themselves of exposure and infanticide before the eighteenth century. Periodic subsistence crises provided incentive to kill or desert children. The widespread famines of the early seventeenth century drove the inhabitants of some areas to cannibalism.[32] It is easy to imagine that in these circumstances people also resorted to exposure and infanticide, all the more so as Russian law before the eighteenth century posed few obstacles to this type of population limitation. But whether infanticide was a commonly accepted practice, a method acceptable in the case of slave populations alone, or an extreme measure resorted to only in desperate times cannot now be determined.

In view of the uncertain knowledge about infanticide in early Russia, it is tempting to attribute the concern expressed for children in the eighteenth century to a shift in values. There is considerable evidence for this hypothesis, but it is also possible that new conditions, particularly those flowing from the reforms of Peter I, may have greatly increased the incidence of infanticide and exposure. Peter changed much in Russia, and some of his measures created conditions which, if they did not augment the actual number of exposures and child murders, certainly increased their visibility and hence their social significance.

One change was the creation of a new category of state serfs known as "assigned peasants" (*pripisnye krest'iane*). This policy arose from the need to provide a supplementary work force for factories, which rapidly increased in number during the early eighteenth century. Many of these factories could not recruit an adequate labor supply from the available pool of unbound workers, and so Peter decided to turn over to them a certain number of villages (or households within a village) to meet their labor needs. The peasants thus assigned had to work off their state tax and labor obligations either by toiling in the factories or, more often, by supplying raw materials and performing auxiliary services . . . V. I. Semevskii, a specialist on the eighteenth-century peasantry, calculated that the number of assigned peasants in state and private industry combined reached approximately 100,000 by the time of the second soul-tax census in the early 1740s and climbed to 190,000 by the third census in 1762. Twenty years later, the number stood at well over a quarter-million (263,899) . . .[33]

The significance of their situation for the question of child abandonment lies in the separation of many of them from their villages and families. Some of the villages concerned were close to the factories they served, but many lay at a considerable distance: as much as six hundred kilometers or more. Since the work normally fell to able-bodied males in the age group from eighteen to forty, young men had to spend long periods far from home. Migration to find work was no novelty in Russia, but this forced draft of tens and even hundreds of thousands of young men to work in factories far from home for periods of a few months to a year and more was unprecedented, and it certainly must have contributed to the number of illegitimate children produced both in the villages of deserted women and near the work sites of the men.

An even greater and more visible impact was produced by another of Peter's programs, the massive recruitment of men for the armed forces. The number of military recruits ran much higher than that of assigned peasants, and the separation of soldiers from home and family was usually permanent . . . Between 1705 and 1713, the army called up 337,196 men, or roughly 11 percent of the pool of men in the age group capable of service . . .[34] For the subsequent period from 1719 to 1745, the demographic historian V. M. Kabuzan has calculated that recruiting levies drew off more than 6 percent of the male population, again with an even higher proportion among the central Great Russian population.[35]

Service in the Russian army lasted twenty-five years or until disablement, and a recruit had little prospect of ever returning to his village, a fact recognized and vividly portrayed in the laments and rituals performed by peasants in taking leave of a recruit. In consequence, military recruitment created another new social category, the soldier's wife (*soldatka*), or the woman left behind. In some cases, especially if she had already produced a child, the soldier's wife found a secure home with her in-laws. But often the presence of an unattached young woman posed a threat to other women of the household and village, who conspired to drive her out. The cities to which the soldiers' wives migrated offered few opportunities for respectable employment and considerable inducement, because of the high proportion of males in the towns, to prostitution. Enough of the soldiers' wives took up this profession to give the whole group an unsavory reputation.[36] More to the point, when one of them became pregnant, she had no place to turn for help. Return to the village was no solution, yet caring for an infant interfered with earning a livelihood. It is in this context that one observes a rising awareness of child exposure and sufficient concern about its magnitude to elicit government intervention to stiffen laws against infanticide and to take other measures to save the children.

The programs initiated by Peter I for assignment of peasants to factories and for military recruitment combined to take as many as 10 to 15 percent of the able-bodied male population either temporarily or permanently away from home. The policies contributed to the social displacement of women and hence to the increased visibility of illegitimacy and child exposure. As noted earlier, it is impossible to calculate whether the incidence of exposures and infanticide increased in comparison with earlier times. If there had been a conscious employment of infanticide earlier to limit population, Peter's policies may merely have added to or abetted the practice while altering its character and locus sufficiently to bring it into public view. If infanticide was rare in the past, Peter's actions gave rise to a new social phenomenon.

A New Sensibility

Whatever role an increased incidence and visibility of infanticide may have played in arousing the concern expressed in the eighteenth century about child murder, the emergence of interest in this problem also owed something to a new appreciation of infant life and sensitivity to children generally. As early as the 1690s, a monk and educator by the name of Karion Istomin produced a radically new and different primer, which included graphic design and the word-object and sentence methods of teaching reading.[37] He thereby revealed his understanding that children occupied a different mental world, perceived their surroundings differently from adults, and had special educational needs. Not long afterward, the government issued large editions of its own civil primer, together with an etiquette book detailing proper behavior in relations between children and adults.[38] These "discoveries of childhood" in the fields of education and manners were paralleled by changes in the organization of charity and the emergence of a system of state-sponsored care for abandoned and homeless children. This expression of a new appreciation of infant life was especially important, because in the field of charity the break with the past was clearest. It was there that the new concern produced major institutional programs and unprecedented efforts to save the lives of unwanted children.

Before the eighteenth century, to judge from the silence of the documentary record, organized charity and public care facilities scarcely existed in Russia. To the extent that any institution could be said to have charge of caring for the poor, ill, crippled, insane, and orphaned, it was the church. From early times, monasteries provided a refuge for people in need, and a midsixteenth-century church council (*Stoglav*) officially imposed this obligation on the church.[39] References later in the century to church-supported almshouses indicate some activity in this area.[40] Further development occurred during the reign of Tsar Mikhail Fedorovich (1613–1645). In establishing a Patriarchal Department in his government, he again laid upon the church the charge of caring for the needy, including now for the first time its responsibility to care for abandoned children.[41] During the remainder of the seventeenth century, patriarchs and other church leaders built a number of almshouses, hospitals, and shelters. There is even a vague reference to "orphan homes."[42] Yet all this work was sporadic and scattered, and it has left little record of its operation or scope.

More significant surely than either monastic charity or facilities provided by the church was local parish help, which was within easy reach of many people and available on a regular basis. Many churches kept on their grounds wooden huts (*izbushki*) or "cells" (evidently small rooms in a dormitory) and took in at parish expense the elderly poor, invalids, and other needy. The number of cells ranged from a few up to fifty or more in large parishes. One Moscow church, St. John the Divine (Ioann-Bogoslov v Bronnoi), had room for one hundred people.[43] No doubt orphans and abandoned children turned up at these refuges, but available records say nothing about their treatment. Even direct references to the care of orphans cannot be taken at face value because of the early Russian practice of calling all unfortunate or displaced persons, even peasants generally, "orphans."[44]

Before the eighteenth century, the financial basis of all charity was private giving. Many assets that the church applied to this work came from private donations, particularly the land and money bequeathed by wealthy patrons in remembrance of their souls. Philanthropy outside the church had the same private character. People of means would set aside large sums of money in their wills for distribution to the poor during the forty-day mourning period following their deaths (*sorokoust*).[45]

[. . .]

The first evidence of a new outlook on welfare came in the reign of Tsar Fedor Alekseevich (1676–1682). This was the period in which Russians began using terms like "state interest" (*gosudarstvennoe delo*) and other abstractions borrowed from the West.[46] Russians were entering a century of rapid and unself-conscious adoption of Western administrative practices, and as part of this process they studied central European *polizei* notions of public welfare. This can be seen clearly in a draft degree drawn up for Tsar Fedor Alekseevich in 1682. Though not implemented at the time, the decree signaled a radical turn in Russian thinking about social policy.

This lengthy document emphasized three basic points. First, it declared the government's intention to develop philanthropy as a public service and obligation and to leave it no longer to haphazard private means or church work. Second, it sought to separate the able-bodied needy from those too old, crippled, or ill to engage in productive labor. Those who could no longer work were to be placed in hospitals, almshouses, and monasteries and supported for life, unless they could be cured, in which case they should be made well. The others, the professional beggars capable of working, would end up in what would later be known as workhouses, institutions that did not yet exist in Russia but which the tsar's advisers hoped to created. The third point concerned homeless children who wandered the streets begging for alms. According to the draft decree, the sovereign was to issue an order requiring, "as in other countries," that homes be built for these waifs.[47] The homes would provide education and training, with separate programs for boys and girls. The boys would acquire basic literacy and then learn a trade in the home or as an apprentice at a master's shop. At maturity, when they proved they could provide for themselves and a wife, they would be released as freemen. The girls were to grow up in the home and then go to convents for schooling. At the proper age, they could buy homes and marry. "Such people," the decree explained, "would in the future contribute to their communities, and there would be no reason to fear robbery from them, because they had been given the means to provide for themselves."[48]

This proposal ran counter to the Russian custom of almsgiving, which assumed the existence of needy receivers in public view. Fedor's advisers wanted to introduce the "well-ordered state," with its regulation of society, repression of the old forms of beggary and almsgiving, and removal of the unsightly crippled, diseased, and derelict from the streets. At the same time, they planned to take the able-bodied poor and street children, who constituted a threat to public safety, and harness them to productive pursuits. It had taken these ideas 150 years to reach Russia after their implementation in western Europe,[49] and Russians would have to wait another 80 years before anything comparable to the program outlined in Fedor's decree could be realized. The decree was nevertheless important as an indication of government thinking, a recognition by the government of its responsibility for public welfare, and an indication of future policy. Fedor's half brother, Peter the Great, definitely wanted to move in the same direction and, despite may obstacles, succeeded in creating some facilities for the care of unwanted children.

In this effort, Peter was preceded and inspired by the work of a churchman. If one discounts the "orphan homes" of the time of Tsar Mikhail Fedorovich, the first shelter specifically for the care of illegitimate children was established by Metropolitan Iov of Novgorod at the Kholmovo-Uspenskii Monastery just outside his diocesan capital. Contemporary sources refer to it as a *domik* or small house, but this could scarcely have been an accurate term. Although no registries from the facility have survived, a Senate document recorded the burial in 1714 of more than 500 children from the shelter.[50] If the mortality rate was similar to the 75 or 80 percent known in Russian foundling homes later in the century, the yearly admissions to Iov's facility may have run as high as 650. This figure could include admissions at more than one location, since one decree referred to Iov's operation as encompassing ten shelters housing up to 3,000 children.[51] The enterprise was large enough to attract the attention of Tsar Peter and move him to furnish Iov's home with additional revenues from other monasteries and with donations from the tsarist family and wealthy nobles.[52]

Peter was not satisfied merely to subsidize the efforts of the church. Once he gained respite from the Northern War, he set out to imitate and extend Iov's facility by establishing his own state-sponsored system of care. It was at this time, early in 1712, that Peter issued a decree calling for the establishment of hospitals for crippled and aged service people no longer fit even for guard duty, and also for the care of "children of shame" so that their mothers would not compound the sin of illegitimacy by committing the greater sin of murder. And he ordered that this be done "on the model of the bishop of Novgorod."[53] This first order appeared somewhat casually as the eighteenth point in a decree covering military recruitment, fortifications, penalties for soldiers absent without leave, and other military affairs. This circumstance shows how closely awareness of child abandonment was bound up with the creation of a standing army and so reinforces speculation about the importance of military recruitment in the problem. Despite this seeming casualness, Peter definitely intended to create the care facilities. He reissued the order on hospitals separately later the same month and again in 1714 and 1715 in an extended form giving more detail on the type of institution desired and its purpose.[54]

These later decrees noted that the hospitals should be built in proximity to churches. Apparently Peter meant to use clergy as administrators and thus forge a link with the established practice of parish help. In Moscow, the facilities were to be of masonry construction; other towns needed only to build in wood. But in all cases they were admonished to use Metropolitan Iov's institution as a model in organizing their work. They should allow mothers of illegitimate children to deposit them at the hospital without having to reveal their identity. The institutions were to employ capable women to care for the children, and Peter ordered that provincial revenues be assigned for the payment of staff and maintenance of the foundling population. The decrees expressed Peter's concern that in the absence of such institutions, shame compelled women to expose their illegitimate infants, and "these children die to no purpose."[55] He also noted that some women simply killed the children, and he issued a stern reminder that the penalty for this crime was execution.

At about the same time as these decrees appeared, Peter was working on the military articles, which increased the punishment for killing a legitimate child. He was obviously much concerned with the question of labor supply. The sight of potentially productive subjects exposed and dying in the streets must have struck him as intolerable. At one point, he even had to scold the Holy Synod about killings of illegitimate infants born in the convents, noting that many bodies of babies had been found at cleanings of the convent cesspools.[56] Concern about this loss of life would explain why he fastened so eagerly on the example of Metropolitan Iov and sought to extend this model of care for unwanted children to the whole country. The further disposition of the children thus saved likewise supports the notion that Peter saw them as raw material for his expanding military forces and construction projects. In 1723, when a number of the youngsters in the hospitals were approaching puberty, orders went out to send the boys over ten years of age to the Admiralty in St. Petersburg for inscription into the navy.[57] The following year, Peter turned others of the children over to craftsmen to be apprenticed in trades.[58]

Within the limits of these objectives, Peter seemed to be interested in supporting and expanding foundling care. He insisted on prompt payment of salaries and maintenance expenses for the hospitals, and he granted churches a monopoly on the sale of candles specifically to assure them of sufficient revenue for running their almshouses and care facilities.[59] But, as with many of his projects, Peter's successors did not share his enthusiasm. After the great reformer's death, the need to bring government expenditures into line with revenues rapidly led to the dismantling of many reforms and institutions, including the foundling shelters.

The extent to which Peter's design for provincial shelters came into being is not known. A Senate decree of 1726 noted that at the time in Moscow province (*guberniia*) alone, 440 children were in foundling care at various shelters, with 120 wet nurses attending them. The Senate apparently had no clear idea of the state of care facilities elsewhere.[60]

By 1729, the persistent problem of displaced adults and abandoned children turning up in the towns and creating a nuisance forced the senators to look more closely into the matter. The issue came up in connection with the case of two boys, ages ten and four, the children of a townsman from Nizhnii Novgorod, who out of dire need brought them to Moscow and then died.[61] The orphaned boys wandered the streets collecting alms. A Senate decree on the matter raised the question of what to do with the large number of runaway soldiers and other people, young and old, who roamed the back alleys of the towns and lodged in taverns, public bathhouses, brothels, and eateries. According to the Senate, they were a public menace and endangered life and property. It ordered that those of suitable age be sent to the military and that youngsters be turned over to the Economic Collegium to be cared for as instructed in Peter I's decrees on "children of shame." At the same time, the government called for the compilation of information about illegitimate children, orphans, and soldiers' children and about the available care facilities (*shpitali*) for illegitimate children.[62] The information must have convinced the authorities that they could not meet the current burden of welfare, for a short time later they moved to discharge the government from any responsibility for the care of girls and women. Young girls went to whoever wished to take them in as servants, and older girls were to be sent to factories or into service work. Boys were apparently still to be reared until old enough to enter the military. Otherwise, the government agreed to maintain only the aged and the mentally or physically disabled.[63]

In making these dispositions, the government was following the practice established in the seventeenth century of trying to fit each subject into a well-defined niche of a castelike society. This objective was explicit in two decrees of 1744 that reiterated the order to empty state care facilities of all but the old and the handicapped. Everyone else was to be attached to some tax-paying group, as a proprietary serf, a town dweller, or a guild member, unless he was entering government or military service.[64] So in one sense this solution marked a regression toward the old family regime, while at the same time the government was searching for corporate bodies beyond the family that could take responsibility for the behavior and obligations of persons who could not be fitted into the old family. But this was the last effort in the eighteenth century to deal with orphaned and abandoned children through the old family regime or the caste system. A few years later, under the influence of Enlightenment values, Catherine II ushered in a new approach which in some respects went beyond anything known in the West.

The available evidence is consistent with all three of the proposed explanations for the emergence in eighteenth-century Russia of public concern and action in regard to child exposure and infanticide. Some combination of the three possibilities may provide the best explanation. The feeble protection given to infant life in early Russian law suggests that infanticide may have been commonplace, especially in rural areas, where often neither the prince's nor the patriarch's writ ran. Hellie has made a strong case for significant levels of female infanticide among slaves, but in the absence of information about other groups, little more can be said. It seems beyond doubt that the social changes wrought by the reforms of Peter the Great and his immediate predecessors increased the incidence of infanticide and the visibility of the victims. The efforts to open up the old Russian family and put its individual members to work for the state led to the uprooting of large numbers of people and their detachment from their familial nests, with attendant increases in illegitimacy. It is difficult, however, to disentangle the issue of increased visibility from the final factor considered, a new sensibility and concern for infant life. In the absence of a visible problem, the concern of the authorities may have remained unexpressed. If it could be shown that exposure and infanticide were common in the past, the argument for an altered sensibility would become much stronger. Even so, there seems to be convincing evidence for the emergence of a new understanding and appreciation of children, influenced by the arrival from the West of humanist learning and populationist economic doctrine.

NOTES

1 *Polnoe sobranie zakonov rossiskoi imperii (PSZ)* 4, no. 2467 (January 16, 1712).

2 *PSZ* 16, no. 11908 (September 1, 1763).

3 Ia. N. Shchapov, ed., *Drevnerusskie kniazheskie ustavy XI–XV vv.*, Moscow, 1976, 17–19. Other references to infanticide may be found in the "commandments" of Metropolitan Georgii, quoted in B. A. Romanov, *Liudi i nravy drevnei Rusi: Istoriko-bytovye ocherki XI–XVVV vv.*, Moscow, 1966, 185–6.

4 Translated from the "Archeograficheskii izvod," in Schapov, *Drevnerusskie kniazzheskie ustavy*, 94.

5 Romanov, *Liudi i nravy*, 186.

6 Schapov, *Drevnerusskie kniazheskie ustavy*, 94.

7 John T. Noonan, Jr., *Contraception: A History of its Treatment by the Catholic Theologians and Canonists*, Cambridge, MA, 1966, 143–300.

8 The killing of deformed infants was not treated as severely as ordinary homicides in nineteenth-century Russian law. It was bracketed in the penal code with death by negligence and justifiable homicides. See

Ulozhenie o nakazaniiakh ugolovnykh i ispravitel'nykh, St Petersburg, 1845, 497, article 1940. I have not discovered if this provision carried over an early Russian value.

9 A. D. Liubavskii, *Iuridicheskie monografii i issledovaniia*, 4 vols, St Petersburg, 1867-8, 4:65.

10 Ibid.

11 M. N. Tikhomirov and P. P. Epifanov, eds, *Sobornoe ulozhenie 1649g.*, Moscow, 1961, ch. 22, art. 3.

12 Ibid., art. 26.

13 See art. 2, ch. 57, in I. I. Lappo, *Litovskii statut v moskovskom perevode-redaktsii*, Yurev, 1916, 341. See also comments by N. Tagantsev, "O detoubiistve," *Zhurnal Ministerstva Iustitsii*, 1868, no. 9, 219-20 and by Liubavskii, *Iuridicheskie monografii*, 4:58.

14 Emily R. Coleman, "L'infanticide dans le Haut Moyen Age," *Annales ESC*, 29 (1974), 326-8.

15 Erik Anners, *Humanitet och rationalism:Studier I upplysningstidens strafflagreformer*, Rättshistoriskt Bibliotek, vol. 10, Stockholm, 1965, 27-30.

16 Oscar Helmuth Werner, *The Unmarried Mother in German Literature, with Special Reference to the Period 1770-1800*, New York, 1917, 29-3.

17 The German text of these articles is in Werner, *Unmarried Mother*, 29-30. For comment, see Anners, *Humanitet och rationalism*, 30-1, 111-12.

18 R. W. Malcolmson, "Infanticide in the Eighteenth Century," in *Crime in England, 1550-1800*, ed. J. S. Cockburn, London, 1977, 187-209.

19 Malcolmson, "Infanticide," 196-200, cites the English law of 1624, which was not repealed until 1803. Others are listed in Anners, *Humanitet och rationalism*, 111-12.

20 Anners, *Humanitet och rationalism*, 30. Frederick William I of Prussia took an especially severe view of the crime and in the 1720s restored the harsh punishments that had begun to be abolished: Werner, *Unmarried Mother*, 33.

21 Peter C. Hoffer and N. E. H. Hull, *Murdering Mothers: Infanticide in England and New England, 1558-1803*, New York, 1981, 64-74. The shift away from the presumption of guilt was noted in England by William Blackstone, who wrote in about 1765 that "it has of late years been usual . . . to require some sort of presumptive evidence that the child was not alive": *Commentaries*, 198.

22 Cited in Malcolmson, "Infanticide," 189.

23 Werner, *Unmarried Mother*, 36-7, 106-7.

24 Susan Janosik McNally, "From Public Person to Private Prisoner: The Changing Place of Women in Medieval Russia," Ph.D. dissertation, State University of New York at Binghampton, 1976.

25 L. V. Cherepnin, ed., *Pamiatniki russkogo prava*, Vol. 7, *Pamiatniki prava perioda sozdaniia absoliutnoi monarkhii vtoraia polovina XVII v.*, Moscow, 1963, 492.

26 Tikhomirov and Epifanov, *Sobornoe ulozhenie*, ch. 22, art. 26. See also the comments on this article in A. G. Man'kov, *Ulozhenie 1649 goda: Kodeks feodal'nogo prava Rossii*, Leningrad, 1980, 222.

27 *PSZ* 5, no. 3003 (March 22, 1716), 369-70.

28 Gosudarstvennaia Publichnaia Biblioteka, Otdel rukopisi, f. 1001, d. 14, p. 215, cited in L. N. Semenova, *Ocherki istorii byta i kul'turnoi zhizni Rossii, pervaia polovina XVIII v.*, Leningrad, 1982, 119.

29 Liubavskii, *Iuridicheskie monografii*, 4:67.

30 Hoffer and Hull, *Murdering Mothers*, 46.

31 Richard Hellie, *Slavery in Russia, 1450-1725*, Chicago, 1982, 442-59.

32 E. D. Maksimov, "Nachalo gosudarstvennogo prizreniia," *Trudovaia pomoshch'*, 1900, no. 1:44.

33 V. I. Semevskii, *Krest'iane v tsarstvovanie imperatritsy Ekateriny II*, vol. 2, St Petersburg, 1901, 295-305.

34 Richard Hellie, "The Petrine Army," paper presented at the Tercentenary Conference on Peter the Great and His Legacy, Chicago, November 18-19, 1972, 9.

35 V. M. Kabuzan, "Izmeneniia v udel'nom vese I territoral'nom razmeshchenii russkogo naseleniia Rossii v XVIII-pervoi polovine XIX vek," in *Problemy istoricheskoi demografii SSSR*, 186-7, Tallinn, 1977, 196. The absolute number of recruits in this period was 513,000: L. G. Beskrovnyi, *Russkaia armiia i flot v XVIII v.*, Moscow, 1978, 33-5.

36 Empress Maria Fedorovna articulated the common view in arguing against allowing the soldatki to adopt foundlings, on the ground that their behavior "can for the most part not be approved of and often it is even quite dissolute": Comment on the case of June 13, 1827, Tsentral'nyi Gosudarstvennyi Istoricheskii Arkhiv goroda Moskvy (TsGIAgM), f. 127, op. 2, d. 7649, pp. 31ob–32. See also the figures on the social background of prostitutes later in the century in Richard Stites, *The Women's Liberation Movement in Russia: Feminism, Nihilism, and Bolshevism, 1860–1930*, Princeton, NJ, 1978, 61.

37 Max J. Okenfuss, *The Discovery of Childhood in Russia: The Evidence of the Slavic Primer*, Newtonville, MA, 1980, 22–35.

38 Ibid., 45–8.

39 L. N. Petrov, "Blagotvoritel'nost' v drevnei Rossii," *Vestnik blagotvoritel'nosti*, 1898, no. 8:31–2.

40 A. D. Stog, ed., *O obshchestvennom prizrenii v Rossii*, 3 vols, St Petersburg, 1818–27, 1:17–18.

41 N. N. Ginzburg, "Prizrenie podkidyshei v Rossii," *Trudovaia pomoshch'*, 1904, no. 4: 499.

42 I. M. Snegirev, *Moskovskie nishchiev XVII veke*, Moscow, 1852, 10–11.

43 M. N. Sokolovskii, "Petr Velikii kak blagotvoritel'," *Vestnik blagotvoritel'nosti*, 1901, no. 7–8:23n.

44 Among the few references to an orphan that can be confirmed as accurate is that in the tale of Archbishop Iona of Novgorod: *Novgorod IV Chronicle*, Dubrovskii spisok, year 6967 (1459), pp. 492–3. (I am grateful to Eve Levine for this reference.)

45 Petrov, "Blagotvoritel'nost'," no. 8, 30–1, 42–3.

46 A. Lappo-Danilevskii, "L'idée de l'état et son evolution en Russie depuis les troubles du XVII siècle jusqu'aux réformes du XVIII," in *Essays in Legal History*, ed. Paul Vinogradoff, London, 1913, 364.

47 Maksimov, "Nachalo gosudarstvennogo prizreniia," 51–3.

48 Ibid., 53.

49 Natalie Zemon Davis, *Society and Culture in Early Modern France*, Stanford, CA, 1975, esp. 17–64; Henry Kamen, *The Iron Century: Social Change in Europe, 1550–1660*, London, 1971, 403–4.

50 *Doklady imp. Prav. Senata v tsarstvovanie Patra I*, vol. 4, book 2, 876–7, cited in Iromonakh Mikhail, "Prizrenie broshennykh detei na Rusi 200 let tomu nazad," *Vestnik blagotvoritel'nosti*, 1902, no. 4:39.

51 This was the decree that established the Moscow Foundling Home: PSZ 16, no. 11908. Snegirev, *Moskovskie nishchie*, 11, mentions one of these shelters, located in Moscow at the church of SS. Kira and Ioann in Kulishki.

52 Piatkovskii, "Nachalo vospitatel'nykh domov v Rossii," *Vestnik Evropy*, 1874, no. 11: 268.

53 PSZ 4, no. 2467 (January 16, 1712).

54 Ibid., no. 2477 (January 31, 1712), 5, no. 2856 (November 4, 1714), and no. 2953 (November 4, 1715).

55 PSZ 5, no. 2856 (November 4, 1714), and no. 2953 (November 4, 1715).

56 Addendum to the Spiritual Regulation, cited in Semenova, *Ocherki istorii byta*, 119–20.

57 PSZ 7, no. 4335 (October 23, 1723).

58 Ibid., no. 4421 (January 20, 1724), repeating an order given by Peter in the Senate on January 14, 1724. See also ibid., no. 4516 (May 29, 1724), concerning schools for instruction in reading and mathematics at "monastery orphanages."

59 PSZ 6, no. 3502 (February 1, 1720), and no. 3746 (February 28, 1721). Peter's orders to use the candle money to develop care facilities further was apparently resisted by the church authorities: P. Avramenko, "Iz Istorii russkoi tserkovnoi blagotvoritel'nosti v sinodal'nom periode," *Trudovaia pomoshch'*, 1916, no. 3:378.

60 PSZ 7, no. 4844 (March 3, 1726).

61 Nizhnii Novgorod was one of a number of relatively large towns without an almshouse as late as 1766. Others included Voronezh, Tambov, Kostroma, Kazan, and Vladimir: Avramenko, "Iz Istorii russkoi tserkovnoi blagotvoritel'nosti," 359.

62 PSZ 8, no. 5450 (July 25, 1729)

63 Ibid., 5584 (June 25, 1730), and no. 5674 (January 20, 1734).

64 PSZ 12, no. 8966 (June 13, 1744), and no. 9011 (August 3, 1744). The same concern that "no one should be wandering about" and that everyone should have a defined position was expressed in instructions for the second soul census: :PSZ 11, no. 8836 (December 16, 1743).

19

Public Leisure and the Rise of Salons

Deborah Hertz

Public Places for Cultivated Persons

K. W. Brumbey, an obscure preacher who was seventeen years old when Frederick the Great became king in 1740, later reflected on the changes that had occurred during Frederick's reign. Brumbey remembered that "when the king ascended to the throne, Berlin had no theater, and there were no public places at which cultivated persons could meet. Residents of almost every class were limited either to domesticity, or searched for their enjoyment in taverns, where was little cultivation to be found."[1] By the time that Frederick died in 1786, Berlin's public life had expanded and diversified greatly.

[. . .]

It was only in the last years of King Frederick's reign that salons appeared in Berlin. Salons were at once far more heterogeneous in their personnel and far more informal in their style than the leisure available in courtly or commercial settings or in the intellectual clubs. It was precisely the volatility of such a diverse group gathering in such an intimate style that made salons such a special adventure at the time. Yet for all the social distance which eventually came to divide courtly, commercial, and club leisure experiences from the salon world, salons actually evolved out of these other three institutions.

Each of these three different settings for leisure experiences contributed in its own way to Berliners' chances to mix with those outside their estate and occupation, and thus eventually to the emergence of salons. The style of courtly leisure was important in the evolution of salons because the court set the tone for those who watched palace life from a distance. As some courtly leisure events were gradually opened to those outside courtly circles, the luxury and glamour of court life came to be shared, however vicariously, by a wider public. Then, too, the leisure avail-

Deborah Hertz, "Public Leisure and the Rise of Salons," pp. 75–77, 95–116 from *Jewish High Society in Old Regime Berlin*. New Haven, CT and London: Yale University Press, 1988.

able for a price at inns, theaters, and coffeehouses made possible some very heterogeneous mixing, although not on very intimate terms. The intellectual clubs, whose members met regularly to discuss books, manuscripts, and ideas, allowed for a deeper level of bonding between men born into different estates and employed in different occupations. Yet these intellectual clubs tended to exclude women, middle-income intellectuals, and Jews.

Although these three leisure opportunities did promote ties across social barriers, neither their structure nor their personnel allowed a miniature society to coalesce that was simultaneously heterogeneous and intimate. Entrance to the socializing at the court itself was strictly limited to those from old noble families. Even the court events open to the public required expensive tickets or a high position on the occupational hierarchy. The commercial leisure institutions, on the other hand, were more accessible than the court, but provided only superficial contact among their consumers. The intellectual clubs, whose format allowed for more intimacy, were attended mainly by older, well-established gentile male intellectuals. It was only in 1780, when salons first appeared among Berliners' leisure choices, that the limited social fusion which had been achieved previously at courtly, commercial, and club events could be deepened and expanded.

The Emergence of Salons

Not all leisure enjoyed by Berliners was as structured as that offered by courts, commercial institutions, and intellectual clubs. There was time in the schedules of most moderately wealthy persons to spend the afternoon or the evening at the home of a friend or acquaintance, time for a purely social event, an event needing no payment, rules, or official membership lists. Indeed, the smaller and the more informal the gathering, the deeper the connections would be between the participants. This was all very clear to the "clean-shaven" Jews who "looked longingly" at gentile high society. But could "clean-shaven" Jewish men and Jewish women with curls and silk dresses really enter high society? Or, for that matter, could Berlin's commoner intellectuals hope to meet with princes and nobles over dinner or at tea?

Before 1760, there was really no high society in Berlin to which Jews or commoner intellectuals might gain an entrée. For during the first half of the eighteenth century, Berlin did not have the kind of heterogeneous social life in which Jews or intellectuals might have participated. Urban nobles still needed the court's help to socialize in the right style. Socializing at the court itself was limited to the small *hoffähig* (courtly) circle. Commoners with high official appointments rarely took the time or money to consume conspicuously. Even if they had, nobles did not deign to visit commoners at their homes even if they worked with them during the day. Rich Jewish and other foreign financiers relaxed mainly with their own kind. Male scholars relaxed at the homes of other scholars or in taverns. Even very prominent and successful Berlin intellectuals were absolutely morose about their social isolation. Friedrich Nicolai, the author, publisher, and bookseller, complained that in Germany, unlike in France or England, the "estate of writers relates only to itself, or to the learned estate."[2] Socializing, in other words, was limited to estate- and occupation-specific groupings. The style, too, was traditional. Only those with invitations arrived at the right door. Women, if they were present at all, did not dominate the event. Except for the scholars' gatherings, conversation was not especially erudite. Neither in personnel nor in structure could the socializing before 1760 ever challenge the status quo, undermine the social structure, or allow for dangerous mixing between young persons of heterogeneous birth.

But as we have seen, as rising land prices and the allure of city living polarized the nobility, as the Seven Years' War enriched the Jewish mercantile elite, and as the educational system allowed young commoner intellectuals to ascend the social ladder, this narrow style of socializing began to loosen. The courtly, commercial, and club leisure activities allowed for some limited social contact across the dissolving social boundaries. But if contacts made at a court-sponsored ball, at a box in the theater, or at an intellectual club were to be deepened, and if those excluded from these three leisure events were ever to meet each other, a new setting was needed. That new setting was the salon.

The coalescence of a lively salon society in Berlin was a gradual process. Two decades before Henriette and Markus Herz opened Berlin's first salon, a few families began to invite guests from different estates to their homes for dinner. The home of Alexander and Wilhelm von Humboldt's parents, for instance, was considered a *gastfreies* or "hospitable" house. Major von Humboldt was the "gentleman of the bedchamber" in the household of the future Frederick William II, and his wife was from a prominent Huguenot family. The Humboldts entertained local French and Jewish friends at their country estate outside of Berlin, and eminent foreign writers called on them too.[3] Friedrich Nicolai, the writer and bookseller, regularly invited scholars traveling through Berlin as well as his own local friends to his home on Sunday evenings. Those passing through town who did not know him well, but who wanted to see or meet him, left their cards at his bookshop. Nicolai's idea of a lively evening was to invite a few scholars each week representing the major fields of scholarship. From the accumulated calling cards left by those who wished to visit him, Nicolai put together a list that included a few intellectual stars with mutually complementary specialties; they were sent invitations for that week. Moses Mendelssohn, Nicolai's close friend, was invited often, as was Eliza von der Recke, a published author and half-sister of the salonière Duchess Dorothea von Courland. Young Daniel Parthey was the tutor in the Nicolai household. His son Gustav recounted in his memoirs the story of Frau Nicolai's initial opposition to Frau von der Recke's first visit on the grounds that she would be "too aristocratic." Frau von der Recke remonstrated to Herr Nicolai that she was "no aristocratic rabble" and eventually became a dear friend of everyone in the Nicolai household.[4]

Mendelssohn himself regularly entertained eminent gentile visitors. Professor Christian Gottfried Schütz, who taught rhetoric at the University of Halle, gave a report on his 1769 visit to the Mendelssohn household in a letter to a friend. He first visited Mendelssohn in his office at the Bernhard silk firm, and received an invitation to call on Herr Mendelssohn at home the next day. Professor Schütz arrived at three, and soon Friedrich Nicolai, Karl Lessing, and a preacher named Eberhard arrived. From 3 until 7 P.M., there was "no slackening of the discussion. . . . At 7 P.M. we dined with Moses, and that was the period of *galanterie*," with the extended Mendelssohn family and with several daughters of the large Itzig family. Gatherings at the Mendelssohn home were thought to be "unique" at the time, since the guests from "all walks of life" conversed there "in a peaceful atmosphere of animated interests." Extravagant provisions were not an attraction: Frau Mendelssohn counted out the necessary number of almonds and hazelnuts before she served them.[5] The Mendelssohn home was not the only Jewish household where gentile guests were received in the 1760s and 1770s. One of the daughters of Daniel Itzig, Blümchen, married Mendelssohn's friend David Friedländer, a wealthy Königsberg merchant who had settled in Berlin and was a prominent reformer within the Jewish community. The Friedländer "palace" was reported to have been a "center of sociability" for enlightened Jews and gentiles. The wealthy Meyer family's "palace" was also described as a "center of sociability." Markus Levin, known to posterity chiefly as the father of the salonière Rahel Levin, also entertained actors and spendthrift young nobles who visited him to arrange for private loans.[6]

The marked change between the socializing styles of the 1760s and 1770s and those of the 1780s is summarized in the memoirs of Berlin's first salonière, Henriette Herz.[7] Describing a sharp break in her social life, Herz isolated the practice of holding an "open house," which she defined explicitly as the home of a scholar at which "uninvited" friends and those "being introduced" could count on a "hospitable reception," as what was distinctive during the era after 1780. Looking back on the two decades before 1780, she observed that Mendelssohn's had indeed been an open house, while Nicolai's had not, and the difference lay not in the means (the Mendelssohn household was comparatively poor) but in that friends of the entire Mendelssohn household came "uninvited."[8]

Unfortunately for us, Herz had other tales whose telling was more pressing, and she devoted no more space in her memoir to informing posterity about whose home was or was not truly "open" in the quarter century between 1780 and 1806. Her silence is all the more lamentable, since, as her own brief discussion illustrates, the word *salon* was infrequently used by participants to designate the new sort of social event which sprung up in Berlin in the 1780s. Nor was any other single term used regularly. In Hamburg, salon-like events were called *Abendgeselschaften*.[9] The letters and memoirs of salon participants are richer in verbal phrases than in nouns illustrating the particular qualities of salon socializing. Herz's good friend Friedrich Schleiermacher, for instance, once referred to the reasons why particular persons "let themselves be introduced" at specific Jewish homes.[10] Instead of "opening a salon," the phrase used was that someone had "opened" their home to "social intercourse."[11] The term *Hausfreund*, "a friend of the household," was sometimes used to describe specific salon guests.[12] Thus, even though contemporaries did not use the word *salon*, their vocabulary does reveal a distinctive style of social life. The phrase "to let oneself be introduced" suggests that the guests themselves chose to visit a particular salon. The same phrase also suggests how important introductions were in the guests' abilities to transform their desire to attend a salon into their actual appearance there. "To open one's home to social intercourse" makes clear that those who wanted to receive frequent and informal visits from friends and from the right strangers could make this desire known without issuing individual invitations to each person on each occasion.

The story of Herz's career as salonière shows that the "making" of an open house could depend as much on the qualities and circumstances of the entire family as it did on the woman's own training and talents. When they married in 1779, Markus Herz was thirty-two and Henriette de Lemos was fifteen. Born the son of a poor Torah scribe in Berlin, Markus Herz had attended medical school in Königsberg, where he also studied philosophy with Immanuel Kant. When he returned to Berlin to practice medicine, he became a close friend and colleague of Mendelssohn's. His work at the Jewish community hospital brought him into contact with his future wife's father, Dr. Benjamin Lemos, the hospital's director. Dr. Lemos's wealthy Portuguese family had come to Berlin via Amsterdam in the previous century. Even before her precocious marriage to Markus Herz, Henriette demonstrated personal qualities which would later prove crucial in her success as a salonière. She was widely known as a spirited child. The children of wealthy Jewish families at the time were allowed to perform secular plays at the small private theaters erected in a few Jewish homes. The Jewish elders, however, frowned on this frivolous habit and planned to forbid it. Twelve-year-old Henriette, in costume, was delegated to plead with the assembled elders and won their permission for the play to go forward. On another occasion, her parents decided to withdraw her from a private girls' day school because her startling beauty attracted so much attention from young men in the streets. But her father continued his daughter's education and taught her French, English, Latin and Hebrew. Later, her husband Markus and her friend Friedrich Schleiermacher continued to guide her reading and language training. Eventually the list of languages she had mastered came to include French, Italian, Portuguese, and Danish, and she also had some competence in Turkish, Malayan, and Sanskrit.[13]

Henriette Herz's classic beauty, intellectual abilities, passion for the newest literary trends, and talent for friendship all contributed to her social successes. Yet Markus's income, professional contacts, and above all, his popular lecture series on natural science held in their home were indispensable in the coalescence of their double salon. As she herself later recalled, it all began as her husband came to have some "very respectable families" as clients in his medical practice. This brought the young couple into "real social relationships" with these unnamed, probably gentile families. Because his lectures took place at home, listeners and clients could gradually and gracefully become friends. The lectures attracted a varied and prestigious audience. Members of the royal family attended as did the French Count Mirabeau and the young von Humboldt brothers, brought there by their tutor, Gottlob Kunth. Kunth had first become acquainted with Markus Herz one day when he sought Markus's advice for a lightning rod the Humboldt family was planning to install. The Herzes began inviting the most interesting persons from the natural history lecture audience to dinner beforehand. In this way their double salon evolved, a salon which was double in ideological style as well as in leadership. Henriette discussed poetry and novels with the young romantics in one room while her husband lectured on reason, science, and enlightenment in the other.[14]

The double salon came to an abrupt end when Markus died suddenly in 1803; because the couple had been spending most of his income on the cost of entertaining, Henriette was far too poor to continue entertaining. Her reluctance to convert to Christianity limited the ways she could support herself. She turned down Count von Dohna's marriage proposal as well as Duchess Dorothea von Courland's invitation for her to join the von Courland household as a governess, because both required a change of religion – a step she refused to take while her mother was still alive. Instead, she boarded students and young country girls who had moved into Berlin to seek employment as domestic servants. She converted after her mother died in 1817, but never remarried. And although many of her friends from the salon days remained loyal, her social life never regained the splendor it had while her husband was alive.

A decade after the Herzes first opened their salon, Henriette's childhood friend Rahel Levin opened the city's second and ultimately most famous salon. Levin's story shows that although a rich and intellectually prominent husband played an important role in Henriette Herz's salon, the absence of such a man need not doom a career as salonière if she had the requisite funds, personal qualities, and friends. Levin's father's French, noble, and theatrical guests exposed her at an early age to an elegant, graceful world. Still, although she sat in on the dinners with this glittering crowd, she felt far distant from it. As she put it herself at the time, she felt like a schlemiehl, a "nobody," around these elegant noble guests.[15] When she was still in her early twenties, Levin was explicit that her Jewishness was to blame for her low status. She complained to her friend David Veit, a medical student at Göttingen, that "it is as if some supramundane being, just as I was thrust into this world, plunged these words with a dagger into my heart: yes, have sensibility, see the world as few see it, be great and noble. . . . But I add one thing more: be a Jewess! And now my life is a slow bleeding to death."[16] She and Veit both concluded that the best way to avoid being treated like a Jew was to avoid cities and situations populated with other Jews.[17] Levin's marginality vis-à-vis the established Jewish community was thus largely her own doing. She prided herself with flaunting its customs, such as breaking the Sabbath by openly riding in a carriage through the streets of Berlin with her friend the actress Marchetti.[18] By refusing to marry the suitable Jewish businessmen proposed by her family, she risked the loneliness which was the consequence of daring to move away from the Jewish world while still suffering rejections by the noble one.

Yet slowly, during the early 1790s, Levin tentatively began to enter the elegant noble circles she had worshipped from afar as an adolescent. During summer trips to the spa at Teplitz she met Josephine von Pachta, a nonconformist noblewoman, and Gustav von Brinkmann, a Swedish diplomat and amateur poet stationed in Berlin. Brinkmann was entranced by the intellectual originality of the "little Levi," as he called her, and introduced her to many of his noble friends; it was he who persuaded his prominent noble friends to visit Levin's salon. Although her mother was convinced that these new friends were ruining her daughter's mental and physical health, for Levin they were a significant accomplishment.[19] She spent the mornings writing long and introspective letters, which also helped to improve her German. In the afternoons, she made up for her lack of formal training by studying English, French, and mathematics with tutors. And in the evenings, she was frequently to be found at the opera or the theater. Afterward, her wide circle of gentile friends had their carriages deliver them at her mother's house in the Jägerstrasse, where they climbed the stairs to her attic apartment. There they gossiped and discussed Iffland's new play, Goethe's novels, and the course of the French Revolution. Levin remained single until she was forty-two, in 1814. After a lonely existence during the French invasion of the city and the War of Liberation, she converted and married a younger gentile admirer, the diplomat and writer Karl August Varnhagen von Ense. Together, they hosted a second salon in Berlin during the second decade of the nineteenth century, but this was a smaller, more formal salon than the gatherings in the Jägerstrasse had been before 1806.

Not all the Jewish salonières were as physically glamorous as Henriette Herz or as socially rebellious as Rahel Levin. Sara Levy was one of nine daughters born to Daniel and Marianne Itzig; her father was the head of the most powerful and most privileged Jewish family in Berlin at the time.[20] Sara's sisters Fanny and Cäcelie both married wealthy Jewish financiers from Vienna, where each hosted a salon.[21] Sara Itzig, too, married within the faith, and neither she nor her husband, a banker named Solomon Levy, ever converted. The Levys' grand home in the center of town across from the stock exchange, with its large adjoining gardens, was an extended family household. Two of Sara Levy's sisters lived there after 1795: her blind sister Recha and her widowed sister Rebekka. The poet Achim von Arnim rented an apartment in the Levy home in 1804, and the daughter of the military preacher Johann Uhden lived there until her death.[22] This heterogeneous household had heterogeneous *Hausfreunde*. Every Thursday a group of ten to fourteen guests were invited for a noon dinner, and on Sunday afternoons, the Levys held an open house for tea. The guests at these occasions included prominent local nobles as well as French diplomats who were visiting Berlin. Frau Levy was praised for her linguistic and musical abilities, if not for her social vivacity or her looks. She apparently spoke French like a native and played the piano for both Hayden and Mozart, two of her most famous visitors. Yet Rahel Levin's husband Karl August Varnhagen found her a bit of a philistine, and Clemens Brentano complained that her salon gatherings were "boring," while others criticized her for name-dropping.[23] But neither her aesthetic, social, and mental limitations nor her professed loyalty to Judaism interfered with Frau Levy's role in high society. She continued to receive regular Sunday visits from the prominent until her death in 1854. For all her purported rigidity in conversation, that year, at the age of ninety-three, she impressed a young nephew by emerging from her carriage and dancing in the street![24]

A glamorous but short-lived salon was hosted by Philippine Cohen, who was born Pessel Zülz in 1776. Her father, who changed his name from Zülz to Bernhard, inherited a silk manufactory that once employed Moses Mendelssohn. His daughter Pessel received a generous dowry of 100,000 taler, and the lucky groom she married was Ephraim Cohen, who moved to Berlin from Amsterdam. Berliners called him the "English Cohen" because he introduced English spinning machines to the city.[25] Husband, wife, and two children all converted together in 1800, and Pessel changed her name to Philippine. The Cohen family lived in an opulent home adjoining Herr

Cohen's wool factory, which was jointly owned by the state and Herr Cohen and employed hundreds of workers. Theirs was a large and varied household. Philippine's mother Madame Bernhard had a house in the country but often stayed with her daughter's family in the city. Philippine's sister, Frau von Boye, who had divorced her Jewish husband and proceeded to marry two different noblemen in succession, was a frequent visitor. Two young aspiring novelists, Wilhelm Neumann and Karl August Varnhagen, were live-in employees, Neumann a clerk in the firm and Varnhagen a tutor for the children. Almost daily, a wider society joined the members of the Cohen household for lunch, gossip, piano-playing, and the reading of novels and personal diaries aloud. Karl August Varnhagen later remembered how he would retire to his room to compose character sketches of the guests and return to the group to read them aloud so that the guests could guess at who was being described. Philippine's sister Frau von Boye was friendly with several prominent intellectuals, including Johann Fichte, Jean Paul (Richter), and Friedrich Schlegel. She occasionally played the patron role and once introduced Neumann and Varnhagen to her famous literary friends by inviting them all to join her at her box at the theater.[26] The Cohen salon dispersed just a year after the Herz salon broke up, in the summer of 1804, when Herr Cohen's years of paying more attention to the charms of salon life than to his factory caught up with him. Mismanagement resulted in the collapse of his business; the court took over the factory and issued a warrant for his arrest. His wife, sister-in-law, and mother-in-law lost their entire fortunes, and Herr Cohen escaped to Holland. Unfortunately, Varnhagen, the main source for the Cohen story, left Berlin soon after he lost his job as tutor, and thus the eventual fate of Frau Cohen's salon remains a mystery.

In 1798, after the Herz, Levin, Levy, and Cohen salons were all well established, Friederich Schleiermacher, a promising young preacher who had moved to the city two years before, wrote to his sister explaining why Berlin's most interesting society gathered at Jewish homes. According to Schleiermacher, it was not just that the richest men in Berlin were Jewish, but also that the Jewish financiers' wives and daughters were cultivated and their style of entertaining informal and lively.[27] Noble complaints about the stiff ceremony of social life at court and the rigidity of noble socializing styles echoed Schleiermacher's emphasis on the distinctiveness of the Jewish elite's lifestyle. Yet the story of a fifth salon, led by the Duchess Dorothea von Courland, shows that entertaining in style was by no means simply a function of one's estate. Indeed, von Courland's story illustrates that if a noblewoman had both enough money and the right attitudes, the problems in the city's social life caused by the rigidity of courtly social styles could in principle have been solved by nobles as well as by Jews.

Von Courland was a member of a prominent noble family from the Baltic provinces. She and her younger half-sister Eliza received a thorough education at home from Dorothea's stepmother, who took learning seriously and enjoyed entertaining intellectual guests and even hired a tutor for the two girls. The young man she chose was Daniel Parthey, who was later employed as a tutor by the Nicolai family and who thus came to introduce Dorothea's half-sister Eliza to the Nicolai family. At eighteen, the beautiful Dorothea was married off to the Duke of Courland. Although much older and quite crochety, the duke encouraged his wife's intellectual interests. They visited cultural shrines in Italy, Immanuel Kant in Königsberg, Frederick the Great in Potsdam, and Moses Mendelssohn in Berlin. But by 1795, when she was thirty-four, the duke had lost his little state of Courland to Russia, in the third division of Poland. He had become increasingly cranky, and Dorothea separated from him. After his death in 1800 she bought a landed estate near Berlin for the summers and a former royal palace on Unter den Linden in Berlin for the winters, where she opened her salon. Von Courland's forthright position as a progressive noble won her admiration from some and disdain from others. She had always been philanthropic and generous, annually spending a quarter of her "pin money" (four thousand taler a year!) on charity. She once canceled a shopping trip to Leipzig in order to loan money to a friend in need. At her estate she raised the wages paid to the peasants and improved the local school; she befriended and provided regular financial support for various impoverished authors. Jean Paul (Richter) and Ludwig Tieck stayed for long periods at her country estate. Dorothea von Courland's noble friends, who included Queen Luise and other women in the royal family, shared her passion for literature, but were frankly shocked at how her egalitarian ideology was expressed in the style of her salon. For von Courland delighted in seating her Jewish and commoner guests next to prominent nobles at the tiny tables she preferred over the usual long ones. This was the duchess' highly self-conscious way of easing the estate barriers that divided wealthy Berliners.[28]

A sixth woman identified by historians as having led a salon was Dorothea Veit. Closer inspection allows us to construct a more nuanced portrait of Veit's role as salonière. Indeed, Veit's ultimate failure to gather a regular salon circle around her shows how delicate the whole endeavor was. Dorothea, the oldest child of Moses Mendelssohn, received a more rigorous education than any other Jewish girl in Berlin at the time. Her father allowed her to join the morning lessons he offered at the Mendelssohn home to a select group of young students, a group which included her younger brothers Joseph and Abraham and the two von Humboldt brothers.[29] But as in the case of Henriette Herz, Moses Mendelssohn's progressive views about his daughter's education did not extend to his daughter's marriage, and Dorothea was wed in late adolescence to a man of her father's choosing – Simon Veit, a kindly but decidedly unintellectual businessman. Dorothea's (or Brendel, as she was still called at the time) efforts to host a salon during her fifteen years as Veit's wife, between 1783 and 1798, culminated in the tiny, all-Jewish Lecture Society that met at the Veits on Thursday evenings. But this intellectual club never developed into a true salon, in part because Simon lacked interest in avant-garde literature, in part because Dorothea was a serious person not altogether at ease in society.

But Veit's failure to succeed as a salonière was the least of her problems in these three years. Almost immediately after her marriage in 1783, she had begun complaining bitterly to her friends about her unhappiness with her husband. Nevertheless, she resisted her friend Henriette Herz's entreaties to leave him and kept the sad news from her father, who died in 1786 believing his daughter to be happily married. For another fourteen years Dorothea stayed with Simon and their two sons, until another man came into her life – Friedrich Schlegel, who had moved to Berlin in 1798. They met at the Herz salon when he was twenty-six and she thirty-four. Veit was by no means a beauty, but she had other qualities more valued by Schlegel: intellectual skills and seriousness, the embodiment of his own pronouncements about the qualities a new generation of women should possess. Moreover, Veit was willing to devote her considerable mental powers to Schlegel's intellectual work. Her sacrifices in this arena were consistent both with Schlegel's view that the new emancipated woman should work alongside her mate and with his less theoretical, more opportunistic need for copyist, translator, admirer, and muse.

And so Dorothea moved to a small apartment in an obscure corner of the city, leaving their two sons with Simon Veit. Although she in fact lived alone, it was rumored that she was living with Friedrich Schlegel. Deserted by her siblings for her open defiance of traditional Jewish values, her isolation was compounded by the snubs of her sophisticated gentile friends. Emancipated though they may have been in principle about the sufferings caused by arranged marriages, many still distanced themselves from the scandal of Dorothea Veit's rebellion. Then, too, Schlegel had made many enemies in various literary feuds. Racked with physical illness as well, Veit's only friends were Schlegel, Friedrich Schleiermacher, and Henriette Herz, who defied her husband's order that she not visit Veit. The publication of Schlegel's erotic novel *Lucinde* in 1799, thought to be a description of the couple's new life together, only deepened her ostracism.[30]

The circumstances of Dorothea Veit's life after she left Berlin in 1801 hardly provided her with the material comfort, geographical stability, or minimum social respectability so useful to salon sponsorship. In Jena, the couple's first home after leaving Berlin, Schlegel was embroiled in bitter literary disputes, and Veit was disliked by Friedrich's powerful sister, Caroline Schlegel. The couple was so poor that Veit set herself to work writing a novel in order to keep food on the table. Her conversion to Protestantism in 1804 and the couple's subsequent marriage provided a minimum of social respectability. But in none of the cities where the couple lived after Jena was Veit ever rich or well connected enough to sponsor a salon.

Not all the salonières were strong, intellectually accomplished personalities. Sara and Marianne Meyer were born into an Orthodox and wealthy family, and their parents provided them with a decorative, fashionable education. Like the household of Rahel Levin, even before 1780 the girls' parents' home was later remembered as a "center of sociability." It was there that the young daughters first met and earned the admiration of a string of esteemed gentile intellectuals. Sara, the oldest, was praised by Lessing, Harder, and Goethe for her lively personality and her talent for languages. At an "early" age, Sara Meyer married Jacob Wulff, but after a decade of marriage, she divorced Wulff and converted to Protestantism – although for unknown reasons, she later converted back to Judaism. But she eventually converted back to Protestantism for a second time, in order to marry again to a nobleman, Baron von Grotthuss. The salon she led as his wife declined in the years after 1806, when Berlin was under foreign rule, because the baron lost his fortune. The elegant Sara von Grotthuss thus ended her days in Oranienburg, where her impoverished husband had found a modest position as a postmaster.

Sara's younger sister Marianne was said to be prettier but less good-hearted than Sara. Her love life was certainly more troubled. First, early in the 1780s, she was courted by Christian von Bernstorff, son of the Danish ambassador in Berlin, but his father forbade the misalliance.[31] Next, Count Gessler, the Saxon ambassador to the Prussian court, publicly announced that he would marry her, but he too humiliated her by failing to uphold his promise. Finally, Marianne Meyer married the Austrian ambassador in Berlin, Prince von Reuss. Her salon must have been open in the years before his death in 1799, while she still enjoyed the material and status comforts of being Princess von Reuss. These perquisites could be enjoyed without having to worry about getting along with her husband, since they had separate households. Despite this physical independence, the rules of his world impinged on the glory of being wedded to a prince. For although she had his title, Marianne was still not considered *hoffähig*, and so was forbidden to visit court circles with her husband.[32] When he died in 1799, she moved to Vienna. But whatever advantages she might have expected to enjoy as his widow were denied to her, as his relatives refused to let her continue using his name and title. Finally, she successfully petitioned the Austrian Emperor Francis II to give her permission to use the noble name "Frau von Eybenberg." Her power as a salonière in Vienna during these years must have been limited indeed, in spite of her friendship with prominent noble families. For in addition to robbing her of her rightful title of "princess," von Reuss's family's rejection of their Jewish daughter-in-law extended to financial deprivation as well, leaving her virtually in poverty.[33]

The ninth woman labeled as a salonière, Rebecca Friedländer, was born Rebecca Solomon, into the same privileged milieu as were the other Jewish salonières, and she shared many of the same social aspirations. Her father was a jewel merchant for the court who changed the family name from Solomon to Saaling. At eighteen, Rebecca married Moses Friedländer, the son of David Friedländer, a wealthy silk entrepreneur active in the reform wing of the Jewish community. But the marriage did not last; she separated from him in 1804, while still only twenty-three.

Friedländer lived alone in Berlin, spending her time corresponding with her best friend Rahel Levin, writing a string of poorly received novels, and hosting "aesthetic teas." She eventually converted and changed her name to Regina Frohberg, hoping this step would enhance her literary career and encourage one of her many noble suitors to ask for her hand in marriage. But none of them did, and Friedländer never remarried.[34]

In the first years after her separation from Moses Friedländer, Rebecca Friedländer's apartment was inside the home of a tenth salonière, Amalie Beer. The heyday of Beer's salon was after the Napoleonic era, but its beginnings can be traced to the pre-1806 years. A descendant of the Liebman family, Berlin's premier court Jewish family early in the eighteenth century, Amalie was married at sixteen to Jakob Herz Beer, who owned sugar factories in Berlin as well as in Italy. Their son, Jacob Meyerbeer, later became a renowned composer. Amalie Beer herself was praised for being "a grand lady from her *Scheitel* [a wig worn by religious Jewish women] to her *Schole* [soles of her shoes], cultivated, clever, charming." Her trips to Italy, both for her husband's business and for her sons' education, only increased her sophistication. She received guests from all circles "majestically, with the most perfect skill" and detested solitude; on her birthdays she welcomed hundreds of guests, who arrived in early morning and remained until late at night. The Beer home was later to become a center for the religiously progressive as well as for the social elite. Isaac Jacobson organized an early, private, "reform" synagogue there in the 1820s, after the Jewish salons had declined.[35]

Another two women have been labeled as salon hosts, but even less is known about their entertaining style than about the women met thus far. An often reproduced sketch of the sculptor Gottfried Schadow, his converted wife Marianne Devidel, and the engravers Jacob Abrahamson and his son gathered around a table at the Abrahamson home has been used as evidence that the Abrahamsons hosted a salon . . .[36] Another home noted by at least one historian as having been a salon is that of J. H. and Helene Unger . . .[37] Yet not only is there no primary source recording of the Ongers hosting salon-like gatherings, but Helene Unger, in her *Briefe über Berlin*, openly condemned the Jewish salonières for their intellectual pretensions.

The last two salons on the roster were both led by men. The bookstore owner Andreas Reimer was noted for hosting regular gatherings of the city's intelligentsia, but no details can be unearthed.[38] The banker and entrepreneur Benjamin Veitel Ephraim, a colorful character, is also reported to have hosted a salon . . .

Herr Ephraim is the last of the fourteen individuals labeled by historians as having hosted salons in Berlin between 1780 and 1806. This wide spectrum makes it clear that holding a salon is best understood as a matter of degree, not an either-or affair – which does not make definitions useless, for a definition sets the parameters. Existing definitions define salons as gatherings hosted by a woman, with intellectual dialogue as the chief entertainment. Two other items noted in existing definitions are that salon guests had diverse social backgrounds and occupations, and that formal invitations were not issued.[39] But a too rigid use of definitions can close us off to the rich diversity of past life. Even if primary-source descriptions of salon life were more abundant, it would be wrong to limit the salon roster to gatherings that strictly met this four-part definition. Even the most well-documented suggest that the borders between the salon, traditional socializing, and the intellectual clubs were hazy. For instance, Rahel Levin, whose gatherings truly fit the hardest, fourth item of existing definitions – hosting without invitations – also entertained the same friends in more formal ways.[40] Salon hosting is thus best understood as a tendency, or an ideal type, that was more pronounced among some gatherings than among others.

Not only are salons elusive of definition retrospectively; they were fragile institutions at the time. The quirks of personality and one's familial circumstances were obviously important in the making of a successful salon. This is best illustrated both by the abrupt end of Henriette Herz's salon in 1803 and by the delicate sort of barriers that made it so difficult for Dorothea Veit to open a real salon. Yet the same twists and turns of individual fate that seem to account for which women became salonières at which moment in their lives actually do little to explain the larger pattern of salon society in Berlin. Personality and family circumstances may have determined which individuals succeeded as salonières at what period of their lives, but the larger scale social needs of members of particular estates and occupations, as well as Prussia's political fate, set the larger scene within which individual salons appeared and disappeared. This is dramatically illustrated by the demise of Rahel Levin's salon, once the most popular salon in the city. Unlike the case of Henriette Herz in 1803, in 1806 Levin's financial situation, and thus her ability to entertain, did not alter dramatically. Yet, beginning in that year the material and ideological conditions in which salons flourished disappeared, and so even the charismatic Levin could not hold her circle together.

The fragility of the ties which bound salon participants to each other is understandable, given the extraordinary heterogeneity of that society. (Because it has not been possible to reconstruct the personnel of each and every salon, the term *salon society* refers to the roughly one hundred persons noted in the sources as having attended at least one salon during this quarter century.) A third of the one hundred were female. The female presence in public leisure events was not entirely new. In the decades before 1780 women had come to participate in court life, in the city's new commercial leisure activities, and even in a few intellectual clubs. Still, although in strictly numerical terms salons were only open to a tiny number of women, the emergence of salons represented a dramatic change for wealthy women. On the stage of symbolic and real cultural power, salons were a far greater opportunity for their lucky female participants than commercial or club leisure. The reason was that salons were almost always formed around specific women. Common admiration of her intellectual and personal qualities was one of the bonds which united the guests. And because salons were informal gatherings which met in homes, participation was not an issue about which male committees could legislate.

Yet considering that eleven of the thirty-one women in salon society were themselves salonières, the comparative size of the public stage salons provided for women shrinks somewhat. Aside from the salonière herself, specific salons did not by any means always include enough non-salonière women to constitute a female literary network or subculture. Rahel Levin's salon included very few women: an 1805 visitor found only one woman there besides Levin herself.[41] Dorothea Veit complained in a 1798 letter that she hated spending the evenings at her friend Henriette Herez's because women were "not allowed to speak," since they would "profane" the philosophical dialogue.[42] Dorothea von Courland, to be sure, did have an unusually large number of female guests. But this was attributed to her high social rank, which allowed her to flout convention by filling her reception room with women.[43]

If the presence of women at the symbolic center of salon life was a sign of emancipation, at first glance it would not seem that salon society was also emancipated by also being dense with Jews. For when the size of the Jewish representation in salons is contrasted with the size of the female representation, it becomes clear that Jews in general did not profit much from salon attendance. Fifteen Jews participated in salon society, and at 15 percent, they were certainly overrepresented in comparison to their proportion of the city at large. But it was mainly Jewish women, not Jewish men, who were overrepresented in salons: the eight Jewish men in salons were a mere 4 percent of the men in salon society, whereas the eleven Jewish women were almost two-fifths of the women in salon society. Jewish women were even more dramatically overrepresented among the salonières, since nine of the twelve women who led salons were Jewish. The noble presence in salons shows a similar pattern. A minority estate was overrepresented among the thirty-one women, but not among the sixty-nine men in salons. A third of all salon participants were noble. Outside of court society, salons had the greatest noble participation of any of the city's leisure activities. Only 6 percent of the members of the intellectual clubs, after all, were noble. But the nobles in salons, like the Jews, were not equally divided among the men and the women. Under a third of the sixty-nine men in salons were noble, whereas over two-fifths of the thirty-one women in salons were noble.

The presence of so many nobles was only one of the aristocratic features of salon life. The custom of having strangers congregating inside large and complex households had long been a part of the noble way of life, in city and in country. Veneration of the salonière resembled the admiration (or literally, the "court") noble courtiers paid to medieval and Renaissance queens. In the Berlin salons of the eighteenth century, as in these earlier courts, homage was paid to the cultivated female with reading of original writing and literary discourse. The leading Jewish salonières founded their salons in conscious imitation of the French noble salon tradition in order to synthesize the best of gallic intellectual form and German intellectual content.[44] Even though not all the Jewish salonières' imitation of an ancient role was so self-conscious, hosting a salon surely did "dust" them with a noble "aura." And acting nobly in this way surely helped to legitimize the Jewish salonières as friends, lovers, and would-be spouses for their noble guests.[45]

It follows from the preponderance of nobles and Jews in female salon society that most of the commoners in salons were men. A quarter of the salon women but over two-thirds of the salon men were commoners. The occupational profile of salon men was not dissimilar to that of the sampled men from the intellectual clubs. Professors were overrepresented in salons, albeit less so than in the intellectual clubs. Both clubs and salons had about as many officials as did the male intelligentsia at large. But both preachers and clerks had as much difficulty arriving in salons as they did in being invited to join an intellectual club. Accordingly, most of the male salon participants were employed in four upper-income occupations: land-owners, officials, merchants, and professors. The strong showing of land-owners, was a consequence of the strong noble representation; many nobles still lived from agricultural profits. Both nobles and well-educated commoners contributed to the number of officials in salons. The few Jewish men in salons were almost exclusively merchants, and the professors, many of whom were arrivistes, had reached the pinnacle of the intellectual institutions.

It is obvious from their comparative youth that the salon men employed in these four occupations had not achieved their positions after long struggles up the social ladder. In 1800 a fifth of all of Berlin's intellectuals, only a tenth of the men in clubs, but almost two-fifths of the men in salon society were under thirty-five. As we shall see, the youth of the salon men had much to do with salon society's distinctive heterogeneity. But this and much else is still mysterious about just how these diverse men came together.

[. . .]

NOTES

1 Brumbey's opinion is cited in the "Zweiter Brief" in the contemporary annual *Jahrbücher der preussischer Monarchie* (hereafter *JPM*) vol. 1 (1800), 171–76.
2 For example, on the male scholars' gatherings which met at the home of Ezechiel von Spannheim see Dorwart, *The Prussian Welfare State, 221*, and Bleich, *Der Hof des König Friedrich Wilhelm III*, 35.

Nicolai's lament is cited in Horst Möller, *Aufklärung in Preussen: Der Verleger, Publizist und Geschichtsschreiber Friedrich Nicolai* (Berlin, 1974), 186.

3 See Sweet, *Wilhelm von Humboldt*, vol. 1, chap. 1, and Bleich, *Der Hof des König Friedrich Wilhelm III*, 42.

4 Gustav Parthey, *Jugenderinnerungen* (Berlin, 1871), 36–7.

5 Altmann, *Moses Mendelssohn*, 159. For another description of social events at the Mendelssohn home see Bach, *The German Jew*, 62.

6 On these families, whose homes Hans Karl Krüger identifies as "centers of sociability," see his *Berliner Romantik and Berliner Judentum* (Bonn, 1939), chap. 1.

7 On the transition between the socializing at the Mendelssohn and Friedländer homes and that of the subsequent generation of "nouveaux-riche" Jews (whose socializing was called salons) see Brunschwig, *Enlightenment and Romanticism*, 262–5.

8 See Julius Furst, ed., *Henriette Herz: Ihr Leben und ihre Erinnerungen* (Berlin, 1858), 124–7.

9 See Wolfgang Nahrstedt, *Die Entstehung der Freizeit* (Göttingen, 1972), 179–83.

10 Friedrich Schleiermacher is quoted in Wilhelm Erman, *Paul Erman: Ein Bereliner Gelehrtenleben 1764–1851* (Berlin, 1927), 96.

11 See Margaretha Hiemenz, *Dorothea von Schlegel* (Freiburg im Breisgau, 1911), 9.

12 One of the many examples of the use of this term, which was still used in the early twentieth century to describe events in the eighteenth century, can be found in Hiemenz, *Dorothea v. Schlegel*, 188. The reference is to Friedrich Schlegel's relationship to various Jewish homes in Berlin.

13 On Herz see Furst, ed., *Henriette Herz*; see also (Mrs.) Vaughn Jennings, *Rahel: Her Life and Letters* (London, 1876), 21–38 and 195–9 and M. Kayserling, *Die jüdischen Frauen in der Geschichte, Literatur und Kunst* (Leipzig, 1879), 199–207. Several of Herz's unpublished letters (few are extant) can be found in the Archive of the Leo Baeck Institute in New York City (V 3/1).

14 Furst, ed., *Henriette Herz*, 96. In Herz's own words: "through his intellect and as a famous doctor [Markus] Herz attracted people, and I attracted them through my beauty and through the understanding I had for all kinds of scholarship." This is a quote from Hans Landsberg, *Henriette Herz: Ihr Leben und Ihre Zeit* (Weimar, 1913), 50.

15 Levin's feelings on this matter, and her use of the term, can be found in Hannah Arendt, *Rahel Varnhagen: The Life of a Jewish Woman* (New York and London, 1957), 6.

16 Translation from ibid., 4.

17 These mutual admonitions can be found on both sides of the Levin-Veit correspondence. See Rahel (Levin) Varnhagen von Ense, *Briefwechsel zwischen Rahel und David Veit* (Leipzig, 1861).

18 Arendt, *Rahel Varnhagen*.

19 Levin's mother's upset was reported in a letter by Gustav von Brinkmann to Julie von Voss, of May 30, 1802, now in packet 2, Berg-Voss Collection, Goethe-Schiller Archive (GSA), Weimar.

20 See the article on the Itzig family in the *Encyclopedia Judaica* (Jerusalem, 1971), vol. 9, 1150–51. See also Wilhelm Erman, *Paul Erman: Ein Berliner Gelehrtenleben 1764–1851* (Berlin, 1927), and Karoline Cauer, *Oberhofbankier und Hofbaurat* (Frankfurt a.M., 1965).

21 The standard work useful for Cäcelie as well is Hilde Spiel, *Fanny von Arnstein, oder die Emanzipation* (Frankfurt a.M., 1962).

22 On von Arnim's stay at the Levy household see Helene Riley, *Ludwig Achim von Arnims Jugend- und Reisejahre* (Bonn, 1978), 108; on Uhden's daughter's sojourn there see Felix Eberty, *Jugenderinnerungen* (Berlin, 1925), 215.

23 On Varnhagen's and Brentano's critiques of Sara Levy see Wilhelm Erman, *Paul Erman*, 96; on Sara Levy's tendency to name-drop see Eberty, *Jugenderinnerungen*, 215.

24 See Eberty, *Jugenderinnerungen*, 251.

25 On Mendelssohn's business relationship with Philippine Cohen's father see Jacob Jacobson, *Jüdische Trauungen in Berlin, 1759–1813* (Berlin, 1968), 150 and 362.

26 Frau von Boye's marital career will not be evaluated. The major source for the discussion here of the Cohen salon is Karl August Varnhagen von Ense, *Denkwürdigkeiten des eigenen Lebens*, Karl Leutner,

ed. (East Berlin, 1954), 81–9. These passages can also be found in vol. 1 of the original, full-length edition of Karl August Varnhagen's memoirs (Leipzig, 1843).

27 Schleiermacher's often-cited letter to his sister about the salons was that of October 22, 1797, in Georg Reimer, ed., *Aus Schleiermachers Leben in Briefen* (Berlin, 1858–63), vol. 1, 160–4. The letter is cited in Jerry F. Dawson, *Friedrich Schleiermacher: The Evolution of a Nationalist* (Austin, 1966), 23.

28 Sources used here on von Courland's life were Baxa, *Friedrich von Gentz*, 156; Jennings, *Rahel*, 38; Christoph August Tiedge, *Anna Charlotte Dorothea, letzte Herzogin von Kurland* (Leipzig, 1823); and Hans Schönfeld, "Die letzte Herzogin von Kurland an brandenbürgischen Höfen," *Sonntags-Verlage der Vitung-Zeitung*, no. 595 (September, 1920). A useful unpublished volume, including original pictures and clippings, was collated by Wolf von Tümpling, *Die Herzogin von Curland und Theodor Körner und die Seinigen: Löbichau 1795–1907* (Thalstein, 1917). The volume is now located in the von Courland collection in the rare manuscript library at the Friedrich Schiller University in Jena, in the German Democratic Republic.

29 On Dorothea Veit see Jennings, *Rahel*, 147–9; Heimenz, *Dorothea v. Schlegel*; M. Kayserling, *Die jüdischen Frauen*, 183–97; and Josef Körner, "Mendelssohns Töchter," *Preussische Jahrbücher* 214 (November, 1928), 167–82. On Mendelssohn's morning lessons see Altmann, *Moses Mendelssohn*. Ludwig Geiger's view on Veit and salons was that Veit really did not want to be a "prominent" woman, but rather to be at home with her loved ones. See Geiger's *Dichtung und Frauen* (Berlin, 1896), 149. Kurt Fervers's view was, on the contrary, that Veit was "jealous" of her friends' salons, in his *Berliner Salons: Die Geschichte einer grossen Verschwörung* (Munich, 1940), 76.

30 On Schlegel's *Lucinde*, see Hans Eichner, *Friedrich Schlegel* (New York, 1970), chap. 4.

31 On the von Bernstorff rejection see Lawrence J. Baack, *Christian Bernstorff and Prussia* (New Brunswick, 1980), 6–8. On both Meyer sisters see Jennings, *Rahel*, 148–50; and Kayserling, *Die jüdischen Frauen*, 218–20.

32 See Jennings, *Rahel*, 148. In addition to the sources noted above see also Varnhagen's views on the two women, in vol. 4 of his *Denkwürdigkeiten*, 635–42.

33 Kayserling, *Die jüdischen Frauen*, 220.

34 On Friedländer see Jacobson, *Jüdische Trauungen*, 440; Arendt, *Rahel Varnhagen*, 107; and the memoirs of her nephew: Paul Heyse, *Jugenderinnerungen und Bekenntnisse* (Berlin, 1901), 6. In 1988 my edited edition (with an introduction) of Rahel Levin's letters to Friedländer will be published by Kiepenheuer and Witsch, Cologne, entitled *Briefe an eine Freundin: Rahel Varnhagen an Rebecca Friedländer*.

35 On the Liebmann (or Liepmann) family see Selma Stern, The *Court Jew*, trans. Ralph Weiman (Philadelphia, 1950), 49ff. One of the rare sources on Amalie Beer is the typescript of an article by Kurt Richter, "Amalie Beer und ihre Söhne," which appeared in the *Centralverein Zeitung* (no. 11, Beilage 3, n.d.). (All quotations are from page one of the typescript.) The typescript is in the Beer Meyerbeer Collection (AR 3194) in the archives of the Leo Baeck Institute, New York City. On Beer's son Michael see the (Nazi-oriented) Wilhelm Grau, *Wilhelm von Humboldt und das Problem des Juden* (Hamburg, 1935), 34, and L. Kahn, "Michael Beer," *Leo Beck Institute Year Book* 12 (1967), 149–60. On Beer's marriage see Jacobson, *Jüdische Trauungen*, 317. On Isaac Jacobson's synagogue in the Beer home see Bach, *The German Jew*, 829–83.

36 The assumption that the depicted gathering at the Abrahamsons was a salon can be found in Bildarchiv Preussischer Kulturbesitz, ed., *Juden in Preussen: Ein Kapitel deutscher Geschichte* (Dortmund, 1981), 150. On the Abrahamsons see the brief article in *The Jewish Encyclopedia* (New York and London, 1901), vol. 1, 123. Kurt Fervers calls the gatherings at the Abrahamson home a salon in his *Berliner Salons*, 96.

37 This claim was made by Brunschwig, *Enlightenment and Romanticism*, 281–2.

38 On Reimer see Varnhagen von Ense, *Denkwürdigkeiten* (Leutner edition), 96.

39 In addition to the definitions of the salon found in note 27, Chap. 1, see Habermas, *Strukturwandel der Öffentlichkeit*. For a useful summary of Habermas's argument in English see Peter Hohendahl, "Introduction to Habermas," and Habermas, "The Public Sphere," both in *New German Critique* 3 (1974),

45–8 and 49–55. I am grateful to Joan Landes of Hampshire College for sharing a chapter, "Eighteenth-Century Sources of the Feminist Public Sphere," of her book-in-progress, *Women and the Public Sphere*, which helped me understand Habermas on this point. For another definition of the salon see Narhrstedt, *Die Entstehung der Freizeit*; see also Karl Haase, "Rahel Varnhagens Brieftheorie," M.A. thesis, Munich, Ludwig Maximilian University, 1977, 14 and 33.

40　For instance, on September 3, 1801, Gustav von Brinkmann wrote to Countess Julie von Voss, describing a *soupé* (dinner) he and "Humboldt" had at Rahel's Levin's. The letter is no. 109 in packet 10 of the Brinkmann-Voss Collection at the GSA.

41　The guest's (one "Grafen S.") narrative describing an evening of Levin's salon is reprinted in C. May, *Rahel: Ein Berliner Frauenleben im 19. Jahrhundert* (Berlin, n.d.), 6–16.

42　See Franz Dcibel, *Dorothea Schlegel als Schriftstellerin im Zusammenbang mit der romantischen Schule*, in *Palaestra* 60 (Berlin, 1905), 158.

43　See Ostwald, *Kultur- und Sittngeschichte Berlins*, 134.

44　See Spiel, *Fanny von Arnstein*, 94.

45　My formulation here is very much indebted to that suggested by Carolyn Lougee in her *Le Paradis des Femmes: Women, Salons, and Social Stratification in Seventeenth-Century France* (Princeton, 1976).

Part V

THE RISE OF THE MODERN STATE SYSTEM

Introduction

The rise of centralized states transformed the political and practical lives of most Europeans more than any institutional change of the seventeenth and eighteenth centuries. These changes flowed naturally from the radical restructuring of religious life, and the concomitant shift in church–state relations. Fifteenth-century Europe contained dozens of political units, ranging in size from tiny city-states in Italy to the massive Grand Duchy of Lithuania. In the Holy Roman Empire, hundreds of towns and Imperial knights claimed effective local sovereignty over territories as small as a few square miles. Some of these entities survived into the eighteenth century, but the trend everywhere led to much larger political units. National states in England, France, the Netherlands, Portugal, and Spain hardened their boundaries, often absorbing the smaller peripheral principalities or kingdoms on their borders. Just as England integrated the Celtic polities of Scotland and Ireland, so, too, Spain absorbed the Basque kingdom of Navarre, and France annexed territories with Breton, Flemish, German, Italian, and Provençal-speaking populations.

In East Central Europe, the process of consolidation took a different form. The great advance of the Ottoman Empire, which had conquered much of the Balkans and parts of Hungary, and extended its authority over the steppes just north of the Black Sea, ceased at the end of the seventeenth century. The Habsburg monarchy slowly conquered the Hungarian Crown lands in the late seventeenth and eighteenth centuries. The Long Turkish War, as the Austrians called it, transferred sovereignty over parts of Hungary, Croatia, Transylvania, and Serbia to the Habsburgs. Further north, the citizens of Poland and Lithuania created the Commonwealth of Many Nations (Union of Lublin, 1569), a state based on layered representative institutions sharing power with the king. This state, which dominated the region until well into the seventeenth century, lost its bearings in the eighteenth century, giving way to two new powers, Prussia and Russia (formerly Muscovy). In the Baltic, the Swedish monarchy rose and fell within the long seventeenth century, providing political structure to a region economically dominated by the Dutch.

Everywhere, little princelings lost power to states that combined some of the features of the later nation-states with the attributes of empires, and, for much of the period, with those of family dynastic corporations. As the essay by Gerhard Oestreich points out, elites and rulers negotiated a key change in this dynamic: "True, in most cases the monarchy was superior to the estates in organizational and governmental talent, but one essential condition for the formation of the state, the integrity of the territory, was defended by the estates [the representative bodies] against the dynastic interests of the ruling house." No longer could ruling houses divide up their principalities: they had to leave the political unit intact for their successor. This simple geographic fact indicates the implicit primacy of the political unit (soon to be called the "nation") over the ruler; in the eighteenth century, the great Atlantic Revolutions – in the British American Colonies, in the Netherlands, in Geneva, in France, in Poland, in Haiti – would make explicit this new political order.

The rapid political changes had close connections to economic, social, and cultural developments. These changed political conditions helped call forth new forms of state organization, institutions, and function. One state function dominated all others: war. European states spent two-thirds or more of their annual income on warfare during conflicts, and paid a third to a half of their revenue in peacetime to cover the interest on the loans they had floated during wars. War became progressively more expensive because armies got larger, arms became more costly, and campaigning became a full-time occupation. Eighteenth-century generals like the English Duke of Marlborough or the Prussian King Frederick the Great thought nothing of attacking in the dead of winter, so their enemies had to maintain full-scale armies throughout the year. These defensive forces required great fortress systems, which, in turn, added dramatically to the cost of the military. Some countries – England and the Netherlands above all, but France, Spain, and the Ottomans, too – had to maintain large navies, making for astronomical expenses in conflicts such as the Seven Years' War (1756–63). French borrowing during that war and the Wars of the American Revolution (1775–83) precipitated the financial crisis that touched off the French Revolution.

Historians now look at these new states, with their military machines, in a global perspective. The fighting within Europe had parallels in the rest of the world, not simply in terms of conflict between colonial powers such as France and England, but in armed confrontations between Europeans and those living in other parts of the globe. The Europeans had a clear military advantage at sea, where their powerful warships generally obliterated opposing naval forces, and along coastlines, where those same ships could enforce blockades and could bombard port towns. On land, it was sometimes a different matter: Amerindian, African, and Asian fighters, some of whose states (like China) dwarfed European ones, inflicted many a defeat on their European foes. These defeats did not stem the European tide, however, because the colonial powers could make such effective use of local rivalries to achieve their goals. Just as Cortez relied heavily on the Tlaxcalans and other Indian allies to defeat the Aztecs, so, too, the Dutch in the East Indies or the British in India or the slave traders on the west coast of Africa made alliances with one local group to defeat another. In the Western Hemisphere, the Europeans also had a formidable biological ally: diseases such as smallpox. Cortez ultimately defeated the Aztecs because smallpox spread from his tiny army into Mexico City (Tenochtitlán), where it annihilated the population. Amerindians had no antibodies for these new diseases: historians estimate that the population of the former Aztec Empire declined by 80 to 90 percent in the first 75 years after European contact. Almost all of these people died of "European" diseases.

Back in Europe, the new financial demands on the state pushed European governments to adopt a range of new policies. First, they had to find ways to borrow money. No state could pay for its wars without loans, and the old borrowing mechanisms, which relied heavily on the credit of the individual prince or, even more often, on the personal credit of his chief financial officer, could not provide enough money. In the sixteenth and early seventeenth centuries, the large states on the Continent declared bankruptcy one after the other. The French and Spanish monarchies, locked in a conflict for supremacy in Western Europe, declared full or partial bankruptcies in the 1550s, the 1590s, and the 1650s. This final bankruptcy marked the end of Spain's role as a great power.

The two rising states of northwest Europe, England (soon to be called the United Kingdom of Great Britain and Ireland) and the United Provinces of the Netherlands, demonstrated the financial future of European states. Both countries moved away from heavy dependence on land taxes, which were difficult (and expensive) to collect, and toward indirect taxes: sales levies, import–export duties, transit fees, manufacturing licenses and surveillance. Under the leadership of controller general Jean-Baptiste Colbert (head of French finances from 1661 to 1683), France followed their lead: in the early seventeenth century, nearly two-thirds of French state revenue came from direct taxes; by the 1670s, 60 percent of state income came from indirect taxes and state monopolies. Other European states – the kingdom of Naples, the Habsburg Empire, Prussia, Russia – slowly shifted their pattern in the eighteenth century, so that by the 1760s all the great powers obtained the largest share of their tax income from indirect levies. This new pattern of taxation indicates to historians the shifting nature of the European economy: as the economies moved away from an emphasis on agriculture and toward the preeminence of commerce and manufacturing, the tax systems shifted, too.

The excerpt from John Brewer's superb study of British state finance, *The Sinews of Power*, demonstrates the extent to which England shared both problems and solutions with its continental rivals. Brewer's work revolutionized our understanding of state development, because he showed that England was not the exception previous historians had claimed it to be. The first sentence of our passage boldly sets forth his thesis: "Between 1688 and 1714 the British state underwent a radical transformation, acquiring all of the main features of a powerful fiscal-military state: high taxes, a growing and well-organized civil administration, a standing army and the determination to act as a major European power."

The practical need to raise more money played an important role in the shift in the nature of the state, but it does little to explain the larger situation. Europeans long believed that they lived in commonwealths: political communities of citizens. Those commonwealths could be towns, like the city-states of Italy or the Imperial towns of the Holy Roman Empire, or they could be monarchies, like France or England. The term derived from the Latin *res publica*, literally public thing, meaning those things common to all. The French used the term *république*, the English called it a commonweale, the Poles *Rzeczpospolita*: everywhere it meant the political community, that is, the collective group of *citizens*, and the public good. In the sixteenth century, no one thought that a republic and a monarchy were different forms of government: a monarchy was a form of republic, not its antithesis. By the eighteenth century, the two words had become antonyms in most European languages. The conflict giving rise to this vocabulary shift, and not a simple expansion of the military and its fiscal apparatus, lies at the heart of the transformation of European states.

Here we need to consider the state as a set of functions. The state regulates the common interests of its citizens: that is how early modern Europeans understood it. The institutions of their common good extended far beyond the central political unit: different aspects of the public good lay within the control of the church, of feudal lords, of towns, of guilds, even of village assemblies. Slowly, these other institutions began to lose their share of stewardship of the *res publica*. Church courts almost everywhere lost jurisdiction to civil courts. In some cases, the central state began to take away responsibility for poor relief or some forms of education, both of which had been virtual monopolies of the Church. James Melton's essay, in Part I, shows the extent to which the eighteenth-century Austrian government, like the Prussian one, sought to use primary education to create a sense of loyalty to the monarchy and the state. Corporate bodies – churches, towns, provincial governments, guilds – increased their leverage over the central state by providing it with money, through underwriting its loans, but then found themselves caught in an intricate web from which they could no longer extricate themselves. States everywhere began to turn on the corporations. Louis XVI abolished French guilds in 1776, only to be forced into retracting the edict (and firing the minister who proposed it) a few months later. Fifteen years later, the Revolutionary National Constituent Assembly repeated Louis's abolition, this time to permanent effect.

Nor were the French in any way exceptional: Joseph II, Emperor of Austria, abolished guilds at virtually the same moment that the French Revolutionaries did. Moreover, Joseph, like the Revolutionaries, also abolished religious orders (except for teaching and nursing orders). Joseph's successor backed down from these radical steps, but they show the extent to which the central state everywhere believed it, not intermediate corporate bodies, had stewardship of the public good, in whose name Louis XVI, the National Assembly, and Joseph II had all claimed to act in their edicts.

Clare Crowston's essay demonstrates that governments could act in seemingly contradictory ways. Although the French government issued edicts attacking the legal rights of women, and, in the late 1680s, published draconian legislation against prostitutes, that same government created new women's guilds and encouraged female labor-force participation. Paid work soon became in France, as elsewhere in Western Europe, a defining characteristic of femininity, provided it was the right sort of work, such as dressmaking. Thus a misogynous government could take actions that strengthened the economic power of women, and weakened patriarchy.

The common thread in virtually every part of Europe was governmental activism, encouraged by a new way of thinking about government. The passage from Felix Gilbert's classic book offers us some insights into the philosophical shift in political thinking at the start of the sixteenth century. Gilbert suggests that Florentine political thinkers, above all Niccolò Machiavelli and Francesco Guicciardini, transformed European conceptions of the role of the state and of the rationale for political action. Gilbert sees Florentine thinkers developing "uncertainties . . . about their trust in reason" and a "growing realization that other qualities were required of a successful statesman":

> In these years, as men were altering their opinions about the qualities needed by a successful leader, there was also a change in the views about the means by which man could control the course of events. Force, which previously had been thought to be just one of the several factors which determined politics, now came to be regarded as the decisive factor . . . This notion – that politics was ruled primarily by force – emerged fully in the second decade of the sixteenth century.

Statesmen and political thinkers in the rest of Europe soon came to follow the Italian lead. The nobility in most places argued for a more republican conception of the commonwealth, one in which they would be the citizens (some nobles admitted a small group of urban elites could be citizens, too). This conception of the commonwealth desired a state that had representative institutions that would vote laws and taxes, an elective judiciary, and an army that bore some resemblance to the citizen militia of ancient Rome. As Gilbert suggests about Florence, the model for the Golden Age shifted from ancient Athens to republican Rome, a state that combined martial virtues with a mixed constitution.

This noble commonwealth actually took shape in Poland, as modern historians such as Robert Frost have explained. They have moved away from the traditional view of the Sejm (parliament) as a backward, selfish body, toward a nuanced view of republican politics in the Polish-

Lithuanian Commonwealth. Their research suggests that the Crown, not the nobility, often undermined the effective functioning of the Sejm. The Polish Sejm thus becomes the mirror image of Brewer's English Parliament, reversing cause and effect: Brewer writes of England: "Paradoxically, a strong parliament effectively resisting much that was proposed by government eventually produced a stronger state."

Everywhere, we see the negotiations between prince and elites. Modern historians have rejected the simplistic version of the backward-looking "feudal" country bumpkins of nineteenth-century middle-class historiography and begun to understand that the early modern nobility, in seeking to defend their own privileges, in fact also stood up for a form of government built on representation of citizens and on consultation. Anthony Feros reminds us that the Kings of Spain, like all rulers, had to challenge this older idea of the polity, "especially those theories that claimed that the king's power was derived directly from the community."[1]

The nobles often had a very narrow definition of citizen (themselves and a few others), but the classical models with which they were familiar had been based on small citizenries. To them, only the politically active class, whose size had been debated since the arguments of Machiavelli and Guicciardini around 1500, needed to be heard: they would "represent" the needs of society as a whole. In the eighteenth century, the expansion of the meaning of the word "citizen" to include large numbers of men radicalized European politics and paved the way for the Atlantic Revolutions.

Thomas Kaiser's innovative article (Part I) on images of "Turkish despotism" in Western Europe enables us to foresee later developments. Europeans reached back to classical models – beginning with Herodotus – to find a dichotomy between their "advanced" form of political organization and the "despotic" form prevalent in "Asia." A sense of cultural superiority had played an enormous role in sixteenth- and seventeenth-century European attacks against the rest of the world, as the work of Anthony Pagden (Part I) and others has shown. Europeans borrowed images from these encounters, as in the case of John Locke's state of nature, heavily influenced by his ideas of Northern Amerindian societies, or Rousseau's "noble savage," a fanciful concoction of Amerindian and African models.

The European encounter with the Ottomans, however, was a different matter. The work of young scholars such as Mitra Brewer has indicated that the trade models used in other parts of the world, which relied on brute military force, could not possibly work in the Ottoman world: the Ottomans held there a clear military superiority over Europeans. When European powers tried gunboat trade tactics in the Levant, the Ottomans invariably forced them to back down, and made European merchants living in the Levant pay enormous fines. Just as Europeans set up a dyad "civilized:barbaric/savage" with those whom they encountered in the Western Hemisphere or Africa, so, too, they set up a dyad "legitimate:despotic" for the "Asian" empires.

Kaiser demonstrates the dual usages of this dichotomy made by the French political philosopher Montesquieu and others. First, they established a "European" mode of government, one that could be traced back to the ancient Greeks. They contrasted this mode of government with an "Asiatic" one that dated back to the Greeks' Persian foes. As King Francis I wrote to Pope Paul III in 1543, "the Turks lacked all humanity and had 'more community with animals and savages than with themselves [European Christians].'"[2] This connection between despotism and the Ottomans was so strong that Antoine Furetière's 1690 French dictionary used the Sultan to illustrate the meaning of the word: "The Grand Seigneur [the Sultan] governs *despotiquement* [despotically]."

Second, Europeans used ostensible critiques of "Turkish" despotism to condemn the arbitrary actions of their own monarchs. Montesquieu transformed the meaning of despotism, making of it a system of government, rather than an individual abuse. Later French writers would use this altered meaning to attack the abuse of their own government, while royal defenders simultaneously tried to dilute the harshness of Ottoman "despotism." They did so, in part, through the fad for Turkish fashion in clothing, household furnishings, and food (known as the *turquerie*).[3] Visitors to French royal palaces can still see the eighteenth-century tapestries woven in honor of visits by various Ottoman ambassadors to the French Court. The royalists also (quite rightly) attacked the dubious factual foundations of claims of Ottoman "despotism," and suggested that the Ottoman Empire actually had an elaborate system of restraints on "royal" power.

These writers alert us to the systems of communication used by all early modern governments. Historians who have claimed the monarchical governments held "absolute" power, even when they admit to the practical limits of "absolutism," tend to overlook the remarkable efforts of such governments to influence public opinion. The relations of domination were, as the French historian Michèle Fogel has written, "demonstrative, unquestioned, and codified."[4] Louis XIV had no more power to change the etiquette at his Versailles dinner table than he did to elevate a peasant over a duke. Anthony Feros's work on Philip III of Spain and his favorites, especially the Duke of Lerma, shows the other side of the coin. One royal favorite, like Lerma, could have a dramatic effect on the life of the country. Feros rightly emphasizes the importance of "public ritual" to the wielding of effective political power in early modern Europe; he reminds us that the stunning paintings still visible in the palace of El Pardo include *The Judgment of Solomon*, *The Triumph of the Eucharist*, and *The Story of Achilles*, three subjects meant to present "Philip III as a just, religious, and prudent monarch." One could say as much of the royal portraiture anywhere in Europe.

Kings made extensive use of parish priests to announce key royal policies. The most "absolute" of kings, Louis XIV, on the verge of catastrophic defeat in June 1709, sent a letter to every parish in his kingdom (about 35,000) asking for the support of the "French people" in the kingdom's hour of desperation. He wrote of his rejection of the peace proposal of the Dutch and English: "I share all the evils that the war has made such faithful subjects suffer . . . [but] I am persuaded that they would themselves oppose the acceptance of conditions equally contrary to justice and to the honor of the name French." Hardly the sort of words we associate with a ruler who simply dictated to his subjects, but very much those of a king who believed himself to be defending justice and something he, and his subjects, could identify as "France." This appeal stands as a fitting testimony to a key moment in the evolution of European nation-states, political entities that would only come to full flower in the next century.

NOTES

1 Thus Charles II strongly objected to Thomas Hobbes's political ideas, even though Hobbes argued for unquestioned royal power. Hobbes rooted that power in the community, not in Divine Right, a position to which Charles II objected.

2 Francis I did not allow his cultural prejudices to get in the way of his political advantage; at the time of this letter, he was an ally of the Ottoman Empire against their common Habsburg foe.

3 Royal palaces in states with closer ties to the Ottomans, like the Polish-Lithuanian Commonwealth and the Habsburg Empire, today bear witness to the influence of goods obtained through the Ottomans, like the magnificent rugs on display in Wawel Castle in Kraków, Poland.

4 M. Fogel, *Les cérémonies de l'information dans la France du XVIe au milieu du XVIIIe siècle* (Paris, 1989), 19.

20

THE CRISIS IN ASSUMPTIONS ABOUT POLITICAL THINKING

Felix Gilbert

Introductory Note

This chapter from Felix Gilbert's classic study, *Machiavelli and Guicciardini*, examines the influence of events in Florence between the death of Lorenzo de' Medici (1492) and the end of the Florentine Republic (1512) on the conceptualization for history. Niccolò Machiavelli is most famous for his tract *The Prince* (1532), written largely to rescue him from the disgrace he suffered when the Medici returned in 1512. An important official of the Republican government, Machiavelli supported the more "democratic" system of 1494–1512, particularly in his longer writings, *The Discourses on Livy* (1531) and the *History of Florence* (1532). Francesco Guicciardini, member of a powerful aristocratic family that had some ties to the Medici, wrote in favor of a more restricted group of citizens, notably in his *History of Italy* (1537–40) and his political maxims (*Ricordi*, 1512–30). Machiavelli and Guicciardini's work as historians and political philosophers had an enormous impact on subsequent European thought, superbly analyzed a decade after Gilbert by John Pocock's magisterial *The Machiavellian Moment: Florentine Political Thought and the Atlantic Republican Tradition* (Princeton: Princeton University Press, 1975).

The death of Lorenzo de' Medici passed power to his incompetent son, Piero, who was driven from Florence in 1494. The city's inhabitants created a far more "democratic" government, based on a Great Council for which 3,000 men were eligible (the largest council of the pre-1494 system had about 300 members). From 1494 to 1498, a famed Dominican preacher, Fra Girolamo Savonarola, dominated Florence. He denounced luxury and decadence, and encouraged considerable iconoclasm; politically, he advocated broad popular participation in assemblies. His key ally, Francesco Valori, elected Gonfaloniere (chief official) in 1497, ruthlessly suppressed a plot by some aristocrats to restore the Medici in 1497, executing several leading citizens.[1] The friar's preaching grew increasingly strident, attacking corruption in the Church, and Pope Alexander

Felix Gilbert, "The Crisis in Assumptions about Political Thinking," pp. 105–111, 115, 117–19, 123, 128–31, 133–4, 136–9, 142–5, 148–52 from *Machiavelli and Guicciardini: Politics and History in Sixteenth-Century Florence*. Princeton, NJ: Princeton University Press, 1965.

VI. In June 1497, the Pope excommunicated Savonarola, banned him from preaching, and forbade all others from listening to him, on pain of excommunication. At first Fra Girolamo obeyed, but when he began preaching again in 1498 matters soon came to a head: in May 1498, a month after an angry mob had murdered Valori and his wife in the street, and nearly seized Savonarola at the Dominican house of St. Marco, the Signoria, now in the hands of his enemies, burned him at the stake in the piazza della Signoria, where a plaque marks the spot of his pyre. Republican government survived until 1512, when the Medici, supported by King Louis XII of France, regained control of the city.

Gilbert uses several technical terms related to Florentine government: the *balìe*, or ad hoc commissions, made recommendations to the Signoria on important policy issues and nominated the *accoppiatori*, or electoral commission. The *accoppiatori* chose the city's officials, who served short terms of office, ranging from two months to a year. Under Lorenzo de' Medici, his clients, serving as *accoppiatori*, regularly stuffed the bags containing the names of eligible candidates solely with names of his supporters, thus ensuring the selection of pro-Medici officials only. The Republican government abolished the *accoppiatori* in 1495, but the Medici brought them back in 1512.

NOTE

1 The Valori were one of the great Florentine aristocratic families. Gilbert cites a work by Niccolò Valori, a regular member of Florentine councils during the Republic, who himself was accused of participating in the February 1513 plot to assassinate the leaders of the restored Medici family. Bartolomeo Valori, a young member of the family, however, sided with the Medici as early as 1508. The Valori had close ties, including those of marriage, to the powerful and wealthy Rucellai, traditional opponents of the Medici; Bernardo Rucellai broke with this tradition because of his distaste for the radicals in the Republican leadership, and supported the return of the Medici in 1512.

Man's approach to the issues of practical politics is dependent on his *a priori* assumptions about two questions: what man is able to do in politics and what he ought to do. The gradual application of new criteria to the evaluation of the forms of political organization was only one aspect of the far-reaching repercussions which the political struggle in Florence had on political thought. Another consequence is perhaps even more important: the change in man's basic assumptions about the nature of politics. It can be observed that men began to alter their views about the forces working in political life and to adumbrate new ideas about the aims of political society.

I

In analyzing the question whether men were changing their views about the forces which they saw working in politics, we might ask what they considered to constitute the presuppositions of political success.

Whom did the Florentines regard as great statesmen? What were the qualities which had enabled them to achieve their successes? An investigation centering on the opinions held about individual leaders reveals more specifically and concretely the changing views about the forces determining the course of politics than would a discussion of theoretical writings which, if they touched on the subject of political leadership at all, treated of it according to traditional literary patterns. The political personality who held the greatest fascination for Florentines of the early sixteenth century was Lorenzo Magnifico de'Medici. The return of the Medici to Florence in 1512, after eighteen years of exile, posed the question: was it possible to restore the system of government by which Florence had been ruled in the previous century? The motives and the actions of Lorenzo Magnifico, under whom the Medicean system of government had been at its zenith, became a topic of intense debate.

In the various political memoranda on the constitutional problems of Florence which were written between 1512 and 1522,[1] the evaluation of Lorenzo Magnifico and of his system of government was a principal issue. Lorenzo was depicted as the prototype of a successful statesman, and he provided an example which his descendants ought to imitate. In Lorenzo's case, as the writers of these political memoranda agreed, the question regularly put in classical literature – whether a man owed his successes to personal virtue or to *Fortuna* – had to be answered that although *Fortuna* had smiled on Lorenzo, his personal qualities had been decisive. Success had come to him because he had pursued a wise and conscious policy.[2] These writers praised Lorenzo for the untiring energy with which he had devoted himself to his political tasks; but they did not ignore the dark sides of his regime. They mentioned that Lorenzo had used public money for personal purposes, but they excused him by explaining that the precarious political situation had absorbed him to such an extent that he could not give sufficient attention to business affairs.[3] These writers emphasized Lorenzo's "simple manners";[4] he had acted not like a prince, but rather he had exerted power within the existing institutional framework. Lorenzo's habit was "to deal with politics in the government palace, to come into the public places every day and to give a friendly hearing to all who came to him, to be an easy companion of the citizens, who saw him as a brother rather than a superior."[5] These writers represented Lorenzo as a leader who kept all groups of the population contented. "He tried to honor and please all citizens: to those who were well-born and powerful, he gave influence and recognition as far as possible."[6]

[. . .]

The portrait of Lorenzo Magnifico delineated in these writings was a purposeful construction rather than the result of a search for historical truth. But it cannot be called an invention because it was the continuation and elaboration of a distortion which had begun much earlier. There is a long and tortuous story behind this glorification of the Magnifico. The view of Lorenzo's contemporaries about him had been very different, almost opposite to that of the aristocrats writing in the second decade of the sixteenth century . . . But the Florentine politicians who had felt constrained by Lorenzo's political eminence judged him with marked reserve . . . In the field of foreign policy, where Lorenzo's successes were most willingly acknowledged, they were ascribed to lucky circumstances – to *Fortuna* – rather than to virtue.[7]

Concerning Lorenzo's domestic policy, the judgment of his contemporaries was much more skeptical, if not entirely negative. Criticism of Lorenzo came not only from the disgruntled politicians who had been slighted by the Magnifico . . . Even men who lacked political ambitions complained in their diaries that Lorenzo acted like a "prince," and they applied to him the word "tyrant."[8]

[. . .]

When the arrogance and recklessness of Lorenzo's son Piero had brought about the fall of the Medici family, the regime was officially condemned as a despotism; because the time of Lorenzo's supremacy had always been regarded as the climax of the Medicean era, his reputation was altered to correspond to that of a typical tyrant. When Savonarola preached his famous sermon on the evils of tyranny, he described a tyrant as a person who rushed his country into war to maintain himself in power, who distracted the masses by festivals and spectacles, who built palaces for himself with the money of the city, and who corrupted the youth and had spies in the magistrates. If personally the tyrant appeared friendly and mild mannered, this, Savonarola said, was only a sign of his devilish cleverness; "he transforms himself into an angel of light to wreak greater damage."[9] The political practices which Savonarola described as characteristic of tyranny had been those of the Magnifico. Although Savonarola may have magnified Lorenzo's weaknesses, all Florence was well aware that fundamentally his picture was taken from life.

[. . .]

Valori's synthesis of the previous evaluations of Lorenzo Magnifico was not the end, however; the climax was reached more than twenty years later with the characterization of Lorenzo in [Francesco] Guicciardini's *History of Italy*. This picture of the Magnifico – more than all others – has influenced the judgments on Lorenzo in the following centuries.

[. . .]

Perhaps because he felt dissatisfied with this evaluation of Lorenzo, Guicciardini remained fascinated by the man and seemed never to tire of discussing his personality and actions. In his *Dialogo del Reggimento di Firenze*, written in the 1520s, a principal topic was an examination of Lorenzo's system of government.[10] The dialogue is divided into two parts. In the second part, Guicciardini outlined what he considered to be the most suitable constitution for Florence. He presented here in a more elaborate form the ideas which he had developed in the *Discorso di Logrogno*. However the ease with which, after 1512, the Medici had discarded the influence of the aristocrats, had impressed Guicciardini and led him to suggest a slight strengthening of the power of the Great Council as a counterweight against the danger of absolutist rule.[11] In this discussion, he focussed on the particular problems of Florence; he believed that it was fruitless to speculate abstractedly about perfect forms of government, and he drew a sharp line between what might seem just and right in theory and what was possible in practice.[12]

This outline of a plan for a good government in Florence is preceded by a long comparison of the Medicean system of government of the fifteenth century and the popular government of 1494. The second part of the dialogue – the presentation of a good government – was necessary because the comparison of the governments existing before and after 1494 illustrated that both had great weaknesses. The first part containing the comparison of the Medici regime and the government established in 1494 is certainly the most interesting[13] because it shows Guicciardini's attempt to shun preconceived ideas and traditional notions. According to Guicciardini, no government can exist without the use of force,[14] and therefore a discussion of whether or not a state is tyrannical is irrelevant. The only criterion which has to be applied is that of the effects which a government will have on the well-being of the community.[15] The efficiency of any form of government depends on the special circumstances which exist in each society; thus a discussion of the working of the government machinery in a particular political society is necessary. The criterion of rational efficiency which Guicciardini applied in the *Discorso di Logrogno* is in the *Dialogo del Reggimento di Firenze* explicitly stated and justified as the only valid method which might lead to practical political results.

[. . .]

Political success in the early sixteenth century appeared to have little connection with rational calculations. Thus the interest in Lorenzo, though originally inspired by a desire to find an example to follow, served now to bring into sharper focus the changed situation of the early sixteenth century, and to throw light on the qualities of leadership required by these new times.

The Florentines were deeply puzzled by the emergence of political personalities and leaders whose conduct did not correspond to their ideas of a policy based on rational calculation. The Florentines tried to penetrate the secret which could explain the success of actions which ought to have led to ruin. Their concern with this problem is evident in the reports with which the Florentine ambassadors followed the career of the *"Papa terrible."* Julius II was one of the demonic personalities of his age, who, because of the long duration of his political influence and activities, astonished his contemporaries more than Cesare Borgia or any other of the "dark heroes" of the time. A phrase which indicates the bewilderment aroused by the personality and actions of Julius II is to be found in a report of the Florentine ambassador, Giovanni Acciaiuoli, written in October 1504; he stated that in the Rome of Julius II things proceed "outside of all reason."[16] Because of the great value which Florentines placed on making political decisions according to reason, this statement was an expression of sharp disapproval.

[. . .]

II

In these years, as men were altering their opinions about the qualities needed by a successful leader, there was also a change in the views about the means by which man could control the course of events. Force, which previously had been thought to be just one of the several factors which determined politics, now came to be regarded as the decisive factor. To be sure, Florentine politicians had never been such visionaries that the importance of force in the political world could have entirely escaped them; but they had considered other factors, such as law and diplomacy, to be equally effective.

This notion – that politics was ruled primarily by force – emerged fully in the second decade of the sixteenth century. Whereas most of the aristocrats stuck to the idea that by acting as mediators between the Medici and the people they could become the "steering wheel" of the government, a certain number of aristocrats believed that all of the aristocrats ought to accept, without reservations, the leadership and the control of the Medici. The former group of aristocrats were mostly older men who had entered politics under Lorenzo Magnifico. The latter group of aristocrats, who favored submission to Medicean domination, were younger men, frequently the sons of the political leaders in the time of Lorenzo and the republic. Although certainly not all of the younger men abandoned the aristocratic camp for that of the Medici, all those who did were young; the split among the aristocrats corresponded to a difference of generations.

The younger men were the prophets of force. Their evaluation of its importance in politics was rooted in the events which took place in the years preceding the return of the Medici. Italian helplessness in the face of foreign invasion since 1494 had been an impressive demonstration of the decisive role of force in politics. The consequence of the Italian defeat was a mounting criticism of the reliance on condottieri and mercenaries. In their writings the humanists had kept alive the idea of a citizen army – because that was the method which Rome had followed.[17] An attempt was made to infuse greater strength into the Florentine military organization by putting into practice the idea of a citizen army. [Niccolò] Machiavelli, then a chancellery official, drafted the law by which the population of the rural areas under Florentine rule was conscripted for military service. There was widespread recognition of the desirability and usefulness of such a measure. Guicciardini approved of it in his *Discorso di Logrogno*. Lodovico Alamanni ascribed, exactly as Machiavelli, "the present shame and serfdom of Italy" to the "habit of using mercenary soldiers"; "the Italians have forgotten how to carry arms themselves."[18]

Military strength became the chief criterion for judging the importance of another power. Machiavelli, reporting from Rome about the first months of the pontificate of Julius II, emphasized the Pope's political impotence because he had neither money nor soldiers.[19] But of the two elements which, according to the frequently used classical adage, a Prince must have – "iron and gold" – the gold became negligible; iron alone determined success.

The significant development which took place after the return of the Medici was that the notion of military force as the exclusive determinant in politics was extended from foreign policy to domestic affairs. Paolo Vettori, a young aristocrat, addressed to Cardinal Giovanni Medici, later Pope Leo X, a memorandum in which he wrote that, while before 1494 "your forefathers, in maintaining their rule, employed skill rather than force; you must use force rather than skill."[20]

[. . .]

The division among the aristocrats, which had come out in the weeks after the overthrow of the republican regime, continued throughout the following ten years. The older generation of aristocrats never abandoned their hopes that they would be able to regain political control; and their hopes were never entirely quashed by the actions of the Medici. Although the manner in which the Medici had seized the government in 1512 showed their disdain for constitutional bodies, and although the Medici continued to rely on force, they did not establish an overtly absolutist regime. They exerted their power behind a republican façade, controlling the offices and councils in much the same manner as had Cosimo and Lorenzo. But the Medici of the sixteenth century did little to conceal the fact that distribution of honors and offices depended on their will. In October of 1512, the *Balìa* elected twenty *Accoppiatori*, mainly the heads of pro-Medici families.[21] Their chief task was to nominate the *Gonfaloniere* and the other members of the Signoria. From the lists of candidates of offices, the names of all those who might be unfriendly to the new regime were removed. In the summer of the next year the basis of the government was broadened by the establishment of deliberative bodies: a Council of the Seventy and a Council of the Hundred, both revivals of councils which had existed in the times of Lorenzo Magnifico. The members of these councils were appointed by the Signoria, but since the Signoria, in turn, was appointed by the pro-Medici *Accoppiatori*, it did nothing but ratify a list of names of prospective council members which Loe X had prepared in Rome and had then transmitted to his nephew, Lorenzo, in Florence for further scrutiny.

[. . .]

The procedures which the Medici used for ruling Florence strengthened the awareness of the differences between form and fact, between appearance and reality in politics. Some of Lorenzo's friends among the younger aristocrats began to regard discussions and speculations about constitutional arrangements as little more than time-wasting intellectual exercises. Lodovico

Alamanni told the Medici that they need not take the constitutional projects and ideas of the older generation seriously: "They are 'wise citizens' and one does not have to bother much about them, because wise men make no revolutions."[22] The reasoning of the older aristocrats – that a broadening of the government and respect for constitutional forms was necessary because of the dissatisfaction of the masses – Alamanni thought silly: "One needs to fear their votes and not their arms; they put their main trust in miracles."[23] In the joy of having discovered in force the real key to the understanding of politics, traditional concepts were arrogantly shoved aside and the picture of politics became simplified to the extreme. It was a sign of the atmosphere which had been created in this time of sham constitutionalism that even an aristocrat who was opposed to Medicean absolutism, Francesco Guicciardini could write: "Every government is nothing but violence over subjects, sometimes moderated by a form of honesty."[24] The distinction between monarchy and tyranny seemed to him meaningless because force is an integral element of all political regimes.

A further logical step would have been to recommend to Lorenzo that he abandon all pretense of maintaining constitutional forms of government and base his regime exclusively on force: that he should become an absolute ruler. Guicciardini reported that "people have not been lacking who have believed and have tried to persuade Lorenzo that it would be safer for him and his adherents to take over absolute rulership in the city, in fact and in title, than to hold the government under some veil of republicanism and freedom." But Guicciardini shrugged off this idea with a brief remark: "Such a procedure would, in the course of time, emerge as being full of difficulties, of suspicion, and finally of cruelty."[25] Alamanni indicated as a possible course of action open to the Medici "to kill all those who might be able and willing to deprive them of their power." But Alamanni rejected such a brutal use of force out of moral considerations as well as out of concern for Lorenzo's reputation: "Killing citizens without reason and dipping one's hands into blood, I am sure, can never find the approval of Your Excellency as a courageous and magnanimous person. . . . You prefer to compete with Caesar and Camillus than with the godless Agathocles, the cruel Sulla and the vicious Liverotto da Fermo."[26] Alamanni's statements show that the enthusiasm for advancing extreme views in theory is frequently not matched by eagerness for seeing them realized. Moreover, in this period men had become conscious that traditional views about politics were deficient, and that a new basis for politics had to be found; but this was all. Men were still groping for a clear and definite formulation of their new insights.

At the end of the fifteenth century, the contrast between *ragione* and *Fortuna* had created different attitudes to politics. *Fortuna*, as the emissary of God, had strengthened the feeling that man was in the hands of uncontrollable forces; man's conduct of affairs ought to remain within the God-given traditional framework. The opposing point of view was that man's reason gave him the power to shape the course of politics; by making use of experience he could impress efficiency and perfection upon the political order. But this latter view had hardly come into its own when political events seemed to demonstrate that reason was only one, and perhaps not even a very effective, instrument in the political struggles. This was the confusing and perturbing situation in which Florentines who thought about politics found themselves in the second decade of the sixteenth centruy.

III

The extent of the crisis in political thinking can be gauged from the deepening of the problem. The foremost issue was, and remained, the form which the Florentine constitution ought to have, but men became aware that this was more than a technical question; it involved the problem of the intrinsic nature of good society.

[. . .]

To many Florentines these brilliantly colored and glittering processions of gods, heroes, and virtues seemed pale and shadowy. The Medici had returned to Florence with the outlook of exiles: for the Medici the world had ended in 1494 and it began again only when they came back to Florence in 1512; for them the intervening period did not exist. But those who had lived in Florence throughout the eighteen years of the republic had a different perspective. They had seen the sudden collapse of Medici rule in 1494 and then they had witnessed the overthrow of another political regime. Many of them must have felt that the restored regime could not last, and that the causes of instability and its cure must be more fundamental.

It seemed to many that Savonarloa, who had admonished the Florentines that political stability and well-being depended on moral reform, came nearer to the truth than all the others with their clever political plans. The persistence of Savonarla's ideas emerged clearly in 1527, when, thirty years after the Frate's death, in a final short-lived attempt to regain freedom, the Florentines threw off the Medici yoke and proclaimed Florence to be a "city of Christ." The process of the survival of Savonarola's ideas throughout the period of the Medici restoration is difficult to trace.[27] The existence of Savonarolians, or of a Savonarolian sect was frequently mentioned, but the expression was used loosely and sometimes it was simply meant to designate all those who wanted to reestablish the Great Council. But there is ample proof that there were many in Florence who adhered to the ideas of the Frate in their entirety, and believed in the interdependence of Christian reform and a stable social order. At the time when the Medici and their followers were parading through the streets of the city in the costumes of pagan antiquity, Florentines crowded the churches whenever a preacher appeared in the pulpit who spoke in the Savonarolian vein, prophesying the end of the world if people did not desist from their sinful life, and promising that if they changed their ways, Florence and Tuscany would become the center of the political and moral renewal of the world. After 1512, hardly a year passed without the appearance in Florence of another preacher of doom and salvation. Some of these preachers were false prophets who used their hold over the people to extort money or to seduce women; but despite these disillusionments, people flocked again and again to the churches in order to hear a new preacher of the Savonarolian stamp raise his voice.[28]

[. . .]

However, even this confirmation of Savonarloa's predictions did not resolve all of Cerretani's doubts; he found it necessary to raise again the question: had Savonarloa been inspired by God? Was he a saintly figure? One of the speakers in [Bartolomeo] Cerretani's dialogue [Istoria Fiorentina] reiterated the objection frequently voiced in the Frate's lifetime, that Savonarola had not been exclusively concerned with saving souls; rather he had intervened in political affairs and had taken an active part in them. He was said to have "wanted to make himself head of our city, both its spiritual and its secular head."[29] Those who refuted these accusations argued that it had been Savonarola's duty to concern himself with the establishment of good laws because religion can flourish only in a well-organized society. "If Savonarola founded a popular regime, if he created laws against vice and against the luxurious dresses of women and youths, if he taught us to live in a republican spirit and required priests, monks, and nuns to conduct themselves like the pious men of olden times, was this an error or did he do right"?[30] Cerretani reinforced this argument by citing the famous proverb that a government cannot be maintained by paternosters. Although Cerretani agreed that this was true for the world as it was constituted, he drew from this proverb the unique conclusion that the political order ought to be changed in such a way that it *could* be ruled by paternosters. Cerretani believed in Savonarola's recommendation that all groups of the population should participate in the government so that one group would not rule over the other. Then the government belonged to everyone, and force would not be needed to maintain it. With the elimination of force, social surroundings would be conducive to the flowering of true religion; there would be a restoration of the society at the time of the foundation of the Christian Church. "To renew the Church means to reintroduce the spiritual and secular regime which existed in the times of the first Christians."[31]

The Savonarolians held to the traditional belief that the only means to political success was obedience to the commandments of God. If the popular regime, which Savonarola had advocated and helped to found, had collapsed – at least temporarily – the reason was that the people had failed God by refusing to give up their sinful ways. If the popular regime was to be restored the people had to change their lives and become true Christians. The spread of the idea of the need for Church reform indicated that these hopes for a good society were not unfounded. However, the central point of the Savonarolians was that political reform – the re-establishment of a popular regime – depended on the moral conversion of man, on the birth of a new spirit among the citizens. The Savonarolians thought little of worldly-wise men who believed that by their own intelligence they could control the course of events; the belief in politics based on reason was anathema to the Savonarolians. Thus a strange link connects the Savonarolians who believed that the world should be ruled by paternosters and those who were advocates of a policy based on force.

These prophets of force were also skeptical about the influence which reason and intelligence could exert on politics; they also believed that the prerequisite for successful political action was a spiritual regeneration of the citizens. Force was viewed, by its advocates, as having a two-fold role in politics: force gave security and stability to those who governed; and force also provided greater coherence and strength for the entire state. The prophets of force recommended the creation of a citizen army not only because of the obvious practical advantage of being less expensive, but also because it was expected these armies would be animated by a new spirit. Citizens defending their homes would fight with greater heroism and develop a greater willingness to undergo sacrifices. The secret of the success of the Romans was, as Alamanni said, their discipline. "What else made the Roman soldiers so perfect but the strictness of their leaders and particularly of Torquato"?[32] The advocates of force wondered, however, whether it was possible to introduce in Florence the radical changes – such as a citizen army – which they believed necessary for the political regeneration of the citizens. Egoism seemed to have become all-pervasive; "one's own interest is master and leads all men." The danger was that men had become too soft for strenuous effort; "they are effeminate and nerveless and inclined to a protected and, considering our resources, a luxurious life; they possess little love for fame or true honour, but much for wealth and money."[33] However these required virtues of discipline and abnegation seemed incompatible with the emphasis on the acquisition of wealth which dominated a commercial city.

In contrast to some of the humanists of the fifteenth century who had recognized business as a useful training for the conduct of affairs of state, the pursuit of commercial interests came to be considered as making man unfit for government and politics.[34] Antonio Brucioli's dialogue *Della Republica* provides the most striking expression of this view held by the advocates of force. Brucioli's work was published in 1526, but its conception had taken place a few years earlier when he had been in Florence and had frequented the meetings in the Rucellai gardens.[35] At the outset of this dialogue one of the speakers presented the accepted view that trade is the mainstay of a republic and that the merchant class is the most important part of a society, but at the end of the discussion he had become convinced that this view was false and that among the professions, trade is "the last, the vilest, and the least necessary."[36] Whereas the speaker had at first spoken of the military profession with contempt, he later recognized that it deserved the first, the most honored place in society. Brucioli was clear-sighted enough to realize that the acceptance of such a new scheme of values required a thorough change in the social order. In an ideal republic great differences of wealth ought not to be allowed. The middle classes ought to predominate as they had predominated in the past. To us it seems illusionary to expect that such a change could ever take place. But to Brucioli and to some of his contemporaries such an ideal republic was not a figment but the restoration of a society that had existed in republican Rome.

If the Medici attempted to legitimate their rule by dangling before the eyes of the Florentines the picture of a past – half recent, half classical – in which peace, wealth, and happiness had existed side by side, if the Savonarolians wanted to return to the times of early Christianity when social conditions had permitted man to live for spiritual ends, even the advocates of force found the justification for their harsh new doctrine in an ideal past: their Golden Age was the Iron Age of Rome.

NOTES

1 The most important are the memoranda by Paolo Vettori, Niccolò Guicciardini, Lodovico Alamanni published by Rudolf von Albertini, *Das Florenitinische Staatsbewusstsein im Uebergang von der Republik zum Prinzipat*, Bern, 1955, pp. 345-77; Francesco Guicciardini's "Del Governo di Firenze dopo la Restaurazione de' Medici," "Del modo di assicurare lo stato alla casa de' Medici," "Dialogo del Reggimento di Firenze," all published in Guicciardini, *Dialogo e Discorsi del Reggimento di Firenze*, ed. R. Palmarocchi, Bari, 1932; Alessandro de' Pazzi's "Discorso al Cardinale Giulio de' Medici," *Archivio Storico Italiano*, vol. I (1842), pp. 420-32; Machiavelli's "Discorso delle cose Fiorentine dopo la morte di Lorenzo." Niccolò Valori's "Vita di Lorenzo," printed in Philippi Villani, *Liber de civitatis Florentiae Famosis Civibus*, ed. G. C. Galletti, Firenze, 1847, pp. 164-82 also has political purposes although it is a eulogy rather than a political memorandum.
2 See particularly Pazzi, *loc. cit.*, p. 423 on the part of virtú and Fortuna in Lorenzo's achievement.
3 Pazzi, *loc. cit.*, p. 422.
4 " . . . Laurentius semper intererat tam comis, et humanus, ut popularius nihil excogitari possit," Valori, *loc. cit.*, p. 177. On Lorenzo's "vita civile," see also Machiavelli's comparison of the older and younger Lorenzo in his letter to Francesco Vettori, February/March 1514 (*Opere* [Biblioteca di Classici Italiani-Feltrinelli Editore], vol. VI, p. 331).
5 " . . . il tenere lo stato in palazzo, il venire in piazza ogni dì et dare facile audientia et grata a chi la voleva, l'esser familiare co' cittadini, faceva che a' cittadini pareva havere un fratello et non uno superiore et per questo più lo amavano . . . ," Alamanni in Albertini, *op. cit.*, p. 369.
6 "Et tutti li ciptadini honorava et carezava, et a quelli che erono nobili et potenti dava authorità et riputatione quanto ragionevole era," Niccolò Guicciardini in Albertini, *op. cit.*, p. 354.
7 "Nell' altre imprese di fuori l'aiutò molte volte la fortuna . . . ," Piero Parenti, *Storia fiorentina* (Florence, 1994) Ms. Biblioteca Nazionale, Florence (BNF) II.IV. 169, f. 127r.
8 As an example may serve Giovanni Cambi, "Istorie," Florence, 1785-6, p. 65: "perchè detto Lorenzo di Piero di Coximo de' Medici s'era fatto chapo di detta Ciptà, et Tiranno . . . ," but also at many other places; Luca Landucci, *Diario Fiorentina*, ed. Jodoco del Badia, Florence, 1883, p. 59, indicates that he regarded Lorenzo's building activities as "princely." The views of contemporaries about the

tyrannical character of Lorenzo's rule are discussed by Joseph Schnitzer, *Savonarola, ein Kulturbild aus der Zeit der Renaissance*, vol. I, Muenchen, 1924, pp. 50 et seq.

9 "E però quanto il tiranno di fuori si dimonstra più costumato, tanto è più astuto e più cattivo e ammaestrato da maggiore e più sagace diavolo, il quale si transfigura nell' Angelo della luce per dare maggiore colpo," Savonarola, *Trattato circa il Reggimento e Governo della Città di Firenze*, Libro II, chapter 2.

10 Francesco Guicciardini, "Dialogo del Reggimento di Firenze," *Dialogo e Discorsi del Reggimento di Firenze*, pp. 3–172; for the date of its composition – 1521-2 – see Roberto Ridolfi, *Vita di Francesco Guicciardini*, Rome, 1960, p. 538; see also Vittorio de Caprariis, *Francesco Guicciardini dalla Politico alla Storia* Bari, 1950, pp. 69–85 for a penetrating analysis of the Dialogo.

11 See *Guicciardini, Dialogo del Reggimento di Firenze*, 231-2, 129.

12 "Ma come si avessi a ordinare e fondare bene uno governo populare, non sarebbe forse difficile el trovare, perché ne sono pieni e' libri antichi di uomini eccellenti che si sono affaticati a scrivere de' governi, e ci è la notizia degli ordini e delle leggi che hanno avuto molte republiche, tra le quali tutte o si potrebbe imitare el migliore, o di ciascuno quelle parte che fussino piú notabili e piú belle. . . . Ma io non so se a noi è a proposito el procedere cosí, perchè non parliamo per ostentazione e vanamente, ma con speranza che el parlare nostro possa ancora essere di qualche frutto, . . . non abbiamo a cercare di uno governo immaginato e che sia piú facile a apparire in su' libri che in pratica, come fu forse la republica di Platone . . . ," Guicciardini, *Dialogo e Discorsi del Reggimento di Firenze*, p. 99.

13 This is also the opinion of de Caprariis, *op. cit.*, p. 81.

14 " . . . tutti gli stati, chi bene considera la loro origine, sono violenti, e dalle republiche in fuora, nella loro patria e non piú oltre, non ci è potestà alcuna che sia legitima . . . ," Guicciardini, *Dialogo e Discorsi del Reggimento di Firenze*, p. 163; but see also the more famous formulation of this idea in the "Discorso di Logrogno," *ibid.*, p. 222: "Non è altro lo stato e lo imperio che una violenzia sopra e' sudditi, palliata in alcuni con qualche titulo di onestá." For the meaning of stato in this period, see below, p. 177.

15 "E però sempre è piú approvato e chiamato migliore governo quello che partorisce migliori effetti. Ed infine, discorrete quanto volete, bisogna, se io non mi inganno, ritornare a quello mio primo fondamento: che gli effetti de' governi sono quegli che danno la sentenzia," Guicciardini, *ibid.*, p. 41; but also p. 15: "a volere fare giudizio tra governo e governo, non debbiamo considerare tanto di che spezie siano, quanto gli effetti loro. . . . "

16 " . . . fuora di ogni ragione . . . ," Archivio di Stato, Florence (ASF), *X di Balìa, Carteggio, Responsive*, vol. 80, c. 1.

17 See C. C. Bayley, *War and Society in Renaissance Florence*, University of Toronto Press, 1961, chapter 5.

18 "Poco obligo habbiamo veramente co'nostri antichi, e quali, deviando Italia da' suoi buoni ordini, la ridussono ad governo di preti et di mercanti, et mettendo in uso la militia mercenaria, l'hanno condotta alla presente ignominia et servitu," Alamanni in Albertini, *op. cit.*, p. 372.

19 November 11, 1503: "Non aver ancora nè genti nè denari conviene di necessità che giocoli di mezzo in fine," Machiavelli, *Opere*, Milano, 1805, vol. V, p. 52; the entire report on pp. 49–53.

20 "Li antecessori vostri . . . usorno in tenere questo Stato piu industria che forza. A voi è necessario usare più forza che industria . . . ," Paolo Vettori in Albertini, *op. cit.*, p. 345.

21 ASF, *Balìe*, vol. 43, f. 59r. (October 19, 1512).

22 " . . . e' sono savii et de' savi non si de' temere, perchè non fanno mai novitá," Alamanni in Albertini, *op. cit.*, p. 370.

23 " . . . et sono da temere le loro fave et non le loro arme, et la loro confidentia è più ne' miraculi che in altro," Alamanni in Albertini, *op. cit.*, p. 366.

24 " . . . tutti gli stati, chi bene considera lo loro origine, sono violenti, e dalle republiche in fuora, nella loro patria e non più oltre, non ci è potesta alcuna che sia legitima . . ." Guicciardini, *Dialogo e Discorsi del Reggimento di Firenze*, p. 163; but see also the more famous formulation of this idea in the "Discorso di Logrogno," *ibid.*, p. 222: "Non è altro lo stato e lo imperio che una violenzia sopra e' sudditi, palliate in alcuni con qualche titulo di onestá."

25 "Non voglio omettere di dire che non è mancato e non manca chi ha avuto opinione ed ha, e forse ha fatto opera di persuaderlo, che sarebbe piú sicurtá di costoro pigliare assolutamente el dominio della cittá in fatti ed in titolo, che tenere el governo sotto questa ombra di civilitá e di libertá; cosa che io non intendo disputare ora, ma io per me giudico che non potrebbono pigliare partito piú pernizioso e per loro e per noi, e che questo maneggio riuscirebbe nel processo del tempo pieno di difficultá, di sospetti ed a ultimo di crudeltá," Guicciardini, "Del modo di assicurare lo stato ai Medici," *Dialogo e Discorsi del Reggimento di Firenze*, p. 281. It was widely said in Florence that Filippo Strozzi and Francesco Vettori, close friends and advisors of Lorenzo Medici, were pushing him towards an absolutist course; see Francesco Vettori's letter to his brother Paolo in Oreste Tommasini, *La vita e gli scritti di Niccolò Machiavelli*, vol. II, Roma, 1911, pp. 1066–8.

26 "Il secondo modo dell'uccidere senza cagione e cittadini et l'insanguinarsi nella sua patria le mani, so che Sua Ex. tia come valorosa et magnanima non approverrà mai . . . vorrà più presto gioastrare non Cesare et Camillo che con lo impio Agathocle, col crudelissimo Sylla et con scelerato Liverocto da Fermo," Alamanni in Albertinin, *op. cit.*, p. 367.

27 An interesting document proving the strength of Savonarola's ideas, is the "Recitazione del caso di Pietro Paolo Boscoli," printed *Archivio Storico Italiano*, vol. I (1842), pp. 283–309, see particularly p. 296; see also the letter from Ulisse da Fano to Lorenzo Strozzi (without date, 1519?), ASF, *Carte Strozziane, 3ª Serie*, vol. 220, c. 163, where Savonarola, in a somewhat ironic way, is called "el gran propheta," and Lorenzo Strozzi is characterized as "uno, e non de' mediocri suoi seguaci." See then, most of all, Cerretani, *Storia in Dialogo*.

28 The most famous of the "false prophets" was the so-called Don Teodoro, see Landucci, *Diario*, p. 349, and Cambi, "Istorie," *loc. cit.*, vol. XXII, pp. 59 et seq. and also, Parenti, *Istoria Fiorentina*, Ms. BNF II.IV.171, f. 112 about Don Teodoro: "ripigl[i]eva certe propositioni di Frate Jeronimo." Parenti gives much material about the religious excitement in Florence, and in Schnitzer's excerpts from Parenti's work (*Quellen und Forschungen zur Geschichte Savonarolas*, ed. J. Schnitzer, vol. IV: *Piero Parenti*) these notices have been published rather extensively.

29 "e' mostrò in molti modi di volersi far capo nella citta nostra, non solo del temporale, ma dello spiri- tuale," Cerretani, *Storia in Dialogo*, II.I.106, f. 142r. (in *Quellen*, ed. Schnitzer, vol. III, p. 100).

30 "Se lui fece et fondò un vivere publico, se creò legge circa l'honestà et vestire di donne, et giovani e fan- ciulle, se lui c'insegnò vivere a uso di republica civilmente et con quella religione, che ne richiede al secolo et a' sacerdoti e monache, la vita di quelli antichi religiosi, o puossi dire, che costui habbi errato o fatto bene?", Cerretani, *Storia in Dialogo*, II.I.106, f. 144v (in *Quellen*, ed. Schnitzer, vol. III, p. 101).

31 "Il rinuovare la Chiesa è rintrodurre il vivere spirituale, temporale come fu al principio di que' primi christani," Cerretani, *Storia in Dialogo*, II.I.106, f. 155v.

32 "Che altro fe' sì perfetta la militia de' Romani che la severità de' lor capi et maxime di Torquato?", Alamanni in Albertini, *op. cit.*, p. 374.

33 " . . . gli animi degli uomini effeminati ed enervati e vòlti a uno vivere delicato e, rispetto alle facultá nostre, suntuoso; poco amore della gloria ed onore vero, assai alle ricchezze e danari," Guicciardini, "Del modo di ordinare il governo popolare" *Dialogo e Discorsi del Reggimento di Firenze*, p. 219.

34 Guicciardini, *ibid.*, pp. 257 et seq.

35 On Brucioli's relation to the Rucellai gardens, see Delio Cantimori, "Rhetoric and Politics in Italian Humanism," *Journal of the Warburg and Coutauld Institutes*, vol. I (1937/8), pp. 83–102 and Alber- tini, *op. cit.*, pp. 79–83. Brucioli and Lodovico Alamanni were friends of Machiavelli, but although some of their ideas might have been influenced by Machiavelli, their writings show that they had their own views and convictions.

36 " . . . dell'ultime, e più vile et di minima necessità . . . ," Antonio Brucioli, "Della Republica," *Dialogi*, Venezia, 1526, p. XVIIIv.

21

FROM CONTRACTUAL MONARCHY
TO CONSTITUTIONALISM

Gerhard Oestreich

After the murder of the Huguenot leadership in the Night of St Bartholomew, 1572, the French Calvinists, struggling for existence, relied on the ancient notion of a polity founded upon a contract. This contract, freely concluded between ruler and people as equal partners, was thought to have established their rights and obligations for all time and to have bound the ruler to an undertaking to govern with justice and piety. Linked with this idea was the Old Testament notion of a covenant; this gave a strong moral backing to the formula of *mutua obligatio* embodied in Roman law. At the same time the Huguenots were attentive to the realities of their own age, the age of representative assemblies, and appealed to the existing compacts and agreements between princes and estates, to the contractual foundation of the European corporative state, and to the right of resistance. The rallying cries of the opponents of monarchy, the "monarchomachs", spread rapidly.[1] The doctrine of contractual government became the basis for future contracts between princes and estates.

The concept of a contract made with the sovereign dates from this period. In the twentieth century it has been attached to the older models of the high or late Middle Ages,[2] the best-known of these being Magna Charta (1215), the Golden Bull of Hungary (1222), the Aragonese Privileges (1283 and 1287), the Joyeuse Entrée of Brabant (1356) and the Treaty of Tübingen (1514). These contracts were concluded before the period of the rise of representative institutions, in its early days or at its height. They represent a reaction to the increased power and efficiency of princely rule and the demands it made on society. The corporative constitution of the estates arose through contractual agreements whose aim was to establish a social order which they had a hand in determining. The corporative state was a product of the transition from feudalism to the early modern state.

A common feature of all these contracts, as regards both their contents and the way they functioned, is seen to be their concern to guarantee and strengthen the law; they are thought, too, to

Gerhard Oestreich, "From contractual monarchy to constitutionalism," pp. 166–77, 179–86 from *Neostoicism and the early modern state*. Cambridge: Cambridge University Press, 1982.

evince an awareness of statehood. However, these are not the only factors: they deal also with the development of government and the participation of the country in its administration. A central issue is that of the contributions and taxes due from the country. In the same spirit they broach questions of legal and administrative organization – not yet separated – and commercial life. All contributions to the government of the prince were considered extraordinary and required the approval of the estates. Increased military imposts, the planning of aggressive war, the striking of new coins, the voting of taxes and the settlement of the prince's debts with financial supervision by the estates – all such matters had been subject to contractual arrangements since Magna Charta. In other words, what was involved was not just the autonomy of the estates, the preservation of their rights and liberties (*jura et libertates*) and the written confirmation of corresponding privileges secured in law, but also an element of supervision over the development of the prince's government and the formation of the state.

True, in most cases the monarchy was superior to the estates in organizational and governmental talent, but one essential condition for the formation of the state, the integrity of the territory, was defended by the estates against the dynastic interests of the ruling house. It was laid down in the contractual instruments that the territory might not be divided or land and populations ceded to another ruler without the consent of the estates. It was particularly important, when a foreign prince took over the country, that its legal system should remain independent and that only indigenous officials should be appointed (the so-called *Indigenatsrecht*). At the same time, as the agreements show, the estates understood that their obligation to give advice and aid included providing financial support for the national administration and its policies, and also for their supervision.[3]

The terms of a contract between the prince and the estates only rarely encroached upon the area of the court and central government. This was reserved to the royal prerogative, the domain of the prince, and was regarded as his cameral sphere. It was only when monarchical government failed – during minorities or dynastic quarrels, at times when the ruler was ill or absent, or when the ruling house was otherwise impeded in the exercise of its functions – that the estates claimed the right to take over the government of the country. This was done, not by means of constitutional agreements which would conform with the concept of a ruling contract, but by special dispositions for governing the country, usually of limited duration.[4]

The theory of contractual rule, as developed by the sixteenth-century monarchomachs, was dominated by the idea of *mutua obligatio*, *mutua pactio*, a reciprocal bond between prince and estates, ruler and people, supported by the biblical doctrine of the covenant, the Old Testament *foedus duplex* between God and the people on the one hand, and between the king and the people on the other. The contracts with the ruler and similar documents which gave reality to the *mutua obligatio* took a number of forms. Whether they were electoral capitulations, recesses of the European assemblies, compacts and agreements, confirmations of privileges or conditions of homage, they regulated and controlled certain areas of public life. No theory characterizes the principal features of the age of the representative constitution more aptly than they do. The Calvinist doctrine of representative institutions matured into a general contractual theory of political life; this subsequently influenced men's thinking about natural law, central to which was the idea of the contractual basis of the state, from early modern times until the Age of Enlightenment. The English absolutists, such as King James I[5] or Thomas Hobbes, discussed the contractual theory in their writings on the state,[6] for the ecclesiastical and political practice of Puritanism in England was dominated by the idea of the covenant. The idea of mutual contracts had its protagonists also in the imperial and national assemblies of the continent. A general atmosphere developed which favoured the drafting of comprehensive *pacta reciproca*, written contracts concerning government, and finally constitutional documents which were more specific versions of the older ruling contracts.

Side by side with the elaboration of religious and legal thinking about contractual arrangements, a development was taking place in the monarchical administration of the state, the growth of which Trevor-Roper describes forcefully and sees as partly responsible for "the crisis of the seventeenth century".[7] The early seventeenth century was a time of change from polyarchic monarchy with estate participation to monistic sovereignty. With its public functions increasing, in both internal and external politics, the control of the state over all social relations and interests made enormous strides. The existing contracts, however, did not adequately guarantee representative participation in the bureaucratic expansion of the early modern state with its consolidation of central government; this was taking place independently of developments in representative institutions. The old agreements had originally dealt in the main with the general *conditions* of late feudal representative monarchy and had provided methods to insure that these conditions were kept; the later contracts of the sixteenth century concerned the immutable *legal and moral relation* between the prince and the estates, guaranteeing local, regional and religious privileges. What mattered now, however, was the influence of the estates over the increasingly solid *institutions* of political rule, centred in the court and the residence. A struggle now began against a power which was trying to set aside the advisory or executive institutions of the estates of the *monarchia mixta* in the spheres of government, administration, and the law. Until now the supervisory function of the estates had been secured on a personal level; now they demanded an active role in central government and the documentation of all governmental and administrative functions in this central area, which was increasingly imbued with the spirit of Bodinian sovereignty.

The further development of these written statements of political functions within the framework of a changing society and economy led, after the periods of representative monarchy and absolutism, to the constitutions of the present day. It has been their function, since the written constitutions of the North American states and the French Revolution,[8] to define "the total structure of the state in a single written document" and to lay down "certain basic propositions concerning its essential structure".[9] Under the constitutional monarchies of the nineteenth century, such instruments were agreed mainly between the ruler and the elected national assembly. They determined the areas of competence proper to the different organs of state, the king, the government, the national assembly and the law, as well as state bodies like the civil service and the army; in addition they laid down the principles underlying the cultural, social and economic order.

As in the case of all historical development, the line from contractual monarchy to modern constitutionalism was not straight. Only in the organization of the government apparatus can one see a purposeful development. The other side of political life, the part played by representative institutions,[10] suffered a severe setback in the age of Absolutism and was realized only piecemeal, in new forms and in a new spirit, by revolutionary acts. In the period of representative constitutions we find the most varied attempts on the part of the estates to secure participation in the organs of state which were evolving under the guidance of the sovereign, in the expanding administrative and legal apparatus, in military affairs, and particularly in the financial and fiscal sphere. We find numerous moves being made in this direction in the grievances and remonstrances, in the ordinances proposed either by individual estates or by the full representative body, in renewals of privileges, in resolutions of the imperial diet and the state assemblies, in the drafting of electoral capitulations, charters, and royal promises.

The *gravamina* or *cahiers* represent a great field for comparative research in representative government, for they contain the actual picture of the state and society seen from the point of view of the estates themselves. It is important that they should be examined, for only when they have been shall we be able to describe the corporative system in its entirety, because only then shall we see fully how the estates understood, both intellectually and politically, the problem of the early modern period, which was (in the words of Näf) "how a government and a country could combine to become a state". Only then shall we be able to document afresh the underlying shift of power towards solidly organized political institutions. It is not enough to analyse and reanalyse the liberties and privileges of the corporations and the standing orders, rights and functions of the assemblies. Instead we must reconstruct from their demands and grievances the legal, economic and social order they sought, the political aims that were envisaged in the corporative state. Only by doing this can we hope to understand and reconstruct the gradual transformation both of the estates and of their comprehension of the state and society during the historical development that took place in the early modern period. We still do not know how the estates and their assemblies saw themselves between the mid-sixteenth and the mid-seventeenth centuries. On the one hand we rely far too much on the great theoreticians of representative government and their abstract models, which are all too often out of step with pragmatic views or at variance with the demands of practical estate politicians; on the other hand we direct our attention too single-mindedly to the onset of the age of monarchical absolutism, which we tend to interpret in an all too monistic manner.

In the period around 1650 there is a striking proliferation of written "forms of government". There are documents from England (1653), Sweden (1634), the Holy Roman Empire (1648), Pomerania (1634) and Ducal Prussia (1661); these have not yet been considered jointly as products of the transition to the modern constitutional state. Four of them, significantly, have the word "government" in their titles: the English "Instrument of Government" or "The Government of the Commonwealth of England", the Swedish *regeringsform*, the Pomeranian *Regierungsform*, and the Prussian *Regierungsverfassung*. However, at this period the German term *Regierung* embraced more than it does now, just as today the English word "government" has a wider meaning than the German word, denoting the total political system, both executive and parliament.[11] The occasion for the emergence of these documents was the confrontation between demands for guarantees of representative government and the ruler's efforts to achieve sovereignty, between the liberty of the nobles and the rule of the king, between corporative opposition and the early modern state. "The seventeenth century is a century of revolts."[12]

The French Fronde (1648–53) was an open civil war against the principle of the absolutist state.[13] It led to various proposals for the organization of the state and society made by the estates and corporations, which were divided among themselves. France's supreme court of law, the Parlement de Paris, expressed its views most clearly in an interesting document of June and July 1648, in association with the *cours souveraines* of finance and accounts; these were firmly in the hands of the *noblesse de robe* through the sale of offices, and they possessed political rights.[14] The document proposed, in twenty-seven articles, "a programme for political and administrative revolution",[15] a plan for a limited government constitution. The very first article demanded the removal of the new *intendants*, the efficient provincial agents of the crown. The consent of the sovereign courts was to be required for the establishment of new offices and the appointment of all officials. This meant that the whole bureaucratic apparatus was to be dependent on the *Messieurs du Parlement*. Thus, separate articles dealt with the areas of administration, jurisdiction, taxes, finance and the economy. The programme of reform was aimed at making the king's government dependent on the *cours souveraines*, especially the Parlement de Paris, which saw itself as representing the Estates General, a kind of Estates General in miniature. The defeat of the Fronde prevented the conclusion of a new contract which would have amounted to a constitution.

In seventeenth-century England the theory of religious and political contracts enjoyed such popularity that laws and other measures passed by Parliament were seen by both King and people as binding contracts between them.[16] In parliamentary debates and discussions in the army, the English revolutionaries gradually evolved the idea of a written constitution. In 1628 Parliament had drawn up a list of constitutional demands in the Petition of Right, a document directed at the alleged illegality of absolute monarchy. Twenty years later the army set itself the task of "creating a stable and lasting relation between King and Parliament whose legal form would embrace all areas of the state and precisely delimit the competence of every organ of power".[17] What was modern about it was the democratic form in which the people's rights were to be defined and guaranteed in relation to those of the government. The army debates of the 1640s[18] led to two draft constitutions, the "Heads of the Proposals" and the "Agreement of the People" in various versions.[19] During the deliberations of the officers' council in Putney, the concept of a constitution in the modern sense emerged with increasing clarity; the exercise of governmental power was to be limited to fixed periods and certain areas, and a description of government organization was worked out. However, it was only in December 1653, and under different circumstances, that the army officers produced the final draft of a written constitution, the "Instrument of Government", consisting of forty-two articles.[20] The first article placed the supreme command of the army, the fleet and the executive firmly in the hands of the Lord Protector and a small Council of State, in whose composition Parliament was accorded a limited right of nomination. The holders of high government offices were to be chosen by Parliament, or by the Council of State with parliamentary ratification. The Lord Protector was guaranteed adequate taxes for the army, the navy and the civil service. The legislative power was to be exercised by Parliament; the term for which it was elected, the composition of the electorate and the procedure for elections were set out in detail. Thus for seven years England had a constitution which took cognizance of the realities of the modern state such as the civil service, the army and the navy. The English republic was a puritan military oligarchy; it was based on a constitution which replaced a contractual agreement with the ruler and older conventions.

In Sweden in the sixteenth and early seventeenth centuries the King made promises to his subjects on his accession; so too did the King of Denmark on his election. These promises were a form of contract between the sovereign and the estates, guaranteeing the personal and material rights of the nobility, especially the higher nobility, and its influence on the life of the state.[21] In 1634, during the minority of Queen Christina, the Swedish diet passed the famous *regeringsform*,[22] consisting of sixty-five paragraphs; this was a fundamental law which regulated and perfected the organization of the higher bureaucracy in the interest of the estates.[23] It is the first constitutional document of our time. It increased the number of colleges from three (the High Court, the Chancery and the Audit Office) to five by creating the Army Council, which was important to Sweden's pursuit of great power politics, and the Admiralty. The structure of each of these offices of government was laid down, and they were controlled by the *Riksråd*, a self-perpetuating college of twenty-five members drawn from the upper nobility. "In reality", remarks Herlitz, the Swedish constitutional historian, "it was the *Riksråd* which conducted government business."[24]

Paragraph 14 laid down that the five colleges should reside permanently in the capital and remain "continually active", regardless of the presence or absence of one or other member of the *Riksråd*. Itinerant government was thus ended; the administration now sat permanently in one place. This was understandable after the long absences of Gustavus Adolphus on military campaigns. The provincial organs, whether courts of law or branches of the general, fiscal, or military administration, were subordinated to the five colleges and obliged to submit reports of their activities (paragraph 36). Civil, military, and legal administration were thoroughly organized and kept strictly separate; their officials were subordinated to the public prosecutor in the highest court and inspected once a year by the five colleges. Other paragraphs laid down regulations for the work of the civil service which were similar to those obtaining in France under absolutist rule at this and later periods, though here all authority was vested in the *Riksråd*, and this was drawn from the estates. Here, then, we have a representative constitution which lays down the expanding form of the early modern state.

Later modifications did not affect the existing principle of organization or its framework. By collaborating closely with the chancellor, the kings gained greater influence. The academic controversy as to whether the instrument of 1634 was really intended to be "perpetual" (*evärdeligen*), as it was called, or only provisional, is peripheral to our investigation into the connection between constitutions and the organization of government.[25] In 1660 the *additament* voted by the *Riksdag* gave greater representation to the commons; it is to be regarded as a part of the constitution. Twenty years later, however, the *regeringsform* of 1634 was repealed by a constitutional declaration of the *Riksdag*, and formal expression was given to the change in 1682, when the *Riksråd* was renamed the "Royal Council" (*Kungligt Råd*). The rule of the upper nobility was terminated, but the organization of the colleges and their lower instances was retained. For the next forty years their presidents were appointed by the King, who by law had sovereign power.[26]

The electoral monarchy of Denmark belongs to the same constitutional area and, though only indirectly relevant to our present concerns, it displays some typical tendencies of the period. In 1648 the throne passed from Christian IV to Frederick III, and the new monarch, in the traditional electoral promises drawn up by the estates, not only confirmed the existing position of the 150 families of the higher nobility in the *Rigsraad*, but was obliged to give them a much greater share in government. Government by the three high offices of state was extended by the creation of three more. For each of these the nobles proposed three of their number, of whom the King chose one. The regional nobility was entitled to propose a successor to any counsellor who died. This fusion of the nobility and the upper bureaucracy is to be found in both central and local government, where officials could be appointed and dismissed only with the approval of the *Rigsraad*. Ten years later, however, the citizens of Copenhagen were placed on a par with the nobility by being allowed to hold offices of state.

In 1660 the fundamental legal shift to absolute rule began.[27] At one of the rare meetings of all the estates – nobles, clergy and towns – the two latter moved to repeal all electoral promises and declare the kingdom a hereditary monarchy. The *Rigsraad* gave way under military pressure; its archives were moved to the royal castle, and the central administration was re-organized by the King. The rule of the aristocracy was over. The new basic law, the *Lex Regia* of 1665,[28] declared, in the first eight of its forty paragraphs, that the King had absolute power in legislation, over home and foreign affairs, the army, the civil service, the church and over questions of war and peace. Paragraph 17 relieved him of any duty incurred by "oath or prescribed obligations", in other words of any contract made with the estates. This constitutional law was kept secret until 1709. We cannot discuss here the national and international background of this revolutionary change. We are concerned only with the way governmental organization was laid down by law: in the one case corporatively, in the promises of 1648, in the other autocratically, in the royal act of 1665.

In two German states on the Baltic there are two more constitutional documents which have not been considered before in this general context. The name of one of them, the *Regierungsform* of the Duchy of Pomerania, is strikingly like that of the Swedish constitution, which was approved in 1634, a mere four months before the Duke of Pomerania was obliged to subscribe to the Pomeranian constitution. The other is from Ducal Prussia, the *Instrument die neue Regierungsverfassung betreffend* ("Instrument concerning the new government constitution") of 1661; its name is not unlike the English constitution of 1653, but there is no similarity of content. It is intriguing to note that its author was a Pomeranian nobleman, who was charged with the task as privy councillor to the Elector of Brandenburg.

Let us consider first the Pomeranian document, which originated during the turmoil of the Thirty Years' War. After the occupation of Pomerania by Gustavus Adolphus in 1630, the military administration of the duchy passed into Swedish control, while the civil administration remained in the hands of the ducal government. In order to ensure an indigenous government and the rights of the estates after the death of the childless duke, when Pomerania was expected to pass to Brandenburg or Sweden, the estates and the ducal government wished to perpetuate the existing régime by giving it a written constitution. There thus arose the jointly drafted *Regierungsform*, which the duke issued in November 1634 as a "recess and constitution".[29]

After establishing Lutheran Protestantism as the religion of the Pomeranian church for all time and after confirming all the national privileges and fundamental laws, the constitution deals *in extenso* with the form of government. Existing institutions are to remain unaltered.[30] For the internal and external policy of the Duke and the estates, however, a new authority is created, a college of government counsellors made up of the former heads of government bodies. The ruler is bound by the decisions of this supreme directorate in ecclesiastical, political and economic affairs. The functions and tasks of the government offices, the High Court and the Church Council (the *Konsistorium*), are specified in precise detail. Finally, the government counsellors are guaranteed the protection, not only of the Duke, but of the "country counsellors" (*Landräte*). This document is a model representative constitution, the ratification of which could have been forced only from a Duke who was incapable of governing, as was later stressed by the King of Sweden and the Elector of Brandenburg, both of whom, as the Duke's successors, were being invited to subscribe to it. The typical institutions of the early modern state are placed under the direction or supervision of the estates, and the entire bureaucracy is placed under their protection. The estates were thinking of themselves, and they made sure of three things: the right to administer their own affairs, the appointment of indigenous officials only, and their own participation in all the rights of sovereignty. At a time when in France Richelieu was building up a central administration independent of the estates, in Sweden and Pomerania the aristocratic or representative state was being secured by official constitutional documents.

[. . .]

The constitutional articles of the Peace of Westphalia made the development of the Holy Roman Empire into an early modern state not only difficult, but impossible; yet at the same time they did not facilitate a representative structure. The next meeting of the Imperial Diet in 1653–4 failed to solve the constitutional problems referred to it. Constitutional reform was broken off; for no viable central or even regional organization for the governance of the Empire took shape. The tasks proper to the Empire as such were in the end carried out by the major princes acting on their own authority.

The Peace of Westphalia is one of the fundamental laws of the Empire and was incorporated into subsequent electoral capitulations. These were in each case negotiated by the Electors in the name of the Empire, and from 1519 onwards they were numbered among the great contractual documents which made up the representative constitution of the Empire; they represented its "fundamental laws" before such a concept existed.[31] The constitutional and legal historian sees them as important precursors of the constitutions of today, as a kind of constitutional instrument. The Peace of Westphalia speaks of the existing *constitutions et leges fundamentales* in the Empire, applying the term to the Golden Bull of 1356, which for four and a half centuries laid down the legal procedure for the election of the Emperor.

Even if the concept of a *constitutio* had a part to play in the seventeenth century, that of the *leges fundamentals* was more important.[32] In France we find the term *lois fondamentales* in use from 1576, in place of the *anciennes lois du Royaume*; in England the term *fundamental law* is applied, for example, to Magna Charta, from the beginning of the seventeenth century. The Swedish chancellor Oxenstierna reckoned the *regeringsform* of 1634, among other items, among his country's fundamental laws (*grundleger*), and we have already encountered the German *Fundamentalgesetz* in the Pomeranian *Regierungsform* of 1634. The term *lex fundamentalis* was known in Germany before 1600. Friedrich Pruckmann, who was professor at Frankfurt an der Oder and later chancellor to the Elector of Brandenburg, speaks in 1591 in his *Paragraphus soluta potestas* of the Salic Law as the *lex fundamentalis florentissimi Galliae regni*.[33] The German combination of the terms "imperial constitution and fundamental laws" has parallels throughout Europe.[34]

The picture that has been sketched here of the transition from ruling contracts to constitutional instruments is one of bewildering variety. The individual developments in the seventeenth century are as varied as their results. Let us try to sum up. We will exclude the programmes of the French Fronde from our summary, since the revolt against the crown, while belonging to the general picture of constitutional agitation in Europe, did not lead to any kind of constitutional settlement. Here the development of the early modern state had already progressed farther than elsewhere and in a direction favourable to the monarchy.

This indicates the essential motive behind the constitutional developments, viz. the struggle for the early modern state, participation of the estates at court and government level, and the determination of the rights of the parties concerned. This is to be seen in a religious and social context. The constitutional documents were attempts to reach lasting settlements in these matters or to perpetuate existing arrangements in documentary form. The motive was the same in all those countries we have considered. The early contracts with the rulers betray little interest in central government proper, which was only then taking shape. These are later modified to become agreements concerned principally with the relations between central government and the estates. The documents now lay down the tasks and structure of the government, the number of government offices there are to be, who is to hold them, and even how members of the government or heads of departments are to be appointed.

The immediate causes vary. In the England of Cromwell it was the struggle between Parliament and the Army that led to the constitution, in Sweden the prolonged absence of the monarch owing to the war and finally the minority of Queen Christina, in Pomerania the anticipated extinction of the local dynasty and the forthcoming accession of a foreign prince, in Prussia the recognition of the new sovereign's rights, in the Empire the experience of a victorious Emperor intent upon absolute monarchy. Behind these various causes a common motive can be discerned, the expansion and strengthening of the state and its administration at the highest level as a result of military requirements. The protracted wars changed the political and social scene. During them the early modern state, in a series of sudden jolts, became institutionalized and consolidated at the central and regional level as a bureaucratic structure. In this situation the privileges of the estates were impaired, and their rights remained under constant threat. Legislation by the monarch and the issuing of ordinances set in motion an authoritative power-mechanism, the continual expansion of state business and state instruments. The imperial and territorial estates sought to protect themselves by means of constitutions. In sovereign East Prussia the principle only seems to have been reversed: the fundamental question remained the same.

The documents deal in the main only with the top level of administration in the composite state or its constituent parts. Administration at the local level, the relation between the central government and the towns and manors is hardly mentioned, if at all. This reflects the view the estates had of themselves and feudal society, at first hardly any different from the one the rulers had as lords of their domains. Hence it reflects also the actual development of the early modern state, which left the towns and manors – the country – to be administered by the authorities of the estates.

In England the constitution drafted by the officers' council in 1653 makes a more clear-cut division between the executive and the legislature, government and parliament. Under the rule of Cromwell a modern government was financially secured. The parliamentary organization and specified election procedures for the property-owning class points forward to new forms of representative government. This constitution and the other English constitutional projects have little formal connection with contracts with the ruler, even though Magna Charta was continually being invoked as a fundamental law. It is a different matter with the Swedish, Pomeranian and Prussian constitutions we have considered, as well as Article VIII of the treaty of Osnabrück affecting the Holy Roman Empire. They go back in a direct line to the early contracts, electoral capitulations and fundamental laws. The terms of the constitutions, especially those of Sweden, Pomerania and Prussia, secure the aristocratic nature of representative government. (This applies also to the Danish charter of 1648.) In these four countries the offices of government were in the hands of the nobles. There was a personal union, constitutionally laid down, between the government and the aristocracy. The same is not true of the highest authorities of the old German Empire. The influence of the Arch-chancellor, the Elector of Mainz, on appointments to the Imperial Court Chancery was controversial. The members of the Aulic Council and the Privy Council were appointed by the Emperor himself, the Imperial Estates being excluded. Direct participation by the Estates was guaranteed only in the Imperial Cameral Court after 1495. However, the Empire never became a typical early modern state with a strong central government.

In the later constitutional moves towards absolutism in Denmark and Sweden we witness the growing tension between the upper and the lower nobility, with the middle class involved in the struggle against the privileges of the nobles. The estates clearly lacked cohesion, and the political and economic interests of the individual classes diverged. This fact was exploited by the monarchy in all those states which were progressing towards absolutism – Sweden, Denmark and the Brandenburg-Prussian monarchy as a whole. In the composite states with absolute monarchies, representative participation in government was eliminated, and the development of the central administration accelerated all the more. The monarch prevented any observation of the workings and functions of his bureaucracy, and his directives were kept secret. The new civil service of the monarchy, drawn from the upper and middle classes, was a uniform social stratum, serving the state, dependent on the monarch, firmly bound to him, and imbued with the spirit of the military and economic state.

The early contracts are viewed by scholars as measures adopted by the estates to counter the growing institutional power of the princes at the end of the feudal period. I should like to regard the continental constitutions of the mid-seventeenth century as parallel phenomena, representing a reaction against monarchical government and the increasing power of the bureaucracy in the early modern state at the end of the period of the participation of the estates in government.

The air was full of contractual ideas, which led to very varied theories and written forms of the mixed constitution. The doctrine of the mixed constitution (*forma mixta, respublica mixta, gouvernement mixte, mixed government,* etc.) was popular throughout Europe in early modern times; it was the theory of the obsolescent corporative state. This theory has yet to be examined in an international context.[35] The Calvinists, especially in England, endeavoured to find "the structure of an ideally formed church constitution"; they were also inspired by a corresponding desire for "a well-considered shaping of the constitution of the state."[36] This was clearly the defensive stance of the estates towards the absolutist tendencies in government produced by the exigencies of war. The corporative state was bound to react against the obvious facts of administrative and military developments. In English history such struggles, together with the documents and constitutions resulting from them, represent a mere episode. In Sweden and Prussia they mark a period of delay before the triumph of absolutism in the closing decades of the seventeenth century. In the Holy Roman Empire, on the other hand, the constitutional provisions of the Peace of Westphalia had a stabilizing effect lasting for a hundred and fifty years amid the changing constitutional scene of modern Europe.

The various constitutions and draft constitutions of the large and small European states thus have a common background. Growing state organization and monarchical bureaucracy, the proliferation of state institutions and increasing centralization and monopolization combined to inaugurate a new period of confrontation between the monarch and the estates. A new problem was added to the existing disputes between the ruler and the representative assemblies, viz. the distribution of power in the developing bureaucracy. This new problem affected the thinking and conduct of both sides. What was involved was the relative weighting of the parties in the unbalanced constitutions of the aristocratic monarchy, *monarchia mixta*. The new European state-system, which was the basis of the European domination of the world, thus began before the period of absolutism; in fact it was one of the factors that made absolutism possible.[37]

If we consider the geographical positions of the four states we have discussed, we are reminded of the models proposed by Otto Hintze with regard to the typology of representative constitutions. This expert in the history of feudalism and the Old Régime divided the states of Europe into those which had belonged to the Carolingian empire and those which had not. Feudalism, in the full sense of the term, was limited to those that had, dissolving all the old forms of local and regional organization and laying the ground for new local régimes. In the countries on the periphery, on the other hand, feudalism was not established completely or permanently, and older regional groupings were preserved. This is the starting point for Hintze's two types of representative constitution. The first type, the two-chamber system of representation, was at home in those countries surrounding the nucleus of the old Carolingian Empire – England, the Scandinavian countries, Poland, Hungary and Bohemia. To this type the constitution of the Empire also belongs. Most of the German states west of the Elbe Hintze regarded as belonging to the tricameral type, represented in western Europe notably by France and Aragon: those to the east belonged to the first, i.e. the two-chamber type.[38] It is striking that the representative systems of the outlying countries, which according to Hintze belonged together, viz. England, Sweden and the duchies east of the Elbe – Pomerania and Prussia – together with the Holy Roman Empire, were the first to experiment with written constitutions. Their constitutional documents seem to lend some support to Hintze's typology.[39]

The existence and development of representative constitutions in the age of absolutism needs to be further illuminated by comparative studies. In addition to the constitutional and political questions discussed here, we must consider the social and economic conditions which I have hitherto left out of account. The rivalries between the French *noblesse d'épée* and the *noblesse de robe*, the unique position of the gentry in the English House of Commons, the forces supporting and opposing the rule of the high nobility in the Swedish *Riksråd*, the ascendancy of the knights in Pomerania and Prussia – in all these instances the estates and political classes were in conflict with the crown, the court and the government: this is the field of forces which Marxist scholars in eastern Europe have investigated in recent years as a socio-economic question in terms of the class war.[40] However, we must beware of plumping for monocausal explanations.

The system of state government was undoubtedly the most important form of organization in society during this century of revolts, this period of transition from contractual monarchy to constitutionalism. Government was the highest institution in the changing political and social scene, and it was a subject of controversy. In each country it possessed a general and a peculiarly national dynamism which, starting from seemingly identical or similar structures, produced differing results in the middle or long term. The constitutional instruments of the seventeenth century do not embody political theories to the same extent as those of the eighteenth, but spring from the pragmatic needs of the state and society, testifying to the shift in organization from the corporative to the sovereign state.[41] The concentration of "governmental authority over the country and its population in the hands of one person or body", an authority which under feudalism and even under the corporative state was dispersed and in each case limited,[42] is the most important development of the early modern period, and it extends to the present day. True, the separate countries of Europe evolved in their own ways, but when all is said and done they were pursuing the same end: they were all working towards the sovereign state and its apparatus of government – *gubernatio et administratio*.

NOTES

1 The texts are found in J. Dennert (ed.), *Beza, Brutus, Hotman. Calvinistische Monarchomachen* (Klassiker der Politik 8), Cologne 1968. See also G. Stricker, *Das politische Denken der Monarchomachen* (diss.), Heidelberg 1967. Althusius summed up the contractual doctrine in one sentence: "Constitutio Magistratus est, qua ille à populo, vel nomine poluil, ab Ephoris, pacto reciproco & mutuo consensu constitutus Imperium & administrationem Reipub. seu regni suscipit" (J. Althusius, *Politica methodice digesta*, Herborn [3]1614, cap. XV, pp. 167f.). The connection between the basic terms *imperium* and *administratio* is important. The conditions of accession are stated as "to rule piously and justly in accordance with the laws".

2 W. Näf, "Herrschaftsverträge und Lehre vom Herrschaftsvertrag", *Schweizer Beiträge zur Allgemeinen Geschichte* 7 (1949) 26–52, esp. 43ff. The texts were edited by Näf under the title *Herrschaftsverträge des Spätmittelalters* (Quellen zur Neueren Geschichte hg. vom Histor. Seminar d. Univ. Bern 17), Berne 1951. The contractual doctrine is traced from ancient times up to Hegel with excerpts from texts by A. Voigt (ed.), *Der Herrschaftsvertrag*. Übersetzungen von P. Badura und H. Hofmann (Politica 16), Neuwied 1965; this contains a bibliography. See also J. Gough, *The Social Contract*, Oxford [2]1957; I.-M. Peters, "Der Ripener Vertrag und die Ausbildung der landständischen Verfassung in Schleswig-Holstein", *Blätter für deutsche Landesgeschichte* 109 (1973) 306ff., esp. notes 5, 6 and 24.

3 For greater detail see G. Oestreich and I. Auerbach, "Ständische Verfassung" in *Sowjetsystem und Demokratische Gesellschaft. Eine vergleichende Enzyklopädie* 6, Freiburg 1972, col. 211ff., esp. 218ff. (reprinted in *Strukturprobleme der frühen Neuzeit*, Berlin 1980, pp. 161–200).

4 Best known are the ordinances of the Holy Roman Empire for 1500 and 1521. (K. Zeumer, *Quellensammlung zur Geschichte der deutschen Reichsverfassung in Mittelalter und Neuzeit*, Tübingen [2]1913, nos. 177 (pp. 297–307) and 182 (pp. 318–24).

5 C. H. McIlwain (ed.), *The Political Works of James I*, New York 1965, p. 68f. James I's treatise *The Trew Law of Free Monarchies: or the Reciprock and Mutuall Dutie Betwixt a Free King, and his Naturall*

Subjects of 1598 indicates the formula in its title. In the text he uses such terms as "mutuall pactation", "contract betwixt two parties" and "contractors".

6 The individual passages are treated by W. Förster, *Thomas Hobbes und der Puritanismus*, Berlin 1969, p. 74ff.

7 Trevor-Roper has more than once described the "Renaissance State", 1500–1600. It is for him 'a great and expanding bureaucracy, a huge system of administrative centralisation, staffed by an ever-growing multitude of "courtiers" and "officers"'. (H. R. Trevor-Roper, "The General Crisis of the 17th Century", *Past and Present* 16 (1959) 42). I cannot go into the extensive discussion arising from Trevor-Roper's Crisis theory, but I regard it as important in the present connection, since the history of institutions and social history are closely related. Cf. T. Aston (ed.) *Crisis in Europe, 1560–1660. Essays from Past and Present*, London 1965.

8 W. Näf, "Der Durchbruch des Verfassungsgedankens im 18. Jahrhundert', *Schweizer Beiträge zur Allgemeinen Geschichte* 11 (1953) 108–20; O. Hintze, "Der Durchbruch des bürgerlinch-demokratischen Nationalstaates in der amerikanischen und der französischen Revolution", id. *Staat und Verfassung, Gesammelte Abhandlungen* 1 (3rd edn. by G. Oestreich), Göttingen 1970, pp. 503–10.

9 H. Heller, *Staatslehre*, Leiden 1934, p. 270.

10 On the meaning of the word "representation" at this period see H. Hofmann, *Repräsentation. Studien zur Wort- und Begriffsgeschichte von der Antike bis ins 19. Jahrhundert*, Berlin 1974, pp. 336ff.

11 The English word "government" still has two senses – "the ruling authority in a state" and "the organization of the state"; see E. Fraenkel, *Das amerikanische Regierungssystem*, Cologne 1960, pp. 181f. and note. On the more extensive sense of "gouvernement" in Bodin and his contemporaries cf. H. Quaritsch, *Staat und Souveränität I, Die Grundlagen*, Frankfurt 1970, pp. 308ff. W. Rothschild, *Der Gedanke der geschriebenen Verfassung in der englischen Revolution*, Tübingen 1903, p. 28, n. I, often uses the word "government" in the sense of "constitution" or "constitutional instrument"; this is suggested to him by Carlyle's interpretation of a speech by Cromwell. For mid-seventeenth century see W. Frotscher, *Regierung als Rechtsbegriff. Verfassungsrechtliche und staatstheoretische Grundlagen unter Berücksichtigung der englischen und französischen Verfassungsentwicklung*, Berlin 1975. Frotscher deals with England on pp. 17ff., France on pp. 44ff. and Germany on pp. 83ff. The term "Regierungsform" goes back to Bodin, who distinguished in 1576 between the state and the government: "L'estat d'une République est différent du gouvernement & administration d'icelle.' Cf. H. Quaritsch, op. cit., pp. 305ff. and H. Denzer, "Bodins Staatsformenlehre', id. (ed.), *Jean Bodin. Verhandlungen der internationalen Bodin-Tagung in München*, Munich 1973, pp. 233–44.

12 R. Mousnier, *L'Assassinat d'Henri IV*, Paris 1964. On the controversy between Porshnev and Mousnier over the significance and character of the popular revolts cf. the literature listed by H. Kretzer, *Calvinismus und französische Monarchie im 17. Jahrhundert*, Berlin 1975, pp. 20 and 42. Also D. Parker, "The Social Foundation of French Absolutism", *Past and Present* 53 (1971).

13 E. H. Kossmann, *La Fronde*, Leiden 1954.

14 "Deliberations arrêtées en l'assemblée des cours souveraines, tenues et commencées en la chambre Saint-Louis le 30 juin 1648" in Isambert, *Recueil général des anciennes lois françaises depuis l'an 420 jusqu'à la révolution de 1789*, 1–29, Paris 1821–33, here 17, pp. 72–84.

15 A. Bourde, "Frankreich vom Ende des Hundertjährigen Krieges bis zum Beginn der Selbstherrschaft Ludwigs XIV. (1453–1661)" in T. Schieder (ed.), *Handbuch der europäischen Geschichte 3*, Stuttgart 1971, p. 813. P. R. Doolin, *The Fonde*, Cambridge, Mass. 1935, p. 11, speaks of "a radical reformation of the institutions of the monarchy . . . a move which touched the government in a vital spot."

16 G. A. Ritter, *Parlament und Demokratie in Grossbritannien*, Göttingen 1972, pp. 52f.

17 W. Rothschild, op. cit., p. 17.

18 Their minutes are printed by A. S. P. Woodhouse (ed.), *Puritanism and Liberty. Being the Army Debates from the Clark Manuscripts (1647/48)*, London [3]1966.

19 S. R. Gardiner, *The Constitutional Documents of the Puritan Revolution 1625–60*, Oxford [3]1906, repr. 1951, pp. 316ff. and 333ff.

20 Ibid., pp. 405ff. On its contents and for an evaluation of it as a written constitution see D. L. Keir, *The Constitutional History of Modern Britain since 1485*, London [9]1969, p. 225f.: "A fundamental and

organic law . . . the Protectoral Power set up by a military junto'. On administration under the Protectorate see G. E. Aylmer, *The State's Servants. The Civil Service of the English Republic 1649–1660*, London 1973, esp. p. 45ff. On the takeover of the administrative business of royal institutions by parliamentary committees, see index under "Committees".

21 N. Herlitz, *Grundzüge der schwedischen Verfassungsgeschichte*, Rostock 1939, pp. 92f.

22 E. Hildebrand (ed.), *Sveriges Regeringsformer 1634–1809 samt Konungaförsäkringar 1611–1800*, Stockholm 1891, pp. 1–41; English translation: M. Roberts (ed.), *Sweden as a Great Power 1611–1697. Government, Society, Foreign Policy* (Documents of Modern History, ed. by A. G. Dickson and A. Davies), London 1968, pp. 18–28. For the older discussions of the *Regeringsform* of 1634 see the literature listed by A. v. Brandt, "Die nordischen Länder 1448–1654", in T. Schieder (ed.), *Handbuch der europäischen Geschichte 3*, Stuttgart 1971, pp. 994 and 1001.

23 On Swedish constitutional history generally see E. Schieche, "Der schwedische Ratskonstitutionalismus im 17. Jahrhundert" in *Spiegel der Geschichte. Festgabe Max Braubach*, Münster 1964, pp. 388–428, esp. 408–11. See also M. Roberts, *Essays in Swedish History*, London 1967, pp. 14–55. Roberts states (p. 25, n. 49) that Oxenstierna interpreted the *Regeringsform* as establishing the existing system legally in an ordered, logical, contemporary government mechanism. On p. 26 the *Regeringsform* is held to be not a triumph of the constitutionalism of the *Riksråd*, but rather the harbinger of its decline. I am grateful to Dr Kersten Krüger for helping me with the Scandinavian literature.

24 N. Herlitz, op. cit., p. 109.

25 The latest discussion of the *regeringsform* from this point of view is by H. A. Olsson, "1634 års regeringsform – lag eller provisorium?", *Histor. Tidskrift* 1972, 2, with a summary in German, pp. 216f. Olsson speaks of the "constitution" which was accepted by the *Riksdag* only as a provisional measure. Queen Christina did not sign it on reaching her majority.

26 On subsequent developments see S. U. Palme, "Vom Absolutismus zum Parlamentarismus in Schweden" in D. Gerhard (ed.), *Ständische Vertretungen in Europa im 17. und 18. Jahrhundert*, Göttingen [2]1974, pp. 368–97. The declaration of sovereignty of 1693 makes the king "responsible to no one on earth for his actions". The Swedish declaration of sovereignty and the Danish *Lex regia* abrogate the representative constitution and introduce absolute rule by law.

27 On this area as a whole see D. Gerhard, "Probleme des dänischen Frühabsolutismus' in *Dauer und Wandel der Geschichte. Festgabe für Kurt von Raumer*, Münster 1965, pp. 269–92.

28 The fundamental work on the subject is still K. Fabricius, *Kongeloven*, Copenhagen 1920. See also E. Wolgast, *Lex Regia. Das dänische und das deutsche Staatsführungsgesetz (1665 bzw. 1934)*, Würzburg 1935 (with a German translation of the Lex Regia by T. Olshausen 1838), English translation by E. Ekman, "The Danish Royal Law", *Journal of Modern History*, 29, 1957, pp. 102–7. The government bodies were streamlined in 1670 by bringing the heads of the colleges into the king's privy council.

29 J. C. Dähnert, *Sammlung Pommerscher und Rügischer Landes-Urkunden 1*, Stralsund 1765, pp. 337–58, printed under the incorrect heading "Die Fürstliche Pommersche Regiments-Verfassung". R. Petsch, *Verfassung und Verwaltung Hinterpommerns im siebzehnten Jahrhundert bis zur Einverleibung in den brandenburgischen Staat*, Leipzig 1907, p. 61 et passim, also speaks of the "Regimentsverfassung".

30 ". . . dass Land und Leute nicht glücklicher und pflegasmer, als unter einer angewöhnten und ihnen hiebevor fürträglich befundenen Regierungs-Form, guberniret werden können" (". . . that the land and the people cannot be governed more happily and more carefully than under a form of government to which they are accustomed and which they have hitherto found acceptable"), Dähnert, op. cit., p. 338.

31 G. Kleinheyer, *Die kaiserlichen Wahlkapitulationen. Geschichte, Wesen und Funktion*, Karlsruhe 1968; F. Hartung, "Die Wahlkapitulationen der deutschen Kaiser und Könige", *Historische Zeitschrift 107* (1911) 306–44 repr. id., *Volk und Staat in der deutschen Geschichte. Gesammelte Abhandlungen*, Leipzig 1940, pp. 67–93.

32 Occurrences of the term in the work of German publicists since 1630 are given by G. Kleinheyer, "Grundrechte" in O. Brunner, W. Conze and R. Koselleck, *Geschichtliche Grundbegriffe 2*, Stuttgart 1975, p. 1055, n. 19. According to this article, Besold in 1625 counted the treaty of Tübingen among the "leges fundamentals". See also R. Grawert, "Leges fundamentals, Wahlkapitulationen", ibid. pp. 887–89 (under the catchword "Gesetz"). The history of the concept is treated by H. Quaritsch, *Staat und*

Souveränität 1, Frankfurt 1970, pp. 364f.; further occurrences of the term are listed in the index under "leges fundamentales'.

33 T. Klein, "Recht und Staat im Urteil mitteldeutscher Juristen des späten 16. Jahrhunderts' in *Festschrift Walter Schlesinger* 1 (*Mitteldeutsche Forschungen* 74, 1), Cologne 1973, p. 456. Petrus Heigius, in his commentary on institutions of 1603, counts the Golden Bull among the "leges fundamentales" of the Empire (ibid. p. 483).

34 Rather than give separate references, I refer in general to the following: A. Lemaire, *Les Lois fondamentales de la monarchie française d'après les théoriciens de l'ancien rèime*, Paris 1907; J. W. Gough, *Fundamental Law in English Constitutional History*, Oxford 1955; H. *Quaritsch*, op. cit. (n. 11), pp. 364ff.; G. Stourzh, *Vom Widerstandsrecht zur Verfassungsgerichtsbarkeit: Zum Problem der Verfassungswidrigkeit im 18. Jahrhundert*, Graz 1974, pp. 6ff.; G. Kleinheyer, op. cit. (n. 32 above). For a general view see H. O. Meisner, *Verfassung, Verwaltung, Regierung in neuerer Zeit* (*Sitzungsberichte der deutschen Akademie der Wissenschaften zu Berlin. Klasse für Philosophie, Geschichte . . .* , Jahrgang 1962, Nr. 1), Berlin 1962, pp. 6ff. Meisner distinguishes the "formal" and the "material" sense of "constitution". Constitutions in the material sense are recorded "in a large number of separate laws, edicts, ordinances, contracts with the estates, etc"; the "constitution" in a formal sense is a single comprehensive document. The combination "constitutioes et leges fundamentales" is found in the constitutional article of the Peace Treaty of Osnabrück, the Instrumentum Pacis Osnabrugensis, Art. VIII, §4.

35 The political doctrine of the mixed constitution was taught in almost all countries. In France it was represented by Seyssel, du Haillan, La Roche-Flavin and Joly. For England see C. C. Weston, "The theory of Mixed Monarchy under Charles I and after", *English Historical Review* 75 (1960) 426–43; id., *English Constitutional Theory and the House of Lords 1556–1832*, London 1965. For Germany see R. Hoke, *Die Reichsstaatslehre des Johannes Limnaeus*, Aalen 1968, pp. 152–209, with references to Gierke and Althusius. For Sweden see N. Runeby, *Monarchia Mixta. Maktfördelningsdebatt i Sverige under den tidigare stormaktstiden* (Studia historica Upsaliensia 6), Stockholm 1962 (summary in German on pp. 544–72). For Italy see R. de Mattei, "La teoria dello 'Stato misto' nel dottrinarismo del Seicento", *Rivista di studi politichi internazionali* 15 (1948) 406–36; id., "Difese ital. del 'governo misto' contro la critica negatrice del Bodin', in *Studi in onore di E. Crossa* 1, Milan 1960, pp. 739–57. The classical origins are discussed by K. v. Fritz, *The Theory of the Mixed Constitution in Antiquity. A Critical Analysis of Polybius's Political Ideas*, New York 1954. On the difference between "mixed government" and "separation of powers" see W. B. Gwyn, *The Meaning of the Separation of Powers*, The Hague 1965. The doctrine of the "status mixtus reipublicae" is briefly treated by O. Gierke, *Das deutsche Genossenschaftsrecht* 4, Berlin 1913, p. 219ff. See also H. Dreitzel, *Protestantischer Aristotelismus und absoluter Staat. Die "Politica" des Henning Arnisäus*, Wiesbaden 1970, pp. 285–97. For seventeenth-century sources see H. U. Scupin and U. Scheuner (eds.), *Althusius-Bibliographie. Bibliographie zur politischen Ideengeschichte und Staatslehre, zum Staatsrecht und zur Verfassungsgeschichte* (rev. by D. Wyduckel), Berlin 1973, nos. 3775, 3890, 4268, 5267, 5339.

36 Rothschild, op. cit. (n. 11 above), p. 2.

37 This is contrary to the older view of Otto Hintze (1901) and W. Mommsen (1938), which is still held by K. Malettke, "Frankreich und Europa im 17. und 18. Jahrhundert. Der französische Beitrag zur Entfaltung des frühmodernen, souveränen Staates", *Francia* 3 (1975) 327 and n. 15. The (early) modern state does not begin in the mid-seventeenth century, as Hintze later showed in 1931 in his article "Wesen und Wandlung des modernen Staates" in id. *Gesammelte Abhandlungen* (n. 9 above), pp. 470–96.

38 O. Hintze, op. cit., pp. 120–39 on the typology of western representative constitutions; pp. 140–85 on the historical conditions for the representative constitution (1930–1). Both articles in id. *Feudalismus – Kapitalismus* (ed. G. Oestreich), Göttingen 1970, pp. 48–113. The latter article in the English edition by F. Gilbert, *cit.* pp. 302–53, under the title of "The Preconditions of Representative Government in the Context of World History". See also G. Oestreich, "Ständestaat und Ständewesen im Werk Otto Hintzes", in D. Gerhard (ed.), *Ständische Vertretungen in Europa im 17. und 18. Jahrhundert*, Göttingen ²1974, pp. 56–71. This article has been reprinted in G. Oestreich, *Strukturprobleme der frühen Neuzeit*, ed. Brigitta Oestreich, Berlin 1980, pp. 145–60.

39 Recently these typological problems of the comparative history of representative government have been taken up again, on the foundations laid by O. Hintze and N. Elias, by H. G. Koenigsberger, *Dominium regale or Dominium politicum et regale. Monarchies and Parliaments in Early Modern Europe* (Inaugural Lecture in the Chair of History at University of London, King's College, 25 February 1975), pp. 4 or 7ff. Koenigsberger's statement that "Dominium politicum et regale was the norm" applies to all the constitutional documents we have considered.

40 Cf. I. Auerbach, "Die marxistisch-sowjetische Forschung" in the article by G. Oestreich and I. Auerbach "Ständische Verfassung" (see n. 3 above).

41 An oddity with regard to its comprehensiveness, durability and content is the constitution of the representative state of Mecklenburg, the agreement of Duke Christian Ludwig with the knights and the country on 18 April 1755 concerning the fundamental law relating to succession (*Landes-Grund-Gesetzlicher Erb-Vergleich*). This remained the constitutional document of the state until 1918. (Printed at Rostock, 1755, 286, 110 folio pages. In addition quarto and octavo. Other editions cited in W. Heess, *Geschichtliche Bibliographie von Mecklenburg* 1, Rostock 1944, pp. 409f. or 184–6.

42 E. W. Böckenförd, *Die verfassungstheoretische Unterscheidung von Staat und Gesellschaft als Bedingung individueller Freiheit* (Rheinisch-Westfälische Akademie der Wissenschaften, Vorträge G 183), Opladen 1973, pp. 10–21 (p. 11) with further literature.

22

THE PARADOXES OF STATE POWER

John Brewer

Between 1688 and 1714 the British state underwent a radical transformation, acquiring all of the main features of a powerful fiscal–military state: high taxes, a growing and well-organized civil administration, a standing army and the determination to act as a major European power. Why did this happen? Why, after a long period of comparative international isolation during which England had been a minor military power, did Britain become a major military and diplomatic actor?

The tendency has been to regard this abrupt and radical change as an inevitable consequence of Britain's successful involvement in the protracted and expensive struggles against Louis XIV. As Charles Tilly's pithy dictum puts it, "war made the state, and the state made war."[1]

And there is certainly no lack of evidence for this interpretation. Seventy-five per cent or more of England's public expenditure in this period went on waging war, and an even higher percentage of tax revenue was spent on military operations and on servicing the debts incurred in wartime. As we have seen, the fiscal and military departments dwarfed the rest of the bureaucracy. Their chief task was not to serve the welfare of the nation but to provide the resources – the money, supplies and manpower – which were the desiderata of an effective military power.

Though there can be little doubt that war was *responsible* for the expansion of the state, it does not follow that war therefore *caused* the expansion of the state apparatus. We have to push the question one stage further and ask why it was that English policy changed so markedly in the late seventeenth century, embroiling in a major European conflict the nation that had previously avoided such terrible conflagrations as the Thirty Years War.

On several occasions during the course of the seventeenth century, the monarch or head of state had attempted to involve his English subjects in European hostilities. Almost invariably he had been restrained by the fiscal conservatism and parsimony of the House of Commons. England did not lack the capacity to become a major belligerent, but the executive was unable to

John Brewer, "The Paradoxes of State Power," pp. 137–54, 161, 265–7 from *The Sinews of Power: War, Money and the English State, 1688–1715*. New York: Alfred A. Knopf, 1989.

overcome the fiscal constraints imposed by a legislature unwilling to provide the financial where-withal for the country to become a great power. Occasionally, of course, the government could call on exceptional resources and circumvent parliamentary restraint but, as both Charles I and Cromwell discovered, such a policy was fraught with difficulty and, in the long term, bound to excite opposition. For much of the seventeenth century the commons successfully limited the government's freedom of movement by keeping a tight rein on the public purse.

After 1688, however, and despite the hostility shown both in and out of parliament towards increased government spending, the crown was able to raise both income and expenditure to unprecedented levels. This is all the more surprising in view of the political independence of the lower house. The commons was far from being the lackey of the administration and frequently overturned or rejected government proposals. What needs to be explained, then, is why the commons was willing both to countenance and to finance a major European war, to embark on a policy which, by the standards of the period, was almost as radical as the deposition of a king.

England's entry, through the eager offices of William of Orange, into the confederation of states determined to hold Louis XIV in check, dragged the nation into more than twenty years of continental warfare. At the outset few Englishmen realized the extent of their commitment, and most parliamentary politicians either wished or assumed that England's role as a European bel-ligerent would be thankfully brief. Even fewer envisaged the transformation that the wars would wreak on the nation's institutions. Those who tried to predict the future were apt to imagine it as most unpalatable. The examples of a militarily beleaguered and highly taxed United Provinces or of a French state dominated by an autocratic monarch with an insatiable appetite for self-aggrandizement were dark auguries for Englishmen who wished for peace and plenty, liberty and the Protestant faith.

The inability of late Stuart politicians to predict the consequences of their nation's entry into war warns us against assuming that the institutional changes of the time were inevitable, a nec-essary consequence of England's becoming a belligerent power. We need to remember that the act of waging war did not inevitably lead to the development of new and more powerful state institutions. Indeed, in early modern Europe war often succeeded in diluting rather than con-centrating state power. The absence of effective public institutions to manage the business of war prompted the growth of *private* military enterprise.[2] The recruitment of troops was handed over to military enterprisers and the collection of revenue assigned to private consortia of financiers. The ruler's grip on his subjects was weakened by venality, the financial burdens of war led to the abandonment of bureaucratic reform, the presence of hostilities on home territory produced administrative breakdown. Fiscal pressures also enhanced the powers of institutions such as par-liaments and estates whose approval was necessary for the levying of taxes. So, though wars might provide opportunities for rulers to consolidate their power and assert themselves against their subjects, they might equally lead to a loss of control, to the growth of private interests which appropriated such public functions as recruitment and tax gathering.

The Nine Years War subjected the English state to all the stresses and strains that accompany involvement in a major war – fiscal crisis, financial scandal, mismanagement and corruption, the virtual collapse of parts of the administration. But what emerged was a *public* fiscal–military appa-ratus, remarkably untainted by private interests. This had not been an inevitable outcome. William's desperate need for cash led him to offer public offices to private financiers with no administrative experience,[3] and there was frequent discussion of a reversion to revenue farming.[4] The rapid, sprawling growth of administration and the remarkable growth in the amount of public moneys increased the temptation to defraud the public and enhanced the opportunity to do so. On occasion in the 1690s it looked as if the administrative system would break down and the money would run out. But, close as the English came to disaster, they succeeded in averting cat-astrophe. Moreover the lessons of the 1690s were learnt remarkably quickly. If the War of Spanish Succession produced a notable number of fortunes for soldiers, sailors, contractors and remit-tance men, it nevertheless saw both a significant reduction in the politicization of administration and in the habit of egregious peculation. The English state managed to avoid the sort of spolia-tion to which other regimes had so often fallen prey.

Why, in what is conventionally viewed as the most unstate-like of states, did the government manage both to cope with the pressures of war and to retain much of its integrity? Two circum-stances were vital. First, William and his followers were the beneficiaries of the administrative reforms initiated by their predecessors. Thus, thanks to Charles and James, the revenue depart-ments were sufficiently well rooted to avoid being swept away by the winds of war. Secondly, the commons restrained malfeasance and secured public accountability. The price the MPs exacted for supporting the war was the opportunity to subject its operations to unparalleled surveillance.[5] This did not prevent peculation and administrative corruption, but it certainly rendered the offences both more risky and more liable to detection. It checked abuse, even if it did not entirely eliminate it.

The commons was not only the watchdog of the state, but also the forum within which the controversial views surrounding the war were debated. The impact of foreign policy, the signifi-cance of war, the repercussions – fiscal, administrative and political – of the struggle against Louis XIV were all discussed with a passion that occasionally approached ferocity. These arguments about the war are of great importance, for they enable us to understand why the commons was prepared, however reluctantly, to support hostilities, and they go far to explain why the admin-istrative and fiscal apparatus assumed the form it did.

Domestic Policy and Foreign Affairs

The overthrow, flight or "abdication" of James II was a watershed in British history. Though there were obvious continuities between the English polity ruled by the Catholic James and the realm governed by the Protestant William and Mary, there were also significant differences. Nearly all political institutions and a good many of those who manned them survived into the new reign, but the new world, though dotted with familiar landmarks – a powerful monarch, a substantial army, a flourishing court and the consummately *politique* Earl of Sunderland – nevertheless con-tained much that was unfamiliar.

Nowhere was this more apparent than in that most jealously guarded of royal prerogatives, the making of foreign policy.[6] After 1688 a royal policy previously marked by acquisitive amity or sympathetic neutrality towards France was replaced by one of active hostility. Despite the rise to power of Louis XIV's France, Charles II had shown remarkably little anxiety about his over-mighty Catholic neighbour. Indeed, Charles had a marked propensity to make himself the client of the French king, and resisted the efforts of his ministers, particularly those of Danby, to develop an anti-French Protestant foreign policy. James II, perhaps because of his preoccupation with domestic affairs, remained equally unperturbed by French aggrandizement.

Such insouciance about the French, which many of Charles and James's subjects did not share, did not survive the Glorious Revolution. William's acquisition of the English crown was, as many Englishmen realized, no philanthropic act. It accorded with his determination to build a European alliance which at best would destroy French hegemony in Europe and which at worst would hold Louis XIV in check.

But the concerns of most Englishmen were far more parochial. They were fighting neither for a Dutch king nor for a balance of power in Europe. They cared little for either. They fought to preserve the revolution of 1688, to avert the return of James II, whom Louis supported, and to avoid the Catholicism and executive intrusion that had been the hallmarks of his reign.

A great many politicians, especially the tories, were therefore concerned to contain the scope of England's military involvement. They wanted to play a subsidiary rather than a leading role in the continental war; they wanted a "blue water" strategy which looked to the navy and to commercial and colonial gains rather than towards the balance of power in Europe. During the war itself they achieved only limited success. But by 1697, with universal war-weariness and the nation in the throes of a major financial crisis, many MPs, as William discovered to his disgust, were also eager to turn their backs on the Continent and to revert to an isolationist foreign policy.

Between 1697 and 1701 it seemed as if the legislature would succeed in expunging many of the effects of nearly a decade of war. The standing army was decimated to a mere 7000 and the war leaders of the whig Junto impeached. The 1701 Act of Settlement – more properly entitled, "An Act for the further limitation of the crown and the better securing the rights of the subject" – introduced a variety of constraints on royal power. Clauses in the Act removed placemen from the commons, made privy councillors more accountable to parliament for their advice to the king, gave judges greater independence, restricted the religion and movement of the monarch, and attempted to prevent his taking foreigners' advice. Many of these measures were aimed personally at William, whose proclivity for Dutch guards, Dutch advisers and European politicking was much disliked. But their effect was to limit the strength of the fiscal–military state as a whole.[7]

But William's opponents had not reckoned with the behaviour of Louis XIV. The French king's conduct in 1701, which included not only provocations over the Spanish Succession and in the Netherlands but the recognition of the Old Pretender and attacks on English trade, convinced all but the most diehard members of the peace party that war, if it were not inevitable, was probably imminent.[8] The dismantling of the English military machine was abruptly reversed. Paradoxically, Louis XIV was one of the greatest allies of those who argued for all-out war against France. He also bears some responsibility for the emergence of England as a fiscal–military power. If William, aided by James, pushed England into the military arena, it was the French king who kept her there.

In 1689, when England first entered the war against France, it was widely recognized that the domestic consequences of losing the war would have been catastrophic. If William had been defeated by James and Louis, if the campaign in Ireland had proved disastrous or Louis's descent on England successful not only would the balance of power in Europe have been transfigured, so would the domestic polity, which would have had to stomach the return of a Catholic king. As Major Wildman reminded the commons in November 1689 "We talk not here for the King, but for the Kingdom. I have heard a doctrine preached here, 'Take Care we be not principals in the war against France' but against King James we are principals in that war to defend us from popery and slavery."[9]

It was this link between the fate of English *domestic* political arrangement and the outcome of the struggle between Louis XIV and his enemies which distinguishes the Nine Years War from earlier European conflicts in which the English had engaged. Apart from the Elizabethan struggle with the Spanish earlier wars had seemed more discretionary, a matter of choosing whether or not the island kingdom would venture forth to enter into a European conflict. But after 1688 the English were involved whether they liked it or not. Moreover, the stakes were exceptionally high. Not everyone might agree with William III's characterization of the war as "not so properly an act of choice as an inevitable necessity in our defence",[10] but it was widely understood that whatever else it might be, the struggle with James and Louis was a war of English succession, fought to preserve a Protestant regime. Indeed the importance of this war aim is borne out by the first clause of the Treaty of Ryswick by which Louis recognized William as England's ruler.

The circumstances of the 1690s – the threat of foreign invasion, William and Mary's tenuous hold on the throne, the fear of domestic plots and insurrection, and the apprehensions about the fate of the Protestant religion both in Britain and Europe – were a boon to those who had long advocated an anti-Catholic and anti-French foreign policy. William's whig supporters pressed home their advantage, portraying high taxes and an expensive war as a lesser evil than the potential loss of domestic and religious liberty. As the whig MP Hampden put it in a series of rhetorical questions,[11]

> what will it avail to say that you are cozened, and, if you give more, you shall be cozened? But are you the better for saving your Money, if Ireland be lost, perhaps England too? Popery, French and Irish, to dwell among you, and govern you; and saving the Taxes will be cold comfort at last, to say "I have saved £100 in taxes, and perhaps my estate will be sequestered, or worse: I must either renounce my religion or lose it."

These words were, of course, the special pleading of an ardent supporter of William, the scion of a famous parliamentary family. The would doubtless have fallen on the deaf ears of Jacobites, Catholics and some of those politicians who dreaded the consequences of England's involvement in a European war. But the rhetoric of Hampden and his colleagues was not without effect. Defence of the new regime or, at least, a desire to avoid a return to the old, does seem to explain why many MPs who might otherwise have been unwilling to fight a war were prepared to support the struggle against France. For once arguments for war based on "state necessity" seemed persuasive. As one commentator conceded,[12]

> Our dear bought experience has taught us what Vast Taxes are absolutely necessary to maintain the armies and Fleet, which are requisite for our security; and for the defence of our religious and civil rights; and provided that we attain those ends, it will not be thought, at long run, we have bought them any too dear.

[. . .]

But critics of the war . . . had, however, to confront an irresoluble paradox. The Glorious Revolution was not only a Protestant but a "country" revolution, concerned both to preserve the true faith as England's official religion and to reduce the powers of central government. But, in order to protect the revolution from its enemies, the powers of the state had perforce to grow as never before. Attempts to solve this contradiction lay at the heart of parliamentary politics of the period. The opponents of higher taxes, deficit financing, an expanding civil administration and a standing army fought bravely to hold big government in check. Yet, at bottom, they recognized that the fiscal–military state protected Englishmen's liberties as much as it threatened them. It was undesirable but necessary. This view, which was slowly and painfully accepted, explains why the focus of opposition to the fiscal–military state gradually shifted away from the attempt to secure its abolition to a policy of containment. For all their brave rhetoric, the opponents of big government knew that though they might win many battles, they could not and, in some cases, did not wish to win the war.

Nevertheless their resistance, as they themselves recognized,[13] was not in vain. If they did not stem the tide of government they were able to reduce its flow or ensure that it ran into what they saw as less harmful channels. The determination to secure accountable government, to root out peculation and graft, and to avoid the indiscriminate expansion of civilian and military offices produced a far more honest and proficient administration than would ever have emerged if such reformist initiatives had been entirely absent. The state apparatus that emerged from this conflict between the advocates of strong government and their opponents was never quite as either side wished or intended: it was never the leviathan that its opponents feared, but neither was it the toothless creature that its apologists apprehended.

The Struggle over Money

At the heart of the struggle over the character and scope of late Stuart government lay the battle over finance. Control over money was the commons' most powerful weapon, albeit one which had been used incompetently in the conflicts between the monarch and the lower house during the 1670s and 1680s. Yet even in this earlier period it had been recognized that, as one MP put it, "tis money that makes a Parliament considerable & nothing else".[14] The Convention and the early parliaments of William and Mary were chastened bodies, determined to learn the lessons their predecessors had overlooked. If the last years of Charles II's reign had reminded them of the fragility of the power of the commons, the reign of James II had demonstrated that disastrous and divisive policies could easily be pursued by a monarch unconstrained by the need to consult "the representative of the people".

Post-Revolutionary politicians knew that they themselves were largely to blame for the follies and disasters that had led to the invitation, signed by both whig and tory, beseeching William of Orange to rescue Englishmen and their liberties from the obduracy and autarchy of a Catholic king. Charles II at the Restoration and James at his succession had been treated with excessive trust. "The heat of loyalty", remarked Sir Robert Howard, a former secretary to the Treasury, "was carried on formerly to excess".[15] Credulous royalism had led parliament to confer a generous financial settlement on both of Charles I's children; parliament itself had granted the monarch the wherewithal "to goven by Arbitrary Power, and abolish Parliaments".[16]

Nearly all MPs – including royal servants as well as back-benchers and radical whigs – were determined to avoid the errors of the past. They hardly needed to be reminded that 1688 gave them such an opportunity. When, in an oft-quoted remark, William Harbord, a West country MP, told the commons that "You have an infallible security for the administration of government; all the revenue is in your hands, which fell with the last King, and you may keep that back,"[17] he was preaching to the converted. Though some, especially amongst William's most fervent admirers, thought it churlish to try to constrain the nation's saviour, many more agreed with William Garraway, the member for Arundel who remarked that, "We have had such violation of our Liberties in the last reigns, that the Prince of Orange cannot take it ill, if we make conditions, to secure ourselves for the future."[18]

The most obvious way to check the power of the crown was through the calling of frequent parliaments, and the way to secure frequent parliaments was to ensure the financial dependence of the monarch. The experiences of the previous reign provided ample information about what paths to avoid and what fiscal routes to follow. James had been financially independent for two reasons. First, parliament had granted him a competency for life, rather than for a limited number of years. Second, this competency took the form of the yield from certain duties. The royal revenue was made up of indirect taxes – customs and excises – on international trade and domestic commerce. Though the monarch could not change the rate of these taxes without the consent of parliament, the yield fluctuated according to the prosperity of the economy. The boom that took place for most of James's reign was therefore an important contributory factor to his fiscal independence.

James had capitalized on these advantages by launching a determined campaign for adminis-trative improvement designed to maximize the returns of the revenues to which he was legally entitled, to reduce local resistance to taxes and to create an effective royal bureaucracy. Though the collection of all indirect taxes became more efficient, the greatest progress was made with the excise. Writing after the Revolution (and with an admittedly large axe to grind) Charles Davenant, the political arithmetician and former Excise commissioner, maintained that a large proportion of the increase in excise returns between 1683 and 1688 was the direct result of administrative reform.[19]

James's financial independence and the bureaucratic initiative, so redolent of French abso-lutism, which accompanied it were burnished on the political memory of William and Mary's early parliaments. They took no chances. Deep as they were in the Dutchman's debt, the commons would not grant him a competency for life. Though William and Mary enjoyed the hereditary excise during their reign, parliament would make up their ordinary income from customs revenues for a period of only four years. Moreover, the commons deliberately increased the crown's fiscal dependence by failing to provide William with extraordinary income to service his wartime borrowing, thereby forcing him to burden his ordinary revenue with debts. At the same time the commons fought back against the administrative initiative begun by James. The last two clauses of the bill of rights took up financial grievances against the hearth tax and the excise. William, no doubt hoping for a generous fiscal present in return, magnanimously aban-doned the hearth tax. Though the measure was popular both in the commons and with the public at large, it failed to elicit the expected response. Instead the lower house proceeded, in the first excise Act after the Revolution to remove a number of administrative innovations that James's excise commissioners had introduced, and to change the rules of evidence to favour those who disputed the duties.[20]

The overall effect of these measures was to end to the possibility of financial independence for the crown. Not even in peacetime could the monarch use his ordinary revenue "to live of his own". In future he had perforce to turn to parliament if he were to remain solvent. The object of securing fiscal dependency was clear: to ensure the regular calling of parliament. This, in turn, would enable the lower house to scrutinize the actions of the executive and redress the grievances of their constituents. The debates of 1689 and 1690, as both Henry Horwitz and Clayton Roberts have shown, leave no doubt that the commons were determined to secure frequent parliaments by holding the power of the purse.[21]

The financial settlement hammered out in 1689 and 1690 meant that in future the ability of the king's ministers to secure parliamentary consent to additional revenues was to be of vital importance to the monarch. From the outset of William and Mary's reign, government ministers sought to initiate an ambitious plan to enable the crown not only to cover its usual expenses but also to wage war on a grand scale. There were two major components in this scheme: a direct tax, a subsidy or assessment equivalent to 2 shillings in the pound; and what was referred to as a "general excise", a tax on the sale of staples. The latter tax would have meant a duty not only on drink but on foodstuffs and such basic items as clothing, leather goods, soap, candles and salt.

A subsidy was, of course, a time-honoured means of supplying the monarch with extraordi-nary revenue;[22] the proposal for a general excise was, however, a more recent and more contro-versial plan. The scheme may have been advocated because William, as a Dutchman, would have been familiar with the fiscal possibilities of a general excise. In the United Provinces in the late seventeenth century about half of the cost of most commodities was attributable to excise duties. But a general excise scheme was just as likely to be of English origin and to be based on the parliamentarian John Pym's excises which had been introduced in July 1643. These taxes had originally been laid on drink – beer, ale, cider and perry – but had spread so quickly that in little more than a year there were excises on soap, cloth, spirits, butcher's meat, salt, poultry, herring, alum, copperas, caps, hats, hops, saffron, silk, tin, iron and wood. The kinds of commodity chosen by the late seventeenth- and eighteenth-century proponents of excises as possible sources of revenue tended to be those which had also been included in Pym's list of excise imposts. To some extent, therefore, there was a (largely unsuccessful) attempt after the Glorious Revolution to revert to the fiscal policies of the parliamentarians during the Civil War.

The government's plan to secure a general excise began immediately after the Glorious Revolution. Late in 1689 a scheme for a general excise on staples failed in a parliamentary committee. In the following year there were many rumours of a plan to introduce a new general excise scheme, although none materialized. In 1691, Charles Davenant helped Sidney Godolphin draft another scheme. In the next two years excise schemes were debated in the commons, and in the spring of 1693 Sir Robert Howard, one of the Lords of the Treasury, worked up a new government proposal. In the following session the government, conscious of the fierce opposition its policy provoked, narrowed its objectives, moving for an excise solely on leather and on soap. For the next two years these proposals were the focus of a protracted battle about taxation in the commons.[23]

A general excise had obvious attractions for the king. Its ubiquity promised to yield large sums yet it was easy to collect. As Charles Davenant put it in his tract of 1695, *An Essay upon Ways and Means of Supplying War*,[24]

> excises seem the most proper Ways and Means to support the government in a long war, because they would lie equally upon the whole, and produce great sums proportionable to the wants of the public. . . . That kind of revenue must needs be very great, where so large a part of the people are every minute paying something towards it; and very easy, when every one, in a manner, taxes himself, making consumption according to his will or ability.

Taxes on production or sales could be assessed less obtrusively and more accurately than duties on wealth or realty; their incidence was less visible than a poll tax, because they were levied not on the public at large but on producers and distributors who passed the costs on to consumers in the form of higher prices. They were also less subject to the fluctuations which plagued customs duties affected by the wartime disruption of trade. A general excise had a further attraction. Thanks to the reforms introduced by James II's commissioners, the Excise employed a body of royal administrators second to none. In short, excises offered the monarch and his ministers the tantalizing combination of administrative simplicity and high returns. They were also the only duties which looked as if they might provide a sufficiently broad tax base to reduce or even, perhaps, to remove the government's need to borrow money. The case for a general excise, it should be remembered, was the case for avoiding a burgeoning public debt.

But many MPs lacked the enthusiasm of the likes of Charles Davenant for such taxes. They feared that a general excise would allow the monarch to reacquire the fiscal independence of which he had been deprived by the revolutionary financial settlement. They were strongly averse to raising supply through taxes with a flexible or unpredictable yield or by imposts that required "an army of officers"[25] to collect the revenue. Such duties raised the prospect reminiscent of James II's reign, of a monarch able, through a combination of good fortune and administrative efficiency, to live off his ordinary revenues. Thus the debate about a general excise was seen by many MPs as part of the larger question of the financial independence of the crown.

The commons worried that a general excise would somehow build itself into the fiscal system and then prove difficult or impossible to dislodge. "We would have taxes so laid", said one commentator, "as when the necessity of taxing ceases, the taxes may cease with them".[26] But, as the whig parliamentary diarist Narcissus Luttrell remarked, "these excises . . . are not likely to be got of[f] again (as the land tax) when the occasion ceases, they take root by their many officers . . . and tho necessity raised them at first, they are apt to find occasion for their continuance".[27]

The early and explicit advocacy of a general excise by the court affected all subsequent debates about excise taxes on specific commodities. A proposal to tax a single item – leather or salt, for instance – was immediately interpreted by many in the house as the thin edge of a thick fiscal wedge. Thus it was reported by Bonnet, the envoy of the court of Brandenburg, that during the debate in 1694 on a leather excise, "quelques uns alléguant que leur condition alloit devenir pire que celle des Hollandois, chez qui rien n'exempt de taxe" "some allege that their condition will be worse than that of the Dutch, for whom nothing is exempt from excises".[28] Or, as Hampden put it somewhat more pungently, "when the serpant gets his head into a hole, it is no hard matter for him to draw his whole body after it".[29] Debates about individual taxes therefore assumed disproportionate importance for individual MPs. A single excise presaged a general one; a general excise promised fiscal independence to the crown; fiscal independence threatened the revolutionary settlement; excises therefore jeopardized the Glorious Revolution.

The land tax, on the other hand, offered no such threat. Voted annually, the tax was of a fixed term and, by the end of the Nine Years War, had a fixed yield of c. £500,000 for every shilling in the pound levied by the lower house. Controlled in the metropolis not by the crown but by the commons, the tax's administration in the field was in the hands of local dignitaries and not in the power of the royal bureaucracy. Land tax assessors, collectors and receivers were all private citizens rather than state employees. They were appointed by local commissioners and were not answerable to a central board or office in London.[30]

Some parliamentary commentators maintained that one of the land tax's most admirable features was that those who were responsible for its imposition were most hurt by it. This guaranteed that, once the tax was no longer essential, it would be sure of a prompt reduction or a swift repeal. In this respect, as in so many others, it differed from excises which "do not immediately touch the members of parliament themselves, who are landed men, and therefore not so directly concerned to get them off".[31] MPs opposed to excises were afraid of the insidious attraction they might hold for the landed classes.[32]

The commons' decided preference for the land tax – its willingness to fund most of the war effort between 1692 and 1713 by a tax which fell primarily on landed wealth – is therefore explained in a single word: control. The tax might fall heavily on the landed classes, but the commons knew that when the time came they could easily (or so they thought) throw off the burden. The tax created no class of insidious bureaucrat, no creatures of the crown ready to support monarchical power and to subvert elections. Though the land tax was in this period the strong arm of the fiscal state, its financial muscle was only exercised at the behest of the commons. It is this that explains why Paul Foley could report to his fellow "country" MP Robert Harley in September 1692 that some MPs preferred to pay 6 shillings in the pound on the land tax rather than support a general excise.[33] The commons were determined not only to limit the monarch's ordinary revenue, but also to keep a tight rein on all extraordinary funding.

Criticism of a general excise was also fuelled by the view, expressed by many MPs, that excises were disproportionately harsh on the poor. Many critics recalled that the Restoration excise had been granted to Charles II to replace royal revenues lost because of the abolition of the Court of Wards. Wardship had penalized the rich; excises, it was argued, encumbered the middling sort and the poor: "it is the generality of the Trading, Working, Industrious and Profitable Part of this Kingdom, that . . . bear the burden. . . . [It falls] upon the backs of the most Industrious part of the Common People."[34] A general excise on drink, victuals and staples, it was maintained, would have been more discriminatory, making the poor

> pay more than the wealthiest of their neighbours, suitable to what they have; for though a rich man spends more in exciseable things than a poor man doth, yet it is as much as he can do to provide the necessaries for his family out of which he pays his proportion.

Such critics saw through the "voluntarist" arguments of Davenant and his colleagues, which claimed that the payment of excises was a matter of choice. They knew perfectly well that a tax on basic commodities left the poor with little or no choice but to pay. They also saw that such taxes consumed a much higher proportion of the poor subject's income.[35]

The defence of their humble constituents served MPs well when they returned to their localities. But their chief concern was undoubtedly the threat posed by the possibility of a monarch able to dispense with parliament. This apprehension, more than any other consideration, explains why MPs like Robert Harley were ready to "pray God direct in the matter, & prevent a General Home Excise".[36]

As it turned out, Harley's supplication was not in vain. Despite the frequency with which the Treasury introduced excise measures during the Nine Years War, the policy of securing a general excise enjoyed very little success. The overall fiscal plan of a general excise and a low land tax was never realized because the government never succeeded in passing a comprehensive excise bill. Repeated efforts secured the passage of only a small body of excise legislation: additional duties on beer, wine and spirits, the salt tax in 1694, the duties on glass, bottles and tobacco pipes of 1696 which proved a failure and were repealed three years later, the malt tax, which became an important feature of the standing revenue, and the leather tax passed in the same year, 1697, which provoked enormous hostility and which was not renewed after it had run its three-year term. The financial labours of an elephant produced a fiscal mouse.[37]

Why did the government's initiative prove such a failure? Why, at a time when the nation seemed in great peril, were ministers unable to secure the fiscal legislation they deemed necessary? We know why many MPs opposed excises, but this does not answer the question of why they enjoyed such success.

Part of the answer lies in the parlous state of political management for much of William's reign. In the years immediately after the Glorious Revolution, the unsuccessful conduct of the war, the administrative difficulties and malfeasance exposed during the rapid expansion of the executive, the political divisions within the king's administration, and the rank mediocrity of some of the crown's ministers – especially of those dealing with finance – meant that the commons lacked incisive leadership and informed guidance from the government front bench. In August 1692, when the privy councillor, the Earl of Rochester prepared a memorandum urging the king to make all speed with preparations for the next parliamentary session, he conceded somewhat disconsolately, "It is perhaps too confident a thing for anyone to say that parliament will, or will not do anything, whatsoever that may be, proposed to them. Lord Camarthen, the president of the council, added an even more pessimistic and defeatist note to Rochester's original comment: "Sir J. Lowther [a Lord of the Treasury] says nobody can know, one day, what the house of Common would do the next, in which all agree with him."[38] This confession reflects, in part, the difficulty of organizing the house in a period when political allegiance were rapidly changing. But it is also, as John Kenyon has pointed out,[39] an astonishing admission of political impotence. Not even the return of Sunder-land – whose skills as a political manager were second to none – nor the emergence of the whig Junto as the dominant and most efficient group in the king's administration could establish a firm and lasting grip on the commons. Between 1694 and 1696 the ministers of the Junto managed to tighten the tenuous grasp, but by 1697 the commons had once again escaped their hold.

Only in the reign of Anne was the Treasury front bench able to assert its control over that most important of government concerns, the passage of financial legislation. If, under William, government fiscal policy was constantly thwarted, after 1702 it was almost never checked by parliamentary opposition. The triumph was reflected in parliamentary procedure. In 1706 a decision was made preventing any MP from introducing a money bill without the recommendation of the crown. This gave the Treasury a monopoly over fiscal legislation. In 1713 this ruling became part of the commons' standing orders.[40] By 1711 such occurrences as the temporary defeat of a leather tax by the group of high tory MPs, the October Club, were sufficiently rare to take most political commentators by surprise.[41] In the previous reign such events had been commonplace.

[...]

The political turbulence of the 1690s pushed the ship of state off course. It also meant that those other than royal officers had the chance to seize the helm. The weak grasp of the king's administration on fiscal policy meant that other groups in the commons were able not only to thwart official policy but to take the legislative initiative. Policy was not coolly formulated at Whitehall but hammered out in the heat of debates at Westminster. From the floor of the house opponents of the government offered fiscal counter-proposals to those of the king's ministers; often the commons preferred these measures to those put forward by the administration. Indeed many of the taxes introduced by the commons in the 1690s were schemes designed to pre-empt or replace government excise proposals. The poll taxes, the wine duty levied on retailers in 1693, the tax on births, marriages and deaths of 1695 and the proposed capitation of 1696 were all introduced as alternative measures to the dreaded excise.[42]

This independent initiative was often led by MPs who sat or who had sat on one of the successive Commissions of Public Accounts which the commons established after 1691 in order to scrutinize government revenue and expenditure . . . The commission was another instance of the commons' determination to set financial constraints on the crown and to ensure that the house exacted the right to detailed scrutiny of public moneys in return for its unprecedented grants of revenue. The commission was also the major source of fiscal ideas and financial information for those who wanted to cut government expenditure and pare government revenue to a bare minimum, "endeavouring to be frugal by good management".[43]

The Commissioners of Accounts have been condemned by some historians as meddlesome, factious and misinformed. But though the commissions formed in Anne's reign have been especially criticized,[44] most recent historians have argued that the commissions of the 1690s performed several valuable services.[45] First, as we have mentioned, their members were actively involved in policy making – formulating fiscal schemes and pressing them in parliamentary debate. Second, they were recognized by MPs, especially those of a "country" persuasion, as an alternative source of financial expertise to the Treasury bench. The commissioners, after all, had examined government accounts in detail – that, indeed, was their chief responsibility – and they often produced figures and estimates that differed from those of the government. They gave back-benchers the confidence and resolve to question the crown's proposals and policy; they bolstered the commons' determination to secure fiscal accountability.

The commissioners also improved fiscal probity. This may seem an excessively credulous claim in view of the 1690s' reputation as a decade remarkable for financial scandal and egregious peculation in all branches of government. Even the commons itself was not untainted: in 1695 the Speaker, Sir John Trevor, was expelled for taking bribes from the East India Company to aid the passage of legislation in which they were an interested party. Such malfeasance was duplicated in many departments. Treasury officials took bribes, naval officers extorted protection money from merchant ships, contractors fiddled their books, victualling commissioners supplied inedible food and undrinkable beer, army officers pocketed their men's pay and tax officials engaged in fraud. No wonder that Robert Harley, always ready with a sententious phrase, could condemn William's reign as "an age of fraud and corruption".[46]

We should, however, put this indubitably reprehensible record in perspective. In William's reign the state apparatus and government spending grew as never before. Yet there was little planning or order to this growth, not the least because of the commons' unwillingness to admit that the war against the former King James and Louis XIV might be a long one. A confused administrative labyrinth took shape in which the nefarious peculator could easily hide. Government expansion meant expanded opportunities for fraud: more money to appropriate, more men with the chance to embezzle it.

But the standards of public misconduct, however deplorable, were no worse than most other European states and were certainly better than they had been in the early seventeenth century. The extent of our knowledge of "corruption" in this period reflects the extent to which it was exposed by contemporaries determined to root out fraud. William's reign would appear to us as a far more virtuous age if it had not been for the assiduous investigations of such reformers as the Commissioners of Accounts. Their work meant that an aggrieved official or a virtuous administrator (quite often the former posing as the latter) could use the commissioners to air a complaint, secure redress or remove an evil.[47] . . .

The activities of the Commissions of Accounts and of their parliamentary supporters are symptomatic of two features of fiscal politics in the reign of William III. First, fiscal policy was the result of various pressures from many political groups, including those outside the administration. Throughout the Nine Years War it was never the monopoly of a single party or interest. In consequence the ship of state, though not rudderless, steered a zig-zag course dictated by the shifting aims of a changing crew. Second, the vagaries of fiscal policy were in large part the result of a clash between two conflicting priorities of the commons. On the one hand, they were determined to secure fiscal accountability; on the other, they were, for all their anxieties and misgivings, prepared to grant the crown unprecedented amounts of money.

[. . .]

In their determination to prevent the crown from establishing a perdurable fiscal apparatus and a standing royal revenue of capacious proportions, the commons tried to restrict both the term of taxes and the extent of government long-term borrowing. Just as they feared duties and imposts which would be difficult to remove once hostilities ended, so they were reluctant to permit public borrowing which would require substantial taxes for many years to come to pay off the interest on long-term loans. They feared that the need to service a long-term debt would erode the distinction between the high taxes which were regrettably necessary in wartime and the low duties which thankfully typified periods of peace. Long-term borrowing, like its handmaiden long-term taxes, threatened the policy of containing the effects of war, a strategy which was dear to the hearts of so many parliamentarians.

The opponents of long-term borrowing were unable to prevent the practice in its entirety. In 1693, 1694 and 1697 the government resorted to long-term loans raised either through public lotteries or the sale of annuities. It also borrowed from the chartered companies, most notably from the Bank of England, which was established, after a bitter political battle, in 1694.[48]

The opponents of the Bank feared both its political ancestry – which was decidedly Dissenting and whig, not to say republican[49] – and its role as a link between an administration bent on prosecuting the war and a financial interest which stood to profit by an escalation of hostilities. Their response was to try to replace the Bank of England by a Land Bank, which they felt would be more representative of and more answerable to the parliamentary classes. This plan almost succeeded in 1696 but eventually foundered on the hostility of the court and on the Land Bank's inability to weather an escalating credit crisis.[50]

Though the Land Bank scheme failed, the opponents of long-term borrowing largely succeeded in their aim of keeping such loans to a minimum. As we have seen, long-term borrowing contributed less than 10 per cent to payments for the cost of the Nine Years War. Unlike all subsequent wars in the eighteenth century, current taxes and short-term borrowing provided the bulk of the funds.

Such a policy clearly served the ends of those who were suspicious of the executive and eager to retain as much parliamentary control of financial affairs as possible. It was also not an intrinsically unsound financial strategy, though it did place a tremendous burden on short-term borrowing. Its greatest weakness was its dependence on a wide variety of short-term fiscal expedients which had been introduced to avoid the general excise. Too many of these taxes suffered from one or both of two major difficulties. First, they failed to produce their estimated yield. Sometimes this was attributable to the impact of the very war the taxes were supposed to fund. Thus the shortfall on successive customs duties[51] was partly a result of the French privateers, operating from St Malo and Dunkirk, who so successfully managed to disrupt British overseas trade. Similarly, the excise commissioners blamed the inadequate returns of the additional beer excise on high prices, tight credit and fall in demand which accompanied the war.[52]

But it was just as likely that a tax failed to produce an estimated yield because the original projections about its return were hopelessly misinformed or wildly optimistic. For all the claims of political arithmeticians, and for all the forecasts of projectors – whose schemes more often resembled the prognostications of the soothsayer than the estimates of an economic analyst – it was extremely difficult to produce accurate calculations about tax yield. In some cases – such as the tax on marriages, births, burials, bachelors and widows – the information on which an estimate could be based could only be properly gathered once the tax had been levied. In others – like the excises on salt, glass, stoneware, earthenware and tobacco pipes – it was hard to assess the impact of the duty on the level of demand for the taxable item. Precise estimates were also inhibited by the way in which tax policy was formulated. The Treasury's lack of control, the eagerness of MPs to embrace taxes which offered an alternative to the dreaded excise, the *ad hoc* character of so much decision-making: these circumstances were not conducive to careful planning and statistical precision, even if they had been possible.

Unreliable yields did not reassure public creditors, who knew that the government relied on tax income to pay the interest on the loans they had extended to the state. Davenant saw the situation quite clearly: "nothing can be so prejudicial to the public credit, as that taxes should not answer what they are given for by parliament".[53] As it became increasingly apparent that so many tax funds were seriously deficient – to the tune of over £5 million by 1697[54] – so government borrowing became more and more difficult. The confidence of public creditors was also affected by the second characteristic of these taxes, namely the short period for which they were voted. How was the creditor to be paid once the tax had lapsed? Could he or she be sure that future funds would be earmarked to service that part of the debt in which they had invested?

By 1697 the proliferation of short-term borrowing – in the form of exchequer tallies, departmental credit and the new exchequer bills – the accumulation of tax deficiencies and the sharp deflation, largely attributable to the Recoinage of 1696–7, were all contributing to a crisis of confidence in public credit. The financial reconstruction that followed involved much that was anathema to opponents of the executive: the extension of existing tax funds, the introduction of new levies and the reorganization of the debt – largely with the help of that *bêtise* of tories and country MPs, the Bank of England – into what was known as "the First General Mortgage", a fund which effectively became part of the long-term debt. Subsequent legislation extended the duties covering these liabilities to the year 1720. In 1711 they were made perpetual.[55]

Though in the short run the proponents of fiscal conservatism had triumphed, in the long term their success in holding down both borrowing and taxes contributed to a fiscal crisis whose resolution guaranteed both permanent debts and perpetual taxes. By 1698 it had become clear that public deficit finance was not an evanescent phenomenon but a long-term part of the workings of the English state. Gradually the opponents of the financial revolution came to recognize that a reversion to earlier days was no longer possible. It was now necessary to harness and tame the forces of public credit, not to seek their abolition.

[. . .]

Historians often regard the opposition to an increase in the size of the armed forces, to an expanding bureaucracy and to high taxes under the later Stuarts as a singular instance of a hopeless and reactionary resistance to inevitable change, which was only able to flourish because of the factiousness of politicians. Typically, this view sees country ideology as the tool of the unscrupulous or the naive belief of the credulous and idealistic. It does not contemplate the possibility that country politics was supported on the pragmatic grounds that, even though its platform stood little chance of wholesale adoption, it preserved the nation from the worst excesses of the state. Yet this is precisely what it succeeded in doing. Nor does this view see the genuine dilemma posed by the larger context of politics after 1688. The wars against Louis XIV were fought for many reasons, but one of their most important aims was the creation or retention of a particular sort of Protestant polity. Yet, as we have seen, the cost of that defence was the creation of a state which threatened that vision of English society and politics. One of the major political concerns of the period was how to steer a safe course between preserving the regime and avoiding its excesses. On the whole, this difficult task was accomplished. Paradoxically, a strong parliament effectively resisting much that was proposed by government eventually produced a stronger state.

NOTES

1 Charles Tilly (ed.), *The Formation of Nation States in Western Europe* (Princeton, 1975), p. 42.
2 These views have been put particularly trenchantly by Tom Ertman in an unpublished paper, "War and statebuilding in early modern Europe" (Harvard University, 1987).
3 Edward Hughes, *Studies in Administration and Finance*, p. 164; Charles Davenant, "Discourses on the Public Revenues, and on the Trade of England, in Two Parts [1698]", *The Political and Commercial*

Works of that Celebrated Writer, Charles Davenant . . . collected and revised by Sir Charles Whitworth (5 vols., London, 1771), vol. 1, pp. 182–98; *Calendar of State Papers Domestic* (1694–5), p. 181; BL Add. Mss 33038 f. 58; *Calendar of Treasury Books (CTB)*, vol. 9, part 2 (1689–90), pp. 366, 369.

4 For these proposals, notably those that led to the offering of the excise for farming in 1700 see PRO T1/58 item 37; T1/69 item 15; T1/71 item 62; T48/88 ff. 235–8; BL Portland Loan 29/278, 29/283; *CTB*, vol. 15, pp. 76–8, 87, 91, 94; *Historical Manuscripts Commission: Le Fleming*, p. 354; James Lowther to Sir John Lowther, 2, 19 March, 3, 20 April, 1, 4 June 1700, Cumbria RO Lonsdale Mss LW2/D 34.

5 Henry Horwitz, *Parliament, Policy and Politics in the Reign of William III* (Manchester, 1977) pp. 87–8.

6 G. C. Gibbs, "The revolution in foreign policy", in Geoffrey Holmes (ed.), *Britain after the Glorious Revolution* (London, 1969), pp. 59–79.

7 These developments are best followed in Henry Horwitz, *Parliament, Policy and Politics*, pp. 222 ff.

8 *Ibid.*, p. 296.

9 *Parliamentary History*, vol. 5, p. 409.

10 *Commons Journals*, vol. 10, p. 104.

11 *Parliamentary History*, vol. 5, p. 567.

12 *Ibid.*, vol. 5, Appendix 6, p. liv; cf. *Taxes no Charge: In A Letter from a Gentleman to a Person of Quality* (London, 1690), A2v.

13 See the remarks of James Stanhope quoted by Geoffrey Holmes in his *British Politics in the Age of Anne*, revised edn (London, 1987), p. 123.

14 Anchitell Grey, *Debates of the House of Commons, from the year 1667 to the year 1694* (10 vols., London, 1769), vol. 4, p. 115.

15 *Ibid.*, vol. 9, p. 125.

16 *Parliamentary History*, vol. 5, pp. lviii–ix.

17 Grey, *Debates*, vol. 9, p. 36.

18 *Ibid.*, vol. 9, p. 30.

19 Davenant, "Discourses on the Public Revenues", pp. 176–80.

20 Henry Horwitz (ed.), *The Parliamentary Diary of Narcissus Luttrell* (Oxford, 1972), p. 78; PRO Treasury 48/88 ff. 243–5, "Some observations on the rise and fall of the revenue of Excise".

21 Henry Horwitz, *Parliamentary, Policy and Politics*, pp. 86–8; Clayton Roberts, "The constitutional significance of the financial settlement of 1690", *Historical Journal*, vol. 20, no. 1 (1977), pp. 59–76.

22 John Beckett, "Land tax or excise: the levying of taxation in seventeenth- and eighteenth-century England", *English Historical Review*, vol. 100 (April 1985), p. 286.

23 *Ibid.*, p. 300; Grey, *Debates*, vol. 9, p. 32; vol. 10, pp. 36–7, 341–3; Foley to Harley, 17 Sept. 1692, BL Portland Loan 29/135; Sunderland to Portland, 3 May 1693, Nottingham University Library, Portland Mss PwF 1212; Horwitz, *Luttrell Diary*, pp. 138, 311; *Calendar of State Papers Domestic* (1690–1), pp. 132, 465; (1691–2), pp. 352–3.

24 Davenant, *Works*, vol. 1, p. 62.

25 History of Parliament Transcripts, House of Lords RO, House of Commons Library Ms. 12 f. 106; [Sir Richard Temple], *An Essay upon Taxes, calculated for the present Juncture of Affairs in England* (London, 1693), p. 12.

26 *Parliamentary History*, vol. 5, p. lxvi.

27 All Souls Mss 167, f. 37v.

28 Quoted in Leopold von Ranke, *A History of England, particularly in the seventeenth century* (6 vols., London, 1875), vol. 6, p. 240.

29 *Parliamentary History*, vol. 5, p. lxiv.

30 Colin Brooks, "Public finance and political stability: the administration of the land tax, 1688–1720", *Historical Journal*, vol. 17, no. 2 (1974), pp. 281–300.

31 *Parliamentary History*, vol. 5, p. lx.

32 But see the alternative view that all taxes eventually fell on land discussed by William Kennedy, *English Taxation, 1640–1799* (London, 1913), pp. 80–1 and John Beckett in his "Land tax or excise", p. 304.

33 Paul Foley to Robert Harley, 17 Sept. 1692, BL Portland Loan 29/135.

34 *Reasons most humbly submitted to the wisdom of Parliament for taking off the present duty of Excise upon Beer and Ale, and laying the Duty upon the Original Malt* (London, 1695), pp. 4, 16–18.

35 John Cary, *An Essay on the State of England* (Bristol, 1695), p. 174.

36 Robert to Sir Edward Harley, 5 Jan. 1691–2, BL Portland Loan 29/79.

37 My emphasis here differs from that of John Beckett who points to the growth in indirect taxes during the Nine Years War. (Beckett, "Land Tax or Excise", pp. 298–9.) But many of these were customs and stamp duties, not excises, and apart from the higher duties on drink, the salt tax and the malt duty introduced at the end of the war, the new excises did not yield substantial amounts of revenue. Moreover as Figure 4.3 shows, the growth in the excise bureaucracy was neglible under William but nearly doubled under Anne.

38 *Calendar of State Papers Domestic* (1691–2), p. 410.

39 John Kenyon, "Lord Sunderland and the king's administration", *EHR*, vol. 71 (1956), pp. 581–2.

40 Peter Thomas, *The House of Commons in the Eighteenth Century* (Oxford, 1971), pp. 69, 72.

41 *The Wentworth Papers 1705–1739*, (ed.) J. J. Cartwright (London, 1883), p. 189, Kaye Parliamentary Diary, History of Parliament Trust, transcript.

42 Colin Brooks, "Projecting, political arithmetic and the act of 1695", EHR, vol. 97 (1982), p. 47.

43 *HMC Portland* III, p. 481.

44 Geoffrey Holmes, *British Politics in the Age of Anne* (revised edn, London 1987), pp. 137–41.

45 J. A. Downie, "The Commission of Public Accounts and the formation of the Country Party", *EHR*, vol. 91 (1976), pp. 33–51; A. MacInnes, *Robert Harley Puritan Politician* (London, 1970), p. 42; Colin Brooks, "The country persuasion and political responsibility in England in the 1690s", *Parliament, Estates and Representation*, vol. 4 (1984), pp. 142–3, 145–6.

46 *HMC Portland* III, p. 596.

47 See, for example, the action of a revenue officer against the Norfolk collector Samuel Dashwood, in 1695. ("Treasury and Excise, 1689–1700", Customs and Excise Library, King's Beam House, ff. 126–8.)

48 Peter Dickson, *The Financial Revolution in England* (London, 1976), pp. 48, 52–7.

49 G. S. de Krey, *A Fractured Society: The Politics of London in the First Age of Party, 1688–1715* (Oxford, 1985), p. 109.

50 Rubini, "The battle of the banks", *EHR*, vol. 85 (1970), pp. 693–714.

51 The relevant acts are 2 W. & M. c.4; 4 W. & M. c.5; 6 & 7 W. & M. c.1; 7 & 8 W. & M. c.10.

52 Excise Commissioners to Treasury, 1 Nov. 1692, PRO Treasury 48/88; Excise Commissioners to Treasury, 23 May 1695, PRO Customs 48/6 f. 26.

53 Davenant, *Works*, vol. 1, p. 139.

54 Dickson, *Financial Revolution*, p. 354.

55 *Ibid.*, pp. 353–5 for details of this episode.

23

THE POWER OF THE KING

Antonio Feros

Political historians have tended to underestimate the influence of the many discourses that helped to define the power of the early modern royal majesty. Primarily concerned with institutional forms, they have concentrated on the juridical language which represented the monarch as the lawmaker and the head of a bureaucratic state. The study of the Spanish monarchy is a case in point. Most modern historians indeed argue that the Spanish monarchy was highly bureaucratic, and that Spanish rulers justified their power using theories and images that were less commanding, less sacred, and more secular than those promoted by their European counterparts. A closer look, however, reveals that Spanish monarchs, in their attempt to construct the royal majesty, used a variety of political languages and no less commanding images of the power and nature of kingship. In Spain, as in other early modern European states, constructing a powerful image of the king was indeed viewed as an essential component of a political ideology that permitted monarchs "to rule, to control and order the world, to change or subdue other men."[1] It is true, however, that Spanish rulers operated in a context peculiar to Spain, where by the late sixteenth century monarchs had become inaccessible and almost invisible to all but a select group of their subjects, thus changing not only the place and political significance of the royal palace but also the function of royal rituals and ceremonies in the constitution of monarchical power.

"The eminent power that the king has," claimed Fray Alonso de Cabrera in a sermon preached in honor of the late king Philip II,

> derives from God and is communicated by Him. Those who resist and rebel against the king, resist God and break God's established order. The king's subjects have to obey their master who has the place of God upon earth. This is the order that will last in the world until the second coming of Christ when He will recover for himself the whole *potestas* and administration of this His realm.[2]

Fray Alonso's sermon is a striking depiction of monarchical power and of the demand for loyalty and obedience from the king's subjects. Yet in a personal monarchy, royal power – even in its

Antonio Feros, "The power of the king," pp. 71–6, 78–88, 90 from *Kingship and Favoritism in the Spain of Philip III, 1598–1621*. Cambridge: Cambridge University Press, 2000.

most absolutist definition – was not the core of the monarchical order. For royal power to be effective, its very nature and characteristics had to become embodied in the person of the monarch, who was the center of the system, the personification of God's will on earth and who as such needed to appear to his subjects "as a divinity, as a hero who has come down from heaven, superior in his nature to the rest."[3]

As in the Balinese court described by Clifford Geertz, in early modern Spain Philip III's contemporaries defined power by defining what kings represented. A monarch – whatever his individual character – exemplified not an individual human but the entire monarchy. Here, too, using Clifford Geertz's words, "the driving aim of higher politics was to construct a state by constructing a king. The more consummate the king, the more actual the realm. . . . If a state was constructed by constructing a king, a king was constructed by constructing a god."[4] In other words, the aim of the king's supporters was to demonstrate that the monarch's power – and thus the monarchical system itself – was not socially created but divinely ordered. The monarch was the possessor of all powers, not because of his office but because of his divine nature.

To construct this mythical monarch, early modern Spanish royalists needed to challenge some aspects of prevailing theories that accepted the human frailty of the king, especially those theories that claimed that the king's power was derived directly from the community. Many political writers agreed that although God was the ultimate origin of power, monarchs obtained their power and authority not directly from Him but through the community. Consequently, they viewed the monarch, not as "a master of the kingdom," but as its administrator and tutor.[5] In accord with these premises, political writers emphasized the monarch's official role and his royal *dignitas* over his human nature, as reflected in the political proposition of the "the king's two persons": one natural, thus weak and perishable; the other public, thus perfect and immortal. These theorists also claimed that the community invested its authority in the king's immortal public person whom they were obliged to obey because he was the possessor of a public office. They also claimed that the monarch's main duty was to prevent his vulnerable natural person, guided by passion and self-interest, from interfering with his responsibilities as tutor of the kingdom.[6]

Monarchs and their supporters began, however, to question some of the central premises of such theories in the last decades of the fifteenth century. Although those serving the Spanish monarch never questioned, at least in theory, the ascendant theory of royal power (that the king's authority comes from the community) or that the king's sacred duty was to serve the common good, they aimed to transform the monarch into a superior human through what Edward Peters has called the "progressive enlargement of the [king's] human character."[7] Indeed, as David Starkey has noted about the English monarchy, Spanish royalists similarly promoted the idea that the king's two persons "fused in the actual person of the king" and, thus, that the king's natural body became endowed with singular qualities justifying, therefore, the transformation of the person of the king (and not the royal insignias representing the public royal *persona*) into "the master-symbol" of monarchical power.[8]

It is possible to find such attempts already during the reign of the Catholic Monarchs (Isabel and Ferdinand) when after their victory in the dynastic civil wars of the late fifteenth century their supporters promoted the idea that although the king's natural person was perishable, the monarch had certain personal qualities that made him unique. The Italian humanist Pietro Martire d'Angheria, who was in Isabel's service at the time, declared in 1488, for example, that Isabel and Ferdinand are like "deities, that came to earth from heaven, inspired by a Holy Spirit and guided by God's hand." They are, he continued, "superhuman . . . and everything they think, say and execute excels human nature."[9] Such royal qualities were also seen as inheritable.

It was said, for example, that Prince John, the Catholic Monarchs' son, although still young, never behaved as a minor because he was "a king's successor." Similarly, Prince Charles, the future emperor and Isabel's grand-child, was depicted as possessing all the qualities of a king "from the moment he was begotten in his mother's womb," and thus "by nature he was an almost divine man."[10] Castiglione was no less enthusiastic when he declared that Prince Charles, despite his young age (ten years), already

> displays such wisdom and such certain signs of goodness, prudence, modesty, magnanimity, and every kind of virtue that if, as everybody expects, the empire of Christendom comes to his hands, it is to be believed that he will eclipse the name of many ancient emperors and equal the fame of many of the most famous men who have ever lived.[11]

Because kings were superior humans who belonged to dynasties selected by God to rule over men, they had an innate good judgment in the ruling of their kingdoms and in choosing the course of action most beneficial to the well-being of their communities. By definition, kings could do no wrong. Francisco de Los Cobos, Charles V's powerful secretary, made this point as he described young Philip II:

> I assure Your Majesty, I not only do not have to reject anything that he decides, but I am astonished at his prudent, well-considered recommendations, which are more fitting in a man trained all his life in state and other affairs than in a ruler who is so new at it, in years and in authority. He is, sir, devoted to virtue and justice, scorning all that is contrary to them. Wherefore we all accept and respect his advice because in the midst of the gravity and restraint with which he gives it and points out the errors, it is accompanied by a natural majesty and authority that is terrifying.[12]

Royal apologists also tried to demonstrate that those who were born to be kings had both physical and psychological qualities that distinguished them from other humans. Juan Huarte de San Juan believed, for example, that kings, in contrast to common mortals, had their various humors in ideal balance and, thus, their constitution achieved "supreme perfection." Men born to be kings had a full memory (*memoria*) to see the past, full imagination (*imaginativa*) to see the future, and great understanding (*gran entendimiento*) "to distinguish, infer, reason, judge, and adopt" the best for their kingdoms. The exterior appearance and behavior of the king reflected such special interior qualities: perfect beauty of the face (to attract the love of his subjects), blond hair (the middle of two extremes, black and white), medium height, and virtuous behavior. Huarte attributed such qualities to the Spanish monarchs and only to three other historical figures: Adam (the first human created in God's image), King David (God's favorite monarch), and Jesus (God and the son of God).[13]

These ideas greatly influenced the ways in which Spanish monarchs were publicly portrayed. Indeed, Charles V and Philip II understood, as did the rulers described by Clifford Geertz, that "the king's ability to project himself (or, better, his kingship) as the stationary axis of the world rested on his ability to discipline his emotions and his behavior with meticulous rigor."[14] In Spain the process of creating a similar public image of the king reached its height during Philip II's reign. Philip II was now described as a king who always showed an imperturbable face, who controlled his feelings, who made everyone tremble in his presence and even his brightest counselors dumb, and who displayed, in private and in public, such greatness that his "authority and glory appear divine," comments which were almost identical to those describing God in Exodus.[15] This personal demeanor was also reproduced in court portraits, which disclose "an imposing, cold, distant, and majestic image" of the king, stripped of any symbols of royal power but easily recognized, as the Italian humanist Pietro Aretino noted, by the "gesto bel di maestà reale."[16]

The presentation of the king as a commanding and sacred person, the epitome of royal power, consumed the energies of Philip III's close servants from the beginning of his reign. There was, in the first place, an urgency to portray the new king as a deserving inheritor of his ancestors' glories and virtues. This task was accomplished in part by suggesting a mystical continuity between Philip II and his son. Philip II, professed the royal chaplain Fray Aguilar de Terrones in a sermon preached to honor the late king, had many virtues, but one summarized them all – his capacity to recreate himself in the person of Philip III. Referring to the fact that Philip II had died in his palace-monastery of El Escorial, Father Terrones noted that: "he [Philip II] built his monastery as a silk worm builds its cocoon, and he died there. But he emerged from this cocoon as the new king [Philip III], whom I believe to be a superior Philip II."[17] Despite its simplicity, this metaphor gave Father Terrones's listeners the powerful impression of being in the very presence of a miraculous event effected by God in the persons of His chosen monarchs. To make this image even stronger Father Terrones ended his sermon by suggesting that Philip III's subjects could worship the new ruler, not because he received his power from God but because the king was himself a god: "Although the king is a god in human flesh . . . if he is religious and just [as everyone knows Philip III to be], he actually will become God (*El rey es un Dios en carne humana . . . el Rey es hombre, pero si es religioso y justiciero, Dios se torna*)."[18]

This image of the transfer of power from Philip II to his son, characterized not as a "succession" but as a "resurrection" of the former in the person of Philip III, was repeated *ad infinitum* during the first few months of the new reign.[19] For example, Lope de Vega in *A la muerte del Rey Filipo Segundo, el Prudente*, presented his readers with the image of a dying Philip II surrounded by personifications of the virtues he had mastered during his life – "Religion, Justice, Mercy, Peace, Prudence, Temperance, Truth, and Fortitude" – which accompanied the king to Heaven. Returning to earth, the Virtues were pleasantly surprised to find themselves in front of "a radiant young Philip III, King of Spain and the new Phoenix, / . . . a divine portrait, / and a glorious printed stamp / of the original soul [Philip II]"[20] – a new Phoenix, "expressly chosen" by God, as demonstrated by the deaths of Philip III's older brothers and his own "miraculous" recovery from poor health in his teenage years.[21]

The words, ideas, and concepts embedded in these sermons and poems reappeared as powerful images during the royal entry of Queen Margaret into Madrid in October 1599. As in other monarchies, the royal entries took place when the king officially visited one of the principal cities of his kingdoms for the first time.[22] In its original form the royal entry represented what Malcolm Smuts calls the "communitarian" facet of kingship,[23] as a reenactment of the union between the king and his kingdom, represented in this case by the city. The king was given the keys to the city as a symbol of its obedience, and by accepting them, he swore to protect the city's privileges. By the end of the sixteenth century, and certainly by the seventeenth, the royal entry had become a celebration of the uniqueness of the monarch and of his privileged position in the body politic.[24]

Queen Margaret's entry into Madrid on 24 October 1599 is illustrative. Patterned after the royal entry of Queen Anne of Austria (the fourth wife of Philip II and Philip III's mother), and approved by Philip III after careful study,[25] this entry deployed a liberal use of mythology or what E. H. Gombrich has referred to as the "mythopoetic faculty."[26] Its designers – the Italian sculptor Pompeo Leoni (also involved in the design for the entry of Anne of Austria), the Italian painter Bartolomé Carducho, the Spanish painter Luis de Carvajal, the architect Francisco Gómez de Mora, and an anonymous poet – spared no analogies, symbols, or images that could enlarge the already mighty image of the Spanish king.[27] In the first arch, referred to as "the principal arch" in a document approved by Philip III and dedicated to "the Royal Power and Majesty," Philip III was depicted as "a robust man supporting two worlds, the old world and the new." He was also depicted as the possessor of the virtues of Jupiter (the ray as a symbol of punishment), Neptune (the trident as the power over the seas), Mars (the shield as a symbol of defense of the realm), Hercules (the mace as a symbol of the king's inner fortitude), and Mercury (the wand as a symbol of wisdom).[28] Entering through two other triumphal arches, the royal procession reached the church of Saint Mary near the royal palace. "Two magnificent statues more than twenty feet high," designed by Pompeo Leoni, covered the façade of the church. One represented King Philip III and the other Atlas carrying a half-globe on his shoulders with the following inscription engraved on its base: *Divisum Imperium cum Jove* (I shared the *imperium* with Jupiter), as a reference to Philip III's youth when he shared the heavy burden of ruling the monarchy with his ailing father (Jupiter).[29]

Public displays of Philip III as the heir of his ancestors' glories and virtues continued throughout his reign. The king himself actively promoted the presentation of a powerful image of previous Spanish rulers and of himself through the decorations he commissioned for El Pardo, a countryside royal palace close to Madrid, and the Alcázar, the royal palace in Madrid. Although many of the paintings Philip III authorized for the halls in El Pardo have disappeared, the iconographical series painted throughout the palace included the "Judgment of Solomon," the "Triumph of the Eucharist," and the "Story of Achilles," allegories that presented Philip III as a just, religious, and prudent monarch. In addition, he commissioned portraits of his ancestors and of himself, the queen, and their children in apparent homage to the dynasty and as a demonstration that he was a capable successor of monarchs of sublime reputation.[30] These iconographical programs were crowned by the placing in the gardens of La Casa de Campo of the magnificent statue of Philip III on horseback, the first of its kind in Spain, and a gift to Philip from Ferdinand I, the Grand Duke of Tuscany.[31]

It could be said that these images and the message they conveyed – that the king's power was sacred and that he alone controlled the lives of his subjects – were very similar to those created and displayed in other European monarchies, thus demonstrating that the Spanish monarchy did not differ from its European counterparts in the images of the royal majesty. What really distinguished the Spanish monarchy was the role that "the master-symbol" of the royal office – the natural person of the king – played in the ritualistic and ceremonial public representation of kingship. Historians of early modern Europe are generally agreed that the French and English monarchies created and perfected the most effective modes of ritualizing kingship to impose the ruler's power over his subjects. As a result, the manipulation of the rulers' public image transformed the French and English monarchies into, in the words of Edward Muir, the "most successful monarchies in late medieval and early modern Europe."[32] In this context, the interest of historians focuses upon the constant public presence of the monarch and the transformation of the court into a public stage where the monarch was the principal actor. According to modern historians, royal power in early modern Europe thus required a splendid *mise-en-scène* where that heavenly creature, the monarch, appeared as the paradigm of absolute power.

The two early modern monarchs who were supreme masters of public ritual were Elizabeth of England and Louis XIV of France. Both understood the need to control, use, and manipulate public ceremonies to transform themselves into the inviolable heads of the court hierarchy and to reinforce the perception that political power was identical to the personal power of the king. Elizabeth's ceaseless travels around her realm, for example, made possible her transformation "into the adored object of her subjects."[33] Monarchs who – like James VI and I, Elizabeth's successor – eschewed public rituals are seen as failures. Muir writes that James VI and I, by avoiding public progresses and ceremonies "for more private ceremonies that asserted the divine right of kings, undermined in practice the sacrality he so ardently advocated."[34]

Not all European monarchies should, however, be analyzed by comparison with the models of Elizabeth and Louis XIV. Modern historians' attempts to reduce the variety of historical experiences to schematic and general paradigms applicable to all polities can lead to a simplistic understanding of monarchies where the ritualization of power took alternative, but not necessarily less successful, forms. One must situate monarchies within their own historical context to appreciate how rituals and ceremonials were employed and, ultimately, to determine how effectively they enhanced the king's power. For example, at least until the mid-seventeenth century, Spanish kings were particularly successful in defending their power and prerogatives, even though the ritualization and representation of their royal majesty differed substantially and in many ways contrasted sharply with the practices of other European monarchs. One sometimes wonders whether Elizabeth's and Louis XIV's constant recourse to public rituals and ceremonials demonstrates their "masterly" use of public means of propaganda or their complete inability to avoid participating in the public ceremonies viewed by many royal supporters in the late sixteenth century as handicaps to effective imposition of the monarch's absolute power.

Indeed, the guiding principle of early modern Spanish rulers' public behavior, since at least the mid-sixteenth century, was, using John H. Elliott's compelling words, the monarchs' "invisibility, and indeed their sheer inaccessibility."[35] This practice was the culmination of a series of challenges to the established views of royal power, especially those concerning the relationship of the ruler to other members of the body politic. Well into the sixteenth century, Spanish rulers were forced to contend with theories according to which the king's sacred duty was to listen to the advice of the members of the body politic and to be open and familiar. The "face of the king not only pleases," a late fifteenth-century anonymous pamphlet alleged, "it inspires, arouses, pleases, and invigorates the king's subjects."[36] The commonly held view was that an open and public monarch gained the loyalty of his subjects, whereas an aloof and private monarch created mistrust and promoted factions and rebellions. As a result, monarchs were advised to give unlimited access to members of the body politic and to transform the royal palace into a public space, "a place where the king exercises justice personally, where he eats and talks with his subjects," according to *Las siete partidas* of Alfonso X the Wise, one of the most influential legal texts in medieval and early modern Spain.[37]

The constant flow of petitioners and others seeking to counsel the king, however, developed into a chronic source of frustration. Already in the late fifteenth century Isabel and Ferdinand had tried to curtail the right of entry into the royal chambers and to restrict it to a select group of servants. But their success appears to have been limited. Queen Isabel, for example, often bitterly complained about the unlimited access her subjects had to her person and private chambers. At the time, available means to limit and regulate access to the queen's private chamber remained primitive and not very effective – "to stay in bed all day, even if I am not sick at all, only because I want to be alone." Even when she was in bed her courtiers failed to leave her alone.[38] The situation began to change with the advent of the Habsburgs. Although Charles, to counteract the mistrust of Spaniards toward a "foreign king," maintained a high level of visibility and accessibility,[39] he challenged old practices by introducing stricter ceremonies of greeting and showing respect to the king. One of his agents in Castile had brought to his attention the political significance of such ceremonies in 1517. "Because authority should descend from the head to the members of the body politic," the king should not allow anyone to become too familiar with him. Instead he should require everyone to observe manners, such as kissing the king's hand and remaining bareheaded in his presence, designed to emphasize the king's superior position.[40]

But even more far-reaching in its impact was the introduction and promotion of a new palace etiquette, one of the first steps in the creation of a new model of Spanish kingship. In 1515 Emperor Maximilian I, Charles's grandfather, had established a new etiquette for Charles's household, which incorporated Maximilian's principle of privacy and certain other elements characteristic of the court of the Austrian and Spanish Habsburgs – a distant king and a strict courtly hierarchy based on one's degree of intimacy with the prince.[41] The primary purpose of the 1515 etiquette was to enforce the prince's privacy by allowing only the *sumiller de corps* to be present when the king went to sleep or got up, and by prohibiting everyone from approaching and talking with the king during his lunch and dinner except for officials in charge of serving his food. The etiquette also instituted a hierarchical degree of intimacy with the prince based on spatial criteria. Only the *sumiller de corps* and palace servants with specific missions were permitted entry into the prince's privy chamber. The rooms closest to the prince's chamber, in turn, were reserved, in the following order, for the "huissiers," and the "pensioners, chambellans, maistres d'hostel et gentilzhommes."[42] That Charles V himself regarded this Burgundian model of a distant and private monarch as best suited to his desire to establish a strong monarchy is reflected in the palace etiquette he himself ordered for his son, the future Philip II, in 1548 despite the opposition of many of his Castilian subjects. Again this etiquette emphasized the king's privacy by giving access to the prince's quarters only to a small number of palace officials.[43]

The most important consequence of these principles was the transformation of the royal household and the king's private quarters into a pivotal center of power and influence, into the "primary sphere of the king's rule."[44] The king's chamber, or as the Spaniards called it at the time, the *retrete* ("the most secret part of the house"), was transformed into a "dreadful place where [invisible] Power lurks."[45] The monarch's inaccessibility also gave new meaning to the royal palace by transforming it into the monarch's private space to which he withdrew accompanied only by a small, select group of servants who helped him to rule his kingdoms and shared his thoughts, his ambitions, and, ultimately, his power.

Writing on the French court during Louis XIV's reign, Norbert Elias asserts that for the king palace etiquette "was an instrument not only of distancing but of power,"[46] something early modern Spanish monarchs clearly understood. In effect, from tentative beginnings in the reign of Charles V, and much more definitely from the time of Philip II, the strict limitations of *entrée* to the king's privy chambers were accompanied by the monarch's increasing withdrawal from public view. During Philip II's reign, the inaccessibility and invisibility of the king came to be viewed as key elements in the practice of kingship, and Philip II's supporters began to defend the idea that the king's invisibility was essential for the promotion of obedience and reverence among the king's subjects. Indeed, as soon as he inherited the throne, Philip II stopped attending the meetings of the various councils and the *Cortes*. As a result, his subjects could only speak with him if they were given access to his person and chambers, a right that was reserved to a limited number of palace officials. The king portrayed by Philip II's contemporaries was a king who never spoke in public, who remained aloof and spent much of his time enclosed in his palaces, especially in the palace at El Escorial. Philip II even avoided participation in the public ceremonies (including royal entries), which many modern historians consider the crucial instrument for imposing the king's power.[47] For Philip II public ceremonials became dutiful performances that kept his subjects content, not instruments of political domination.

As with other aspects of kingship, Philip II tried to instill similar behavior in his son, Philip III, and it was during Philip III's reign that the king's inaccessibility was turned into an enduring political axiom, a sort of religion of state and an essential component in the constitution of royal power. Although both English and French rulers also attempted to isolate themselves by retreating into an aristocratic milieu, this practice never replaced the accepted principle that a real king should remain a public king.[48] As the Frenchman Pierre Matthieu observed, the French needed a visible and accessible king because otherwise they would believe that there was no king, whereas Spaniards believed that the power of the royal majesty would increase when the king was invisible and inaccessible.[49] Early seventeenth-century Spanish political authors also noted this distinctive character of the Spanish kingship. Juan Fernández de Medrano, for example, advised the king that "it is a certain kind of religion to retire from your subjects. You should not become familiar with anyone, except with the person who is your oracle [meaning 'favorite'], because *continuus aspectus minus verendos magnos homines ipsa satietate facit.*"[50] Medrano could choose many historical examples to support his views, but he settled on Emperor Tiberius, who according to Medrano had lived "*Occultum, ac subdolum fingendis virtutibus*" ("Hidden and deceitful, feigning virtue").[51]

Tiberius and others among the ancients were not the only examples evoked by early seventeenth-century Spanish writers to justify their king's inaccessibility and invisibility. As important as these historical models were those taken from Christian doctrine and traditions, including the doctrine of the Holy Sacrament. Diego de Guzmán, Queen Margaret's biographer, for example, criticized those who advocated that the Holy Sacrament be publicly exposed all day, thus visible to everyone at all times. Such exhibition, he feared, would result in a loss of "the respect, reverence, and love due to Him" by transforming the holy representation of Jesus Christ into an ordinary custom. "Those who see me will die, our Lord said. In this way God imposed respect and fear among men," and, according to Guzmán, a monarch, God's representative on earth, should behave similarly by limiting his public exposure and by prohibiting his subjects from attempting to see him outside established (and increasingly exceptional) public ceremonies.[52]

In addition, as these precepts suggest, the king's invisibility meant that the monarch should speak only with a small group of select individuals. If the king were to speak with everyone, he would lose the respect and obedience of his subjects, the author of "Discurso de las privanzas" advised. Taking Tiberius as his example, he further noted that "in [Tiberius's] times the only permitted way to address the prince was by writing, even when the prince was present."[53] Silence was thus considered an ideal way for the Spanish king to establish his preeminence, to protect his power and reputation.[54] In 1598, the year of Philip II's death, Giovanni Botero advocated exactly such behavior when he proposed that a monarch should always keep his thoughts secret and not speak too much. "Men somewhat taciturn and melancholic are more revered than the merry and loquacious; and in sum where the Prince can make himself understood with deeds he ought not to use words."[55] To Philip III and his favorite, to use the words of Frank Whigham, "speech and other significations revealed not power but powerlessness, a pleading with the audience for a hearing, for recognition, for ratification."[56]

Philip III's silence in public, his aloofness, and his tendency to be "in solitude with very little court," accompanied always by his favorite, caught the imagination of his contemporaries almost from the start of his reign.[57] Queen Margaret's entry into Madrid late in 1599 was, for example, distinguished by the fact that no one could see the king, who remained hidden from public view accompanied only by Lerma,[58] offering his subjects a still more compelling image of the king, now imagined and depicted as a god and a hero in the triumphal arches and statues displayed in Madrid at the time. Philip III's withdrawal from public view in the company of his favorite continued throughout his reign. This custom met both the king's need to remain aloof from his subjects and Lerma's desire to exercise control over access to the king. After all, Lerma had been told that Philip II "was obeyed and feared even when he had locked himself into his rooms" and that he should promote the king's inaccessibility to establish Philip III's authority and his own influence.[59]

Such principles inspired one of the less understood measures taken early in the reign: the relocation of the royal court from Madrid to Valladolid for what proved to be a period of six years
(1601–6). Modern historians have interpreted this event as a manifestation of Lerma's economic
self-interest because his Castilian lands were closer to Valladolid than to Madrid. The presence
of the royal court – the richest and largest internal market – increased demand for local products
of all kinds, and the move clearly benefited Lerma's estates. Only apparently motivated by
Lerma's interests, however, the relocation of the court to Valladolid occurred primarily for political reasons. In fact, Philip III had inherited a bankrupt, dysfunctional, and overpopulated court-
city, and Madrid's defects "became an emblem for the *mal gobierno* [bad government] of the old
regime."[60] Almost immediately after his accession, Philip III created a special committee to
examine the situation in Madrid and the possible relocation of the court to an alternative site and
requested the committee to recommend measures that might be taken to create a new court for
a new king.[61] Madrid, as depicted in the committee's report, was an over-populated, confronta-
tional, and noisy court full of "vices and sins," where it was impossible to protect the king's
privacy because the offices of the councils were located in the royal palace. The committee saw
few advantages in keeping the court in Madrid and recommended that it relocate to one of several
Castilian cities that in the past had hosted the royal court: Valladolid, Toledo, or Burgos. In the
end Philip III chose Valladolid, arguing that he had received reports stating that there was sufficient infrastructure to host the royal family.

The committee also presented Philip III with a set of recommendations to help him avoid a
fate for the court in Valladolid similar to the one in Madrid. The king was told to establish rigid
controls over who should have the right to live at the court and to remember that it was important to have not "a populous court but a populous kingdom." The committee thus proposed that
residence at Valladolid be limited to those who had lived there prior to the relocation of the court
and to those who held court or palace offices. Nobles should live on their estates; the councils
should be relocated to other cities, with the exception of the Council of State. The dispersal of
the councils would mean that those searching for rewards or justice need not go to the court,
thereby weakening the power of the councils by separating them from the king's person.

Philip III did not, however, follow all of the committee's recommendations. The councils, for
example, were permitted to remain at the court, although their chambers were no longer located
in the royal palace as they had been in Madrid. The new rulers did try to restrict the number of
residents permitted to live at the court. Immediately before the court's relocation, a royal order
was issued prohibiting the entry of all individuals who did not have a letter-patent signed by the
committee in charge of relocating the court to Valladolid.[62] According to Luis Cabrera de
Córdoba, this measure seems to have succeeded, at least initially, because the new rulers were
able to prevent the entry of many "insignificant" individuals – widows, beggars, and idle persons
without business or office at the court.[63] Success did not last, however, and soon the problems
of Valladolid were similar to those experienced by the court in Madrid. Furthermore, despite
assurances of an infrastructure adequate to a royal court, it soon became obvious that it was
impossible to maintain the royal family at Valladolid in the decorum to which they were accustomed. This inadequacy was the main reason why Philip III decided to return the court to Madrid
in 1606.[64]

Notwithstanding their failure to control unruliness at the court, Philip III's and Lerma's behavior at Valladolid established the style of the new regime regarding the king's public presence.
Lerma had taken upon himself to arrange the new royal quarters in Valladolid, which he bought,
redecorated, and later sold to the king. The buildings housing the royal family were a complex
set of edifices connected through second-floor passages to protect the royal family's privacy, trans-

forming the royal palace into a private space that was opened to the public only on selected ceremonial occasions.[65] Lerma also made available to the king his own palace in Valladolid, La Huerta de la Ribera, an enormous residence located just outside the city on the banks of the Pisuerga River. There the monarch, his family, and entourage could rest and attend the masques, theatrical performances, banquets, naval ballets, and bullfights that Lerma organized to entertain his master.[66] The routine established in Valladolid was followed once the court returned to Madrid. Lerma bought and reconditioned the Quinta del Prior, also known as Huertas del Duque de Lerma, an enormous *hacienda* located in the Paseo del Prado, a suburb of Madrid, where he again organized many spectacles to entertain the king and the royal entourage.[67]

In addition to enjoying the protected spaces at the court, Philip III, accompanied by Lerma, spent as much time as possible in his or Lerma's countryside residences. Lerma, firm in his belief that such retreats were essential to maintain his political independence and to hold the king's favor, was undeterred by criticism accusing him of taking "the king to the countryside to prevent everyone from speaking with him."[68] Thus, Philip – always in Lerma's company but often without members of his own family – spent long periods in El Pardo, which was rebuilt and redecorated under the king's supervision after a fire in 1604, in Aranjuez, and, particularly after 1606, in El Escorial or in Lerma's residences, including the town of Lerma, ostentatiously rebuilt after 1606, and in La Ventosilla, a hunting palace located near Valladolid.[69] These residences were private spaces where indiscreet individuals who did not belong to Lerma's inner circle were forbidden,[70] leaving Philip III, Lerma, and their entourage to hunt, entertain themselves, and attend to the affairs of state free from outside influence.

NOTES

1 Stephen Orgel, *The Illusion of Power* (Berkeley, 1975), p. 47.

2 "Sermón predicado en el funeral por Felipe II," in Fray Alonso de Cabrera, *Sermones del maestro Fray Alonso de Cabrera*, ed. Manuel Mir (Madrid, 1906), p. 699.

3 Mariana, *De rege*, p. 154.

4 Clifford Geertz, *Negara. The Theatre State in Nineteenth-Century Bali* (Princeton, 1980), p. 124.

5 For a survey of these theories see Fernández Albaladejo, *Fragmentos de monarquía*, pp. 72–85.

6 The implications of the Spanish theory of the king's two persons has not yet been explored in its entirety; for some aspects of this theory see Bartolomé Clavero, "*Hispanus Fiscus, Persona Ficta*: concepción del sujeto político en la época Barroca," in Clavero, *Tantas personas como estados* (Madrid, 1986), pp. 53–105. The most important general reference remains Ernst H. Kantorowicz, *The King's Two Bodies* (Princeton, 1957).

7 Edward Peters, *The Shadow King. Rex Inutilis in the Medieval Law and Literature, 751–1327* (New Haven, 1970), p. 214.

8 David Starkey, "Representation through Intimacy," in Ioan Lewis, ed., *Symbols and Sentiments* (London, 1977), p. 188.

9 Pietro Martire d'Angheria, *Epistolario de Pedro Mártir de Anglería*, ed. J. López Toro, 4 vols. (Madrid, 1953–7), vol. 1, pp. 6, 7, Martire de Angheria to Juan Borromeo and Teodoro Papiense, 2 Feb. 1488.

10 *Ibid.*, vol. 111, pp. 101–2, and IV, p. 86, Angheria to Luis Hurtado de Mendoza, 1 Jan. 1513, and to the Duke of Mondéjar and the Duke of Vélez, 13 Nov. 1520. See also the words of the Bishop of Badajoz in *Cortes de los Antiguos Reinos de Castilla y León*, 5 vols. (Madrid, 1857), vol. IV, p. 293.

11 Castiglione, *El cortesano*, vol. II, p. 149.

12 Francisco de los Cobos to Charles V, 1543?; cf. Hayward Keniston, *Francisco de los Cobos, Secretary of the Emperor Charles V* (Pittsburgh, Pa., 1960), pp. 269–70. On Philip II's image see Fernando Bouza

Alvarez, "La majestad de Felipe II. Construcción del mito real," in José Martínez Millán, ed., *La corte de Felipe II* (Madrid, 1994).

13 Juan Huarte de San Juan, *Examen de ingenios para las ciencias* [1575], ed. Esteban Torre (Madrid, 1977), chap. 14, pp. 288, 291–3 and 302–8. Huarte's book was frequently translated into other languages: French (twenty-two editions from 1580 to 1675); Italian (seven editions between 1582 and 1604); English (five editions between 1594 and 1698); Latin (1622), and so on; see Torre's edn., pp. 51–2. See also Castiglione, *El cortesano*, vol. I, p. 149.

14 Geertz, *Negara*, p. 130.

15 Cabrera de Córdoba, *Historia de Felipe II*, vol. I, pp. 323–4. Exodus 19:22–4, 20:18–21.

16 Cf. H. E. Wethey, *The Paintings of Titian. 11: The Portraits* (London, 1971), p. 42. On the portraits of the Spanish kings see Fernando Checa Cremades, *Pintura y escultura del Renacimiento en España, 1450–1600* (Madrid, 1983), pp. 349–57, and Jonathan Brown, "Enemies of Flattery: Velázquez' Portraits of Philip IV," *Journal of Interdisciplinary History*, 17 (1986), pp. 137–54.

17 "Sermón que predicó a la Majd. del Rey don Felipe III el doctor Aguilar de Terrones su predicador, en las honras que su Majd. hizo al católico Rey d. Felipe Segundo, que sea en gloria, en San Gerónimo de Madrid, a 19 del mes de octubre de 1598," in Juan Iñíguez de Lequerica, ed., *Sermones funerales en las honras del rey nuestro señor don Felipe II, con el que se predicó en las de la serenísima infanta doña Catalina duquesa de Saboya* (Madrid, 1599), fol. 21r.

18 *Ibid.*, fol. 23v. On Father Aguilar de Terrones's sermon and in general on preachers and preaching during Philip III's reign see Hilary Dansey Smith, *Preaching in the Spanish Golden Age. A Study of Some Preachers of the Reign of Philip III* (Oxford, 1978); pp. 48–9 on Terrones's sermon.

19 Iñíguez de Lequerica, the editor of Terrones's sermon and other funeral sermons dedicated to Philip II, reminded his readers that Philip II "has bequeathed us a son so equal to himself in his name and deeds" that the transmittal of power "was not a simple succession but a resurrection of Philip II as Philip III [*que no pareciese sucesión sino resurección*]" in *ibid.*, "Prologue of Lequerica," n.p.; see also "Sermón que predicó el padre Maestro Fray Agustín Dávila de la Orden de los Predicadores, calificador del Santo Oficio, en 8 de noviembre de 1598 a las honras que la ciudad de Valladolid hizo en su iglesia mayor al rey Felipe II nuestro señor," fol. 80v.

20 "A la muerte del Rey Filipo Segundo, el Prudente," in Lope Félix Vega Carpio, *Obras escogidas de Lope de Vega*, ed. Federico Carlos Sainz de Robles, 3 vols., 2nd edn. (Madrid, 1987), vol. II, p. 98.

21 Biblioteca Nacional, Madrid (BNM) Mss 8526, "Discurso sobre el gobierno que ha de tener Su Majd. en su monarquía para conservarla," anon., Madrid, 15 Oct. 1599, fol. 19v.

22 Gonzalo Fernández de Oviedo, *Libro de la cámara real del príncipe don Juan y oficios de su casa y servicio ordinario* [1530?], ed. J. M. Escudero (Madrid, 1870), p. 102.

23 R. Malcolm Smuts, "Public Ceremony and Royal Charisma: the English Royal Entry in London, 1485–1642," in A. L. Beier, David Cannadine, and James M. Rosenheim, eds., *The First Modern Society. Essays in English History in Honour of Lawrence Stone* (Cambridge, 1989), p. 76; a good summary of this ceremony is in Roy Strong, *Art and Power* (Berkeley, 1984), pp. 7–11, 44–50.

24 *Ibid.*, p. 48; on the royal entry in Spain and its evolution, see Checa Cremades, *Pintura y escultura*, pp. 371–83; and Alicia Cámara Muñoz, "El poder de la imagen y la imagen del poder. La fiesta en el Madrid del Renacimiento," in *Madrid en el Renacimiento* (Madrid, 1986), pp. 66–77.

25 José Martí y Monsó, *Estudios histórico-artísticos relativos principalmente a Valladolid* (Valladolid, 1898), pp. 277–8. The royal approval is dated in Valencia, on 8 Mar. 1599. In this authorization the king also ordered that nothing should be done without his prior permission. On Queen Margaret's entry see also Virginia Tovar Martín, "La entrada triunfal en Madrid de doña Margarita de Austria (24 de octubre de 1599)," *Archivo Español de Arte*, 61 (1988), pp. 385–403.

26 E. H. Gombrich, "Icones Symbolicae. Philosophies of Symbolism and their Bearing in Art," in his *Symbolic Images. Studies in the Art in the Renaissance* (Chicago, 1985), pp. 128–30.

27 The different reports on the preparation of this entry mentioned a poet or poets charged with creating the "soul" of the triumphal arches, but they never mentioned who those poets were: Martí y Monsó, *Estudios histórico-artísticos*, pp. 277, 281.

28 Tovar Martín, "La entrada triunfal," pp. 390–5.

29 *Ibid.*, p. 402. The texts that described this entry do not explain the meaning of the statue of Atlas; it is important to remember, however, that Pompeo Leoni also designed the last statue of Anne of Austria's royal entry in 1570, representing Philip II as Atlas bearing the world on his shoulders. See López de Hoyos, *Real aparato*, fol. 40.

30 On decorations in El Pardo see Vicente Carducho, *Diálogos de la pintura* [*c.* 1636], ed. Francisco Calvo Serraller (Madrid, 1979), Dialogue 7, pp. 328–33; José Miguel Morán, "Felipe III y las Artes," *Anales de Historia del Arte*, I (1989), pp. 159–75; Rosa López Torrijos, *La mitología en la pintura española del siglo de oro* (Madrid, 1985), pp. 198–203; and Mary Newcome, "Genoese Drawings for the Queen's Gallery in El Pardo," *Antichità Viva*, 29 (1990), pp. 22–30. On the collection of portraits of Philip III's ancestors and relatives see "Memoria de los retratos que sean hecho para la casa Real del Pardo [por Pantoja de la Cruz]," a document published in Maria Kusche, *Juan Pantoja de la Cruz* (Madrid, 1964), pp. 65–7; and J. Moreno Villa and F. J. Sánchez Cantón, "Noventa y siete retratos de la familia de Felipe III por Bartolomé González," *Archivo Español de Arte y Arqueología*, 38 (1937). On the plans to redecorate El Alcázar commissioned by Philip III from Vicente Carducho, which were abandoned when Philip III died in 1621, see Carducho, *Diálogos*, pp. 326–7; and Steven N. Orso, *Philip IV and the Decoration of the Alcázar de Madrid* (Princeton, 1986), pp. 121ff.

31 The statue was commissioned by Ferdinand I in 1600; Giambologna designed the statue and worked on it from 1606 until his death in 1608 when Pietro Tacca replaced him. See Walter A. Liedtke, *The Royal Horse and Rider. Painting, Sculpture and Horsemanship, 1500–1800* (New York, 1989), pp. 70, 204–5. On the origins of this statue see Edward L. Goldberg, "Artistic Relations between the Medici and the Spanish Courts, 1587–1621: Part I," *The Burlington Magazine*, 138 (1996), p. 114. On contemporary references to this statue see Antonio Liñán y Verdugo, *Guía y avisos de forasteros que vienen a la corte* [1620], ed. Edisons Simons (Madrid, 1980), p. 177. Today the statue is situated in the Plaza Mayor of Madrid, the most important architectural improvement in Madrid during Philip III's reign.

32 Edward Muir, *Ritual in Early Modern Europe* (Cambridge, 1997), p. 249.

33 *Ibid.*, p. 246.

34 *Ibid.* On Louis XIV, see Louis Marin, *Portrait of the King*, trans. Martha M. Houlé (Minneapolis, Minn., 1988); and Peter Burke, *The Fabrication of Louis XIV* (New Haven, 1992).

35 "The Court of the Spanish Habsburgs: A Peculiar Institution?", in John H. Elliott, *Spain and its World, 1500–1700* (New Haven, 1989), p. 148. See also Fernando Checa Cremades, "Felipe II en el Escorial: la representación del poder real," in *El Escorial: arte, poder y cultura en la corte de Felipe II* (Madrid, 1989), pp. 17–20.

36 BNM, Mss 6020, "Advertencias del buen govierno," fol. 77v.

37 *Las siete partidas del rey Don Alfonso el Sabio* (Madrid, 1989), pt. II, tit. 9, law 29, "Qué cosa es palacio."

38 Ochoa, *Epistolario*, vol. II, p. 17, Queen Isabel to her confessor, Hernando de Talavera, 30 Dec. 1494; on Ferdinand and Isabel's contradictory behavior toward access to the royal chambers see Ladero Quesada, *La hacienda real*, pp. 372–3; and *ibid.*, *Los Reyes Católicos*, pp. 82–3.

39 For a few contemporary references see Antonio Rodríguez Villa, ed., "El emperador Carlos V y su corte (1522–1539): Cartas de D. Martín de Salinas," *Boletín de la Academia de la Historia*, 93 (1903), pp. 55, 93; and Francisco López de Villalobos, *Algunas obras*, 2 vols. (Madrid, 1886), vol. I, pp. 144–5.

40 Fernández Alvarez, *Corpus documental*, vol. I, p. 69, Cardinal Cisneros? to Adrian of Utrecht, 1517?; on the importance of keeping one's head covered in the presence of the king and the changes introduced by Charles see Elliott, "The Court of the Spanish Habsburgs," p. 152.

41 For the "Burgundian style" see C. A. F. Armstrong, "The Golden Age of Burgundy," in A. G. Dickens, ed., *The Courts of Europe. Politics, Patronage and Royalty* (New York, 1977), pp. 55–75; and Werner Paravicini, "The Court of the Dukes of Burgundy. A Model for Europe?" in R. G. Asch and A. M. Birke, eds., *Princes, Patronage and the Nobility. The Court at the Beginning of the Modern Age, c. 1450–1650* (Oxford, 1991), pp. 69–102.

42 "Ordonnance de Charles, prince d'Espagne, archiduc de Bourgogne . . . pour le governement de sa maison," in M. Gachard, *Collection des voyages des souverains des Pays-Bas*, 3 vols. (Brussels, 1874), vol. II, app. I.

43 On the new etiquette of the royal palace see Antonio Rodríguez Villa, *Etiquetas de la casa de Austria* (Madrid, 1913); for an excellent analysis of palace etiquette in early modern Spain see Elliott, "The Court of the Spanish Habsburgs," pp. 143–54. On the opposition to this palace etiquette see Helen Nader, "Habsburg Ceremony in Spain: The Reality of the Myth," *Historical Reflections/Réflexions Historiques*, 15 (1988).

44 Norbert Elias, *The Court Society*, trans. Edmund Jephcott (New York, 1983), p. 119. Elias's words refer to the royal court in general, but given the conditions in the Spanish monarchy the real center of power, the center from which the Spanish monarch imposed his will, was the royal palace, and throughout the early modern period Spanish monarchs concerned themselves more with the royal household and palace than with the royal court in general.

45 These are the words used by Roland Barthes in his analysis of Racine's plays; see Roland Barthes, *On Racine*, English trans. Richard Howard (Berkeley, 1992), pp. 3–4. On the meaning of the word *retrete* see Sebastián de Covarrubias Orozco, *Tesoro de la lengua castellana o española* [1611], facsimile edn. (Madrid, 1984), *s. v.* "retrete."

46 Elias, *The Court Society*, p. 117; see also his *The Civilizing Process: The History of Manners and State Formation and Civilization*, trans. Edmund Jephcott (Oxford, 1994), p. 267.

47 See Parker, *Philip II*, pp. 20–2, 82.

48 On this topic, see Smuts, "Public Ceremony," p. 85; Orest Ranum, "Courtesy, Absolutism, and the Rise of the French State, 1630–1660," *Journal of Modern History*, 52 (1980), pp. 426–51. For the Russian case, see Valerie A. Kivelson, "The Devil Stole His Mind: The Tsar and the 1648 Moscow Uprising," *American Historical Review*, 98 (1993), pp. 733–56.

49 BNM, Mss 9078, "Breve compendio I elogio de la vida del rey Don Phelipe segundo de felicissima memoria escrito en francés por Pierre Matiu," fols. 32r–v; cf. Bouza Alvarez, "La majestad de Felipe II," p. 52. See also Conde de Salinas, "Dictamen del conde de Salinas en que se examinan las prerogativas de la corona y de las cortes de Portugal" [1612], ed. Erasmo Buceta, in *Anuario de Historia del Derecho Español*, 9 (1932), p. 378.

50 This Latin sentence, meaning "if great men are seen often they are less revered," was included by Giovanni Botero (*The Reason of State*, ed. P. J. Waley and D. P. Waley [London, 1956], p. 57) in the Italian version of his *Ragion di Stato*. Antonio de Herrera y Tordesillas did not include this sentence in his Spanish translation of Botero's work.

51 Juan Fernández de Medrano, *República mixta* (Madrid, 1602), p. 32. The aloofness of Tiberius, a ruler who moved his headquarters far from Rome to distance himself from Senate pressure, is a crucial element in Tacitus's *Annals*, 4.41, 57–8, 67, in Tacitus, *Complete Works*, ed. Moses Hadas (New York, 1942). See also Alamos de Barrientos, *Aforismos*, vol. I, pp. 99–100; Lorenzo Ramírez de Prado, *Consejo y consejeros de príncipes* [1617], ed. Juan Beneyto (Madrid, 1958), p. 24. These three books were dedicated to the Duke of Lerma. See also Antonio de Herrera, "Discurso de cómo se ha de entender que cosa es Majestad, decoro y reputación," in BNM, Mss 3011, Antonio de Herrera, "Primera parte de las varias epístolas, discursos, y tratados dirigidos al rey nro. señor don Felipe IV," fols. 16rff. On the "invisibility" of Philip III as the result of the image of the royal majesty created by Philip II see Javier Varela, *La muerte del rey. El ceremonial funerario de la monarquía española (1500–1850)* (Madrid, 1990), pp. 53ff.

52 Diego de Guzmán, *Vida y muerte de doña Margarita de Austria, reina de España* (Madrid, 1617), fols. 229v–230. See also Juan Pablo Mártir Rizo, *La Poética de Aristóteles traducida del latín* [1623], ed. Margerete Newels (Cologue, 1965), pp. 44–5, 75.

53 "Al rey don Felipe III: discurso de las privanzas," in Quevedo y Villegas, *Obras*, vol. II, p. 1393.

54 Francisco de Gurmendi, *Doctrina física y moral de príncipes* (Madrid, 1615), bk. 1, chap. 6: "De la importancia y excelencia del silencio," fol. 22v; Francisco de Gurmendi, too, dedicated his book to Lerma.

55 "Aggiunte," in Botero, *Practical Politics*, p. 240. See also "Imagen del silencio y descripción de lo que sus partes representa," in Juan de Jarava, *Problemas o preguntas problemáticas* (Alcalá de Henares, 1546), fols. 156v–168v; and Pliny the Elder, *Historia natural de los animales*, trans. Jerónimo de Huerta (Madrid, 1603), bk. 7, chap. 23, fol. 57.

56 Frank Whigham, *Ambition and Privilege. The Social Tropes of Elizabethan Courtesy Theory* (Berkeley, 1984), pp. 39, 51.

57 Simeone Contarini to the Venetian senate 1605; cf. Elliott, "The Court of the Spanish Habsburgs," p. 148. On the treatment of these characteristics by the literature of the period see Antonio Feros, "Vicedioses pero humanos: el drama del rey," *Cuadernos de Historia Moderna*, 14 (1993), pp. 103–31.

58 Cabrera de Córdoba, *Relaciones*, p. 47.

59 BNM, Mss 18275, "Memorial que dieron al Duque de Lerma, cuando entró en el valimiento del sr. Rey Felipe III," fol. 2r.

60 The situation of Madrid, the scandals created by "prostitutes," the increase in the population, the relaxation of customs, and so on, were the subject of considerable debate during the reign of Philip II; see, for example, BFZ, *carp.* 132, fol. 54: report of the *junta* in charge of the "reformation" of customs in Madrid, 4 Sept. 1586. See also Claudia Sieber, "Madrid: A City for a King," paper presented at the meeting of the Society for Spanish and Portuguese Historical Studies, St. Louis, 1987, p. 1.

61 Archivo General de Simancas (AGS) GJ, *leg.* 897, a report without date and author; I thank Dr. Claudia Sieber for drawing my attention to this important document. On the debate over the removal of the court and the constitution of this special committee see Sieber, "Madrid: A City for a King," pp. 4–7.

62 Luisa de Carvajal to Magdalena de San Jerónimo, letters of 16 Oct. 1600, 29 Jan. and 29 May 1601, in Carvajal y Mendoza, *Epistolario y poesías*, pp. 107, 109, 113.

63 Cabrera de Córdoba, *Relaciones*, p. 99.

64 Lerma and his followers justified this move by suggesting that the local government in Valladolid had failed to transform the city into an attractive and well-appointed court. See AGS Est., *leg.* 201/n.p., "Ordenes del duque de Lerma de parte de su Majd. a don Pedro Franqueza sobre diferentes materias," Dec. 1605.

65 Lerma bought all the buildings from various nobles between 1599 and 1600 and sold them to the king in December 1601. On the royal quarters at Valladolid see the excellent article by Jesús Urrea, "La Plaza de San Pablo como escenario de la corte," in *Actas del 1 Congreso de Historia de Valladolid* (Valladolid, 1999), pp. 15–29; Luis Cervera Vera, *El conjunto palacial de la villa de Lerma* (Valencia, 1967), chaps. 1–3; José J. Rivera Blanco, *El palacio real de Valladolid* (Valladolid, 1981), chaps. 4–6; Agustín Bustamante García, *La arquitectura clasicista del foco vallisoletano (1561–1640)* (Valladolid, 1983), pp. 395–402.

66 That La Huerta was useful for Lerma only as far as it could be used to impose his dominion over the king's activities is demonstrated by the fact that Lerma sold it to the king in June 1606 when the court's return to Madrid was a *fait accompli*. On the conditions of this sale, see AGS CC ME, *leg.* 920, *exp.* 8, Memorandum of Lerma, 11 July 1607. See also Cervera Vera, *El conjunto palacial*; and Bustamante García, *La arquitectura clasicista*, pp. 402–3; for a contemporary account of the activities of Lerma and the king at Valladolid see the memoirs of Tomé Pinheiro da Veiga, a Portuguese who lived in Valladolid until the court returned to Madrid: Tomé Pinheiro da Veiga, *Fastiginia o fastos geniales* [1605], ed. Narciso Alonso Cortés (Valladolid, 1916).

67 On the Quinta del Prior, demolished at the end of the nineteenth century to build the Palace Hotel, see Archivo de los Duques de Lerma, Toledo (ADL), *leg.* 1/*exp.* 9, and *leg.* 40/*exp.* 8, and AGS CC, Libros de Cédulas, bk. 172, royal decree, 10 Oct. 1605; see also María Isabel Gea Ortigas, *El Madrid desaparecido* (Madrid, 1992), p. 118. In the *relaciones* written by Cabrera de Córdoba are numerous references to the activities organized by Lerma in his residence.

68 BNM, Mss 1492, "Papel que escribió el Cardenal Sandoval, arzobispo de Toledo, al duque de Lerma," for. 32v.

69 On Philip III's preference for El Pardo, see Fernando Checa Cremades and José Miguel Morán, *El coleccionismo en España* (Madrid, 1985), pp. 228–30; on La Ventosilla and Lerma, see Cervera Vera, *El conjunto palacial*.

70 See, for example, Cabrera de Córdoba, *Relaciones*, pp. 163–4, 253–4, 286; and AGS Est., *leg.* 200/n.p., report of Pedro de Franqueza, Valladolid, 23 May 1605.

24

THE ROYAL GOVERNMENT, GUILDS, AND THE
SEAMSTRESSES OF PARIS, NORMANDY, AND PROVENCE

Clare Haru Crowston

Scholars of women's work have tended to agree that female labor opportunities declined in Europe from the late Middle Ages through the end of the seventeenth century. According to this argument, as guilds grew in strength across the early modern period they gradually excluded women, with the active support of local and royal authorities. Those who retained guild privileges, notably masters' wives and widows, found their privileges drastically reduced over time. These limitations were but one aspect of an overall loss of independence for women, who became increasingly confined by law and male family authority. As Natalie Zemon Davis has written: "Women suffered for their powerlessness in both Catholic and Protestant lands in the late sixteenth to eighteenth centuries as changes in marriage laws restricted the freedom of wives even further, as female guilds dwindled, as the female role in middle-level commerce and farm direction contracted, and as the differential between male and female wages increased."[1]

The seamstresses pose a striking challenge to the thesis of a linear decline in women's economic and legal status during the early modern period. In 1675, when the triumph of absolutism, corporatism, and patriarchal marriage legislation might lead one to expect the nadir of women's experience, one discovers instead the creation of new independent seamstresses' guilds in Paris and Rouen. Moreover, after this date female needleworkers in many provincial cities and towns became members of tailors' guilds. By the 1750s, seamstresses held the title of guild mistress in at least fifteen cities and towns in the regions of Brittany, Normandy, Provence, Ile-de-France, Picardy, and Auvergne. In all of these cases, seamstresses were allowed to work for women and children only, and were explicitly prohibited from working for men. Using the cities of Paris, Caen, and Marseilles as case studies, in this chapter I seek to explain and account for the guild status achieved by French seamstresses and show its evolution over time.

A range of factors was responsible for the entry of seamstresses into the guild system. Among the most important was the royal government's efforts, under the ministry of Jean-Baptiste

Clare Haru Crowston, "The Royal Government, Guilds, and the Seamstresses of Paris, Normandy, and Provence," pp. 173–5, 213–16, 442–5 from *Fabricating Women: The Seamstress of Old Regime France, 1675–1791*. Durham, NC and London: Duke University Press, 1997.

Colbert, to encourage and rationalize the French economy in the 1670s. The decision to award a guild to the Parisian seamstresses thus belonged to a wider effort to extend corporate association to hitherto unorganized sectors of the economy. The choice of the seamstresses, however, was not accidental. In defiance of the tailors' guild monopoly, seventeenth-century seamstresses had established themselves as the most important labor force in the production of made-to-measure women's and children's clothing. Legalizing their work promised to remove a source of dissension from the labor market and provide a new outlet for the domestic cloth industries that Colbert was eager to foster. This female trade was also large and coherent enough to support the burden of incorporation. Encouraged by the strong cultural association between sewing and femininity, women had streamed into the seamstresses trade during the first three quarters of the seventeenth century.

Gender was both crucial and tangential to the seamstresses' inclusion in guilds. By the mid-seventeenth century, a strong sexual division of labor already characterized the garment trades. Female needleworkers produced articles of clothing for women and children, while most tailors specialized in men's clothing. When it brought seamstresses into the corporate system, the royal government in some ways merely institutionalized the preexisting sexual division of labor. The king did not sanction the guild's creation because of new ideas about women and work; instead the royal government used ostensibly natural sexual divisions to divide a growing trade sector equitably. By granting legal and institutional status to this sexual division of labor, however, royal administrators inadvertently created a new and influential model of sexual difference. This model suggested that a woman's sex should determine all aspects of the work she performed, from the products she made to the people she worked with to the clients she served. Appropriate "women's work" was intrinsically and essentially tied to femininity. These were not new ideas, but rarely had they received the force of royal privilege and the full power of the law to enforce them.

The Parisian seamstresses' guild was thus born of the intersection of administrative, socio-economic, and cultural factors. Once it was established in 1675, the guild became a model for reorganizing the garment trades in cities across France. For provincial seamstresses, the Parisian example was a source of inspiration, emboldening them to seek expanded corporate privileges. When they arbitrated conflicts between tailors and seamstresses, administrators also looked to the Parisian example, although they had to compromise between central initiatives and local guild traditions and practices.

[. . .]

Women and Guilds in Seventeenth-Century France

Almost every woman engaged in economically productive work in Old Regime France. Like men, most women performed agricultural and domestic labor either on their own land, as share-croppers, or as day laborers for richer peasants. Within the cities, domestic service employed the largest number of women, with servants of both sexes representing between 5 and 15 percent of the urban population.[2] Another large group of women worked as street or market traders, hawking vegetables, dairy products, fish, and other foodstuffs, or peddling trinkets, used bits of clothing, and other inexpensive articles. The least fortunate supplied their brute force in exchange for minimal wages, serving as porters or unskilled laborers on building sites.

With very few exceptions, French guilds restricted their membership to adult males of the Catholic religion. The vast majority of women were therefore excluded from the economic and social benefits of guild membership. This did not mean, however, that they had no place in the guild world. On the contrary, they were a constant presence in corporate workshops and boutiques, as mistresses in a handful of female guilds, as relatives of male guild members, or as hired workers. Women in the corporate sphere occupied the summit of female labor, possessing specialized skills that enhanced their family businesses or won them independent salaries.

Out of approximately sixty Parisian guilds prior to 1673, only two were composed exclusively of women.[3] These were the linen-drapers (*marchandes maîtresses toilières lingères canevassières*), who sold linen cloth and finished goods, and the hemp merchants (*maîtresses linières filassières chanvrières*), who sold flax, tow, and hemp. The linen-drapers' 1645 statutes gave them a quasi-monopoly on the sale of all linen cloth and finished goods, which they traded in the Halle aux Toiles. Their statutes also authorized mistresses to travel or send representatives to all "cities or places where both new and used Linen Cloth, Sheets and Thread are made, fabricated, traded, and sold."[4] This was a striking affirmation in a society with strong legal and social restrictions on female autonomy.[5] With their control of the trade in linen cloth and goods, linen-drapers occupied a central position in the Parisian garment trades, employing hundreds of female workers to sew the finished articles they sold. The royal edict of 1691, which established a hierarchy of four "classes" of Parisian guilds, ranked them in the second level. A government study accompanying this edict estimated the guild to number four hundred mistresses, stating: "This community is very well-regulated and in good order; several mistresses conduct a quite considerable trade; those of the Palace and the Cemetery of Saints-Innocents are quite poor".[6]

The *filassières* were merchants of flax, tow, and hemp, materials used in the manufacture of rope and coarse cloth. They served as intermediaries between provincial suppliers and weavers or ropemakers in the capital city. Like the linen-drapers, the *filassières* monopolized the import of these goods to Paris. The *filassières'* guild, however, was much smaller and played only a minor role in Parisian commerce. The report prepared for the 1691 edict described them as numbering only sixty mistresses, who practiced their trade conjointly with their husbands: "They are the ones who sell tow. And all of the mistresses of this trade . . . are wives of master ropemakers and these two trades are poor."[7] The edict of 1691 assigned them to the fourth class of Parisian guilds.

Apart from exclusively female guilds, a small number of Parisian corporations accepted both men and women. One was the guild of small grain and seed dealers (*maîtres-maîtresses grainiers-grainières*) created in 1595. The masters and mistresses of this corporation controlled the retail sale of seeds and legumes, as well as secondary cereals such as barley, millet, and buckwheat. Members of the Parisian bourgeoisie, traveling merchants, and master gardeners could conduct a wholesale trade in these items, but their goods were subject to inspection by corporate officials. In this guild, female mistresses shared the same status as male masters and its statutes reserved two of the four elected leadership positions for women. This was the only example of a truly mixed-sex guild in Paris.[8]

Women played a less prominent role in two unusual corporate bodies, the barbers-surgeons' community and the painters-sculptors' academy of Saint Luke. Female midwives composed a distinct and subordinate subdivision of the first group. They elected their own officials to oversee their affairs, but the surgeons controlled the corporation as a whole. Female membership candidates were examined "by the king's first surgeon or his lieutenant, by the four provosts of the College of Surgery, by the king's four surgeons at his Châtelet and by the four mid-wives' officials [*jurées*]."[9] The second organization, the painters-sculptors' academy of Saint Luke, also accepted female members. Its administrators appear to have been exclusively male, however, and women entered the community in relatively small numbers across the eighteenth century. In

1736, for example, only seven of sixty new members of the corporation were female. In 1762, nine out of fifty-seven were women.[10]

Outside Paris, the city of Rouen in Normandy possessed the only known additional women's guilds of seventeenth-century France. Rouen was a major industrial and commercial center, with perhaps the longest history of guild organization in France.[11] Drawing on this vigorous corporate tradition, women had obtained five independent guilds in this city, compared to only two in Paris. These included two linen-drapers' guilds – the new linen-drapers and the merchants of used linen – as well as the ribbon merchants (*marchandes rubannières*), the tow merchants, and the stocking- and feathersworkers (*maîtresses bonnetières-plumassières*).[12]

"Women's Work" in the Late Seventeenth Century: The Ambiguities of Law, Custom, and Practice

To judge from the short list of female guilds in Paris and Rouen, contemporary notions of appropriate "women's work" included needlework, textile preparation and sales, food vending, and assistance in childbirth. The feminine codification of such activities was not new, but an inheritance from classical and Christian traditions. In 1672, the playwright Molière used needlework to symbolize a traditional domestic and virtuous femininity, abandoned by outspoken *précieuses* of his day. In *Les Femmes savantes*, the "good bourgeois" Chrysale declares that in his father's time, women's "households were their learned speech, and their books a thimble, thread and needles." He thus contrasted the intellectual pretensions of contemporary women unfavorably with the modesty and homeliness of previous generations.[13]

If the gender codifications of certain tasks was well known and deeply rooted, it was manifested in the late seventeenth century in a complicated mixture of law, custom, and practice. In some sectors, as we have seen, women drew on the acknowledged "femininity" of certain tasks to acquire independent guild privileges. This was a rare achievement. In most cities, professional needlework was off-limits to women, as were food-preparation trades and entire sectors of textile production. Male guilds enjoyed monopolies over these crafts, excluding women from activities nonetheless viewed as typically feminine. Every year, guild officials invested considerable time and money pursuing illegal female workers and the masters who hired them. In April 1692, for example, the Parisian embroiderers' guild successfully prosecuted a group of its own masters for having hired female workers (*fausse-ouvrières*). In the future, masters were enjoined to conform to guild rules and hire only qualified male workers. The fact that needlework and other skills were so strongly associated with femininity, therefore, did not entitle women to practice them for economic gain.[14]

As this example demonstrates, however, women could often be found as hired employees or illegal entrepreneurs in trades where they had no legal right to work. *Encyclopédie* engravings from the mid-eighteenth century depict women working alone or alongside male colleagues in a number of crafts ostensibly ruled by male guilds. These included the embroiderers, stocking-makers, manufacturers of buttons and decorative trim, fanmakers, enamelers, makers of artificial flowers, papermakers, wigmaker-barbers, saddlers, and makers of silk and golden thread. The editors of the *Encyclopédie* presented female labor in these trades as a simple fact, which apparently required no textual commentary.[15] Cultural notions of appropriate female tasks – sewing, making textiles and decorative objects, or decorating small objects – could thus overcome legal strictures, encouraging male employers to hire women in sectors where they were theoretically forbidden.

To make this picture even more complicated, one must also acknowledge the importance of female labor in myriad trades that had no association with typical "female" tasks. The wives and daughters of guild masters in many different trades participated in the family business on a daily basis, and their labor could be crucial to its survival. In many cases, the husband focused on productive labor with his journeymen, while his wife waited on customers and kept accounts. In other circumstances, wives and daughters played an integral role in the production of finished goods. Recognizing the importance of this contribution, some guilds authorized their members to hire their colleagues' female relatives. In 1692, the sentence pronounced against the embroiderers explicitly reaffirmed masters' capacity to hire other masters' daughters. Guilds also acknowledged women's stake in the family economy by allowing widows to continue their husbands' business in limited conditions and letting them transmit guild membership through marriage. Any task that women performed in the context of a family concern could therefore be considered an appropriate form of "women's work."

At least one late-seventeenth-century observer, conscious of the gaps among legal stricture, cultural codification, and practice, complained that male guilds should not be permitted to monopolize the few economic activities that were intrinsically appropriate for women:

> This liberty of certain works which do not depend on trade apprenticeship or the constraints of a guild [*jurande*] should be preserved even more for women and girls since we know the dangers to which necessity exposes the weakness of their sex[;] the greatest number know how to wash clothes, to do linen work, sewing[;] some make needlework tapestries, others mourning head-dresses, masks of hair[;] can we envy a widow, sometimes a lady, charged with several children, if she finds in one of these small works that with which to feed her family, and he who would wish to reduce them to begging for their bread in order to profit from the gift of such masterships would [he] not be entirely guilty?[16]

This passage underlines the ambiguity surrounding women's work in the late seventeenth century. The author did not problematize the question of how or why women performed certain tasks; he believed simply that women "knew" how to wash clothes or use a needle. His understanding of "women's work" drew on implicit assumptions about female skill, but he did not explicitly link them to women's essential or biological nature. Instead, he seemed to believe that these were skills women usually acquired in the course of everyday life. The moral focus of "women's work" therefore did not lie in a claim that women should perform certain types of activities, and refrain from others, at risk of violating their essential femininity. He argued merely that women who needed to earn a living should be permitted to exercise the few skills that they most likely already possessed. His goal was to provide succor to the poor and prevent the disorder and degradation inherent in idleness and poverty. These views reflected broader attitudes toward women's work in late-seventeenth-century France, in which the relationship between ideology, law, and practice remained largely unarticulated and unexamined. Notions of tradition and custom vied with explicit legal strictures, which in turn rubbed against everyday practices. Administrators and members of the world of work dealing with this complicated amalgam produced an array of local and strategic compromises without attempting to sort out the contradictions inherent in them.

Women both benefited and suffered from this situation. On the one hand, the gendered codification of trade skills enhanced women's economic position in the labor market, allowing them to acquire guild privileges or to work in certain trades regardless of legal restrictions. Women were likely to acquire the skills in sewing or textile production that enabled them to seek work in such trades, and male masters were likely to hire them, even though they could be prosecuted for doing so. On the other hand, the existence of recognized domains of "women's work" also discouraged women from entering other sectors. Their privileged relationship to certain trades thus stifled alternate possibilities of employment. Acquiring guild privileges in 1675, the seamstresses' trade perhaps best embodies the paradoxical strengths and weaknesses of "women's work." Once they acquired a guild their example did much to crystallize existing notions of "women's work," contributing to a new articulation and rigidification of the traditional sexual division of labor.

Seamstresses in Seventeenth-Century France

Prior to 1675, the Parisian garment trades furnished an excellent example of the clash between ideas about women's work and legal constraints obstructing it. Until this date, the tailors' guild held a monopoly over the production of made-to-measure clothing for men, women, and children. As their 1660 statutes stated, the guild held exclusive rights

> to make and sell all kinds of Suits and other ordinary articles of clothing, for the use of men, women and children, custom-made or ready-made, to display for sale, sell, [and] market them in all kinds of fabrics and leathers, and other materials if appropriate, and which may be appropriate in the future for the fabrication and perfection of the said garments.[17]

Despite this monopoly, seamstresses had established a strong presence in the trade by the mid-seventeenth century at least. The tailors' statutes indirectly acknowledged this situation by prohibiting masters from employing them: "No Master of the said trade may maintain two boutiques, nor receive any illegal worker [chambrelan], nor seamstress [couturière], nor associate himself with used-clothes dealers nor anyone but a master of the said craft and trade."[18] The statutes also forbade journeymen, at risk of imprisonment, from entering the employ of illegal tailors and seamstresses. A collection of several hundred seventeenth-century apprenticeship contracts held in Parisian notarial archives sheds further light on the seamstresses' trade before incorporation. The existence of this large group of contracts is in itself surprising, because seamstresses in this period constituted an illegal trade group. One might have expected formal, notarized contracts to be prohibitively public endeavors for artisans who risked prosecution for their work. Moreover, notaries should have refused to draw up the contracts, because their professional regulations forbade them from aiding illicit transactions. The large number of surviving contracts thus testifies to the vigor, size, and audacity of the seamstresses' trade prior to incorporation.[19]

To judge from these contracts, the pre-1675 seamstresses were already a strongly gender-specific trade group. The term couturière is found in apprenticeship contracts as an exclusively female trade appellation. No examples exist of male couturiers, although the tailors' guild had used the term up to the sixteenth century, and one scholar has found equal numbers of male couturiers and female couturières in sixteenth-century training contracts.[20] Moreover, the seamstresses accepted only girls and young women as their apprentices, never boys. The gender of the seamstresses' clients was not explicitly indicated in these apprenticeship contracts, but it is likely that most of them were women as well.

Pre-1675 apprenticeship contracts also reveal the emergence of distinct forms of specialization in the trade. Many women called themselves simply "seamstresses," while others specified that they were seamstresses in woolen cloth, in linens, in children's clothing, or in mourning garments. A small number of the women had family ties with tailors. Out of a sample of forty-five contracts, four seamstresses were married to Parisian master tailors, one to a tailor with no guild affiliation, and another woman's father was a master tailor. The rest were independent business-women who seem to have run their own enterprises.

Above all, the contracts underline the development of standardized training procedures in this trade. Seamstresses did not acquire skills at home from female relatives, but through several years of formal training outside the home. Relations between apprentice and mistress were governed by a notarized contract, which followed the standard guild model for apprenticeship agreements. Some seamstresses appeared several times, taking on a series of apprentices during careers of long duration.

Apprenticeship contracts thus reveal a well-established, large, and thriving female trade niche. At least two factors must explain the seamstresses' success in defying the tailors' monopoly. The first was the cultural association between women and needlework. Like embroidery, contempo-raries may well have perceived seamstresses' work as a legitimate female activity and been willing to disregard legal strictures against it. The fact that seamstresses worked primarily for their own sex further situated their labor within the private, unregulated domain. The second factor aiding seamstresses was the sheer practical obstacles involved in expelling them from the trade. Because most worked in their own homes, guild officials would have faced severe difficulty in locating and prosecuting them. The lower wages that women received for their labor also made them more attractive than male tailors to their clients. Both ideological and practical considerations thus encouraged the success of seamstresses against the tailors.[21]

Colbert and the Edict of 1673

The catalyst for changes in the legal framework of the garment trades issued from events in the realm of high politics. In 1669, Controller General Jean-Baptiste Colbert issued a series of ordi-nances for the woolen cloth and textile dying industries. These ordinances contained detailed regulations for every step of production, which he intended to become a new national standard. He also took steps to encourage the domestic manufacture of high-quality silk cloth and lace, in order to eliminate expensive foreign importation and to provide new products for export. Turning from manufacture to commerce, Colbert promulgated a *Code du commerce* (commercial code) for trade and commerce across France in 1673, offering national rules for the conduct of merchants and traders. Throughout his tenure, the controller general took measures to encourage French economic development by establishing a handful of new commercial companies and granting exclusive monopolies on new techniques or products to royally sponsored manufacturers.[22]

In March 1673, Colbert trained his energies on the guild system, issuing a royal edict that ordered the incorporation of all unincorporated trades in cities and towns where guilds existed. The edict noted that artisans working outside the guild system suffered harassment and legal sanctions from local corporations. It also asserted that the lack of supervision over these trades posed a serious threat to public well-being. Without corporate officers to police production and commercial standards, consumers fell victim to shoddy merchandise and fraudulent trade prac-tices. The extension of the guild system to all trades, the edict suggested, would resolve the prob-lems of producer and consumer alike.[23]

This was not the first time that a French king had issued such an order; the edict's preamble recalled previous royal edicts of 1581 and 1597, which made similar demands. The edict of 1673, however, appeared at a time when the royal government held a particular interest in its success.

Louis XIV had undertaken war with the Dutch in 1672 and he urgently required new sources of income to fight it. The edict stated explicitly that revenue generated by the new guilds would be directed "without any diversion towards the pressing expenses of the war."[24] Half of the fees paid by masters and mistresses in the new guilds would accrue to the royal treasury. As a supplementary measure, the 1673 edict ordered all existing guilds to update their statutes and pay to have them confirmed by the crown. A second edict assigned responsibility for these payments to municipal authorities. If the guilds could not furnish the necessary money, the municipalities would have to pay for them.

These stipulations underline the fiscal interests behind the 1673 edict. They have led some historians to dismiss it as a hasty and superficial grasp at an easily plundered source of revenue. It is clear, indeed, that monetary needs weighed heavily in the controller general's mind as he drafted the edict. Nevertheless, intense fiscal concerns do not preclude the existence of economic and administrative motives as well. Taxation and administrative reform had always been intertwined in the government's relationship with the guilds. With the 1673 edict, Colbert sought to generate new income as quickly as possible, but he also took the opportunity to increase efficiency and quality standards in production. This would not only help in the short-term war effort, it would further his twin goals of freeing France from foreign imports and expanding the country's export capacity. It would also help fulfil his desires to create new forms of employment for otherwise idle and impoverished French subjects, reduce social disarray and increase potential tax revenue. Ultimately, a strong French economy – favored by well-organized and regulated trades – would provide the foundation for a stronger monarchy. Seen in this perspective, the 1673 edict was wholly compatible with Colbert's other legislative projects, such as the *Code du commerce* or his series of regulations for the textile industry.[25]

The application of the edict offers perhaps the best clues to the intentions behind it. In its aftermath, members of the royal government drew up a report titled "Table of the Arts and Crafts to Establish as Guilds in the City and Suburbs of Paris Following the Edict of the Month of March 1673." This document targeted thirty-seven different Parisian trades for incorporation. It listed the population of each trade, the amount to be charged for mastership in each of the new guilds, and the sums that the royal government could expect from its half-share of new masters' fees. Among the thirty-seven trades, we find innkeepers, millers, and merchants of diverse goods such as firewood, wheat, coal, horses, wholesale leather, spirits, butter, and waxed cloth. Two occupations were indicated to be exclusively female, the seamstresses and the fresh-flower sellers.[26]

Judging from the information included in this list, the revenue that each trade could offer to the crown was an important criterion of selection, but it was not the only one. The seamstresses, it is true, would offer an impressive ninety thousand livres from their three-thousand-strong workforce. Each woman would pay sixty livres, half of which would go to the royal government. This was the largest sum calculated for any trade. Other professions, however, would provide much smaller amounts. The two hundred fresh-flower sellers, for example, would produce only an estimated six thousand livres. Aside from fiscal considerations, the predominance of merchants of important basic goods suggests a desire to regulate traffic in major items of public consumption. The millers' presence in the list supports this suggestion, given the tremendous sensitivity of subsistence issues in this period and the constant fear of dearth and the urban riots it could inspire. In the case of the innkeepers and boardinghouse keepers, a desire for greater surveillance of the Parisian itinerant population may have been at work. Overall, the crucial prerequisites for incorporation appear to have been a level of prosperity sufficient to support the financial burdens of guild status and a sufficiently stable and coherent workforce to make a success of corporate organization, with its elections, assembly meetings, and regulations. Desire from the trades' practitioners probably also played a significant role in their inclusion on this list.[27]

Unlike its predecessors, the legislation of 1673 produced remarkable results. According to Emile Levasseur, the Parisian guilds rose in number from 60 in 1672 to 83 several months after the edict, and finally to 129 in 1691. A similar response occurred in provincial towns and cities.[28] French artisans and merchants clearly perceived the 1673 edict as a legitimate invitation to enter the corporate world, and they responded with enthusiasm. Despite the new fees they would encounter, they judged the benefits of guild status to outstrip the drawbacks. The needs of the state therefore succeeded in fostering a substantial propagation of corporate organization among urban artisans in the 1670s, including some groups of female workers.

The Creation of the Parisian Seamstresses' Guild

In response to the possibilities offered by the 1673 edict, a group of seamstresses quickly organized to draft statutes for a new guild, and then submitted them to the king with a letter requesting incorporation. As the king stated in his letters patent:

> In execution of which Edict, several Women and Girls, having shown Us that in all times they have worked at sewing, to clothe young children and make Skirts, Dressing Gowns, Mantuas, Skirt Bodices and other clothes of convenience [*habits de commodité*] for persons of their sex and that this work was the only manner in which they could gain their living honestly: They entreated Us to establish them as a guild [*communauté*], and to accord them the Statutes that they had presented Us to exercise their Profession.[29]

This request adds weight to the impression given by the apprenticeship contracts, suggesting that by 1675 seamstresses had developed a strong professional identity, based on a set of precisely delimited products and the common gender of both workers and clients. Some form of association existed among them, which permitted a rapid response to the new legislation. The framing of their request also indicates some sophistication with the legal procedures and rhetoric of the guild world. Seamstresses were not only conscious of the gender composition of their trade; they were capable of manipulating it by emphasizing the precarious moral situation of working women. Their statement carried the tacit warning that if they could not work in this "honest" trade they might turn in desperation to less honorable forms of income.

The king transmitted these statutes to his procurator at the Châtelet of Paris and the lieutenant general of police, Nicolas de la Reynie, for their approval. In their report, these officials noted the tailors' utter failure to eliminate seamstresses from their trade, concluding that the establishment of a female guild could not cause any further harm. They thus informed the king that:

> The practice of using Seamstresses to make their Skirts, Dressing Gowns, Skirt Bodices and other clothes of convenience [*habits de commodité*] had introduced itself among Women and Girls of every condition to such an extent; that regardless of the seizures undertaken by the Tailors' Officials and the condemnations that had been pronounced against the Seamstresses, they continued working as previously. That this severity exposed them to suffer great vexations, but did not make them cease exercising their Commerce, and that their establishment as a Guild therefore did not greatly prejudice the Master Tailors' [guild], because up to the present they did not work less, even though they have no right to do so.[30]

Beyond practical considerations, the royal letters patent raised moral concerns, not for the female artisans in question, but for their elite female clients. The king's letters stated that he had consented to the new corporation: "Having moreover considered that it was quite within propriety and suitable for the decency and modesty of Women and girls to permit them to be clothed by persons of their sex, when they judge it appropriate."[31] Concerns for female modesty were thus an explicit motivation for the guild's creation.

In addition to these directly expressed explanations, we may identify a number of tacit considerations at work. Garment-making offered a source of employment to working women, who might otherwise be idle, indigent, and a source of social disorder. Disputes between tailors and seamstresses generated disarray in the labor market and legal expenses within the male guild. Properly organized and regulated, needleworkers would provide new outlets for French textile production, the most important industry in France and a particular object of Colbert's concern. It was no use pouring effort and subventions into silk, woolen, and lace manufacture if French women did not have sufficient access to finished goods made with these products. Incorporating the seamstresses also offered a new and highly lucrative source of revenue. Creating a seamstresses' guild thus promised to aid urban labor markets, stimulate the growth of domestic industry, and – not the least of considerations – provide ninety thousand livres to the crown.

The king granted the seamstresses' letters patent as a new guild on March 30, 1675, and the Parisian Parlement registered the letters in September of the same year. This document granted the seamstresses the same legal status as other Parisian guilds. New mistresses were sworn in before the king's procurator at the Châtelet of Paris and thereby acquired the official title of *maîtresses couturières* (mistress seamstresses). As established by the new statutes, the guild's administrative structure and regulations were similar to those of other Parisian guilds. An electoral body composed of guild mistresses elected three of six administrative officers each year. With the authorization of the Archbishop of Paris, a guild confraternity was established in the parish church of Saint-Gervais under the patronage of Saint-Louis. The guild's basic regulations corresponded entirely with corporate norms. It was no more responsible to outside authority than any male corporation.

The seamstresses' trade privileges, however, did set them apart. The tailors' guild had possessed for centuries a monopoly on the fabrication of men's and women's clothing. The royal government could not simply dismantle these privileges, which had been repeatedly confirmed by the king's predecessors. As arbiter of the corporate sphere, the state therefore sought a compromise that would permit seamstresses to work in the trade with the least possible diminishment of the tailors' position. Royal officers found a solution by permitting seamstresses to work for women and children only. Tailors not only retained their rights to make women's and men's clothing, they also maintained a monopoly over the most expensive female attire of the period, the two-piece dress worn by court noblewomen.[32]

With this compromise, the royal government denied the seamstresses a monopoly on their sector of commerce, placing them in a situation of direct competition with the tailors. This was a highly unusual situation, because the guild system usually functioned to eliminate or at least minimize competition, not to foster it. Once again, we encounter the paradoxical effects of gender on female labor. The royal government could not have imposed such unequal trade rights on a male rival to the tailors' guild; however, it would have been impossible for a male trade to acquire even these limited privileges. The seamstresses' female gender both rendered possible and restricted their legal rights.

The sexual division imposed on the product market carried over to policies for hiring and guild administration. The 1675 statutes forbade mistress seamstresses from hiring journeymen

tailors and barred master tailors from employing female workers. They also prohibited seamstresses' and tailors' elected officials from conducting inspection visits on the other guild's
members. A gender barrier thus ran through all aspects of the new guild's constitution. Adopted
in some ways as a simple institutionalization of preexisting practice, the new legal status accorded
to sexual segregation in the garment trades would become a model for provincial towns and cities.

[. . .]

Conclusion

Before 1675, the Parisian tailors' guild held a monopoly over the production of made-to-measure
clothing. In defiance of this prerogative, seventeenth-century seamstresses established a growing
trade niche. A long tradition of formal apprenticeship existed among them, which transmitted
different forms of specialization. The seamstresses' trade resembled other forms of "women's
work" in seventeenth-century France in making use of skills culturally coded as "feminine" that
were nonetheless legally restricted to male guild members. The strong cultural association
between needlework and femininity helped seamstresses to challenge the tailors' monopoly,
creating a situation in which women routinely violated the law to practice a stereotypically
"female" trade.

On its own, the combination of cultural codification and everyday practice did not suffice to
change the law. This opportunity resulted from Colbert's 1673 edict calling for the creation of
new guilds in all unincorporated trades. If not for the fiscal and managerial needs of the centralizing state, the seamstresses would probably have remained an illegal labor force. In 1675, the
seamstresses obtained the same legal rights as male guilds, but sexual difference nonetheless lay
at the heart of the new guild's constitution. Seamstresses were allowed to make clothing only for
other women and children and could hire only female workers. These stipulations stemmed in
part from concerns about the purity of elite female clients, but they were not part of an attempt
on the government's part to reshape gender ideologies. Instead, sexual segregation offered the
easiest way to compromise between the centuries-old privileges of the tailors and the new claims
of the seamstresses. It offered seamstresses' legal status for their labor, while restricting them to
an easily delimited sector of the garment trades. Royal officials probably saw this as a fair and
reasonable compromise, because seamstresses already worked predominantly for women. This
settlement had the additional advantage of preventing seamstresses' husbands or fathers from
encroaching on the tailors' trade through their wives' or daughters' privileges. As seniors in the
corporate world, tailors retained their full gamut of privileges.

After 1675, the Parisian seamstresses' guild served as both a positive and a negative model for
provincial towns and cities. As the demand for women's clothing rose beyond tailors' ability to
satisfy it, their guilds began to accept seamstresses as subordinate members. The Parisian
example warned of the possibility of an independent female guild, encouraging tailor's guilds to
accept women before they acquired sufficient clout to obtain guild status on their own. When
seamstresses entered tailors' guilds they acquired the same privileges as their Parisian colleagues,
with the right to work for women and children only and to hire female workers.

Over time, seamstresses in Paris and the provinces successfully augmented their privileges.
Once they had entered the guild system and acquired the right to press lawsuits and represent
themselves to authorities, the logic of seamstresses' corporate status allowed them to push for
equal rights with male guilds. They did not claim to make clothes for men, but they successfully
expanded their rights over women's apparel. . . .

Several points raised by the seamstresses' encounter with the guild system from 1675 to 1791 should be underlined. First, this case study demonstrates the lack of official prejudice against female labor. Far from restricting or discouraging women's work, royal and municipal administrators felt that it needed to be encouraged and protected to prevent widespread female destitution and the social disorder it generated. They also valued female trades as a means to satisfy the needs of the urban populace and to stimulate domestic production and consumption. Administrators were less sure of the proper way to regulate women's work. In many cases, female trades seemed too humble or disorganized to form guilds; they also faced the obstacle of resistance from established male guilds. During certain periods of economic and political reform, however, royal ministers agreed to grant women new guilds, with all of the privileges and obligations that accompanied corporate status. The regularizing and centralizing tendencies of the state in the late seventeenth century could thus serve to create greater equality for women rather than reducing it.

The seamstresses' varied experience in French cities and towns highlights important regional variation in the guild system itself. This diversity suggests that provincial guilds continued to function within a regional and municipal dynamic, despite efforts at centralized royal control. The contrast between Normandy and Provence, moreover, indicates that existing corporate traditions – including the prior existence of female guilds – had a powerful influence on women's capacity to acquire guild status. Where the corporate tradition was strong, seamstresses could attain formal mistress status, with the privileges and constraints inherent in it. Where guilds were weaker, and women had no previous corporate role, they remained auxiliary and largely voiceless members of tailors' guilds. Ironically, therefore, the incorporation of women was not a symptom of the weakness or decline of the guild system, but a sign of its strength. It was the vitality of the guild tradition within northern cities that furnished women with the conceptual and legal tools to argue for their autonomous corporate rights.

For advocates of the guild system, the seamstresses offered proof that women were not incompatible with guilds and that, on the contrary, they might thrive within them. . . .

Proving women's aptitude for corporate organization was not the seamstresses' most widespread legacy. More important was their contribution to a new articulation of the sexual division of labor. The traditional haziness of women's work disappeared in a trade explicitly defined by the gender of its practitioners, products, and clients. The task of the law was no longer to impose a vision of social, economic, and moral exigency on the world of work, but to allow a natural division of labor based on sex to emerge. The seamstresses' example therefore helped to naturalize and essentialize women's association with needlework. From being a traditional connection, subject to condemnation by guild rules, it became an innate aspect of femininity. . . .

This new way of looking at women's work must be understood in the broader context of changing ideas about nature, the human body, the individual, and of labor itself. These ideas came from the general conceptual shift of the Englightenment, from the corporation to the individual, and from laws and customs governing social conduct to "natural" ways of life and behavior. Shifting women's work from an ambiguous mixture of custom, law, and practice to an essentialized notion of innate female skill was one part of much larger cultural and political changes, which surfaced in the realm of fashion as well.

NOTES

1 Natalie Z. Davis, "City Women and Religious Change," in *Society and Culture in Early Modern France* (Stanford, 1975), 94. This passage is cited in James B. Collins, "The Economic Role of Women in Seventeenth-Century France," *French Historical Studies* 16, no. 2 (1989): 436–70. For early and

influential versions of this argument, see Alice Clark, *The Life of Working Women in the Seventeenth Century* (1919; London: Routledge and K. Paul, 1982); and Ivy Pinchbeck, *Women Workers and the Industrial Revolution, 1750–1850* (New York: Routledge, 1930). More recently, see Merry Wiesner, *Working Women in Renaissance Germany*, and *Gender, Church, and State in Early Modern Germany*; Martha Howell, *Women, Production, and Patriarchy in Late Medieval Cities*, and *The Marriage Exchange: Property, Social Place, and Gender in Cities of the Low Countries, 1300–1550* (Chicago: University of Chicago Press, 1998); Jean H. Quataert, "The Shaping of Women's Work in Manufacturing: Guilds, Households, and State in Central Europe, 1648–1870"; and Lindsey Charles and Lorna Duffin, eds., *Women and Work in Preindustrial England* (London: Croom Helm, 1985). These historians have challenged Clark's idealized view of female economic opportunities in the Middle Ages, but agreed that a significant decline in the scope and autonomy of female labor occurred through the early modern period. For a provocative argument about the "compact" between the patriarchal family and monarchical power in this period, see Sarah Hanley, "Social Sites of Political Practice in France: Lawsuits, Civil Rights, and the Separation of Powers in Domestic and State Government, 1500–1800," *American Historical Review* 102, no. 1 (1997): 27–52; "Engendering the State: Family Formation and State Building in Early Modern France," *French Historical Studies* 16, no. 1 (1989): 4–27.

2 For numerical evaluations of female domestic servants in Paris, see Roche, *The People of Paris*, 65–9; Fairchilds, *Domestic Enemies: Servants and Their Masters in Old Regime France* (Baltimore: Johns Hopkins University Press, 1984), 2; and Sarah Maza, *Servants and Their Masters in Eighteenth-Century France: The Uses of Loyalty* (Princeton: Princeton University Press, 1983), 26–8.

3 At first glance, women's place in the early modern guild world appears to have declined significantly from the Middle Ages. Etienne Boileau's thirteenth-century catalogue of Parisian guilds, the *Livre des Métiers*, listed at least four guilds dominated by women: two silk-spinning trades, the silk ribbonmakers, and the makers of silk headdresses (*coiffures*). Boileau also listed trades composed of both men and women, including the makers of flower garlands and the makers of silk wimples (*coiffes*). The comparison between the medieval and the early modern situations, however, is deceptive. First, medieval women's guilds were less autonomous than their seventeenth-century counterparts. The statutes transcribed by Boileau show they were administered by male overseers (*prud'hommes*), rather than their own mistresses. Second, if women had lost this handful of medieval corporations by the end of the fifteenth century, they had also established control over two new trades. The linen-drapers' guild was created in 1485, after the female practitioners of the trade successfully eradicated a male guild of linen and canvas merchants. By 1645, their privileges included the sale of linen cloth as well as the manufacture and retail sale of finished linen goods. A similar process took place among hemp merchants, where women took over the guild's membership and administrative structures in the fifteenth and sixteenth centuries. For the medieval period, see R. de Lespinasse and F. Bonnardot, eds., *Le livre des métiers d'Etienne Boileau* (Paris, 1879). For the hemp merchants, see Lespinasse, *Les Métiers et corporations de la ville de Paris*, vol. 3, 45. Useful review essays on European women and guilds include Olwen Hufton's review article in *Signs*, 14, no. 1 (autumn 1988): 223–34; J. Bennett, "'History that Stands Still': Women's Work in the European Past," *Feminist Studies* 14 (1988): 269–83; and Maryanne Kowaleski and Judith M. Bennett, "Crafts, Guilds, and Women in the Middle Ages: Fifty Years after Marian K. Dale," *Signs* 14, no. 2 (winter 1989): 474–87.

4 AN (Archives nationales) AD XI 20, "Statuts, ordonnances et articles que les marchandes maîtresses toilières, lingères, canevassières . . ." (Paris, 1645). See the articles pertaining to the *lingères* in Lespinasse, *Les Métiers et Corporations de la ville de Paris*, 3 vols. (Paris, 1886), vol. 3; and Jaubert, *Dictionnaire raisonné universel des arts et métiers*, vol. 2. Cynthia Truant is currently completing a book-length study of the Parisian linen-drapers.

5 BN (Bibliothèque nationale) MSS Delamare 2179 f. 58, "Estat des corps de marchands et des arts et métiers de la ville de Paris." A branch of the mercers' guild traded in wholesale linen cloth in competition with the linen-drapers, although they had no rights to sell in the Halle aux Toiles.

6 BN MSS Joly de Fleury 1728, fols. 186–99.

7 Ibid.

8 Lespinasse, *Les métiers et corporations de la Ville de Paris*, vol. 1, 228–39.

9 Martin Saint-Léon, *Histoire des corporations de métier*, 495. See also Lespinasse, *Les métiers et corporations de la ville de Paris*, vol. 3, 622–36. Administratively tied to the Parisian Faculty of Medicine and royal medical officers, the barber-surgeons' corps was not a guild in the strict sense of the word. It did, however, possess statutes similar to those of the Parisian guilds and was included along with them in many acts of royal legislation. For an account of the most famous eighteenth-century midwife, see Nina Rattner Gelbart, *The King's Midwife: A History and Mystery of Madame du Coudray* (Berkeley: University of California Press, 1998).

10 Lespinasse, *Les métiers et corporations de la ville de Paris*, vol. 2, 187–223. In 1648, the royal government created a royal academy for painting and sculpture, which merged with the existing painter-sculptors' guild in 1652. In 1663, the monarchy granted the academy a monopoly over instruction in painting and sculpture.

11 Martin Saint-Léon, *Histoire des corporations de métier*, 73: "Mais entre toutes les villes du nord de la France et de la Belgique, c'est peut-être à Rouen que la corporation professionnelle ou plus exactement le guilde d'artisans apparaît pour la première fois avec les caractères de la plus indiscutable authenticité."

12 See Ouin-Lacroix, *Histoire des anciennes corporations et des confréries réligieuses de la capitale de la Normandie*; and Hafter, "Métiers féminins à Rouen au XVIIIe siècle," *French Historical Studies* (forthcoming).

13 Molière, *Le Bourgeois gentilhomme*, 164–5.

14 Letter from the royal procurator at the Châtelet of Paris to the controller general, April 4, 1692, Arthur-Michel de Boislisle, ed., *Correspondance des contrôleurs généraux des finances avec les intendants des provinces*, vol. 2, no. 1069 (Paris: Imprimerie nationale, 1874–97).

15 See *Encyclopédie, ou Dictionnaire raisonné des sciences, des arts et des métiers*, vols. 23–6, 29–32.

16 BN MSS Delamare 2179. The text was written anonymously in 1688.

17 BA (Bibliothèque de l'Arsenale) 80 J 4710, "Statuts et ordonnances des marchands-maîtres tailleurs d'habits, pourpointiers-chaussetiers de la ville, fauxbourgs et banlieue de Paris," article 4. Despite the tailors' claim to a monopoly on ready-to-wear clothing, the *fripiers*' guild also possessed the right to sell ready-to-wear garments, if made from cloth beneath a specified value.

18 BA 80 J 4710, "Statuts et ordonnances des marchands-maîtres tailleurs d'habits, pourpointiers-chaussetiers de la ville, fauxbourgs et banlieue de Paris."

19 The contracts are held in the Minutier Central at the Archives nationales in Paris. A card catalogue in the Salle des Inventaires contains references to several hundred of these contracts.

20 Loats, "Gender and Work in Sixteenth-Century Paris," Ph. D. diss., University of Colorado, 1993.

21 See de Vries, "Between Purchasing Power and the World of Goods," in *Consumption and the World of Goods*, ed. J. Brewer and R. Porter, London, 1993. With regard to the timing of the female trade's emergence, several factors were probably involved. One might posit the rise of seamstresses as an indirect result of the growth of the French army in the second half of the seventeenth century. If tailors shifted their activities to meet the tremendous demand for new army uniforms, the lack of adequate suppliers of women's clothing may have opened a niche for female artisans. One might also consider the possible effects of an "industriousness" revolution, which Jan de Vries claims preceded the consumer and industrial revolutions. According to de Vries, seventeenth-century European families began to reorient their labor toward the market, leading to a new intensity and frequency of employment for women and children. The growth of seamstresses in this case would represent a redeployment of female labor away from the household economy toward an additional and independent source of remuneration.

22 A vast literature exists on Colbert and mercantilism. Classics include Pierre Clément, *Histoire de Colbert et de son administration*, 2 vols. (1874; Geneva: Slatkine, 1981); Charles W. Cole, *Colbert and a Century of French Mercantilism*, 2 vols. (New York, 1939); Eli F. Heckscher, *Mercantilism*, 2 vols. trans. Mendel Shapiro (London: G. Allen and Unwin, 1935); and Henri Sée, "Que faut-il penser de l'oeuvre economique de Colbert?" *Revue historique* 152 (1926): 181–94. More recently, see Philippe Minard, *La Fortune du colbertisme* (Paris: Fayard, 1997); Roland Mousnier, ed., *Un Nouveau Colbert: Actes du*

colloque pour le tricentaire de la mort de Colbert (Paris: S.E.D.E.S., 1985); and Julian Dent, *Crisis in Finance: Crown, Financiers, and Society in Seventeenth-Century France* (Newton Abbot, Eng.: David and Charles, 1973).

23 Lespinasse, *Les Métiers et corporations de la ville de Paris*, vol. 1, 117.
24 Ibid.
25 For a highly skeptical reading of the 1673 edict, see Jean-Louis Bourgeon, "Colbert et les corporations: l'exemple de Paris," in *Un Nouveau Colbert: Actes du colloque pour le tricentenaire de la mort de Colbert*, ed. R. Mousnier (Paris, 1985). In this article, Bourgeon attacks the "general false idea" that Colbert's aim was to generalize the guild system, insisting that Colbert deliberately established separate spheres of production to compete with the guild system. While Bourgeon's argument usefully underlines Colbert's openness to variation and experimentation in economic organization, I believe he overstates his case in denying any administrative intent whatsoever to the 1673 edict.
26 BN MSS Delamare 21 791, "Table des arts et mestiers à etablir en communauté en la ville et faubourgs de Paris suivant l'édit du mois du Mars 1673."
27 Jean-Claude Perrot cites a Caen lieutenant general of police who suggested that desire from the trade was the most important criterion for incorporation: "Pour avoir les prérogatives de communauté et acquérir ou conserver à l'exclusion des autres ou concurremment avec elles, une portion de commerce, il faut une volonté actuelle de composer une communauté, une espèce d'association, des réglements autorisés, une prestation de serment, des préposés du corps pour veiller à l'observation du bon ordre." Perrot, *Genèse d'une ville moderne: Caen au XVIIIe siècle* (Paris, 1975), 322.
28 Levasseur, *Histoire des classes ouvrières et de l'industrie en France avant 1789*, 184.
29 AN AD XI 16, "Statuts, ordonnances et declaration du Roy, confirmative d'iceux, pour la communauté des couturières de la ville, fauxbourgs et banlieue de Paris."
30 Ibid.
31 Ibid.
32 The royal government's care to protect the tailors' preexisting privileges echoed clearly in the seamstresses' letters patent, which ordered that the women's new statutes be enforced: "Sans néanmoins que lesdits. Statuts ni l'érection des Couturières en Corps de Métier puissent faire préjudice au droit et à la faculté qu'ont eu jusqu'ici les Maîtres Tailleurs de faire des Jupes, Robes de Chambre, toutes sortes d'habits de Femmes et d'Enfans, que Nous voulons leur être conservés en son entier, ainsi qu'ils en ont joui jusqu'à présent." See "Statuts, ordonnances et déclaration du Roy, confirmative d'iceux, pour la communauté des couturières de la ville, fauxbourgs et banlieue de Paris."

Part VI

RESEARCH PARADIGMS, OLD AND NEW

INTRODUCTION

"There is only one science of humankind, in time and in space." So wrote the great French medievalist, Marc Bloch, in *The Historian's Craft* (1946), one of the Patristic texts of the writing of history since the Second World War. Bloch set a standard few historians can hope to reach, but his holistic methods have defined the research agenda of the past 50 years. He had a peerless knowledge of archival documents, whether in Latin or the various forms of "French" used in medieval and early modern times. To his skills in paleography and diplomatics, and his knowledge of legal forms, political events, and institutions, Bloch added insights drawn from geography, demography, linguistics, archeology, sociology, and even from his visits to the French countryside. He reminded historians that we must work from the present backwards – examining, for example, the structure of fields as laid out today – as well as from the past forwards.

Bloch and his friend and collaborator, Lucien Febvre (Part III), established the *Annales* school, which took its name from the journal they had founded in 1929. The journal ceased publication during World War II – Bloch, a leader in the French Resistance, was tortured and shot by the Gestapo in 1944 – but reappeared in 1946. Bloch and Febvre soon came to be identified as the godfathers of its two main interests, Bloch with socioeconomic history viewed through the eyes of ordinary people; Febvre with the history of *mentalités*, collective states of mind. In fact, each of them had worked extensively in both areas: Bloch, for example, wrote a superb book on the "Royal Touch," the belief that the King of France had the capacity to cure scrofula simply by touching its victims.

Bloch and Febvre, and their most famous disciples, like Fernand Braudel, helped provide a bridge between the underlying nineteenth-century intellectual origins of modern scholarship, the historiography of the late nineteenth century, and the multidisciplinary explosion in historical writing that began in the 1960s. Nineteenth-century philosophers such as G. W. F. Hegel and Friedrich Nietzsche established foundational intellectual principles for modern historians. Historians have drawn heavily on the insights of Karl Marx, above all his ideas about class conflict and history; Max Weber, on social structure, institutions, and religion; Emile Durkheim, a founder of modern sociology, and Sigmund Freud, to cite only a few of the key influences.

Modern historians took their basic chronology of European development from the nineteenth-century founding fathers of modern historiography, people like Leopold von Ranke in Germany, Jules Michelet in France, Lord Macaulay in England, Jacob Frijn in the Netherlands, or Jakob Burckhardt, a Swiss who wrote on the Italian Renaissance. These historians created what are now called "master narratives," the basic chronologies that divide history into manageable eras – like the Renaissance, an historical moment clearly defined by Burckhardt's *Civilization of the Renaissance in Italy* (1860; translated 1868) – and into stories, one might say myths, that modern scholarship has increasingly viewed as tautological constructs rather than historical truths. Ranke could seek to write history as it actually happened; modern scholars would argue that Ranke and all other historians create history. History has thus come to derive meaning from two linguistic origins, from the Greek *historein*, to relate, implying an impartial narrative of truth, and the French *histoire*, story. History becomes a collective story, as much a creation as individual memory.

The innovation of Bloch and Febvre, or the English historian R. H. Tawney, was to break away from the political narrative that dominated historiography in their time, and to look at underlying social and economic structures. They did so not from the perspective of those on top and at the center, but from the perspective of those on the bottom and at the periphery. This perspective encouraged their students to look to other disciplines, such as demography and sociology, for new methodologies. The work of the historical demographer Louis Henry on reconstruction of families, and that of the Cambridge Population Project on English population trends, had an overwhelming impact on the generation of scholarship produced in the 1960s and early 1970s. These trends spread quickly to other countries, as in the case of the *Alltaggeschichte* (everyday history) movement in Germany (West and East) and Austria during the 1970s and 1980s. Scholars to the east of the Iron Curtain pursued these same topics within a Marxist framework, often hamstrung by political interference, but producing intellectually exciting work, like the writings of the Polish historians Witold Kuła and Marian Małowist. The older traditions, like the Kraków School in Poland, also evolved, under the leadership of Iosef Gierowski.

The collapse of Marxism as the central organizing intellectual force of European life, and among American historians of Europe, during the 1970s, created an extraordinary vacuum at the core of historical inquiry.[1] Consciously or unconsciously, historians work from underlying intellectual premises, and, by the late 1960s, those premises desperately needed renewal. Moreover, the historical profession itself underwent profound change around 1965, with the exponential expansion of the professoriate (in response to mass higher education), and the entry into it of many men from social classes rarely represented in earlier times among historians. In the late 1970s, the number of women entering the profession began to rise sharply, today, women earn 35 to 40 percent of all history Ph.D.s awarded in the United States, and their numbers are rising sharply in Europe, too.

These developments profoundly affected historiography. The epistemology of history changed, in that historians sought out new sources, rejecting "facts" created by elites, above all by governments. Here, the postmodernists, above all the French scholar Michel Foucault, have had the greatest influence. Historians have taken Foucault's ideas on sexuality, on language, on the "birth of the prison," on "civility," and on knowledge itself and used them to create models they test with empirical research. In the last two decades, the work of Pierre Bourdieu has had the same impact, above all his construct of the "habitus," which enables historians to move beyond simplistic ideas of culture. The contrast between the crude models of elite vs. popular culture in the historiography of the 1970s and the Bourdieu-influenced models of cultural fluidity and adaptability of the 1990s could not be more stark. The works of Bourdieu, Michel de Certeau, Dominique Julia, David Sabean, Roy Porter, Carlo Ginzburg, and other pioneers have essentially rendered unutilizable much of the scholarship about "popular culture" written in the 1970s and even in the 1980s.[2]

Bourdieu and Foucault are widely available elsewhere, so we have here chosen a passage from the German sociologist Norbert Elias, whose books *The Court Society* (1969; translated 1983) and *The Civilizing Process* have provided the theoretical framework for virtually every recent study of a European court or for the "creation of modern man."[3] Scholars increasingly reject Elias's emphasis on the role of the Court, but his model remains the starting point for inquiry. Since the late 1980s, the work of another German sociologist, Jürgen Habermas, above all *The Structural Transformation of the Public Sphere* (1969; translated 1989), has underlain much of the historical scholarship about the birth of modern political culture. Here again, recent research has called into question many of Habermas's assumptions, but the model he created – of a sphere of political debate public both because it was printed and because it took place in open venues, such as cafés – remains fundamental to most scholarship about the political transformations of the seventeenth through nineteenth centuries.

The new methodologies of historians have come overwhelmingly, as the examples of Foucault, Bourdieu, Elias, and Habermas suggest, from other disciplines. In addition to the scholars from other disciplines, however, we must also emphasize in this transition the role of the pioneering historians who first use the new methods. Their transformation of a sociological or anthropological method into an historiographical one often determines the manner in which later historians will use the technique. Natalie Zemon Davis's article "Women on Top" straddles the line between a new methodology, feminist studies, and an historian adapting that methodology. One can make a strong case that Davis's articles helped create a methodology of feminist studies.[4] Her innovative use of new sources to establish roles for women in everyday life enabled her then to reread traditional sources in a new light, revealing the staggering blindness of virtually all male historians who had written before her. Scholars like Davis or the English medievalist Joan Thirsk were voices in a wilderness so vast that today we imagine with difficulty its extent. Her work led directly to a new generation of scholarship, like that of Judith Bennett or Merry Wiesner, herself a pioneer. In the excerpt from Wiesner's first book (1986!) provided in Part IV, one is struck by the fact that she cannot refer the reader to historiography about women's work in other parts of the Holy Roman Empire, because no such literature then existed. The explosion of scholarship about women has provided historians with a more well-rounded model of early modern societies, and, like the work of Bourdieu or Foucault, called into question the "knowledge" accumulated on many fundamental issues, such as the economies of peasant households. No modern scholar, for example, could discuss the medieval English economy without reference to Bennett's work, yet scholarship produced before the 1980s invariably ignored women's substantial contribution to the English economy.

Alfred Crosby, who wrote in the early 1970s, pioneered yet another methodological innovation: the intrusion of ecosystems into human history. Nothing could seem more self-evident than the idea that humans live in a broader ecosystem, yet *The Columbian Exchange* made historians realize how remiss they had been in integrating the history of humankind into the history of the Earth. The *Annales* School, as in the case of Braudel or Pierre Goubert, had been a rare exception, building as it did on the great tradition of French historical geography.[5] Crosby's look across the Atlantic, at the impact of the exchange of plants, animals, and microbes, has revolutionized our understanding of many elements of history. In the late 1980s, a classroom discussion of the Spanish conquest of Mexico would have begun its search for the reason for Cortez's triumph with his superior technology (guns and metal swords), whereas today that discussion would start with smallpox.

Europe's exchange with the rest of the world began at the biological level. Animals, plants, and microbes that had been confined to one area of the world, now spread to others. Europeans brought the horse, cattle, sheep, and pigs to the Western Hemisphere. Europeans and Africans also brought their diseases: smallpox, against which Amerindians had no antibodies, enabled Cortes to conquer Mexico City, and soon annihilated the populations of the West Indies and Central America. The best estimates suggest that ten million people died in the Aztec Empire during the first decade of the Spanish presence. In 75 years, the population of the region may have dropped by as much as ninety percent, due almost entirely to imported diseases.

The Americas provided the Eastern Hemisphere with some critical new crops, above all corn (maize), potatoes, beans, and manioc (cassava). Soon crops that had flourished in Africa, such as coffee and sugar (brought by Columbus himself, in 1493), became staples of the Western Hemisphere's economy. Crops brought to eat – oranges, lemons, bananas, melons, lettuce, the list goes on and on – also transformed the Western Hemisphere's environment. When the Spanish moved away from their original bases in tropical climates, they were able to add grapes (for wine), wheat, and olives to the list, in regions such as modern-day California or Chile (for olives and grapes), and even in the central Andes, in the case of wheat. Crosby points out, however, that these deliberate transfers were only the tip of the iceberg, because most "proletarian" plant immigrants, like daisies or dandelions, crossed the Atlantic "as informally as did the smallpox virus. Their seeds arrived in the folds of textiles, in clods of mud, in dung, and in a thousand other ways."

Where will the historiography of early modern Europe go from here? We offer three texts that may indicate the future. Two of them, by Victor Lieberman and Kenneth Pomeranz, expand the geographic framework, while the third, by Paula Findlen, transgresses formerly sacrosanct intellectual boundaries. Lieberman's essay, part of his introduction to *Beyond Binary Histories*, suggests that European state development can no longer be viewed so narrowly. The false dichotomy of East–West, Asia–Europe, obscures the reality that the Eurasian land mass had many similar developments in early modern times. States became larger everywhere, often coalescing into "national" units. Local, vernacular languages replaced the old "imperial" tongues, be they Arabic, Chinese, Pali, or Latin. At the same time, local dialects often lost ground to "national" languages, like French or Japanese. Everywhere, religious organizations came under closer state control.

> In sum, between c. 1450 and 1830 across mainland Southeast Asia, in what became the Russian empire, in those territories that cohered as France, and in the Japanese islands we find parallel tendencies towards the consolidation of fragmented political units, more efficient systems of extraction and control, and more uniform cultural expression.

The use of transnational comparisons of state development within Europe has been relatively rare, but such an historiography – Jeremy Duindam's new book on European Courts, for example – is emerging. The next wave will take us into a comparison broader still, the Eurasian context. That comparison has already begun in the work of historical sociologists, whose source base is resolutely secondary (work of other scholars); the coming innovation may well be comparisons made by historians, using the historian's method of examining primary sources.

Pomeranz not only moves the dialogue about economic development into the world context, but he forces historians to deal with the methodology of economists. Although not relying on the heavily econometric models favored in work about the contemporary world, Pomeranz does show historians how the worldwide comparison of the sort of fundamental indicators used in comparison of contemporary economies can be used for historical purposes. Like Bloch, he urges us to move from the present to the past, as well as the past to the present. His findings suggest that historians of the European economy have been driven more by assumptions inherited from the nineteenth century than by historical reality. As Lieberman's title suggests, the binary assumption, West–East, looks increasingly irrelevant, indeed misleading. Here we can see the impact of intellectual trends in other fields: Edward Said's *Orientalism* (1977), which posited the artificial creation of the "Orient" by Western scholars, has fundamentally altered all comparisons of Europe and Asia.

Paula Findlen breaks down an intellectual barrier, rather than a geographic one. Since World War II, the idea of the "Scientific Revolution," a concept essentially invented in the 1940s by scholars such as Herbert Butterfield, has dominated Western consciousness of the development of "modern" ways of thinking. As the selection from Kathleen Wellman (Part III) suggests, the historical reality of the acceptance of "scientific" ideas differs pretty dramatically from the lovely little myth we have promulgated for the past half-century. Findlen takes us onto new ground, into a world in which the origins of modern science are "seriocomic," as much as scientific. Her work, and that of scholars such as Wellman or Patricia Seed (Part III), encourages us to deconstruct existing categories of analysis and to try to deal with early modern society on its own terms, not those we have created for it, or, more often those created for it by nineteenth-century writers.

These essays provide examples of the different ways in which historians find new paradigms to structure their research. Intellectuals, whether through philosophical insight or general questioning, provide the most common source. Writers such as Foucault, Bourdieu, or Elias transcend disciplines, just as Marx and Durkheim did. Intellectual assumptions can come from nineteenth-century philosophers like Hegel, or from twentieth-century thinkers like John Rawls or Martin Heidegger. Historians today increasingly question formerly assumed categories, like memory. The publication over a decade ago of the volumes edited by Pierre Nora, *Les lieux de mémoire* (1984; translated into English as *The Realms of Memory*, 1996) marks the arrival of a critical mass of study on memory, a base point from which to start. Here historians of Europe can look to those working on other areas, like Jonathan Spence on China (*Treason by the Book*, 2001, or *The Memory Palace of Matteo Ricci*, 1985), or those from another discipline, like the anthropologist Joanne Rapaport, who examines the uses of history among indigenous peoples in Colombia. Within European studies themselves, literary scholars like Mary Carruthers (*The Book of Memory*, 1990) have reconfigured our understanding of memory in medieval European culture, and hence in our own. Historians can learn, too, from master storytellers, like José Saramago, whose Portuguese novel, *The History of the Siege of Lisbon* (1987; translated 1996), raises fundamental questions about the nature of human memory and the creation of history.

Closer to home, the community of historians can look within, to see whose work points in new directions. Just as Natalie Zemon Davis pointed the way in the 1960s or Alfred Crosby in the 1980s, so, too, an historian today will break down traditional barriers, and ask questions so novel they force a reconceptualization of the fundamental outlines of early modern European history. We believe the strongest such initiative will come in global history, reconceptualizing Europe as one place among many. The Reformation, for example, simply must become part of a larger story of Christianity in the sixteenth-century world. The Catholic offensive – in the east, leading to the Uniate Church in the borderlands between Muscovy and the Polish-Lithuanian Commonwealth, in the West, to the conversion of the Amerindians, and in China, to the efforts of the Jesuits, Franciscans, and Dominicans – needs to be assessed in its global dimension. Only then can we make sense of religious developments within Western Europe itself.

Whither early modern European history? The next generation of historians will want to study broadly, in time and in space, as Bloch suggested. Be archaeologists of knowledge, by reading earlier historians and thinkers, to know whence our current ideas came (Febvre). Be culturally inclusive, comparing Spain not simply to France but to the Ottoman Empire and even to China (Lieberman). Think globally, because early modern people transformed our planet by connecting the divided hemispheres (Crosby). Be nonhierarchical, studying subordinate groups like women, or sailors, or slaves, eschewing assumptions that cultural change moves from the dominant to the dominated (Davis, Macfarlane). Be intellectually inquisitive, seeking out new ideas in anthropology and other disciplines (Findlen, Sabean). Be fluid in time, using many of the tools of analysis of contemporary societies to examine early modern ones (Pomeranz).

Above all, as the range of essays provided here demonstrates, combine the linear and non-linear approaches to history. The linear method, like a snake following the jellied path to the river of forgetfulness, is led more often by instinct than reason, and "knows" its destination before it starts. The nonlinear one can easily lose the forest for the trees. Paradigms help us avoid the "poverty of empiricism" (C. Wright Mills), hard data help us avoid the folly of assumptions disguised as "historical fact." The events of our own day, sadly reveal the consequences of simplistic historical analogies. The theorist in Marx could say that history repeats itself; the historian in Bloch suggested rather that "misunderstanding of the present is the inevitable consequence of ignorance of the past."

NOTES

1 Marxist historians remained more prominent in English history, in part because of the colossal achievements of Christopher Hill and Edward Thompson, but the trend in studies of seventeenth-century English history since the 1980s has been sharply away from Hill's interpretation.
2 One of Ginzburg's contributions to this evolution, *The Night Battles*, appeared in 1961, truly a work ahead of its time.
3 The French scholar Robert Muchembled used this phrase as the title of a 1988 book that essentially repudiated his work of the 1970s on the defeat of popular culture by elite culture between the sixteenth and eighteenth centuries. Muchembled relied, like so many other historians, on the intellectual framework provide by Foucault and Elias. Several essays in this volume, such as that of Anthony Feros, explicitly cite Elias's theories.
4 Foucault straddled this same line. He did little work with documents, but his analysis of printed primary sources fits into one traditional form of historiography.
5 The great monographs of Braudel, Goubert, Emmanuel Le Roy Ladurie and other scholars of the first generation of *Annalistes* invariably begin with an extensive discussion of the geography – broadly defined – of the area they study: Mediterranean, Beauvaisis, or Languedoc, in their three cases.

25

THE COURTIZATION OF THE WARRIORS

Norbert Elias

The court society of the seventeenth and eighteenth centuries, and above all the court nobility of France that formed its centre, occupied a specific position within this whole movement of inter-penetration of the patterns of conduct of ever-wider circles. The courtiers did not originate or invent the muting of affects and the more even regulation of conduct. They, like everyone else in this movement, were bending to the constraints of interdependence that were not planned by any individual person or group of persons. But it is in this court society that the basic stock of models of conduct was formed which then, fused with others and modified in accordance with the posi-tion of the groups carrying them, spread, with the compulsion to exercise foresight, to ever-wider circles of functions. Their special situation made the people of court society, more than any other Western group affected by this movement, specialists in the elaboration and moulding of social conduct. For, unlike all succeeding groups in the position of an established upper class, they had a social function but no occupation.

Not only in the Western civilizing process, but in others such as that of eastern Asia, the moulding which behaviour receives at the great courts, the administrative centres of the key monopolies of taxation and physical force, is of equal importance. It is first here, at the seat of the monopoly ruler, that all the threads of a major network of interdependencies run together; here, at this particular social nexus, more and longer chains of action intersect than at any other point in the web. Even long-distance trade links, into which urban-commercial centres are inter-woven here and there, never prove lasting and stable unless they are protected for a considerable period by strong central authorities. Correspondingly, the long-term view, the strict control of conduct which this central organ demands of its functionaries and of the prince himself or his representatives and servants, are greater than at any other point. Ceremony and etiquette give this situation clear expression. So much presses directly and indirectly on the central ruler and his close entourage from the whole dominion, each of his steps, each of his gestures may be of such momentous and far-reaching importance, precisely because the monopolies still have a strongly

Norbert Elias, "The Courtization of the Warriors," pp. 387–97, 422–9 from *The Civilizing Process: Sociogenetic and Psychogenetic Investigations*. Oxford: Blackwell, 2000 [1994].

private and personal character, that without this exact timing, these complex forms of reserve and distance, the tense balance of society on which the peaceful operation of the monopoly administration rests would rapidly lapse into disorder. And, if not always directly, then at least through the persons of the central ruler and his ministers, every movement or upheaval of any significance in the whole dominion reacts on the bulk of the courtiers, on the whole narrower and wider entourage of the prince. Directly or indirectly, the intertwining of all activities with which everyone at court is inevitably confronted, compels him to observe constant vigilance, and to subject everything he says and does to minute scrutiny.

The formation of monopolies of tax and physical force, and of great courts around these monopolies, is certainly no more than one of several interdependent processes which provide the momentum of this gradual process of "civilization". But their formation provides one of the keys by which we can gain access to the driving forces of these processes. The great royal court stands for a period at the centre of the social networks which set and keep the civilizing of conduct in motion. In tracing the sociogenesis of the court, we find ourselves at the centre of a civilizing transformation that is both particularly pronounced and an indispensable precondition for all subsequent spurts and counter-spurts in the civilizing process. We see how, step by step, a warrior nobility is replaced by a tamed nobility with more muted affects, a court nobility. Not only within the Western civilizing process, but as far as we can see within every major civilizing process, one of the most decisive transitions is that of *warriors to courtiers*. But it need scarcely be said that there are widely differing stages and degrees of this transition, this inner pacification of a society. In the West the transformation of the warriors proceeded very gradually from the eleventh or twelfth centuries until it slowly reached its conclusion in the seventeenth and eighteenth centuries.

How it came to pass has already been described in detail: first, the wide landscape with its many castles and estates; the degree of integration was slight; the everyday dependence and thus the horizon of the bulk of the warriors, like that of the peasants, was restricted to their immediate district:

> Localism was writ large across the Europe of the early Middle Ages, the localism at first of the tribe and the estate, later shaping itself into those feudal and manorial units upon which medieval society rested. Both politically and socially these units were . . . nearly independent, and the exchange of products and ideas was reduced to a minimum.[1]

Then, from the profusion of castles and estates in every region, arose individual houses whose rulers had attained, in many battles and through the growth of their landed possessions and military power, a position of predominance over the other warriors in a more extended area. Their residences became, as a result of the greater confluence of goods arriving at them, the homes of a larger number of people, "courts" in a new sense of the word. The people who came together here in search of opportunities, always including a number of poorer warriors, were no longer as independent as the free warriors ensconced in their more or less self-sufficient estates; they were all placed in a kind of monopolistically controlled competition. And even here, in a circle of people that was still small compared to the absolutist courts, the co-existence of a number of people whose actions constantly intertwined, compelled even the warriors who found themselves thus in closer interdependence to observe some degree of consideration and foresight, a more strict control of conduct and – above all towards the mistress of the house on whom they depended – a greater restraint of their affects, a transformation of their drive economy. The *courtois* code of conduct gives us an idea of the regulation of manners, and the *Minnesang*[2] an impression of the drive-control, that became necessary and normal at these major and minor territorial courts. They bear witness to a first spurt in the direction which finally led to the complete transformation of the nobility into courtiers, and an enduring "civilizing" of their conduct. But the web of interdependence into which the warrior entered was not yet very extensive or closed. If he had to adopt a certain restraint at court, there were still countless people and situations in respect of which he needed to observe no special restraint. He might escape the lord and the lady of one court in the hope of finding lodgings at another. The country road was full of sought and unsought encounters which required no very great control of impulses. At court, towards the mistress, he might deny himself violent acts and affective outbursts; but even the *courtois* knight was first and foremost still a warrior, and his life an almost uninterrupted chain of wars, feuds and violence. The more peaceful constraints of social interweaving which tend to impose a profound transformation of drives, were not yet bearing constantly and evenly on his life; they intruded only intermittently, and were constantly breached by military compulsions which neither tolerated nor required any restraint of the affects. Correspondingly the self-restraint which the *courtois* knights observed at court was only slightly consolidated into half-unconscious habits, into the almost automatic pattern characteristic of a later stage. The *courtois* precepts were mostly addressed, in the heyday of knightly court society, to adults and children alike; conformity to them by adults was never taken so much for granted that one might cease to speak about them. The conflicting impulses never disappeared from consciousness. The structure of self-constraints, especially the "super-ego", was not yet very strongly or evenly developed.

In addition, one of the main motive forces which later, in the absolutist-court society, played an important part in consolidating polite manners in the individual and in continuously refining them, was as yet still lacking. The upward pressure of urban-bourgeois strata against the nobility was still relatively slight, as correspondingly was the competitive tension between the two estates. To be sure, at the territorial courts themselves, warriors and town-dwellers sometimes competed for the same opportunities. There were bourgeois as well as noble *Minnesänger*; and in this respect too the *courtois* court showed to some extent the same structural regularities which later appeared, fully developed, in the absolutist court: it brought people of bourgeois and noble origin into constant contact. But later, in the era of fully developed monopolies of the means of ruling, the functional integration of nobility and bourgeoisie, and thus the possibility of constant contacts as well as permanent tensions, was already quite highly developed even outside the court. Contacts between bourgeois and warriors such as occurred at the *courtois* courts, were still relatively rare. In general, the intertwining of dependencies between bourgeoisie and nobility was still slight compared to the later period. The towns and the feudal lords in their immediate or wider neighbourhood still stood opposed as alien political and social units. How little the division of functions was developed, and how great the relative independence of the different estates still was, is clearly demonstrated by the fact that the spread of customs and ideas between town and town, court and court, monastery and monastery, i.e. relationships within the same social stratum, even over long distances, was often greater than contacts between castles and towns in the same district.[3] This is the social structure which – by way of contrast – we must keep in mind in order to understand the different structure, the different social processes through which there gradually emerged an increasing "civilization" of the way in which individuals steer themselves.

Here, as in every society with a barter economy, exchange and thus mutual dependence and integration between different classes was still slight as compared to the following phases. Society's whole mode of life was therefore less uniform. The power of arms, military potential and property were then extremely closely and directly related. Thus the unarmed peasant lived in an abject condition. He was at the mercy of the armed lord to a degree that no person was exposed to others in the everyday life of later phases, when public or state monopolies of force had deve-loped. The lord and master, on the other hand, the warrior, was functionally so little dependent on his inferiors (though of course such dependency was never entirely lacking), he was, through the overwhelming physical threat normally emanating from him, untrammelled in relation to them to an extent which surpassed by far the relative power surplus of any upper class in relation to lower classes at the later stages of social development. Similarly with the standard of living: then, too, the contrast between the highest and lowest classes of this society was extremely great, par-ticularly in the phase when a decreasing number of especially mighty and wealthy lords was emerging from the mass of the warriors. We encounter similar contrasts today in areas where the social structure is nearer to that of Western medieval society than that of the West today, for example in Peru or Saudi Arabia. Members of a small élite have an immense income of which a far larger part than is the case with high incomes in the West today, is used for the personal con-sumption of its owner, luxuries of his "private life", robes and jewellery, residence and stables, utensils and meals, feasts and other pleasures. The members of the lowest class, the peasants, by contrast, live wretchedly under the constant threat of bad harvests and starvation; even under normal circumstances the produce of their work just suffices to provide them with subsistence; their standard of living is considerably lower than that of any class in "civilized" societies. And only when these contrasts are reduced, when through the competitive pressure affecting this society from top to bottom the division of functions and interdependence over large areas gra-dually increases, when the functional dependence even of the upper classes grows while the social power and living standards of the lower class rise, only then do we find the constant foresight and self-control in the upper classes, the continuous upward movement of the lower ones, and all the other changes which one can observe in any civilizing spurt encompassing broader strata.

To begin with – at the starting-point of this movement as it were – the warriors lived their own lives and the burghers and peasants theirs. Even in spatial proximity the gulf between the estates was deep; customs, gestures, clothes or amusements differed, even if mutual influences were not entirely lacking. On all sides social contrast – or, as people in a more uniform world like to call it, the variety of life – was greater. The upper class, the nobility, did not yet feel any appreciable social pressure from below; even the bourgeoisie scarcely contested their function and prestige. They did not yet need to hold themselves constantly in check and on the alert in order to maintain their position as the upper class. They had their land and their swords: the primary danger for each warrior was other warriors. And so the mutual control the nobles imposed on their conduct as a means of class distinction was correspondingly less, so that in this respect too the individual knight was subjected to a lower degree of self-control. He occupied his social position far more securely and as a matter of course than the courtly noble. He did not need to banish coarseness and vul-garity from his life. There was nothing disturbing for him in thinking about the lower classes; they were not permanently associated with anxiety, and thus there was no social taboo on anything recalling the lower classes in upper-class life, as happened later. No repugnance or embarrassment was aroused by the sight of the lower classes and their behaviour, but a feeling *contempt*, which was expressed openly, untroubled by any reserve, uninhibited and unsublimated. The "Scenes from the Life of a Knight" discussed earlier in this book give a certain impression of this attitude, although the documentation was taken from a later, courtly period of knightly existence.[4]

How the warriors were drawn step by step into the vortex of increasingly stronger and closer interdependencies with other classes and groups, how an increasing part of them fell into func-tional and finally institutional dependence on others, has already been described in detail from various aspects. These are processes acting in the same direction over centuries: loss of military and economic self-sufficiency by all warriors, and the conversion of a part of them into courtiers.

One can detect the operation of these forces of integration as early as the eleventh and twelfth centuries, when territorial dominions consolidated themselves and a number of people, particularly less favoured knights, were forced to go to the greater and lesser courts to seek service.

Then, slowly, the few great courts of princely feudality rose above all the others; only members of the royal house now had the chance to compete freely with one another. And above all the richest, most brilliant court of this period of competing feudal princes, the Burgundian court, gives an impression of how this transformation of warriors into courtiers gradually advanced.

Finally, in the fifteenth and above all the sixteenth century, the whole momentum maintaining this transformation, the differentiation of functions, the increasing interdependence and integration of ever-larger areas and classes, increased. This is seen particularly clearly in the circulation of money, a social instrument the use of and changes in which indicate most accurately the degree of division of functions, and the extent and nature of social interdependence. The volume of money grew more quickly, and at a corresponding rate the purchasing power or value of money fell. This trend towards the devaluation of minted metal began, like the transformation of warriors into courtiers, early in the Middle Ages. What is new at the transition from medieval to modern times is not monetarization, with the decrease in the purchasing power of minted metal as such, but the pace and extent of this movement. Here, as so often, what first appears as merely a quantitative change, is on closer inspection an expression of qualitative changes, transformations in the structure of human relationships, of society.

Certainly, this accelerating devaluation of money is not by itself the cause of the social changes that emerge more and more clearly at this time; it is part of a larger process, a lever in a more complex system of intertwining trends. Under the pressure of competitive struggles of a particular stage and structure, the demand for money increased at this time; to satisfy it new ways and means were sought and found. But, as was pointed out earlier, this trend had a very different meaning for different sectors of society; this is precisely what shows how great the functional interdependence of different strata had become. Favoured by this trend were all those groups whose functions permitted them to compensate for the falling purchasing power of money by acquiring more money, especially bourgeois groups, and the kings as controllers of the tax monopoly; disadvantaged were groups of warriors or nobles who had an income which nominally remained the same but constantly diminished in purchasing power with the accelerating devaluation of money. It was the pull of this trend that in the sixteenth and seventeenth centuries drew more and more warriors to the court and thus into direct dependence on the king, while conversely the kings' tax revenues grew to such an extent that they could maintain an ever-larger number of people at their court.

If one contemplates the past as a kind of aesthetic picture book, if one's gaze is directed above all at changes of "styles", one may easily have the impression that from time to time the tastes or minds of people changed abruptly through a kind of inner mutation: now we have "Gothic people" before us, now "Renaissance people", and now "Baroque people". If we try to gain an idea of the structure of the whole network of relationships in which all the individual people of a certain epoch were enmeshed, if we try to follow the changes in the institutions under which they lived, or in the functions on which their social existence was based, our impression that at some moment the same mutation suddenly and inexplicably took place in many minds independent of each other, is increasingly dispelled. All these changes take place quite slowly over a considerable period, in small steps and to a large extent noiselessly for ears capable of perceiving only the great events heard far and wide. The explosions in which the existence and attitudes of individual people are changed abruptly and therefore especially perceptibly, are nothing but particular events within these slow and often almost imperceptible social shifts, whose effects are grasped only by comparing different generations, by placing side by side the social destinies of fathers, sons and grandsons. Such is the case with the transformation of the warriors into courtiers, the change in the course of which an upper class of free knights was replaced by one of courtiers. Even in the last phases of this process, many individuals may still have seen the fulfilment of their existence, of their wishes, affects and talents, in the life of a free knight. But all these talents and affects were now becoming increasingly impossible to put into practice because of the gradual transformation of human relations; the functions that gave them scope were disappearing from the fabric of society. And the case is no different, finally, with the absolutist court itself. It too was not suddenly conceived or created at some moment by individuals, but was formed gradually on the basis of a specific transformation of social power-relationships. All individuals are driven by a particular dependence on others into this specific form of relationship. Through their interdependence they hold each other fast within it, and the court was not only generated by this interweaving of dependencies, but created itself over and again as a form of human relationships outlasting individuals, as a firmly established institution, as long as this particular kind of mutual dependence was continuously renewed on the basis of a particular structure of society at large. Just as, for example, the social institution of a factory is incomprehensible unless we try to explain why the entire social field continuously generates factories, why people in them are obliged to perform services as employees or workers for an employer, and why the employer is in turn dependent on such services, so the social institution of the absolutist court is just as incomprehensible unless we know the formula of needs, the nature and degree of mutual dependence, by which people of different kinds were bound together in this way. Only thus does the court appear before our eyes as it really was; only thus does it lose the aspect of a fortuitously or arbitrarily created grouping, about which it is neither possible nor necessary to ask the reason for its existence, and only thus does it take on meaning as a network of human relationships which, for a period, continuously reproduced itself in this way, because it offered many individual people opportunities of satisfying certain needs generated over and again in their society.

The constellation of needs out of which the "court" constantly reproduced itself as an institution over generations has been shown above: the nobility, or at least parts of it, needed the king because, with advancing monopolization, the function of free warrior was disappearing from society; and because, with increasing monetary integration, the produce from their estates – measured against the standards of the rising bourgeoisie – no longer allowed them more than a mediocre living and frequently not even that, and certainly not a social existence that could maintain the nobility's prestige as the upper class against the growing strength of the bourgeoisie. Under this pressure a part of the nobility – whoever could hope to find a place there – entered the court and thus into direct dependence on the king. Only life at court opened to individual nobles within this social field access to economic and prestige opportunities that could in any way satisfy their claims to an existence of upper-class distinction. Had the nobles been concerned solely or even primarily with economic opportunities, they would not have needed to go to the court; many of them could have acquired wealth more successfully through a commercial activity – such as a rich marriage. But to gain wealth through commercial activity they would have had to renounce their noble rank; they would have degraded themselves in their own eyes and those of other nobles. It was this very distance from the bourgeoisie, their character as nobles, their membership of the upper class of the country, that gave their lives meaning and direction. The desire to preserve their class prestige, to "distinguish" themselves, motivated their actions far more than the desire to accumulate money. They therefore not only remained at court because they were dependent on the king, but they remained dependent on the king because only life amid courtly society could maintain the distance from others and the prestige on which depended their salvation, their existence as members of the upper class, the establishment or the "Society" of the country. No doubt, at least a part of the courtly nobility could not have lived at court had they not been offered many kinds of economic opportunities there. But what they sought were not economic possibilities as such – they were, as noted above, to be had elsewhere – but possibilities of existence that were compatible with the maintenance of their distinguishing prestige, their character as a nobility. And this double bond through the necessity for both money and prestige is to varying degrees characteristic of all upper classes, not only the bearers of "civilité" but also of "civilization". The compulsion that membership of an upper class and the desire to retain it exert on the individual is no less strong and formative than that arising from the simple necessity of economic subsistence. Motives of both kinds are wound as a double and invisible chain about the individual members of such classes; and the first bond, the craving for prestige and fear of its loss, the struggle against the obliteration of social distinction, is no more to be explained solely by the second, as a masked desire for more money and economic advantages, than it is ever to be found lastingly in classes or families that live under heavy external pressure on the borderline of hunger and destitution. A compulsive desire for social prestige is to be found as the primary motive of action only among members of classes whose income under normal circumstances is substantial and perhaps even growing, and at any rate is appreciably over the hunger threshold. In such classes the impulse to engage in economic activity is no longer the simple necessity of satisfying hunger, but a desire to preserve a certain high, socially expected standard of living and prestige. This explains why, in such elevated classes, affect-control and self-constraint are generally more highly developed than in the lower classes: fear of loss or reduction of social prestige is one of the most powerful motive forces in the transformation of constraints by others into self-restraints. Here, too, as in many other instances, the upper-class characteristics of "good society" were particularly highly developed in the courtly aristocracy of the seventeenth and eighteenth centuries, precisely because, within its framework, money was indispensable and wealth desirable as a means of living, but certainly not, as in the bourgeois world, the basis of prestige as well. To those belonging to it, membership of courtly society meant more than wealth; for just this reason they were so entirely and inescapably bound to the court; for just this reason the pressure of courtly life shaping their conduct was so strong. There was no other place where they could live without loss of status; and this is why they were so dependent on the king.

The king for his part was dependent on the aristocracy for a large number of reasons. For his own conviviality he needed a society whose manners he shared; the fact that the people who served him at table, on going to bed or while hunting belonged to the highest nobility of the land, served his need to be distinguished from all the other groups in the country. But above all he needed the nobility as a counterweight to the bourgeoisie, just as he needed the bourgeoisie to counterbalance the nobility, if his scope to manipulate the key monopolies were not to be reduced. It is the inherent regularities of the "royal mechanism" that placed the absolutist ruler in dependence on the nobility. To maintain the nobility as a distinguishing class, and thus to preserve the balance and tension between nobility and bourgeoisie, to allow neither estate to grow too strong or too weak: these were the fundamentals of royal policy.

The nobility – and the bourgeoisie, too – were not only dependent on the king; the king depended on the existence of the nobility. But without doubt the dependence of the individual noble on the king was incomparably greater than that of the king on any individual noble; this is very clearly manifested in the relation between king and nobility at court.

The king was not only the nobility's oppressor, as part of the courtly nobility felt; nor was he only their preserver, as large sections of the bourgeoisie believed; he was both. And the court,

NORBERT ELIAS

therefore, was likewise both: an institution for taming and preserving the nobility. "If a noble," La Bruyère says in a passage on the court, "lives at home in the provinces, he is free, but without support; if be lives at Court, he is protected, but a slave."[5] In many respects this relationship resembles that between a small independent businessman and a high employee in a powerful family concern. At court a part of the nobility found the possibility of living in accordance with their status; but the individual nobles were not now, as the knights were earlier, in free military competition with each other: they were in monopoly-bound competition for the opportunities the monopoly ruler had to allocate. And they not only lived under the pressure of this central lord; they were not only subjected to the competitive pressure which they, together with a reserve army of country aristocracy, exerted on each other; they were above all under pressure from rising bourgeois strata. With the latter's growing social power the noblemen at court had constantly to contend; they lived from the duties and taxes that came primarily from the third estate. The inter-dependence and interweaving of different social functions, above all between nobility and bour-geoisie, was very much tighter than in preceding phases. All the more omnipresent, therefore, were the tensions between them. And as the structure of human relationships was changed in this way, as the individual was now embedded in the human network quite differently from before and moulded by the web of his dependencies, so too did the structure of individual conscious-ness and affects change, the structure of the interplay between drives and drive-controls, between conscious and unconscious levels of the personality. The closer interdependence on every side, the heavy and continuous pressure from all directions, demanded and instilled a more even self-control, a more stable superego and new forms of conduct between people: warriors became courtiers.

Wherever we encounter civilizing processes of any scope, we also find structural similarities within the wider socio-historical context in which these changes in mentality occur. They may take place more or less quickly, they may advance, as here, in a single sweep or in several spurts with strong counter-spurts; but as far as we can see today, a more or less decisive courtization of warriors, whether permanent or transitory, is one of the most elementary social preconditions of every major movement of civilization. And however little importance the social formation of the court may at first sight have for our present life, a certain understanding of the structure of the court is indispensable in comprehending civilizing processes. Some of its structural characteris-tics may also throw light on the life at centres of power in general.

[. . .]

In the course of this study it was indicated by means of a number of examples how from the sixteenth century onwards the standard of social conduct was caught up in a quicker movement, how it remained in motion during the seventeenth and eighteenth centuries and then, during the eighteenth and nineteenth centuries, spread – transformed in some respects – throughout the whole of western society. This advance of restrictions and libidinal transformations set in with the conversion of the knightly into a court nobility. It is very closely bound up with the change already discussed in the relationship of the upper class to other functional groups. The "cour-tois" warrior society is not remotely under the same pressure, does not live in anything like the same interdependence with bourgeois strata, as the court aristocracy. This court upper class is a formation within a much denser network of interdependencies. It is held in a pincer comprising the central lord of the court on whose favour it depends on the one hand, and the leading bour-geois groups with their economic advantages on the other, groups which are forcing their way upwards and contesting the aristocracy's position. Tensions between court aristocratic and bourgeois circles do not increase only at the end of the eighteenth or the beginning of the nineteenth century; from the first the existence of the court aristocracy is strongly and constantly threatened by the aspiring bourgeois classes. Indeed, the courtization of the nobility takes place only in conjunction with an increased upward thrust by bourgeois strata. The existence of a high degree of interdependence and tension between nobles and bourgeois is a basic constituent of the courtly character of the leading groups of the nobility.

We should not be deceived by the fact that it took centuries for this continuous tug of war between noble and bourgeois groups to be decided in favour of some of the latter. Nor should we be misled by the fact that the constraints on the upper class, the functional interdependence and latent tension between different strata in the absolutist society of the seventeenth and eighteenth centuries, were less than in the various national societies of the nineteenth and twentieth centuries. As compared with the functional constraints on the free medieval warrior nobility, those on the court aristocracy were already very great. Social tensions, particularly between the nobility and bourgeoisie, take on a different character with increasing pacification.

As long as control of the instruments of physical violence – weapons and troops – is not very highly centralized, social tensions lead again and again to warlike actions. Particular social groups, artisan settlements and their feudal lords, towns and knights, confront each other as units of power which – as only states do later – must always be ready to settle their differences of interest by force of arms. The fears aroused in this structure of social tensions can still be discharged easily and frequently in military action and direct physical force. With the gradual consolidation of power monopolies and the growing functional interdependence of nobility and bourgeoisie, this changes. The tensions become more even. They can be resolved by physical violence only at infrequent climaxes or turning points. And they therefore express themselves in a continuous pressure that each individual member of the nobility must absorb within him or herself. With this transformation of social relationships, social fears slowly cease to resemble flames that flare rapidly, burn intensely and are quickly extinguished, only to be rekindled just as quickly, becoming instead like a permanently smouldering fire whose flame is hidden and seldom breaks out directly.

From this point of view as well, the court aristocracy represents a type of upper class different from the free warriors of the Middle Ages. It is the first of the more constrained upper classes, which is followed in modern times by even more heavily fettered ones. It is threatened more directly and strongly than the free warriors by bourgeois classes in the whole basis of its social existence, its privileges. As early as the sixteenth and seventeenth centuries there is in France, among certain leading bourgeois groups, particularly the high judicial and administrative courts, a strong desire to establish themselves in place of, or at least alongside, the nobility of the sword as the upper class of the country. The policy of these bourgeois strata is largely aimed at increasing their own privileges at the expense of the old nobility, even though they are at the same time – and this gives their relationship its peculiarly ambivalent character – bound to the old nobility on a number of common social fronts. For just this reason the fears that such continuous tensions bring with them express themselves, in these leading bourgeois strata, only in a concealed form controlled by strong super-ego impulses. And this applies all the more to the genuine nobility who now find themselves on the defensive, and in whom the shock of the defeat and loss they have suffered with pacification and courtization, long shows its after-effects. The court aristocrats too must more or less contain within themselves the agitation aroused by the constant tug of war with bourgeois groups. With this structure of interdependencies, the social tension produces a strong *inner* tension in the members of the threatened upper class. These fears sink down in part, though never entirely, into the unconscious zones of the personality and re-emerge from them only in changed form, as specific automatisms of self-control. They show themselves, for example, in the special sensitivity of the court aristocracy to anything that remotely touches the hereditary privileges on which their existence is based. They manifest themselves in the affect-laden gestures of revulsion from anything that "smells bourgeois". They are partly responsible for the fact that the court aristocracy is so much more sensitive to lower-class gestures than were the warrior nobility of the Middle Ages, that they strictly and emphatically exclude everything "vulgar" from their sphere of life. Finally, this permanently smouldering social fear also constitutes one of the most powerful driving forces of the social control that every member of this court upper class exerts over himself and other people in his circle. It is expressed in the intense vigilance with which members of court aristocratic society observe and polish everything that distinguishes them from people of lower rank: not only the external signs of status, but also their speech, their gestures, their social amusements and manners. The constant pressure from below and the fear it induces above are, in short, one of the strongest driving forces – though not the only one – of that specifically civilized refinement which distinguishes the people of this upper class from others and finally becomes second nature to them.

For it is precisely the chief function of the court aristocracy – their function for the mighty central ruler – to distinguish themselves, to maintain themselves as a distinct formation, a social counterweight to the bourgeoisie. They are completely free to spend their time elaborating the distinguishing social conduct of good manners and good taste. The rising bourgeois strata are less free to elaborate their conduct and taste; they have professions. Nevertheless, it is at first their ideal, too, to live like the aristocracy exclusively on annuities and to gain admittance to the court circle; this circle is still the model for a large part of the ambitious bourgeoisie. They become "Bourgeois Gentilhommes". They ape the nobility and its manners. But precisely this makes modes of conduct developed in court circles continually become useless as means of distinction, and the noble groups are forced to elaborate their conduct still further. Over and again customs that were once "refined" become "vulgar". Manners are polished and polished and the embarrassment-threshold constantly advances, until finally, with the downfall of absolutist-court society in the French Revolution, this spiral movement comes to an end or at least loses its force. The motor which, in the courtly phase, drives forward the civilizing transformation of the nobility – and with it the shame and repugnance threshold, as the examples in the first volume showed – is propelled both by the increased competition for the favour of the most powerful within the courtly stratum itself, and by the constant pressure from below. In this phase the *circulation of models* proceeds, as a result of the greater interdependence and therefore closer contact and more constant tension between different classes, far more quickly than in the Middle Ages. The "good societies" that come after the courtly one are all interwoven directly or indirectly, into the network of professional occupations, and even though "courtly" orientations are never entirely lacking in them, these no longer have remotely the same influence; from now on profession and money are the primary sources of prestige, and the art, the refinement of social conduct ceases to have the decisive importance for the reputation and success of the individual that it had in court society.

In every social stratum that area of conduct which is functionally of most vital importance to its members is the most carefully and intensively moulded. The exactitude with which, in court society, each movement of the hands while eating, each piece of etiquette and even the manner of speech is fashioned, corresponds to the importance which all these functions have for court people both as means of distinction from below, and as instruments in the competition for royal favour. The tasteful arrangement of house or park, the ostentatious or intimate – depending on the fashion – ornamentation of rooms, the witty conduct of a conversation or even a love affair, all these are in the courtly phase not only the private pleasures of individuals, but vital demands of their social position. They are pre-conditions for the respect of others, for the social success which here plays the same role as professional success in bourgeois society.

In the nineteenth century, with the gradual ascendancy of economic – commercial and industrial bourgeois – strata and their increasing pressure for access to the highest power positions in the state, all these skills cease to hold the central place in the social existence of people; they cease to be of primary significance for success or failure in their status and power struggles. Other skills take their place as primary skills on which success or failure in life depends – capacities such as occupational skills, adeptness in the competitive struggle for economic chances, in the acquisition or control of capital wealth, or the highly specialized skill needed for political advancement in the fierce though regulated party struggles characteristic of an age of increasing functional democratization. While the aristocratic courtiers personality structure is to a large extent determined by the need to compete for status and power chances within one of the ruling court establishments of their age, the social personality structure of the rising bourgeois strata is determined by the competition for a greater share of the growing capital wealth, or else for jobs or for positions which endow their occupants with greater political or administrative chances of power. These and related competitive struggles now become the main factors of constraint which leave their imprint upon the personality of individuals. Even though certain strata of the new economic and political bourgeoisie again and again form "good societies" of their own, and thus develop, or take over, some of the skills more highly cultivated in aristocratic societies, the pattern of social constraints acting upon the members of bourgeois "good societies" is in one decisive respect different from that acting upon aristocratic courtiers and gentlemen. The social existence of the latter is not only *de facto* founded upon unearned income of one kind or another, but living on unearned income and thus without any occupational work, in these circles, has a very high value. It is an almost indispensable condition for those who wish to "belong". With the rise of the economic and political bourgeoisie this aristocratic ethos changes. Its members, or at least its male members, are expected to work for a living, even if they form "good Societies" of their own. Forms of sociability, the ornamentation of one's house, visiting etiquette or the ritual of eating, all are now relegated to the sphere of private life. They preserve their vital function most strongly in that national society where, despite the rise of bourgeois elements, aristocratic social formations remained longest and most vigorously alive: in England. But even in the peculiar amalgam that developed here from the interpenetration over centuries of aristocratic and bourgeois models of conduct, middle-class traits gradually move into the foreground. And generally in all Western societies, with the decline of the purer aristocracy, whenever and however this takes place, the modes of conduct and affective forms which are developed are those necessary to the performance of money-earning functions and the execution of precisely regulated work. This is why professional bourgeois society, in everything that concerns social conduct, takes over the ritual of court society without developing it with the same intensity. This is why the standard of affect-control in this sphere advances only slowly with the rise of the professional bourgeoisie. In court society, and partly in English society too, this division of human existence into professional and private spheres does not exist. As the split becomes more general a new phase begins in the civilizing process; the pattern of drive-control that professional work necessitates is distinct in many respects from that imposed by the function of courtier and the game of court life. The exertion required by the maintenance of bourgeois social existence, the stability of the super-ego functions, the intensity of drive-control and drive-transformation demanded by bourgeois professional and commercial functions, are in sum considerably greater, despite a certain relaxation in the sphere of social manners, than the corresponding social personality structure required by the life of a court aristocrat. Most obvious is the difference in the regulation of sexual relationships.

However, the court-aristocratic moulding of the personality passes over in this or that form into the professional bourgeois one and is propagated further by it. We find this impregnation of broader strata by behavioural forms and drive-controls originating in court society particularly in regions where the courts were great and wealthy and their influence as style-building centres correspondingly strong. Paris and Vienna are examples of this. They are the seats of the two great rival absolutist courts of the eighteenth century. An echo of this can still be heard in the present day, not only in their reputation as centres of "good taste" or of luxury industries whose products are intended particularly for the use of "ladies", but even in the cultivation of sexual relationships, the erotic character of the population, even though reality in this respect may no longer quite match the reputation so frequently exploited by the film industry.

In one form or another, however, the models of conduct of court-aristocratic *bonne compagnie* have penetrated industrial society at large even where the courts were less rich, powerful and influential. That the conduct of the ruling Western groups, the degree and kind of their affect-control, show a high degree of uniformity despite all national variations, is certainly, in general terms, a result of the closely knit and long-ranging chains of interdependence linking the various national societies of the West. But within this general framework the phase of the semi-private power monopolies and of court-aristocratic society, with its high interdependence all over Europe, plays a special part in the moulding of Western civilized conduct. This court society exercised for the first time, and in a particularly pure form, a function which was afterwards transmitted in differing degrees and with various modifications to broader and broader strata of Western society, the function of a "good society", an upper class under pressure from many sides, from the organized monopolies of taxation and physical force on the one hand, and from the rising middle and lower classes on the other. Court society was indeed the first representative of the particular form of upper class which emerged more clearly the more closely, with the advancing division of functions, the different social classes became mutually dependent, and the larger the number of people and the geographical areas that were placed in such interdependence. It was a highly constricted upper class, whose situation demanded constant self-restraint and intense drive-control. Precisely this form of upper class from now on predominated in Western countries. And the models of this self-restraint, first developed in court-aristocratic society for the sphere of sociability, were passed on from class to class, adjusted and modified, like the upper-class function itself. The heritage of aristocratic society had greater or lesser importance depending on whether its character as "good society" played a greater or lesser role for a class or a nation. As we have said, this was the case to a greater or lesser degree with increasingly broad classes and finally entire nations in the West, particularly nations which, having early developed strong central institutions, early became colonial powers. In such nations there was an increase – under the pressure of social integration embodied both in the intensity of competition within the upper class itself and in the necessity of preserving its higher living standard and prestige *vis-à-vis* lower strata – in the strength of a particular kind of social control, in sensitivity to the behaviour of other members of one's own class, in individual self-control and in the strength of the individual "super-ego". In this way modes of conduct of a court-aristocratic upper class were amalgamated with those of various bourgeois strata as these rose to the position of upper classes; *civilité* was incorporated and perpetuated – with certain modifications depending on the situation of its new host – in what was now called "civilization" or, more precisely, "civilized conduct". So, from the nineteenth century onwards, these civilized forms of conduct spread across the rising lower classes of Western society and over the various classes in the colonies, amalgamating with indigenous patterns of conduct. Each time this happens, upper-class conduct and that of the rising groups interpenetrate. The standard of conduct of the rising class, its pattern of commands and prohibitions, reflects in its structure the history of the rise of this class. So it comes about that the typical "drive- and conduct-pattern" of the different industrial nation states, their "national character", still represents the nature of the earlier power-relationships between nobility and bourgeoisie and the course of the century-long struggles between them, from which a specific type of middle-class groups in the end emerged for a time as the dominant establishment. Thus, to give one out of many examples, the national code of conduct and affect-control in the United States has to a greater extent middle-class characteristics than – in spite of many similarities – the corresponding English code. In the making of this English code features of aristocratic descent fused with those of middle-class descent – understandably, for in the development of English society one can observe a continuous assimilating process in the course of which upper-class models (especially a code of good manners) were adopted in a modified form by middle-class people, while middle-class features (as for instance elements of a code of morals) were adopted by upper-class people. Hence, when, in the course of the nineteenth century, most of the aristocratic privileges were abolished, and England with the rise of the industrial working classes became a nation state, the English national code of conduct and affect-control showed very clearly the gradualness of the resolution of conflicts between upper and middle classes in the form, to put it briefly, of a peculiar blend between a code of good manners and a code of morals. Analogous processes were shown by the example of the difference between the German and French national characters. And it would not be difficult to add further illustrations relating to the national characters of the other European nations.

In each case, the waves of expansion of the standards of civilized conduct to a new class went hand in hand with an increase in the social power of that class and a raising of its standard of living to that of the class above it, or at least of that direction. Classes living permanently in danger of starving to death or of being killed by enemies can hardly develop or maintain those stable restraints characteristic of the more civilized types of conduct. To instil and maintain a more stable super-ego agency, a relatively high standard of living and a fairly high degree of security are necessary.

NOTES

1 C. H. Haskins, "The Spread of Ideas in the Middle Ages", in *Studies in Mediaeval Culture* (Oxford, 1929), pp. 92ff.
2 Apart from the *Minnelieder* there is a wealth of material showing this standard, in some cases even more clearly, e.g. the small prose piece by Andreas Capellanus in Marie de Champagne's cycle "De Amore", and the whole literature of the medieval controversy over women. The *Minnesänger* were medieval (12th–14th-century) German lyric poets/singers who carried on in German-speaking lands the troubadour tradition created by Occitan/Provençal poets in the 11th and 12th centuries. Their songs (*Minnelieder*) dealt with themes of romantic or courtly love, as indicated by their name, derived from the medieval German words for "love" and "singer." Elsewhere in his text, Elias contrasts sharply the attitudes toward women expressed in the *Minnesänger's* lover songs and "the more brutal ones prevalent in the chansons de geste," such as the Song of Roland (12th century) that praised, and recounted in gory detail, the brave deeds of knights on the field of battle.
3 Haskins, op. cit., p. 94.
4 J. de la Bruyère, *Caractères* (Paris, Hachette, 1922).
5 N. Elias, *The Civilizing Process*, vol. 1 (Oxford: Basil Blackwell, 1976; originally published in Switzerland as *Über den Prozess der Zivilisation*, 1939).

26

WOMEN ON TOP

Natalie Zemon Davis

I

The female sex was thought the disorderly one par excellence in early modern Europe. "*Une beste imparfaicte*," went one adage, "*sans foy, sans loy, sans craincte, sans constance*." Female disorderliness was already seen in the Garden of Eden, when Eve had been the first to yield to the serpent's temptation and incite Adam to disobey the Lord. To be sure, the men of the lower orders were also believed to be especially prone to riot and seditious unrest. But the defects of the males were thought to stem not so much from nature as from nurture: the ignorance in which they were reared, the brutish quality of life and conversation in the peasant's hut or the artisan's shop, and their poverty, which led to envy.[1]

With the women the disorderliness was founded in physiology. As every physician knew in the sixteenth century, the female was composed of cold and wet humors (the male was hot and dry), and coldness and wetness meant a changeable, deceptive, and tricky temperament. Her womb was like a hungry animal; when not amply fed by sexual intercourse or reproduction, it was likely to wander about her body, overpowering her speech and senses. If the Virgin Mary was free of such a weakness, it was because she was the blessed vessel of the Lord. But no other woman had been immaculately conceived, and even the well-born lady could fall victim to a fit of the "mother," as the uterus was called. The male might suffer from retained sexual juices, too, but (as Doctor François Rabelais pointed out) he had the wit and will to control his fiery urges by work, wine, or study. The female just became hysterical.[2] In the late seventeenth century, when vanguard physicians were abandoning humoral theories of personality in favor of more mechanistic notions of "animal spirits" and were beginning to remark that men suffered from emotional ills curiously like hysteria, they still maintained that the female's mind was more prone to be disordered by her fragile and unsteady temperament. Long before Europeans were asserting flatly

Natalie Zemon Davis, "Women on Top," pp. 124–42, 150–1, 310–15 from *Society and Culture in Early Modern France*. Stanford, CA and Cambridge: Stanford University Press and Polity Press, 1975.

that the "inferiority" of black Africans was innate, rather than the result, say, of climate, they were attributing female "inferiority" to nature.[3]

The lower ruled the higher within the woman, then, and if she were given her way, she would want to rule over those above her outside. Her disorderliness led her into the evil arts of witch-craft, so ecclesiastical authorities claimed; and when she was embarked on some behavior for which her allegedly weak intellect disqualified her, such as theological speculation or preaching, that was blamed on her disorderliness, too. The rule of a queen was impossible in France by the Salic law, and mocked by the common proverb *"tomber en quenouille."* For Pastor John Knox it was a "monstrous regimen," "the subversion of good order . . . all equitie and justice," whereas the more moderate Calvin "reckoned it among the visitations of God's anger," but one that should be borne, like any tyranny, with patience. Even a contemporary defender of queenship, John Aylmer, still had to admit that when he thought of the willfulness of women, he favored a strong role for Parliament. As late as 1742, in the face of entomological evidence to the contrary, some apiologists pretended that nature required the rule of a King Bee[4]

What were the proposed remedies for female unruliness? Religious training that fashioned the reins of modesty and humility; selective education that showed a woman her moral duty without enflaming her undisciplined imagination or loosing her tongue for public talk; honest work that busied her hands; and laws and constraints that made her subject to her husband.[5]

In some ways, that subjection was gradually deepening from the sixteenth to the eighteenth centuries as the patriarchal family streamlined itself for more efficient property acquisition, social mobility, and preservation of the line, and as progress in state-building and the extension of commercial capitalism were achieved at a cost in human autonomy. By the eighteenth century, married women in France and England had largely lost what independent legal personality they had formerly had, and they had less legal right to make decisions on their own about their dowries and possessions than at an earlier period. Propertied women were involved less and less in local and regional political assemblies. Working women in prosperous families were beginning to withdraw from productive labor; those in poor families were increasingly filling the most ill-paid positions of wage labor. This is not to say that females had no informal access to power or continuing vital role in the economy in these centuries; but the character of those relations was in conflict.[6]

Which side of the conflict was helped by the disorderly woman? Since this image was so often used as an excuse for the subjection of women, it is not surprising to find it opposed by one counter-strain in early feminist thought, which argued that women were *not* by nature more unruly, disobedient, and fickle than men. If anything it was the other way around. "By nature, women be sober," said the poet Christine de Pisan, "and those that be not, they go out of kind."[7] Women are by nature more modest and shamefaced than men, claimed a male feminist, which is demonstrated by the fact that women's privy parts are totally covered with pubic hair and are not handled by women the way men's are when they urinate. Why, then, did some men maintain that women were disorderly by nature? Because they were misogynists – vindictive, envious, or themselves dissolute.[8]

These claims and counterclaims about sexual temperament raise questions not merely about the actual character of male and female behavior in preindustrial Europe, but also about the varied uses of sexual symbolism. Sexual symbolism, of course, is always available to make statements about social experience and to reflect (or conceal) contradictions within it. At the end of the Middle Ages and in early modern Europe, the relation of the wife – of the potentially disorderly woman – to her husband was especially useful for expressing the relation of all subordinates to their superiors, and this for two reasons. First, economic relations were still often perceived in the medieval way as a matter of service. Second, the nature of political rule and the newer problem of sovereignty were very much at issue. In the little world of the family, with its conspicuous tension between intimacy and power, the larger matters of political and social order could find ready symbolization.[9]

Thus, Jean Calvin, himself a collapser of ecclesiastical hierarchies, saw the subjection of the wife to the husband as a guarantee of the subjection of both of them to the authority of the Lord. Kings and political theorists saw the increasing legal subjection of wives to their husbands (and of children to their parents) as a guarantee of the obedience of both men and women to the slowly centralizing state – a training for the loyal subject of seventeenth-century France or for the dutiful citizen of seventeenth-century England. "Marriages are the seminaries of States," began the pre-amble to the French ordinance strengthening paternal power within the family, For John Locke, opponent of despotic rule in commonwealth and in marriage, the wife's relinquishing her right of decision to her husband as "naturally . . . the abler and stronger" was analogous to the individual's relinquishing his natural liberties of decision and action to the legislative branch of government.[10]

Indeed, how could one separate the idea of subordination from the existence of the sexes? Gabriel de Foigny's remarkable fictitious land of Australie (1673), a utopia of hermaphrodites, shows how close the link between the two was perceived to be. The Australian, in whom the sexes were one, could not understand how a conflict of wills could be avoided within the "mutual pos-session" of European marriage. The French traveler answered that it was simple, for mother and child were both subject to the father. The hermaphrodite, horrified at such a violation of the total autonomy that was the sign of complete true "men." dismissed the European pattern as bestial.[11]

The female's position was used to symbolize not only hierarchical subordination but also vio-lence and chaos. Bruegel's terrifying *Dulle Griet*, painted during the occupation of the Nether-lands by Spanish soldiers, makes a huge, armed, unseeing woman, Mad Meg, the emblem of fiery destruction, of brutal oppression and disorder. Bruegel's painting cuts in more than one way, however, and shows how female disorderliness – the female out of her place – could be assigned another value. Next to Mad Meg is a small woman in white on top of a male monster; it is Saint Margaret of Antioch tying up the devil. Nearby other armed women are beating grotesque animals from Hell.[12]

Bruegel's Margarets are by no means alone in preindustrial Europe. In hierarchical and con-flictful societies that loved to reflect on the world-turned-upside-down, the *topos* of the woman-on-top was one of the most enjoyed. Indeed, sexual inversion – that is, switches in sex roles – was a widespread form of cultural play in literature, in art, and in festivity. Sometimes the reversal involved dressing and masking as a member of the opposite sex – the prohibitions of Deuteron-omy 22, Saint Paul, Saint Jerome, canon law, and Jean Calvin notwithstanding.[13] Sometimes the reversal involved simply taking on certain roles of forms of behavior characteristic of the opposite sex. Women played men; men played women; men played women who were playing men.

It is the uses of sexual inversion, and more particularly of play with the image of the unruly woman in literature, in popular festivity, and in ordinary life, that will be the subject of the rest of this essay. Evidently, the primary impulse behind such inversion in early modern Europe was not homosexuality or disturbed gender identity. Although Henri III expressed special wishes of his own when he and his male "mignons" masked as Amazons in the 1570s, and although the seventeenth-century Abbé de Choisy, whose mother had dressed him as a girl through adoles-cence, had special reasons for using a woman's name and wearing female clothes until he was thirty-three,[14] still most literary and festive transvestism at this time had a wider psychosexual and cultural significance than this.

Anthropologists offer several suggestions about the functions of magical transvestism and ritual inversion of sex roles. First, sexual disguise can ward off danger from demons, malignant fairies, or other powers that threaten castration or defloration. Second, transvestism and sexual reversal can be part of adolescent rites of passage, either to suggest the marginality of the transitional state (as when a male initiate is likened to a menstruating woman) or to allow each sex to obtain something of the other's power (as in certain initiation and marriage customs in early Greece). Third, exchange of sex can be part of what Victor Turner has called "rituals of status reversal," as when women in certain parts of Africa usurp the clothing, weapons, or tasks of the superior males and behave in lewd ways to increase the chance for a good harvest or to turn aside an impending natural catastrophe. Finally, as James Peacock has pointed out, the transvestite actor, priest, or shaman can symbolize categories of cosmological or social organization. For instance, in Java the transvestite actor reinforces by his irregularity the importance of the categories high/low, male/female.

However diverse these uses of sexual inversion, anthropologists generally agree that they, like other rites and ceremonies of reversal, are ultimately sources of order and stability in a hierarchical society. They can clarify the structure by the process of reversing it. They can provide an expression of, and a safety value for, conflicts within the system. They can correct and relieve the system when it has become authoritarian. But, so it is argued, they do not question the basic order of the society itself. They can renew the system, but they cannot change it.[15]

Historians of early modern Europe are likely to find inversions and reversals less in prescribed rites than in carnivals and festivities. Their fools are likely to escape the bounds of ceremony,[16] and their store of literary sources for inversion will include not only the traditional tales of magical transformation in sex, but also a variety of stories in which men and women *choose* to change their sexual status. In addition, there are comic conventions and genres, such as the picaresque, that allow much play with sexual roles. These new forms offered increased occasions and ways in which topsy-turvy could be used for explicit criticism of the social order. Nevertheless, students of these festive and literary forms have ordinarily come to the same conclusion as anthropologists regarding the limits of symbolic inversion: a world-turned-upside-down can only be righted, not changed. To quote Ian Donaldson's recent study Comedy from Jonson to Fielding: "The lunatic governor . . . , the incompetent judge, the mock doctor, the equivocating priest, the hen-pecked husband: such are the familiar and recurrent figures in the comedy of a society which gives a general assent to the necessity of entrusting power to its governors, judges, doctors, priests, and husbands."[17]

I would like to argue, on the contrary, that comic and festive inversion could *undermine* as well as reinforce that assent through its connections with everyday circumstances outside the privileged time of carnival and stage-play. Somewhat in contradistinction to Christine de Pisan and the gallant school of feminists, I want to argue that the image of the disorderly woman did not always function to keep women in their place. On the contrary, it was a multivalent image that could operate, first, to widen behavioral options for women within and even outside marriage, and, second, to sanction riot and political disobedience for both men and women in a society that allowed the lower orders few formal means of protest. Play with the unruly woman is partly a chance for temporary release from the traditional and stable hierarchy; but it is also part of the conflict over efforts to change the basic distribution of power within society. The woman-on-top might even facilitate innovation in historical theory and political behavior.

II

Let us begin with a review of the major types of sexual inversion we find in literary sources – sources sober and comic, learned and popular. Then we will consider the disorderly woman in more detail. What kinds of license were allowed through this turnabout? First of all, we have stories of men who dress as women to save themselves from an enemy or from execution, to sneak into the opponent's military camp, or to get into a nunnery or women's quarters for purposes of seduction. In all of these cases, the disguise is not merely practical but exploits the expected physical frailty of women to prevent harm to the male or to disarm his victim. A more honorable trickery is ventured by Pyrocles in Sidney's *Arcadia*, by Marston's Antonio, and by d'Urfé's Céladon, for they dress as brave Amazons or as a Druid priestess in order to have access to the woman they wish to woo. Here no more than in the first case does the inversion lead to criticism of social hierarchy. Rather Pyrocles is rebuked by his friend for "his effeminate love of a woman," for letting his "sensual weakness" rebel against his manly reason.

Only with the male fool or clown do we find literary examples of male transvestism serving to challenge order. In the seventeenth-century *commedia dell'arte*, a black-faced Harlequin dolls himself up as a ridiculous Diana, goddess of the chase, replete with crescent-moon ruff, fancy clothes, and a little bow. The result is so absurd that not only are boundaries between high and low effaced, but, as William Willeford has suggested, reality itself seems to dissolve.[18]

The stories, theater, and pictorial illustration of preindustrial Europe offer many more examples of women trying to act like men than vice versa, and more of the time the sexual inversion yields criticism of the established order. One set of reversals portrays women going beyond what can ordinarily be expected of a mere female; that is, it shows women ruling the lower in themselves and thus deserving to be like men. We have, for instance, tales of female saints of the early Church who lived chastely as male monks to the end of their lives, braving false charges of fathering children and withstanding other tests along the way. Five of these transvestite ladies appear in Voragine's *Golden Legend*, which had wide circulation in manuscript and printed editions in both Latin and the vernacular.[19]

Other uncommon women changed their roles in order to defend established rule or values associated with it. Disguised as men, they prove fidelity to lovers whom they wish to marry or, as in the case of Madame Ginevra in Boccaccio's tale, prove their chastity to doubting husbands. Disguised as men, they leave Jewish fathers for Christian husbands and plead for Christian mercy over base Jewish legalism. Disguised as men, they rescue spouses from prison and the family honor from stain. For example, in *The French Amazon*, one of Mademoiselle l'Héritier's reworkings of an old French tale, the heroine maintains her father's connections with the court by fighting in the place of her slain and rather incompetent twin brother. She, of course, ultimately marries the prince. Along with Spenser's Britomart, Tasso's Clorinda, and others, the French Amazon is one of a line of noble women warriors, virtuous viragos all, magnanimous, brave, and chaste.[20]

To what extent could such embodiments of order serve to censure accepted hierarchy? They might reprove by their example the cowardice and wantonness of ordinary men and women. But they used their power to support a legitimate cause, not to unmask the truth about social relationships. By showing the good that could be done by the woman out of her place, they had the potential to inspire a few females to exceptional action and feminists to reflection about the capacities of women (we will see later whether that potential was realized), but they are unlikely symbols for moving masses of people to resistance.

It is otherwise with comic play with the disorderly woman, that is, inversion that can be expected of the female, who gives rein to the lower in herself and seeks rule over her superiors. Some portraits of her are so ferocious (such as Spenser's cruel Radagunde and other vicious viragos) that they preclude the possibility of fanciful release from, or criticism of, hierarchy. It is the same with those tales, considered humorous at the time, that depict a savage taming of the shrew, as in the fabliau of *La Dame escoillée*, where the domineering lady is given a counterfeit but painful "castration" by her son-in-law, and in the sixteenth-century German cartoon strip *The Ninefold Skins of a Shrewish Woman*, which are stripped off one by one by various punishments. The legend of the medieval Pope Joan also has limited potential for mocking established order. As told by Boccaccio, it is a hybrid of the transvestite saint and the cruelly tamed shrew: Joan wins the papacy by her wits and good behavior, but her illicit power goes to her head, or rather to her womb. She becomes pregnant, gives birth during a procession, and dies wretchedly in the cardinals' dungeon.[21]

There are a host of situations, however, in which the unruly woman is assigned more ambiguous meanings. For our purposes we can sort out three ways in which the multivalent image is used. First, there is a rich treatment of women who are happily given over to the sway of their bodily senses or who are using every ruse they can to prevail over men. There is the wife of Bath, of course, who celebrates her sexual instrument and outlives her five husbands. And Rabelais' Gargamelle – a giant of a woman, joyously and frequently coupling, eating bushels of tripe, quaffing wine, joking obscenely, giving birth in a grotesque fecal explosion from which her son Gargantua somersaults shouting "Drink, drink." Then the clever and powerful wife of the *Quinze joies de mariage* – cuckolding her husband and foiling his every effort to find her out, wheedling fancy clothes out of him, beating him up, and finally locking him in his room. Also Grimmelshausen's Libuschka, alias Courage, one of a series of picaresque heroines – fighting in the army in soldier's clothes; ruling her many husbands and lovers; paying them back a hundredfold when they take revenge or betray her; whoring, tricking, and trading to survive or get rich. Husband-dominators are everywhere in popular literature, nicknamed among the Germans St. Cudgelman (Sankt Kolbmann) or Doktor Siemann (she-man). The point about such portraits is that they are funny and amoral: the woman are full of life and energy, and they win much of the time; they stay on top of their fortune with as much success as Machiavelli might have expected for the Prince of his political tract.[22]

A second comic treatment of the woman out of her place allows her a temporary period of dominion, which is ended only after she has said or done something to undermine authority or denounce its abuse. When the Silent Wife begins to talk and order her husband about in Ben Jonson's *Epicoene*, she points out that women cannot be mere statues or puppets; what her husband calls "Amazonian" impudence in her is simply reasonable decorum.[23] When the Woman-Captain of Shadwell's comedy puts aside her masculine garb and the sword with which she has hectored her jealous and stingy old husband, she does so only after having won separate maintenance and £400 a year. The moral of the play is that husbands must not move beyond the law to tyranny. In *As You Like It*, the love-struck Rosalind, her tongue loosed by her male apparel and her "holiday humor," warns Orlando that there is a limit to the possession he will have over a wife, a limit set by her desires, her wit, and her tongue. Though she later gives herself to Orlando in marriage, her saucy counsel cannot be erased from the real history of the courtship.

The most popular comic example of the female's temporary rule, however, is Phyllis riding Aristotle, a motif recurring in stories, paintings, and household objects from the thirteenth through the seventeenth centuries. Here Aristotle admonishes his pupil Alexander for his excessive attention to a certain Phyllis, one of his new subjects in India. The beautiful Phyllis gets revenge before Alexander's eyes by coquettishly persuading the old philosopher to get down on all fours and, saddled and bridled, carry her through the garden. Here youth overthrows age, and sexual passion, dry sterile philosophy; nature surmounts reason, and the female, the male.[24]

Phyllis' ambiguous ride brings us to a third way of presenting the woman-on-top, that is, where the license to be a social critic is conferred on her directly. Erhard Schoen's woodcuts (early sixteenth century) portray huge women distributing fools' caps to men. This is what happens when women are given the upper hand; and yet in some sense the men deserve it. Erasmus' female Folly is the supreme example of this *topos*. Stultitia tells the truth about the foibles of all classes and defends the higher folly of the Cross, even though paradoxically she's just a foolish gabbling woman herself.[25]

These varied images of sexual topsy-turvy – from the transvestite male escaping responsibility and harm to the transvestite fool and the unruly woman unmasking the truth – were available to city people who went to the theater and to people who could read and afford books. They were also familiar to the lower orders more generally in both town and country through books that were read aloud and through stories, poems, proverbs, and broadsheets.[26]

In addition, popular festivals and customs, hard though they are to document, show much play with switches in sex roles and much attention to women-on-top. In examining these data, we will notice that sexual inversion in popular festivity differs from that in literature in two ways. Whereas the purely ritual and/or magical element in sexual inversion was present in literature to only a small degree, it assumed more importance in the popular festivities, along with the carnivalesque functions of mocking and unmasking the truth. Whereas sexual inversion in literary and pictorial play more often involved the female taking on the male role or dressing as a man, the festive inversion more often involved the male taking on the role or garb of the woman, that is, the unruly woman – though this asymmetry may not have existed several centuries earlier.

The ritual and/or magical functions of sexual inversion were filled in almost all cases by males disguised as grotesque cavorting females. In sections of Germany and Austria, at carnival time male runners, half of them masked as female, half as male, jumped and leaped through the streets. In France it was on St. Stephen's Day or New Year's Day that men dressed as wild beasts or as women and jumped and danced in public (or at least such was the case in the Middle Ages). The saturnalian Feast of Fools, which decorous doctors of theology and prelates were trying to ban from the French cathedrals in the fifteenth and sixteenth centuries, involved both young clerics and laymen, some of them disguised as females, who made wanton and loose gestures. In parts of the Pyrénées at Candlemas (February 2), a Bear Chase took place[27] involving a lustful bear, costumed hunters, and young men dressed as women and often called Rosetta. After an amorous interlude with Rosetta, the bear was killed, revived, shaved, and killed again.[28]

In England, too, in Henry VIII's time, during the reign of the Boy Bishop after Christmas some of the male children taken from house to house were dressed as females rather than as priests or bishops. The most important English examples of the male as grotesque female, however, were the Bessy and Maid Marian. In the northern counties, a Fool-Plough was dragged about the countryside, often on the first Monday after Epiphany, by men dressed in white shirts. Sword dances were done by some of them, while old Bessy and her fur-clad Fool capered around and tried to collect from the spectators. Maid Marian presided with Robin Hood over the May games. If in this capacity she was sometimes a real female and sometimes a disguised male, when it came to the Morris Dance with Robin, the Hobby Horse, the dragon, and the rest, the Marian was a man. Here again the Maid's gestures or costume might be licentious.[29]

All interpreters of this transvestism see it, like the African example mentioned earlier, as a fertility rite – biological or agricultural[30] – embedded into festivities that may have had other meanings as well. In the European context the use of the female garb was especially appropriate, for it drew not merely on the inevitable association of the female with reproduction, but on the contemporary definition of the female as the lustier sex. Did it also draw on other features of sexual symbolism in early modern Europe, e.g. the relation of the subordinate to the superior? Did it (as with our transvestite Harlequin of the *commedia dell'arte*) suggest to peasants or city folk the blurring or reversing of social boundaries? Perhaps. When we see the roles that the woman-on-top was later to play, it is hard to believe that some such effect was not stimulated by these rites. In the urban Feast of Fools, in any case, the fertility function of the transvestism was already over-shadowed by its carnivalesque derision of the celibate priestly hierarchy.

Along with these instances of festive male transvestism, we have some scanty evidence of a more symmetrical switch. During the Twelve Days of Christmas or on Epiphany, mummers and guisers in northern England, the Scottish Lowlands, and northern France might include men *and* women wearing the clothes of the opposite sex. At Fastnacht in fifteenth-century Nuremberg men dressed as women and women as men, and the same was the case at Shrovetide in sixteenth-century England and perhaps at Mardi Gras in early modern France. Possibly here too there is some old relation to fertility rites, but the exchange may well be connected with the more flex-ible license of carnivalesque inversion. At least in the case of "goose-dancing" at Eastertime on the Scilly Islands in the mid-eighteenth century, we know the license was used to tell the truth: "the maidens are dressed up for young men and the young men for maidens: thus disguised they visit their neighbours in companies, where they dance, and make jokes upon what has happened on the island; when everyone is humorously told their own without offense being taken."[31]

The truth-telling of Europe's male festive societies was much less gentle than that of the Scilly geese. These organizations were the Kingdoms and Abbeys of Misrule discussed in [another] essay.[32] (In England and Scotland we have Lords of Misrule and Abbots of Unreason, though the exact character of their bands remains to be studied.) Among other roles in town and countryside, the Abbeys expressed the community's interest in marriages and their outcome much more overtly than the cavorting Bessy or Rosetta. In noisy masked demonstrations – chari-varis, scampanete, katzenmusik, cencerrada, rough music, and the like – they mocked newlyweds who had not produced a baby soon enough and people marrying for the second time, especially when there was a gross disparity in age between bride and groom. Indeed, any local scandal might be made the target for their pots, tambourines, bells, and horns.

The unruly woman appeared in the Abbeys' plays in two forms. First as officers of Misrule. In rural areas, these were usually called Lords and Abbots; in the French cities, however, they took all kinds of pompous titles. Among these dignitaries were princesses and Dames and espe-cially Mothers: we find Mère Folle in Dijon, Langres, and Chalon-sur-Saône; Mère Sotte in Paris and Compiègne; and Mère d'Enfance in Bordeaux. In Wales, though I know of no female festive titles, the men who conducted the *ceffyl pren*, as the local rough music was called, blackened their faces and wore women's garb.[33] In all of this there was a double irony: the young villager who became an Abbot, the artisan who became a Prince directly adopted for their Misrule a symbol of licit power; the power invoked by the man who became Mère Folle, however, was already in defiance of natural order – a dangerous and vital power, which his disguise made safe for him to assume.

The unruly woman not only directed some of the male festive organizations; she was some-times their butt. The village scold or the domineering wife might be ducked in the pond or pulled through the streets muzzled or branked or in a creel.[34] City people from the fifteenth to the eighteenth centuries were even more concerned about husband-beating, and the beaten *man* (or a neighbor playing his part) was paraded through the streets backward on an ass by noisy revel-ers. In the English Midlands the ride was known as a Skimmington or a Skimmety, perhaps from the big skimming ladle sometimes used by women in beating their husbands. In northern England and Scotland, the victim or his stand-in "rode the stang" (a long hobbyhorse), and a like steed was used in the *ceffyl pren* in Wales. In some towns, effigies of the offending couple were prom-enaded. In others, the festive organization mounted floats to display the actual circumstances of the monstrous beating: the wives were shown hitting their husbands with distaffs, tripe, sticks, trenchers, water pots; throwing stones at them; pulling their beards; or kicking them in the genitals.[35]

With these last dramatizations, the Misrule Abbeys introduced ambiguities into the treatment of the woman-on-top, just as we have seen in the comic literature. The unruly woman on the float was shameful, outrageous; she was also vigorous and in command. The mockery turned against her martyred husband. And the message of the urban carnival was mixed: it both exhorted the henpecked husband to take command and invited the unruly woman to keep up the fight.

Real women in early modern Europe had less chance than men to initiate or take part in their *own* festivals of inversion. To be sure, a female fool named Mathurine flourished at the courts of Henri IV and Louis XIII and, dressed as an Amazon, commented on political and religious matters; but there is no sign of festive organizations for young women. Confraternities for young unmarried women, where they existed at all, stayed close to religious devotion. Queens were elected for special occasions, such as Twelfth Night or Harvest, but their rule was gentle and tame. The young May queens in their flowers and white ribbons begged for money for dowries or for the Virgin's altar, promising a mere kiss in return. Some May customs that were still current in early modern Europe, however, point back to a rowdier role for women. In rural Franche-Comté during May, wives could take revenge on their husbands for beating them by ducking the men or making them ride an ass; wives could dance, jump, and banquet freely without permission from their husbands; and women's courts issued mock decrees. (In nearby Dijon by the sixteenth century, interestingly enough, Mère Folle and her Infanterie had usurped this revenge from the woman; May was the one month of the year when the Misrule Abbey would charivari a man who had beaten his wife.) Generally, May – Flora's month in Roman times – was thought to be a period in which women were powerful, their desires at their most immoderate. As the old saying went, a May bride would keep her husband in yoke all year round. And in fact marriages were not frequent in May.[36]

In Nuremberg it was at carnival time that women may have assumed some kind of special license in the sixteenth and seventeenth centuries. Illustrated proclamations in joking pompous language granted every female with "a wretched dissolute husband" the right to deny him his freedom and to beat him till "his asshole [was] roaring." Another decree, issued by Foeminarius, the Hereditary Steward of Quarrel and Dispute Valley, gave three years of Privileges to the suffering Company of Wives so that they might rule their husbands: they could bear arms, elect their own mayor, and go out and entertain as they wished while their spouses could buy nothing or drink no wine or beer without the wives' permission. And, of course, the men did all the housework and welcomed any bastards that the wives might bear.[37]

The woman-on-top was a resource for private and public life in the fashions we have described only so long as two things were the case: first, so long as sexual symbolism had a close connection with questions of order and subordination, with the lower female sex conceived as the disorderly lustful one; second, so long as the stimulus to inversion play was a double one – traditional hierarchical structures *and* disputed changes in the distribution of power in family and political life. As we move into the industrial period with its modern states, classes, and systems of private property, and its exploitation of racial and national groups, both symbolism and stimuli were transformed. One small sign of the new order is the changing butt of domestic charivaris: by the nineteenth century, rough music in England was more likely to be directed against the wife-beater than against the henpecked husband, and there are signs of such a shift in America and even in France.[38]

The woman-on-top flourished, then, in preindustrial Europe and during the period of transition to industrial society. Despite all our detail in this essay, we have been able to give only the outlines of her reign. Variations in sexual inversion from country to country or between Protestants and Catholics have been ignored for the sake of describing a large pattern over time. Cultural play with sex roles intended to explore the character of sexuality itself (Where did one sex stop and the other begin?) has been ignored to concentrate on hierarchy and disorder. The timing and distribution of transvestite riots, and the nature of play with sex roles before the fourteenth century, need to be investigated. (Is it not likely that there were female transvestite rituals in areas where hoeing was of great consequence? Can the unruly woman have been so much an issue when sovereignty was less at stake?) The asymmetry between male and female roles in festive life from the fifteenth through the eighteenth centuries remains to be explored, as do some of the contrasts between literary and carnivalesque inversion. What has been established are the types of symbolic reversal in sex roles in early modern Europe and their multiple connections with orderliness in thought and behavior. The holiday rule of the woman-on-top confirmed subjection throughout society, but it also promoted resistance to it. The Maid Marian danced for a plentiful village; the Rosetta disported with the doomed old bear of winter; the serving women of Saint Giles threw stools for the Reformed Kirk; Ghostly Sally led her Whiteboys in a new kind of popular justice. The woman-on-top renewed old systems, but also helped change them into something different.

NOTES

1 Pierre Grosner, *Les motz dorez De Catbon en francoys et en latin . . . Proverbes, Adages, Auctoritez et ditz moraulx des Saiges* (Paris, 1530/31), f. F. vii^r. Claude de Rubys, *Les privileges franchises et immunitez octroyees par les roys . . . aux consuls . . . et habitans de la ville de Lyon* (Lyon, 1574), p. 74. Christopher Hill, "The Many-Headed Monster in Later Tudor and Early Stuart Political Thinking," in C. H. Carter, ed., *From the Renaissance to the Counter-Reformation. Essays in Honour of Garrett Mattingly* (London, 1966), pp. 296–324.

2 Female medical practitioners also accepted the theory of the "wandering womb" and provided remedies for female hysteria. See *A choice Manual of . . . Select Secrets in Physick . . . Collected and Practised by . . . the Countesse of Kent* (London, 1653), pp. 114, 145; *Recueil des Remedes . . . Recueillis par les Ordres Charitables de . . . Madame Fouquet* (4th ed.; Dijon, 1690), pp. 168–89; Jean de Rostagny, *Traité de Primerose sur les erreurs vulgaires de la medecine* (Lyon, 1689), p. 774; Angélique Du Coudray, *Abrégé de l'art des Accouchemens* (Paris, 1759), p. 173.

3 Laurent Joubert, *Erreurs populaires au fait de la medecine* (Bordeaux, 1578), pp. 161ff. François Poullain de La Barre, *De l'excellence des hommes contre l'egalité des sexes* (Paris, 1675), pp. 136ff., 156ff. Ilza Veith, *Hysteria, The History of a Disease* (Chicago, 1965). Michael Screech, *The Rabelaisian Marriage* (London, 1958), Chap. 6. Thomas Sydenham, in his important *Epistolary Dissertation to Dr. Cole* (1681), connects the delicate constitution of the woman with the irregular motions of her "animal spirits" and hence explains her special susceptibility to hysteria. Winthrop Jordan, *White over Black. American Attitudes toward the Negro, 1550–1812* (Chapel Hill, N.C., 1968), pp. 11–20, 187–90.

4 Heinrich Institoris and Jacob Sprenger. *Malleus Maleficarum* (ca. 1487), trans. M. Summers (London, 1928), Part I, question 6: "Why it is that Women are chiefly addicted to Evil Superstitions." Florimond de Raemond, *L'histoire de la naissance, progrez et decadence de l'hérésie de ce siècle* (Rouen, 1623), PP. 847-8, 874-7. Fleury de Bellingen. *L'Etymologie ou Explication des Proverbes françois* (La Haye, 1656), pp. 311ff. James E. Phillips, Jr., "The Background of Spenser's Attitude toward Women Rulers," *Huntington Library Quarterly* 5 (1941–42): 9-10. [John Aylmer], *An Harborowe for Faithfull and Trewe Subiectes, agaynst the late blowne Blaste, concerninge the Government of Wemen* (London, 1559). J. Simon, *Le gouvernement admirable ou la République des Abeilles* (Paris, 1742), pp. 23ff. John Thorley, in *The Female Monarchy. Being an Enquiry into the Nature, Order and Government of*

Bees (London, 1744), still finds it necessary to argue against those who cannot believe in a queen bee (pp. 75–86).

5 See, for instance, Juan Luis Vives, *The Instruction of a Christian Woman* (London, 1524). and François de Salignac de la Mothe Fénelon, *Fénelon on Education*, trans. H. C. Barnard (Cambridge, 1966).

6 P. C. Timbal, "L'esprit du droit privé," *XVIIe siècle* 58–9 (1963): 38–39. P. Ourliac and J. de Malafosse, *Histoire du droit privé* (Paris, 1968), 3: 145–52, 264–8. L. Abensour, *Le femme et le féminisme avant la Révolution* (Paris, 1923), Part 1, chap. 9. Alice Clark, *The working Life of Women in the Seventeenth Century* (London, 1919; reprint 1968). E. Le Roy Ladurie, *Les paysans de Languedoc* (Pairs, 1966), pp. 271–80 and *Annexe 32*, p. 859.

7 Some female writers from the sixteenth to the early eighteenth centuries, such as Marguerite de Navarre, Madame de Lafayette, Aphra Behn, and Mary de la Rivière Manley, did not accept this view. Although they did not portray women as necessarily more lustful than men, they did give females a range of sexual appetites at least equal to that of males.

8 Christine de Pisan, *The Boke of the Cyte of Ladyes* (a translation of *Le Tresor de la Cité des Dames*, 1405; London, 1521), f. Ee i^v. Henry Cornelius Agrippa of Nettesheim, *Of the Nobilitie and Excellencie of Womankynde* (translation from the Latin edition of 1509; London, 1542), f. B iv^{r-v}.

9 The English characterization of a wife's killing of her husband as petty treason rather than as homicide may be an early example of the kind of symbolism being described here. Petty treason appeared as a crime distinct from high treason in the fourteenth century, and lasted as such till the early nineteenth century. It included the killing of a master by his servant, a husband by his wife, and a prelate by a secular cleric or religious. As Blackstone presents the law, it seems to differ from earlier Germanic practice, which treated the murder of *either* spouse by the other as an equally grave crime. The development of the concept and law of treason was closely connected with the development of the idea of sovereignty. J. G. Bellamy, *The Law of Treason in England in the Later Middle Ages* (Gambridge, Eng., 1970), pp. 1–14, 225–31; William Blackstone, *Commentaries on the Laws of England* (Oxford, 1770), Book IV, chap. 14, including note t. The use of male/female as an expression of social relationships (master/servant, sovereign/subject, and the like) is not the only kind of sexual symbolism in early modern Europe, thought it is the basis for discussion in this essay. Eric Wolf considers male/female as an expression of the relationships public/domestic and instrumental-ordering/expressive-ordering in "Society and Symbols in Latin Europe and in the Islamic Near East," *Anthropological Quarterly* 42 (July 1968): 287–301. For an attempt at a very broad theory of sexual symbolism, see Sherry B. Ortner, "Is Female to Male as Nature Is to Culture?" in Michelle Zimbalist Rosaldo and louise Lamphere, eds., *Woman, Culture, and Society* (Stanford, Calif., 1974), pp. 67–87.

10 Jean Calvin, *Commentaries on the Epistles of Paul the Apostle to the Corinthians*, trans. J. Pringle (Edinburgh, 1848), 1: 353–61 (1 Cor. 11:3–12). William Gouge, *Domesticall Duties* quoted in W. and M. Haller, "The Puritan Art of Love," *Huntington Library Quarterly* 5 (1941–42): 246. John G. Halkett. *Milton and the Idea of Matrimony* (New Haven, 1970), pp. 20–4. Gordon J. Schocher, "Patriarchalism, Politics and Mass Attitudes in Stuart England," *Historical Journal* 12 (1969): 413–41. Catherine E. Holmes, *L'éloquence judiciaire de 1620 à 1660* (Paris, 1967), p. 76. Ourliac and de Malafosse, *Droit Privé*, 3: 66 ("*L'époque des rois absolus est ausscelle des pères absolus.*"). John Locke, *The Second Treatise of Government*, ed. T. P. Peardon (Indianapolis, Ind., 1952), chap. 7, par. 82; chap. 9, pars. 128–31.

11 [Gabriel de Foigny], *Les avantures de Jacques Sadeur dans la découverte et le voyage de la terre australe* (Amsterdam, 1732), chap. 5, especially pp. 128–39.

12 Robert Delevoy, *Bruegel* (Lausanne, 1959), pp. 70–5.

13 Deut. 22:5; 1 Cor. 11: 14–15. Saint Jerome, *The Letters of Saint Jerome*, Trans. C. C. Mierow (London, 1963), 1: 161–62 (Letter 22 to Eustochium). Robert of Flamborough, *Liber Penitentialis*, ed. J. F. Firth (Toronto, 1971), Book 5, p. 164. (I am grateful to Carolly Erickson and Stephen Horowitz for the last two references.) Jean Calvin, "Sermons sur le Deutéronome," in *Ioannis Calvini opera quae supersunt omnia*, ed. G. Baum, E. Cunitz, and E. Reuss (Brunswick, 1863–80), 28: 17–19, 234 (hereafter cited as *Calvini opera*). Vern Bullough, "Transvestites in the Middle Ages," *American Journal of Sociology* 79 (1974): 1381–94.

14 Pierre de l'Estoile, *Mémoires-journaux*, ed. Brunet et al. (Paris, 1888–96). 1: 142–3. 157, 180. François-
    Timoléon de Choisy, *Mémoires*, ed. G. Mongrédien (Paris, 1966), pp. 286–360. Bullough's "Transves-
    tites in the Middle Ages," which I have read as this essay goes to press, also discusses male cross-dressing
    in social rather than in psychopathological terms, that is, in terms of the higher and lower qualities
    assigned to male and female traits: males who dress as women have a temporary or permanent desire
    for status loss (p. 1393). I think this is accurate as a very preliminary formulation. My essay shows the
    varied functions of role inversion and transvestism as well as the gains in power and the options they
    brought to males.

15 Max Gluckman, *Order and Rebellion in Tribal Africa* (New York, 1963), Introduction and chap. 3.
    Victor Turner, *The Forest of Symbols. Aspects of Ndembu Ritual* (Ithaca, N.Y., 1967), chap. 4. *Idem. The
    Ritual Process. Structure and Anti-Structure* (Chicago, 1968), chaps. 3–5. Gregory Bateson, "Culture
    Contact and Schismogenesis," *Man* 35 (Dec. 1935): 199. J. C. Flügel, *The Psychology of Clothes*
    (London, 1930), pp. 120–1. Marie Delcourt, *Hermaphrodite. Myths and Rites of the Bisexual Figure in
    Classical Antiquity* (London, 1956), chap. 1. James Peacock, "Symbolic Reversal and Social History:
    Transvestites and Clowns of Java," in Barbara Babcock-Abrahams, ed., *Forms of Symbolic Inversion*
    (forthcoming). See also Rodney Needham's discussion of symbolic reversal and its relation to classifi-
    cation in his introduction to E. Durkheim and M. Mauss, *Primitive Classifications*, trans. R. Needham
    (Chicago, 1972), pp. xxxviii–xl.

16 William Willeford, *The Fool and His Scepter* (Evanston, Ill., 1969), especially pp. 97–8.

17 Ian Donaldson, *The World Upside-Down, Comedy from Jonson to Fielding* (Oxford, 1970), p. 14.

18 Stith Thompson, *Motif-Index of Folk Literature* (rev. ed.; Bloomington, Ind., 1955–58), K310, K514,
    K1321, K1836, K2357.8. Sir Philip Sidney. *The New Arcadia*, Book I, chap. 12. Honore d'Urfé,
    Astrée (1609–19). John Marston, *The History of Antonio and Mellida* (1602). Willeford, *The Fool*,
    pp. 58–62.

19 Delcourt, *Hermaphrodite*, pp. 84–102. John Anson, "The Female Transvestite in Early Monasticism:
    The Origin and Development of a Motif," *Viator* 5 (1974), S.1 (I am grateful to Mr. Anson for several
    bibliographic suggestions). The transvestite saints appearing in Voragine's *Golden Legend* are St. Mar-
    garet, alias Brother Pelagius (Oct. 8); Saint Pelagia, alias Pelagius (Oct. 8); Saint Theodora, alias Brother
    Theodore (Sept. 11); Saint Eugenia (Sept. 11); and Saint Marina, alias Brother Marinus (June 18). See
    also Bullough, "Transvestites," pp. 1385–7.

20 Thompson, *Motif-Index*, K3.3, K1837. A. Aarne and Stith Thompson. *The Types of the Folktale* (2d rev.
    ed.: Helsinki, 1964), 88A 890, 891A. Giovanni Boccaccio. *Decameron,* Second Day, Story 9. William
    Shakespeare, *The Merchant of Vneice*, Act II, scenes 4–6; Act IV, scene 1. M. J. L'Héritier de Villandon,
    Les caprices du destin ou Recueil d'histoires singulieres et amusantes. Arrivées de nos jours (Paris, 1718),
    Avertissement and tale "L'Amazone Françoise." Celeste T. Wright. "The Amazons in Elizabethan Liter-
    ature," *Studies in Philology* 37 (1940): 433–45. Edmund Spenser, *The Faerie Queen*, Book III, Canto 1.

21 Spenser, *Faerie Queene*, Book V, Cantos 4–5; Wright, "Amazons," pp. 449–54. "The Lady Who Was
    Castrated," in Paul Brians, ed. and trans., *Bawdy Tales from the Courts of Medical France* (New York,
    1972), pp. 24–36. David Kunzle, *The Early Comic Strip. Narrative Strips and Picture Stories in the
    European Broadsheet from 1450 to 1825* (Berkeley and Los Angeles, 1973), pp. 224–5. Giovanni
    Boccaccio, *Concerning Famous Women*, trans. G. G. Guarino (New Brunswick, N.J., 1963), pp.231–4.

22 Chaucer, *The Canterbury Tales*, "The Wife of Bath's Prologue." François Rabelais, *La vie très horri-
    fique du Grand Gargantua. Père de Pantagruel*, chaps. 3–6. Mikhail Bakhtin, *Rabelais and His World*
    (Cambridge, Mass., 1968), pp. 240–1. *Les quinze joies de mariage*, ed. J. Rychner (Geneva, 1963). Harry
    Baxter, "The Waning of Misogyny: Changing Attitudes Reflected in *Les Quinze Joyes de Mariage*."
    Lecture given to the Sixth Conference on Medieval Studies, Western Michigan University, Kalamazoo,
    Michigan, 1971. H. J. C. von Grimmelshausen, *Courage. The Adventuress and the False Massiah, trans.
    Hans Speier* (Princeton, 1964). Johannes Janssen, *History of the German People at the Close of the Middle
    Ages*, trans. A. M. Christie (London, 1896–1925), 12: 206, n. 1. Kunzle, *Early Comic Strip*, p. 225. *Mari
    et femme dans la France rurale* (catalogue of the exhibition at the Musée national des arts et traditions
    populaires, Pairs, September 22–November 19, 1973), pp. 68–9.

23 The ambiguities in *Epicoene* were compounded by the fact that the Silent Wife in the play was a male playing a female, that is, a male actor playing a male playing a female. Professional troupes, of course, always used males for female parts in England until the Restoration and in France until the reign of Henri IV. See J. H. Wilson, *All the King's Ladies. Actresses of the Restoration* (Chicago, 1958) and Léopold Lacour, *Les premières actrices françaises* (Paris, 1921).

24 Ben Jonson, *Epicoene*, Act IV. See Donaldson, *World Upside-Down*, chap. 2, and Edward B. Partridge, *The Broken Compass* (New York, 1958), chap. 7. Thomas Shadwell. *The Woman-Captain* (London, 1680). William Shakespeare, *As You Like It*, Act III, scenes 2, 4, Act IV, scene 1. For an interesting view of Shakespeare's treatment of Katharina in *The Taming of the Shrew*, see Hugh Richmond, *Shakespeare's Sexual Comedy* (Indianapolis, Ind., 1971), pp. 83–101. Henri d'Andei, *Le Lai d'Aristote de Henri d'Andeli*, ed. M. Delboville (Bibliothèque de la Faculté de Philosophie et letters de l'Université de liège, 123; Paris, 1951). Hermann Schmitz, *Hans Baladung gen. Grien* (Bielefeld and Leipzig, 1922), Plate 66. K. Oettinger and K.-A. Knappe, *Hans Baldung Grien und Albrecht Dürer in Nürnberg* (Nuremberg, 1963), Plate 66. Kunzle, *Early Comic Strip*. p. 224.

25 *Erasmus en zijn tijd* (Catalogue of the exhibition at the Museum Boymans – van Beuningen, Rotterdam, October–November 1969), nos. 151–2. See also no. 150, *The Fools' Tree* (ca. 1526), by the "Petrarch-Master" of Augsburg, reproduced here as Plate 10. Willeford, *The Fool*, Plate 30, drawing by Urs Graf. Erasmus, *The Praise of Folly*. See also Dame Folly leading apes and fools in H. W. Janson, *Apes and Ape Lore in the Middle Ages and Renaissance* (London, 1952), pp. 204–8 and Plate 36.

26 See, for instance, John Ashton, ed., *Humour, Wit and Satire in the Seventeenth Century* (New York, 1968; republication of the 1883 ed.), pp. 82ff. John Wardroper, ed., *Jest upon Jest* (London, 1970). chap. 1. Aarne and Thompson. *Folktale*, 1375, 1366A. Kunzle, *Early Comic Strip*, pp. 222–3.

27 Though evidence for the Candlemas Bear Chase is fullest and clearest from the French and Spanish Pyrénées, there are suggestions that it was more widespread in the Middle Ages. In the ninth century, Hincmar of Reims inveighed against "shameful plays" with bears and women dancers. Richard Bernheimer has argued for the connection between the bear hunt and the wild-man hunt, performed in several parts of Europe, and this has been confirmed by Claude Gaignebet, who relates it further to the popular play of Valentin and Ourson. Bruegel represented this game in an engraving and in his painting of the Battle of Carnival and Lent: a male, masked and dressed as a female, holds out a ring to the wild man. See R. Bernheimer, *Wild Men in the Middle Ages* (Gambridge, Mass., 1952), pp. 52–6; C. Gaignebet, "Le combat de Carnaval et de Carême de P. Bruegel (1559)," *Annales. Economics, Sociétés, Civilisations* 27 (1972): 329–31.

28 S. L. Sumberg, *The Nuremberg Schembart Carnival* (New York, 1941), especially pp. 83–4, 104–5. Maria Leach, ed., *Funk and Wagnalls Standard Dictionary of Folklore, Mythology and Legend* (New York, 1949–50), "Schemen." Jean Savaron, *Traitté contre les masques* (Paris, 1608), p. 10. M. du Tilliot, *Mémoires pour servir à l'histoire de la Fête des Foux* (Lausanne and Geneva, 1751), pp. 8, 11–12. Arnold Van Gennep, *Manuel du folklore français* (Pairs, 1943–49), 1.3: 908–18. Violet Alford, *Pyrenean Festivals* (London, 1937), pp. 16–25. Compare the Pyrénées Bear and Rosetta with the Gyro or grotesque giant woman, played by young men on Old Candlemas Day in the Orkney Islands (F. M. McNeill, *The Silver Bough* [Glasgow, 1961], 3: 28–9). Curt Sachs, *World History of the Dance* (New York, 1963), pp. 335–9.

29 Joseph Strutt. *The Sports and Pastimes of the People of England* (new ed.; London, 1878), pp. 449–51, 310–11, 456. C. L. Barber, *Shakespeare's Festive Comedy* (Princeton, 1951), p. 28. Leach, *Dictionary of Folklore*, "Fool plough," "Morris."

30 Leach, *Dictionary of Folklore*, "Transvestism." Willeford, *The Fool*, p. 86. Van Gennep. *Manuel*, 1.8: 910. Alford, *Festivals*, pp. 19–22. Sachs, *Dance*, pp. 335–9.

31 Henry Bourne, *Antiquitates Vulgares; or the Antiquities of the Common People* (Newcastle, 1725), pp. 147–8. McNeill, *Silver Bough*, 4: 82. Roger Vaultier, *Le Folklore pendant la guerre de Cent Ans* (Paris, 1965), pp. 93–100. J. Lefebvre, *Les fols et la folie* (Paris, 1968). p. 46, n. 66. A. Holtmont, *Die Hosenrolle* (Munich, 1925), pp. 54–5. Donaldson, *World Upside-Down*, p. 15. Van Gennep, *Manuel*, 1.3: 884. Strutt, *Sport*, p. 125.

32 For full documentation and bibliography on this material, see Chap. 4 of Davis, *Society and Culture*, "The Reasons of Misrule," and E. P. Thompson, "'Rough Music': Le Charivari anglais," Annales ESC 27 (1972): 285–312.

33 P. Sadron. "Les associations permanentes d'acteurs en France au moyen-age." *Revue d'histoire de théâtre* 4 (1952): 222–31. Du Tilliot, *Mémoires*, pp. 179–82. David Williams, *The Rebecca Riots* (Cardiff, 1955), pp. 53–4. Willeford, *The Fool*, pp.175–9.

34 See "The Reasons of Misrule," n. 34. J. W. Spargo, *Juridical Folklore in England Illustrated by the Cucking-Stool* (Durham, N.C., 1944). McNeill, *Silver Bough*, 4: 67.

35 In addition to the sources given in n. 33, see Hogarth's illustration of a Skimmington Ride made about 1726 for Samuel Butler's *Hudibras* ("Hudibras encounters the Skimmington").

36 Enid Welsford, *The Fool, His Social and Literary History* (London, 1935), pp. 153–4. Van Gennep. *Manuel*, 1.4: 1452–72, 1693–4. Lucienne A. Roubin, *Chambrettes des Provençaux* (Paris, 1970), pp. 178–9, Chap. 4, "The Reasons of Misrule," n. 13. Jean Vostet, *Almanach ou Prognostication des Laboureurs* (Paris, 1588), f. 12^{r-v}. Erasmus, *Adagiorum Chiliades religieuse* (Paris, 1955), 1: 44. On the women's revenge at Saint Agatha's day in the Savoie, see A. Van Gennep, "Le culte populaire de Sainte Agathe en Savoie," *Revue d'ethnographie* 17 (1924): 32.

37 Kunzle, *Early Comic Strip*. pp. 225, 236.

38 Thompson. "'Rough Music,'" especially pp. 296–304. For examples of charivaris against wife-beaters in France in the early nineteenth century, see Cl. Xavier Girault, "Etymologie des usages des principales époques de l'année et de la vie," *Mémoires de l'Académie Celtique* 2 (1808): 104–6 (mentions charivari *only* against men who beat their wives in May; Girault lived in Auxonne, not far from Dijon, where the May prohibition was in effect in the sixteenth century); J. A. Du Laure, "Archeographe au lieu de La Tombe et de ses environs," *Mémoires de l'Académie Celtique* 2 (1808): 449 (mentions charivaris only against wife-beaters and against neighbors who do not go to the wife's aid; La Tombe is in the Seine-et-Marne); Van Gennep, *Manuel*, 1.3: 1073 (Van Gennep also gives examples of the older kind of charivari against the beaten husband, p. 1072).
An example from the American colonies is found in J. E. Culter, *Lynch-Law* (London, 1905), pp. 46–7: a group of men in Elizabethtown, New Jersey, in the 1750s called themselves Regulars and went about at night with painted faces and women's clothes, flogging men reported to have beaten their wives. I am grateful to Herbert Gutman for this reference.

27

The Contrasts

Alfred W. Crosby, Jr.

The Contrasts

On the evening of October 11, 1492, Christopher Columbus, on board the *Santa Maria* in the Atlantic Ocean, thought he saw a tiny light far in the distance. A few hours later, Rodrigo de Triana, lookout on the *Pina's* forecastle, sighted land. In the morning a party went ashore. Columbus had reached the Bahamas. The connection between the Old and New Worlds, which for more than ten millennia had been no more than a tenuous thing of Viking voyages, drifting fishermen, and shadowy contacts via Polynesia, became on the twelfth day of October 1492 a bond as significant as the Bering land bridge had once been.[1]

The two worlds, which God had cast asunder, were reunited, and the two worlds, which were so very different, began on that day to become alike. That trend toward biological homogeneity is one of the most important aspects of the history of life on this planet since the retreat of the continental glaciers.

The Europeans thought they were just off the coast of Asia – back to Eurasia again – but they were struck by the strangeness of the flora and fauna of the islands they had discovered. The record kept by Columbus is full of remarks like:

> I saw neither sheep nor goats nor any other beast, but I have been here but a short time, half a day; yet if there were any I couldn't have failed to see them. . . .
>
> There were dogs that never barked. . . .
>
> All the trees were as different from ours as day from night, and so the fruits, the herbage, the rocks, and all things.[2]

The distinctiveness of the human inhabitants of these islands struck Columbus, as well. He found the Indians unlike even black Africans, the most exotic people he had ever met with before.

Alfred W. Crosby, Jr., "The Contrasts," pp. 3–6, 165–173 from *The Columbian Exchange: Biological and Cultural Consequences of 1492*. Westport, CT: Greenwood Press, 1972.

The Indians' hair was "not kinky, but straight and coarse like horsehair; the whole forehead and head is very broad, more so than any other race that I have ever seen." These Arawak Indians were so impressed with the Europeans – their vessels, clothing, weapons, shapes, and colors – that they thought them demigods and gathered around to kiss the Spaniards' "hands and feet, marvelling and believing that they came from the sky . . . [and] feeling them to ascertain if they were flesh and bones like themselves."[3]

The differences between the life forms of the two worlds have amazed men ever since 1492. Most nonbotanists are inclined to pay more attention to animals than plants, so the contrast between the flora of the eastern and western hemispheres has never excited as much interest as that between the fauna, but the contrast is a marked one. It is not absolute – some 456 species of plants, for instance, are indigenous to both North America and Japan – but the uniqueness of American flora must be acknowledged. Cacti, for instance, are exclusively American in origin. Despite hundreds of years of contact via shipping between the northeastern part of the United States and adjacent Canada and the rest of the world, only about 18 percent of the total number of plant species growing in this part of America are of non-American origin.[4]

The pre-Columbian agriculturalists developed the American food plants from an assemblage of wild plants which was very different from that which the inventors of agriculture in the Old World had. Even the most optimistic of the early colonists of Virginia had to admit that the flora was alien more often than it was familiar. This difference becomes more and more pronounced as one moves south into Mexico and beyond. Jean de Léry, who was a member of the abortive French colony at Río de Janeiro in the 1550s, found only three plants with which he was familiar: purslane, basil, and a kind of fern. All the others were strange, leading to all sorts of difficulties. With no grapes, how were the Europeans to make the wine needed to celebrate the Lord's Supper? Was it better to forego the ceremony until wine could be obtained from Europe or to operate on the theory that Jesus used wine only because it was common in Palestine, and that, therefore, His sacrifice of Himself on the Cross could be commemorated with one of the local Indian beverages?[5]

The contrast between the Old and New World fauna has impressed everyone who has ever crossed the Atlantic or Pacific. Some species are common to both worlds, especially in the northern latitudes, but sometimes this only serves to point up other contrasts. In South and Central America the biggest native quadruped is the tapir, an animal also present in southeast Asia, but by no means the most impressive animal there.[6] The Old World elephant has a much more useful nose and is many times larger. Tropical America's four-legged carnivores are more impressive than the herbivorous tapir, but here, too, the strange disparity between New and Old World mammals appears. The jaguar is not an animal to treat with contempt, but compared to a lion or tiger, he is one of the middle-sized cats.

The early explorers wondered at the smallness of the American mammals they came upon in their early expeditions, most of which were limited to the torrid zone. It was the reptiles, snakes, birds, and insects that really impressed them. Europe has no reptile as big as the iguana; there is probably no animal quite as ugly. The iguana reminded Amerigo Vespucci of the flying serpent of legend, except for the lack of wings. Vespucci and his comrades reacted to the iguanas exactly as nature intended that the enemies of these harmless beasts should: "Their whole appearance," he wrote of the reptiles, "was so strange that we, supposing them to be poisonous, did not dare approach them." Many of the fellow jungle-dwellers of the iguanas were at least as strange, often as terrifying, and frequently a good deal more dangerous. In the rivers there were eels that defended themselves with electricity, and rays and piranhas. There were monkeys – no oddity in itself, but these swung by their tails! Who had ever seen a bird as strange as the toucan, who seemed more beak than body, and who had ever seen a land bird as large as the Andean condor actually fly? And who, outside of a nightmare, had ever seen bats that drank blood or a snake quite as long as the anaconda?[7]

[. . .]

New World Foods and Old World Demography

The fact that Old World diseases devastated the aboriginal peoples of America and the fact that venereal syphilis in Europe, Asia, and Africa has killed millions and crippled the reproductive capacities of legions seem relatively unimportant when placed alongside the statistics on population growth of the post-Columbian era. It is this latter phenomenon, and not the other two, which is the most impressive single biological development of this millennium. In the last three hundred years the number of human beings on this planet has quadrupled, doubling between 1650 and 1850 and then once again in the last century . . .[8]

It is provocative to those engaged in an examination of the biological consequences of the voyages of Columbus and his generation to note that this population growth has occurred since 1492. Rapid worldwide human population growth probably occurred only twice before in all history: once when man, or protoman, first developed tools and again when man invented agriculture. And then it happened again, after the century in which Europeans made high ways of the oceans. Is there a connection between Christopher Columbus and the population explosion?[9]

[. . .]

The causes of the increase are usually given as follows: a decrease in the number and severity of wars; advances in medical science and hygiene; the establishment of stable governments over large areas; improvement in transportation, which permits rapid transfer of food from areas of surplus to areas of famine; and an increase and improvement of food supply. There are others which have also been suggested, but the above are the most widely circulated. How valid are they? Birth and death rates are the result of such myriad factors that demographers agree that all of the given reasons for population expansion are, if taken one by one, invalid. Some, however, have less general validity than others, whatever their significance may be in specific cases. It seems likely that wars, by and large, have increased, rather than decreased, in their destructiveness in the last three hundred years. It is certain that few of the mothers and babies since 1650 have enjoyed the benefits of hygienic surroundings or decent medical treatment. Stable governments probably do enhance population increase, but what about China's rapid population growth in the nineteenth and twentieth centuries, a period on which chaos became increasingly the rule rather than the exception within that empire? Improved transportation certainly helps to limit the number and duration of famines, but it is hard to believe that this is a factor of major importance; and it is certainly true that world population growth began to accelerate generations before the engine – steam, gasoline, or other fuel – replaced human and animal muscle in transportation.

The one factor that will promote population growth and that has been nearly universally influential over the past three hundred years is the increase and improvement of the food supply. We have come full circle, all the way back to Thomas Malthus. Of course, his theory that population increase follows upon increase in food supply is a grossly oversimplified explanation of an extremely complicated matter, but he was basically right about that phenomenon in preindustrial societies, a category which included the entire human race of his time a century and a half ago. In such societies starvation and malnutrition are usually significant checks on the population growth: therefore, an increase in the food supply will produce an increase of people.

[. . .]

The most obvious way in which a people can improve food production is by raising more of its standard crops. But this is not always easy; often most of the land suitable for the traditional crops is already planted with them, and often an increase in the sowing of traditional crops will only bring on an increase in the pests and diseases that prey on them.

An entirely new food plant or set of food plants will permit the utilization of soils and seasons which have previously gone to waste, thus causing a real jump in food production and, therefore, in population. But before we accept this statement as gospel, let us acknowledge that we are taking much for granted. How can we be *sure* that a population which simultaneously switches from wheat to maize and increases in size could not have accomplished the increase without every having heard of maize? Perhaps the switch to maize came not because of its greater productivity but because the people in question simply liked the way it tasted. Perhaps the increase in population stemmed from a dozen or a hundred factors having nothing whatever to do with maize.

But let us proceed. Hypotheses about past events are not susceptible to scientific proofs, and the historian can never hope to have a hypothesis certified as anything better than reasonable. He must lope along where scientists fear to tread. It seems reasonable to say that human beings, in matters of diet, especially of the staples of diet, are very conservative, and will not change unless forced. No coercion is as generally effective as hunger. And when hunger is assuaged – even by the products of alien seed – babies are conceived, are born, thrive, and live to have their laps full of grandchildren.

All the basic food plants are the products of careful cultivation and breeding practiced by the neolithic farmer. Although he never saw or heard of genes, he produced wheat, barley, rice, maize, potatoes, manioc, and other foods – the chief supports of human life on this planet – from wild species so unpromising that only the professional botanist can see the resemblance between today's plant and its ancestor.

[. . .]

But the claim that there were *almost* entirely different groups of food plants cultivated in the Old and New Worlds in pre-Columbian times is still acceptable to historians, archeologists and paleo-botanists. There is no doubt whatsoever that no crop of one hemisphere was a significant source of food for large numbers of people of the other hemisphere before 1492.[10]

The great Russian botanist Nikolai Ivanovich Vavilov, in the course of his research on the geographical origins of various cultigens, made up a list of the 640 most important plants cultivated by man. Roughly speaking, five hundred of them belonged to the Old World and one hundred to the New.[11] Driven by the fact that America provided so few domesticated animals for food, the Indian produced some of the most important of all food plants. He also gave humanity such nonfoods as tobacco, rubber, and certain cottons, but let us restrict ourselves to a list of his most valuable food crops.[12]

The botanists' assurance that these foods are of American origin is supported by the testimony of the etymologists: all but three of the listed names are derived from American Indian words. Collectively these plants made the most valuable single addition to the food-producing plants of the Old World since the beginnings of agriculture.[13]

Maize	Pumpkin
Beans of many kinds (*Phaseolus* *vulgaris* and others)	Papaya
	Guava
Peanuts	Avocado
Potato	Pineapple
Sweet potato	Tomato
Manioc (also called cassava and tapioca)	Chile pepper (*Capsicum* *annuum* and others)
Squashes	Cocoa

Of these crops, maize, potatoes, sweet potatoes, beans, and manioc have been most abundantly cultivated and eaten in the last four hundred years. The others have had great significance in restricted areas, but have never become staple foods for as large a part of the human race as the five above.

If maize were the only gift the American Indian ever presented to the world, he would deserve undying gratitude, for it has become one of the most important of all foods for men and their live-stock. Ears of ancient wild maize, recently unearthed in Mexico, enable us to measure the achievement of the American Indian agriculturalist. The mature ear of wild maize was about as thick as a pencil and an inch long. The food value of the whole ear was probably less than a single kernel of twentieth-century maize.[14]

Many types of maize existed when the European arrived in America and many more exist today. As a result, maize will produce good crops in an extreme variety of climates. Its advantage over equivalent Old World plants is that it will prosper in areas too dry for rice and too wet for wheat. Geographically, it has fitted neatly between the two. Its supremely valuable characteristic is its high yield per unit of land which, on world average, is roughly double that of wheat. For those to whom famine is a reality, maize has the additional benefit of producing food fast. Few other plants produce so much carbohydrate, sugar, and fat in as short a growing season.[15]

Despite the fact that the potato does not grow well in the tropics, it is one of the crops raised in greatest quantity by man. Only wheat competes with it as the most important plant food of the temperate zones, and the potato produces several times as much food per unit of land as wheat or any other grain. Furthermore, it can be, and so often has been, cultivated very successfully in tiny plots of poor land in a great variety of temperate zone climates, at altitudes from sea level to well over 10,000 feet, and by the most inept farmers using the most primitive tools.[16]

Although there are few parts of the world where the sweet potato is the primary crop, its unusually high yield – three to four times that of rice, for instance – and its resistance to drought and tolerance of poor soils make it a vitally important secondary crop throughout a wide band of the warmer lands. A good example is to be found in Indonesia, which produced 13.4 million metric tons of rice in 1962–1963 – and also over three million metric tons of sweet potatoes.[17]

The bean was one-third of the alimentary trinity that supported Meso-American civilization when the Spaniard arrived – the other two members being maize and squash – and plays a role of similar, if not equal, importance in the diets of millions throughout the world today. The bean family contains over one thousand species – some New, some Old World in origin – and since most writers and statisticians have been satisfied that "beans is beans," it is difficult to make precise statements of the importance of *American* beans. The most important single kind of bean is the eastern hemisphere's soybean, but the lima, sieva, Rangoon, Madagascar, butter, Burma, pole, curry, kidney, French, navy, haricot, snap, string, common, and frijole bean are all American. Often called the "poor man's meat," American beans are especially rich in protein, as well as in oils and carbohydrates.[18]

When the European arrived in America, the American beans already existed in varieties suitable to almost every climate, and they were so obviously superior to many Old World pulses that they quickly spread to Europe, Africa and Asia.[13] Because they have often been a private garden crop rather than a field crop, they have escaped the official censuses; when they are listed in censuses, they are often grouped under the general heading "Pulses" with a number of other kinds of beans. Their importance defies exact statistical description, but that importance is still there. Any world traveler will tell you that the visitor-from-far-away may be treated to gourmet delights for his first few meals in a strange new country, but eventually he will find himself confronted – in Norway, Siberia, Dahomey, and Australia – with a plate of beans – American beans,

NOTES

1 The theoretical basis of this chapter is neatly summed up in George Gaylord Simpson, *The Geography of Evolution* (Philadelphia: Chilton Books, 1965), 69–132.

2 Christopher Columbus, *Journals and Other Documents on the Life and Voyages of Christopher Columbus*, trans. Samuel Eliot Morison (New York: Heritage Press, 1963), 72–3, 84.

3 Ibid., 66, 90.

4 Hui-Lin Li, "Floristic Relationships Between Eastern Asia and Eastern North America," *Transactions of the American Philosophical Society* 42 N.S. (1952), 403; Henry A. Gleason and Arthur Cronquist, *The Natural Geography of Plants* (New York: Columbia University Press, 1964), 34; Ronald Good. *The Geography of Flowering Plants* (New York: John Wiley, 1964), 64.

5 Jean de Léry, *Journal de Bord de Jean de Léry en la Terre de Brésil*, ed. M. R. Mayeux (Paris: Editions de Paris, 1957), 129, 293; William Strachey, *The Historie of Travell unto Virginia Britania* (London: Hakluyt Society, 1953), 117–33; Stefan Lorant, ed., *The New World* (New York: Duell, Sloan, & Pearce, 1965), 230–62.

6 Carl H. Lindroth, *The Faunal Connections Between Europe and North America* (New York: John Wiley, 1957), 15–134; Léry, *Journal*, 239. The tapir is an odd sort of animal with a stubby semi-prehensile nose; at the most, it is only three feet high and six feet long. The best that Léry could say of the Brazilian tapir was that it was something like a cow, and entirely unlike either.

7 Martin Waldseemüller, *Cosmographiae Introductio by Martin Waldseemuller . . . To Which are Added the Four Voyages of Amerigo Vespucci*, ed. and trans. Joseph Fischer and Franz von Wiesser (Ann Arbor: University Microfilms, 1966), 106. Simpson, *Geography of Evolution*, 167–208.

8 Dennis H. Wrong, *Population and Society* (New York: Random House, 1965), 13.

9 William H. McNeill, *The Rise of the* West (New York: Mentor, 1965), 627–8, suggests the Columbian exchange as one of the chief causes of the population explosion. The exchange of diseases between and within the Old and New Worlds at first limited population growth; then, as resistance to those maladies built up all over the globe, the population began to expand: "age-old epidemic checks upon population faded into merely endemic attrition."

10 George Carter, "Plant Evidence for Early Contacts with America," *Southwestern Journal of Anthropology* 6 (Summer 1950), 162–82; George Carter, "Plants Across the Pacific," *Memoirs for the Society of American Archaeology*, 9, Supplement to *American Antiquity* 18(3), part 2 (January 1953), 62–71; George Carter, "Maize to Africa," *Anthropological Journal of Canada* 1(2) (1963), 3–8; Carl O. Sauer, "Maize into Europe," *Akten des 34. Internationalen Amerikanisten Kongresses* (Vienna: Verlag

Ferdinand Berger, Horn, 1962), 777–8; Thor Heyerdahl, "Merrill's Reappraisal of Ethnobotanical Evidence for Prehistoric Contact Between South America and Polynesia," *Proceedings of the 34th International Congress of Americanists (Vienna, 1960)*, 1962, 789–96.

11 Nikolai Ivanovich Vavilov, *The Origin, Variation, Immunity and Breeding of Cultivated Plants* (New York: Ronald Press, 1951), 44. See also C. D. Darlington, *Chromosome Botany and the Origins of Cultivated Plans* (New York: Hafner, 1963), 132–80.

12 Vavilov, *Cultivated Plants*, 39–43.

13 Uncultivated plants, such as cacti, made the journey from the New to the Old World, also, but their impact seems less than that of their Old World counterparts on the New. As always, "weeds" take hold when the ecology of a give area has been disturbed. Henry N. Ridley found Singapore Island to be entirely covered with dense forest in 1822. Man had stripped the jungle off by his return in 1888, and he found a number of alien invaders among the new growth: "thirty-nine came from South America and the West Indies, nineteen from other parts of tropical Asia, three from China, seven from Africa, four from Europe, and fourteen were typical weeds now so widely distributed that their homes of origin is uncertain." Henry N. Ridley, *The Dispersal of Plants Throughout the World* (Ashford, Kent, UK: L L. Reeve, 1930), 639.

14 Vance Bourjaily, "The Corn of Coxcatlán," *Horizon* 7 (Spring 1966), 55; Richard S. MacNeish, "Ancient Mesoamerican Civilization," *Science* 143 (February 7, 1963), 531–7; Paul C. Mangelsdorf, Richard S. MacNeish, and Walton C. Galinat, "Domestication of Corn," *Science* 143 (February 7, 1964), 538–45.

15 Food and Agricultural Organization of the United Nations, *Production Yearbook, 1963* (Rome: FAO, 1964), 17:37–8; 46–8; David Mitrany. *The Land and the Peasant in Rumania* (London: Oxford University Press, 1930), 304.

16 Désiré Bois, *Les Plantes Alimentaires Chez Tous les Peuples et à Travers les Ages* (Paris: Paul Lechevalier, 1927), 1:331; William L. Langer, "Europe's Initial Population Explosion," *American Historical Review* 69 (October 1963), 11; Cecil Woodham-Smith, *The Great Hunger: Ireland 1845–1849* (New York: New American Library of World Literature, 1964), 30; Berthold Laufer, *The American Plant Migration, part I: The Potato*, Anthropological Series, vol. 28 (Chicago: Field Museum of Natural History), 1938, 11.

17 FAO Production Yearbook, 1963, 52, 79; Ping-Ti Ho, *Studies on the Population of China, 1368–1953* (Cambridge, MA: Harvard University Press, 1959), 186; A. Hyatt Verrill, *Foods America Gave the World* (Boston: L. S. Page, 1937), 46, 48; Ruth McVey, ed., *Indonesia* (New Haven, CT: Southeast Asia Studies, Yale University, 1963), 131.

18 Herbert J. Spinden, "Thank the American Indian," *Scientific American* 138 (April, 1928): 330–2, 331; William H. Youngman, "America – Home of the Bean," *Agriculture in the Americas* 3 (December, 1943): 228–32, 228; Carl O. Sauer, *Agricultural Origins and Dispersals* (New York, 1952), 65; W. R. Arkroyd, *Legumes in Human Nutrition*, Food and Agricultural Organization of the United Nations Study No. 19 (1964) vi, 38, 109; Atemas Ward, *Encyclopedia of Food* (New York, 1941), 29; D. Bois, *Les Plantes Alimentaires Chez Tous les Peuples et à Travers les Ages* (Paris, 1927), 1 : 142.

28

Transcending East–West Dichotomies: State and Culture Formation in Six Ostensibly Disparate Areas

Victor Lieberman

Binary Histories

Although the question has assumed at least two principal forms, most scholars who would compare the history of Europe and Asia have long been absorbed with a single query: Why was Asia different?

On the one hand, a tradition of macrohistorical sociology starting with Montesquieu, John Stuart Mill, Karl Marx, and Max Weber sought to establish "despotism" as a general form of Oriental civilization whose historic immobility contrasted with the restless innovation of Europe. In more recent years Immanuel Wallerstein, Jean Baechler, John A. Hall, Michael Mann, E. L. Jones, Daniel Chirot, and Geoffrey Parker, among others whose expertise is in Western history, have pursued implicitly or explicitly the same theme of European, or more precisely West European, exceptionalism. If we may extract an explanation common to many of these later observers, it is that of cultural entelechy, the peculiar centuries-old legal-cum-political heritage of the West: its multiplicity of competing power networks, its unusually strong legal guarantees for personal property, the consequent strength of market mechanisms and commercial institutions.[1]

On the other hand, influenced by these broad concerns but usually focusing on more circumscribed problems of institutional or social history, scholars of early modern Asia have explored the degree to which specific European features had analogues in the East. The most popular candidates, not surprisingly, have been "feudalism" and "capitalism," followed more recently by European concepts of the "public sphere." Among historians of Japan, even those who opt for narrow definitions usually concede that the late Muromachi period, in particular, exhibited many characteristics of European-style feudalism, while the Tokugawa era produced capitalist features.[2] Scholars of pre-1800 China, South, and Southeast Asia have also marshalled evidence of commercial intensification and greater specialization in production and exchange,

Victor Lieberman, "Transcending East–West Dichotomies: State and Culture Formation in Six Ostensibly Disparate Areas," pp. 19–38 from *Beyond Binary Histories: Re-imagining Eurasia to c. 1830*. Ann Arbor: University of Michigan Press, 1999.

features which in some respects recall early modern Europe.[3] Yet on the whole, it is safe to say that the search for recognizably European analogies has yielded rather modest results. With the doubtful exception of Japan, all concede that Asia in 1800 was not moving towards an industrial revolution on the Western model; much effort therefore has gone into finding the culprits responsible for this "failure."[4] Nor did European notions of individual and corporate autonomy have any close resonance. Although late Ming/Qing China (where the issue has been most closely examined) saw growing extrabureaucratic activity by organizations concerned with public welfare on the local level, the notion of an autonomous "public sphere," characterized by critical debate on issues of national policy by individuals enjoying defined rights vis-à-vis the state, had no parallel, certainly not before the twentieth century.[5] In the image of E. L. Jones' widely-received book, Europe was indeed a "miracle."[6]

But given the choice of criteria, was any other conclusion possible? Could one really expect to link European and Asian historical experiences by means of phenomena whose definitions were, at bottom, culture specific? How profitable would a discussion of English social organization prove if the template were Indian *varnas*? By and large, the search for European elements outside Europe has been structured to yield the same result as the dynamism–immobility contrast. In both cases we are necessarily left with an image of incomparability, and by implication, Asian deficiency.

Although Russian institutions, particularly after Peter, could hardly be described as static, Russia too has often been assimilated to a binary discourse. Exposed to sustained Mongol–Tatar influence, lacking a powerful bourgeoisie, subject to an extraordinary level of state direction, her educated classes obsessed by a sense of inferiority vis-à-vis the West, Russia has appeared to many indigenous and foreign observers alike as a variant of Asian despotism, an exception, if not the antithesis, to normative Western patterns. Peter Chaadaev's characterization of his homeland as a kind of historic swamp ("Talking about Russia one always imagines that one is talking about a country like the others; in reality, this is not so at all.") inaugurated an approach which in successive Slavophile, Weberian, and Cold War incarnations, has remained remarkably vital into the late twentieth century.[7]

One hardly need rehearse the political benefits – directed as much against self-doubt as against colonial and semi-colonial subjects – that accrued from describing the non-Western world as awaiting the Western kiss of life. Not infrequently "Asia" as an emblem for unwise policy was also defined by domestic European political debates. But more basically, Eurocentrism said less about political sensibilities per se than about the overwhelming intellectual – nay, emotional – need to explain ever widening power inequalities between Euro-America and the rest of the world during the eighteenth to mid-twentieth centuries. To assimilate comparative historiography to an Orientalist mode; to portray European patterns as some sort of norm whose absence (invariable, yet somehow still puzzling) in other areas had to be explained; to hypostatize and essentialize asymmetries was all too irresistible. Hence the compression of societies that were enormously varied but comparably vulnerable into a single category, "Asia."[8] Hence too the contrast between European dynamism and Asian/Russian stasis even among historians with impeccable anti-imperialist credentials. We see this later tendency, for example, in the intellectually bankrupt, but long-lived Marxist notion of the Asiatic Mode of Production as a non-linear, regionally-specific formation.[9] We see it among post-war Japanese academics who held Tokugawa repression and xenophobia responsible for Japan's "retardation." We see it in the call by J. C. van Leur and John Smail for an Indies-centered history of Southeast Asia, a call which although strongly anti-colonial, ironically mirrored colonial historiography in its insistence on the autonomy and extreme conservatism of Southeast Asian civilization.[10]

New Criteria, New Affinities

In the post-imperial, post-Cold War late twentieth century, less dichotomous approaches to Eurasian history seem feasible, if not obligatory. In part the pressure of accumulated empirical studies encourages revision. But most basically the retreat of American power in Asia, East Asia's spectacular economic success, the globalization of information and consumer culture, and the (possibly temporary) erosion of regionally-based political ideologies have combined to weaken the self-confidence, the sensibilities, the psychological assumptions of Eurocentric historiography. Not unlike those sixteenth-century genealogists who furnished upwardly mobile English commoners with aristocratic ancestries, now we may be tempted to reward the latest success stories by emphasizing the early evidence of their achievement. As John W. Hall some thirty years ago observed of Japanese historiography, novel interpretations normally arise less from new evidence than from the preoccupations of a new generation.[11] Such revisionism is in fact already far advanced in Japanese studies. Once despised as an era of backwardness and isolation, the Tokugawa period is now widely praised for having engendered those very patterns of social solidarity, capital accumulation, and agricultural innovation on which Japan's modern industrial success has rested.[12] John P. Powelson, writing over a decade after E. L. Jones, has now accorded early modern Western Europe and Japan the apotheosis which Jones once allowed only Western Europe as exceptions to universal agrarian stasis.[13]

This essay seeks, in preliminary and schematic fashion, to widen the geographic scope of such revisionist approaches, and at the same time to shift their thematic focus. Useful correctives though they may be, the new views of Tokugawa history provide a basis for Eurasian comparisons no more adequate than classical Eurocentrism, and for the same reason: they employ a criterion, namely the ability to support a precocious industrialization, that by definition was restricted to one or two societies. Preserving intact the chasm between Europe and the rest of the world, such an approach merely shifts Japan from one side to the other.

I propose to substitute what I believe are more neutral, capacious, and ultimately more revealing standards of comparison. In particular, I am interested in the little noted Eurasian pattern between c. 1450 and 1830 whereby localized societies in widely separated regions coalesced into larger units – politically, culturally, commercially. I seek both to describe these parallel evolutions, and to relate such departures to changes in demography, markets, urbanization, literacy, military technology, and interstate competition. Now obviously, as intellectual constructs all such categories and processes derive from the Western historical imagination no less clearly than "feudalism" and the "public sphere." But as demonstrable patterns within this now universal mode of viewing the past, sustained integrative patterns were not restricted to Europe, and in some cases found fullest and most dramatic expression outside Western Europe. Such an approach is not incompatible with – nor have I any desire to minimize – European exceptionalism, arguably the central feature of early modern world history. Yet such an approach also permits us to begin viewing European and other regional experiences as peculiar variants of more general Eurasian patterns. Instead of "failure" or "success," we find numerous idiosyncratic sites along very broad continua.

The six geographic areas on which I concentrate are discordant, and for that very reason, instructive. I include the chief realms of mainland Southeast Asia (Burma, Siam, Vietnam), omitted from most world histories, both because I am eager to contextualize my region of expertise and because this region offers truly novel perspectives on global simultaneity. In turn I juxtapose Southeast Asia with Western Europe as typified here by France (but which could have been represented as easily by Britain, Sweden, Portugal, Spain, Prussia, etc.), with the Russian empire, and with Japan. That these regions spanned the northern and eastern rimlands of Eurasia, generally had minimal contact with one another, differed profoundly in demography, popular culture, high religion, administrative and economic structures – but nonetheless experienced remarkably synchronized political rhythms illustrates in stark fashion the thesis of Eurasian interdependence.

These six areas were in fact part of a Eurasian subcategory sharing the following features: (a) Lying on the periphery of older civilizations (in India, the Mediterranean, China), all imported world religions, developed urban centers, and underwent what Barbara Price calls "secondary state" formation during the latter part of the first or the early second millennium C.E.[14] Principalities founded in this period provided a novel charter for subsequent local states in so far as their religious, cultural, and in some cases, dynastic and territorial traditions were regarded as normative and legitimizing. (b) Following the decay/disruption of these charter principalities, a renewed process of political and cultural integration began at some point between 1450 and 1590 and, in key dimensions, continued to gain in scope and vigor well into the nineteenth century. (c) In partial explanation of this accelerating solidity, each polity enjoyed relatively good internal communications and/or an economic/demographic imbalance between districts that was markedly favorable to the capital area. (d) Throughout the period c. 1400–1830 each also enjoyed substantial protection from external invasion, whether overland from Central Asia or by sea from Europe. In their common possession of such features, these six societies constituted an intermediate category between, on the one hand, China, which experienced a uniquely precocious and durable integration, and on the other, Mughal India and island Southeast Asia, where political integration proved less intense and continuous. Among these six case studies the juxtaposition of similarities and divergences allows us to identify variables governing particular outcomes, while the concluding section explores some of the larger contrasts with other sectors of Eurasia. Conceivably societies ignored in the present essay could be assimilated to the same continuum, with the Ottomans perhaps intermediate between the Russian and the Mughal empires, and so forth.

Why use for Eurasian comparison this criterion of political and cultural coalescence rather than, say, broad changes in economic, urban, or intellectual structure? In part, I hasten to acknowledge, because these concerns are most congenial to existing Southeast Asian historiography, whose focus remains political and cultural; and in part, I have suggested, because synchronized integration provides a sensitive index of global connections. Is it not puzzling that the multistate systems of Europe and of mainland Southeast Asia, at opposite ends of Eurasia, should have experienced more or less simultaneous oscillations and consolidation? And does not a recognition of such similarities invite reconsideration of processes usually interpreted in a purely regional context? At the same time, a concern with integration can suggest novel connections between ostensibly disparate phenomena – demographic, military, literary, religious – all of which reflected a wider, more rapid circulation of goods and ideas. Note that higher exchange velocities, so to speak, transformed not only the most successful polities within each region, but also less durable contenders – Burgundy, Lithuania, Chiang Mai, Cambodia, and so forth – so that the patterns with which we are concerned are of yet wider application. Beyond this and perhaps most fundamental, trends towards political, cultural, and commercial integration merit attention because for centuries prior to c. 1830 they helped to define the political aspirations, self-images, ethnicities, and conceptions of sanctity available to local elites, and also to growing sectors of the general population. Nor is early modern state and culture formation without contemporary implications, although here one must be wary of essentialism.

I am the first to acknowledge, however, that these concerns hardly exhaust the possibilities for what I shall term early modern classification. In its West European context, "early modern" refers to a complex of traits usually said to include not only standardization within emergent national units – but also an increased emphasis on rationality and secularism, growing literacy, and in the wake of urbanism and denser market relations, a halting movement from familiarity to impersonality, from inherited status to individual merit, from social solidarity and public honor to self-interest and privacy.[15] These six case studies focus on the first element in the above list, that of consolidation. I also emphasize that across much of Eurasia literacy rapidly expanded, popular religions became subject to an unprecedented degree of textually-sanctioned reform, political authority became far more routinized, and particularly after 1750, economic growth encouraged social mobility, an erosion of ascriptive categories, and greater commercial influence in elite society. All served to give this era in Eurasian history a distinctive character. But other intellectual and social components of European early modernity – rationalist critiques of religious tradition, elaborated theories of social organization, autonomous associations in the space between family and state, the legal abstraction of authority from the specifics of lordship – receive less attention, chiefly because these features had little or no purchase in Southeast Asia or pre-Petrine Russia.

Yet if one were to examine the most economically developed sectors of Asia, including coastal China and India as well as Japan, other possibilities might open. I have cautioned against efforts at mechanical duplication of European patterns, but one might well find a range of preeminently urban intellectual and cultural developments worthy of broad comparison.[16] Likewise, if one were to use as organizing principles proto-industrialization, commercial networks, marriage and family systems, or tensions between high religion and popular beliefs, groupings of Eurasian regions rather different from those presented in this essay might well emerge. (Clearly, however, many of these also would eschew a simple East–West dichotomy.) In short, this essay approaches the problem of Eurasian coherence from a particular and, I believe, revealing set of perspectives without in any sense pretending to an exclusive prerogative.

In seeking to treat Eurasia as an interactive, loosely synchronized ecumene, I employ William H. McNeill's seminal study of Eurasian epidemiology,[17] climate reconstructions hinting at hemispheric regimes of agricultural productivity,[18] Alfred Crosby, Jr. and James Lee's studies of Columbian exchanges,[19] and a growing literature on international trade, including post-Wallersteinian world systems theories promoted by André Gunder Frank, Barry K. Gills, and Janet L. Abu-Lughod.[20] I also build on Jack Goldstone's pregnant theory of demographically-driven revolts in Western Europe, the Ottoman empire, and China.[21] However, in contrast to most epidemiological, climatic, and world systems theorists, I am as concerned with internal social and institutional evolution as with external linkages, and I adopt an open-ended multifactoral approach. By extension, the Wallersteinian theory of unequal exchange within a global or regional hegemonic system seems to me less useful than the notion of overlapping trade circuits with multiple, fluid centers. I differ as well from Goldstone, both because demography is but one of several key variables and because I am not primarily concerned with periodic collapse. Rather, my six studies focus on secular construction, to which periodic breakdown often provided an acceleratory stimulus.

As for the chronological limits of early modernity: Although I shall refer to early charter polities, the great Eurasian-wide economic upsurge of the mid and late 1400s – and attendant innovations in warfare, politics, and culture – recommend this period as a rough point of departure. A terminal date is more difficult to coordinate across Eurasia and more arbitrary in so far as we have after *c.* 1720 a continuously accelerating series of changes, but the second quarter of the nineteenth century has some claim to attention as the era which saw the irruption of European colonialism in mainland Southeast Asia, more adumbrative external pressures on Japan, and the onset of profound railroad-borne transformations in France. Within this broad era, in some locales one could claim that the mid-sixteenth and mid-eighteenth centuries inaugurated major subperiods.

Territorial Consolidation

What then were the chief parallels among the areas under consideration?

Most visible was the sustained movement between *c.* 1450 and 1830 towards the political and administrative integration of what had been fragmented, localized units. Thus in Europe west of the Dniester and Vistula five to six hundred more or less independent polities in 1450 were reduced to some 25 by the late nineteenth century. In northeastern Europe, Siberia, and the Caucasus, over thirty city-states, princedoms, and khanates yielded to a single Russian imperial suzerainty. In mainland Southeast Asia, some 22 genuinely independent states in 1350 were reduced to three – Burma, Siam, and Vietnam – by 1825, when Europeans began to freeze an ongoing process. In Japan a very large, if fluid, number of proto-daimyo domains and autonomous religious and merchant communities in 1500 had come under unified rule by century's end.

[...]

Administrative Centralization and Social Regulation

At the same time as privileged cores extended their territorial writ, they commonly sought to strengthen their extractive, judicial, and military functions and systems of provincial control. As just indicated, external expansion and internal reform were mutually reinforcing in so far as larger domains required more efficient control, while the concentration of resources that flowed from better coordination facilitated colonization and conquest.

If all these polities, Russia apart, were of comparable size in 1800, their populations and internal geographies differed substantially, along with the potential for centralization. Each Southeast Asian realm contained a population in 1800 of between 4 and 7.5 million, which, despite a respectable proportion of city-dwellers, could not support urban and commercial networks comparable to those of the larger states. Vietnam was also disadvantaged in that its elongated domain lacked a central river artery. On the other hand, although the highlands of western and central mainland Southeast Asia were relatively inaccessible, the Irrawaddy and Chaophraya basins tended to concentrate the population in easily-monitored clusters. France, Russia, and Japan in 1800 each had between 30 and 37 million people, including urban communities considerably larger than in Southeast Asia. With no major mountain barriers, extensive roads, and at least four major rivers, in France problems of control and communication were relatively modest. The extraordinary vastness of the Russian plain posed more obvious problems, but these were offset to some extent by the western concentration of population and by Russia's excellent river systems. The Japanese islands had no central river, but the seas provided regular coastal links, while demographic-transport concentrations in the Kinai region and the Kanto created natural political foci.

At times reinforcing, at times contradicting these geographic and demographic patterns, diverse local imaginations, external models, and interstate pressures produced wide discrepancies in administrative form and penetration . . .

To complicate further Eurasian comparisons, lest one assume that we can effortlessly rank all six societies according to one or two indices of "state power," consider that spheres of government vigor could be quite distinct. By the late 1700s, for example, the Russian state was effective in organizing up-to-date military forces, but not particularly interested in local religious observance. In Burma, the situation was more or less reversed.

Notwithstanding such differences in geography, structure, and focus, between c. 1400 and 1830 the administrative systems of France, Russia, Burma, Siam, Vietnam, and Japan experienced certain general parallels . . .

In each polity, as consolidation resumed or began after 1450 or 1500, we find a long-term, if halting tendency for peripheral zones and autonomous enclaves to assimilate to the status of intermediate or core provinces, and for systems of extraction and coordination in the core to improve. Thus, for example, independent kingdoms that fell under Burmese and Siamese rule were converted to governor-ruled provinces, while control of governorships and apanages within the core also strengthened. Supervision in the French *pays d'États* gradually approached that in north-central France. Southern Hokkaido and Kyushu by 1650 were tied to the center as effectively as outer areas of Honshu had been in 1400. In Vietnam during the era of division the northern and southern seigneuries steadily modified internal operations, while, as noted, from 1830s the new Nguyen dynasty sought to standardize provincial administration.

[. . .]

Animating and complementing institutional elaboration were expanded systems of patronage. Although administrative procedure became more routinized, even in France until the late 1700s clientelism remained basic to the operation of the polity. Authorities everywhere sought not to destroy factions, but to balance and incorporate them through centrally-administered pensions, blocs of offices, tax privileges, guarantees of status, concessions of all sorts. Sharon Kettering's description of French patron–broker–client ties as "interstitial, supplementary, and parallel" to more formal structures can easily be generaized.[22] In lieu of an earlier historiography that saw the early modern state in France, Russia, and Southeast Asia crushing and displacing local elites, this perspective allows for a substantial degree of accommodation between central and regional leaders whose interests in patronage, social regulation, and military effectiveness were basically congruent.[23]

But if the state was less autonomous, more subject to faction, negotiation, and paralysis than earlier historians conceded, it is also true that over the long term local prerogatives were substantially modified. Most basic, princes and other regional leaders in France, Russia, and lowland Southeast Asia gradually lost the right to tax without permission, to build private fortifications, to run some independent judicial systems, and – apropos the Weberian definition of the state – to employ unauthorized violence against one another or their subjects. As royal income grew, as status came to be defined in relation to uniform hierarchies, as central armies achieved a clear superiority, ambitious leaders tended to abandon rebellion and "mighty neighbor patronage" in return for improved access to royal patronage and stronger support for their rights vis-à-vis local rivals and/or over the local peasantry.[24]

In all six societies between c. 1500 and 1830 religious organizations likewise came under more effective regulation. Personnel and, in some cases, doctrine were monitored more closely by appointed officials. In Burma, Russia, Japan, and France (the latter most dramatically, but not exclusively, from 1789), church lands or income were reduced, at times severely. State resources widened accordingly, while religious groups were curtailed or eliminated as institutionalized political actors. Ironically, in some cases efforts to increase religious conformity intensified even as the power of the church waned, because the state assumed wider responsibility for monitoring social behavior.[25]

Indeed, typically from the seventeenth century, authorities in Russia, France, Burma, Japan, and Vietnam attempted to regulate more aspects of daily life, not least as these affected lower social strata. Determined in varying degrees to increase revenue, to assure cheap grains, and/or to coopt powerful merchants, virtually every rimland state fixed prices, standardized weights and measures, and granted monopolies (at least until the late 1700s, when a liberalizing trend appeared in many countries). To cement ties with local powerholders, to promote order, to defend hierarchy, to ensure service and tax payments, and to advertise the power of central authorities, vigorous attempts also were made to strengthen hereditary status divisions, to integrate them into a theoretically universal system, to define deviance, and to extend legal regulation and criminal punishment, at least in those cities and core provinces subject to effective control . . .

In turn the growing scope of government action, the extension of authority to new territories, the sheer increase in the volume of documents joined with wider literacy (see below) to encourage changes in political culture. In all six countries secretariats gradually expanded, the court as it outgrew the ruler's household became more elaborate, and the royal (or shogunal) position became more elevated. In varying degrees, in Burma, Siam, (pre-1600 and post-1800) Vietnam, Russia, and France, the prerogatives of the royal family as a whole were curtailed in favor of those of the paramount ruler. At the same time, most visibly but by no means only in Western Europe, government procedures tended to grow more impersonal, routinized, and professional.

Cultural Integration

This discussion of political culture leads to a third general index of integration within each rimland society: a growing, if highly imperfect and uneven, uniformity of religious, ethnic, and other cultural symbols.

Following Ernesto Laclau, Chantal Mouffe, and Tessa Morris-Suzuki, I regard regional or national culture not as a "coherently structured whole," but as an "unsutured" complex of identities that normally fluctuated according to locale, class, corporate group, even individual.[26] At the same time, within any stable population, by definition, rituals, symbols, vocabularies, and practices permitted a measure of intercourse and common identification. The main point is that in the early modern societies under review, such features became more standardized.

In theory standardization could be of two types: (a) lateral, elite standardization, in which a complex of linguistic, ritual, and stylistic practices spread from central to provincial elites; elite practices as whole thus remained more or less distinct from those of subordinate classes; and (b) vertical, demotic standardization, in which some features characteristic of elites spread to lower social strata (or vice versa), so that the entire population of the country/kingdom became more distinct from people in adjacent countries.[27] Lateral integration often involved the partial absorption of one literate complex by another. Nobles and bourgeois in Languedoc assimilated to north French styles, Lao and Khmer tributaries adopted (even as they helped to modify) select elements of central Thai culture. Although vertical, demotic integration also could involve literate displacements, more frequently it exposed illiterate folk traditions to literate norms. Popular dialects, identities, and religious practices were marginalized, or at least challenged. Oftentimes as well, demotic change had a misogynist thrust, rejecting females' claims to supernatural access, subordinating women more completely to male legal power.

Put baldly, we see tendencies towards lateral standardization in all six countries; reasonably sustained movements of vertical, demotic integration in Japan, France, and Vietnam; and weaker vertical tendencies in Burma, Siam, and Russia. It is at once apparent that these complex patterns, like the rhythm of territorial consolidation, showed scant respect for East–West divisions. Moreover, in almost every case ethnic self-definitions underwent rapid change starting in the fifteenth or sixteenth century.

[. . .]

NOTES

1 See Weber, *Economy and Society* (Berkeley, 1978), II, chs 10–15; Perry Anderson, *Lineages of the Absolutist State* (London, 1974), 397–402, 462–549; Wallerstein, *The Modern World-System*, I (Orlando, FL, 1974); Baechler, Hall, and Mann (eds), *Europe and the Rise of Capitalism* (Oxford, 1988); John A. Hall, *Powers and Liberties* (Oxford, 1985); Jones, *The European Miracle* (Cambridge, 1987); Chirot, "The Rise of the West," *American Sociological Review* 50 (1985): 181–95; Parker, *The Military Revolution* (Cambridge, 1988); Karl Wittfogel, *Oriental Despotism* (New York, 1981), 374–89.

2 Rushton Coulborn (ed.), *Feudalism in History* (Princeton, 1956); Edmund Leach *et al.* (eds), *Feudalism: Comparative Studies* (Sydney, 1985); John W. Hall and Marius B. Jansen (eds), *Studies in the Institutional History of Early Modern Japan* (Princeton, 1968), 3–51; Gary P. Leupp, *Servants, Shophands and Laborers in the Cities of Tokugawa Japan* (Princeton, 1992); Yasukazu Takenaka, "Endogenous Formation and Development of Capitalism in Japan," *The Journal of Economic History [JEH]* 29, 1 (1969): 141–62 [this entire journal issue is devoted to examining the early extent of extra-European capitalism]; Karen Wigen, "The Geographic Imagination in Early Modern Japanese History," *The Journal of Asian Studies [JAS]* 51, 1 (1992): 3–29; David L. Howell, "Proto-Industrial Origins of Japanese Capitalism," *JAS* 51, 2 (1992): 269–86.

3 Evelyn Rawski, "Research Themes in Ming-Qing Socioeconomic History – The State of the Field," *JAS* 50, 1 (1991): 84–111; Susan Naquin and Evelyn Rawski, *Chinese Society in the Eighteenth Century* (New Haven, 1987); Lloyd E. Eastman, *Family, Fields, and Ancestors* (New York, 1988); Philip C.C. Huang, *The Peasant Family and Rural Development in the Yangzi Delta, 1350–1988* (Stanford, 1990); Albert Feuerwerker, "Presidential Address: Questions about China's Early Modern Economic History that I Wish I Could Answer," *JAS* 51, 4 (1992): 757–69; Frank Perlin, "Proto-Industrialization and Pre-Colonial South Asia," *Past and Present [PP]* 98 (1983): 30–95; D.A. Washbrook, "Progress and Problems: South Asian Economic and Social History *c.* 1720–1860," *Modern Asian Studies [MAS]* 22, 1 (1988): 57–96; Sanjay Subrahmanyam, "Rural Industry and Commercial Agriculture in Late Seventeenth-Century South-Eastern India," *PP* 126 (1990): 76–114; *idem* (ed.), *Merchants, Markets and the State in Early Modern India* (Delhi, 1990); Anthony Reid, *Southeast Asia in the Age of Commerce, 1450–1680*, 2 vols (New Haven, 1988, 1993); Victor Lieberman, "Secular Trends in Burmese Economic History, *c.* 1350–1830," *MAS* 25, 1 (1991): 1–31; Peter Carey, "Waiting for the 'Just King'," *MAS* 20, 1 (1986): 59–137.

4 The chief suspects are cultural impediments, political sins of commission (market interference), political sins of omission (failure to provide capital-friendly institutions), and demographically-based equilibrium traps. See previous notes, plus Ramon H. Myers, "How Did the Modern Chinese Economy Develop?" *JAS* 50, 3 (1991): 604–28; Albert Feuerwerker, "The State and the Economy in Late Imperial China," *Theory and Society* 13, 3 (1984): 297–326; William T. Rowe in Olivier Zunz (ed.), *Reliving the Past* (Chapel Hill, NC, 1985), 236–96; Mark Elvin, *The Pattern of the Chinese Past* (Stanford,

1973); Tapan Raychaudhuri in Raychaudhuri and Irfan Habib (eds), *The Cambridge Economic History of India*, I (Cambridge, 1982), 261–307, esp. 295; Jeyamalar Kathirithamby-Wells in Anthony Reid (ed.), *Southeast Asia in the Early Modern Era* (Ithaca, NY, 1993), 123–48; Thomas C. Smith, *Native Sources of Japanese Industrialization, 1750–1920* (Berkeley, 1988).

5 On the public sphere debate, William T. Rowe, "The Public Sphere in Modern China," *Modern China* 16, 3 (1990): 309–29; "Symposium: 'Public Sphere' 'Civil Society' in China?" *Modern China* 19, 2 (1993); Bin Wong, "Great Expectations: The 'Public Sphere' and the Search for Modern Times in Chinese History," *Chugoku shigakkai* 3 (1993): 7–50; C.A. Bayly, "Rethinking the Origins of the Indian Public Sphere," Univ. of Michigan lecture, Sept. 15, 1995. A similar test of European categories in Asia involves the search for a "17th-century crisis," *MAS* 24, 4 (1990), special issue.

6 Jones, *Miracle*. Cf. his later argument for sustained growth in Song China and Tokugawa Japan, *Growth Recurring* (Oxford, 1988).

7 Quote from Richard Pipes, *Russia under the Old Regime* (New York, 1992), 266. Pipes' book itself offers an essentialist Cold war view. Cf. Liah Greenfeld, *Nationalism* (Cambridge, MA, 1992), ch. 3; Marshall Poe, "Russian Despotism" (PhD, UC Berkeley, 1993); Valerie Kivelson, *Autocracy in the Provinces* (Stanford, 1996), Intro.

8 See Edward Said, *Orientalism* (New York, 1978); Anderson, *Lineages*, Note B; Michael Adas, *Machines as the Measure of Men* (Ithaca, 1989); K.N. Chaudhuri, *Asia Before Europe* (Cambridge, 1990), 19–24.

9 Anderson, *Lineages*, Note B, 462–549.

10 J. C. van Leur, *Indonesian Trade and Society* (The Hague, 1955), e.g., 95–6; John R. W. Smail, "On the Possibility of an Autonomous History of Modern Southeast Asia," *Journal of Southeast Asian History* 2:2 (1961): 72–102.

11 Hall, "The New Look of Tokugawa History," in Hall and Jansen, *Institutional History*, 55, corroborating C. Vann Woodward.

12 On Japanese revisionism, now in fact a new orthodoxy, see *supra* nn. 2, 4, plus Thomas C. Smith, *The Agrarian Origins of Modern Japan* (Stanford, 1959); Chie Nakane and Shinzaburo Oishi (eds), *Tokugawa Japan* (Tokyo, 1991).

13 Powelson, *Centuries of Economic Endeavor* (Ann Arbor, MI, 1994).

14 Price, "Secondary State Formation: An Explanatory Model," in Ronald Cohen and Elman R. Service (eds), *Origins of the State* (Philadelphia, 1978), 161–86. Conceivably parts of West Africa could be included in this schema.

15 Marvin Becker, *Civility and Society in Western Europe, 1300–1600* (Bloomington, IN, 1988); *idem, The Emergence of Civil Society in the Eighteenth Century* (Bloomington, IN, 1994); Robin Briggs, *Early Modern France 1560–1715* (Oxford, 1977); Isser Woloch, *Eighteenth-Century Europe* (New York, 1982).

16 See previous references to the "public sphere" debate, which takes on added significance when one compares urban publishing industries in Japan and Europe: Henry D. Smith II, "The History of the Book in Edo and Paris," in James L. McClain *et al.* (eds), *Edo and Paris* (Ithaca, NY, 1994), 332–52, and Mary Elizabeth Berry, this volume. According to Karen Wigen, "Mapping Early Modernity: Geographic Meditations on a Comparative Concept" (MS), the conjuncture of urbanization, wider literacy, voluntary associations, evidential philosophy, and an emphasis on the autonomous self in the arts suggests cultural analogies between late Ming/Qing China and the early modern West. Cf. David Johnson, "Communication, Class, and Consciousness in Late Imperial China," in Johnson *et al.* (eds), *Popular Culture in Late Imperial China* (Berkeley, 1985), 34–72.

17 McNeill, *Plagues and Peoples* (Garden City, NY, 1976).

18 H.H. Lamb, *Climate Present, Past, and Future*, II (London, 1977), ch. 17; *idem, The Changing Climate* (London, 1966); T.M.L. Wigley *et al.* (eds), *Climate and History* (Cambridge, 1981); Takehiko Mikami, "The Climate Reconstruction of East Asia in the Period *c.* 1500–1850" (MS); T. Mikami (ed.), *Proceedings of the International Symposium on the Little Ice Age Climate* (Tokyo, 1992).

19 Crosby, *The Columbian Exchange* (Westport, CT, 1972); Lee, "Migration and Expansion in Chinese History," in William H. McNeill and Ruth S. Adams (eds), *Human Migration: Patterns and Policies*

(Bloomington, IN, 1978), 20–47; *idem*, "Food Supply and Population Growth in Southwest China, 1250–1850," *JAS* 41, 4 (1982): 711–46.

20 Frank and Gills (eds), *The World System* (London, 1993); Abu-Lughod, *Before European Hegemony* (New York, 1989); Philip D. Curtin, *Cross-cultural Trade in World History* (Cambridge, 1984); Jerry H. Bentley, *Old World Encounters* (New York, 1993); Wolfram Fischer *et al.* (eds), *The Emergence of a World Economy 1500–1914*, I (Wiesbaden, 1986); John F. Richards (ed.), *Precious Metals in the Later Medieval and Early Modern Worlds* (Durham, NC, 1983); William Atwell, "Some Observations on the 'Seventeenth-Century Crisis' in China and Japan," *JAS* 45, 2 (1986): 223–44.

21 Goldstone, *Revolution and Rebellion in the Early Modern World* (Berkeley, 1991). Cf. Roland Mousnier, *Peasant Uprisings in Seventeenth Century France, Russia, and China* (New York, 1970).

22 Kettering, *Patrons, Brokers, and Clients in Seventeenth-Century France* (New York, 1986), 5.

23 For such views, and contrasts with earlier historiography, see Michael Mann, *The Sources of Social Power*, I (Cambridge, 1986), 458–63; Nicholas Henschall, *The Myth of Absolutism* (London, 1992); François-Xavier Emmanuelli, *Un mythe de l'absolutisme bourbonien* (Aix-en-Provence, 1981); David Parker, *The Making of French Absolutism* (New York, 1983); William Beik, *Absolutism and Society in Seventeenth-Century France* (Cambridge, 1985); Robert Harding, *Anatomy of a Power Elite* (New Haven, 1978); Roger Mettam, *Power and Faction in Louis XIV's France* (Oxford, 1988); Nancy Shields Kollmann, *Kinship and Patronage: The Making of the Muscovite Political System 1345–1547* (Stanford, 1987); Robert Crummey, *Aristocrats and Servitors* (Princeton, 1983); Kivelson, *Autocracy*.

24 Previous note, plus Ronald G. Asch and Adolf M. Birke (eds), *Princes, Patronage, and The Nobility* (Oxford, 1991); Wyatt, *Thailand*, chs 4–6; Busakorn Lailert, "The Ban Phlu Luang Dynasty" (PhD, Univ. of London, 1972); Akin Rabibhadana, *The Organization of Thai Society in the Early Bangkok Period 1782–1873* (Ithaca, NY, 1969); *CHJ*, III, chs 1–6, IV, chs 1–5; Mary Elizabeth Berry, *Hideyoshi* (Cambridge, MA, 1982), chs 4–6.

25 Victor Lieberman, "The Political Significance of Religious Wealth in Burmese History," *JAS* 39, 4 (1980): 753–69; Pipes, *Russia*, ch. 9; Donald Ostrowski, "Church Polemics and Monastic Land Acquisition in Sixteenth-Century Muscovy," *Slavic and East European Review [SEER]* 64, 3 (1986): 355–75; Paul Bushkovitch, *Religion and Society in Russia* (New York, 1992), chs 3–5; Eugenii V. Anisimov, *The Reforms of Peter the Great* (Armonk, NY, 1993), 203–17; Isabel de Madariaga, *Russia in the Age of Catherine the Great* (New Haven, 1981), 111–27, 515; Edwin O. Reischauer and Albert M. Craig, *Japan* (Sydney, 1979), 77, 87; *CHJ*, IV, 359–72; R. J. Knecht, *Francis I*, 51–65; Roland Mousnier, *Institutions*, I, ch. 7; François Furet, *Revolutionary France 1770–1880* (Oxford, 1992), 80–5, 226–8. Of course, the French church remained a key political actor to 1789. On Vietnamese controls, Nguyen Ngoc Huy & Ta Van Tai, *The Le Code*, 3 vols (Athens, OH, 1987), Articles 152, 215, 288, 301.

26 Laclau and Mouffe, *Hegemony and Socialist Strategy* (London, 1985), chs 3, 4; Morris-Suzuki, "The Invention and Reinvention of 'Japanese Culture'," *JAS* 54, 3 (1995): 759–80. Cf. Clifford Geertz, *The Interpretation of Cultures* (New York, 1973).

27 Cf. Anthony D. Smith, *The Ethnic Origins of Nations* (Oxford, 1986), 76–89, opposing lateral and vertical *ethnies* as stable communities, rather than as evolutionary processes.

29

Introduction to *The Great Divergence.* *China, Europe, and the Making of the Modern World Economy*

Kenneth Pomeranz

Much of modern social science originated in efforts by late nineteenth- and twentieth-century Europeans to understand what made the economic development path of western Europe[1] unique; yet those efforts have yielded no consensus. Most of the literature has focused on Europe, seeking to explain its early development of large-scale mechanized industry. *Comparisons* with other parts of the world have been used to show that "Europe" – or in some formulations, western Europe, Protestant Europe, or even just England – had within its borders some unique homegrown ingredient of industrial success or was uniquely free of some impediment.

Other explanations have highlighted relations between Europe and other parts of the world – particularly various forms of colonial extraction – but they have found less favor with the majority of Western scholars.[2] It has not helped matters that these arguments have emphasized what Marx called the "primitive accumulation" of capital through the forcible dispossession of Amerindians and enslaved Africans (and many members of Europe's own lower classes). While that phrase accurately highlights the brutality of these processes, it also implies that this accumulation was "primitive" in the sense of being the *beginning* step in large-scale capital accumulation. This position has become untenable as scholarship has shown the slow but definite growth of an investible surplus above subsistence through the retained earnings of Europe's own farms, workshops, and countinghouses.

This book will also emphasize the exploitation of non-Europeans – and access to overseas resources more generally – but not as the sole motor of European development. Instead it acknowledges the vital role of internally driven European growth but emphasizes how similar those processes were to processes at work elsewhere, especially in east Asia, until almost 1800. Some differences that mattered did exist, but I will argue that they could only create the great transformation of the nineteenth century in a context also shaped by Europe's privileged access to overseas resources. For instance, western Europe may well have had more effective institutions

Kenneth Pomeranz, "Introduction," pp. 3–17 from *The Great Divergence. China, Europe, and the Making of the Modern World Economy*. Princeton, NJ: Princeton University Press, 2000.

for mobilizing large sums of capital willing to wait a relatively long time for returns – but until the nineteenth century, the corporate form found few uses other than for armed long-distance trade and colonization, and long-term syndicated debt was primarily used within Europe to finance wars. More important, western Europe had by the eighteenth century moved ahead of the rest of the world in the use of various labor-saving technologies. However, because it continued to lag behind in various land-saving technologies, rapid population growth and resource demands might, in the absence of overseas resources, have forced it back onto a path of much more labor-intensive growth. In that case it would have diverged far less from China and Japan. The book thus calls upon the fruits of overseas coercion to help explain the *difference* between European development and what we see in certain other parts of Eurasia (primarily China and Japan) – not the whole of that development or the differences between Europe and *all* other parts of the Old World. A few other factors that do not fit firmly into either category, such as the location of coal supplies, also play a role. Thus the book combines comparative analysis, some purely local contingency, and an integrative or global approach.

Moreover, the comparative and integrative approaches modify each other. If the same factors that differentiate western Europe from, say, India or eastern Europe (e.g., certain kinds of labor markets) are shared with China, then comparisons cannot simply be the search for a European difference; nor can patterns shared at both ends of Eurasia be explained as unique products of European culture or history. (Nor, of course, can they be explained as outgrowths of universal tendencies, since they distinguish some societies from others.) The resemblances between western Europe and other areas that force us to turn from a purely comparative approach – one that assumes essentially separate worlds as units of comparison – to one that also looks at global conjunctures[3] have another significance as well. They imply that we cannot understand pre-1800 global conjunctures in terms of a Europe-centered world system; we have, instead, a polycentric world with no dominant center. Global conjunctures often worked to western Europe's advantage, but not necessarily because Europeans created or imposed them. For instance, the remonetization of China with silver from the fifteenth century on – a process that predated the European arrival in the Americas and the export of its silver – played a crucial part in making Spain's far-flung New World empire financially sustainable; and horrific, unanticipated epidemics were crucial to creating that empire in the first place. Only after nineteenth-century industrialization was well advanced does it make sense to see a single, hegemonic European "core."

Most of the existing literature, however, has remained set in an either/or framework – with either a Europe-centered world system carrying out essential primitive accumulation overseas[4] *or* endogenous European growth called upon to explain almost everything. Given those choices, most scholars have leaned toward the latter. Indeed, recent scholarship in European economic history has generally reinforced this exclusively internal focus in at least three ways.

First, recent research has found well-developed markets and other "capitalist" institutions further and further back in time, even during the "feudal" period often thought to be the antithesis of capitalism.[5] (A similar sort of revision has occurred in analyses of medieval science and technology, where what was once disparaged as the "Dark Ages" has now come to be seen as quite creative.) This has tended to reinforce the notion that western Europe was launched on a uniquely promising path well before it began overseas expansion. In some recent treatments, industrialization itself disappears as a turning point, subsumed into centuries of undifferentiated "growth."

To put matters slightly differently, older literatures – from the late nineteenth-century classics of social theory to the modernization theory of the 1950s and 1960s – stressed a fundamental opposition between the modern West and its past, and between the modern West and the non-

West. As more recent literature has tended to narrow the first gap, it suggests that the second gap – European exceptionalism – goes back even further than we thought. But it is a central contention of this book that one can just as easily find grounds to narrow the gap between the eighteenth-century West and at least some other parts of Eurasia.

Second, the more market dynamics appear even amid supposedly hostile medieval culture and institutions, the more tempting it has been to make market-driven growth the *entire* story of European development, ignoring the messy details and mixed effects of numerous government policies and local customs.[6] And if legislative fiat at home added only small detours or occasional slight shortcuts to European development paths, why should coercion overseas – in places far from the main action of the story – be worth much attention? Meanwhile, an increasingly exclusive focus on private initiatives has not only provided an enviably clear story line, but a story line compatible with currently predominant neoliberal ideas.

Third, since this ongoing process of commercialization touched much of preindustrial western Europe, much recent literature treats whatever is left of the Industrial Revolution as a *European* phenomenon, rather than, as used to be common, as a British phenomenon spreading later to the rest of Europe.[7] Such a move is challenged, not only by a mass of older scholarship, but also by more recent work suggesting that England had already diverged from the continent in crucial respects centuries before the Industrial Revolution.[8] But the shift from a British to a European focus has been facilitated by the aforementioned tendencies to deemphasize politics and to minimize the conflict between "traditional" practices and rationally self-interested individuals, making it easier to minimize variation within western Europe.

Positing a "European miracle" rather than a British one has important consequences. For one thing, it again makes extra-European connections seem less important. Most of western Europe was far less involved in extracontinental trade than Britain was: so if it was "Europe" rather than "Britain" whose commercial growth led smoothly to industrial growth, then domestic markets, resources, and so forth must have been adequate for that transition. Moreover, if growth was largely achieved through the gradual perfection of competitive markets, then it seems implausible that colonies beset by mercantilist restrictions and unfree labor, to name just two problems, could possibly have been dynamic enough to significantly affect their mother countries. Thus Patrick O'Brien, a leading exponent of a "European" view, concedes that *British* industrialization, in which cotton played such a crucial role, is hard to envision without colonies and slavery, but then continues:[9]

> Only a simplistic growth model with cotton as a leading sector and with British innovation as the engine of Western European growth could support an argument that the Lancashire cotton industry was vital for the industrialization of the core. That process proceeded on too broad a front to be checked by the defeat of an advanced column whose supply lines stretched across the oceans to Asia and the Americas.

He then concludes that "for the economic growth of the core, the periphery was peripheral."[10]

Such arguments make Europe's overseas expansion a minor matter in a story dominated by emerging economic superiority. Empire might be explained *by* that superiority or might be independent of it, but had little to do with creating it. The resulting narratives are largely self-contained in two crucial senses: they rarely require going either beyond Europe or beyond the model of free, competing buyers and sellers at the heart of mainstream economics. For those scholars who also explain the increased speed of technological change largely in terms of a patent system granting more secure property in creativity, this closure becomes almost complete.

The emphasis on "European" industrialization has also tended to shape the units used in our comparisons, often in unhelpful ways. In some cases, we get comparative units based simply on contemporary nation-states, so that Britain is compared to India or China. But India and China are each more comparable in size, population, and internal diversity to Europe as a whole than to individual European countries; and a region within either subcontinent that by itself might be comparable to Britain or the Netherlands is lost in averages including Asian equivalents of the Balkans, southern Italy, Poland, and so on. Unless state policy is the center of the story being told, the nation is not a unit that travels very well.

A second durable approach has been to first search for things that made "Europe" as a whole distinct (though the particulars chosen often really describe only part of the continent) and then, once the rest of the world has been dropped from the picture, to look within Europe for something that made Britain distinct. These continental or "civilizational" units have so powerfully shaped our thinking that it is hard to shake them; they will appear here, too. But for many purposes, it seems more useful to try a different approach, anticipated in important ways by my colleague R. Bin Wong.[11]

Let us grant the following: few essential characteristics unite, say, Holland and the Ukraine, or Gansu and the Yangzi Delta; a region like the Yangzi Delta (population 31,000,000–37,000,000 circa 1750, depending on the precise definition) is certainly big enough to be compared to eighteenth-century European countries; and various core regions scattered around the Old World – the Yangzi Delta, the Kantō plain, Britain and the Netherlands, Gujarat – shared some crucial features with each other, which they did not share with the rest of the continent or subcontinent around them (e.g., relatively free markets, extensive handcraft industries, highly commercialized agriculture). In that case, why not compare these areas directly, before introducing largely arbitrary continental units that had little relevance to either daily life or the grand patterns of trade, technological diffusion, and so on?[12] Moreover, if these scattered cores really had much in common – and if we are willing to allow some role for contingencies and conjunctures – it makes sense to make our comparisons between them truly reciprocal: that is, to look for absences, accidents, and obstacles that diverted England from a path that might have made it more like the Yangzi Delta or Gujarat, along with the more usual exercise of looking for blockages that kept non-European areas from reproducing implicitly normalized European paths.

Here, too, I am following a procedure outlined in Wong's recent *China Transformed*. As Wong points out, much of classic nineteenth-century social theory has been rightly faulted for its Eurocentrism. But the alternative favored by some current "postmodern" scholars – abandoning cross-cultural comparison altogether and focusing almost exclusively on exposing the contingency, particularity, and perhaps unknowability of historical moments – makes it impossible even to approach many of the most important questions in history (and in contemporary life). It seems much preferable instead to confront biased comparisons by trying to produce better ones. This can be done in part by viewing both sides of the comparison as "deviations" when seen through the expectations of the other, rather than leaving one as always the norm. It will be my procedure in much of this book, though my concrete application of this reciprocal comparative method has some significant differences from Wong's, and I carry the approach onto rather different terrain.[13]

This relatively untried approach at least generates some new questions that put various parts of the world in a different light. For instance – and here again I largely agree with Wong – I will argue that a series of balanced comparisons show several surprising similarities in agricultural, commercial, and proto-industrial (i.e., handicraft manufacturing for the market rather than home use) development among various parts of Eurasia as late as 1750. Thus the explosion of further growth in western Europe alone during the nineteenth century again becomes a rupture to be explained. By contrast, some recent literature, by limiting itself to intertemporal European comparisons and finding similarities there (which are real enough), tends to obscure this rupture, Thus, such literature also often barely passes over important contributions to industrialization – especially conjunctural ones – which may appear as taken-for-granted "background" in a comparison limited to different periods in Europe.

A strategy of two-way comparisons also justifies linking what may at first seem two separate issues. The point at which western Europe became the richest economy need not be the same as the point at which it broke out of a Malthusian world into one of sustained per capita growth. Indeed, most of what I have called the "Europe-centered" approaches argue that western Europe had become uniquely rich long before its industrial breakthrough. And if our only question were whether China (or India, or Japan) could have made its own breakthrough to such a world – i.e., if we normalize the European experience and make it the pattern one would expect in the absence of "blockages" or "failures" – it would no longer be very important to ask when Europe actually escaped a Malthusian world: it would matter far more that it had been for a long time on a path bound to lead to that breakthrough eventually. Meanwhile, the dates by which it had definitively surpassed other places would tell us little about other possibilities for Europe and only about when those other places had taken their detours into stagnation.

But if we make reciprocal comparisons and entertain the possibility that Europe could have been a China – that no place was bound to achieve dramatic and sustained per capita growth – the link between the two becomes closer. If we further argue – as I will in subsequent chapters – that some other parts of the eighteenth-century world were roughly as close as Europe was to maximizing the economic possibilities available to them without a dramatic easing of their resource constraints (like that made possible for Europe by fossil fuels and the New World), then the link between the two issues becomes closer still.

The two questions are still separable: differences in climate, soil, etc., might have given different areas different preindustrial possibilities. But it seems unlikely that Europe enjoyed a substantial edge in those possibilities over all other densely settled regions, particularly since the evidence presented later in this book suggests that it did not in fact become much better-off than east Asia until industrialization was well under way. Or it might turn out that although Europe did not pull ahead of east Asia until the eve of industrialization, certain institutions were in place by a much earlier date that did make industrialization bound to happen after all; that even without the Americas and favorably located fossil fuels, technological inventiveness was already sufficient to sustain growth in the face of any particular local resource shortages, and without resorting to the extremely labor intensive solutions which sustained aggregate, but not per capita, growth elsewhere. But the strong assumptions that such an assertion of inevitability would require begin to look shaky once we actually hold Europe up against the standard of some other preindustrial economies – especially since the last few centuries of European economic history before industrialization do not show consistent and robust per capita growth. Thus, two-way comparisons both raise new questions and reconfigure the relationships among old ones.

Thus, we will emphasize reciprocal comparisons between *parts* of Europe and parts of China, India, and so on that seem to me to have been similarly positioned within their continental worlds. We will return to continental units and to still larger units, such as the Atlantic world, when our questions – such as those about the relationships of cores to their hinterlands – require it. And in some cases we will need to take the entire world as our unit, requiring a somewhat different kind of comparison – what Charles Tilly calls the "encompassing comparison," in which rather than comparing two separate things (as classical social theory did) we look at two parts of a larger whole and see how the position and function of each part in the system shape their nature. At this level, which I emphasize more than Wong does, comparison and the analysis of connections become indistinguishable. The importance of keeping the analysis reciprocal, however, remains. Our perception of an interacting system from which one part benefited more than others does not in itself justify calling that part the "center" and assuming that it is the unshaped shaper of everything else. We will see, instead, vectors of influence moving in various directions.

Variations on the Europe-Centered Story: Demography, Ecology, and Accumulation

The arguments positing that western Europe's economy was uniquely capable of generating an industrial transformation generally fall into two clusters. The first, typified by the work of E. L. Jones, argues that beneath a surface of "preindustrial" similarity, sixteenth- through eighteenth-century Europe had already moved far ahead of the rest of its world in the accumulation of both physical and human capital.[14] A central tenet of this view is that various customary checks on fertility (late marriage, a celibate clergy, etc.) allowed Europe to escape from the otherwise universal condition of a "pre-modern fertility regime" and thus from a similarly universal condition in which population growth absorbed almost all of any increase in production. Consequently, Europe was uniquely able to adjust its fertility to hard times and to increase its per capita (not just total) capital stock over the long haul.

Thus, in this view, differences in the demographic and economic behavior of ordinary farmers, artisans, and traders created a Europe that could support more non-farmers; equip its people with better tools (including more livestock); make them better nourished, healthier, and more productive; and create a larger market for goods above and beyond the bare necessities. The central arguments underlying this position were laid out over thirty years ago by John Hajnal:[15] they have been elaborated since then, but not radically altered. However, recent work on birthrates, life expectancy, and other demographic variables in China, Japan, and (more speculatively) Southeast Asia has made what Hajnal thought were unique European achievements look more and more ordinary.

The significance of these findings has not yet been fully appreciated, but they have been partially acknowledged in the one important recent addition to the demographically driven story line: the recognition that there were economic booms and rising living standards in preindustrial settings outside Europe. However, these are always treated as temporary flowerings that either proved vulnerable to political shifts or played themselves out as productivity-enhancing innovations proved unable to stay ahead of the population increases that prosperity encouraged.[16]

Such stories are an important advance over much earlier literature, which argued either implicitly or explicitly that the whole world was poor and accumulation minimal until the early modern European breakthrough; among other things, it has forced scholars to look at "the fall of Asia"[17] as well as the "rise of Europe." However, these versions of the story are often anachronistic in at least two crucial ways.

First, they tend to read too much of the nineteenth- and twentieth-century ecological disasters that have afflicted much of Asia (and the underlying problem of dense population) back into earlier periods and present eighteenth-century Asian societies as having exhausted all the possibilities available to them. Some versions attribute this condition to all of an artificial unit called "Asia" circa 1800; but India, Southeast Asia, and even parts of China still had a good deal of room to accommodate more people without either a major technological breakthrough or a decline in the standard of living. Probably only a few parts of China and Japan faced such a situation.

Second, such stories often "internalize" the extraordinary ecological bounty that Europeans gained from the New World. Some do so by assimilating overseas expansion to the pattern of "normal" frontier expansion within Europe (e.g., the clearing and settlement of the Hungarian plain or the Ukraine, or of German forests). This ignores the exceptional scale of the New World windfall, the exceptionally coercive aspects of colonization and the organization of production there, and the role of global dynamics in ensuring the success of European expansion in the Americas.[18] The clearing of new agricultural lands in Hungary and the Ukraine had parallels in Sichuan, Bengal, and many other Old World locales; what happened in the New World was very different from anything in either Europe or Asia. Moreover, because nineteenth-century Europe found enormous ecological relief beyond its borders – both acquiring resources and exporting settlers[19] – such accounts rarely consider whether some densely populated core regions in sixteenth- through eighteenth-century Europe faced ecological pressures and options not radically different from those of core regions in Asia.

Thus, the literature that incorporates the "fall of Asia" tends to do so with the aid of an oversimplified contrast between an ecologically played-out China, Japan, and/or India, and a Europe with plenty of room left to grow – a Europe that, in one formulation, had the "advantages of backwardness"[20] because it had not yet developed enough to make full use of its internal resources.

In an attempt to move beyond such impressionistic claims, one needs to offer a systematic comparison of ecological constraints in selected key areas of China and Europe. This inquiry shows that although some parts of eighteenth-century Europe had some ecological advantages over their east Asian counterparts, the overall pattern is quite mixed. Indeed, key Chinese regions seem to have been better-off than their European counterparts in some surprising ways, such as available fuel supply per capita. Moreover, Britain, where industrialization in fact began, had few of the underutilized resources that remained in various other parts of Europe. Indeed, it seems to have been no better-off than its rough counterpart in China – the Lower Yangzi Delta – in timber supply, soil depletion, and other crucial ecological measures. Thus, if we accept the idea that population growth and its ecological effects made China "fall," then we would have to say that Europe's internal processes had brought it very close to the same precipice – rather than to the verge of "take-off" – when it was rescued by a combination of overseas resources and England's breakthrough (partly conditioned by geographic good luck) in the use of subterranean stores of energy. If, on the other hand, Europe was not yet in crisis, then in all likelihood China was not either.

In making this argument I parallel some of the arguments in work on global development by Sugihara Kaoru – work I discovered too late in my writing to deal with in great detail.[21] Sugihara emphasizes, as I do, that the high population growth in east Asia between 1500 and 1800 should not be seen as a pathology that blocked "development." On the contrary, he argues, this was an "East Asian miracle" of supporting people, creating skills, and so on, which is fully comparable as an economic achievement to the "European miracle" of industrialization. Sugihara also emphasizes, as I do, the high standard of living in eighteenth-century Japan and (to a lesser extent in his view) China, as well as the sophistication of institutions that produced many of the beneficial effects of markets without the same state guarantees for property and contract that many Westerners believe is the precondition of markets.[22] He also argues – a point consistent with my argument though beyond the scope of this book – that in the long run it has been a combination of western European and east Asian types of growth, allowing Western technology to be used in societies with vastly more people, which has made the largest contribution to world GDP, not a simply diffusion of Western achievements.

Sugihara does, however, suggest that a basic difference between these two "miracles" is that as far back as 1500, western Europe was on a capital-intensive path and east Asia on a labor-intensive path. By contrast, I argue – in keeping with the finding of surprising similarities as late as 1750 and with my determination to take the question "Why wasn't England the Yangzi Delta?" as seriously as "Why wasn't the Yangzi Delta England?" – that Europe, too, could have wound up on an "east Asian," labor-intensive path. That it did not was the result of important and sharp discontinuities, based on both fossil fuels and access to New World resources, which, taken together, obviated the need to manage land intensively. Indeed, there are many signs that substantial regions in Europe were headed down a more labor-intensive path until dramatic late eighteenth- and nineteenth-century developments reversed that path. We will find such evidence in aspects of agriculture and proto-industry throughout Europe (including England) and in almost everything about Denmark.[23] The East-West difference that developed around labor-intensity was not essential but highly contingent; the distribution of population growth (as opposed to its aggregate size) turns out to be one crucial variable, which in turn has much to do with market *distortions* in sixteenth- through eighteenth-century Europe and with migration to the New World in the nineteenth century.

In both China and Japan population growth after 1750 was heavily concentrated in less-developed regions, which then had smaller surpluses of grain, timber, raw cotton, and other land-intensive products to "vent" through trade with resource-hungry cores; and since part of the increased population of these peripheral areas went into proto-industry, they also had less need to trade with core regions. In Europe, on the other hand, it was largely areas that were already relatively advanced and densely populated that had large population increases between 1750 and 1850. Most of eastern Europe, for instance, only began to experience rapid population growth after 1800, and southern Europe (especially southeastern Europe) began to catch up even later . . . Meanwhile, it is worth emphasizing that they are not differences that reflect a greater *overall* strain on resources in east (much less south) Asia as compared to Europe. Let us move, then, from arguments about quantities of resources available – either those already accumulated or those left untapped – to arguments claiming that European institutions *allocated* resources in ways more conducive to long-term self-sustaining growth.

Other Europe-Centered Stories: Markets, Firms, and Institutions

A second group of arguments – evident in somewhat different ways in the work of Fernand Braudel, Immanuel Wallerstein, and K. N. Chaudhuri, and in a very different way in that of Douglass North – pays less attention to *levels* of wealth. Instead, these arguments emphasize the emergence of institutions in early modern Europe (or some part of it) said to be more conducive to economic development than those existing elsewhere. The focus of these arguments is generally on the emergence of efficient markets and property-rights regimes that rewarded those who found more productive ways to employ land, labor, and capital. A common, though not universal, companion to these arguments is the claim that economic development was stifled elsewhere (especially in China and India) by a state that was either too strong and hostile to private property or too weak to protect rationalizing entrepreneurs when the latter clashed with local customs, clergy, or strongmen.[24]

Potentially consistent with these arguments – though quite distinct from them – is the work of Robert Brenner, who explains divergent development paths within Europe as the result of class struggles that altered property-rights regimes. In Brenner's interpretation, western European peasants won the first round of a struggle with their lords in the century or so after the Plague, establishing their freedom from forced labor; eastern European peasants lost, and the ruling class lived for centuries thereafter by squeezing peasants harder, without ever modernizing agriculture or introducing labor-saving innovations. Within western Europe, Brenner continues, a second round of struggle ensued, with lords who now owned only the land seeking the freedom to manage it so as to maximize profits, often by removing unproductive or "excess" tenants. French elites lost this battle, according to Brenner, and France was stuck thereafter with an agricultural system based on millions of smallholders neither able nor very interested in innovations that would make some of them unnecessary. But in England the lords won, invested in innovations that made it possible to cut labor costs, and expelled huge numbers of unneeded workers from the land. At least some of these dispossessed farmers eventually became England's industrial workforce, buying food from the agrarian surplus created by their expulsion and marketed by their former lords.

In Brenner's argument, class struggle, rather than either Malthusian pressures or the "natural" emergence of more perfect markets, supplies the motor of the story; the destination, however, is similar. How much a society winds up resembling neoclassical models determines how productive it will be thereafter; in particular, England, the country where land and labor wound up most sharply separated (and most completely commodified) is presumed to have *therefore* developed the most dynamic economy. In this, Brenner winds up rather oddly aligned with Douglass North, who – while rejecting class struggle as the explanation of property-rights regimes – also argues that economies became increasingly capable of development as they evolved increasingly competitive markets for commodified land, labor, capital, and intellectual property.

Both North's and Brenner's arguments focus on the institutional settings in which the great majority of people operated: markets for day labor, tenancy contracts, and for products that ordinary people both produced and consumed. In this they resemble the arguments discussed above, which argue that preindustrial Europeans were already uniquely prosperous and productive, and tend to merge with those arguments.

However, the other major set of institutionalist arguments – those of Braudel and his school – focuses more on the profits accumulated by a few very wealthy people; the institutions that facilitated this kind of accumulation often involved special privileges that interfered with neoclassical markets. Consequently, these scholars have paid more attention to profits based on the use of coercion and collusion. And because many of the great merchants they focus on were involved in long-distance trade, these scholars have paid more attention to international politics and Europe's relations with other areas. Wallerstein, in particular, treats the growth of trade between "feudal" eastern Europe and "capitalist" western Europe as the real beginning of a world economy, and he emphasizes that continued accumulation of profits in the free-labor "core" of that economy has required the continued existence of poor, generally unfree "peripheries."

But nonetheless, the motor of Wallerstein's story is western Europe's unique combination of relatively free labor, large and productive urban populations, and merchants and governments that facilitated long-distance trade and the reinvestment of profits. The international division of labor that emerged from this trade increased the difference in wealth between western Europe and everyone else, since peripheries increasingly specialized in those goods for which cheap, often coerced, labor was more important than the tools and institutions needed for high productivity – but it was based on preexisting socioeconomic differences that enabled western Europe to impose on others in the first place.

Problems with the Europe-Centered Stories

This work borrows from these arguments – mostly those of the various "institutionalists" – but ultimately argues for different propositions. First, no matter how far back we may push for the origins of capitalism, *industrial* capitalism, in which the large-scale use of inanimate energy sources allowed an escape from the common constraints of the preindustrial world, emerges only in the 1800s. There is little to suggest that western Europe's economy had decisive advantages before then, either in its capital stock or economic institutions, that made industrialization highly probable there and unlikely elsewhere. The market-driven growth of core areas in western Europe during the preceding centuries was real enough and was undoubtedly one crucial precursor of industrialization – but it was probably no *more* conducive to industrial transformation than the very similar processes of commercialization and "proto-industrial" growth occurring in various core areas in Asia.[25] The patterns of scientific and technical development that were taking shape in early modern Europe were more unusual, but we shall see that they still did not, by themselves, guarantee that western Europe would wind up on a fundamentally different economic path from, for instance, east Asia.

Second, European industrialization was still quite limited outside of Britain until at least 1860. Thus, positing a "*European* miracle" based on features common to western Europe is risky, all the more so since much of what was widely shared across western Europe was at least equally present elsewhere in Eurasia.

Instead of contending that Europe had an internally generated economic edge before 1800, one might paint a picture of broad similarities among the most densely populated and commercialized parts of the Old World. There is evidence from numerous places to show that Europe had not accumulated a crucial advantage in physical capital prior to 1800 and was not freer of Malthusian pressures (and thus more able to invest) than many other large economies. People in various other areas seem to have lived as long and as well as Europeans and to have been at least equally willing and able to limit fertility in the interest of household-level accumulation. [One must then examine] the possibility that Europe had a crucial technological edge even before the Industrial Revolution. Here we do find some differences that mattered – but which would have had smaller, later, and probably qualitatively different effects without both the fortunate geographic accidents essential to the energy revolution and Europe's privileged access to overseas resources. Technological inventiveness was necessary for the Industrial Revolution, but it was not sufficient, or uniquely European. It is unclear whether whatever differences existed in the *degree* of technological inventiveness were crucial to exiting a Malthusian world (technological breakthroughs could have been spread over a slightly longer period), but it is clear that the differences in global context that helped ease European resource constraints – and so made innovation along particular (land-using, energy-using, and labor-saving) paths a fruitful, even self-reinforcing, process – were significant.

. . . western European land, labor, and product markets, even as late as 1789, were on the whole probably *further* from perfect competition – that is, less likely to be composed of multiple buyers and sellers with opportunities to choose freely among many trading partners – than those in most of China and thus less suited to the growth process envisioned by Adam Smith. . . .

Some scholars have argued that Chinese families were more prone than western European ones to keep women and children working beyond the point at which their marginal output sank below the value of a subsistence wage, thus producing an "involuted economy" . . .[26] Rather, labor deployment in Chinese families seems to closely resemble the reorientation of labor, leisure, and consumption toward the market that Jan DeVries has called Europe's "industrious revolution."[27] In sum, core regions in China and Japan circa 1750 seem to resemble the most advanced parts of western Europe, combining sophisticated agriculture, commerce, and nonmechanized industry in similar, arguably even more fully realized, ways. Thus we must look outside these cores to explain their subsequent divergence.

NOTES

1 It should be noted here that "western Europe," for most authors, is a social, economic, and political construct, not an actual geographic entity: Ireland, southern Italy, and most of Iberia, for instance, did not have much of the economic development usually held to be characteristically European or western European. I will generally use the term in a geographical sense, while pointing out that the areas often taken to stand for "Europe" in these comparisons (e.g., the southern Netherlands, or northern England), might be better compared, in both size and economic characteristics, with such units as China's Jiangsu province, rather than with entire subcontinents such as China or India.

2 Note, for instance, the generally negative current mainstream verdicts on the arguments of E. Williams, *Capitalism and Slavery* (New York: Russell & Russell, 1944), A. G. Frank, *Capitalism and Underdevelopment in Latin America: Historical Studies of Chile and Brazil* (New York: Monthly Review Press, 1969), S. Amin, *Accumulation on a World Scale* (New York: Monthly Review Press, 1978), etc. A good general critique of the overseas extraction thesis is Jan de Vries, *The Economy of Europe in an Age of Crisis, 1600–1750* (New York: Cambridge University Press, 1976): 139–46, 213–14.

3 For a discussion of comparisons between entities that are assumed to be systemically interrelated rather than truly separate (which he calls the "encompassing comparison"), see C. Tilly, *Big Structures, Large Processes, Huge Comparisons* (New York: Russell Sage Foundation, 1984).

4 E.g., J. Blaut, *The Colonizer's Model of the World: Geographic Diffusionism and Eurocentric History* (New York: Guilford, 1993).

5 For a good recent example, see R. H. Britnell, *The Commercialization of English Society, 1000–1500* (Cambridge: Cambridge University Press, 1993).

6 For a good example of the tendency to minimize the importance of both legislative changes and popular custom, see the large literature reinterpreting the decline of English open fields. These fields were once thought to represent a collective ethic hostile to nascent capitalism and to have been destroyed by legislation as more individualist, less paternalist ideas became dominant in Parliament. It is now common in fact to argue that open fields in fact represented a rational strategy for individuals in a world of fluctuating harvests and no insurance and disappeared largely because gradually declining interest rates made another form of harvest insurance – namely grain storage – cheaper and more effective than keeping one's land in many scattered plots likely to have slightly different soils and micro-climates (e.g., D. McCloskey: "The Persistence of the English Common Fields," in *European Peasants and Their Markets: Essays in Agrarian Economic History*, ed. E. L. Jones and W. Parker (Princeton, NJ: Princeton University Press), 73–119; "The Economics of Enclosure: A Market Analysis," in ibid., 123–60; and "The Open Fields of England: Rent, Risk and the Rate of Interest, 1300–1815," in *Markets in History: Economic Studies of the Past* (Cambridge: Cambridge University Press, 1989), 5–49. A further consequence of this view is the claim that the absence of any comparable successful government assault on traditional open fields in France was not as important an impediment to French development as earlier historians had generally held.

7 For two classic, though very different, statements of the British-centered view, see D. Landes, *The Unbound Prometheus: Technological Change and Industrial Development in Western Europe from 1750 to the Present* (Cambridge: Cambridge University Press, 1969) and E. Hobsbawm, *Industry and Empire* (London: Penguin, 1975). One of the most explicit and trenchant critiques of this view is P. O'Brien and C. Keyder, *Economic Growth in Britain and France, 1780–1914* (London: George Allen & Unwin, 1978).

8 See, e.g., G. Snookes, "New Perspectives on the Industrial Revolution," in *Was the Industrial Revolution Necessary?*, ed. G. Snookes (London: Routledge, 1994), 1–26; E. Wrigley, "Brake or Accelerator? Urban Growth and Population Growth before the Industrial Revolution," in *Urbanization in History*, ed. A. D. Van der Woude, A. Hayami, and J. De Vries (Oxford: Clarendon Press, 1990), 101–12.

9 P. O'Brien, "European Economic Development: The Contribution of the Periphery," *Economic History Review* 35:1 (February 1982): 1–18.

10 Ibid. In his work with Keyder on Britain and France, O'Brien makes the much more convincing but different point that European industrialization was not *simply* the diffusion of British innovations to the rest of the continent. France, for instance, concentrated on different industries, which often involved finishing British semi-finished goods. But the very complentarity between Britain and France that shows the possibility of different routes to industrialization also suggests that we cannot simply remove British industrialization from the story and say that had that not happened, the continent would have industrialized anyway. And the British story, as we shall see, is unimaginable without two crucial discontinuities – one created by coal and one by colonies.

11 R. Bin Wong, *China Transformed: Historical Change and the Limits of European Experience* (Ithaca, NY: Cornell University Press, 1997).

12 On the limited utility of "civilizations" as a unit, see J. Fletcher, *Studies in Chinese and Islamic Inner Asia*, ed. B. Forbes Manz (Brookfield, VT: Variorum, 1995), 3–7; M. Hodgson, *Rethinking World History: Essays on Europe, Islam, and World History*, ed. E. Burke III (Cambridge: Cambridge University Press, 1993), 17. On continents, see K. Wigen and M. Lewis, *The Myth of Continents* (Berkeley: University of California Press, 1997).

13 For example, I place greater stress than Wong does on global conjunctures and reciprocal influences and bring more places besides Europe and China into the discussion; I also say little about some of his topics, such as state formation, and much more about some he does not treat extensively, such as environmental change.

14 E. Jones, *The European Miracle: Environments, Economics, and Geopolitics in the History of Europe and Asia* (Cambridge: Cambridge University Press, 1981) and *Growth Recurring: Economic Change in World History* (New York: Oxford University Press, 1988).

15 J. Hajnal, "European Marriage Patterns in Perspective, in *Population in History*, ed. D. V. Glass and D. E. C. Eversley (Chicago: Aldine Publishing, 1965), 101–46, and "Two Kinds of Preindustrial Household Formation System," *Population and Development Review* 8:3 (September 1982): 449–94.

16 Jones, *Growth Recurring*; M. Elvin, *The Pattern of the Chinese Past* (Stanford, CA: Stanford University Press, 1975); J. Powelson, *Centuries of Economic Endeavor: Parallel Paths in Japan and Europe and Their Contrast with the Third World* (Ann Arbor: University of Michigan Press, 1994).

17 J. Abu-Lughod, *Before European Hegemony: The World System, A.D. 1250–1350* (New York: Oxford University Press, 1989); A. G. Frank, *ReOrient: The Silver Age in Asia and the World Economy* (Berkeley: University of California Press, 1998).

18 See, e.g., Jones, *The European Miracle*, 70–4.

19 A. Crosby, *Ecological Imperialism: The Biological Expansion of Europe, 900–1900* (Cambridge: Cambridge University Press, 1986), 2–5, 294–308.

20 Frank, *ReOrient*, 283, playing on Gerschenkron.

21 K. Sugihara, "Agriculture and Industrialization: the Japanese Experience," in *Agriculture and Economic Growth*, ed. P. Mathias and J. Davis (Oxford: Blackwell, 1997), 148–66.

22 It is worth noting, however, that in recent years many Western economic historians have also become interested in describing institutional arrangements that made contracts easily enforceable, and thus permitted efficient markets, even in the absence of much state involvement in guaranteeing property rights. For a helpful summary, see A. Grief, "Théorie des jeux et analyse historique des institutions," *Annales HSS* 3 (May–June 1998): 597–633.

23 See for instance M. Ambrosoli, *The Wild and the Sown* (Cambridge: Cambridge University Press, 1997); D. Levine, *Family Formation in an Age of Nascent Capitalism* (New York: Academic Press, 1977); and T. Kjaergaard, *The Danish Revolution, 1500–1800* (Cambridge: Cambridge University Press, 1994).

24 K. Wittfogel, *Oriental Despotism: A Comparative Study of Total Power* (New Haven, CT: Yale University Press, 1957); Jones, *European Miracle*, 66–7, 118, 125; Jones, *Growth Recurring*, 130–46; J. Mokyr, *The Lever of Riches: Technological Creativity and Economic Progress* (New York: Oxford University Press, 1990), 233–4; and Powelson, *Centuries of Economic Endeavor*.

25 Sugihara, "Agriculture and Industrialization," and A. Hayami, "Kinsei Nihon no keizai hatten to Industrious Revolution," in *Tokugawa shakai kara no tenbo: hatten, kozo, kokusia kankei*, ed. H. Akira, S. Osamu, and S. Chuya (Tokyo: Dobunkan, 1989), 19–32, see the "industrial" and "industrious" revolutions diverging already in the seventeenth century; G. Arrighi, *The Long Twentieth Century: Money, Power, and the Origins of Our Times* (New York: Verso, 1994) in the eighteenth century. Although there are indeed signs of such a divergence that far back, I will argue that it was not sealed until the turn of the nineteenth century, when the New World plus coal made it clear that such as land-using, resource-intensive path would remain sustainable for a prolonged period.

26 Philip Huang, *The Peasant Family and Rural Development in the Lower Yangzi Region*, 1350–1988 (Stanford, 1990), 1–17; for a related argument see Jack Goldstone, "Gender, Work and Culture: Why the Industrial Revolution Came Early to England but Late to China," *Sociological Perspectives* 39:1 (1996): 1–21.

27 Jan de Vries, "The Industrious Revolution and the Industrial Revolution," *Journal of Economic History* 54:2 (June 1994): 249–70.

30

BETWEEN CARNIVAL AND LENT: THE SCIENTIFIC REVOLUTION AT THE MARGINS OF CULTURE

Paula Findlen

How curious, after all, is the way in which we moderns think about the world! And it is all so novel, too.

E. A. Burtt

In the half-century since the "Scientific Revolution" became a meaningful description of the transformation of attitudes toward nature in the sixteenth and seventeenth centuries, it seems to have enjoyed more lives than the Cheshire cat and to have remained as enigmatic.[1] Since its original formulation in the late 1940s, it has been the topic of a lively debate about the origins and character of modern approaches to nature and, more generally, knowledge. The result has been not only increased skepticism that the Scientific Revolution could be reduced to any single narrative, but also a profusion of narratives about what constituted its fundamental characteristics. As Hayden White observes, "any given set of real events can be emplotted in a number of ways, can bear the weight of being told as any number of different stories."[2] In the process, the Scientific Revolution, perhaps more than any other area of science studies, has become a testing ground for new approaches to the historical understanding of science and new ways of understanding the process of scientific change.

Why should we feel so compelled to tell and retell this particular story in the history of science, when there are so many other episodes worthy of our attention? Surely part of the fascination lies in the sense that the Scientific Revolution is, in many respects, *the* original story in the history of science. From the sixteenth century onward, humanist natural philosophers – from the anatomist Andreas Vesalius to the astronomer Johannes Kepler – wrote the histories of various sciences in order to publicize the importance of their reformation of knowledge. By the

Paula Findlen, "Between Carnival and Lent: The Scientific Revolution at the Margins of Culture," pp. 243–67 from *Configurations* 6 (2). Johns Hopkins University Press, 1998.

eighteenth century they had become the story, protagonists of a narrative rewritten by new scholarly communities in search of modern ruptures with the past.[3] The crafting of scientific narrative
has been a prolonged and self-conscious exercise in which scientists as well as historians have
participated over the centuries – all the more so because neither the scientist nor the historian
enjoyed distinct intellectual identities until fairly recently (quite often, as the case of the seventeenth-century statesman, historian, and natural philosopher Francis Bacon demonstrates well,
they were the same person). Accordingly, we might see the Scientific Revolution as one of the
fundamental experiments in narrating the history of science.

While the grand narrative of the Scientific Revolution has largely been a story of the rise of
modern science that takes science in a fairly defined sense as its focal point, cultural approaches
to the history of science suggest a variety of other possibilities that explore in greater detail the
imagery that early modern Europeans had at their disposal when they attempted to describe
nature. Such imagery was not simply an afterthought to the study of nature; often it was so deeply
embedded in the act of seeing and understanding nature that it would be impossible to separate
how a particular natural philosopher viewed nature from how he viewed culture.[4] Defining nature
and defining culture were complementary activities in the sixteenth and seventeenth centuries.
If we wish to truly understand what it meant to do early modern science, then we need to think
more carefully about what it meant to be early modern.

The approach I am suggesting has already had a number of advocates. Several years ago, John
Schuster remarked that "the Scientific Revolution consisted of a process of change and displacement among and within competing *systems of natural philosophy*," and he recommended that historians look more carefully at the "privileged images, metaphors or models" that defined
these different approaches to knowledge.[5] The literature exploring the fundamental cultural
themes of the early modern period can be a rich resource for expanding our interpretations of the
Scientific Revolution.[6] Since nature was never an isolated subject of study during this period
but always part of some larger project, we should examine more closely those features of early
modern society that best illuminate the place of science in that world. What were the defining
images of knowledge? How did interpretations of nature play out these larger intellectual themes?
As Hans Blumenburg wrote, "The absolute necessity of science in the contemporary world does
not license any inferences about the process by which it began."[7] We need to be open to new possibilities about what motivated and shaped the intense investigation of nature toward the end of
the Renaissance.

Science was a *mobile* subject that intersected with many different facets of early modern
culture, never resting securely in any one place but constantly at play in society. For this very
reason, it is hard to envision one single narrative encompassing the richness of the enterprise of
investigating nature. Historians of science might profit from making greater use of techniques of
analysis that celebrate the tensions and pluralities of the early modern world. To paraphrase the
medievalist Caroline Walker Bynum, we may wish to consider science in a *comic mode*: "A
comic stance knows that there is, in actuality, no ending (happy or otherwise) – that doing history
is, for the historian, telling a story that could be told in another way."[8] Such an ironic philosophy of knowledge has not often enjoyed a comfortable place in the study of science, which tends
to be seen as a subject beyond the boundaries of irony and humor. Yet comedy in all its
forms was one of the central expressions of the society that initiated the transformation of Western
science. This essay is an experiment in inserting this particular strand of Renaissance values into
the narrative of the Scientific Revolution. What would a comic narrative of the Scientific Revolution look like? What would it add to our understanding of new interpretations of nature in this
period?

Huizinga, Bakhtin, and the History of Science

One of the key images defining the sixteenth and seventeenth centuries is the battle between Carnival and Lent. It is one of the central emblems of the early modern period, most famously illustrated in Peter Brueghel's eponymously named painting of 1559 in which pale, censorious Lent, virtually done in by its austerity, battles corpulent Carnival revelers in the streets of an imaginary Flemish city.[9] In Brueghel's sixteenth-century interpretation, we have no doubt who he believes is winning the contest. Like his contemporaries Erasmus and Rabelais, Brueghel clearly understood the power of the ludic over its graver alternatives. And yet it is the *coexistence* of these two themes that he celebrates and immortalizes. Carnival has no meaning without Lent; locked in an eternal contest, they enact the battle between passion and reason, appetite and intellect, pleasure and piety, excess and scarcity that encompasses so many of the questions that guided and shaped the lives of early modern Europeans.[10]

The dialectic relationship between Carnival and Lent, and the Renaissance predilection toward Carnival, has been the subject of some of the most interesting and enduring cultural analyses of the early modern period. Such work has been virtually ignored in the study of the Scientific Revolution, and yet it has much to offer historians of science interested in cultural perspectives on knowledge. As Fernand Hallyn remarked, "The history of irony as a companion to the history of science has not yet been written."[11] But irony was just one facet of the Renaissance celebration of the ludic. Laughter, copiousness, and materiality all enjoyed strong connections that had ramifications for understanding nature as well as interpreting humanity. Attempts to deny and suppress these impulses created a competing aesthetic, the other side of the telescope through which early modern Europeans gazed at the world. "Carnival is the most capital and mortal enemy of Lent," wrote the anonymous author of the *Discourse against Carnival* (1607) at the height of the Catholic Reformation.[12] The strength and universality of these themes in narrations of culture suggests that they should be equally evident and important in scientific and philosophical writings. In the following pages I offer a brief account of ludic interpretations of the Renaissance and then suggest how they might be relevant to the study of science.

In 1938, on the verge of the Second World War, the Dutch historian Johan Huizinga published *Homo ludens*. Huizinga's essay on the "play element" in culture did not focus exclusively on the Renaissance but made it a pivotal moment in the history of the ludic.[13] For Huizinga, the history of civilization was a history of the gradual displacement of play from key aspects of human endeavor, as societies evolved. "The great archetypal activities of human society are all permeated with play from the start," he wrote.[14] The demands of more modern societies seemed to erode this impulse:

> As a civilization becomes more complex, more variegated and more overladen, and as the technique of production and social life itself become more finely organized, the old cultural soil is gradually smothered under a rank layer of ideas, systems of thought and knowledge, doctrines, rules and regulations, moralities and conventions which have all lost touch with play. Civilization, we then say, has grown more serious; it assigns only a secondary function to playing.[15]

Elaborating on Vico's theory of the stages of civilization, from gods to heroes to men, Huizinga saw play as humanity's first impulse, nurtured to its height in the Renaissance: "the whole mental attitude of the Renaissance was one of play."[16]

Huizinga's ludic image of the Renaissance was perfected by the Russian literary scholar Mikhail Bakhtin, who in 1965 composed *Rabelais and His World*.[17] For Bakhtin, exploring the role of laughter in the Renaissance offered an opportunity to comment on the problems of totalitarianism through a historically specific investigation of the relationship of laughter to "official" culture. Laughter represented an unofficial and subversive means of expression, a freedom in the midst of restrictions. In his interpretation of the writings of Rabelais, it became virtually synonymous with the Renaissance: "A boundless world of humorous forms and manifestations opposed the official and serious tone of medieval ecclesiastical and feudal cultures."[18] At the same time, Bakhtin argued that it was a privileged philosophical perspective: "Certain essential aspects of the world are accessible only to laughter."[19]

Like Huizinga, Bakhtin viewed the Renaissance as the pinnacle of human playfulness, though he argued elsewhere that there was also a more universal dialectic between play and seriousness that existed apart from history.[20] The society that gave Rabelais the intellectual resources to write *Gargantua and Pantagruel*, to prefer Democritus's laughter to Heraclitus's tears, became a talisman of the possibilities of freedom in times of adversity. Laughter, Bakhtin remarked, "liberates from the fear that developed in man during thousands of years: fear of the sacred, of prohibitions, of the past, of power."[21] It produced a different form of knowledge that eschewed dogmas in favor of more opaque truths. As Rosalie Colie perceptively observed in her study of Renaissance paradoxes, "the paradoxical form denies commitment."[22] Paradoxes were one of many forms of knowledge used by Rabelais and his contemporaries as a means of critiquing prevailing institutions and behaviors without committing themselves to any new orthodoxy.

Bakhtin offered his own version of the theory of civilization's decline proposed by Huizinga. In his interpretation, laughter ceased to enjoy its universal (one is tempted to say metaphysical) status in the seventeenth century and became more "narrow and specific."[23] Not coincidentally, Michel Foucault's "classical age" marked an important watershed in the history of laughter, producing a political and intellectual aesthetic that no longer favored the jocose, abundant humor of Rabelais but a more restrained style (leading writers such as Jean de La Bruyère to describe the French humanist's books as a "monstrous assemblage").[24] The Cartesian worldview, Bakhtin argued, thrived on singular, specific meanings, suppressing the ambiguities of Renaissance interpretations. It diminished the dialectic of culture in order to affirm the unity of the absolutist state.

Similarly, we might roughly divide the emergence of alternative philosophies of nature into two stages: an earlier phase in which it seemed important and even enjoyable to propose as many different interpretations of nature as possible, and a later phase in which it became crucial to decide which systems and methodologies to prefer, to commit oneself to a particular vision of knowledge. When the Jesuit Antonio Viera participated in a 1674 Roman debate about the preferability of Heraclitus's tears to Democritus's laughter, he summed up the philosophical underpinnings of this new approach with a simple statement: "Laughter is improper to reason."[25] Laughter, with all of its ambivalence and irony about the stage of the world, was indeed human, but it was no longer the hallmark of the thinking individual who came to define the scientist.

Neither Huizinga nor Bakhtin made science a central subject in the study of Renaissance culture. At the same time, they did not ignore the place of science in society. For Huizinga, science was one of those "archetypal activities of human society" that began as a cosmic game and became something quite different in modern times; citing Plato, he located the origins of philosophy in sacred riddles and identified key elements of scientific thought that demonstrated traces of the ludic: "Thus, for instance, the scientist's continued penchant for systems tends in the direction of playing."[26] Theoretical knowledge was, unto itself, learned sport because many of its tools – models, hypotheses, rhetorical arguments – were inherently playful.

In offering this assessment, Huizinga undoubtedly drew inspiration from the Dutch humanist Erasmus's witty portrait of natural philosophers in his *Praise of Folly* (1511). "Theirs is certainly a pleasant form of madness," wrote Erasmus, which sets them building countless universes and measuring the sun, moon, stars and planets by rule of thumb or a bit of string, and producing reasons for thunderbolts, winds, eclipses and other inexplicable phenomena. They never pause for a moment, as if they'd access to the secrets of Nature, architect of the universe, or had come to us straight from the council of the gods. Meanwhile Nature has a fine laugh at them and their conjectures, for their total lack of certainty is obvious enough from the endless contention amongst themselves on every single point.[27]

Natural philosophy, in Erasmus's ironic portrait, was an example of the presence of Folly in many areas of human endeavor. It was a deliberately ludic creation of Nature for the amusement of humanity: "how wisely mother Nature, the parent and creator of the human race, has seen to it that some spice of folly shall be nowhere lacking."[28]

In this particular interpretation, science was the study not simply of nature but of the secrets of an ironic, laughing goddess who revealed herself in full Rabelaisian splendor. She was the Roman naturalist Pliny's *Natura* – a fecund, pagan deity who humorously watched God's supreme creation, mankind, attempt to understand her creative activity in the world. Such imagery, as Horst Bredekamp has shown, had Christian as well as Platonic significance since the act of creation was a divine game played by God himself, "at play everywhere in the world, delighting to be with the sons of men."[29] While God's game belonged primarily to the heavens and in the original Creation, nature's resided on earth in a series of daily creations that occurred in imitation of the original moment in which the universe was made. Science, as Erasmus suggested in his witty satire, was a divinely inspired guessing game in which natural philosophers attempted to infer what neither God nor nature would ever tell them.

Yet other features of science resisted play, and Huizinga saw these characteristics as predominant in modern science. "By way of conclusion," he wrote,

we might say that modern science, so long as it adheres to the strict demands of accuracy and veracity, is far less liable to fall into play as we have defined it, than was the case in earlier times and right up to the Renaissance, when scientific thought and method showed unmistakable play-characteristics.[30]

Certain forms of truth-telling were not ludic – in fact, *could not be* in order to render one singular truth in nature visible. As Huizinga suggested in this casual statement, an afterthought in a long and complex account of the constitutive elements of human society, many of the practices we associate with science since the seventeenth century depended on the suppression of the ludic in order to function. They belonged not to the world of Carnival but to the triumph of Lent.

Bakhtin also noted the peculiar role of science in the Lenten world of the Cold War era, which, in his view, had not quite replaced the dogmatic seriousness of theology: "In the culture of modern times a specific form of seriousness, strict and scientific, has acquired considerable importance. In principle, this form is exempt from all intolerant dogmatism and presents, by its very nature, the form of a problem, is self-critical and uncompleted."[31] Science, when untainted by any allegiances to those older forms of power that Bakhtin indicted, offered the public a reflective seriousness that underscored its ability to be objective and impartial. The post-Cartesian world had produced at least one form of seriousness that Bakhtin did not view solely in light of the struggle between official and unofficial cultures (though he surely placed science in the realm of the official by underscoring its seriousness). Nonetheless, such sensibilities were alien to the Rabelaisian world of Carnival that he described and celebrated, just as they played no innate role in the make-up of *homo ludens*.

In their interpretations of Renaissance society, both Huizinga and Bakhtin presented science as a learned activity dependent on certain cognitive qualities that humanity, particularly in western

Europe, developed and came to value in or around the seventeenth century. These values created a new moral code for intellectual life, celebrating the ideal scholar as a grave, rational, and disciplined individual who viewed himself in the pious mirror of Nature.[32] Science, as Robert Hooke optimistically proclaimed in the introduction to his *Micrographia* (1665), deserved the attention of "the most *serious* part of men."[33] Furthermore, such attitudes were historically contingent and culturally specific. They emerged from a society engaged in a conscious struggle over the place of traditional and pagan values in many aspects of human endeavor, in the wake of the Reformation. Revising the image of knowledge and its makers was not purely an academic exercise but an active struggle to reclaim knowledge for the pious.

The triumph of Lent and the struggle to maintain Carnival, in other words, did not occur only in the Rabelaisian marketplace. As Peter Burke observes, "This cultural reformation was not confined to the popular, for the godly disapproved of all forms of play."[34] Pious elites, both Protestant and Catholic, increasingly viewed Carnival as unchristian; more generally, they imagined Carnival to be a talisman of many other forms of indulgence, excess, and error that led one away from God. Reformers such as the archbishop of Milan, Carlo Borromeo, decried the "grave offenses that are made against God during Carnival," urging parishioners to purify themselves in order to properly celebrate Lent.[35] Given the currently accepted view that natural philosophers in the seventeenth century were even more pious than their predecessors, as the examples of Boyle and Newton amply demonstrate, should it surprise us that many of their criticisms of Renaissance approaches to nature employed the metaphors and images also prevalent in simultaneous attacks on Carnival?[36] Certainly this is an instance in which we can observe many different iterations of a widely debated social and philosophical issue that affected interpretations of nature as much as any other subject.

Playing the Game of Knowledge

By the sixteenth century, play enjoyed enormous status among humanist scholars. Paradoxes, enigmas, encomia, learned witticisms, and other forms of elaborate jokes had become a central part of social and intellectual life, preferred modes of expression for many learned authors. "I'm not sure anything is learned better than when it is learned as a game," observed Erasmus in his *Colloquies*.[37] Games were not merely child's play but an important feature of the Renaissance tradition of *serio ludere* (playing seriously), which viewed play as a divine activity. "Trifling may lead to something more serious," remarked Erasmus in *Praise of Folly*, though he never guaranteed that it would.[38]

Influenced by such writers as Erasmus and Thomas More, whose ludic *Utopia* was eagerly read by scholars such as Johannes Kepler, Renaissance natural philosophers made *serio ludere* one of the dominant images of knowledge. This philosophical choice seemed to transcend any one approach to nature, creating a discursive style that Aristotelians, Neoplatonists, and adherents of various new natural philosophies shared. Different approaches to nature celebrated the ludic in their own peculiar ways. Renaissance naturalists reread the book of nature in search of evidence of nature's jokes, compiling long lists of phenomena, from lodestones to fossils to flowers, imprinted with *lusus naturae*.[39] Even as late as the 1690s, the German encyclopedist Johann Zahn celebrated asbestos's inflammability as "among the innate miracles of Nature, in which divine Wisdom plays."[40] There seemed to be no end to the amusement and pleasure that nature, a corpulent, carnivalesque deity, could offer.

Mathematicians examined the classic problems of their discipline for instances of geometric, cabalistic, and numerological play, while astronomers debated whether play extended as far as the heavens themselves, alternately including and excluding such phenomena as comets in the category of *lusus naturae*. So great was the desire to play that one could not achieve wisdom without participating in the game of knowledge. "I have here before my eyes the infinity of mysteries," wrote John Dee in his *Monas hieroglyphica* (1564), "but I wanted to interrupt the speculation by this sport."[41] Twenty years later, the Italian philosopher and heretic Giordano Bruno invited readers of his *Ash Wednesday Supper* (1584) to "a banquet . . . so trifling and serious" where they might discuss Copernicus's theories of the heavens; surely it is no coincidence that the first public statement advocating Copernicus's heliocentrism appeared in the form of a ludic dialogue, guaranteed (according to Bruno) to "make monkeys split their sides with laughter."[42] Bruno's work lay at the paradoxical beginnings of the new science, rather than at its more sober conclusion. "Natural law is ribaldry," he proclaimed in his *Expulsion of the Triumphant Beast* (1584), a mythological dialogue of the gods in which he confessed to eating meat during Lent.[43] Within a decade such statements led him into the hands of the Inquisition, who found nothing funny about his ironic approach to knowledge and faith, condemning him to be burned as a heretic in 1600.

No natural philosopher played more elegantly or more profoundly than the German mathematician Johannes Kepler. While Bruno declared himself a reincarnation of Momus, the god of laughter, Kepler saw himself as destined for a seriocomic existence. At age twenty-six, in 1597, he wrote that his horoscope had predetermined this Erasmian fate: "In this man there are two opposite tendencies: always to regret any wasted time, and always to waste it willingly. For Mercury makes one inclined to amusements, games and other light pleasures."[44] Kepler subsequently became a master of all the various forms of literary and philosophical expression that sated his ludic impulses. He characterized himself as someone "fond of riddles and subtle witticisms" who "made much play with allegories which he worked out to the most minute detail, dragging in farfetched comparisons."[45] These impulses produced entertaining pamphlets such as *The Six-Cornered Snowflake* (1611) and *Somnium* (1634), which celebrated the trivial, the fantastic, and the imaginary in nature through Kepler's talent to "reason jocularly."[46]

Yet play was not simply a leisurely pastime and entertainment for the imperial courtiers with whom Kepler associated in Prague. For Kepler, as for Erasmus, it revealed the pattern of the universe, conveyed by God through the artistry of nature. Unlike Bruno, who saw mathematics as a limited approach to the truth, scoffing that "it is one thing to play with geometry, and quite another to verify things with nature,"[47] Kepler felt that God's primary identity was that of a geometer; accordingly, one could only understand his game through numbers. In the *Cosmic Mystery* (1596), Kepler used the ludic to discern the inscription of the Trinity in the heavens, searching for its physical and mathematical traces "as if at a game" (*quasi lusu*); drawing on his reading of such works as J. C. Scaliger's *Exoteric Exercitations*, an erudite attack on the work of the sixteenth-century physician Girolamo Cardano filled with natural paradoxes, Kepler presented the order of the universe as a divine game, a luxurious dessert course for princes whose noble minds needed such rich food in order to be sated.[48] The culmination of such play was his nesting of the planets within the five Pythagorean solids, which he described as "an astrological game" (*lusus astrologicus*).[49] How the heavens went – one of the most serious subjects of the seventeenth century – occurred to Kepler in a moment of ludic ecstasy.

Kepler's use of the ludic in the development of his astronomy and natural philosophy attracted the attention of other philosophers. When Philipp Feselius attacked judicial astrology as yet another example of the "imagined signatures of things," a "jolly fantasy of idle heads,"[50] Kepler responded with a reasoned defense of this form of knowledge that expanded on the theories of play put forth in his *Cosmic Mystery*. In *Tertius interveniens* (1610), he argued that the Paracelsian doctrine of signatures was both an occupation for God to keep him from idleness after the initial Creation, and a means of signifying his continued presence in and supervision of the world. Play was the ultimate form of mimesis, a divine art passed down from God to nature to humanity: "Just as God the creator has played, so he has taught Nature, his image, to play, and indeed to play the same game that he has played before her."[51] Understanding and participating in the cosmic game was a means of approaching the deity, sharing in his wisdom.

While defining play as a form of truth, Kepler also criticized other natural philosophers who played indiscriminately. In a famous debate with the English physician and occultist Robert Fludd in 1619–1622, he chastised Fludd for subscribing to a hieroglyphic and hermetic approach to nature that did not conform to any physical reality.[52] Instead, Kepler's play was a game with evidence. In the fourth book of his *Epitome of Copernican Astronomy* (1618–1621) he critiqued "the game of inventing doctrines that are contrary to true."[53] The source of truth lay in the interaction between geometric knowledge and physical causes. "Everything is corrected according to the laws of nature," he asserted in *The Harmonies of the World* (1619).[54] Nature answered two truths, one divine and the other human. "Naturally, I too play with symbols, and I have planned to write a little work, *Geometrical Cabbala*, which would treat the ideas of natural things in geometry," Kepler confessed: "But I play in such a way that I do not forget that I am playing. For we can prove nothing by symbols, we can discover no secret in natural philosophy by geometric symbols, unless they agree with established facts."[55]

Kepler's seriocomic vision of the world was not the unbridled passion of Carnival but a more tempered engagement with ludic creation that kept truth always in sight. Like the German chemist and humanist schoolmaster Andreas Libavius who remarked, in the midst of his debate with the Paracelsian Oswald Croll in 1615, "but perhaps we are only playing at games,"[56] Kepler understood that the human mind could invent forms of signification that answered to no higher judge of truth. While able to entertain Rudolphine courtiers with accounts of how Nothing (a snowflake) evidenced "the Creator's design" through its geometric form, he also allowed that some subjects were beyond the realm of play.[57] In 1598 he confided to a correspondent, "I am earnest about Faith and I do not play with it."[58] Theology delimited a realm of absolute seriousness for Kepler; thus his inscription of the Trinity was no human game but divine revelation. In affirming the truth of religion and the necessity of treating it with a gravity unnecessary in other domains of knowledge, he hoped to avoid the mistakes of More and Erasmus, who had been censured for their public celebration of folly and free will, and – let us imagine – Bruno, who would die for it two years later.[59] As Kepler – a Lutheran with Calvinist leanings in the Catholic regions of the Holy Roman Empire – understood well, playing seriously was not without its consequences.

Yet Kepler could not feel entirely safe even by restricting his play to nature. By the early decades of the seventeenth century the theological debate over free will that had been one of the touchstones of the early Reformation extended from humanity's relationship to God to address the place of nature in the cosmos. As nature became an important location for the resolution of key theological debates, it, too, was reshaped by the seriousness of faith. Writing in the aftermath of the religious turmoil in England, Francis Bacon proclaimed an absolute separation of the ludic from theology, recording his advice in Latin and English so that no reader might miss its import: "*Non est major confusio, quam serii et joci; There is no greater confusion than the confounding of jest and earnest.*"[60] The contrast with a figure such as Bruno, who described his philosophy as "mixing up all kinds of discourse, grave and serious, moral and natural, ignoble and noble, philosophic and comic," could not have been more extreme.[61] In the *Description of the Intellectual*

Globe, Bacon extended this dictum to natural philosophy, explicitly rejecting the image of knowledge created by Erasmus and celebrated by such followers of the Erasmian tradition as Kepler: "For an apotheosis of Folly . . . is a thing not to be endured."[62] The Carnival of nature was over, and Lent was just around the corner.

The Seriocomic Origins of Modern Science

In subsequent decades Bacon's approach to natural philosophy gained wider currency. Toppling those Carnival deities, Nature and Folly, became an important symbol of the ascendancy of new experimental and mathematical philosophies, both of which embraced theological and philosophical seriousness (combining strictures about faith with Stoic admonitions about the disciplined mind). Descartes went so far as to imagine knowledge as a reluctant participant in a Carnival revel that he needed to enter in order to remove it from a licentious and delusory world: "The sciences are at present masked," he remarked in his *Preambula* (1619), "but if their masks were taken off, they would be revealed in all their beauty."[63] Like Bacon, he encouraged other philosophers to respond to the idolatry of nature with iconoclasm, stripping false ornaments away from God's handiwork.

By the 1660s the triumph of Lent had acquired some powerful and vocal advocates among the members of the early Royal Society. Readers of Bacon and Descartes, the early Royal Society members attempted to purge their interpretations of nature of any traces of the ludic, which they associated with paganism, atheism, and an excessive love of rhetoric. In this new vision, Renaissance interpretations of nature appeared increasingly like remnants of those jocose pagan gods with whom Bruno had laughed in the midst of his Carnival revel. "For the works of God are not like the Tricks of Iuglers or the Pageants that entertain Princes," wrote Robert Boyle in *Some Considerations Touching the Usefulnesse of Natural Philosophy* (1663).[64] That same year, as Charles II prepared to make an official visit to the Royal Society, Christopher Wren wrote anxiously to the current president, William Brouncker, about the sort of demonstrations appropriate for a king. Charles II might not enjoy an arid presentation of experimental philosophy, but he would be equally unimpressed with "knacks only, and things to raise wonder, such as Kircher, Schottus, and even jugglers abound with," which would "scarce become the gravity of the occasion."[65] Contrasting the experimental style of the Royal Society to that of the Jesuits, who drew inspiration from the natural magic tradition, Boyle and Wren removed natural philosophy from the marketplace to place it in the true temple of God.

Boyle's views on the seriousness of nature owed a great deal to his reading and writing of religious and ethical treatises in his youth. In *The Aretology*, written around 1645, he argued for a new kind of seriousness that was not the somber despair of the melancholic, but a gravity that came from seriousness of purpose: "Men oftentimes in the Vertuus mistake seriousness, and employedness of Mind for Melancholy humors, as if the h[e]art could not be merry within without hanging out the flag of lafter at the Mouth"; no Rabelaisian laugher, Boyle described the things "that tickle the Spleene of deluded mortals, and begets their mirth" as "worthless trifles."[66] He imagined that pursuing geometry, as Descartes advocated, might discipline the mind adequately so that it would no longer be drawn to wantonly pleasurable subjects. Science was a chaste passion removed from the world of Carnival, its antidote rather than its complement.

Removing the ludic from natural philosophy was no easy task. Centuries of assumptions about nature needed to be revised, from the smallest phenomenon to the largest theoretical structure, and reason needed to supplant the imagination. The early Royal Society made this one of its primary goals: "For the main intendment of this *Society* is to erect a well-grounded *Natural History* which takes of the *heats of wanton Phantasie*, hinders its *extravagant excursions*, and ties it down to *sober Realities*," wrote Joseph Glanvill in his 1668 defense of the Royal Society.[67] Indeed, the definition of nature itself underwent significant changes. Nature's place as a "semi-Deity" in philosophical systems such as the ones expounded by Bruno, Fludd, and Kepler diminished the glory of God; it reduced him, Boyle felt, "to Play *After-Games*."[68] For if God had given the principal game to nature, what really was left for him to do?

Gradually the creative impulses ascribed to nature were either revealed to be delusions of the human intellect playing with nature, or subsumed within nature's laws. This, at least, was what many experimental philosophers hoped would happen, and they aggressively argued the principle of order in many of their publications. Hooke, for example, placed Kepler's snowflake under the microscope in order to reveal "the most simple and plain operation of Nature."[69] We might contrast this account with Kepler's explanation, a half-century earlier: "formative reason does not only act for a purpose," he affirmed, "but also to adorn. It does not strive to fashion only natural bodies, but is in the habit of playing with the passing moment . . . I transpose the meaning of all such from playfulness (in that we say Nature *plays*) to this serious intention."[70] While Kepler found the snowflake sublime, Hooke insisted that it was ordinary.

During the next two decades, Hooke systematically reinterpreted an array of extraordinary phenomena, insisting that there was no play in any of these acts of nature. Three years after the publication of his views on snowflakes, he lectured the members of the Royal Society on the causes of earthquakes. This topic provided an opportunity to return to the problem of *lusus naturae*, picking up where Bacon had left off. In his writings, Bacon had explicitly condemned this category of nature – not as a site of privileged insight, as Kepler argued, but as an example of the problem with Renaissance intepretations of nature. Moralizing about this vision of nature, he declared *lusus naturae* "sports and wanton freaks of nature," lascivious products of nature's courtesanry.[71] These were the baubles with which a false goddess enticed undisciplined philosophers into her midst. They yielded great pleasure but no knowledge. Hooke argued that the idea of nature's play was "contrary to her general Method of acting in all other Bodies"; he could not envision nature "idely mocking herself, which seems contrary to her Gravity."[72] Twenty years later, as Hooke and other natural philosophers bound tricky phenomena such as comets to the new laws of nature, he still was concerned enough about ludic interpretations of nature to exhort his audience not to subscribe to a theory that promoted the "needless formation of useless Beings."[73] Nature had become a Lenten tool of a sober deity who preferred to work rather than play.

Even proponents of the theory of nature's "plastic virtue," such as the Cambridge Neoplatonists Henry More and Ralph Cudworth (and later Leibniz), carefully presented the role of nature in the formation of beings as an act of obedience to God rather than a spontaneous expression of free will. Since God had many tasks to supervise, wrote Cudworth in *The True Intellectual System of the Universe* (1678), he allowed "stupid, unconscious nature" to execute his most simple commands, and this drudging servant enjoyed a simple, vegetative existence that shared nothing with higher forms of life; chastising those philosophers who exalted nature's creativity, Cudworth presented them as sportive miscreants who played a Carnival game: "But this hath always been the sottish humor and guise of the atheists, to invert the order of the universe and hange the picture of the world as of a man with his heels upwards."[74] The ludic was indeed a "world turned upside down," where high traded its place with low. Cudworth's task was to reassert the natural order of things.

The efforts of a handful of English natural philosophers to suppress the ludic in science joined forces with attempts by Continental savants to create new forms of natural philosophy that, regardless of their many specific differences, were united in their desire not to play with nature. By the 1690s, Leibniz condemned *lusus naturae* as "a term void of meaning"; he was supported by many Italian naturalists, from Agostino Scilla to Antonio Vallisneri, who also expressed distaste at this term.[75] Yet no official pronouncement on the need to separate play from science appeared until 1720, when Bernard le Bovier de Fontenelle finally declared a moratorium on jokes at the Paris Academy of Sciences, in his capacity as editor of the annual *Histories of the Royal Academy of Sciences*. Upon receipt of a foetus of a monstrous lamb, he wrote: "Ordinarily one considers monsters as jokes of nature but the *philosophes* are very persuaded that nature never jokes, that she always follows inviolably the same rules, and that all her works are, so to speak, equally serious."[76] Playing with nature was fun, but, as Bacon had long ago insisted, it was "of no serious use towards science."[77]

The decision of the secretary of one of the leading scientific societies to refuse ludic accounts of nature, relegating them to more popular publications such as his well-known *Conversations on the Plurality of Worlds* (1686), brought the debate about the ludic to a temporary close. Increasingly the use of the ludic demarcated the divide between learned and popular discussions of science. Play was an attractive means of making science enjoyable for women, children, and the unlettered masses of humanity, but it demeaned the public pursuit of knowledge by scholars. Women, advised the great French educator François Fénelon, were bored by "whatever is grave and serious."[78] Such presuppositions indicate the many ways in which attitudes toward play and seriousness formed the nascent culture of science in early modern Europe.

As I have suggested in this essay, natural philosophers did not intend to make science serious when they accelerated investigations of nature in the sixteenth and seventeenth centuries. This result was an interesting by-product of the struggle to interpret nature and to find a meaningful place for scientific activities in early modern and modern societies. Kepler was not the only philosopher to stand at the crossroads between playful and serious interpretations of nature: he was joined there by one of his most renowned correspondents, the Italian mathematician Galileo. Galileo's outlook on the place of natural philosophy in his society can aptly be characterized as seriocomic. Writing to Kepler in August 1610, with the announcement of his discovery of the four moons of Jupiter on everyone's lips, he queried: "What is to be done now? Shall we follow Democritus or Heraclitus?"[79] Galileo's inability to answer this question decisively proved disastrous for his relations with the Catholic Church, which increasingly, as the activities of reforming bishops to suppress Carnival as a pagan ritual demonstrate, exhibited little tolerance for laughter – a pagan, not a Christian, virtue. Yet at times Galileo seemed to understand the shifting climate of the world that he and his contemporaries inhabited. In his *Dialogue Concerning the New Star* (1605), published under the pseudonym of Cecco di Ronchitti, he imagined his Aristotelian opponents selling their books, filled with foolish systems, in the midst of Carnival; in response, he penned the following warning: "it's nearly Lent."[80]

NOTES

1 For an introduction of the different histories of the Scientific Revolution, see H. Floris Cohen, *The Scientific Revolution: A Historiographic Inquiry* (Chicago: University of Chicago Press, 1994); Andrew Cunningham and Perry Williams, "De-Centring the 'Big Picture': *The Origins of Modern Science* and the Modern Origins of Science," *British Journal for the History of Science* 26 (1993): 407–32; David C. Lindberg and Robert S. Westman, eds., *Reappraisals of the Scientific Revolution* (Cambridge: Cambridge University Press, 1990); Roy Porter, "The Scientific Revolution: A Spoke in the Wheel?"

in *Revolution in History*, ed. Roy Porter and Mikulás Teich (Cambridge: Cambridge University Press, 1986), pp. 290–316; and Steven Shapin, *The Scientific Revolution* (Chicago: University of Chicago Press, 1996).

2 Hayden White, *The Content of the Form: Narrative Discourse and Historical Representation* (Baltimore: Johns Hopkins University Press, 1987), p. 44. In invoking this concept, I am especially interested in the choices made by early modern natural philosophers in describing new ways of seeing nature as well as knowledge.

3 See Nicholas Jardine, *The Birth of the History and Philosophy of Science: Kepler's "A Defense of Tycho Against Ursus" with Essays on Its Provenance and Significance* (Cambridge: Cambridge University Press, 1984); and Donald R. Kelley, ed., *History and the Disciplines: The Reclassification of Knowledge in Early Modern Europe* (Rochester, NY: University of Rochester Press, 1997).

4 This particular issue has been an underlying premise of much work in the cultural history of science: see esp. Joseph Rouse, "What Are Cultural Studies of Scientific Knowledge?" *Configurations* 1 (1993): 1–22; and Peter Dear, "Cultural History of Science: An Overview with Reflections," *Science, Technology, and Human Values* 20 (1995): 150–70. For a broader view of cultural methodologies, see Roger Chartier, *Cultural History: Between Practices and Representations*, trans. Lydia G. Cochrane (Ithaca, NY: Cornell University Press, 1988); and Lynn Hunt, ed., *The New Cultural History* (Berkeley: University of California Press, 1989).

5 John Schuster, "The Scientific Revolution," in *Companion to the History of Modern Science*, ed. R. C. Olby, G. N. Cantor, J. R. R. Christie, and M. J. S. Hodge (London: Routledge, 1990), pp. 224–5. James Bono, *The World of God and the Languages of Man* (Madison: University of Wisconsin Press, 1995), is one of the few examples of recent scholarship to take up this call, emphasizing semiotic approaches to scientific texts.

6 Historians of science have already made good use of the work of sociologists such as Max Weber and Norbert Elias in order to explore such themes as the "Protestant ethic" and the "civilizing process." This essay instead focuses on ways of understanding early modern society that derive more from literary and cultural analysis.

7 Hans Blumenburg, *The Legitimacy of the Modern Age*, trans. Robert M. Wallace (Cambridge, Mass.: MIT Press, 1983), p. 230.

8 Caroline Walker Bynum, "In Praise of Fragments: History in the Comic Mode," in idem, *Fragmentation and Redemption: Essays on Gender and the Human Body in Medieval Religion* (New York: Zone Books, 1991), p. 25.

9 Claude Gaighebet, "Le combat de Carnaval et de Carême de P. Bruegel (1559)," *Annales ESC* 27 (1972): 313–45.

10 Peter Burke, *Popular Culture in Early Modern Europe* (New York: Harper Torchbook, 1978). See also Natalie Zemon Davis, "The Reasons of Misrule," in idem, *Society and Culture in Early Modern France* (Stanford: Stanford University Press, 1975), pp. 97–123; Robert Scribner, "Reformation, Carnival, and the World Turned Upside Down," *Social History* 3 (1978): 234–64; and Martine Grinberg and Sam Kinser, "Les combats de Carnaval et de Carême: Trajets d'une métaphore," *Annales ESC* 38 (1983): 65–98.

11 Fernand Hallyn, *The Poetic Structure of the World: Copernicus and Kepler*, trans. Donald M. Leslie (New York: Zone Books, 1990), p. 35. While historians of science have not explored the role of the ludic in science, art historians and literary critics have remarked on the potential of this subject: see esp. Rosalie Colie, *Paradoxia Epidemica: Renaissance Traditions of Paradox* (Princeton: Princeton University Press, 1966); Ernest B. Gilman, *The Curious Perspective: Literary and Pictorial Wit in the Seventeenth Century* (New Haven, Conn.: Yale University Press, 1978); and Barbara Stafford, *Artful Science: Enlightenment Entertainment and the Eclipse of Visual Education* (Cambridge, Mass.: MIT Press, 1994).

12 *Discorso contro il Carnevale* (anonymous), in Ferdinando Taviani, *La Commedia dell'Arte e la società barocca* (Rome: Bulzoni, 1969), p. 73. This may be the treatise attributed to Giovan Antonio Parlasca in 1608.

13 We should not have expected otherwise from Johan Huizinga, the author of *The Autumn of the Middle Ages*, trans. Rodney J. Payton and Ulrich Mammitzsch (Chicago: University of Chicago Press, 1996), and of *Erasmus* (New York: Scribner, 1924). On Huizinga, see W. R. H. Koops, E. H. Kossman, and Gees van der Platt, eds., *Johan Huizinga, 1872–1972* (The Hague: Nijhoff, 1973); and Anton van der Lem, *Johan Huizinga: Leven en werk in beelden en documenten* (Amsterdam: Werelbibliotheek, 1993).

14 Johan Huizinga, *Homo ludens: A Study of the Play-Element in Culture* (1950; Boston: Beacon Press, 1955). p. 4.

15 Ibid., p. 75. See also pp. 119, 134.

16 Ibid., p. 180.

17 On Bakhtin, see Katarina Clark and Michael Holquist, *Mikhail Bakhtin* (Cambridge: Mass.: Belknap, 1984); Michael Holquist, *Dialogism: Bakhtin and His World* (London: Routledge, 1990); Ken Hirschkop and David Shepherd, eds., *Bakhtin and Cultural Theory* (Manchester: Manchester University Press, 1989); and Amy Mandelker, ed., *Bakhtin in Contexts: Across the Disciplines* (Evanston, Ill.: Northwestern University Press, 1995). The only study that focuses on Bakhtin's approach to the Renaissance is Richard M. Berrong, *Rabelais and Bakhtin: Popular Culture in Gargantua and Pantagruel* (Lincoln: University of Nebraska Press, 1986).

18 Mikhail Bakhtin, *Rabelais and His World*, trans. Hélène Iswolsky (1968; Bloomington: Indiana University Press, 1984), p. 4.

19 Ibid., p. 66. As these quotes indicate, Bakhtin was more explicitly concerned about the relations between laughter and power than was Huizinga.

20 Mikhail Bakhtin, *The Dialogic Imagination: Four Essays*, ed. Michael Holquist, trans. Caryl Emerson and Michael Holquist (Austin: University of Texas Press, 1981).

21 Bakhtin, *Rabelais* (above, n. 18), p. 94.

22 Colie, *Paradoxia Epidemica* (above, n. 11), p. 38.

23 Bakhtin, *Rabelais* (above, n. 18), p. 67.

24 Ibid., p. 109. See also p. 101, where Bakhtin equates classical culture with the suppression of the grotesque. Indeed, one can draw some intriguing conclusions when reading Michel Foucault's *The Order of Things: An Archeology of the Human Sciences* (New York: Random House, 1970) in conjunction with Bakhtin's work. Certainly the doctrine of signatures celebrated by Foucault as the paradigmatic expression of Renaissance modes of thought resonates with the grotesque of Rabelais: both celebrate an excessive, exaggerated form of materiality.

25 Antonio Viera, *Plaidoyer en faveur des larmes d'Héraclite*, as quoted by Jean Delumeau, "The Rejection of Amusement," in idem, *Sin and Fear: The Emergence of a Western Guilt Culture, 13th–18th Centuries*, trans. Eric Nicholson (New York: St. Martin's Press, 1990), p. 456.

26 Huizinga, *Homo ludens* (above, n. 14), p. 203.

27 Desiderius Erasmus, *Praise of Folly*, trans. Betty Radice (London: Penguin, 1971), p. 151.

28 Ibid., p. 87.

29 Prov. 8: 30–1; the original in the Latin Vulgate reads: "Cum eo eram, cuncta componens. / Et delectabar per singolos dies, / Ludens coram eo omni tempore, Ludens in orbe; / Et deliciae meae esse cum filiis hominum." See Horst Bredekamp, "The Playfulness of Natural History," in idem, *The Lure of Antiquity and the Cult of the Machine*, trans. Allison Brown (Princeton: Markus Weiner, 1995), pp. 63–80; quote on p. 67. See also Paula Findlen, "Jokes of Nature and Jokes of Knowledge: The Playfulness of Scientific Discourse in Early Modern Europe," *Renaissance Quarterly* 43 (1990): 292–331. For a general discussion of changing views of nature, see R. G. Collingwood, *The Idea of Nature* (Oxford: Clarendon, 1945).

30 Huizinga, *Homo ludens* (above, n. 14), p. 203.

31 Bakhtin, *Rabelais* (above, n. 18), p. 122.

32 This subject has been most recently discussed in Steven Shapin, *A Social History of Truth: Civility and Science in Seventeenth-Century England* (Chicago: University of Chicago Press, 1994), though Shapin does not explicitly emphasize the importance of *gravitas* to Boyle's philosophical persona. Earlier works have also identified these traits as essential features of seventeenth-century society, but their attempts to

tie them too closely to any one discursive formulation limit them. See Max Weber, *The Protestant Ethic and the Spirit of Capitalism*, trans. Talcott Parsons (London: Allen and Unwin, 1930); Albert O. Hirschman, *The Passions and the Interests: Political Arguments for Capitalism Before Its Triumph* (Princeton: Princeton University Press, 1977); and Robert Merton, *Science, Technology, and Society in Seventeenth-Century England* (1938; New York: Harper and Row, 1970). For an interesting new discussion of this subject, see Michael Heyd, "Be Sober and Reasonable": *The Critique of Enthusiasm in the Seventeenth and Early Eighteenth Centuries* (Leiden: Brill, 1995).

33 Robert Hooke, *Micrographia* (London, 1665), pref. Such language was lifted almost directly from many passages in Francis Bacon where he alluded to the sobriety and severity of the new experimental philosophy; see Paula Findlen, "Francis Bacon and the Reform of Natural History in the Seventeenth Century," in Kelley, *History and the Disciplines* (above, n. 3), pp. 239–60. Boyle also described experimenters as "sober and modest men": see Steven Shapin and Simon Schaffer, *Leviathan and the Air-Pump: Hobbes, Boyle, and the Experimental Life* (Princeton: Princeton University Press, 1985), p. 65.

34 Burke, *Popular Culture* (above, n. 10). p. 208.

35 Carlo Borromeo, *Lettera a Mons. Giambattista Castagna* (1571), in Taviani, *Commedia dell'Arte* (above, n. 12), p. 18.

36 See Amos Funkenstein, *Theology and the Scientific Imagination from the Middle Ages to the Seventeenth Century* (Princeton: Princeton University Press, 1986); and David C. Lindberg and Ronald L. Numbers, eds., *God and Nature: Historical Essays on the Encounter between Christianity and Science* (Berkeley: University of California Press, 1986), esp. pp. 136–237.

37 Erasmus, *Colloquies*, in Walter Gordon, *Humanist Play and Belief: The Seriocomic Art of Desiderius Erasmus* (Toronto: University of Toronto Press, 1990), p. 94.

38 Erasmus, *Praise of Folly* (above, n. 27), p. 59.

39 I have discussed this in greater detail in Findlen, "Jokes of Nature" (above, n. 29).

40 Johann Zahn, *Specula physico-mathematico-historica notabilium ac mirabilium sciendorum* (Nuremberg, 1696), vol. 2, p. 92.

41 C. H. Josten, "A Translation of John Dee's 'Monas Hieroglyphica' (Antwerp, 1564), with an Introduction and Annotations," *Ambix* 12 (1964): 192. The sport in question regards the multiplicity of shapes formed by the letter *B*.

42 Giordano Bruno, *The Ash Wednesday Supper*, ed. and trans. Edward A. Gosselin and Lawrence S. Lerner (Hamden, Conn.: Archon Books, 1977), pp. 67–8. On the seriocomic aspects of Bruno's philosophy, see Nuccio Ordine, *Giordano Bruno and the Philosophy of the Ass*, trans. Henryk Baranski with Arielle Saiber (New Haven, Conn.: Yale University Press, 1996).

43 Giordano Bruno, *Expulsion of the Triumphant Beast*, trans. Arthur D. Imerti (New Brunswick, N.J.: Rutgers University Press, 1964), pp. 54 (quote), 59 (on Lent).

44 Johannes Kepler, *Opera omnia* (Frankfurt and Erlangen, 1858–71), vol. 5, p. 477, as translated in Arthur Koestler, *The Watershed* (Garden City, NY: Anchor Books, 1960), p. 31.

45 Ibid., p. 35.

46 *Kepler's Somnium*, ed. and trans. Edward Rosen (Madison: University of Wisconsin Press, 1967), p. 65n60.

47 Bruno, *Ash Wednesday Supper* (above, n. 42), p. 150; I have modified the translation.

48 Johannes Kepler, *Mysterium cosmographicum (The Secret of the Universe)*, trans. A. M. Ducan, ed. E. J. Aiton (New York: Abaris Books, 1981), p. 63. Elsewhere Kepler wrote: "The same things do not suit the people and the princes, and these heavenly matters are not nourishment for everyone indiscriminately, but just for a noble mind. . . . Princes usually have something very expensive kept for the dessert course, which they use only if they are satiated, to relieve the monotony" (ibid., p. 55).

49 Ibid., p. 119. For more on this form of mathematical and cosmological play, see S. K. Heninger, *Touches of Sweet Harmony: Pythagorean Cosmology and Renaissance Poetics* (San Marino, Calif.: Huntington Library, 1974).

50 Kepler quotes from Philipp Feselius's *Discurs von der Astrologia iudiciaria* in Johannes Kepler, *Tertius interveniens*, in his *Gesammelte Werke* (Munich: C. H. Beck'sche Verlagsbuchhandlung, 1940), vol. 4.

51 Kepler, ibid., p. 246, as translated by D. P. Walker, "Kepler's Celestial Music," in idem, *Studies in Musical Science in the Late Renaissance*, Studies of the Warburg Institute, 37 (London: Warburg Institute, 1978), p. 56. On the doctrine of signatures, see Massimo Luigi Bianchi, *Signature rerum: Segni, magia e conoscenza da Paracelso a Leibniz* (Rome: Edizioni dell'Ateneo, 1987); and Paula Findlen, "Empty Signs? Reading the Book of Nature in Renaissance Science," *Studies in the History and Philosophy of Science* 21 (1990): 511–18.

52 In this respect, we should see Fludd as another proponent of the "emblematic worldview" described by William Ashworth, and Kepler as a self-critical participant who had begun to make categorical distinctions between culturally generated symbols and symbols that conform to evidence in nature. See William Ashworth, "Natural History and the Emblematic World View," in Lindberg and Westman, *Reappraisals of the Scientific Revolution* (above, n. 1), pp. 303–32.

53 Johannes Kepler, *Epitome of Copernican Astronomy and Harmonies of the World*, trans. Charles Glenn Wallis (Amherst, NY: Prometheus Books, 1995), p. 10 (*Gesammelte Werke*, vol. 7, p. 254).

54 Johannes Kepler, *Harmonice mundi*, in *Gesammelte Werke*, vol. 6, p. 374.

55 Kepler, *Gesammelte Werke*, vol. 16, p. 158, cited in Hallyn, *Poetic Structures* (above, n. 11), p. 167. This exchange has been the subject of many interesting analyses: see esp. Robert Westman, "Nature, Art, and Psyche: Jung, Pauli, and the Kepler-Fludd Polemic," in *Occult and Scientific Mentalities in the Renaissance*, ed., Brian Vickers (Cambridge: Cambridge University Press, 1984), pp. 179–86; and Brian Copenhaver, "Natural Magic, Hermeticism, and Occultism in Early Modern. Science," in Lindberg and Westman, *Reappraisals of the Scientific Revolution* (above, n. 1), pp. 282–6. Both interpretations highlight the different uses of languages and images by Kepler and Fludd, but I instead would like to underscore the use of such tools in a *shared* endeavor: cosmic play.

56 Andreas Libavius, *Examen philosophiae novae* (1615), cited in Owen Hannaway, *The Chemists and the World: The Didactic Origins of Chemistry* (Baltimore: Johns Hopkins University Press, 1975), p. 106.

57 Johannes Kepler, *The Six-Cornered Snowflake*, ed. and trans. Colin Hardie (Oxford: Clarendon Press, 1966), p. 33.

58 Kepler, *Gesammelte Werke*, vol. 13, p. 264, cited in Koestler, *Watershed* (above, n. 44), p. 82.

59 On December 4, 1623, in the midst of composing his *Somnium*, Kepler wrote to Matthias Bernegger: "More in his *Utopia* and Erasmus in his *Praise of Folly* ran into trouble and had to defend themselves. Therefore let us leave the vicissitudes of politics alone and let us remain in the pleasant, fresh green fields of philosophy" (Carola Baumgardt, *Johannes Kepler: Life and Letters* [New York: Philosophical Library, 1951], p. 156). For a fascinating discussion of the theological ramifications of *serio ludere* in the debates about free will, see Marjorie O'Rourke Boyle, *Rhetoric and Reform: Erasmus' Civil Dispute with Luther* (Cambridge, Mass.: Harvard University Press, 1983).

60 Francis Bacon, "An Advertisement Touching the Controversies of the Church of England" (1589), in *The Works of Francis Bacon*, ed. James Spedding, Robert Leslie Ellis, and Douglas Denon Heath (London: Longmans, 1857–74), vol. 8, p. 77. Italics in original.

61 Giordano Bruno, *Cause, Principle, and Unity*, trans. Jack Lindsay (New York: International Publishers, 1962), p. 60.

62 Francis Bacon, *Descriptio globi intellectualis*, in *Works*, vol. 5, pp. 523–4.

63 René Descartes, *Preambula*, in *The Philosophical Writings of René Descartes* (Cambridge: Cambridge University Press, 1985), vol. 1, p. 3. Such imagery evokes the ideal of a "naked Christ" celebrated, for example, by Puritans.

64 Robert Boyle, *Some Considerations Touching the Usefulness of Natural Philosophy*, 2nd ed. (London, 1664), vol. 1, p. 51. For a classic study of paganism in Renaissance thought, see Jean Seznec, *The Survival of the Pagan Gods: The Mythological Tradition and Its Place in Renaissance Humanism and Art*, trans. Barbara F. Sessions (New York: Harper Torchbooks, 1953).

65 Christopher Wren to William Brouncker, 30 July/9 August 1663 in Thomas Birch, *A History of the Royal Society*, vol. 1, p. 288, cited in Shapin and Schaffer, *Leviathan and the Air-Pump* (above, n. 33), p. 31.

66 John T. Harwood, ed., *The Early Essays and Ethics of Robert Boyle* (Carbondale: Southern Illinois University Press, 1991), pp. 68–9.

67 Joseph Glanvill, *Plus Ultra, or the Progress and Advance of Knowledge Since the Days of Aristotle*, ed. Jackson I. Cope (1668; Gainesville, Fla.: Scholars' Fascimiles and Reprints, 1958), pp. 89–90 (italics in original).

68 Boyle, *A Free Enquiry Into the Vulgarly Receiv'd Notion of Nature* (London, 1686), pp. 15, 10 (italics in original). See Michael Hunter and Edward B. Davis, "The Making of Robert Boyle's *Free Enquiry into the Vulgarly Receiv'd Notion of Nature* (1686)," *Early Science and Medicine* 1 (1996): 245–271. For an excellent discussion of a parallel transformation in attitudes toward wonder, see Lorraine J. Daston and Katharine Park, *Wonders and the Order of Nature, 1150–1750* (New York: Zone Books, 1998).

69 Hooke, *Micrographia* (above, n. 33), p. 88.

70 Kepler, *Six-Cornered Snowflake* (above, n. 57), pp. 33. For an interesting discussion of Hooke's use of the microscope to redeem nature and its interpreters, see Catherine Wilson, "Visual Surface and Visual Symbol: The Microscope and the Occult in Early Modern Science," *Journal of the History of Ideas* 49 (1988): 85–108.

71 Bacon, *Parasceve*, in *Works*, vol. 4, p. 255.

72 Hooke, "A Discourse of Earthquakes" (1668), in *The Posthumous Works of Robert Hooke* (London, 1705), pp. 289, 318.

73 Hooke, "A Lecture Read Feb. 15 1687/8," in ibid., p. 403.

74 Ralph Cudworth, "On Plastic Nature," in *The Cambridge Platonists*, ed. Gerald R. Craig (Oxford: Oxford University Press, 1968), p. 252.

75 Leibniz, *Protogaea* (1691/92, pub. in 1749), in Paolo Rossi, *The Dark Abyss of Time: The History of the Earth and the History of Nations from Hooke to Vico*, trans. Lydia G. Cochrane (Chicago: University of Chicago Press, 1984), p. 59. Other examples are discussed in greater detail in Findlen, "Jokes of Nature" (above, n. 29).

76 *Historie de l'Académie Royale des Sciences* (Paris, 1720), p. 28. This episode is briefly mentioned in Lorraine Daston, "The Factual Sensibility," *Isis* 79 (1988): 464.

77 Bacon, *Novum Organum*, in *Works*, vol. 4, p. 166.

78 H. C. Barnard, ed. and trans., *Fénelon on Education* (Cambridge: Cambridge University Press, 1966), p. 65. On the use of play to educate in the eighteenth century, see Stafford, *Artful Science* (above, n. 11); and James Secord, "Newton in the Nursery," *History of Science* 23 (1985): 127–51.

79 Galileo to Kepler, Padua, August 19, 1610, in Baumgardt, *Johannes Kepler* (above, n. 59), p. 86. This subject will be treated in greater detail in Paula Findlen, "Galileo's Laughter," in *When Science Became Serious* (forthcoming).

80 *Galileo Against the Philosophers in His Dialogue of Cecco di Ronchitti (1605) and Considerations of Alimbert Mauri (1606)*, trans. Stillman Drake (Los Angeles: Zeitlin and Ver Brugge, 1976), p. 51.

INDEX

abbayes folles 211, 212, 405–6
Abbeys of Misrule 211, 212, 105 6
abolitionism, rise 16, 35, 36, 37–8
abortion, and infanticide 270
absolutism 319, 326
  English 318, 321
  Florentine 311
  French 69–77, 92, 188–91, 194, 304, 320
  and Roman empire 21, 22
  and royal court 387, 390–4, 396
  Scandinavian 322, 325
Abu-Lughod, Janet L. 423
Académie des Sciences 187–8
accoppiatori (electoral commission; Florence) 306, 310
Achillini, Alessandro 162
Act in Restraint of Appeals (1533) 19–20
Act of Settlement (1701) 335
acts of mercy 101–13, 115–16
administration: centralization 424–6
  and government 318–27, 332–4, 336–43
Africa, and slavery 32–8, 300
Agricola, Georg 164
Alamanni, Lodovico 310–11, 313
Albert of Saxony 162
Alberti, Leon Battista 175, 181–2
  Four Books on the Family 87
Albertus Magnus 27
Albuquerque, Luís de 205 n.29
Aleksei Mikhailovich of Russia 270
Alembert, Jean d' 157, 187, 192, 194
Alexander VI, Pope 305–6
Alfonso VI of Castile 20
Alfonso X of Castile, *Siete Partidas* 19, 102, 353
algebra 165
All Saints' Day, ceremonies 115
Alltaggeschichte movement 380
almsgiving 102, 104–5, 108, 114–16, 277
Althusius, J. 327 n.1
Ambrose of Milan, St, and burial of the dead 114
America, Constitution (1787) 13, 16
American Revolutionary Wars 300
Americas: and Atlantic slave systems 32–8
  conquest 2, 13, 15–16, 18, 430
  and European industrialization 436
  and food supply 382, 414–16
  and international trade 33–4
Amerindians: conversion 13
  and European disease 13, 300, 381–2, 414, 431
  and food crops 415–16
  humanity 15–16
Annales school 207, 379, 381
Anne, Queen of England 342
Anquetil-Duperron, M. Abraham-Hyacinthe 74–6
anti-Semitism 14, 200–12, 222
apprentices: and education 57
  female 367–8, 370, 372
Aquinas, St Thomas 23, 27
Aretino, Pietro 351

Argens, Jean-Baptiste de Boyer, marquis d' 74
Ariès, Philippe 119 n.65
Aristotle: and civil society 19, 23, 24, 25–6, 28
  and science 162
  and slavery 24–6, 35
  and women 217–18
armies: citizen 310, 313
  cost 300
  standing 332, 334–6
Asia: and Catholicism 13
  early charter polities 422–3
  and Europe 419–27, 430–40
Aubigné, Agrippa d' 3
Augsburg: and citizenship 228
  and guardianship 231
  and legal rights of women 232
Augsburg, Peace (1555) 85, 227
Augustine of Hippo: and burial of the dead 102, 114, 119 n.65
  De Civitate Dei 23, 27, 31 n.59
  Enchiridion 102
Austria: and France 77
  General School Ordinance 57, 58, 59–62, 64
  and Kressel commission 56
  non-German territories 16, 63–5
  and school reform (1774) 16, 55–65, 301–2
  and suppression of Jesuits 55–6
  see also Habsburg Empire
authority: obedience to 25, 85–7
  paternal 4, 28, 86–7, 139, 250–2, 269, 273, 362
  religious 192
Aylmer, John 399
Aztec Empire 15, 300, 382

Bacon, Francis 19, 156, 194, 444, 450–3
Baechler, Jean 419
Bakhtin, Mikhail 115, 445–6, 447
Baldus de Ubaldis 28
balìa (commission; Florence) 306, 310
Banat, and school reforms 60, 63, 64–5
barbarians 24–6, 27, 48–9
Barbier, Edmond Jean François 74
Barlaeus, Caspar 148
Barnard, Sir Francis 19
Barnavi, E. 90
Barthes, Roland 360 n.45
Basnage, Henri 242
Bayle, Pierre 73
beans 416–17
Beckett, John 347 n.37
Beer, Amalie 291
behavior: manuals 87–8
  and social order 88–9
Belges, Lemaire de 170 n.4
Belon, Pierre 164
Bennett, Judith 381
Berlin: public leisure 282–3
  salons 219–20, 282–93
Bernard of Clairvaux, St 28, 108

Bernheimer, Richard 410 n.27
Bernier, François 72
Betskoi, Ivan 268
Beutelsbach (Württemberg), and bull sacrifice 14, 88, 121–36
Blackstone, William 280 n.21, 408 n.9
Blanco, Manuel García 117 n.26
Blanning, T. C. W. 69
Bloch, Marc 379–80, 382, 383–4
Blumenburg, Hans 444
Bodin, Jean 3, 10, 44–5, 72, 253
Boemus, J. 162
Bohemia: and educational reform 61–2
    and German language 64
    and Habsburg empire 16
Boileau, Etienne 374 n.3
Bolley, Canzlei Advocat 14, 121–31, 134–5
Borromeo, Carlo 175, 184, 448
Botero, Giovanni 355, 360 n.50
Boulainvilliers, Henri comte de 73
Bourdieu, Pierre 380–1, 383
bourgeoisie: Europe and Asia compared 420
    and nobility 387–8, 390–7
    and salon culture 218–19
Bourgeon, Jean-Louis 376 n.25
Boye, Frau von 288
Boyer, Marjorie N. 107, 118 n.42
Boyle, Robert 448, 451–2
Brantôme, Pierre de Bourdeille 168
Braudel, Fernand 379, 381, 437, 438
Brazil, and Portugal 200
Bredekamp, Horst 447
Brenner, Robert 437–8
Brewer, John 4, 301, 303, 332–45
bridges, maintenance 107–8
Brinkmann, Gustav von 287, 296 n.40
Britain: colonies 18–19, 20, 432
    see also England
brotherhoods 12
Brougham, Henry 39 n.9
Brown, Peter 27
Broyard, Anatole 138, 150 n.2
Brucioli, Antonio, Della Republica 313–14
Bruegel, Pieter 400, 445
Brumbey, K. W. 282
Brunelleschi, Filippo 177
Brunfels, Otto 163
Bruno, Giordano 449, 450, 451, 452
Bücher, Karl 238 n.9
Buffet, chronicler 97
bull, village sacrifice 14, 88, 121–36
Burckhardt, Jakob 380
burial of bull 14, 88, 121–36
burial of the dead: as act of mercy 102, 103, 112–15
    and offerings of food 114–15
Buridan, Jean 162
Burke, Edmund 20
Burke, Peter 448
Burma 424–5, 426–7
Burns, J. H. 28
Burtt, E. A. 443
Butterfield, Herbert 3, 157, 383
Bynum, Caroline Walker 444

Cabrera de Córdoba, Luis 356
Cabrera, Fray Alonso de 348
cahiers de doléances 86
Calasso, Francesco 19
Calvin, John 9, 168, 399, 400
Calvinism 10–11, 159
    and representative institutions 317, 318, 326
Cambridge Population Project 380
Campanella, Tomasso, De Monarchia hispanica 28
Campbell, Mildred 263
capitalism: and colonialism 430–1, 436
    early 431
    Europe and Asia compared 419–20, 421, 427, 430–1, 439

    and Protestantism 10–11
    and rise of individualism 259–60, 262, 265
    and slavery 33, 35–6, 430
    and status of women 220, 237
Cardano, Girolamo 165, 168, 449
Caribbean, and Atlantic slave systems 32–3, 36
Carnival: and Lent 158–9, 208, 211, 445, 447–8, 450–3
    and masks 213–14 n.11, 404
    and sex role inversion 401, 404–7
Carra, Jean-Louis 69
Carrara, Alberti 162
Carruthers, Mary 383
cartography 160–1, 201–2
Castiglione, Baldassari 155, 350
catechisms 62–3, 103–4
Catherine II of Russia 268, 279
Catholic League, France 90–4, 97
Catholicism: in Austria 55–65
    and catechism 62–3, 103–4
    and Eastern Orthodoxy 85
    and empire 27, 85
    and humanist education 42–3, 46
    and laity 86–7
    and reform 61, 62–3
    and Reformation 12–13, 86
    and uniformity 88
    and visual arts 159, 173, 175–8, 183
    see also Catholic League; confraternities; Counter Reformation; Trent, Council
Cats, Jacob 148
cattle epidemic, and superstition 14, 88, 121–36
Central Europe, and Habsburg dynasty 15
Cerretani, Bartolomeo 312–13
Certeau, Michel de 380
Chaadaev, Peter 420
change: in identities 1–2, 9–17, 85
    in intellectual life 2–3
    in religious and social life 2, 85–9
charity: and care for infants 275–6
    and confraternities 88, 101–16
charivari 12, 212, 405–6
Charles the Bald of Burgundy 20
Charles I of England 333
Charles II of England 304 n.1, 334, 337, 341, 451
Charles V, Emperor 16, 167, 168, 271, 350, 353–4
Chartier, Roger 158–9, 207–13
Chaucer, Geoffrey, Canterbury Tales 10, 403
Chaudhuri, K. N. 437
Chaunu, Pierre 101
children: appreciation of 275–9
    parent–child relationships 138, 260–2, 263–4, 266, 272
    see also infanticide
China: compared with Europe 431, 433, 434, 435–7, 439–40
    and public sphere 420
Chirot, Daniel 419
Choisy, abbé de 400
Christianity: and conversion 13, 18, 85
    and dominium 16, 26–7, 28–9, 31 n.56, 202
    and Islam 15, 70, 71–2
    and laicization 172–3, 176–7
    and material culture 182–3
    and unity 2, 9, 13, 16, 85
    and works of charity 101–2
Christina, Queen of Sweden 321, 324
Chuquet, Nicolas 166
church: and charity 88, 275–6, 277–8
    and empire 26–8, 85
    and fêtes 209–11
    material culture 172–84
    and state 299, 302, 312–13, 323
Cicero, Marcus Tullius 16, 19, 22, 23–6, 41, 42, 46, 87
cities: free ducal 225
    free imperial 222–5, 299, 301
    and political power 226
citizenship: and education 42–6
    in German cities 226–7, 230

and history 42, 51
of nobility 302–3
Roman 23, 25
and women 226–8, 230
city states 299, 301
and civil society 23
and historiography 45
civil society 10, 23, 25–6, 93
civility 87–8, 398
civilization: and empire 24–6, 396
and play 445–8
and royal court 386–7, 391–4, 396–7
civitas 23, 25 6, 27, 28–9
Clark, Alice 220–1, 373–4 n.1
class: and property 438
see also bourgeoisie; nobility
Claudian (Claudius Claudianus) 18
cleanliness, and social order 89
Clement XIV, Pope 55–6
clergy: and fêtes 209–11
and laity 86, 172
and role of women 272
and voyages of discovery 200–1
clientelism, French 91–2, 425
clocks 167
clubs, intellectual 282–4, 289, 291, 293
Cohen, Philippine 287–8
Colbert, Jean-Baptiste 72, 301, 362–3, 368–9, 371, 372
Colie, Rosalie 446
Collins, James B. 1–5, 253
Cologne: female guilds 235
medieval churches 174
colonialism, and capitalism 430–1
colonies: colonial wars 300
and empire 18–19, 20
and European diseases 300, 381–2, 414, 431
and industrialization 432, 436
Columbus, Christopher 9, 155–6, 382, 412–13, 414
comedy, and Scientific Revolution 444, 445–7
commerce: Europe and Asia compared 419, 423
and politics 313–14
commonwealths 10, 301
and nobility 302–3
community, intellectual 186–95
conduct, social, and court nobility 385–97
Confessio Tetrapolitana 224
confraternities 88, 101–16
and bridge-keeping 107–8
and burial of the dead 103, 112–15, 181
and care for the young 108–9
female 371, 406
and fêtes 211, 212
and hospitals 104–6
and laicization of religion 172–3, 174
and provision of dowries 103, 109–11
and ransoming of prisoners 103, 111–12
and rivalries 177
as welfare providers 88, 101–6, 115–16
Conring, Hermann 50
Constant, J.-M. 91–2
Constantine the Great, and empire 21, 22, 28
Constitutio Criminalis Carolina 271
constitutions: American 16, 319
English 321, 324, 325, 326
Florentine 311–12
French 319
and Holy Roman Empire 323–4, 325
mixed 319, 326
and monarchy 319, 321–5, 327
Polish 16
Pomeranian 322–3, 325
Prussian 323, 324, 325
Swedish 321–2, 325
consumption: and demand 175–8
and lay religion 173, 175–8
and material culture of the church 173, 183

role of women 3
and slavery 33
Contarini, Gasparo 162
contract: contractual monarchy 317–19, 320–1, 324–7, 349
social 10, 34
contracts, by women 231–4, 245, 248, 253
control, social: and education 157
and religion 86
conversion, forced 13, 15, 201
conversos 201
Copernicus, Nicolas 9, 155, 156, 161, 449
core and periphery 35, 422, 431–2, 434–5, 438, 439
corruption, England 334, 343
Cortez, Hernán 15–16, 300, 381 2
Counter Reformation: and clarification of dogma 86–7
and education 61
increase in austerity 111, 175, 177, 183
and Jesuits 55
and laity 86–7, 172
court, royal: growth 426
and leisure 282–3, 288
and nobility 92, 381, 385–97
women's role 219
courts, legal see law
covenant, and contractual monarchy 317, 318
Cracow, and humanist education 41–2, 45
Cromwell, Oliver 324, 325, 333
Crosby, Alfred Jr. 5, 381–2, 383–4, 412–17, 423
cross-dressing 400–1, 402–5
crosses, as markers of discovery 199–200
crossroads, and sacrifice of bull 88, 121, 123–8, 130, 132
Crouzet, Denis 2, 88, 90–7
Crowston, Clare Haru 3, 4, 302, 362–73
Cudworth, Ralph 452
culture: Europe and Asia compared 426–7
pictorial 178–84
popular 121–36, 158–9, 207–13
précieuse 218–19
and science 188–95, 444
Turkish 73–4

Da Gama, Vasco 9, 199, 201
dance, and the Church 210
Danzig: and citizenship 15
and humanist education 42, 45
Darnton, Robert 193
Daston, Lorraine 190
Davenant, Charles 22, 338, 339, 341, 344
Davis, David Brion 36, 37
Davis, Natalie Zemon 3, 5, 219, 362, 381, 383–4, 398–407
De Pisan, Christine 241, 242, 399, 401
De Vries, Jan 375 n.21, 440
debts, responsibility for 231–5
Dee, John 449
deMause, Lloyd 138
democracy: Florentine 305
and Ottoman Empire 75
Denmark, constitutional monarchy 322, 325
Descartes, René 11–12, 156, 188–9, 196 n.21, 451
Descimon, Robert 90, 92, 93
despotism: domestic and foreign 69–70, 303–4
Medici 307–8
"Oriental" 70, 419–20
and Ottoman Empire 15, 69–77, 303
determinism, economic 260–1
Díaz, Bernal 2, 15
Diderot, Denis 157, 187, 191
Diet of Augsburg 224
Digest 21, 24
diplomacy, and Ottoman Empire 69–70, 71–4
discovery: and dominion 16, 197–9, 202–3
markers of 199–200
disease, spread 13, 300, 381–2, 414, 431
division of labor: international 438
sexual 14, 221, 363–7, 371–2, 373
Długosz, Jan 49

Domenichino (Domenico Zampieri) 179
domesticity, and role of women 217–18, 220–1, 272
Donaldson, Ian 401
Donatello 159
Dönhoff, Ernst 43
Douglass, Frederick 36
dowries: control 218, 232–3
    and customary law 244, 245, 247, 254
    provision 14, 103, 109–11
Drescher, Seymour 36, 37, 39 n.9
dress: democratization 11
    Turkish 74
Drouot, H. 90
Du Pan, Jacques Mallet 78 n.9
Dubarry, Madame 74
Duhem, Pierre 162
Duindam, Jeremy 382
Dupin, Charles 74
Dupront, Alphonse 208
Durkheim, Émile 4, 379, 383

Eannes, Gil 199
Eastern Orthodoxy, and Catholicism 85
economy: comparative studies 432–9
    and economic method 382–3
    Europe and Asia compared 423–4
    late sixteenth-century crisis 90–2
    and role of women 11, 218, 220, 222, 226, 232–7, 272, 302, 362–73, 381, 399
ecosystems theory 381–2, 412–17, 436
Edict of Nantes (1598) 85
education: compulsory 56–7, 58–9, 62
    and Enlightenment 56, 156, 157
    exclusions 58–9
    and family relationships 141–2, 145, 148–9
    and gender 62, 218, 241, 289, 290
    Habsburg reforms 16, 55–65
    and history 45–6, 50
    legal 241
    and linguistic diversity 16
    political 42–4
    role of state 301
    role of women 4, 218, 399
    and social control 157
    textbooks 56, 57, 61, 64
egalitarianism: and individuality 10
    and salon culture 219–20, 289
    and science 188–9, 193–4
Elbing, and humanist education 42, 45
elect 10–11
Eliade, Mircea 117 n.37
Elias, Norbert 5, 354, 360 n.44, 381, 383, 385–97, 454 n.6
Elizabeth I of England 198, 352–3
Elliott, John H. 353
Eltis, David 16, 32–8
empire 18–29
    and Church 26–8, 85
    and civilization 24–6, 396
    and civitas 23, 25–6
    and economy 432
    and law 21, 23–4
    meanings 19–22
    and military rule 21
    and monarchy 21–2
    and Roman Empire 18–19, 20–1, 22–6
    and state 19–20
    and universalism 28–9
Encyclopédie 157, 187, 194, 365
England: civil war 85, 87
    constitution 321, 324, 325, 326
    and contract 321
    exports 34
    fiscal policy 301, 332–3, 337–45
    foreign policy 334, 335–7
    and fundamental law 324, 325
    and industrialization 432, 436, 438
    and infanticide 271

labor market 34, 36
    and marriage and family 258–66
    as nation-state 299, 395, 397
    paradoxes of state power 332–45
    and property law 246
    slave system 37
    state development 301, 332–45
    trade 33–4
    and voyages of discovery 198–9
    and women in trade 240 n.59
Enlightenment 3, 155
    antecedents 186–95
    and despotism 69
    and educational reform 56
    and faith and reason 156–7
    and national origins 46
    and salon culture 219
    and secularism 191–2
    and superstition 88, 131, 136
Ephraim, Benjamin Veitel 291
equality: in marriage 10
    and reason 11–12, 15–16
    religious 11
    and slavery 35
Erasmus, Desiderius 167–8, 404
    Manners for Children 87, 155
    and play 445, 446–7, 448, 450–1
Erikson, Erik 267 n.8
estates, and monarchy 299–300, 317–27
Estienne, Robert 162
Etaples, Lehèvre de 162, 168
etiquette, court 354, 385–97
Eugene IV, Pope 108
Europe: and Asia 419–27, 430–40
    and economic growth 32, 36, 431–4, 437–8
    and industrialization 430–6, 439
    overseas expansion 432
exceptionalism, European 419, 421, 431–40
exempla literature 209
exploration, voyages 5, 9, 15, 155–6, 162, 197–200

faith, and reason 27, 156–7
family: and child-rearing responsibility 148
    and education and training 141–2, 145, 148–9
    and lineage property 245–8, 252, 254, 264
    and marriage choices 146
    nuclear 89, 259–60, 264
    parent–child relationships 89, 138–50, 260–2, 263–4, 266, 272
    and patriarchy 4, 220, 259, 399–400
    in recent history 220, 258–66
    and rise of individualism 9–10, 258–66
    and role of women 217, 235
    size and spacing 89, 139–40, 142–3, 145
    see also infanticide
father, and authority 4, 28, 86–7, 139, 250–2, 268, 273
Favart, Charles, Soleiman II 74
fear, eschatological 90, 93
Feast of Fools 210, 404–5
Febvre, Lucien 3, 158, 160–70, 379, 383
Fedor Alekseevich of Russia 276–7
Felbiger, Johann Ignaz 56–8, 59, 62–3, 65
femininity, and women's work 269, 363, 365–6, 372–3
feminist studies 381, 398–407
Fénelon, François de Salignac de 241, 242, 453
Feros, Anthony 303, 304, 348–57, 384 n.3
fertility rites 404–5
Feselius, Philipp 449
festival see fête
fête 158–9, 207–13
    and the Church 209–11
    of John the Baptist 86, 95, 159, 210–11, 212
    municipal control 211–13
Fête de Fous 210, 404–5
feudalism: and capitalism 431
    and Carolingian empire 326
    and Catholic League 91–2
    Europe and Asia compared 419

Findlen, Paula 158, 382, 383, 384, 443–53
Florence: army 310, 313
   churches and cathedral 173, 177
   and constitutionalism 311–12
   and Medicis 305, 306, 307–12, 314
   and political thought 302, 305–14
   republic 305–6, 309–11, 312–13
Fludd, Robert 450, 452
Flynn, Maureen 88, 101–16
Fogel, Michèle 304
Foigny, Gabriel de 400
Foley, Paul 340
Fontenelle, Bernard le Bovier 191, 193, 453
food supply, and population growth 413–16
Foppa, Vicenzo 176
force see violence
foreign policy: English 334, 335–7
   French 69, 70, 74
Foucault, Michel 87, 93, 115, 380–1, 383, 446
foundlings, care for 108–11, 275–9
Fox, Charles James 38
France: and the church 426
   colonies 18–19, 35
   compared with Southeast Asia 421, 424–5, 427
   and early modern science 186–95
   and economic development 438
   and Enlightenment 157
   and female litigation 241–54
   and fundamental laws 324
   medieval churches 174
   as nation-state 299
   and Ottoman Empire 4, 15, 69–77, 303–4
   and peasant religious traditions 86
   penitential processions 88, 90, 94–7
   revenues 91, 300–1, 368–9
   trade 38–9 n.4
   and voyages of discovery 199
   and Wars of Religion 91, 92–3
   women and guilds 362–73
   see also absolutism; fête; Fronde; Huguenots; nobility
Francis I of France 170 n.4, 303
Frank, André Gunder 423
Frankfurt: churches 174
   and citizenship 228
   guilds 222–3
   as imperial free city 222
   and legal rights of women 232–3
Frederick II "the Great" of Prussia 55, 56, 271–2, 282, 288, 300
Frederick III of Denmark 322
Frederick William I of Prussia 280 n.20
Fredro, Andrzej Maksimilian 46
freedom: and absolutism 72
   and slavery 16, 32–8
Freitas, Seraphin de 199
French Revolution: and abolition of guilds 302
   causes 300
   and constitution 319
   and the individual 219
   and rights of women 11, 217
Freud, Sigmund 379
Friedländer, David 284, 290
Friedländer, Rebecca 290–1
Friedrich, Karin 2, 16, 41–51
Frijn, Jacob 4, 380
Froissart, Jean 167
Fronde (France) 189, 320–1, 324
Frost, Robert 302
Fuchs, Leonhard 163
funerals, and confraternities 112–15
Furetière, Antoine 73, 303

Galileo Galilei 9, 155, 156, 161, 162, 164, 453
Galland, Auguste 73
Garraway, William 337
Gebler, Tobias 56
Geertz, Clifford 115, 349, 350
Geiler von Kaiserberg, Johannes 230

Gelasian I, Pope 26
gender: and citizenship 226–8
   and division of labor 221, 363–7, 371–2, 373
   and education 62, 218, 241, 289, 290, 399
   and equality 11–12
   in family relationships 150
   and inheritance 245
   and sex-role reversal 291, 400–8
genealogies, and family relationships 142–4, 150
geography, historical 381–2, 412–17
German language, in Habsburg empire 63–4, 65
Germany: economic role of women 220, 222–37
   fundamental laws 324
   and infanticide 271–2
   medieval churches 174
   and religion of states 85
Gesner, Konrad von 163
Ghirlandaio, Domenico 176, 181
Gierowski, Iosef 380
Giesey, Ralph 247
Gilbert, Felix 4, 302, 305–14
Gills, Barry K. 423
Ginzburg, Carlo 181, 380
Giotto di Bondone 182
Glaber, Raul 176
Glanvill, Joseph 452
Glick, Thomas 205 n.22
Glorious Revolution (1688) 85, 334, 335–6, 338–41
Gnapheus, Wilhelm 42
God, as father 4, 28
godparents 143–5, 144
Goldgar, Anne 193
Goldsmith, Oliver 20
Goldstone, Jack 423
Goldthwaite, Richard 159, 172–84
Gombrich, E. H. 351
Goody, J. 244, 255 n.13
Goubert, Pierre 381
government: forms 303–4, 308, 310–13, 320, 323
   representative 317, 318, 319–20, 322, 324–7
   and revenues 91, 300–1, 332–3, 425
   see also contract, social; democracy; monarchy; republic
Gramsci, Antonio 36
Gregory I the Great, Pope 27
Grosrichard, Alain 69
Grosseteste, Robert 28
Grotius, Hugo 198
Grunau, Simon, Prussian Chronicle 47
guardianship 229–31, 235
Guer, Jean-Antoine 70, 78 n.7
Guicciardini, Francesco 4, 302, 303
   Dialogo del Reggimento di Firenze 308, 311
   Discorso di Logrogno 308, 310
   History of Italy 305, 308
   Ricordi 305
guilds: abolition 302
   female 236, 362–3, 364, 365–6, 367–8, 370–2, 373
   French edict of 1673 302, 368–70, 372
   male, and role of women 218, 220, 226, 235–7, 302, 362, 366
   and political power 220, 222–4, 235–6
Guise family 92, 100 n.30
Gustavus Adolphus of Sweden 321, 323
Guzmán, Diego de 355
gymnasia: Austria 58–9, 60
   Polish-Lithuanian Commonwealth 42–3

Habermas, Jürgen 381
Habsburg Empire: and ethnic diversity 16
   and France 71–2, 77
   and Hungary 299
   and linguistic diversity 16
   and palace etiquette 354
   and papacy 56
   and school reform (1774) 55–65
   and taxation 301
Hajnal, John 435

Hall, John A. 419, 421
Hallyn, Fernand 445
Hamburg, and salons 285
Hamilton, Alexander 22
Hampden, John 336, 340
Harbord, William 337
Harley, Robert 340–1, 343
Hartknoch, Christoph 46, 48
Hazard, Paul 192
Hegel, G. W. F. 4, 86, 379, 383
Heidegger, Martin 383
Hellie, Richard 273, 279
Hélyot, Hippolyte 112
Henry III of France 92, 400
Henry, Louis 380
Herlitz, N. 321
Hertz, Deborah 219–20, 282–93
Herz, Henrietta and Markus 284–6, 289, 291–2
Hess, Mathes Ignaz von 58–9
hierarchy, and sex role reversal 402–3, 406
Hill, Christopher 384 n.1
Hintze, Otto 326, 330 n.37
history: of Catholic League 90–4
    comparative 419–27, 430–40
    and the festive explosion 207
    medieval 169
    and national origins 15, 41, 44–6
    and political education 43–4, 46
    Prussian and Polish 47–8
    research paradigms 379–84
Hobbes, Thomas 10, 259, 304 n.1, 318
Holy League see Catholic League
Holy Roman Empire: and constitutional reform 323–5, 326
    imperial cities 222–5, 299, 301
    and Prussia 48, 51
    and Roman Empire 45
homosexuality, and Ottoman Empire 70
hoof and mouth disease, village remedy 14, 88, 121–36
Hooke, Robert 448, 452
Horwitz, Henry 338
hospitals, and confraternities 104–6
Houard, David 244, 246, 253
House of Commons (British) 327, 332–5, 337–43
household: as basic unit of production 10, 259, 266
    as microcosm 89
    and women 11, 12, 217–18, 272
Howard, Sir Robert 337, 339
Huarte de San Juan, Juan 350
Hubatsch, Walter 45
Huguenots 72, 85, 91, 317
Huizinga, Johan 178–9, 445–7
human sciences see social sciences
humanism: in Cracow 41–2
    and education 89, 145–6
    and history 41–2, 44–6, 48, 49
    and imperium 19
    Italian 3, 41, 309–10
    and play 448
    and science 160–2, 193
    and symbolism 182
humanity: of Amerindians 15–16
    and Christianity 27, 28–9
    of Ottomans 15, 72
    in Roman Empire 24–6
Humboldt, Alexander and Wilhelm von 284, 286
Hume, David 18, 157
Hungary: and Habsburg monarchy 16, 299
    and school reforms 16, 60, 63, 64, 65
Huppert, George 195 n.8

identity: changes 1–2, 9–17, 85
    gender 11, 14
    individual 9–11, 87, 155
    linguistic 16–17
    and myth and history 41–51
    and name 12
    national 2, 16

noble 92
    and religion 13–14
    urban/rural 14–15
illegitimacy, and infanticide 268, 270–1, 272, 273, 274–5, 277–9
imagery: religious 159, 178, 179–83
    secular 159, 178, 179–81, 182
    and symbolism 178–9, 182
imperium 19–26, 352
    and Church 26–8
India, compared with Europe 433, 434, 436
individual: as basic unit of political society 10, 259
    and court society 390–1, 396
    and laicization of religion 173
    and rights 219
    and state 13, 220
individualism: affective 89, 138
    and French Revolution 219
    and the group 9–13, 38, 87, 89, 373
    and Reformation 86, 155
    rise 219, 220, 258–66
    and women 4, 11, 14
indulgences 106, 108, 112–13
industrialization 259, 265
    comparative studies 420, 421, 430–6, 439
    and labor 33
    and work of women 220–1, 237, 399
infanticide: and appreciation of children 275–9
    European views 270–3
    in France 250, 253
    increase in 273–5
    legal evidence 269–70
    in Russia 220
inheritance: by children 139
    by women 232, 242, 244–5, 247–8, 249, 250–3, 254
Innocent III, Pope 29 n.3
Inquisition 14, 156, 201
institutions: and economic development 437–8, 439
    representative 317, 318, 319–20, 325–6
"Instrument of Government" (England) 320, 321
international relations, France and Ottoman Empire 69–77
intimacy 87
Iorgovici, Paul 65
Iov, Metropolitan of Novgorod 277–8
Isabel and Ferdinand of Spain 106, 349, 353
Isidore of Seville 21
Islam: and Christianity 15, 70, 71–2
    see also Ottoman Empire
Italy: material culture of the church 172–84
    medieval churches 173–5
Itineraries 202
Ivan IV of Russia 270, 272

Jacquart, J. 91
James I of England 318
James II of England 334–6, 337–8, 339
James VI of Scotland and I of England, and public ritual 352–3
Janković, Theodor 62, 64–5
Jansenism 73, 77
Japan: compared with Europe 419, 424–5, 426, 431, 434, 435–7, 440
    revisionist history 421
    and slavery 39 n.8
    and Southeast Asia 422, 427
Jesuits: and education 42–3, 58, 60
    suppression 13, 55–6
Jews: attacks on 200
    expulsion 14, 201–2, 222
    and salon culture 220, 283, 284–93
João II of Portugal 199, 201
João III of Portugal 197, 201
Johann von Posilge 47
Johannesson, Kurt 44
John the Baptist: feast day 95, 159, 210–11
    in visual art 159
John of Paris 27

Jones, E. L. 419–20, 435
Jonson, Ben, *Epicoene* 403
Jordanes, 6th-c. historian 48–50
Joseph II of Austria 56, 60, 66 n.22, 302
Josselin, Ralph 263–4
journals 87
journeymen 12, 223, 236–7, 367, 371
Julia, Dominique 380
Julius II, Pope 309–10
just war theory 2, 27
Justinian, *Institutes* 23, 31 n.53

Kabuzan, V. M. 274
Kadlubek, bishop of Cracow 49
Kaiser, Thomas E. 4, 15, 69–77, 303
Kant, Immanuel 192, 285, 288
Kaunitz, W. A., Prince von 56, 66 n.13
Keckermann, Barthel 42, 45, 46
Kenyon, John P. 258, 342
Kepler, Johannes 9, 156, 161, 443, 448, 449–53
Kettering, Sharon 425
Kindermann, Ferdinand 59, 60–2
kinship, and rise of individualism 259, 266
knowledge: and experience 156, 188, 191–2
    and play 448–53
    and power 134–6
    and progress 157
    and reason 88, 156
    scientific 186–95, 444, 447–8
    and voyages of discovery 198–9
Knox, John 399
Koebner, R. 78 n.11
König, Ernst 45
Kraków School 380
Krantz, Albert 49
Kressel von Qualtenberg, Franz 56, 58, 65–6 n.7
Kromer, Marcin 50–1
Kuła, Witold 380
Kundera, Milan 217, 219

La Bruyère, Jean de 392, 446
La Tour, Georges de 159
labor: waged 266, 399, 437–8
    and slave system 32–8
Laclau, Ernesto 426
Ladurie, E. Le Roy 208, 213 n.2
laity: and Counter Reformation 86–7, 172
    and laicization of religion 172–3, 176–7
land tax 340–1
language: and education 16, 63–4
    and identity 16–17
    scientific 164–6
Lasch, Christopher 267 n.8
law: canon 269–70
    customary 139, 242–8, 249, 251, 253–4
    and empire 21, 23–4
    fundamental laws 323–4, 325
    and history 43–4
    and infanticide 269–74, 279
    Islamic 71, 75
    natural 27, 43, 318
    Roman 16, 23–4, 43, 139, 317
    Russian 269–74, 279
    and women 220, 228–35, 237, 241–54, 399
Lazarillo de Tormes 10
Le Bras, Gabriel 116 n.1
leadership, and state 302, 306–9
Lee, James 423
Leeuwenhoek, Antonie van 164
Leibniz, G. W. 24, 166, 452–3
leisure, public 219–20, 282–93
    commercial 282–4
    courtly 282–4, 288
    intellectual clubs 282–4, 289, 291, 293
Lent: and Carnival 158, 208, 211, 445, 447–8, 450–3
    and *fête* 158
Leo I the Great, Pope 27

Leo X, Pope 310
Leoni, Pompeo 351–2
Lerma, Duke of 304, 355–7
Levasseur, Emile 270
Lévi-Strauss, Claude 25
Levin, Rahel 284, 286–7, 290–2
Levy, Sara 287
lex fundamentalis 324
Lex Rhodia 26
Libavius, Andreas 450
Lieberman, Victor 5, 382–3, 384, 419–27
Linguet, Simon-Nicolas Henri 74, 75–6
Linschoten, Jan 202
literacy 423
    female 14, 249
litigation: by women 241–54, *243*
    criminal charges 248
    and property 242, 244–53
    and royal offices 252–3
Locke, John 10, 156, 157, 303, 400
Long Turkish War 299
Los Cobos, Francisco de 350
Louis XIV of France: and absolutism 72–3, 188–90, 194, 304
    and guilds 368–9, 370–1
    and public ritual 352–3
    and science 187–9
    and war with England 332, 333, 334–6, 343, 345
Louis XVI of France 302
Loyseau, Charles 72
Lübeck, and legal rights of women 232, 233
Luther, Martin 9, 12, 85–6, 131, 168
Lutheranism, German 222–5, 323
Luttrell, Narcissus 340
Lyons, *fêtes* 212–13

Macaulay, Thomas Babbington, Lord 262, 380
Macfarlane, Alan 10, 220, 221, 258–66, 384
Machiavelli, Niccolò 4, 22, 23, 302, 303, 310
    The Prince 19, 29 n.5, 305, 403
McNeill, William H. 423
magic: and Scientific Revolution 156
    and village remedies 122, 128, 134
Magna Charta 317, 318, 324, 325
maize 415–16
Małowist, Marian 380
Malthus, Thomas 414–15, 438
Mann, Michael 419
manners 386–7, 393–5, 397
Manuel of Portugal 200–1
maps and mapping 160–1, 199–200, 202
Marana, Jean-Paul 73
Margaret, Queen of Spain 351, 355
Margot, Alain 248
Marguerite de Navarre 155, 168, 208 n.7
Maria Fedorovna of Russia 281 n.36
Maria Theresa, Empress, and school reform 16, 55–65
market: and European development 437–9
    and visual arts 175–8
    and women 3, 218, 220–1, 232–4, 363
Marlot, Dom Guillaume 96
Marnix von St. Aldegonde, Philip 145
marriage: affective 260–1, 263, 266
    contracts 245, 246, 247
    and individual choice 10, 14, 146, 148
    and legal rights of women 218, 362
    and property 245–8, 252, 254, 264
    regulation 86
Marshall, Sherrin 89, 138–50
Martini, Karl Anton von 56, 59
Martire d'Angheria, Pietro 349
Marx, Gratian 59
Marx, Karl 4, 259, 266, 379, 383–4, 419, 430
Mary, Blessed Virgin, and White Processions 96
Mary Magdalene, in visual art 159
masks, carnival 213–14 n.11, 404
Mason, Roger A. 44
Master John (navigator) 200, 201

mathematics 165–6, 188, 191
Matthieu, Pierre 355
Maximilian I, Emperor 354
Mead, Margaret 267 n.10
mechanism, Cartesian 188–9, 191, 192
Medici, Lorenzo de' 305, 306, 307–9, 310–11
Medici, Piero de' 305, 307
Medrano, Juan Fernández de 355
Melton, James van Horn 16, 55–65, 301–2
Memmingen: and citizenship 227, 228
    as free imperial city 224–5
    and guilds 224, 235
memory 383
men, and cross-dressing 400–1, 402, 404–5, 407
Mendelssohn, Moses 284–5, 287, 288–9
mendicant movement 172, 176, 179
mentalités, study 3
mercantilism 35–6, 432
Mercator, Gerardus 202
merchants: and city government 235, 314
    and economic crisis 91, 92
    women as 3
mercy, acts of, and confraternities 101–13, 115–16
Merian, Maria Sibylla 219
method, scientific 156, 157–8
Meurier, Hubert 96, 97
Meyer, Sara and Marianne 290
Mézeray, François Eudes de 71, 72
Michelangelo 183
Michelet, Jules 5, 380
Miechowita, Maciej 49
Mikhail Fedorovich of Russia 275
Mill, John Stuart 419
Mills, C. Wright 384
Minnesäng 386
mirrors 11, 14
Misericordias, and burial of the dead 112–13
missionaries, Catholic 85
Mitchison, Rosalind 258
mobility: geographic 14, 227, 259, 266
    social 399, 423
Modern Devotion 87
Molière (Jean Baptiste Poquelin) 218, 365
Mommsen, W. 330 n.37
monarchy: accessibility 353–5
    and administration 318–27, 337–43
    constitutional 319, 321–5, 327
    contractual 317–19, 320–1, 324–7, 349
    Danish 322, 325
    and despotism 303–4
    and empire 21–2
    English 321, 332–3
    and estates 299–300, 317–27
    French 4, 92, 300, 320–1, 355
    mixed 319, 326
    Ottoman 71, 72, 75–6
    as patriarchal 4, 11
    power 348–57
    and public ritual 352–4
    representative 319–20, 324–5, 337
    and republic 31n.51
    Spanish 21, 300–1, 303, 348–57
    Swedish 321–2
    see also absolutism; court
money, social impact 389
monopoly, commercial 197–8
Montel, Paul 166
Montesquieu, Charles Louis de Secondat 22
    and despotism 69, 71, 73, 76, 77, 303–4, 419
More, Henry 452
More, Thomas, Utopia 9, 448, 450
Morelli, Giovanni 181
Morgan, Edmund S. 36, 37, 40 n.20
Morris-Suzuki, Tessa 427
mortality, infant and child 140, 140, 260–1, 270
Moser, Hugh 121, 136 n.2
mother, and parent–child relationships 141–3

Mouffe, Chantal 427
Mousnier, R. 320, 328 n.12
Muchembled, Robert 384 n.3
Muir, Edward 352–3
Müller, Ignaz 56
Munich: and citizenship 227
    as free ducal city 225
    and legal rights of women 232, 234
murder see infanticide
Musset, Jacqueline 245
Mylius, Michael 43
mythology, and national origins 44, 46, 48–51

Näf, W. 320
names 12
Napier, John 166
nature: and play 448–53
    and science 190–1, 192, 195, 444, 446–8
navies: cost 300
    English 335
navigation, scientific 197–8, 201–3
Necker, Jacques 38, 40
needlework, as women's work 363, 365–7, 368, 370–1, 372–3
Netherlands: and education 141–2
    as nation-state 299
    and national origins 44
    and navigational skills 201–2
    and parent–child relationships 138–50
    and political education 44
    and slave system 37
    and social order 89
    taxation 301
    and visual arts 159
Neunachbar, Jan 43
New Christians 201
Newton, Isaac 9, 156–7, 190, 448
Nicholas of Cusa 162
Nicolai, Friedrich 283, 284–5
Nicolet, Claude 26
Nietzsche, Friedrich 4, 379
Nine Years War 333, 335–6, 340–1, 343–4
nobility: and commonwealth 302–3
    and courtly leisure 283
    and education 59, 145–6
    English 395, 397
    Florentine 309, 310–11
    French 91–2, 189, 320, 326–7, 385–97
    and group and individual identity 10
    Ottoman 70
    Polish 41, 46, 50
    Prussian 50–1
    and representative government 320–3, 325
    and salons 292–3
    Swedish 321–2
    as warriors and courtiers 92, 381, 385–97, 425
Nora, Pierre 383
Normandy: female litigants 241–54, 243
    literacy rates 249
North, Douglass 437, 438
Northern Piety 87
novels, "oriental" 73–4
Nunes, Pedro 201, 202, 203
Nuremberg: churches 174
    and citizenship 227
    economy 223–4
    as free imperial city 224
    and guilds 235
    and legal rights of women 229, 232–3
    and political power 224
    and sex-role inversion 405, 406
Nye, Robert A. 157

O'Brien, Patrick 432
Oestreich, Gerhard 299–300, 317–27
offices, royal, women's rights in 219, 244, 250, 252–3, 254
order, social 88–9, 179, 183, 219

orders: religious 172, 302
  social 7, 11–12, 20, 219
  and visual arts 176, 183
orientalism 70, 383, 419–20
orphans, care for 109–11, 275–9
Orthodox Church 64–5
Orzechowski, Stanisław 50
Ottoman Empire: armies 71, 303
  and despotism 15, 69–77, 303
  extent 299
  and France 4, 15, 69–77, 303–4
  legitimacy of war on 2, 27
Oughtred, William 166

Pacheco Pereira, Duarte 198
Pacioli, Lucas 165–6
pagans 27, 41, 159
Pagden, Anthony 2, 16, 18–29, 303
painting: altarpieces 176, 177, 179
  demand for 173, 175–8, 183
  frescoes 176, 179, 180, 181
  panel 178, 180–1
  portraits 181–2
Paleotti, Gabriel 183
Panaetius of Rhodes 24
papacy: and Habsburg Empire 56
  and Reformation 85
parent–child relationships 89, 138–50, 260–2, 263–4, 266,
  272
Paris: female guilds 364–5, 370
  seamstresses' guild 362–3, 367–8, 370–2
Parker, Geoffrey 419
Parlement de Paris 209, 320–1, 371
parliament, English 303, 321, 324, 325, 332–45
Parthey, Daniel 284, 288
Paruta, Paolo 26
Pascal, Blaise 159, 165
Pastorius, Joachim 42, 43, 46, 50
patriarchy 4, 220, 259, 399–400
patrons: and court politics 219
  as godparents 144–5
  in Southeast Asia 425
Patterson, Orlando 36, 37, 40 n.20
Paul III, Pope 108
Paz, Octavio 41
Peacock, James 401
peasants: assigned 274–5
  and European development 438
  as litigants 248–9
  and nobility 387–8
  and remedy for hoof and mouth disease 14, 88, 121–36
  and time 168–9
Peasants' War (1525) 85–6, 224
Peeters, H. F. M. 145
penance, and superstition 131–2
penitents: and burial of the dead 112–13
  processions 88, 90, 94–7
Pergen, Johann Anton 58
periphery and core 35, 422, 431–2, 434–5, 438, 439
Perrot, Jean-Claude 376 n.27
Peter I of Russia 268, 272–3, 274–5, 277–9, 420
Peter von Dusburg 47
Peters, Edward 349
Philip II of Spain 350–1, 354
Philip III of Spain 349–57
  and favorites 304, 355–6
  inaccessibility 354–6
  qualities 351–2
  and relocation of court 356–7
Phillips, Ulrich Bonnell 35
philosophes 157, 190–4, 453
philosophy, political 302, 305–14
pilgrims, and charity 105, 106, 108, 113–14
plantation system 33–5
Plato 218, 446
Platter, Thomas 168
play, and the Renaissance 158, 445–9, 451

Pocock, J. G. A. 20, 305
Poland, partition 69
Polish Constitution (1791) 16
Polish-Lithuanian Commonwealth: and citizenship 15, 42–3
  and Gothic mythology 48–9
  as nation-state 299
  and national origins 41, 44, 47–8
  and political education 43–6
  and politics 302–3
  and religions 13
  and Sarmatian mythology 44, 48, 49–51
politics: and commerce 313–14
  crisis in political thought 302, 305–14
  and empire 23
  and force 309–10, 313
  and moral reform 312–13
  and religion 92–3
  research paradigms 381
  and role of women 217
Politiques 92
Polybius 22, 23, 27
Pomerania
  constitution 322–3, 324
  and Polish-Lithuanian Commonwealth 51
Pomeranz, Kenneth 5, 382–3, 430–40
Pompadour, Madame de 74
poor relief: and confraternities 101–4, 107, 108, 115–16
  and state 301
population: control by infanticide 270, 273, 274
  effects of war 222–5, 228
  growth 173–4, 223, 224–5, 414–16
Porter, Roy 380
portraiture, royal 304, 350–1
Portugal: colonies 18, 35
  as nation-state 299
  and religious toleration 200–1
  and scientific navigation 5, 197–203
Possevino, Antonio 44
potatoes 416
Poullain de la Barre, François 12
poverty: and confraternities 88, 101–4, 107
  and religious art 183
  and social order 88–9, 91
Powelson, John P. 421
power: and knowledge 134–6
  paradoxes 332–45
  and women 87, 253–4
Pownall, Thomas 20
Price, Barbara 422
Přichovský, Anton Peter 61, 62
printing: and intellectual change 155, 160, 163–4
  print culture 193
  spread 3, 9, 87
  and traditional ritual 158, 207–13
processions: and fêtes 211
  penitential 88, 90, 94–7
professionalization of science 188, 193–4
progress, and Enlightenment 157
property: of children 139
  common 245, 259
  and customary law 244–8
  in early modern England 259, 266
  and industrialization 437–8
  lineage 245–8, 252, 254
  in Ottoman Empire 70, 72, 75
  and political rights 10–11
  of women 218, 226–7, 230–2, 242, 244–8, 249, 250–4,
    399
Protestantism: and capitalism 10–11
  and Catholicism 12, 86
  and empire 27
  and humanist education 42–3, 46
  and individualism 155
  and religious art 182–3
  and women 87
Pruckmann, Friedrich 324
Prudhomme, Louis-Marie 217

Prussia: and constitution 323, 324, 325, 326
    and historiography 15, 41–2, 45–6, 47–8
    and mythology 44, 48–51
    as nation-state 299
    and political education 43–4, 46
    and school reform 56, 58, 301
    and taxation 301
public sphere, Europe and Asia compared 419–20
purgatory 172
Pussot, Jean 94

Rabelais, François 398, 403, 445–6
    and science 164, 165–6, 168, 169, 170 n.4
Ranke, Leopold von 4, 380
Ransel, David 220, 268–79
ransoming of prisoners 103, 111–12
Rapaport, Joanne 383
Raphael (Raffaello Sanzio) 176
Rawls, John 383
reason: and belief 27, 156–7, 423
    and equality 11–12, 16
    and humanity 24
    and knowledge 88, 156
    and politics 309, 311, 313, 423
    and science 188, 446, 451–2
    and slavery 25–6
    and truth 155
reciprocity, in relationships 89, 138–40, 148–50
Recorde, Robert 166
Reformation: and changing identities 2, 12–13, 85
    and geographic mobility 227
    global context 5, 383
    and individualism 86, 155
    and intellectual change 155–6
    and political power 220, 222–4
    and visual arts 182–3
regeringsform (Sweden) 320, 321–2, 324
Regierungsform (Pomerania) 320, 322–3, 324, 325
Regierungsverfassung (Prussia) 320, 323
Regiomontanus (Johannes Müller) 170 n.7
Reimer, Andreas 291
Reims, and penitential processions 95–6, 97
religion: and citizenship 227
    and division of Europe 2, 85
    and family relationships 150
    and identity 2, 13–14
    and imagery 159
    individual 173
    and reason 423
    and role of women 3, 226
    and science 156–7, 191–2
    and state 13, 92–3, 382, 423, 425–6
    see also Christianity; Islam
Renaissance: and church building and adornment 176–9
    and demand for visual art 179–81
    and intellectual change 2–3, 155–6
    and national origins 41–4
    and play 158, 445–9, 451
    and political society 4
    and science 160–3, 444, 445, 446–8, 452
Renaudot, Théophraste 186
representation, in early modern state 317, 318, 319–20, 322, 324–6, 337
republic: and empire 21–2
    English 321
    Florentine 305–6, 310–11, 312–13
    and monarchy 301
republic of letters, French 193–4
research paradigms 379–84
resistance, right of 317
Ricaut, Paul 73
Rice, Eugene 1
Richardson, J. S. 30 n.17
Richelieu, Armand Jean du Plessis, cardinal 187, 253, 323
Ridley, Henry N. 418 n.13
rights: female 12, 16, 217–18, 235, 302
    legal 229–34, 399

political 10–11, 16, 27
ritual 158–9
    court 385
    fertility 404–5
Roberts, Clayton 338
Robertson, William 18
Roman Empire 18–19, 20–6
    and Christianity 26–9, 85
    and Holy Roman Empire 45
Romanov, B. A. 269
Rondibilis, Guillaume 163–4
Ronsard, Pierre de 3
Rösner, Johann Gottfried 45
Rosu, Michael 65
Rouen, female guilds 365
rough music 12, 212, 405–6
Rousseau, Jean-Jacques 10, 303
Royal Prussia see Prussia
Royal Society 451–2
Ruiz, Juan 102–3
Rumeu de Armas, Antonio 107
Russia: compared with Europe 420
    compared with Southeast Asia 422, 424–7
    illegitimacy and infanticide 220, 268–79
    as nation-state 299
    and role of women 272
    and taxation 301
Ryswick Treaty 336

Sabean, David 2, 14, 88, 121–36, 380, 384
sacrifice, as village remedy 14, 88, 121–36
Said, Edward 383
Saint-Pierre, Charles Irénée de Castel, abbé de 73
saints, cult 172
Sales von Greiner, Franz 56
Salic Law 253, 324, 399
Sallust (Gaius Sallustius Crispus) 20, 22, 44
salons 218–19
    in Berlin 282–93
salvation: and Catholic League 88, 92–4
    and confraternities 88, 101
Saramago, José 383
Sarmatians, in Prussian mythology 44, 48, 49–51
Savonarola, Fra Girolamo 305–6, 308, 312–14
Scaliger, Joseph Justus 44, 167, 449
Schadow, Gottfried and Marianne 291
Schlegel, Friedrich 288, 289–90
Schleiermacher, Friedrich 285, 288, 289
Schneider, Zoë A. 3, 220, 241–54
Schoen, Erhard 403–4
Schönwald, Samuel 46
schools: elementary/minor 57–8, 59, 61, 301–2
    major 57–8, 59
    normal 55, 56, 57–8, 60–1
Schurtzfleisch, Samuel 50–1
Schuster, John 444
Schütz, Caspar 45, 47
Schütz, Christian Gottfried 284
science: Cartesian 188
    and experiment 188, 191–2
    and humanism 160–2, 193
    mathematical 188, 191
    and nature 190–1, 192, 195, 444, 446–8
    professionalization 188, 193–4
    and religion 156–7, 191–2
    and Renaudot's conferences 186–95
    scientific language 164–6
    scientific method 156, 157–8, 191
"Scientific Revolution" 3, 5, 9, 14, 155, 157–8, 383
    and equality 11
    and faith 156–7
    history of 443–4
    and mechanical science 188–9
    and play 158, 444, 445–53
Scotland, and national origins 44
seamstresses, in France 362–73
secularism 191–2, 423

Seed, Patricia 3, 5, 197–203, 383
Sejm (Poland) 42, 302–3
Semevskii, V. I. 274
Seneca, Lucius Annaeus 26
Seraglio, Turkish 70–1, 73–4
Serbo-Croatian language 16, 64
serfdom 16, 37, 274–5
Seven Years' War 283, 300
sexuality: control 110–11, 228, 261, 269–71, 272
    and role reversal 219, 400–8
    symbolism 399–400, 404–7
Sforza, Bona 41
Shadwell, Thomas, *The Woman-Captain* 403
Shakespeare, William, *As You Like It* 403
Shapin, Steven 455–6 n.92
Siam 424–7
Siete Partidas 19, 102, 353
Sigismund I of Poland 41
Sigismund III of Poland 48
Signoria (Florence) 306, 310
Signot, Jacques 162
Skimmington ride 12, 405
Skocpol, Theda 78 n.3
slavery: Atlantic slave systems 16, 32–8
    of children 269
    and empire 2, 24–6, 430, 432
    in Ottoman Empire 71
Smail, John 420
smallpox, spread 300, 381–2
Smith, Adam 18, 22, 439
Smuts, R. Malcolm 351
social sciences 430
    and Enlightenment 188–9, 190–5
societies, secret 219
society: court 385–97
    and *fête* 207–13
    and individual 87, 155, 259
    and natural function 12
    and political reform 312–14
sociology, historical 382
Sorel, Charles 168, 186
Soupirs de la France esclave 72
Southeast Asia: compared with Europe 421–2, 424–7, 435
    and state formation 422–3
Souza, Martim Afonso da 202
sovereignty: and empire 19, 22
    local 299
    and property 72
    and representation 320
    rise 4
    Turkish 75
space, liturgical 173–5
Spain: and American conquests 15
    colonies 18–19, 20, 29, 35, 199
    confraternities 88, 101–16
    and France 72, 77
    and monarchy 21, 300–1, 303, 348–57
    as nation-state 299
    and Ottoman Empire 72
    and religious minorities 200
    revenues 300–1
Spanish Succession War 332, 333–5
Spence, Jonathan 383
spirituality: lay 172–3
    and uniformity 87
    and visual arts 159, 173, 175, 178, 180–1, 183
Starkey, David 349
Starowolski, Szymon 44, 45, 50
state: and administration 318–27, 332–4, 336–43
    and church 299, 302, 312–13, 323
    and corporate institutions 301–2, 333
    and empire 19–20
    and finances 300–1
    and force 308, 309, 311, 313–14
    and individual 13, 220
    and leadership 302, 306–9
    and monarch 299–300, 349

paradoxes of power 322–45
    and religion 13, 92–3, 382, 423, 425–6
    and science 187
    in Southeast Asia 422–3
    and territorial integrity 300, 318, 424
    and war 300, 318, 332–5
    see also government; taxation
state system, emergence 4, 299–304, 326, 382
Steiff, Karl 121, 136 n.1
Steinfeld, Robert J. 37
Stella, Erasmus 47–9
Stevin, Simon 202
Stone, Bailey 69
Stone, Lawrence 138, 220, 221, 258–66
Strasbourg: churches 174
    and citizenship 227, 228, 230
    as free imperial city 223
    and guilds 223, 235
    and legal rights of women 229–31, 233–4
Stuttgart: as free ducal city 225
    and legal rights of women 232
Suetonius (Gaius Suetonius Tranquillus) 24
sugar, consumption 33
Suger, abbot 176
Sugihara, Kaoru 436–7
superstition: and Enlightenment 88, 131, 157
    and *fêtes* 210–11
    and village remedies 14, 88, 121–36
Sweden: fundamental laws 324
    monarchy 299, 321–2, 324, 325, 326
    and national origins 44, 48, 50
Sydenham, Thomas 407 n.3
symbolism: and imagery 178–9, 182
    sexual 399–400, 404–7

Tacitus, Publius Cornelius 20, 22, 41, 48–50
taste: courtly 394–6
    Renaissance 175, 177–8
Tavernier, Jean-Baptiste 70, 78 n.10
Tawney, R. H. 259, 266, 380
taxation 318, 425
    and excise 337–42, 344–5
    indirect 223, 301, 337–8
    land tax 340–1
    and war 91, 332, 336, 337–45
Taylor, Karen L. 1–5
teacher training, Austria 60
Temple, Sir William 20
Terrones, Fray Aguilar de 351
Teutonic Knights, and historiography 45, 47–8
textbooks 56, 57, 61, 64
theater 219, 283–4
    and sex role reversal 402, 403–4
Thiers, Jean-Baptiste 209, 210
Thirsk, Joan 258, 381
Thirty Years' War 222–5, 228, 323
Thomas, Keith 258
Thompson, E. P. 258, 259, 262, 265, 384 n.1
Thorn, and humanist education 42–3, 45
Thorndike, Lynn 161
Tilly, Charles 332, 434
time: and festivals 209
    measurement 167–70
Tischindeal, Dmitrie 65
Titian (Tiziano Vecellio) 159
toleration, religious 64, 75, 150, 200–1, 223
Tomas de Trujillo 102
Tommaso de Vio (Caejetan) 31 n.56
Tory, Geoffroy 170 n.4
towns: and churches 173–4
    and *fêtes* 211
trade: Asian 423, 437
    England 33–4
    European 431, 432, 438
    Ottoman Empire 303
    and politics 313–14
    women in 240 n.59, 362

transvestism 400–1, 402–7
Trent, Council (1543–63) 9, 12, 86–7, 97
    and sumptuary legislation 177, 183
Trevor-Roper, Hugh 319
Trexler, Richard 181
trigonometry 202
truth, and science 158, 187, 447, 450
Tuck, Richard 27
Turkey see Ottoman Empire
Turner, Victor 104, 401

Ugo de Fleury 29 n.3
Ullman, Walter 19
Unger, J. H. and Helene 291
United States of America: as empire 22
    and slavery 37
universalism, and empire 28–9

Valori, Francesco 305–6, 308
Valori, Niccolò 306 n.1
Van der Mylen 52
Van Leur, J. C. 420
Van Loo, Carle 74
Vasari, Giorgio 178
Vavilov, Nikolai Ivanovich 415
Vega Carpio, Lope Félix de 351
Veit, Dorothea 289–90, 292
Veneziano, Domenico 177–8
Veragüe, Pedro de 103
Vergennes, Charles Gravier, comte de 69, 74
vernaculars, in Austrian territories 64–5
Vesalius, Andreas 161, 443
Vespucci, Amerigo 413
Vezelić, Alexsije 65
Vienna Normal School 55, 56–8, 65
Viera, Antonio 446
Viète, François 165, 166
Vietnam 424–7
villages: as collectivity 132–3
    and knowledge 134–6
    and leadership 133–4
    and peasant remedy for epidemic 14, 88, 1
violence: domestic 246
    religious 85
    state 308, 309, 311, 313–14, 425
Viret, Pierre 167
Vitruvius (Marcus Vitruvius Pollio) 162
Voltaire (François Marie Arouet) 74, 75–6
Von Courland, Dorothea 284, 286, 288–9, 29?
Von der Recke, Eliza 284, 288
Vujić, Joakim 65

Wackernagel, Martin 183
wages: female 17 n.10, 362, 368, 399
    and slavery 33–4, 36
Wallerstein, Immanuel 419, 423, 437, 438
war: economic impact 300, 332, 343–4
    and state 300, 318, 332–5
warriors: as courtiers 92, 381, 385–97, 425
    women as 402
wars, religious: France 91, 92–3, 189
    Germany 85
Weber, Max 4, 11, 259, 266, 379, 419, 454 n.6
weiblichte Freiheit 231–2, 234

welfare system: and confraternities 88, 101–6, 115–16
    early modern Germany 223, 224
    early modern Russia 275–9
Wellman, Kathleen 3, 5, 9, 158, 186–95, 383
Wende, Georg 43
Westphalia, Peace 323–4, 326
wet nurses 138, 143, 278
Whigham, Frank 355
White, Hayden 443
White Processions (1583) 88, 90, 94–7
Widman, Johannes 166
widows: in business 11, 218
    and dower 245, 246, 253
    and guardianship 229–31
    and guilds 236, 362, 366
    as heads of households 11, 22
    and property 246–7, 249, 252–3
Wiesener, Merry E. 3, 220, 222–37, 381
Willeford, William 402
William III of Orange 333–6, 337–8, 341–3
Williams, Bernard 25
wills: and charity 103, 110, 276
    and parent–child bonds 89, 140, 146, 147, 149–50
    of women 111, 229, 245, 246–7
Wilson, James 26
witchcraft 271–2, 399
witnesses, women as 249–50
women 3–4
    and citizenship 226–8, 230
    and court patronage 219
    and dependence 11, 217, 235
    and domesticity 217–18, 220–1, 272
    economic role 11, 218, 220, 222, 226, 232–7, 272, 382,